SMALL GROUPS

Key Readings in Social Psychology

General Editor: ARIE W. KRUGLANSKI, University of Maryland at College Park

The aim of this series is to make available to senior undergraduate and graduate students key articles in each area of social psychology in an attractive, user-friendly format. Many professors want to encourage their students to engage directly with research in their fields, yet this can often be daunting for students coming to detailed study of a topic for the first time. Moreover, declining library budgets mean that articles are not always readily available, and course packs can be expensive and time-consuming to produce. *Key Readings in Social Psychology* aims to address this need by providing comprehensive volumes, each one of which will be edited by a senior and active researcher in the field. Articles will be carefully chosen to illustrate the way the field has developed historically as well as current issues and research directions. Each volume will have a similar structure to include:

- an overview chapter, as well as introduction to sections and articles
- questions for class discussion
- annotated bibliographies
- full author and subject indexes

Published Titles

The Self in Social Psychology	Roy F. Baumeister
Stereotypes and Prejudice	Charles Stangor
Motivational Science	E. Tory Higgins and Arie W. Kruglanski
Social Psychology and Human Sexuality	Roy F. Baumeister
Emotions in Social Psychology	W. Gerrod Parrott
Intergroup Relations	Michael A. Hogg and Dominic Abrams
The Social Psychology of Organizational Behavior	Leigh L. Thompson
Social Psychology: A General Reader	Arie W. Kruglanski and E. Tory Higgins
Social Psychology of Health	Peter Salovey and Alexander J. Rothman
The Interface of Social and Clinical Psychology	Robin M. Kowalski and Mark R. Leary
Political Psychology	John T. Jost and James Sidanius
Close Relationships	Harry T. Reis and Caryl Rusbult
Social Neuroscience	John T. Cacioppo and Gary G. Berntson
Social Cognition	David L. Hamilton
Small Groups	John M. Levine and Richard L. Moreland

Titles in Preparation

Attitudes	Richard E. Petty and Russell Fazio
Language and Communication	Gün R. Semin
Persuasion	Richard E. Petty and Russell Fazio
Social Comparison	Diederik Stapel and Hart Blanton

For continually updated information about published and forthcoming titles in the Key Readings in Social Psychology series, please visit: **www.keyreadings.com**

SMALL GROUPS
Key Readings

Edited by

John M. Levine
University of Pittsburgh, Pennsylvania

Richard L. Moreland
University of Pittsburgh, Pennsylvania

Psychology Press
New York and Hove

Published in 2006
by Psychology Press
270 Madison Avenue
New York, NY 10016
www.psypress.com

Published in Great Britain
by Psychology Press
27 Church Road
Hove, East Sussex BN3 2FA
www.psypress.co.uk

Psychology Press is an imprint of the Taylor & Francis Group

Typeset in 10/12, Times by Macmillan India, Bangalore, India
Printed and bound in the USA by Sheridan Books, Inc., Ann Arbor, MI, on acid-free paper
Paperback cover design by Hybert Design

10 9 8 7 6 5 4 3 2 1

Library of Congress Cataloging-in-Publication Data
Small groups : key readings / edited by John M. Levine & Richard L. Moreland.
    p. cm. – (Key readings in social psychology)
  Includes bibliographical references and index.
  ISBN-10: 0-86377-593-4 (hardback : alk. paper)
  ISBN-10: 0-86377-594-2 (pbk. : alk. paper)
  ISBN-13: 978-0-86377-593-2 (hbk)
  ISBN-13: 978-0-86377-594-9 (pbk)
    1. Small groups—Research. 2. Communication in small groups. I. Levine, John M. II. Moreland, Richard L. III. Series.

 HM736.S65 2006
 302.3′4–dc22

                                                                                2005034118

ISBN-13: 978-0-86377-593-2 (hbk)
ISBN-13: 978-0-86377-594-9 (pbk)

ISBN-10: 0-86377-593-4 (hbk)
ISBN-10: 0-86377-594-2 (pbk)

Contents

About the Editors

John M. Levine is Professor of Psychology and Senior Scientist at the Learning Research and Development Center at the University of Pittsburgh. His research focuses on small group processes, including majority and minority influence, group socialization, shared reality, and group loyalty. He is a Fellow of the American Psychological Association and the American Psychological Society. Professor Levine has served as Editor of the *Journal of Experimental Social Psychology* and Executive Committee Chair of the Society of Experimental Social Psychology. He co-edited *Perspectives on Socially Shared Cognition* (with L. B. Resnick and S. D. Teasley) and *Shared Cognition in Organizations: The Management of Knowledge* (with L. L. Thompson and D. M. Messick).

Richard L. Moreland is a Professor of Psychology and Management at the University of Pittsburgh. He studies many aspects of small groups, with a special focus on how those groups change over time. Such changes include group formation and dissolution, group development, and group socialization. He is a Fellow of the American Psychological Society and of Division 8 (Society of Personality and Social Psychology), Division 9 (Society for the Psychological Study of Social Issues), and Division 49 (Group Psychology and Group Psychotherapy) of the American Psychological Association. He has served on the Executive Boards of Divisions 9 and 49, and as President of Division 49.

Acknowledgments

The editor and publisher are grateful to the following for permission to reproduce the articles in this book:

Reading 1: Ennett, S. T., & Bauman, K. E. (1994). The contribution of influence and selection to adolescent peer group homogeneity: The case of adolescent cigarette smoking. *Journal of Personality and Social Psychology*, *67*, 653–663. Copyright © 1994 by the American Psychological Association. Reprinted with permission.

Reading 2: Kanter, R. M. (1977). Some effects of proportions on group life: Skewed sex ratios and responses to token women. *The American Journal of Sociology*, *82*, 695–990. Copyright © 1977 by the University of Chicago Press. Reprinted with permission.

Reading 3: Tziner, A., & Eden, D. (1985). Effects of crew composition on crew performance: Does the whole equal the sum of its parts? *Journal of Applied Psychology*, *70*, 85–93. Copyright © 1985 by the American Psychological Association. Reprinted with permission.

Reading 4: Driskell, J. E., & Mullen, B. (1990). Status, expectations, and behavior: A meta-analytic review and test of the theory. *Personality and Social Psychology Bulletin*, *16*, 541–553. Copyright © 1990 by Sage Publications, Inc. Reprinted with permission.

Reading 5: Prentice, D. A., Miller, D. T., & Lightdale, J. R. (1994). Asymmetries in attachments to groups and to their members: Distinguishing between common-identity and common-bond groups. *Personality and Social Psychology Bulletin*, *20*, 484–493. Copyright © by Sage Publications, Inc. Reprinted with permission.

Reading 6: Zurcher, Jr., L. A. (1970). The "friendly" poker game: A study of an ephemeral role. *Social Forces*, *49*, 173–186. Copyright © 1970 by the University of North Carolina Press. Reprinted with permission.

Reading 7: Kramer, R. M., & Brewer, M. B. (1984). Effects of group identity on resource use in a simulated commons dilemma. *Journal of Personality and Social Psychology*, *46*, 1044–1057. Copyright © 1984 by the American Psychological Association. Reprinted with permission.

Reading 8: Gruenfeld, D. H. (1995). Status, ideology, and integrative complexity on the U.S. Supreme Court: Rethinking the politics of political decision making. *Journal of Personality and Social Psychology*, *68*, 5–20. Copyright © 1995 by the American Psychological Association. Reprinted with permission.

Reading 9: Marques, J. M., Abrams, D., & Serôdio, R.G. (2001). Being better by being right: Subjective group dynamics and derogation of in-group deviants when generic norms are undermined. *Journal of Personality and Social Psychology*, *81*, 436–447. Copyright © 2001 by the American Psychological Association. Reprinted with permission.

1998 by the American Psychological Association. Reprinted with permission.

Reading 24: Arrow, H. (1997). Stability, bistability, and instability in small group influence patterns. *Journal of Personality and Social Psychology*, 72, 75–85. Copyright © 1997 by the American Psychological Association. Reprinted with permission.

Reading 25: Moreland, R. L. & Levine, J. M. (2001). Socialization in organizations and work groups. In M. E. Turner (Ed.), *Groups at work* (pp. 69–112). Mahwah, NJ: Lawrence Erlbaum Associates, Inc. Copyright © 2001 by Lawrence Erlbaum Associates, Inc., Publishers. Reprinted with permission.

Reading 26: Ancona, D. G., & Caldwell, D. F. (1988). Beyond task and maintenance: Defining external functions in groups. *Group & Organization Studies*, 13, 468–494. Copyright © 1988 by Sage Publications, Inc. Reprinted with permission.

Small Groups: An Overview

John M. Levine and Richard L. Moreland

Why study groups? The answer is simple—it is impossible to understand human behavior without considering the role that groups play in people's lives. Most people belong to an array of informal and formal groups that influence them in both obvious and subtle ways. These groups include families, friendship cliques, work crews, sports teams, bridge clubs, bible study circles, therapy groups, and so on. Many (perhaps most) daily activities are carried out in such groups, which are not only important in their own right, but also connect people to larger social institutions, such as business organizations and religious denominations. In many cases, group influence is easy to recognize, as when an air crew responds to an in-flight emergency or a gang attacks someone from a rival gang. These examples involve coordinated responses by people with common goals, so it seems obvious that they cannot be adequately understood by analyzing the thoughts, feelings, and behaviors of isolated individuals. But in other cases, observers may be fooled into thinking they have been seeing a strictly individual phenomenon, when in fact that phenomenon was heavily influenced by past or present group experience. Examples include such diverse behaviors as using a slang expression, choosing a hair style, smoking a cigarette, and working hard in school.

The impact of groups derives from their ability to satisfy members' needs (cf. Baumeister & Leary, 1995; Forsyth, 1999; Mackie & Goethals, 1987). Many such needs have been identified, but they can be organized into four major categories. First, groups satisfy the *survival* needs of members by facilitating their ability to conceive and rear offspring, obtain food and shelter, and protect themselves against enemies. Second, groups satisfy the *psychological* needs of members by allowing them to develop intimate relations with others, avoid loneliness, and exert influence and power. Third, groups satisfy the *informational* needs of members by clarifying their physical and social environments and allowing them to evaluate their opinions, abilities, and outcomes through social comparison. Finally, groups satisfy the *identity* needs of members by providing a social, or collective, basis for their beliefs about themselves (e.g., Hell's Angel, Michael Jackson fan). These group functions are so powerful and widespread that some analysts believe the human propensity for group membership has evolved through natural selection and thus represents a fundamental part of our genetic makeup (e.g., Baumeister & Leary, 1995; Caporael, 2001). Because groups have the potential to satisfy the needs of their members does not mean, of course, that they always do so.

Nevertheless, the rewards of group membership are sufficient to ensure that most people belong to groups throughout their lives.

Defining Groups

Many definitions have been offered for the term "group," emphasizing such diverse characteristics as interdependence (e.g., Cartwright & Zander, 1968), communication (e.g., Homans, 1950), influence (e.g., Shaw, 1981), structure (e.g., Sherif & Sherif, 1956), and shared identity (Brown, 2000). Each of these definitions captures something important about groups, but using them to make hard-and-fast distinctions between "groups" and "nongroups" seems misguided. Instead, a better approach is to view "groupiness," or social integration, as a dimension along which sets of people can vary (Moreland, 1987). According to McGrath (1984), a set of people is high in groupiness to the extent that it contains just a few members who interact freely in a wide range of activities and who have both a history of past interaction and an expectation of future interaction. On the basis of these criteria, families and football teams are "groupier" than crowds and classrooms.

Even if we think of groupiness as a continuum rather than a dichotomy, qualitative differences between groups of different sizes can still be identified. For example, unlike groups containing three or more people, groups containing just two persons (dyads) are destroyed by the loss of a single member and cannot exhibit several phenomena that occur in larger groups, such as third-party mediation, coalition formation, and majority-minority relations (Mills, 1958; Simmel, 1950). And some phenomena that occur in both dyads and larger groups, such as self-disclosure, are often different in the two contexts (Solano & Dunham, 1985). By the same token, very large groups, such as organizations, often develop formal role systems, status hierarchies, and norms that are seldom if ever observed in smaller groups. Given these differences, as well as the extensive literatures on dyads (Berscheid & Reis, 1998) and organizations (Pfeffer, 1998), this book focuses primarily on small face-to-face

groups containing at least three members (Levine & Moreland, 1998).

Does anything special happen to people when they join groups? Many early observers (e.g., Durkheim, 1938/1966; LeBon, 1895/1960; McDougall, 1920) were impressed by the apparent differences in how people act when they are together versus alone. They noted, for example, that groups often exhibit more antisocial and aggressive behavior than do isolated individuals. This led them to claim that groups possess emergent properties that cannot be predicted from the individual characteristics of their members. This claim, however, did not go unchallenged. Its most influential critic was Floyd Allport (1924), who argued that "There is no psychology of groups which is not essentially and entirely a psychology of individuals" (p. 4). According to Allport, questions about how people behave in groups can (and must) be answered by studying the characteristics of individual members. Although debates about the reality of groups and the existence of emergent group properties have never been completely settled (see Steiner, 1974, 1986), most contemporary researchers believe groups are distinct social entities that deserve to be studied in their own right.

This consensus is based on three primary lines of argument. First, groups are frequently perceived as real by both members and nonmembers (e.g., Campbell, 1958; Hamilton & Sherman, 1996). Not surprisingly, perceived "entitativity" is greater for some kinds of groups than others. For example, researchers (Lickel, Hamilton, Wieczorkowska, Lewis, Sherman, & Uhles, 2000) have shown that intimacy groups (e.g., families, close friends) seem more entitative than task groups (e.g., committees, project teams), which in turn are seem more entitative than social categories (e.g., women, Americans) and loose associations (e.g., neighbors). Second, people often behave differently as group members than as either (a) isolated individuals or (b) participants in dyadic interactions. In the former case, people who observe fellow group members give incorrect responses to simple stimuli give more incorrect responses themselves than do people who answer alone (Asch, 1956), and people working on effortful tasks expend less energy when their output will be combined with the output of others than when it will not (Latané, Williams, & Harkins, 1979). In the latter case, people behave less competitively in interpersonal situations (involving two competing individuals) than in intergroup situations (involving two competing groups). This "interpersonal-intergroup discontinuity effect" (Schopler & Insko, 1992) rests on two motives—fear, based on the perception that another group cannot be trusted, and greed, based on the desire to exploit another group. Finally, the characteristics of individual group members often do not predict how the group as a whole will perform on a collective task (Moreland & Levine, 1992). In some cases, the group performs better than expected on the basis of its members' abilities, and in other cases it performs worse. Stated differently, a group can be either more or less than the sum of its parts.

A Brief History of Group Research

The 1930s marked the beginning of systematic research on small groups by social psychologists, and several notable research projects were conducted prior to World War II. These included Sherif's (1936) laboratory experiments on the development of group norms under conditions of uncertainty; Lewin, Lippitt, and White's (1939) field experiments on how leadership styles influenced children's aggressive behavior; and Whyte's (1943) participant observation research on the social dynamics of street gangs. According to Cartwright and Zander (1968), the development of group research during this period was facilitated by three key factors. First, cultural and economic conditions in the United States were favorable, in particular the widespread belief that social problems could be solved through scientific research and the willingness of academic institutions, governmental agencies, and business organizations to provide funds for such research. Second, several professions that dealt with groups (social work, group psychotherapy, education, and business administration) strongly encouraged research on group processes. Finally, social scientists acknowledged

that groups are "real" and worthy of study, and they provided methodological techniques for group research (e.g., statistical tools for analyzing data, methods for observing social interaction).

Interest in small groups surged after the war and remained strong during the 1950s, as indicated by many important theoretical, empirical, and methodological advances during that period. Several new theories about groups were proposed (e.g., Festinger, 1950; Thibaut & Kelley, 1959), and interesting research was done on a wide variety of topics, including leadership (Chowdry & Newcomb, 1952), conflict within and between groups (e.g., Deutsch, 1949), and conformity (e.g., Asch, 1956). By the early 1960s, however, many social psychologists lost their enthusiasm for group research. Several hypotheses for this decline have been offered, including the claim that theoretical developments did not keep pace with empirical findings (McGrath, 1984) and the argument that societal conditions were not ripe for group research (Steiner, 1986). Though important work on groups was done during the next 30 years, the field as a whole languished until the middle 1980s. Since that time, there has been a substantial increase in the amount of research on groups (Moreland, Hogg, & Hains, 1994). In social psychology, much of that work has focused on intergroup processes. In contrast, organizational psychologists have devoted most of their attention to intragroup processes, particularly the performance of work teams (Sanna & Parks, 1997).

Studying Groups

The first step in studying group processes is formulating a research question. In some cases, these questions are based on hunches derived from one's own or others' experiences in groups. For example, an historical account of reduced interracial tension between black and white soldiers in the same unit following combat might lead a researcher to investigate when cooperation under stress improves intergroup relations. In most cases, however, research questions are derived from theories about groups. Although there is no single, unified theory of group processes, group research is by no means atheoretical. Instead, many "midrange" theories have been developed to explain specific aspects of group behavior. Such theories are the major source of research hypotheses in most areas of social psychology. The absence of grand theories can be frustrating if one seeks the "big picture" of a particular field, but efforts to develop such theories for group phenomena have met with little success. This is not surprising, given the complexity of group phenomena and the fact that they have been systematically studied for only a few decades.

Once a research question has been generated, a methodology for answering it is needed. As McGrath (1984) points out, group researchers seek to maximize three things when choosing a methodology—the ability to generalize findings across populations, precision in measuring behavior (and controlling extraneous variables), and the realism of the research context. In light of these criteria, let us examine three major methodologies that group researchers often use.

Case Studies

One important methodology for investigating group processes is the case study, which involves an indepth examination of one or more groups. Case studies can involve several kinds of data, including interviews with group members, archival analyses of documents about the group, and observations of members' interactions. Typically, case studies obtain qualitative information about group life with the goal of providing a rich descriptive account of how members interact. Few case studies try to test specific hypotheses, and they rarely contain numerical data or statistical tests.

A classic observational case study was conducted by Whyte (1943), who spent over three years investigating Italian American gangs in Boston. Whyte was a participant observer in the groups he studied, and group members knew that he was a social scientist interested in their behavior. His study yielded valuable information about many facets of group life, including group norms and roles, relations between leaders and followers, and techniques members used to manage conflict. Case

studies have been used to investigate other group phenomena as well. Examples in this volume include papers by Kanter (1977) on the effects of skewed sex ratios in business groups, Zurcher (1970) on roles and norms in recreational groups, and Ancona and Caldwell (1988) on how groups relate to their social environments.

Like all methodologies, case studies have both strengths and weaknesses. In participant observation studies, such as the one Whyte conducted, the researcher can obtain detailed information about group processes that is typically inaccessible to outsiders. However, when an observer reveals his or her presence, as Whyte did, group members may become self-conscious and behave differently than they would if they did not think they were being watched (cf. Roethlisberger & Dickson, 1939). This problem can be eliminated if the observer keeps his or her research secret, pretending to be an ordinary group member, but such covert observation is problematical on ethical grounds. Both kinds of participant observation share some weaknesses, namely that researchers may (a) unintentionally influence the group activities they are observing, (b) become so personally involved in the group that they lose their objectivity, and (c) fail to record information about group processes in real time, so they must later reconstruct what they saw from memory. Data obtained by external observers may be more reliable than those of participant observers, because external observers are less likely to influence group activities, can maintain a more detached perspective on what happens in the group, and are able to collect data during interaction (e.g., by videotaping members' behavior). However, such researchers typically have access to less information than do participant observers, so they produce less informative accounts of group activities.

Rather than observing how group members behave during interaction, researchers sometimes interview them afterwards or obtain documents reporting group activities. Interviews can provide useful information about members' beliefs, motives, and feelings during interaction without influencing or disrupting their behavior. However, this information is necessarily retrospective and thus subject to some of the same biases that affect participant observers' recollections. Archival analyses of documents about the group, including minutes of meetings, speeches, and memoirs, can also yield a detailed and nuanced portrait of group activities. But these kinds of documents have their own problems—minutes may be written to provide a particular (and biased) picture of what happened at a meeting; speeches may reflect members' political goals rather their true feelings; and memoirs may be distorted by memory errors or the desire to portray actions favorably.

In terms of McGrath's (1984) three methodological goals for group research, case studies generally get high marks for the realism of the research context, because they are conducted in natural rather than laboratory groups. However, case studies typically get lower marks for the ability to generalize findings across populations and precision in measuring behaviors (and controlling extraneous variables). Because case studies are often conducted on single groups, it is difficult to know whether their findings can be generalized to other groups. Moreover, such studies often measure behaviors in imprecise ways and fail to control extraneous variables.

Correlational Studies

Another useful methodology for studying group processes is the correlational study. Like case studies, correlational studies can employ various kinds of data. These include observations of group behavior, members' responses to questionnaires and interviews, and documents about the group. Case studies and correlational studies are similar in that neither involves random assignment of participants to different conditions, manipulation of independent variables, or control of extraneous variables (the hallmarks of true experiments). One difference between case studies and correlational studies is that the latter more often use data from multiple groups than from a single group. Of greater importance is the fact that correlational studies, unlike most case studies, generate quantitative (numerical) information about the direction and strength of relationships between particular variables.

A classic correlational study was conducted by Newcomb (1943), who spent several years investigating how the integration of students into a college community (Bennington) affected their attitudes on political issues. Newcomb was intrigued by the fact that first-year students, who came from politically conservative families and held conservative views when they entered college, generally became more liberal as time went on. By examining students' responses to questions about their relations with peers and their political views, Newcomb found that students who became more liberal were more likely to accept Bennington (with its liberal political climate) as their reference group than were those who remained conservative. Interestingly, in a follow-up study conducted some two decades later, Newcomb and his colleagues discovered that the political attitudes of Bennington graduates were stable over the years—these students were more liberal (as indicated by their voting preferences in subsequent presidential elections) than were demographically similar women who did not graduate from Bennington (Newcomb, Koenig, Flacks, & Warwick, 1967).

Correlational studies have been used to investigate other group phenomena as well. Examples of correlational research in this book include the papers by Ennett and Bauman (1994) on adolescent cigarette smoking; Prentice, Miller, and Lightdale (1994) on attachments in different kinds of groups; Gruenfeld (1995) on status, ideology, and integrative complexity in Supreme Court decisions; Fiedler (1965) on leadership effectiveness (with the exception of the experiment presented later in the paper); Meindl, Ehrlich, and Dukerich (1986) on the "romance" of leadership (Studies 1–3); and McKenna and Bargh (1998) on identity "demarginalization" through group participation on the Internet.

In discussing case studies, we mentioned some pluses and minuses associated with observational, interview, and archival data. These comments are equally applicable to correlational studies using these kinds of data. As noted earlier, however, correlational studies differ from cases studies in that they generate quantitative information about the direction and strength of relationships between variables. Such information is useful if one's goal is *prediction*. However, correlational studies seldom allow conclusions about *causation*, which is problematic because most group researchers want to draw causal inferences from their data. The thorny issue is that a correlation between two variables (A and B) can reflect any of three possible causal scenarios. First, variations in A might cause variations in B. Second, variations in B might cause variations in A. Finally, variations in some unmeasured variable (C) might cause variations in both A and B, creating the false impression that one causes the other. However, certain statistical techniques using correlational data, such as cross-lagged panel designs and structural equation modeling, can provide some information about causality (Campbell & Stanley, 1966; Kenny, Kashy, & Bolger, 1998).

In terms of McGrath's (1984) goals for group research, correlational studies often have high generalizability across populations, because data can be obtained from multiple groups. Such studies present a mixed picture, however, regarding McGrath's other two goals, namely realism of the research context and precision in measuring behavior and controlling extraneous variables. For example, correlational studies assessing ongoing behavior in natural groups are relatively high in realism, whereas studies asking people to predict how they might vote in a future election are relatively low. Moreover, correlational studies using carefully designed survey instruments are relatively high in precision, whereas those relying on documents are relatively low.

Experiments

A final methodology for studying group processes is the experiment. The hallmarks of an experiment are (a) random assignment of participants to conditions, (b) manipulation of independent variables, and (c) control of extraneous variables that might also affect the dependent variables. By ensuring that all participants have an equal probability of assignment to each condition, systematically manipulating independent variables, and holding constant extraneous variables, researchers guarantee that any relationship between variations

in the level of an independent variable and responses on a dependent variable are caused by the independent variable. Thus, in contrast to case studies and correlational studies, experiments allow a researcher to make strong inferences about causality.

A classic experimental study was conducted by Aronson and Mills (1959), who were interested in how the severity of initiation into a group affects subsequent evaluations of that group. The researchers hypothesized that people who undergo an unpleasant initiation will experience *cognitive dissonance* (i.e., discomfort arising from the realization that they performed an action inconsistent with their self image), which in turn will cause them to exaggerate the positive qualities of the group they are entering. To test this hypothesis, Aronson and Mills randomly assigned college women, who had volunteered to participate in group discussions on the psychology of sex, to three conditions. In the severe initiation condition, participants were required to read aloud (to the male experimenter) a list of obscene words and some vivid descriptions of human sexual activity in order to join the group. In the mild initiation condition, participants had to read aloud five sexually-related, but not obscene, words. In the control condition, participants were not required to read aloud any material before joining the group. Next, participants were asked to listen to what they believed was an ongoing discussion among the members of the group they would soon enter. This discussion, which was tape recorded to control extraneous variables (e.g., group members' appearance), was a very boring conversation about the sexual behavior of lower animals. Finally, participants were asked to rate the discussion and the group members on several scales (e.g., dull–interesting, intelligent–unintelligent). The results indicated, consistent with the hypothesis, that participants in the severe initiation condition rated both the discussion and the group members more favorably than did participants in the mild initiation and control conditions, who gave similar ratings.

Because of their value in establishing causality, experiments are the most widely used methodology in group research (Moreland et al., 1994). So it is not surprising that most of the papers included in this book (all the studies not identified above) describe experiments. It is important to note that although most group experiments are done in laboratory settings, experiments also can be conducted in field settings (e.g., Arrow, 1997; Tziner & Eden, 1985). The results of laboratory and field experiments, as well as correlational studies, can be statistically summarized and evaluated using meta-analytic procedures, as in Driskell's and Mullen's (1990) review of research on status, expectations, and behavior.

In terms of McGrath's (1984) three goals for group research, laboratory experiments get high marks on their precision in measuring behavior and controlling extraneous variables. Questions are often raised, however, about whether experiments satisfy McGrath's other goals, namely realism and generalizability. In order to maximize measurement precision, experimental researchers often create highly artificial environments that lack many features of natural settings. Because these environments do not mirror what participants encounter in their everyday lives, they are low in "mundane realism" (Aronson & Carlsmith, 1968). However, mundane realism may be less important than two other kinds of realism (Aronson, Wilson, & Brewer, 1998). One of these is "experimental realism," or the degree to which the experimental situation is involving and meaningful to participants. The other is "psychological realism," or the degree to which the psychological processes produced in the experiment are similar to those that occur in everyday life. Although group experiments are often low in mundane realism, they can be high in experimental and psychological realism. As for generalizability across populations, laboratory experiments are typically weak, because researchers seldom try to replicate their studies with different kinds of participants (e.g., adolescents and middle-aged people, Americans and Asians). By focusing on just one population (frequently college students), experimental researchers run the risk of producing results with limited generalizability (but see Mullen & Copper, 1994).

Finally, it is important to mention ethical problems that can arise in experimental research. The most important of these involve psychological discomfort to participants and deception concerning the purposes of the experiment. In recent years, guidelines for protecting the welfare of research participants developed by the American Psychological Association and government-mandated Institutional Review Boards for evaluating university research have increased investigators' sensitivity to ethical issues associated with experimental (and nonexperimental) studies. Group researchers typically take great pains to minimize psychological distress to participants, to avoid deception whenever possible, and to debrief participants about the purposes and procedures of experiments.

What to Do?

Clearly, case studies, correlational studies, and experiments all have weaknesses as well as strengths. According to McGrath (1984), this situation is inevitable because it is impossible for a study simultaneously to achieve precision, realism, and generalizability (e.g., attempts to increase precision invariably decrease realism). The implication of this argument is sobering: There is no one "right" way to do group research. Given that every methodology is flawed in one way or another, what can a researcher do? From McGrath's perspective, the saving grace is that different methodologies have different flaws. The trick, then, is to use multiple methodologies, so that the advantages of one offset the disadvantages of another. Unfortunately, because of the time and energy this strategy requires, McGrath's advice is rarely followed by individual researchers. However, because different researchers with different methodological preferences are often interested in the same phenomena, the kind of methodological triangulation that McGrath advocates sometimes occurs across researchers.

Paper Selection for this Book

Research on small groups is diverse, because people who study such groups come from several disciplines and vary in their methodological preferences and substantive interests. The goal of this book was to capture that diversity and the excitement of small group research, rather than to showcase classic papers in the field, which are probably familiar to most readers. Although most of the papers in the book were written by social psychologists, several papers by sociologists and organizational scientists are also included. And all three of the major methodologies used to investigate groups are represented. Finally, the diverse substantive interests of group researchers are reflected in the five part headings used to organize the book (see Levine & Moreland, 1998). These are group composition (the number and type of people who belong to the group); group structure (the status systems, norms, roles, and cohesion that constrain interactions among group members); group conflict (competition between members to obtain scarce resources, both tangible and intangible); group performance (cooperation among members to create joint products and achieve common goals); and group ecology (the physical, social, and temporal environments in which a group operates). Although these five aspects of groups are all important, they have not received equal research attention. To reflect this fact, more space was devoted to conflict and performance papers than to papers on composition, structure, and ecology.

REFERENCES

Allport, F. (1924). The group fallacy in relation to social science. *American Journal of Sociology*, *29*, 688–706.

Ancona, D. G., & Caldwell, D. F. (1988). Beyond task and maintenance: Defining external functions in groups. *Group and Organization Studies*, *13*, 468–494.

Aronson, E., & Carlsmith, J. M. (1968). Experimentation in social psychology. In G. Lindzey & E. Aronson (Eds.), *The handbook of social psychology* (2nd ed., Vol. 2, pp. 1–79). Boston, MA: McGraw-Hill.

Aronson, E., & Mills, J. (1959). The effect of severity of initiation on liking for a group. *Journal of Abnormal and Social Psychology*, *59*, 177–181.

Aronson, E., Wilson, T. D., & Brewer, M. B. (1998). Experimentation in social psychology. In D. Gilbert, S. Fiske, & G. Lindzey (Eds.), *The handbook of social psychology* (4th ed., Vol. 1, pp. 99–142). Boston, MA: McGraw-Hill.

Arrow, H. (1997). Stability, bistability, and instability in small group influence patterns. *Journal of Personality and Social Psychology*, *72*, 75–85.

Asch, S. E. (1956). Studies of independence and submission to group pressure: I. A minority of one against a unanimous majority. *Psychological Monographs*, *70*, No. 9 (Whole No. 417).

Baumeister, R. F., & Leary, M. R. (1995). The need to belong: Desire for interpersonal attachments as a fundamental human motivation. *Psychological Bulletin*, *117*, 497–529.

Berscheid, E., & Reis, H. T. (1998). Attraction and close relationships. In D. Gilbert, S. Fiske, & G. Lindzey (Eds.), *The handbook of social psychology* (4th ed., Vol. 2, pp. 193–281). Boston, MA: McGraw-Hill.

Brown, R. (2000). *Group processes* (2nd ed.). Oxford, UK: Blackwell.

Campbell, D. T. (1958). Common fate, similarity, and other indices of the status of aggregates of persons as social entities. *Behavioral Science*, *3*, 14–25.

Campbell, D. T., & Stanley, J. C. (1966). *Experimental and quasi-experimental designs for research*. Chicago: Rand-McNally.

Caporael, L. R. (2001). Evolutionary psychology: Toward a unifying theory and a hybrid science. *Annual Review of Psychology*, *52*, 607–628.

Cartwright, D., & Zander, A. (1968). *Group dynamics: Research and theory* (3rd ed.). New York: Harper & Row.

Chowdry, K., & Newcomb, T. M. (1952). The relative abilities of leaders and non-leaders to estimate the opinions of their own groups. *Journal of Abnormal and Social Psychology*, *47*, 51–57.

Cook, T. D., & Campbell, D. T. (1979). *Quasi-experimentation: Design and analysis issues for field settings*. Boston: Houghton-Mifflin.

Deutsch, M. (1949). An experimental study of the effects of cooperation and competition upon group process. *Human Relations*, *2*, 199–232.

Driskell, J. E., & Mullen, B. (1990). Status, expectations, and behavior: A meta-analytic review and test of the theory. *Personality and Social Psychology Bulletin*, *16*, 541–553.

Durkheim, E. (1938/1966). *The rules of sociological method*. New York: Free Press.

Ennett, S. T., & Bauman, K. E. (1994). The contribution of influence and selection to adolescent peer group homogeneity: The case of adolescent cigarette smoking. *Journal of Personality and Social Psychology*, *67*, 653–663.

Festinger, L. (1950). Informal social communication. *Psychological Review*, *57*, 271–282.

Fiedler, F. E. (1965). The contingency model: A theory of leadership effectiveness. In H. Proshansky & B. Seidenberg (Eds.), *Basic studies in social psychology* (pp. 538–551). New York: Holt, Rinehart, and Winston.

Forsyth, D. R. (1999). Group dynamics (3rd ed.). Belmont, CA: Wadsworth.

Gruenfeld, D. H. (1995). Status, ideology, and integrative complexity on the U.S. Supreme Court: Rethinking the politics of political decision making. *Journal of Personality and Social Psychology*, *68*, 5–20.

Hamilton, D. L., & Sherman, S. J. (1996). Perceiving persons and groups. *Psychological Review, 103,* 336–355.

Homans, G. C. (1950). *The human group.* New York: Harcourt Brace.

Kanter, R. M. (1977). Some effects of proportions on group life: Skewed sex ratios and responses to token women. *American Journal of Sociology, 82,* 965–990.

Kenny, D. A., Kashy, D. A., & Bolger, N. (1998). Data analysis in social psychology. In D. Gilbert, S. Fiske, & G. Lindzey (Eds.), *The handbook of social psychology* (4th ed., Vol. 1, pp. 233–268). Boston, MA: McGraw-Hill.

Latané, B., Williams, K. D., & Harkins, S. (1979). Many hands make light the work: The causes and consequences of social loafing. *Journal of Personality and Social Psychology, 37,* 822–832.

LeBon, G. (1895/1960). *The crowd: A study of the popular mind.* New York: Viking Press.

Levine, J. M., & Moreland, R. L. (1998). Small groups. In D. Gilbert, S. Fiske, & G. Lindzey (Eds.), *The handbook of social psychology* (4th ed., Vol. 2, pp. 415–469). Boston, MA: McGraw-Hill.

Lewin, K., Lippitt, R., & White, R. (1939). Patterns of aggressive behavior in experimentally created (social climates). *Journal of Social Psychology, 10,* 271–299.

Lickel, B., Hamilton, D. L., Wieczorkowska, G., Lewis, A., Sherman, S. J., & Uhles, A. N. (2000). Varieties of groups and the perception of group entitativity. *Journal of Personality and Social Psychology, 78,* 223–246.

Mackie, D. M., & Goethals, G. R. (1987). Individual and group goals. In C. Hendrick (Ed.), *Group processes* (pp. 144–166). Newbury Park, CA: Sage.

McDougall, W. (1920). *The group mind.* New York: Putnam.

McGrath, J. E. (1984). *Groups: Interaction and performance.* Englewood Cliffs, NJ: Prentice-Hall.

McKenna, K. Y. A., & Bargh, J. A. (1998). Coming out in the age of the Internet: Identity "demarginalization" through virtual group participation. *Journal of Personality and Social Psychology, 75,* 681–694.

Meindl, J. R., Ehrlich, S. B., & Dukerich, J. M. (1985). The romance of leadership. A*dministrative Science Quarterly, 30,* 78–102.

Mills, T. M. (1958). Some hypotheses on small groups from Simmel. *American Journal of Sociology, 63,* 642–650.

Moreland, R. L. (1987). The formation of small groups. In C. Hendrick (Ed.), *Group processes* (pp. 80–110). Newbury Park, CA: Sage.

Moreland, R. L., Hogg, M. A., & Hains, S. C. (1994). Back to the future: Social psychological research on groups. *Journal of Experimental Social Psychology, 30,* 527–555.

Moreland, R. L., & Levine, J. M. (1992). The composition of small groups. In E. J. Lawler, B. Markovsky, C. Ridgeway, & H. A. Walker (Eds.), *Advances in group processes* (Vol. 9, pp. 237–280). Greenwich, CT: JAI Press.

Mullen, B., & Copper, C. (1994). The relation between group cohesiveness and performance: An integration. *Psychological Bulletin, 115,* 210–227.

Newcomb, T. M. (1943). *Personality and social change.* New York: Dryden.

Newcomb, T. M., Koenig, K. E., Flacks, R., & Warwick, D. P. (1967). *Persistence and change: Bennington College and its students after twenty-five years.* New York: Wiley.

Pfeffer, J. (1998). Understanding organizations: Concepts and controversies. In D. Gilbert, S. Fiske, & G. Lindzey (Eds.), *The handbook of social psychology* (4th ed., Vol. 2, pp. 733–777). Boston, MA: McGraw-Hill.

Prentice, D. A., Miller, D. T., & Lightdale, J. R. (1994). Asymmetries in attachments to groups and their members: Distinguishing between common-identity and common-bond groups. *Personality and Social Psychology Bulletin, 20,* 484–493.

Roethlisberger, F. J., & Dickson, W. J. (1939). *Management and the worker.* Cambridge, MA: Harvard University Press.

Sanna, L. J., & Parks, C. D. (1997). Group research trends in social and organizational psychology: Whatever happened to intragroup research? *Psychological Science, 8,* 261–267.

Schopler, J., & Insko, C. A. (1992). The discontinuity effect in interpersonal and intergroup relations: Generality and mediation. In W. Stroebe & M. Hewstone (Eds.), *European review of social psychology* (Vol. 3, pp. 121–151). Chichester, England: Wiley.

Shaw, M. E. (1981). *Group dynamics: The psychology of small group behavior* (3rd ed.). New York: McGraw-Hill.

Sherif, M. (1936). *The psychology of social norms.* New York: Harper & Row.

Sherif, M., & Sherif, C. (1956). *An outline of social psychology* (rev. ed.). New York: Harper and Row.

Simmel, G. (1950). *The sociology of Georg Simmel.* Glencoe, IL: Free Press.

Solano, C. H., & Dunnam, M. (1985). Two's company: Self-disclosure and reciprocity in triads versus dyads. *Social Psychology Quarterly, 48,* 183–187.

Steiner, I. D. (1974). Whatever happened to the group in social psychology? *Journal of Experimental Social Psychology, 10,* 94–108.

Steiner, I. D. (1986). Paradigms and groups. In L. Berkowitz (Ed.), *Advances in experimental social psychology* (Vol. 19, pp. 251–289). New York: Academic Press.

Tziner, A., & Eden, D. (1985). Effects of crew composition on crew performance: Does the whole equal the sum of its parts? *Journal of Applied Psychology, 70,* 85–93.

Whyte, W. F. (1943). *Street corner society.* Chicago: University of Chicago Press.

Zurcher, L. A. (1970). The "friendly" poker game: A study of an ephemeral role. *Social Forces, 49,* 173–186.

SUGGESTED READINGS

Forsyth, D. R. (2006). *Group dynamics.* Belmont, CA: Brooks/Cole.

Hogg, M. A., & Tindale, S. (Eds.) (2001). *Blackwell handbook of social psychology: Group processes.* Malden, MA: Blackwell.

Kenny, D. A., Mannetti, L. Pierro, A., Livi, S., & Kashy, D. A. (2002). The statistical analysis of data from small groups. *Journal of Personality and Social Psychology, 83,* 126–137.

Levine, J. M., & Moreland, R. L. (1998). Small groups. In D. Gilbert, S. Fiske, & G. Lindzey (Eds.), *The handbook of social psychology* (4th ed., Vol. 2, pp. 415–469). Boston, MA: McGraw-Hill.

McGrath, J. E. (1984). *Groups: Interaction and performance.* Englewood Cliffs, NJ: Prentice-Hall.

PART 1

Group Composition

From the viewpoint of outsiders, the most striking aspect of a group may be its composition—the number and types of people who belong. Unfortunately, research on group composition is relatively scarce, and even when it is done, researchers are often more interested in other aspects of group life that are affected by composition, rather than in composition itself. Nevertheless, some interesting and important research on group composition has been done. This work can be organized along three dimensions (see Moreland & Levine, 1992). First, different characteristics of group members can be studied. Some researchers study the size of a group, noting the simple presence or absence of members, whereas others study the types of people who belong, focusing on their demographic characteristics (e.g., age, race, sex), abilities (e.g., intelligence, skills), opinions (e.g., beliefs, values), or personalities (e.g., traits, motives, neuroses). Second, group members' characteristics can be measured in different ways. Some researchers prefer measures of central tendency, assessing the proportion of group members who have a characteristic or the mean level of that characteristic within the group. Other researchers prefer measures of variability, assessing the range of a characteristic in a group or classifying the group as heterogeneous or homogeneous for that characteristic. A few researchers even examine special configurations of characteristics among group members, such as the compatibility of their psychological needs (Schutz, 1958). Finally, different analytical perspectives on group composition can be taken.

Some researchers view the composition of a group as a *consequence* that depends on the operation of various sociological or psychological processes. A few researchers view it as a *context* that moderates other phenomena. Most researchers, however, view group composition as a *cause* that can influence other aspects of groups, such as their structure, dynamics, and performance. Because of their importance, these analytical perspectives deserve further commentary.

Group Composition as a Consequence

Research on groups often occurs in laboratories, where group composition can be controlled. Researchers who *want* to study composition effects do so by creating groups of different types. But for many researchers, composition effects are just a nuisance that must somehow be controlled. Standardization often serves that purpose. A researcher can make every group the same size, for example, and other member characteristics (e.g., sex) that might affect the research results can be held constant through restricted sampling. The random assignment of people to groups can also be used to distribute the effects of member characteristics (e.g., abilities) evenly across groups. All of this contrasts sharply with the world outside of laboratories, where group membership is rarely controlled by a central authority. Even when such control is exerted, the creation of interchangeable groups is rarely the goal. Natural groups thus can and do vary in their composition. Some groups are larger than others, and different groups contain distinct types of

members. There is evidence, for example, that groups tend to be small (Desportes & Lemaine, 1988) and that members of the same group are similar (Jackson, Brett, Sessa, Cooper, Julin, & Peyronnin, 1991; Maccoby, 1998) and different from the members of other groups (Carroll, 1993; McPherson & Rotolo, 1996). Several theories offer possible explanations for these findings (see Moreland & Levine, 2003).

Group Composition as a Context

Every psychological phenomenon occurs in some context, and many (maybe most) phenomena occur in the context of friendship cliques, families, and other groups. Thus, it would not be surprising if those phenomena were shaped by the composition of such groups. Consider the intellectual development of children, which occurs in the context of families (and other groups to which children belong). As they age, children get smarter, and the general rate of their development is well known. But what about the families in which children grow up? Those families vary in their composition—some are larger than others, some contain mostly boys rather than girls, and some contain a child with special needs. These composition differences among families could alter the rate of intellectual development in their children. In larger families, for example, children might interact less often, or in more superficial ways, with their parents, which could suppress their rates of intellectual development and prevent them from becoming as smart as they could have been if their families were smaller (Zajonc & Markus, 1975).

Group Composition as a Cause

Many researchers study group composition as a cause, maybe because such work promises to reveal how groups could be formed or altered to produce better outcomes, such as greater cohesion and performance. Consider, for example, efforts by lawyers to shape trial verdicts by selecting some potential jurors and rejecting others during the *voir dire* process, or efforts by coaches and owners of sports teams to improve their teams' win/loss records by changing player rosters during the off-season. Anyone who relies on groups, and who can control at least some aspects of their composition, would be eager to know how those groups should be composed.

Research that reflects this analytical perspective can be organized by the member characteristics that one might try to control. The most basic of these is the presence or absence of group members, which determines a group's size. Many studies comparing groups of different sizes have been performed, and they have revealed several important differences. Some of these differences favor larger groups; others favor smaller groups. Larger groups, for example, may perform better because they have access to more member resources, such as time, money, expertise, and contacts. Larger groups also tend to be more diverse, which could improve their performance as well. Finally, larger groups often seem more legitimate, which may discourage interference and encourage support from outsiders. Larger groups can also suffer from many problems, however. For example, they may experience coordination problems (e.g., scheduling difficulties, confusion about task responsibilities), as well as

motivation problems (e.g., free riding, social loafing, "sucker effects"), all of which can harm their performance. There is also greater conflict in larger groups, their members are generally less cooperative with one another, and several forms of member misbehavior (e.g., cheating) occur more often in larger groups. Finally, participation levels tend to be lower and more variable in larger groups, where a few people tend to dominate all the rest. Membership in larger groups is often less satisfying as a result.

All of this suggests that there may be no "optimal" group size. So instead of making a group larger or smaller, it might be wiser for its members to develop coping methods that maximize the strengths and minimize the weaknesses associated with its size. Planning and process coordination, for example, could help solve coordination problems in larger groups, and team building and goal setting could help solve their motivational problems.

The demographic characteristics of group members can also be important and have thus been studied by many researchers. Much of their work has focused on the issue of *diversity* (Williams & O'Reilly, 1997), often through comparisons between homogeneous and heterogeneous groups. For example, groups containing only males or females may be compared with groups that contain both sexes. This research, especially as applied to school and work groups, has been motivated in part by moral and legal pressures that are weakening the barriers around many groups, allowing people who were excluded in the past (because of their sex or race, handicaps, or lifestyles) to become members.

The evidence on diversity is mixed, just as it is for group size. The main advantage of diversity (noted earlier) is that it can improve the performance of a group, especially on tasks that require creative thinking and a broad range of knowledge and skills. The main disadvantage of diversity is that it can produce conflict among group members. As a result, group cohesion may be weakened, tempting some members to leave. Those who leave are often the people who differ most from other group members (Tsui, Egan, & O'Reilly, 1992), so their departure makes the group less diverse. It could be argued, in fact, that people generally prefer homogeneous to heterogeneous groups, and they only join or remain in heterogeneous groups if external pressures force them to do so.

The advantages and disadvantages of diversity are not independent, because the performance of a group can be affected by conflict among its members. To complicate matters further, many factors can moderate the effects of diversity on group performance and conflict among group members. The optimal type or level of diversity for a group is thus unclear. So, rather than trying to change the membership of a group, it might be wiser (again) for members to develop coping methods that maximize the strengths and minimize the weaknesses associated with whoever already belongs.

One general strategy for minimizing the weaknesses associated with diversity is to train group members to control whatever conflicts diversity creates. Some conflicts can be prevented by educating people about their similarities and differences, encouraging greater tolerance, and improving social skills. It is also possible to build cohesion and trust through team building, and people can be taught to resolve their conflicts more effectively. One general strategy for maximizing the strengths associated with diversity, without actually changing who belongs to a group, involves a variety of tactics that just *simulate* diversity. These include seeking input from outsiders (e.g., consultants), and changing the group's structure. Structural changes may involve creating new roles in a group (e.g., a "devil's advocate" who criticizes standard operating procedures) or altering group norms (e.g., encourage people to evaluate plans more critically). When these and similar tactics succeed, they improve the performance of a group without creating conflicts among its members.

Finally, much research has been done on the abilities, opinions, and personalities of group members. Most of this work reveals simple *additive effects*—as the level of some individual characteristic rises in a group, its impact on that group's structure, dynamics, or performance becomes correspondingly larger. Thus, sports teams win more games when players are more skilled (Jones, 1974), juries render harsher verdicts when jurors are more conservative (Bersoff & Ogden, 1987), and work groups develop more rigid, hierarchical structures when members have stronger safety needs (Aronoff & Messe, 1971). Additive effects suggest that groups are like machines whose components are individual members. Each person, through his or her own characteristics, influences the group independently and would thus affect every group the same way, regardless of their members. An intelligent person, for example, would improve the task performance of any group, and his or her impact would be the same in every group.

But what about the notion of "chemistry" among group members? As noted earlier, groups sometimes exhibit emergent properties that do not reflect the characteristics of their members in any simple way. Sports teams, for example, occasionally perform far better or worse than expected, given the skills of their players. And consider some of the decisions that the Supreme Court has made, decisions that were far more liberal or conservative than expected, given the political orientations of the justices who wrote them. Although these *interactive effects* are rare, some researchers have found them, especially in field research on natural groups (rather than laboratory research on artificial groups). Interactive effects suggest that groups could be viewed as organisms rather than machines. In some cases, the influence of different members on a group may thus be interdependent, rather than independent. If so, then someone could affect different groups in different ways, depending on who else belonged. For example, an intelligent person might improve the task performance of one group more than that of another, if the intellectual mix in the former group were somehow better.

Research on group composition as a cause tends to be fragmented. Researchers who study one member characteristic seldom study other characteristics, nor do they often consider research by others on those characteristics. This seems unfortunate, because research on one characteristic of group members could clarify the effects of their other characteristics on the group. To address this problem, Moreland and Levine (see, for example,

Moreland, Levine, & Wingert, 1996) developed a "generic model" of group composition effects that offers answers to three important questions.

First, which characteristics of group members are likely to be important at a given moment? A key variable here, according to Moreland and Levine, is *salience*, or the extent to which group members are thinking about a characteristic. Salience can vary both across characteristics and over time. Some characteristics of group members (e.g., race) are more salient than others (e.g., personality traits) because they are more readily apparent. The salience of a characteristic can also be affected by its distribution within a group. As the variance of a characteristic in a group increases (e.g., women join a group whose other members are all men), it attracts more attention. Finally, a characteristic can become salient if it seems relevant to people's outcomes or lends meaning to their experiences. Family members become more aware of one another's camping skills, for example, if their summer vacation takes them to a wilderness area.

When a characteristic is salient, relevant composition effects can occur. Everyone in the group possesses some level of that characteristic and can thus contribute to such effects. This raises a second important question, namely which members are likely to have the greatest impact on the group? A key variable here, according to Moreland and Levine, is *visibility*, or the extent to which other members of the group notice a particular person's characteristics. Members who participate more often in group activities or who have more status or seniority in the group tend to be more visible. As a result, the group is more likely to reflect their characteristics. And situational factors could once again be important. These include the type of task that a group must perform (e.g., a "disjunctive task," where the performance of a group depends entirely on the performance of its best member, can make that person more visible) and the relationships group members have with outsiders (e.g., someone's visibility can increase if he or she has friends or relatives with special resources that the group needs).

Finally, an important question is how the characteristics of group members combine to affect a group. Because additive effects occur more often than interactive ones, and interactive effects occur primarily in natural groups, *social integration* is a key variable here, according to Moreland and Levine. Social integration is the tendency for people who belong to a group to think, feel, and act as a group, rather than as individuals (see Moreland, 1987). As its level of social integration rises, a group becomes more "real," and so simple additive effects are soon joined by more complex, interactive effects.

REFERENCES

Aronoff, J., & Messe, L. A. (1971). Motivational determinants of small-group structure. *Journal of Personality and Social Psychology, 17*, 319–324.

Bersoff, D. N., & Ogden, D. W. (1987). In the Supreme Court of the United States, Lockhart v McCree: Amicus curiae brief for the American Psychological Association. *American Psychologist, 42*, 59–68.

Carroll, G. R. (1993). A sociological view on why firms differ. *Strategic Management Journal, 14*, 237–249.

Desportes, J. P., & Lemaine, J. M. (1988). The sizes of human groups: An analysis of their distributions. In D. Canter, J. C. Jesuino, L. Soczka, & G. M. Stephenson (Eds.), *Environmental social psychology* (pp. 57–65). Dordrecht, The Netherlands: Kluwer Academic.

Jackson, S. E., Brett, J. F., Sessa, V. I., Cooper, D. M., Julin, J. A., & Peyronnin, K. (1991). Some differences make a difference: Individual dissimilarity and group heterogeneity

as correlates of recruitment, promotions, and turnover. *Journal of Applied Psychology, 76*, 675–689.

Jones, M. B. (1974). Regressing group on individual effectiveness. *Organizational Behavior and Human Performance, 11*, 426–451.

Maccoby, E. E. (1998). *The two sexes: Growing up apart, coming together*. Boston: Harvard University Press.

McPherson, J. M., & Rotolo, T. (1996). Testing a dynamic model of social composition: Diversity and change in voluntary groups. *American Sociological Review, 61*, 179–202.

Moreland, R. L. (1987). The formation of small groups. In C. Hendrick (Ed.), *Review of personality and social psychology* (Vol. 8, pp. 80–110). Newbury Park, CA.: Sage.

Moreland, R. L., & Levine, J. M. (1992). The composition of small groups. In E. Lawler, B. Markovsky, C. Ridgeway, & H. Walker (Eds.), *Advances in group processes* (Vol. 9, pp. 237–280). Greenwich, CT: JAI Press.

Moreland, R. L., & Levine, J. M. (2003). Group composition: Explaining similarities and differences among group members. In M. A. Hogg, & J. Cooper (Eds.), *Sage handbook of social psychology* (pp. 367–380). London: Sage.

Moreland, R. L., Levine, J. M., & Wingert, M. L. (1996). Creating the ideal group: Composition effects at work. In J. Davis & E. Witte (Eds.), *Understanding group behavior* (Vol. 2, pp. 11–35). Hillsdale, NJ: Erlbaum.

Schutz, W. C. (1958). FIRO: *A three-dimensional theory of interpersonal behavior*. New York: Rinehart.

Tsui, A. S., Egan, T. D., & O'Reilly, C. A. (1992). Being different: Relational demography and organizational attachment. *Administrative Science Quarterly, 37*, 549–579.

Williams, K. Y., & O'Reilly, C. A. (1998). Demography and diversity in organizations: A review of 40 years of research. In B. Staw & R. Sutton (Eds.), *Research in organizational behavior* (Vol. 20, pp. 77–140). Greenwich, CT: JAI Press.

Zajonc, R. B., & Markus, G. B. (1975). Birth order and intellectual development. *Psychological Review, 82*, 74–88.

Readings

The first paper in this set, by Ennett and Bauman (1994), illustrates research on group composition as a consequence. The paper describes a field study of smoking behavior in friendship cliques of adolescent boys at several schools. Cliques were identified through surveys of the boys. The cliques were numerous, but generally small in size. Whereas most of the boys belonged to cliques, some did not. The latter boys included isolates, who had few or no friends, and liaisons, who were friends with clique members but did not belong to cliques themselves. The research focused on the boys' smoking behavior, which was also identified through surveys. Most of the boys did not smoke, but some did. Cliques tended to be homogeneous for smoking— clique members were more similar to one another in their smoking behavior than they were to other boys. Most of the cliques were actually non-smoking; smokers were less likely than other boys to belong to cliques.

What role did friendship cliques play in smoking (and thus clique membership)? Ennett and Bauman identified two processes in this regard, namely influence (socialization) and selection. The influence process, which occurs within cliques, involves social pressure on boys to conform to the smoking norms of their cliques. A boy who belongs to a nonsmoking clique would thus feel pressure to avoid smoking, whereas a boy who belongs to a smoking clique would feel pressure to smoke. The selection process involves entering and/or leaving cliques. A boy decides to join a clique, and a clique decides to admit a boy, partly on the basis of whether the boy's smoking behavior matches that of the clique. A variant of this process is deselection—a boy who belongs to a clique is more likely to leave it if his smoking behavior does not match that of the clique.

Ennett and Bauman found that both influence and selection could explain why some boys smoked and others did not, and the two processes were roughly equal in strength. Deselection seemed weaker, operating primarily for nonsmokers. These results help to balance the general tendency among parents and others to attribute adolescent smoking solely to "peer pressure" (influence). Selection is important as well and thus deserves more attention.

The second paper, by Kanter (1977), illustrates research on group composition as a cause. Kanter studied a special gender configuration, namely male groups that contain token female members. A token is someone of a type that is rare in a group—often the token is the only group member of that type. Kanter interviewed several token women, along with their male coworkers and managers, from small sales teams in a large corporation. She also observed how team members interacted with one another, both at work and at informal social gatherings. Note that this research was qualitative rather than quantitative—there are no numerical data or statistical tests in the paper. Kanter offers instead a detailed description of the teams, accompanied by some insights into their dynamics.

According to Kanter, three special perceptual phenomena arise in groups with token members. First, tokens are more "visible" than others, in the sense that group members pay more attention to them. This visibility produces performance pressures. For example, Kanter found that token women often felt self-conscious, which interfered with their performance. And they worried that their performance would be viewed by other team members as evidence regarding the abilities of *all* women. The women responded to these performance pressures by seeking "invisibility" in various ways (e.g., dressing blandly, behaving meekly) or (conversely) by trying to outperform everyone in the team.

Second, tokens produce "polarization" in groups. The boundaries between tokens and other group members are strengthened because those other members exaggerate how much they differ from the tokens. Kanter found, for example, that male coworkers acted more coarsely when token women were present, isolated those women by conducting certain activities (work-related and otherwise) only when token women were absent, and asked token women to pass various "loyalty tests," such as laughing at sexist jokes or joining in when other women in the company were criticized. The women responded to this polarization by accepting their social isolation from male coworkers, or (conversely) by becoming more masculine in their appearance and behavior, hoping to be treated as "insiders."

Finally, tokens experience "assimilation" when their unique personal qualities are overlooked or ignored by other group members, who rely instead on broad stereotypes about the type of person the tokens represent. Kanter found, for example, that token women were often misidentified by male coworkers as lower status female workers (e.g., secretaries), rather than colleagues. And role entrapment occurred when token women were viewed and treated by male coworkers as occupants of a few stereotypical feminine roles, such as "mothers" or "cheerleaders." Some token women responded to this assimilation by actually becoming who other members of their team perceived them to be, changing not only their appearance and behavior but also their self-perceptions.

The final paper in this set, by Tziner and Eden (1985), also illustrates group composition as a cause, but offers a rare example of interactive composition effects. Tziner and Eden performed a field experiment using tank crews in the Israeli Army. A crew of this sort contains three soldiers, who play different roles in operating the tank. The researchers began by assessing the ability and motivation levels of many soldiers, using questionnaire measures. This enabled them to classify every soldier as high (above average) or low (below average) in each quality. The Army then allowed the researchers to create tank crews representing every possible combination (64 in all) of ability and motivation levels across the three work roles. Over a training period of about two months, these crews were observed by their commanders, who recorded how well the crews performed a variety of combat tasks (e.g., speed and accuracy at firing tank weapons). At the end of that time, the commanders produced general evaluations of each crew's performance.

Tziner and Eden analyzed their data by regressing crew performance on predictors representing additive and interactive composition effects. They began with six simple predictors representing the ability and motivation levels of each crew's three members. Five of these six predictors were significant, and all of them were positive, revealing strong additive composition effects—crews performed better when their members had higher levels of ability and motivation. A second set of predictors, representing possible interactions between the ability or motivation levels for different pairs of crew members, was then added, followed by a third set of predictors representing possible interactions among the ability or motivation levels for all three crew members. These additional sets of predictors tested for interactive composition effects—did the impact of one soldier's ability or motivation on the crew's performance change depending on the ability or motivation levels of other soldiers in the crew? One predictor from the second set and another predictor from the third set proved to be significant, indicating that interactive composition effects did occur, above and beyond the additive composition effects revealed by the first set of predictors. Both of the significant interactive predictors involved ability rather than motivation and showed that crews performed unusually well when high ability members worked together, but unusually poorly when low ability members worked together. This led the researchers to suggest that in forming new tank crews, the Army should not "spread the talent around," but rather create as many crews as possible whose members are all high in ability. Any remaining soldiers with high ability should then be distributed broadly, so that there are few or no crews in which every member is low in ability.

Discussion Questions

1. Even in a heterogeneous group, members could separate themselves into cliques that are homogeneous. Is there any harm in this? If so, then what is it and how can it be avoided?
2. Being a liaison between groups can create special problems and opportunities for a person. Describe some of them.
3. Do you think quantitative or qualitative research on groups is better? Why?
4. Have you ever belonged to a group with good (or bad) "chemistry?" What was that like? Do you think such chemistry can be managed? How?
5. Imagine that you are forming a new group and that you have a clear image in mind of the kind of group you want. What problems would you face in composing that group?

Suggested Readings

Harrison, D. A., Price, K. H., Gavin, J. H., & Florey, A. T. (2002). Time, teams, and task performance: Changing effects of surface-and deep-level diversity on group functioning. *Academy of Management Journal, 45,* 1029–1045.

Lau, D. C., & Murnighan, J. K. (1998). Demographic diversity and faultlines: The compositional dynamics of organizational groups. *Academy of Management Review, 23,* 325–340.

McPherson, J. M., & Rotolo, T. (1996). Testing a dynamic model of social composition: Diversity and change in voluntary groups. *American Sociological Review, 61,* 179–202.

Moynihan, L. M., & Peterson, R. S. (2001). A contingent configuration approach to understanding the role of personality in organizational groups. In B. Staw (Ed.), *Research in organizational behavior* (Vol. 23, pp. 327–378). Oxford, UK: Elsevier.

Watson, W., Michaelsen, L. K., & Sharp, W. (1991). Member competence, group interaction, and group decision making: A longitudinal study. *Journal of Applied Psychology, 76,* 803–809.

The Contribution of Influence and Selection to Adolescent Peer Group Homogeneity: The Case of Adolescent Cigarette Smoking

Susan T. Ennett and Karl E. Bauman

Understanding the homogeneity of peer groups requires identification of peer groups and consideration of influence and selection processes. Few studies have identified adolescent peer groups, however, or examined how they become homogeneous. This study used social network analysis to identify peer groups (cliques), clique liaisons, and isolates among adolescents in 5 schools at 2 data collection rounds ($N = 926$). Cigarette smoking was the behavior of interest. Influence and selection contributed about equally to peer group smoking homogeneity. Most smokers were not peer group members, however, and selection provided more of an explanation than influence for why isolates smoke. The results suggest the importance of using social network analysis in studies of peer group influence and selection.

Many theories of social psychology, such as reference group theory (Newcomb, 1950; Sherif, 1948), small group theory (Festinger, Schachter, & Back, 1950; Hare, 1964; Homans, 1950), social learning theory (Bandura, 1977; Burgess & Akers, 1966; Sutherland & Cressey, 1978), social impact theory (Latané, 1981), and, more recently, social network theory (Smelser, 1988; Wellman, 1988)

Susan T. Ennett, Research Triangle Institute, Center for Social Research and Policy Analysis, Research Triangle Park, North Carolina; Karl E. Bauman, Department of Health Behavior and Health Education, University of North Carolina at Chapel Hill.

This research was supported by Grant 5 RO1 DA2480 from the National Institute on Drug Abuse of the U.S. Department of Health and Human Services and Grant 3 RO1 CA45997-04S1 from the National Cancer Institute of the U.S. Department of Health and Human Services.

Correspondence concerning this article should be addressed to Susan T. Ennett, Research Triangle Institute, Center for Social Research and Policy Analysis, P.O. Box 12194, Research Triangle Park, North Carolina 27709.

identify peer groups as a major source of attraction and influence. Many theories of adolescence similarly identify the peer group as central to adolescent behaviors, attitudes, and values (e.g., Blos, 1962; J. C. Coleman, 1980; J. S. Coleman, 1961; Douvan & Adelson, 1966; Hartup, 1983). Accordingly, the peer group has been used to explain a variety of adolescent attributes and behaviors, including orientation toward school (J. S. Coleman, 1961; Davies & Kandel, 1981), popular teen culture (Ball, 1981; Dunphy, 1963; Eder, 1985), and drug use (Jessor & Jessor, 1977; Kandel, 1978a).

Fundamental to all theoretical considerations of peer groups is that peer group members have similar characteristics; that is, members are homogeneous. The homogeneity of peer groups has been broadly explained by two processes: influence and selection (Billy & Udry, 1985; Cohen, 1977; Fisher & Bauman, 1988; Kandel, 1978a). The distinction between these processes is fundamental: One (influence) suggests that peer groups cause behavior, whereas the other (selection) indicates that behavior causes the formation of homogeneous groups. Influence contributes to peer group homogeneity when individuals who join groups are socialized to be more similar to group members. Moreland and Levine (1992) suggested that group homogeneity results from reciprocal influence processes in which the group attempts to change the individual in ways that improve his or her value as a member, whereas the individual attempts to change the group in ways that make it more satisfying. Selection processes result in group homogeneity when individuals who are similar in certain attributes purposefully select each other as friends (Kandel, 1978a). A more sociologically based selection explanation for homogeneity suggests that people who are drawn to the same activities interact with each other and become friends (Feld, 1981). More credence is commonly given to influence than selection in explaining similarity among friends. However, influence and selection processes are not mutually exclusive; both may contribute to peer group homogeneity (Fisher & Bauman, 1988; Kandel, 1978a).

Empirical considerations of the relative importance of influence and selection to peer group homogeneity rarely have been addressed, perhaps because the data and analysis demands are substantial. The purpose of this article is to report research that used social network analysis to study the contribution of influence and selection to cigarette smoking homogeneity in adolescent peer groups. A large literature suggests that adolescent peer groups play a crucial role in the initiation and maintenance of cigarette smoking as evidenced by the observation that adolescents who smoke are likely to have friends who smoke (e.g., Bauman, Fisher, Bryan, & Chenoweth, 1984; Huba & Bentler, 1980; Lanese, Banks, & Keller, 1972; McAlister, Krosnick, & Milburn, 1984; Sussman et al., 1990; van Roosmalen & McDaniel, 1989). The importance of the peer group to adolescent smoking is widely attributed to peer pressure (Urberg, Cheng, & Shyu, 1991), an assumption reflected in the many smoking prevention programs that teach adolescents how to resist pressures to smoke (e.g., Flay, d'Avernas, Best, Kersell, & Ryan, 1983; Glynn, 1989; Moskowitz, 1983). Consideration is given less frequently to the role of selection, that is, friendship choice based on smoking behavior, in accounting for smoking homogeneity among peers.

In spite of the centrality of peer groups to the voluminous research literature on adolescent smoking etiology and to smoking prevention programs, few studies have been based on analysis of systematically constructed peer groups. Furthermore, the contribution of influence and selection to smoking homogeneity in peer groups, as groups, has been little studied. Without consideration of cigarette smoking within the context of empirically formed peer groups, conclusions about the relevance of the peer group to adolescent smoking initiation and maintenance are incomplete.

Our study adds to research in this area by identifying adolescent peer groups and by examining influence and selection as mechanisms of group homogeneity. We used the most direct approach to identification of peer groups by applying formal social network analysis. Network analysis uses aggregated data on the relationships among individuals, such as the friendship links among adolescents who go to the same school, to identify groups. Friendship links are identified by asking adolescents questions like "who are your best friends?" Peer groups are revealed through analysis of overlapping links among adolescents. This approach to group identification differs completely from inferring peer group membership from the behavior adolescents attribute to friends or from friendship pairs. Prior to our own investigations (Ennett & Bauman, 1993; Ennett, Bauman, & Koch, 1994), studies using formal network analysis to study the relationship between peer groups and cigarette smoking had not been reported. The more common approach has been to focus on friendship pairs. Most studies of influence and selection also have been focused on friendship pairs (except, as described later, Cohen, 1977); we are unaware of earlier use of network analysis to investigate these processes.

If peer groups are homogeneous with respect to cigarette smoking, then that similarity may occur as a result of influence, selection, or both processes. Influence occurs when peers cause adolescents to adopt their behavior, as when adolescents initiate smoking in response to the direct pressure or example of their peers. Selection could account for peer homogeneity through two conceptually distinct processes. It might operate through adolescents choosing peers whose behavior is similar to their own (e.g., as when nonsmokers chose nonsmokers for friends), or it could operate through deselection. Deselection contributes to homogeneity when adolescents drop peers whose behavior is unlike their own, as when peer relationships dissolve when smoking behavior becomes dissimilar. Longitudinal data with adequate numbers of respondents with changed and stable behavior, and with changed and stable peer affiliations, are needed to separate influence and selection effects.

Several studies, including one using data from the study reported in this article, have focused on friendship pairs. They have provided detailed rationales for the distinct contributions of influence and selection to peer homogeneity, disentangled influence and selection effects in longitudinal data, and pointed out the problems of overattributing homogeneity to peer influence (Billy & Udry, 1985; Cohen, 1977; Fisher & Bauman, 1988; Jussim & Osgood, 1989; Kandel, 1978a). A conclusion from the previous research is that, contrary to common wisdom, selection is the major determinant of friend similarity with respect to a variety of attitudes and behaviors (e.g., drug use, sexual behavior, deviant values, and academic aspirations) and,

therefore, that it is incorrect to attribute most of the association between friend and adolescent behavior to peer influence.

Few studies of peer homogeneity have focused explicitly on cigarette smoking, and only one considered peer groups. Cohen (1977) studied 49 high school friendship groups to determine the relative contributions of pressures toward conformity (influence), selection, and group departure by deviates (deselection) to group homogeneity according to 18 individual characteristics, including smoking. Cohen found that initial peer group selection based on common characteristics, and not peer influence, was the major determinant of group homogeneity. Because of the broad focus of this analysis, however, findings specific to smoking apart from other attributes (e.g., alcohol consumption, dating frequency, and church attendance) are limited. In addition, the measure of smoking, smoking frequency, was not defined; different smoking behaviors (e.g., initiation and quitting) were not studied; and no information was provided about the extent of smoking by adolescents in the sample or within peer groups. Fisher and Bauman (1988) concluded that selection is markedly stronger than peer influence in accounting for smoking homogeneity in friendship pairs. Comparison of the findings showed support for all three processes, but was weaker for peer influence than for selection and weakest for deselection. Recent studies by Urberg (Urberg et al., 1991; Urberg, Shyu, & Liang, 1990), also based on best friend pairs, indicate that peer influence contributes to smoking homogeneity. However, selection was not assessed in these studies, although its confounding with influence was minimized by controlling for initial behavior.

In earlier analyses of data from the present study we used formal network analysis to identify peer group (clique) members, clique liaisons, and isolates among ninth-grade adolescents in five junior high schools (Ennett & Bauman, 1993; Ennett et al., 1994). Adolescents are assigned to these social positions depending on the extent and pattern of their friendship links with others. Clique members belong to a cluster of adolescents who share more friendship ties among themselves than with others (e.g., Brown, 1989; Hallinan, 1980). We consider cliques to be identical to peer groups. Liaisons are friends with other adolescents, but they are not members of a clique. They provide bridging ties between cliques by having friendships with members of different cliques (Granovetter, 1973; Hansell, 1981; Shrum & Cheek, 1987). Isolates have few or no friendship links with others.

Our findings showed that smoking varied by social position, with significantly higher rates of current smoking among isolates than clique members or liaisons (Ennett & Bauman, 1993). In addition, we found that adolescents in the same friendship clique were more like one another in their smoking behavior than they were like adolescents in other friendship cliques (Ennett et al., 1994). This yielded a majority of cliques characterized as predominantly nonsmoking and a significant minority as predominantly smoking. Whether influence, selection, or both contributed to clique homogeneity was not addressed.

The results of these analyses provide the foundation for our present study of influence and selection in the broad context of adolescents' social networks and with reference to their social positions in networks. We focus on the processes by which cliques become homogeneous in smoking. In so doing, we focus on the contribution of influence and selection to the smoking behavior of adolescents who are clique members. In addition, we investigate these processes with respect to clique liaisons and isolates. We examine two types of smoking behaviors: current smoking and quitting current smoking. Unlike many previous studies, data concerning peers' smoking behavior are based on peers' direct reports rather than on adolescents' perceptions of friend behavior. This avoids the problem of artificially inflating the positive association between the behavior of friends by adolescents' projection of their own attributes to others (Bauman & Fisher, 1986; Iannotti & Bush, 1992).

Method

Subjects

The data presented here are from a panel study of cigarette smoking by adolescents conducted in 1980 and 1981 (Bauman et al., 1984). Network analysis

of these data and examination of influence and selection are possible because friendship links at two rounds of data collection were identified and the smoking behavior of adolescents and their friends was measured at both rounds.

Subjects were adolescents at five schools in a one school system. A separate network analysis was conducted for each school to identify adolescents as clique members, liaisons, or isolates in a network of their peers. Analyses were conducted separately by school rather than all schools combined because schools are the primary locus of adolescent friendships (Blythe, Hill, & Thiel, 1982; J. S. Coleman, 1961; Kandel, 1978b). Subjects then were combined across schools to study influence and selection processes.

There were 1,326 8th graders enrolled in the five schools in the Guilford County North Carolina School System in Spring 1980, and 1,092 (82%) completed self-administered questionnaires between July 29 and November 30, 1980 (Round 1), when they were 9th graders. Of those, 945 (87%) completed questionnaires 1 year later between July 10 and October 15, 1981, when they were 10th graders (Round 2). Although some questionnaires were completed at both rounds just before the start of school, analysis suggested that this did not bias the network data. There were no significant differences in number of friendships or number of reciprocated friendships for subjects who completed the questionnaire before and after the beginning of the school year (Ennett, 1991). At both rounds of data collection, trained data collectors administered questionnaires in private settings in the subjects' homes. The sample for these analyses includes subjects who were surveyed at both rounds of data collection and for whom measures of smoking behavior are available at both rounds ($n = 926$).

Adolescents in Guilford County were similar to adolescents in the state of North Carolina and the United States on available demographic variables at the time of the study (Bauman et al., 1984). The average age of subjects at Round 1 was 14.1 years ($SD = .51$). Approximately 50% were female; about 85% were White, with most of the remainder Black/African American; and 62% had mothers with low education (i.e., high school graduate or less).

Social Network Analysis

The network analyses were based on subjects' responses to a series of sociometric items. Subjects named their three best friends, in order of best friend, second best friend, and third best friend, who were around their same age and not siblings. The names were written on a sheet of paper that was kept separate from the questionnaire and left with the subject. Identification numbers were recorded for friends who were in the subject's grade at school and attended one of the schools in the system, and therefore would also be eligible to complete questionnaires. This allowed linking the data of friends who participated in the study. Each friend named by an adolescent defined a friendship link. Friendship links between adolescents in the same school provided the raw data for the network analyses.

Although adolescents were not restricted to naming friends from school, at both rounds of data collection approximately 95% of friendship links were between adolescents in the same school. The fact that such a large percentage of friendship choices were between subjects in the same school confirms the appropriateness of using schools to form network boundaries.

For the Round 1 network analyses, links to schoolmates who were not surveyed were excluded (i.e., friends not in the study but named by subjects). For the Round 2 analyses, links to schoolmates surveyed at Round 1 but not at Round 2 were included; links to schoolmates not surveyed at either data collection point were excluded. Therefore, as shown in Table 1.1, the number of subjects available for the Round 2 network analyses (1,032) was larger than the Round 2 sample size (945) but slightly smaller than the Round 1 sample (1,092). Although the links to schoolmates surveyed at Round 1 but not at Round 2 were one-sided (i.e., we know who named them as friends, but it is impossible to know whom they would have named as friends at Round 2), excluding them would limit the data available for the Round 2 network analyses. Despite the larger samples used for the network analyses, our findings concerning influence and selection are reported, as described earlier, only for subjects represented in

TABLE 1.1. Sample Sizes for Network Analyses

Sample	%	n
Round 1 subjects surveyed at Round 2	86.5	945
Round 1 subjects included in Round 2 network analysis	94.5	1,032
Round 1 subjects included in influence and selection analyses	84.8	926[a]

Note: Round 1 = 1,092 subjects.
[a] 19 subjects surveyed at Round 2 were eliminated because of missing information on their smoking behavior at Round 2.

both the Round 1 and Round 2 network analyses and for whom complete information was available ($N = 926$), as shown in row 3 of Table 1.1.

The network analyses were conducted using the NEGOPY (negative entropy) program (Richards, 1989; Richards & Rice, 1981). NEGOPY assigns every individual in the network to a set of mutually exclusive social positions; the three major positions are group (clique) member, liaison, and isolate. NEGOPY detects cliques, liaisons, and isolates on the basis of patterns of friendship links and characteristics of those links. The program allows consideration to be given to whether friendships are reciprocated (i.e., A names B as friend and B names A as friend), whether friendship pairs are also linked by common friendships to other adolescents (i.e., A and B are friends, and both are friends with C), and the direction of friendship nominations (i.e., A names B as friend). In keeping with the assumption that cliques are likely to be made up of adolescents with many friendships in common, we set the program to recognize both reciprocated friendships and friendships linked by other common friendships. These were weighted so that reciprocated friendships represented twice the interaction of nonreciprocated friendships; that is, reciprocated friendships were given a weight of 2 and nonreciprocated friendships were given a weight of 1. A similar weighting scheme was used for pairs with common friends. The weights reflect the presumed greater interaction among these adolescents than those adolescents joined only by a single link (i.e., A names B as friend, and A and B have no friends in common). Slightly less than half of all friendships were reciprocated at the two rounds of data collection (43% at Round 1 and 40% at Round 2).

These percentages are almost identical to the percentage of reciprocated friendships among high schoolers (41%) reported by Kandel (1978b).

NEGOPY defines cliques as being made up of individuals who interact more with each other than with individuals in other groups; this definition is consistent with descriptions of cliques provided by many adolescent researchers (e.g., J. S. Coleman, 1961; Dunphy, 1963; Hollingshead, 1949). Cliques have a minimum size of three members. After tentatively detecting cliques, the program applies several confirmatory tests. Clique members are required to have most of their interaction (>50%) with members of the same clique and at least two links with others. As defined above, the extent of an adolescent's interaction with others reflects both reciprocated friendships and friendships in common with other clique members. Each clique also is tested to see if the clique members are all connected by some path lying entirely within the group from each member to each of the other members of the clique. Other tests split cliques to determine if they actually represent more than one clique. These tests help ensure that each adolescent identified as a clique member is truly a participating member of the clique and that each clique represents a single clique.

Measures

The definitions of social position follow from the NEGOPY program and are illustrated in Figure 1.1. The arrowheads indicate the direction of the links reported by adolescents; double-headed arrows indicate reciprocated links. Clique members are adolescents belonging to a friendship clique, as defined earlier.

Liaisons are not members of a clique, but through their friendship links they connect cliques to one another. They have at least two links that provide either direct or indirect connections between cliques. Liaisons provide indirect (multistep) connections between cliques by connecting liaisons who have direct connections with cliques. In Figure 1.1, Persons F and H are direct liaisons; Person G is an indirect liaison. Thus, liaisons are characterized by a relatively high degree of peer interaction, but outside of rather than within particular cliques.

Isolates are only minimally connected to other adolescents in the network. This position category includes adolescents with no friends at all, isolated dyads (i.e., adolescents with only one friendship that may or may not be reciprocated), and tree nodes (i.e., adolescents who are connected in

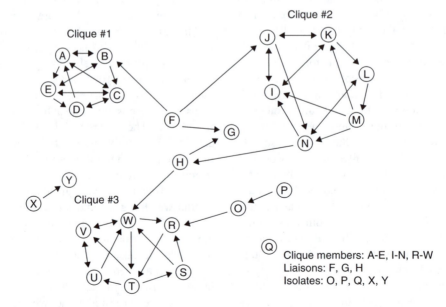

FIGURE 1.1 ■ Social network positions.

a chain structure, such that if any one link is removed the rest are separated from the network). In Figure 1.1, Persons X and Y represent an isolated dyad and Person O represents a tree node. It is important to note that only isolated dyads are categorized as isolates; most dyads are integrated into a friendship clique. Thus, although some isolates have friends, they are not integrated into peer cliques nor do they primarily associate with adolescents who are clique members.

The percentage of subjects who were clique members, liaisons, and isolates at Round 1 and at Round 2 are shown in Table 1.2. The results show that a larger percentage of subjects were clique members (approximately 41% at both rounds) than either liaisons or isolates. In the schools combined, there were 87 cliques at Round 1 and 82 cliques at Round 2. Clique size at both rounds was approximately 5 members ($M = 5.3$, $SD = 3.3$ at Round 1; $M = 5.0$, $SD = 2.9$ at Round 2). Fifty-seven of the Round 2 cliques were cliques that survived from Round 1 to Round 2, whereas 25 cliques were formed at Round 2. Following Cohen (1977), we defined cliques as surviving if (a) 50% or more of the Round 1 membership was present in the Round 2 clique or (b) if 50% or more of the Round 2 clique members were from the same Round 1 clique. In Cohen's study, 76% of cliques survived from the fall to the spring of the same school year. The survival rate in the present study was only slightly less

(67% of Round 1 cliques), despite the fact that there was a longer, 1-year interval between data collection rounds and students changed from 9th to 10th grade.

Cigarette smoking measures included both individual and clique-level smoking. The measures of adolescent smoking included current smoking and quitting, were based on adolescents' self-reported use of cigarettes and carbon monoxide content in alveolar breath samples, and were constructed as dichotomous measures. Adolescents who answered yes to the question "Do you smoke cigarettes now?" and who also indicated they had smoked one or more packs of cigarettes in their lifetime were defined as current smokers. All adolescents with 9 parts per million or higher carbon monoxide in their breath also were classified as current smokers (Bauman & Dent, 1982). Self-report validity of smoking was increased by informing subjects before completing questionnaires that their answers would be checked by a biochemical measure (Bauman & Dent, 1982). The self-report and biochemical measures were in agreement for 92% of adolescents. Quitters were defined as adolescents who were current smokers at Round 1 but not at Round 2.

The percentages of clique members, liaisons, and isolates who were current smokers at Round 1 and Round 2 are shown in Table 1.2. As the table indicates, a larger percentage of isolates than either clique members or liaisons were smokers. The differences in smoking by social position were statistically significant at both rounds of data collection.

Clique smoking was measured by the presence of smokers in the clique and was constructed as a dichotomous measure. We defined cliques as nonsmoking if they were composed of all nonsmokers or, for some analyses, if they were made up of all nonsmokers except the focal adolescent. For example, to analyze quitting, a smoker's clique was considered nonsmoking if all other members were nonsmokers. Smoking cliques included one or more smokers or, for some analyses (as above), other smokers in addition to the focal adolescent. The definition of a smoking clique is necessarily broad (i.e., the number of smokers ranges from 1 to many or from 4% to 100%) because there were relatively

TABLE 1.2. Social Network Position and Smoking Distribution at Round 1 and Round 2 ($N = 926$)

Measure	Round 1		Round 2	
	n	%	n	%
Social position				
Clique member	388	41.9	383	41.4
Liaison	279	30.1	242	26.1
Isolate	259	28.0	301	32.5
Smokers[a]				
Clique member	39	10.1	53	13.8
Liaison	25	9.0	37	15.3
Isolate	66	25.5	84	27.9

Note: For Round 1 smokers, $\chi^2(2, N = 926) = 39.2$, $p < .001$; for Round 2 smokers, $\chi^2(2, N = 926) = 24.5$, $p < .001$.
[a] Percentages represent clique members, liaisons, and isolates who are smokers.

few cliques with smokers and the number of smokers within cliques tended to be small. Of 28 cliques defined as smoking at Round 1, more than three fourths were made up of half or fewer smokers. A less liberal definition of clique smoking would have limited the sample for analyses.

At both rounds of data collection the majority of cliques were composed entirely of nonsmokers: 68% of cliques at Round 1 and 63% of cliques at Round 2 were nonsmoking. Of the remaining cliques, 2% at both rounds were all smoking cliques, and 30% at Round 1 and 34% at Round 2 were composed of smokers and nonsmokers.

Study Attrition

As described earlier, more subjects were included in the network analyses than in the samples used to test the hypotheses because of study attrition. Current smokers at Round 1 were less likely than nonsmokers to be present at Round 2, $\chi^2(1, N = 1,092) = 5.45, p < .05$. Subjects whose mothers were less educated also were underrepresented at Round 2, $\chi^2(3, N = 1,076) = 14.51, p < .01$. There were no differences, however, in social position, race, or gender.

Change in Peer Affiliations and Smoking Behavior From Round 1 to Round 2

For us to examine the influence and selection hypotheses, some subjects had to change social position between Round 1 and Round 2, and some had to change smoking behavior, including changing from nonsmoker to smoker and smoker to nonsmoker. Approximately 50% of subjects changed social position from Round 1 to Round 2, indicating sufficient change in peer affiliations to test the hypotheses. This percentage includes subjects who moved from one clique to another.

The current smoking rate at Round 1 was 14.0% and 18.8% at Round 2. From Round 1 to Round 2, 7.2% of subjects who were Round 1 nonsmokers became current smokers ($n = 67$) and 17.7% of Round 1 smokers quit smoking ($n = 23$). Although the percentages of subjects who changed smoking behavior are small, they are adequate for our analyses.

Data Analysis

Ten hypotheses guided the study: Four concern influence, four concern selection, and two concern deselection. Different subsamples were used to test the hypotheses. The subsamples, described with the results, applied restrictions that minimized the possibility of confounding one set of effects with another. The results are presented in contingency tables that generally cross-classify adolescent smoking behavior at one round with the smoking characteristics of their social position at the other round (e.g., clique smoking composition). Each table is described by the contingency coefficient and Fisher's exact test or the chi-square statistic (χ^2). The contingency coefficient is the most widely used measure of association in contingency tables and provides an estimate of the strength of the association (Cohen, 1988). The value of the Fisher's exact test for small samples and the chi-square statistic for large samples provides a measure of the statistical significance of the association (Fleiss, 1981). Because of the small sizes of some of the subsamples, we present results at the $p < .1$ level. Attention to the magnitude of the contingency coefficient may be more meaningful, however, in interpreting the results. According to Cohen (1988), contingency coefficients of .10, .29, and .45 represent small, medium, and large degrees of association, respectively.

Results

Influence

We tested four hypotheses to determine whether influence on smoking occurs within the context of adolescent peer groups. We consider influence on both current smoking initiation and quitting for clique members and liaisons. The analyses were restricted to clique members and clique liaisons because clique members and liaisons either belong to or have direct ties with a peer group and therefore only they can be directly influenced by their peer group. Liaisons with only indirect ties to cliques were excluded. We further restricted the sample by considering only cliques that survived from Round 1 to Round 2 to ensure that selection did not operate. We predicted that influence should be strongest in surviving cliques because adolescents are subject to their effect for a longer period of time. For completeness, we also report results that include all Round 1 cliques that did not survive to Round 2.

We hypothesized that Round 1 nonsmokers in smoking cliques would be more likely to become smokers than Round 1 nonsmokers in nonsmoking cliques. The analogous hypothesis for liaisons was that Round 1 liaison nonsmokers with links to smoking cliques would be more likely to smoke at Round 2 than Round 1 liaison nonsmokers with links to nonsmoking cliques. For quitting, we hypothesized that Round 1 smokers in cliques without other smokers would be more likely to be Round 2 nonsmokers (to quit) than Round 1 smokers in cliques with other smokers. Similarly, Round 1 liaison smokers with links to nonsmoking cliques would be more likely to be Round 2 nonsmokers (to quit) than liaisons with links to smoking cliques.

The results are presented in Tables 1.3–1.6 and support the influence hypotheses for smoking initiation (Tables 1.3 and 1.4) but not for smoking cessation (Tables 1.5 and 1.6). As shown in Table 1.3, nonsmokers in smoking cliques were significantly more likely to become smokers than nonsmokers in nonsmoking cliques; the effect of influence was stronger for subjects in surviving cliques (contingency coefficient = .32) than for subjects in all cliques (contingency coefficient = .12). In surviving cliques, 22.9% of nonsmokers in smoking cliques became smokers, whereas only 2.2% of nonsmokers in nonsmoking cliques became smokers. As shown in Table 1.4, nonsmoking liaisons to smoking cliques were more likely to become smokers than nonsmoking liaisons to nonsmoking cliques. The effect was about the same when the sample was restricted to surviving cliques and when all Round 1 cliques were included. In both samples, approximately 17% of nonsmoking liaisons to smoking cliques became smokers compared with approximately 6% of nonsmoking liaisons to nonsmoking cliques.

The percentage of smokers among clique members who quit did not vary by whether other

TABLE 1.3. Round 2 Smoking Behavior of Round 1 Nonsmokers in Smoking and Nonsmoking Cliques (in Percentages)

| Round 2 behavior | Type of Round 1 clique | | | |
| | Surviving only | | All | |
	Smoking	Nonsmoking	Smoking	Nonsmoking
Smoker	22.9	2.2	12.8	5.5
n	8	3	12	14
Nonsmoker	77.1	97.8	87.2	94.5
n	27	131	82	241
Total	100.0	100.0	100.0	100.0
n	35	134	94	255

Note: For subjects in *surviving only* cliques, $p < .001$, contingency coefficient = .32; for subjects in *all* cliques, $\chi^2(1, N = 349) = 5.27$, $p < .05$, contingency coefficient = .12.

TABLE 1.4. Round 2 Smoking Behavior of Round 1 Liaison Nonsmokers ($N = 136$) with Links to Smoking and Nonsmoking Cliques (in Percentages)

| Round 2 smoking behavior | Type of Round 1 clique | | | |
| | Surviving only | | All | |
	Smoking	Nonsmoking	Smoking	Nonsmoking
Smoker	17.1	5.5	17.2	6.0
n	6	6	10	9
Nonsmoker	82.9	94.6	82.7	94.0
n	29	104	48	140
Total	100.0	100.0	100.0	100.0
n	35	110	58	149

Note: For subjects linked to *surviving only* cliques, $\chi^2(1, N = 145) = 4.78$, $p < .05$, contingency coefficient = .18; for subjects linked to *all* cliques, $\chi^2(1, N = 207) = 6.25$, $p < .05$, contingency coefficient = .17.

smokers were present in the clique (Table 1.5) or among liaisons by whether their ties were to smoking or nonsmoking cliques (Table 1.6). The results for cessation did not vary by whether the sample included only surviving cliques or all cliques. Although not statistically significant, it is noteworthy that 25% of smokers in surviving smoking cliques quit by Round 2, whereas no smokers in nonsmoking cliques were quitters (Table 1.5). Given the small sample, however, this contradictory finding may not be particularly meaningful.

TABLE 1.5. Round 2 Smoking Behavior of Round 1 Smokers in Smoking and Nonsmoking Cliques (in Percentages)

Round 2 smoking behavior	Type of Round 1 clique			
	Surviving only		All	
	Smoking	Nonsmoking	Smoking	Nonsmoking
Smoker	75.0	100.0	78.3	81.3
n	9	12	18	3
Nonsmoker	25.0	0.0	21.7	18.7
n	3	0	5	3
Total	100.0	100.0	100.0	100.0
n	12	12	23	16

Note: The focal subject is the only smoker in nonsmoking cliques. Fisher's exact p was nonsignificant for subjects in *surviving only* (contingency coefficient = .35) and *all* (contingency coefficient = .04) cliques.

TABLE 1.6. Round 2 Smoking Behavior of Round 1 Liaison Smokers with Links to Smoking and Nonsmoking Cliques (in Percentages)

Round 2 smoking behavior	Type of Round 1 clique			
	Surviving only		All	
	Smoking	Nonsmoking	Smoking	Nonsmoking
Smoker	80.0	50.0	78.6	66.7
n	8	1	11	2
Nonsmoker	20.0	50.0	21.4	33.3
n	2	1	3	1
Total	100.0	100.0	100.0	100.0
n	10	2	14	3

Note: Fisher's exact p was nonsignificant for subjects linked to *surviving only* (contingency coefficient = .25) and *all* (contingency coefficient = .11) cliques.

Selection

We evaluated four selection hypotheses that propose that adolescents choose a peer group by matching their smoking behavior to that of the group. For the first three hypotheses we reasoned that clique members who change cliques and liaisons and isolates who join cliques select cliques with smoking behavior congruent to their own. The fourth hypothesis proposed that among isolates who become liaisons, smokers are more likely than nonsmokers to become linked with smoking cliques.

As before, we used two samples for the analyses; one had more stringent sample restrictions and the other was more inclusive. The first included adolescents who joined or were linked to only those cliques that survived from Round 1 to Round 2 and where the clique smoking behavior was the same at both rounds; the second sample included adolescents who joined either surviving or new Round 2 cliques (i.e., all Round 2 cliques). The first sample was used to ensure that the smoking behavior of the clique did not change over the period of time when selection took place, and therefore it is the sample of primary interest for assessing selection.

Because the selection hypotheses examine subjects who change social position from Round 1 to Round 2, we conducted preliminary analyses to determine whether smoking differentially affected change in social position. Round 1 smokers were significantly less likely to change social position than Round 1 nonsmokers: 38% of smokers compared with 52% of nonsmokers changed social position, $\chi^2(2, N = 926) = 9.6$, $p < .01$. As discussed later, the greater stability of smokers relative to nonsmokers may reflect selection processes that favor nonsmoking over smoking.

The results, presented in Table 1.7, show that adolescents in all three social positions joined cliques with adolescents of similar smoking behavior. The contingency coefficients were stronger for clique members and isolates than for liaisons. The results also generally are stronger when the sample is restricted to surviving cliques with stable smoking behavior. However, despite the strong tendency for clique members who smoke to join a smoking clique (contingency coefficient = .48), the results did not reach the $p < .1$ level of significance in the smaller restricted sample of clique members.

We found no support for the hypothesis that isolates who become liaisons select cliques on the basis of common smoking behavior (Table 1.8). The sample size was small, however. Of 27 Round 1 isolates who became Round 2 liaisons, only 3 were smokers at Round 1. It should be noted that because liaisons can have multiple links to cliques, the total number of links for the two samples (34 and 36) was greater than the sample size. Even so, the 3 smokers only had four links to cliques.

TABLE 1.7. Type of Round 2 Clique Joined by Round 1 Smokers and Nonsmokers by Social Position (in Percentages)

| | Round 1 social position | | | | | |
| | Clique member[a] (n = 38) | | Liaison (n = 117) | | Isolate (n = 38) | |
Type of Round 2 clique joined	Smoker	Nonsmoker	Smoker	Nonsmoker	Smoker	Nonsmoker
Surviving cliques[b]						
Smoking[c]	100.0	11.1	55.6	24.5	85.7	32.1
n	1	2	5	24	6	9
Nonsmoking[d]	0.0	88.9	44.4	75.5	14.3	67.9
n	0	16	4	74	1	19
Total	100.0	100.0	100.0	100.0	100.0	100.0
n	1	18	9	98	7	28
Fisher's exact *p*	ns		<.1		<.05	
Contingency coefficient	.48		.19		.43	
All cliques						
Smoking[c]	80.0	21.2	55.6	25.0	75.0	36.7
n	4	7	5	27	6	11
Nonsmoking[d]	20.0	78.8	44.4	75.0	25.0	63.3
n	1	26	4	81	2	19
Total	100.0	100.0	100.0	100.0	100.0	100.0
n	5	33	9	108	8	30
Fisher's exact *p*	<.05		<.1		<.1	
Contingency coefficient	.40		.18		.30	

[a] Sample restricted to clique members who change cliques from Round 1 to Round 2.
[b] Sample restricted to surviving cliques with the same smoking behavior at Round 1 and Round 2.
[c] Smoking cliques have at least one smoker other than the focal subject, who may or may not smoke.
[d] Nonsmoking cliques have no smokers except the focal subject, who may or may not smoke.

TABLE 1.8. Type of Round 2 Clique Links of Round 1 Isolate Smokers and Nonsmokers (n = 27) Who Become Liaisons (in Percentages)

| | Type of Round 2 clique | | | |
| | Surviving only | | All | |
Type of Round 2 clique link	Smoking	Nonsmoking	Smoking	Nonsmoking
Smoking	50.0	36.7	50.0	37.5
n	2	11	2	12
Nonsmoking	50.0	63.3	50.0	62.5
n	2	19	2	20
Total	100.0	100.0	100.0	100.0
n	4	30	4	32

Note: Fisher's exact *p* was nonsignificant for subjects linked to *surviving only* (contingency coefficient = .09) and *all* (contingency coefficient = .08) cliques.

Deselection

We evaluated two deselection hypotheses to determine whether cliques drop members or members drop cliques when member and clique behavior is dissimilar. We tested whether nonsmokers are more likely to leave smoking than nonsmoking cliques and whether smokers are more likely to leave cliques with no other smokers than ones with other smokers. We compared the following two samples: (a) subjects in only surviving cliques and cliques where the smoking behavior did not change from Round 1 to Round 2 and (b) subjects in all cliques at Round 1 regardless of whether they survived at Round 2. In both samples, only subjects whose smoking behavior did not change from Round 1 to Round 2 were used. The restrictions imposed on the first sample ensured that dissimilarity between the subject and clique could not have disappeared before deselection took place.

The results suggest that deselection operates for nonsmokers but not for smokers. In both samples, nonsmokers were more likely to be dropped or to leave cliques when there were smokers than

TABLE 1.9. Round 2 Clique Membership Status of Round 1 Nonsmokers in Smoking and Nonsmoking Cliques (in Percentages)

| Round 2 clique status | Type of Round 1 clique | | | |
| | Surviving only | | All | |
	Smoking	Nonsmoking[a]	Smoking	Nonsmoking
Left	42.4	24.3	67.1	45.6
n	14	35	55	110
Stayed	57.6	75.7	32.9	54.4
n	19	109	27	131
Total	100.0	100.0	100.0	100.0
n	33	144	82	241

Note: Only cliques with the same smoking behavior at Round 1 and Round 2 are included. For subjects in *surviving only* cliques, $\chi^2(1, N = 177) = 4.4$, $p < .05$ (contingency coefficient = .16); for subjects in *all* cliques, $\chi^2(1, N = 323) = 11.2$, $p < .001$ (contingency coefficient = .18).
[a] All subjects remained nonsmokers at Round 2.

TABLE 1.10. Round 2 Clique Membership Status of Round 1 Smokers in Smoking and Nonsmoking Cliques (in Percentages)

| Round 2 clique status | Type of Round 1 clique | | | |
| | Surviving only[a] | | All | |
	Smoking	Nonsmoking	Smoking	Nonsmoking
Left	21.4	0.0	38.9	53.9
n	3	0	7	7
Stayed	78.6	100.0	61.1	46.2
n	11	6	11	6
Total	100.0	100.0	100.0	100.0
n	14	6	18	13

Note: All subjects remained smokers at Round 2. Fisher's exact *p* was nonsignificant for subjects in *surviving only* (contingency coefficient = .27) cliques; $\chi^2(1, N = 31) = .68$, *ns* (contingency coefficient = .15) for subjects in *all* cliques.
[a] Only cliques with the same smoking behavior at Round 1 and Round 2 are included.

when there were no smokers (Table 1.9). Smokers, however, were not differentially dropped from, nor did they choose to leave, otherwise nonsmoking or smoking cliques (Table 1.10).

Discussion

This study is the first to use formal social network analysis to identify adolescent peer groups in order to study the contribution of influence and selection on peer group homogeneity. Most previous research in this area has studied pairs rather than groups, despite the clear centrality of groups to a wide range of social psychological theories, the saliency of peer groups in adolescence, and the focus on groups as the locus of explanation for a variety of adolescent behaviors. The social network approach provides a needed match of methods to research questions concerning peer groups. Measuring networks represents a distinct advancement over assuming the existence of peer groups from other data sources, such as pairs.

We focused on cigarette smoking as the behavior of interest, but our findings may generalize to other drugs as well, such as to alcohol and marijuana. Cigarette smoking among adolescents is widely attributed to peer group influence, whereas selection explanations are typically ignored. That peer influence is a major cause is a ubiquitous feature of considerations of adolescent drug use in general. We found that selection provides much of the explanation for similarity in smoking among adolescents in the same peer group. Indeed, comparison of the significant contingency coefficients suggests that selection contributes as much as influence to clique smoking homogeneity. Deselection is less important than either influence or selection in explaining the similarity in smoking among clique members. Because selection and influence contribute about equally to peer group homogeneity in adolescent smoking, the relative importance of influence is less than commonly assumed. Although our findings contradict the popular wisdom that peer group influence is largely responsible for adolescent smoking, they substantiate previous research that found that both influence and selection processes contribute to smoking homogeneity among peers (Cohen, 1977; Fisher & Bauman, 1988).

An important exception to our general findings concerns adolescents who are already smokers. Our results suggest that friends do not cause their smoking friends to quit smoking. Perhaps among smokers the strong influence of addiction supersedes any impact that might otherwise be attributable to friend influence. However, our sample for studying quitting was small, which limited our ability to adequately explore this behavior.

Our results suggest that peer group influence plays a smaller role in causing smoking than generally thought because selection appears to be at least equal to influence in peer group homogeneity. Other findings derived from our network analysis substantiate this conclusion. Specifically, the vast majority of peer group members were shown to be nonsmokers, yielding a majority of peer groups at both data collection rounds composed entirely of nonsmokers. Within peer groups, therefore, influence must favor nonsmoking rather than smoking for most adolescents.

Whereas influence provided about half of the explanation for the small number of adolescent smokers in peer groups, influence provided less explanation for smoking among nonpeer group members. This is important because most smoking occurred outside the context of peer groups: The majority of smokers were isolates. By definition, these adolescents cannot be directly influenced by a peer group. Nevertheless, peer groups might influence isolate smoking if isolates model the behavior of cliques characterized by smoking. However, because the prototypic behavior of most peer groups was nonsmoking, vastly more nonsmoking than smoking models were available to isolates, suggesting that indirect influence was not strong.

In contrast, selection might provide a greater explanation than influence for why smokers were overrepresented among isolates. This would be the case if cliques tended to keep smokers from joining. Indeed, we found that smokers were less likely than nonsmokers to change social position from the first to the second round of data collection. Perhaps cliques excluded smokers and limited interactions with liaison smokers, and this resulted in the majority of smokers being isolates. Deselection also could contribute to the explanation for isolate smoking if cliques also tend to expel smoking members. However, our findings do not suggest this. Adolescent smokers who were members of cliques were no more likely to leave nonsmoking than smoking cliques.

Although selection may be a more important explanation than influence for how isolates become smokers, other explanations may be needed. It could be that smoking is a result of social isolation.

Perhaps isolates have social inadequacies, and smoking is a coping mechanism. Another possible explanation is that the relationship between smoking and isolation is spurious. Perhaps both are manifestations of some other factor, such as school maladjustment or tendencies toward deviance. These are important areas for future research.

The findings from this study are not surprising from a theoretical perspective even though most previous empirical studies have not examined peer groups: The homogeneity of adolescent peer groups with respect to cigarette smoking results from both influence and selection processes. The findings are surprising, however, in light of the structure of adolescent peer relations and how adolescent cigarette smoking is commonly portrayed. That is, we did not find smoking to be primarily a peer group phenomenon largely caused by peer influence. Most smoking occurred among isolates, and selection provides a more likely explanation than influence for smoking by these adolescents. The results suggest the importance of other adolescent peer structures than cliques to adolescent behavior. If we had not used a social network approach, which allowed investigation of influence and selection processes within peer groups and vis-à-vis nonpeer group members, we would not have arrived at this conclusion. An earlier study of influence and selection processes using these same data but using friendship pairs (Fisher & Bauman, 1988) did not suggest the importance of network isolation to adolescent smoking. Clearly, other determinants of adolescent smoking than peer group influence are needed to advance our understanding of this behavior, and perhaps other adolescent behaviors as well.

Our findings have practical relevance to the prevention of adolescent cigarette smoking, which is a priority health objective for the nation (U.S. Department of Health and Human Services, 1990). Many smoking prevention programs reflect the assumption that peer group influence is a major cause of adolescent smoking and tailor activities toward helping adolescents recognize and resist peer pressures to smoke. Evaluation of these programs suggests that they have weak to moderate influence on adolescent smoking (Bruvold, 1993; Kozlowski,

Coambs, Ferrence, & Adlaf, 1989). Perhaps greater effectiveness would be achieved if more emphasis were placed on fostering the natural conditions of the peer group and in considering the peer group an ally in smoking prevention. Activities might focus more on helping adolescents join and function in cliques than on resisting peer influence. In addition, perhaps isolates should be considered high risk targets for smoking prevention programs.

More research is needed on influence and selection processes beyond the scope of this study. Our analysis of these processes was based on measures of peer groups derived from data collected at two occasions. These "snapshots" do not capture the dynamic nature of interactions within peer groups that contribute to homogeneity. They do not reveal, for example, whether influence and selection processes operate simultaneously, in some special order, or differently for some groups than others. The total complexity of influence and selection processes undoubtedly is not reflected by our findings. In addition, our results are simplistic in that we did not consider a range of factors that could interact with influence and selection processes. A number of studies, for example, have shown that peer groups inevitably recognize a leader (e.g., Dunphy, 1963; Sherif & Sherif, 1964), whose behavior might be a stronger source of attraction and influence than the peer group as a whole. Latané's (1981) social impact theory specifies that social influence processes are a function of the strength, immediacy, and number of other people present, suggesting several factors, such as clique size, that warrant further investigation.

Our study was limited in other ways. We did not investigate differences in influence and selection processes by differences in group composition; for example, according to characteristics along which the cliques tended to be homogeneous, such as gender, race, and socioeconomic status (Ennett et al., 1994). Our previous research indicated that cliques are more pertinent to smoking for girls, White adolescents, and adolescents with lower socioeconomic status. Therefore, it may be possible that the influence and selection processes described in this study might be less important for boys, Black adolescents, and those with higher socioeconomic status. Unfortunately, analyzing this possibility was not feasible because, given the low prevalence of smoking, partitioning the sample by demographic characteristics would have resulted in insufficient cases for study. This is an area for future investigation.

Although study attrition was not great (13.5%), significantly more current smokers at Round 1 were lost to follow-up than nonsmokers. It is difficult to know how the disproportionate loss of smokers might have biased the study findings. Because we studied natural groups rather than artificial groups in a laboratory setting, we were not able to manipulate or control characteristics of groups that might affect influence and selection processes. Although an experimental approach would be inappropriate in this context, our inferences concerning causes of smoking homogeneity should be interpreted accordingly.

A final limitation is that we did not consider other adolescent characteristics than smoking. Indeed, because smoking is relatively unusual among adolescents, difficult to quit, and perhaps less visible than many behaviors, other attributes may be more informative for studying influence and selection. Peer group influence is considered to be fundamental to many more behaviors than those involving cigarettes or other drugs (Bandura, 1977; Brown, 1989; Clausen, 1968; Douvan & Adelson, 1966; Savin-Williams & Berndt, 1990). That influence can be confused for selection has been suggested for adolescent sexual behavior, political orientation, delinquency, educational aspirations, value similarity, and a host of other variables (Billy & Udry, 1985; Cohen, 1977; Jussim & Osgood, 1989; Kandel, 1978a). Here again, however, most research has focused on friendship pairs rather than peer groups. Studies of the contribution of influence and selection to a wide variety of adolescent behaviors might benefit from using a social network approach.

REFERENCES

Ball, S. J. (1981). *Beachside comprehensive*. Cambridge, England: Cambridge University Press.

Bandura, A. (1977). *Social learning theory*. Englewood Cliffs, NJ: Prentice Hall.

Bauman, K. E., & Dent, C. W. (1982). Influence of an objective measure on self-reports of behavior. *Journal of Applied Psychology, 67*, 623–628.

Bauman, K. E., & Fisher, L. A. (1986). Findings from longitudinal studies of adolescent smoking and drinking. *Journal of Youth and Adolescence, 15*, 345–353.

Bauman, K. E., Fisher, L. A., Bryan, E. S., & Chenoweth, R. L. (1984). Antecedents, subjective expected utility, and behavior: A study of adolescent cigarette smoking. *Addictive Behaviors, 9*, 121–136.

Billy, J. O. G., & Udry, J. R. (1985). Patterns of adolescent friendship and effects on sexual behavior. *Social Psychology Quarterly, 48*, 27–41.

Blos, P. (1962). *On adolescence.* New York: Free Press of Glencoe.

Blythe, D. A., Hill, J. P., & Thiel, K. S. (1982). Early adolescents' significant others: Grade and gender differences in perceived relationships with familial and nonfamilial adults and young people. *Journal of Youth and Adolescence, 11*, 425–445.

Brown, B. B. (1989). The role of peer groups in adolescents' adjustment to secondary school. In T. G. Berndt & G. W. Ladd (Eds.), *Peer relationships in child development* (pp. 188–215). New York: Wiley.

Bruvold, W. H. (1993). A meta-analysis of adolescent smoking prevention programs. *American Journal of Public Health, 83*, 872–880.

Burgess, R. L., & Akers, R. L. (1966). A differential association–reinforcement theory of criminal behavior. *Social Problems, 14*, 128–147.

Clausen, J. (1968). *Socialization and society.* Boston: Little, Brown.

Cohen, J. M. (1977). Sources of peer group homogeneity. *Sociology of Education, 50*, 227–241.

Cohen, J. (1988). *Statistical power analysis for the behavioral sciences.* Hillsdale, NJ: Erlbaum.

Coleman, J. C. (1980). Friendship and the peer group in adolescence. In J. Adelson (Ed.), *Handbook of adolescent psychology* (pp. 408–431). New York: Wiley.

Coleman, J. S. (1961). *The adolescent society.* New York: Free Press of Glencoe.

Davies, M., & Kandel, D. B. (1981). Parental and peer influences on adolescents' educational plans. *Psychological Bulletin, 52*, 177–193.

Douvan, E., & Adelson, J. (1966). *The adolescent experience.* New York: Wiley.

Dunphy, D. C. (1963). The social structure of urban adolescent peer groups. *Sociometry, 26*, 230–246.

Eder, D. (1985). The cycle of popularity: Interpersonal relations among female adolescents. *Sociology of Education, 58*, 154–165.

Ennett, S. T. (1991). *A social network analysis of adolescent cigarette smoking.* Unpublished doctoral dissertation, University of North Carolina at Chapel Hill.

Ennett, S. T., & Bauman, K. E. (1993). Peer group structure and adolescent cigarette smoking: A social network analysis. *Journal of Health and Social Behavior, 34*, 226–236.

Ennett, S. T., Bauman, K. E., & Koch, G. G. (1994). Variability in cigarette smoking within and between adolescent friendship cliques. *Addictive Behaviors, 19*, 295–305.

Feld, S. L. (1981). The focused organization of social ties. *American Journal of Sociology, 86*, 1015–1035.

Festinger, L., Schachter, S., & Back, K. (1950). *Social pressures in informal groups.* Stanford, CA: Stanford University Press.

Fisher, L. A., & Bauman, K. E. (1988). Influence and selection in the friend–adolescent relationship: Findings from studies of adolescent smoking and drinking. *Journal of Applied Social Psychology, 18*, 289–314.

Flay, B. R., d'Avernas, J. R., Best, J. A., Kersell, M. W., & Ryan, K. B. (1983). Cigarette smoking: Why young people do it and ways of preventing it. In P. McGrath & P. Firestone (Eds.), *Pediatric and adolescent behavioral medicine* (pp. 132–183). New York: Springer-Verlag.

Fleiss, J. L. (1981). *Statistical methods for rates and proportions.* New York: Wiley.

Glynn, T. J. (1989). Essential elements of school-based smoking prevention programs. *Journal of School Health, 59*, 181–188.

Granovetter, M. S. (1973). The strength of weak ties. *American Journal of Sociology, 78*, 1360–1380.

Hallinan, M. T. (1980). Patterns of cliquing among youth. In H. C. Foot, A. J. Chapman, & J. R. Smith (Eds.), *Friendship and social relations in children* (pp. 321–342). New York: Wiley.

Hansell, S. (1981). Ego development and peer friendship networks. *Sociology of Education, 54*, 51–63.

Hare, A. P. (1964). Interpersonal relations in the small group. In R. E. L. Faris (Ed.), *Handbook of modern sociology* (pp. 217–271). Chicago: Rand McNally.

Hartup, W. W. (1983). Peer relations. In P. H. Mussen (Ed.), *Handbook of child psychology* (Vol. 4, pp. 103–196). New York: Wiley.

Hollingshead, A. B. (1949). *Elmtown's youth.* New York: Wiley.

Homans, G. C. (1950). *The human group.* New York: Harcourt, Brace & World.

Huba, G. J., & Bentler, P. M. (1980). The role of peer and adult models for drug taking at different stages in adolescence. *Journal of Youth and Adolescence, 9*, 449–465.

Iannotti, R. J., & Bush, P. J. (1992). Perceived vs. actual friends' use of alcohol, cigarettes, marijuana, and cocaine: Which has the most influence? *Journal of Youth and Adolescence, 21*, 375–389.

Jessor, R., & Jessor, S. L. (1977). *Problem behavior and psychosocial development. A longitudinal study of youth.* San Diego, CA: Academic Press.

Jussim, L., & Osgood, D. W. (1989). Influence and similarity among friends: An integrative model applied to incarcerated adolescents. *Social Psychology Quarterly, 52*, 98–112.

Kandel, D. B. (1978a). Homophily, selection, and socialization in adolescent friendships. *American Journal of Sociology, 84*, 427–436.

Kandel, D. B. (1978b). Similarity in real-life adolescent friendship pairs. *Journal of Personality and Social Psychology, 36,* 306–312.

Kozlowski, L. T., Coambs, R. B., Ferrence, R. G., & Adlaf, E. M. (1989). Preventing smoking and other drug use: Let the buyer beware and the intervention be apt. *Canadian Journal of Public Health, 80,* 452–456.

Lanese, R. R., Banks, P. R., & Keller, M. D. (1972). Smoking behavior in a teenage population: A multivariate conceptual approach. *American Journal of Public Health, 62,* 807–813.

Latané, B. (1981). The psychology of social impact. *American Psychologist, 36,* 343–356.

McAlister, A. L., Krosnick, J. A., & Milburn, M. A. (1984). Causes of adolescent cigarette smoking: Tests of a structured equation model. *Social Psychology Quarterly, 47,* 24–36.

Moreland, R. L., & Levine, J. M. (1992). The composition of small groups. In E. J. Lawler, B. Markovsky, C. Ridgeway, & H. A. Walker (Eds.), *Advances in group processes* (Vol. 9, pp. 237–280). Greenwich, CT: JAI Press.

Moskowitz, J. M. (1983). Preventing adolescent substance abuse through drug education. In T. J. Glynn, C. G. Luekefeld, & J. P. Ludford (Eds.), *Preventing adolescent drug abuse: Intervention strategies* (NIDA Research Monograph 47; DHHS Publication No. ADM 86–1280). Washington, DC: U.S. Government Printing Office.

Newcomb, T. M. (1950). *Social psychology.* Hinsdale, IL: Dryden Press.

Richards, W. D. (1989). *The NEGOPY network analysis program.* Burnaby, British Columbia, Canada: Department of Communications, Simon Fraser University.

Richards, W. D., & Rice, R. E. (1981). The NEGOPY network analysis program. *Social Networks, 3,* 215–223.

Savin-Williams, R. C., & Berndt, T. J. (1990). Friendship and peer relations. In S. S. Feldman & G. R. Elliott (Eds.), *At the threshold: The developing adolescent* (pp. 277–307). Cambridge, MA: Harvard University Press.

Sherif, M. (1948). *An outline of social psychology.* New York: Harper & Row.

Sherif, M., & Sherif, C. W. (1964). *Exploration into conformity and deviation of adolescents.* New York: Harper & Row.

Shrum, W., & Cheek, N. H. (1987). Social structure during the school years: Onset of the degrouping process. *American Sociological Review, 52,* 218–223.

Smelser, N. J. (1988). Social structure. In N. J. Smelser (Ed.), *Handbook of sociology* (pp. 103–129). Newbury Park, CA: Sage.

Sussman, S., Dent, C. W., Stacy, A. W., Burciaga, C., Raynor, A., Turner, G. E., Charlin, V., Craig, S., Hansen, W. B., Burton, D., & Flay, B. R. (1990). Peer-group association and adolescent tobacco use. *Journal of Abnormal Psychology, 99,* 349–352.

Sutherland, E. H., & Cressey, D. R. (1978). *Criminology* (10th ed.). Philadelphia: Lippincott.

Urberg, K. A., Cheng, C. H., & Shyu, S. J. (1991). Grade changes in peer influence on adolescent cigarette smoking: A comparison of two measures. *Addictive Behaviors, 16,* 21–28.

Urberg, K. A., Shyu, S. J., & Liang, J. (1990). Peer influence in adolescent smoking. *Addictive Behaviors, 15,* 247–255.

U.S. Department of Health and Human Services. (1990). *Healthy people 2000.* Washington, DC: U.S. Government Printing Office.

van Roosmalen, E. H., & McDaniel, S. A. (1989). Peer group influence as a factor in smoking behavior of adolescents. *Adolescence, 24,* 801–816.

Wellman, B. (1988). Structural analysis: From method and metaphor to theory and substance. In B. Wellman & S. D. Berkowitz (Eds.), *Social structures: A network approach* (pp. 19–61). Cambridge, England: Cambridge University Press.

Received April 9, 1993
Revision received February 18, 1994
Accepted March 3, 1994 ■

Some Effects of Proportions on Group Life: Skewed Sex Ratios and Responses to Token Women[1]

Rosabeth Moss Kanter*

Proportions, that is, *relative* numbers of socially and culturally different people in a group, are seen as critical in shaping interaction dynamics, and four group types are identified on the basis of varying proportional compositions. "Skewed" groups contain a large preponderance of one type (the numerical "dominants") over another (the rare "tokens"). A framework is developed for conceptualizing the processes that occur between dominants and tokens. Three perceptual phenomena are associated with tokens: visibility (tokens capture a disproportionate awareness share), polarization (differences between tokens and dominants are exaggerated), and assimilation (tokens' attributes are distorted to fit preexisting generalizations about their social type). Visibility generates performance pressures; polarization leads dominants to heighten their group boundaries; and assimilation leads to the tokens' role entrapment. Illustrations are drawn from a field study in a large industrial corporation. Concepts are extended to tokens of all kinds, and research issues are identified.

* Yale University and Harvard Law School.

[1] Thanks are due to the staff of "Industrial Supply Corporation," the pseudonymous corporation which invited and provided support for this research along with permission for use of the data in this paper. The research was part of a larger project on social structural factors in organizational behavior reported in Kanter (in press). An early version of this article was prepared for the Center for Research on Women in Higher Education and the Professions, Wellesley College, which provided some additional financial support. Barry Stein's colleagueship was especially valuable. This article was completed while the author held a Guggenheim fellowship.

In his classic analysis of the significance of numbers in social life, Georg Simmel (1950) argued persuasively that numerical modifications effect qualitative transformations in group interaction. Simmel dealt almost exclusively with the impact of absolute numbers, however, with group size as a determinant of form and process. The matter of relative numbers, of proportion of interacting social types, was left unexamined. But this feature of collectivities has an impact on behavior. Its neglect has sometimes led to inappropriate or misleading conclusions.

This paper defines the issues that need to be explored. It addresses itself to proportion as a significant aspect of social life, particularly important for understanding interactions in groups composed of people of different cultural categories or statuses. It argues that groups with varying proportions of people of different social types differ qualitatively in dynamics and process. This difference is not merely a function of cultural diversity or "status incongruence" (Zaleznick, Christensen, and Roethlisberger 1958, pp. 56–68); it reflects the effects of contact across categories as a function of their proportional representation in the system.

Four group types can be identified on the basis of various proportional representations of kinds of people. *Uniform* groups have only one kind of person, one significant social type. The group may develop its own differentiations, of course, but groups considered uniform are homogeneous with respect to salient external master statuses such as sex, race, or ethnicity. Uniform groups have a "typological ratio" of 100:0. *Skewed* groups are those in which there is a large preponderance of one type over another, up to a ratio of perhaps 85:15. The numerically dominant types also control the group and its culture in enough ways to be labeled "dominants." The few of another type in a skewed group can appropriately be called "tokens," because they are often treated as representatives of their category, as symbols rather than individuals. If the absolute size of the skewed group is small, tokens can also be solitary individuals or "solos," the only one of their kind present. But even if there are two tokens in a skewed group, it is difficult for them to generate an alliance that can become powerful in the group. Next, *tilted* groups

begin to move toward less extreme distributions and less exaggerated effects. In this situation, with a ratio of perhaps 65:35, dominants are just a majority and tokens a minority. Minority members are potentially allies, can form coalitions, and can affect the culture of the group. They begin to become individuals differentiated from each other as well as a type differentiated from the majority. Finally, at a typological ratio of about 60:40 down to 50:50, the group becomes *balanced*. Culture and interaction reflect this balance. Majority and minority turn into potential subgroups which may or may not generate actual type-based identifications. Outcomes for individuals in such a balanced peer group, regardless of type, will depend on other structural and personal factors, including formation of subgroups or differentiated roles and abilities. Figure 2.1 schematizes the four group types.

The characteristics of the second type, the skewed group, provide a relevant starting point for this examination of the effects of proportion, for although this group represents an extreme instance of the phenomenon, it is one encountered by large numbers of women in groups and organizations in which numerical distributions have traditionally favored men.

At the same time, this paper is oriented toward enlarging our understanding of male-female interaction and the situations facing women in organizations by introducing structural and contextual effects. Most analyses to date locate male-female interaction issues either in broad cultural traditions and the sexual division of labor in society or in the psychology of men and women whether based on biology or socialization (Kanter 1976c). In both macroscopic and microscopic analysis, sex and gender components are sometimes confounded by situational and structural effects. For example, successful women executives are almost always numerically rare in their organizations, whereas working women are disproportionately concentrated in low-opportunity occupations. Conclusions about "women's behavior" or "male attitudes" drawn from such situations may sometimes confuse the effect of situation with the effect of sex roles; indeed such variables as position in opportunity and power structures account for a large number of phenomena related to work behavior that

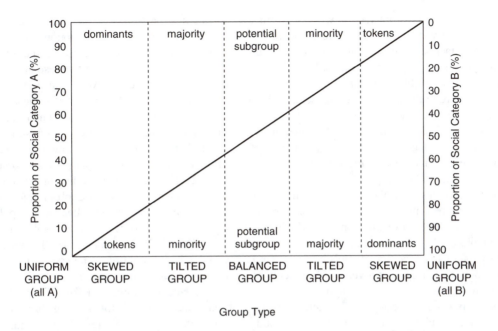

FIGURE 2.1 ■ Group types as defined by proportional representation of two social categories in a membership.

have been labeled "sex differences" (Kanter 1975, 1976a, 1976d, and in press). Therefore this paper focuses on an intermediate-level analysis: how group structures shape interaction contexts and influence particular patterns of male-female interaction. One advantage of such an approach is that it is then possible to generalize beyond male-female relations to persons-of-one-kind and person-of-another-kind interaction in various contexts, also making possible the untangling of what exactly *is* unique about the male-female case.

The study of particular proportions of women in predominantly male groups is thus relevant to a concern with social organization and group process as well as with male-female interaction. The analysis presented here deals with interaction in face-to-face groups with highly skewed sex ratios. More specifically, the focus is upon what happens to women who occupy token statuses and are alone or nearly alone in a peer group of men. This situation is commonly faced by women in management and the professions, and it is increasingly faced by women entering formerly all-male fields at every level of organizations. But proportional scarcity is not unique to women. Men can also find

themselves alone among women, blacks among whites, very old people among the young, straight people among gays, the blind among the sighted. The dynamics of interaction (the process) is likely to be very similar in all such cases, even though the content of interaction may reflect the special culture and traditional roles of both token and members of the numerically dominant category.

Use of the term "token" for the minority member rather than "solo," "solitary," or "lone" highlights some special characteristics associated with that position. Tokens are not merely deviants or people who differ from other group members along any one dimension. They are people identified by ascribed characteristics (master statuses such as sex, race, religion, ethnic group, age, etc.) or other characteristics that carry with them a set of assumptions about culture, status, and behavior highly salient for majority category members. They bring these "auxiliary traits," in Hughes's (1944) term, into situations in which they differ from other people not in ability to do a task or in acceptance of work norms but only in terms of these secondary and informal assumptions. The importance of these auxiliary traits is heightened if members of the majority group have a history of interacting with the token's category in ways that are quite different from the demands of task accomplishment in the present situation—as is true of men with women. Furthermore, because tokens are by definition alone or virtually alone, they are in the position of representing their ascribed category to the group, whether they choose to do so or not. They can never be just another member while their category is so rare; they will always be a hyphenated member, as in "woman-engineer" or "male-nurse" or "black-physican."

People can thus be in the token position even if they have not been placed there deliberately for display by officials of an organization. It is sufficient to be in a place where others of that category are not usually found, to be the first of one's kind to enter a new group, or to represent a very different culture and set of interactional capacities to members of the numerically dominant category. The term "token" reflects one's status as a symbol of one's kind. However, lone people of one type among members of another are not necessarily tokens if their presence is taken for granted in the group or organization and incorporated into the dominant culture, so that their loneness is merely the accidental result of random distributions rather than a reflection of the rarity of their type in that system.[2]

While the dynamics of tokenism are likely to operate in some form whenever proportional representation in a collectivity is highly skewed, even if the dominant group does not intend to put the token at a disadvantage, two conditions can heighten and dramatize the effects, making them more visible to the analyst: (1) the token's social category (master status) is physically obvious, as in the case of sex, and (2) the token's social type is not only rare but also new to the setting of the dominants. The latter situation may or may not be conceptually distinct from rarity, although it allows us to see the development of patterns of adjustment as well as the perception of and response to tokens. Subsequent

tokens have less surprise value and may be thrust into token roles with less disruption to the system.

With only a few exceptions, the effects of differences in proportional representation within collectivities have received little previous attention. Hughes (1944, 1946, 1958) described the dynamics of white work groups entered by a few blacks, pointing out the dilemmas posed by status contradictions and illuminating the sources of group discomfort as they put pressures on the rare blacks. There are a few studies of other kinds of tokens such as Segal's (1962) observations of male nurses in a largely female colleague group. Reports of professional women in male-dominated fields (e.g., Epstein 1970; Hennig 1970; Lynch 1973; Cussler 1958) mention some special issues raised by numerical rarity. More recently, Laws (1975) has developed a framework for defining the induction of a woman into token status through interaction with a sponsor representing the numerically dominant group. Wolman and Frank (1975) reported observations of solo women in professional-training groups; Taylor and Fiske (1975) have developed experimental data on the perception of token blacks in a white male group. The material in all of these studies still needs a theoretical framework.

With the exceptions noted, research has generally failed to take into account the effects of relative numbers on interaction. Yet such effects could critically change the interpretation of familiar findings. The research of Strodtbeck and his colleagues (Strodtbeck and Mann 1956; Strodtbeck, James, and Hawkins 1957) on mock jury deliberations is often cited as evidence that men tend to play initiating, task-oriented roles in small groups, whereas women tend to play reactive, socioemotional roles. Yet a reexamination of these investigations indicates that men far outnumbered women as research subjects. There were more than twice as many men as women (86 to 41) in the 12 small groups in which

---

[2] As an anonymous reviewer pointed out, newness is more easily distinguished from rarity conceptually than it may be empirically, and further research should make this distinction. It should also specify the conditions under which "accidental loneness" (or small relative numbers) does not have the extreme effects

noted here: when the difference is noted but not considered very important, as in the case of baseball teams that may have only one or two black members but lack token dynamics because of the large number of teams with many black members.

women were found to play stereotypical expressive roles.[3] The actual sex composition of each of the small groups is not reported, although it could have important implications for the results. Perhaps it was women's scarcity in skewed groups that pushed them into classical positions and men's numerical superiority that gave them an edge in task performance. Similarly, in the early kibbutzim, collective villages in Israel that theoretically espoused equality of the sexes but were unable fully to implement it, women could be pushed into traditional service positions (see Tiger and Shepher 1975) because there were often more than twice as many men as women in a kibbutz. Again, relative numbers interfered with a fair test of what men or women can "naturally" do (Kanter 1976b).

Thus systematic analysis of the dynamics of systems with skewed distributions of social types— tokens in the midst of numerical dominants—is overdue. This paper begins to define a framework for understanding the dynamics of tokenism, illustrated by field observations of female tokens among male dominants.

The Field Study

The forms of interaction in the presence of token women were identified in a field study of a large industrial corporation, one of the *Fortune 500* firms (see Kanter [in press] for a description of the setting). The sales force of one division was investigated in detail because women were entering it for the first time. The first saleswoman was hired in 1972; by the end of 1974, there had been about 20 in training or on assignment (several had left the company) out of a sales force of over 300 men. The geographically decentralized nature of sales meant, however, that in training programs or in field offices women were likely to be one of 10 or 12 sales workers; in a few cases, two women were together in a group of a dozen sales personnel. Studying women who were selling industrial goods had particular

advantages: (1) sales is a field with strong cultural traditions and folklore and one in which interpersonal skills rather than expertise count heavily, thus making informal and cultural aspects of group interaction salient and visible even for members themselves; and (2) sales workers have to manage relations not only with work peers but with customers as well, thus giving the women two sets of majority groups with which to interact. Sixteen women in sales and distribution were interviewed in depth. Over 40 male peers and managers were also interviewed. Sales-training groups were observed both in session and at informal social gatherings for approximately 100 hours. Additional units of the organization were studied for other research purposes.

Theoretical Framework

The framework set forth here proceeds from the Simmelian assumption that form determines process, narrowing the universe of interaction possibilities. The form of a group with a skewed distribution of social types generates certain perceptions of the tokens by the dominants. These perceptions determine the interaction dynamics between tokens and dominants and create the pressures dominants impose on tokens. In turn, there are typical token responses to these pressures.

The proportional rarity of tokens is associated with three perceptual phenomena: visibility, polarization, and assimilation. First, tokens, one by one, have higher visibility than dominants looked at alone: they capture a larger awareness share. A group member's awareness share, averaged over shares of other individuals of the same social type, declines as the proportion of total membership occupied by the category increases, because each individual becomes less and less surprising, unique, or note-worthy; in Gestalt terms, they more easily become "ground" rather than "figure." But for tokens there is a "law of increasing returns": as individuals of their type come to represent a *smaller* numerical proportion of the group, they potentially capture a *larger* share of the group members' awareness.

---

[3] The 17 least active subjects (out of a total of 144) were dropped from the analysis; their sex is not mentioned in published reports. Those 17 might have skewed the sex distribution even further.

Polarization or exaggeration of differences is the second perceptual tendency. The presence of a person bearing a different set of social characteristics makes members of a numerically dominant group more aware both of their commonalities with and their differences from the token. There is a tendency to exaggerate the extent of the differences, especially because tokens are by definition too few in number to prevent the application of familiar generalizations or stereotypes. It is thus easier for the commonalities of dominants to be defined in contrast to the token than it would be in a more numerically equal situation. One person can also be perceptually isolated and seen as cut off from the group more easily than many, who begin to represent a significant proportion of the group itself.

Assimilation, the third perceptual tendency, involves the use of stereotypes or familiar generalizations about a person's social type. The characteristics of a token tend to be distorted to fit the generalization. If there are enough people of the token's type to let discrepant examples occur, it is possible that the generalization will change to accommodate the accumulated cases. But if individuals of that type are only a small proportion of the group, it is easier to retain the generalization and distort the perception of the token.

Taylor and Fiske's (1976; Taylor 1975) laboratory experiments provide supportive evidence for these propositions. They played a tape of a group discussion to subjects while showing them pictures of the group and then asked them for their impressions of group members on a number of dimensions. The tape was the same for all subjects, but the purported composition of the group varied. The pictures illustrated either an otherwise all-white male group with one black man (the token condition) or a mixed black-white male group. In the token condition, the subjects paid disproportionate attention to the token, overemphasized his prominence in the group, and exaggerated his attributes. Similarly, the token was perceived as playing special roles in the group, often highly stereotypical ones. By contrast, in the integrated condition, subjects recalled no more about blacks than whites and evaluated their attributes in about the same way.

Visibility, polarization, and assimilation are each associated with particular interaction dynamics

that in turn generate typical token responses. These dynamics are similar regardless of the category from which the token comes, although the token's social type and history of relationships with dominants shape the content of specific interactions. Visibility creates performance pressures on the token. Polarization leads to group boundary heightening and isolation of the token. And assimilation results in the token's role entrapment.

Performance Pressures

The women in the sales force I studied were highly visible, much more so than their male peers. Managers commonly reported that they were the subject of conversation, questioning, gossip, and careful scrutiny. Their placements were known and observed throughout the sales unit, while those of men typically were not. Such visibility created a set of performance pressures: characteristics and standards true for tokens alone. Tokens typically perform under conditions different from those of dominants.

1. Public Performance

It was difficult for the women to do anything in training programs or in the field that did not attract public notice. The women found that they did not have to go out of their way to be noticed or to get the attention of management at sales meetings. One woman reported, "I've been at sales meetings where all the trainees were going up to the managers—'Hi, Mr. So-and-So'—trying to make that impression, wearing a strawberry tie, whatever, something that they could be remembered by. Whereas there were three of us [women] in a group of 50, and all we had to do was walk in, and everyone recognized us."

Automatic notice meant that women could not remain anonymous or hide in the crowd; all their actions were public. Their mistakes and their relationships were known as readily as any other information. It was impossible for them to have any privacy within the company. The women were always viewed by an audience, leading several to complain of "over-observation."

2. Extension of Consequences

The women were visible as category members, and as such their acts tended to have added symbolic consequences. Some women were told that their performance could affect the prospects for other women in the company. They were thus not acting for themselves alone but carrying the burden of representing their category. In informal conversations, they were often measured by two yardsticks: how *as women* they carried out the sales role and how *as salesworkers* they lived up to images of womanhood. In short, every act tended to be evaluated beyond its meaning for the organization and taken as a sign of "how women do in sales." The women were aware of the extra symbolic consequences attached to their acts.

3. Attention to a Token's Discrepant Characteristics

A token's visibility stems from characteristics—attributes of a master status—that threaten to blot out other aspects of the token's performance. While the token captures attention, it is often for discrepant characteristics, for the auxiliary traits that provide token status. No token in the study had to work hard to have her presence noticed, but she did have to work hard to have her achievements noticed. In the sales force, the women found that their technical abilities were likely to be eclipsed by their physical appearance, and thus an additional performance pressure was created. The women had to put in extra effort to make their technical skills known, to work twice as hard to prove their competence. Both male peers and customers would tend to forget information women provided about their experiences and credentials, while noticing and remembering such secondary attributes as style of dress.

4. Fear of Retaliation

The women were also aware of another performance pressure: to avoid making the dominants look bad. Tokenism sets up a dynamic that makes tokens afraid of outstanding performance in group events and tasks. When a token does well enough to show up a dominant, it cannot be kept a secret, because all eyes are on the token. Therefore it is difficult in such a situation to avoid the public humiliation of a

dominant. Thus, paradoxically, while the token women felt they had to do better than anyone else in order to be seen as competent and allowed to continue, they also felt in some cases that their successes would not be rewarded and should be kept secret. One woman had trouble understanding this and complained of her treatment by managers. They had fired another woman for not being aggressive enough, she reported; yet she, who succeeded in doing all they asked and had brought in the largest amount of new business during the past year, was criticized for being too aggressive, too much of a hustler.

Responses of Tokens to Performance Pressures

There are two typical ways tokens respond to these performance pressures. The first involves overachievement. Aware of the performance pressures, several of the saleswomen put in extra effort, promoted themselves and their work at every opportunity, and let those around them know how well they were doing. These women evoked threats of retaliation. On the gossip circuit, they were known to be doing well but aspiring too high too fast; a common prediction was that they would be cut down to size soon.

The second response is more common and is typical of findings of other investigators. It involves attempts to limit visibility, to become socially invisible. This strategy characterizes women who try to minimize their sexual attributes so as to blend unnoticeably into the predominant male culture, perhaps by adopting "mannish dress" (Hennig 1970, chap. 6). Or it can include avoidance of public events and occasions for performance—staying away from meetings, working at home rather than in the office, keeping silent at meetings. Several of the saleswomen deliberately kept such a low profile, unlike male peers who tended to seize every opportunity to make themselves noticed. They avoided conflict, risks, and controversial situations. Those women preferring social invisibility also made little attempt to make their achievements publicly known or to get credit for their own contributions to problem solving or other organizational tasks. They are like other women in the research literature who have let others assume visible leadership (Megaree 1969) or take credit for their accomplishments (Lynch 1973; Cussler 1958). These women did blend into the background, but they also limited recognition of their competence.

This analysis suggests a reexamination of the "fear of success in women" hypothesis. Perhaps what has been called fear of success is really the token woman's fear of visibility. The original research identifying this concept created a hypothetical situation in which a woman was at the top of her class in medical school—a token woman in a male peer group. Such a situation puts pressure on a woman to make herself and her achievements invisible, to deny success. Attempts to replicate the initial findings using settings in which women were not so clearly tokens produced very different results. And in other studies (e.g., Levine and Crumrine 1975), the hypothesis that fear of success is a female-linked trait has not been confirmed. (See Sarason [1973] for a discussion of fear of visibility among minorities.)

Boundary Heightening

Polarization or exaggeration of the token's attributes in contrast to those of the dominants sets a second set of dynamics in motion. The presence of a token makes dominants more aware of what they have in common at the same time that it threatens that commonality. Indeed it is often at those moments when a collectivity is threatened with change that its culture and bonds become evident to it; only when an obvious outsider appears do group members suddenly realize their common bond as insiders. Dominants thus tend to exaggerate both their commonality and the token's difference, moving to heighten boundaries of which previously they might not even have been aware.[4]

1. Exaggeration of Dominants' Culture

Majority members assert or reclaim group solidarity and reaffirm shared in-group understandings by emphasizing and exaggerating those cultural elements which they share in contrast to the token. The token becomes both occasion and audience for the highlighting and dramatization of those themes that differentiate the token as outsider from the insider. Ironically, tokens (unlike people of their type represented in greater proportion) are thus instruments for under*lining* rather than under*mining* majority culture. In the salesforce case, this phenomenon was most clearly in operation in training programs and at dinner and cocktail parties during meetings. Here the camaraderie of men, as in other work and social settings (Tiger 1969), was based in part on tales of sexual adventures, ability with respect to "hunting" and capturing women, and off-color jokes. Secondary themes involved work prowess and sports. The capacity for and enjoyment of drinking provided the context for displays of these themes. According to male informants' reports, they were dramatized more fervently in the presence of token women than when only men were present. When the men introduced these themes in much milder form and were just as likely to share company gossip or talk of domestic matters (such as a house being built), as to discuss any of the themes mentioned above, this was also in contrast to the situation in more equally mixed male-female groups, in which there were a sufficient number of women to influence and change group culture in such a way that a new hybrid based on shared male-female concerns was introduced. (See Aries [1973] for supportive laboratory evidence.)

In the presence of token women, then, men exaggerated displays of aggression and potency: instances of sexual innuendo, aggressive sexual

---

[4] This awareness often seemed to be resented by the men interviewed in this study, who expressed a preference for less self-consciousness and less attention to taken-for-granted operating assumptions. They wanted to "get on with business," and questioning definitions of what is "normal" and "appropriate" was seen as a deflection from the task at hand. The culture in the managerial/technical ranks of this large corporation, like that in many others, devalued introspection and emphasized rapid communication and ease of interaction. Thus, although group solidarity is often based on the development of strong in-group boundaries (Kanter 1972), the stranger or outsider who makes it necessary for the group to pay attention to its boundaries may be resented not only for being different but also for giving the group extra work.

teasing, and prowess-oriented "war stories." When one or two women were present, the men's behavior involved showing off, telling stories in which masculine prowess accounted for personal, sexual, or business success. The men highlighted what they could do, as men, in contrast to women. In a set of training situations, these themes were even acted out overtly in role plays in which participants were asked to prepare and perform demonstrations of sales situations. In every case involving a woman, men played the primary, effective roles, and women were objects of sexual attention. In one, a woman was introduced as president of a company selling robots; she turned out to be one of the female robots, run by the male company sales manager.

The women themselves reported other examples of testing to see how they would respond to the "male" culture. They said that many sexual innuendos or displays of locker-room humor were put on for their benefit, especially by the younger men. (The older men tended to parade their business successes.) One woman was a team leader and the only woman at a workshop when her team, looking at her for a reaction, decided to use as its slogan "The [obscenity] of the week." By raising the issue and forcing the woman to choose not to participate in the workshop, the men in the group created an occasion for uniting against the outsider and asserting dominant-group solidarity.

2. Interruptions as Reminders of "Difference"

Members of the numerically dominant category underscore and reinforce differences between tokens and themselves, insuring that the former recognize their outsider status by making the token the occasion for interruptions in the flow of group events. Dominants preface acts with apologies or questions about appropriateness directed at the token; they then invariably go ahead with the act, having placed the token in the position of interrupter or interloper. This happened often in the presence of the saleswomen. Men's questions or apologies were a way of asking whether the old or expected cultural rules were still operative—the words and expressions permitted, the pleasures and forms of release indulged in. (Can we still swear? Toss a football? Use technical jargon? Go drinking? Tell in jokes? See Greenbaum [1971, p. 65] for other examples.) By posing these questions overtly, dominants make their culture clear to tokens and state the terms under which tokens interact with the group.

The answers almost invariably affirm the understandings of the dominants, first because of the power of sheer numbers. An individual rarely feels comfortable preventing a larger number of peers from engaging in an activity they consider normal. Second, the tokens have been put on notice that interaction will not be "natural," that dominants will be holding back unless the tokens agree to acknowledge, permit, and even encourage majority cultural expressions in their presence. (It is important that this be stated, of course, for one never knows that another is holding back unless the other lets a piece of the suppressed material slip out.) At the same time, tokens have also been given the implicit message that majority members do *not* expect those forms of expression to be natural to the tokens' home culture; otherwise majority members would not need to raise the question. (This is a function of what Laws [1975] calls the "double deviance" of tokens: deviant first because they are women in a man's world and second because they aspire inappropriately to the privileges of the dominants.) Thus the saleswomen were often in the odd position of reassuring peers and customers that they could go ahead and do something in the women's presence, such as swearing, that they themselves would not be permitted to do. They listened to dirty jokes, for example, but reported that they would not dare tell one themselves. Via difference-reminding interruptions, then, dominants both affirm their own shared understandings and draw the cultural boundary between themselves and tokens. The tokens learned that they caused interruptions in "normal" communication and that their appropriate position was more like that of audience than full participant.

3. Overt Inhibition: Informal Isolation

In some cases, dominants do not wish to carry out certain activities in the presence of a token; they have secrets to preserve. They thus move the locus of some activities and expressions away from public settings to which tokens have access to more private settings from which they can be excluded. When information potentially embarrassing or damaging to dominants is being exchanged, an outsider audience is not desirable because dominants do not know how far they can trust tokens. As Hughes (1944, 1958) pointed out, colleagues who rely on unspoken understandings may feel uncomfortable in the presence of "odd kinds of fellows" who cannot be trusted to interpret information in just the same way or to engage in the same relationships of trust and reciprocity (see also Lorber 1975). The result is often quarantine—keeping tokens away from some occasions. Thus some topics of discussion were never raised by men in the presence of many of the saleswomen, even though they discussed these topics among themselves: admissions of low commitment to the company or concerns about job performance, ways of getting around formal rules, political plotting for mutual advantage, strategies for impressing certain corporate executives. As researchers have also found in other settings, women did not tend to be included in the networks by which informal socialization occurred and politics behind the formal system were exposed (Wolman and Frank 1975; O'Farrell 1973; Hennig 1970; Epstein 1970). In a few cases, managers even avoided giving women information about their performance as trainees, so that they did not know they were the subject of criticism in the company until they were told to find jobs outside the sales force; those women were simply not part of the informal occasions on which the men discussed their performances with each other. (Several male managers also reported their "fear" of criticizing a woman because of uncertainty about how she would receive it.)

4. Loyalty Tests

At the same time that tokens are often kept on the periphery of colleague interaction, they may also be expected to demonstrate loyalty to the dominant group. Failure to do so results in further isolation; signs of loyalty permit the token to come closer and be included in more activities. Through loyalty tests, the group seeks reassurance that tokens will not turn against them or use any of the information gained through their viewing of the dominants' world to do harm to the group. They get this assurance by asking a token to join or identify with the majority against those others who represent competing membership or reference groups; in short, dominants pressure tokens to turn against members of the latter's own category. If tokens collude, they make themselves psychological hostages of the majority group. For token women, the price of being "one of the boys" is a willingness to turn occasionally against "the girls."

There are two ways by which tokens can demonstrate loyalty and qualify for closer relationships with dominants. First, they can let slide or even participate in statements prejudicial to other members of their category. They can allow themselves to be viewed as exceptions to the general rule that others of their category have a variety of undesirable or unsuitable characteristics. Hughes (1944) recognized this as one of the deals token blacks might make for membership in white groups. Saleswomen who did well were told they were exceptions and were not typical women. At meetings and training sessions, women were often the subjects of ridicule or joking remarks about their incompetence. Some women who were insulted by such innuendos found it easier to appear to agree than to start an argument. A few accepted the dominant view fully. One of the first saleswomen denied in interviews having any special problems because she was a woman, calling herself skilled at coping with a man's world, and said the company was right not to hire more women. Women, she said, were unreliable and likely to quit; furthermore, young women might marry men who would not allow them to work. In this case, a token woman was taking over "gate-keeping" functions for dominants (Laws 1975), letting them preserve their illusion of lack of prejudice while she acted to exclude other women.

Tokens can also demonstrate loyalty by allowing themselves and their category to provide a source of humor for the group. Laughing with others, as Coser (1960) indicated, is a sign of a common definition of the situation; to allow oneself or one's kind to be the object of laughter signals a further willingness to accept others' culture on their terms. Just as Hughes (1946, p. 115) found that the initiation of blacks into white groups might involve accepting the role of comic inferior, the saleswomen faced constant pressures to allow jokes at women's expense, to accept kidding from the men around them. When a woman objected, men denied any hostility or unfriendly intention, instead accusing the woman by inference of lacking a sense of humor. In order to cope, one woman reported, "you learn to laugh when they try to insult you with jokes, to let it roll off your back." Tokens thus find themselves colluding with dominants through shared laughter.

Responses of Tokens to Boundary Heightening

Numerical skewing and polarized perceptions leave tokens with little choice about whether to accept the culture of dominants. There are too few other people of the token's kind to generate a counterculture or to develop a shared intergroup culture. Tokens have two general response possibilities. They can accept isolation, remaining an audience for certain expressive acts of dominants, in which case they risk exclusion from occasions on which informal socialization and political activity take place. Or they can try to become insiders, proving their loyalty by defining themselves as exceptions and turning against their own social category.

The occurrence of the second response on the part of tokens suggests a reexamination of the popularized "women-prejudiced-against-women" hypothesis or the "queen bee syndrome" for possible structural (numerical) rather than sexual origins. Not only has this hypothesis not been confirmed in a variety of settings (e.g., Ferber and Huber 1975); but the analysis offered here of the social psychological pressures on tokens to side with the majority also provides a compelling

explanation for the kinds of situations most likely to produce this effect, when it does occur.

Role Entrapment

The third set of interaction dynamics centering around tokens stems from the perceptual tendency toward assimilation: the distortion of the characteristics of tokens to fit preexisting generalizations about their category. Stereotypical assumptions and mistaken attributions made about tokens tend to force them into playing limited and caricatured roles in the system.

1. Status Leveling

Tokens are often misperceived initially as a result of their statistical rarity: "statistical discrimination" (U.S. Council of Economic Advisers 1973, p. 106) as distinguished from prejudice. That is, an unusual woman may be treated as though she resembles women on the average. People make judgments about the role played by others on the basis of probabilistic reasoning about the likelihood of what a particular kind of person does. Thus the saleswomen like other tokens encountered many instances of mistaken identity. In the office, they were often taken for secretaries; on the road, especially when they traveled with male colleagues, they were often taken for wives or mistresses; with customers, they were usually assumed to be substituting for men or, when with a male peer, to be assistants; when entertaining customers, they were assumed to be wives or dates.

Such mistaken first impressions can be corrected. They require tokens to spend time untangling awkward exchanges and establishing accurate and appropriate role relations, but they do permit status leveling to occur. Status leveling involves making adjustments in perception of the token's professional role to fit the expected position of the token's category—that is, bringing situational status in line with master status, the token's social type. Even when others knew that the token saleswomen were not secretaries, for example, there was still a tendency to treat them like secretaries or to make demands of them appropriate to secretaries. In the most blatant case, a woman was a sales trainee along with three men; all four were to be given positions as summer replacements. The men were all assigned to replace salesmen; the woman was asked to replace a secretary—and only after a long, heated discussion with the manager was she given a more professional assignment. Similarly, when having professional contacts with customers and managers, the women felt themselves to be treated in more wife-like or datelike ways than a man would be treated by another man, even though the situation was clearly professional. It was easier for others to make their perception of the token women fit their preexisting generalizations about women than to change the category; numerical rarity provided too few examples to contradict the generalization. Instances of status leveling have also been noted with regard to other kinds of tokens such as male nurses (Segal 1962); in the case of tokens whose master status is higher than their situational status, leveling can work to their advantage, as when male nurses are called "Dr."

2. Stereotyped Role Induction

The dominant group can incorporate tokens and still preserve their generalizations about the tokens' kind by inducting them into stereotypical roles; these roles preserve the familiar form of interaction between the kinds of people represented by the token and the dominants. In the case of token women in the sales force, four role traps were observed, all of which encapsulated the women in a category the men could respond to and understand. Each centered on one behavioral tendency of the token, building upon this tendency an image of her place in the group and forcing her to continue to live up to the image; each defined for dominants a single response to her sexuality. Two of the roles are classics in Freudian theory: the mother and the seductress. Freud wrote of the need of men to handle women's sexuality by envisioning them as either madonnas or whores—as either asexual mothers or overly sexual, debased seductresses. (This was

perhaps a function of Victorian family patterns, which encouraged separation of idealistic adoration of the mother and animalistic eroticism [Rieff 1963; Strong 1973].) The other roles, termed the pet and the iron maiden, also have family counterparts in the kid sister and the virgin aunt.

A. Mother.—A token woman sometimes finds that she has become a mother to a group of men. They bring her their troubles, and she comforts them. The assumption that women are sympathetic, good listeners, and can be talked to about one's problems is common in male-dominated organizations. One saleswoman was constantly approached by her all-male peers to listen to their domestic problems. In a variety of residential-sales-training groups, token women were observed acting out other parts of the traditional nurturant-maternal role: cooking for men, doing their laundry, sewing on buttons.

The mother role is a comparatively safe one. She is not necessarily vulnerable to sexual pursuit (for Freud it was the very idealization of the madonna that was in part responsible for men's ambivalence toward women), nor do men need to compete for her favors, because these are available to everyone. However, the typecasting of women as nurturers has three negative consequences for a woman's task performance: (1) the mother is rewarded by her male colleagues primarily for service to them and not for independent action. (2) The mother is expected to keep her place as a noncritical, accepting, good mother or lose her rewards because the dominant, powerful aspects of the maternal image may be feared by men. Since the ability to differentiate and be critical is often an indicator of competence in work groups, the mother is prohibited from exhibiting this skill. (3) The mother becomes an emotional specialist. This provides her with a place in the life of the group and its members. Yet at the same time, one of the traditionally feminine characteristics men in positions of authority in industry most often criticize in women (see Lynch 1973) is excess emotionality. Although the mother herself might not ever indulge in emotional outbursts in the group, she remains identified with emotional matters. As long as she is in the minority, it is unlikely that nurturance, support, and expressivity will be valued or that a mother can demonstrate and be rewarded for critical, independent, task-oriented behaviors.

B. Seductress.—The role of seductress or sexual object is fraught with more tension than the maternal role, for it introduces an element of sexual competition and jealousy. The mother can have many sons; it is more difficult for a sex object to have many lovers. Should a woman cast as sex object, that is, seen as sexually desirable and potentially available ("seductress" is a perception, and the woman herself may not be consciously behaving seductively), share her attention widely, she risks the debasement of the whore. Yet should she form a close alliance with any man in particular, she arouses resentment, particularly because she represents a scarce resource; there are just not enough women to go around.

In several situations observed, a high-status male allied himself with a seductress and acted as her "protector," not only because of his promise to rescue her from the sex-charged overtures of the rest of the men but also because of his high status per se. The powerful male (staff member, manager, sponsor, etc.) can easily become the protector of the still "virgin" seductress, gaining through masking his own sexual interest what other men could not gain by declaring theirs. However, the removal of the seductress from the sexual marketplace contains its own problems. Other men may resent a high-status male for winning the prize and resent the woman for her ability to the high-status male that they themselves could not obtain as men. While the seductress is rewarded for her femaleness and insured attention from the group, then, she is also the source of considerable tension; and needless to say, her perceived sexuality blots out all other characteristics.

Men may adopt the role of protector toward an attractive woman, regardless of her collusion, and by implication cast her as a sex object, reminding her and the rest of the group of her sexual status. In the guise of helping her, protectors may actually put up further barriers to a solitary woman's full acceptance by inserting themselves, figuratively speaking, between the woman and the rest of a group. A male sales trainer typically offered token women in training groups extra help and sympathetically attended to the problems their male peers might cause, taking them out alone for drinks at the end of daily sessions.

C. Pet.—The pet is adopted by the male group as a cute, amusing little thing and taken along on group events as symbolic mascot—a cheerleader for the shows of male prowess that follow. Humor is often a characteristic of the pet. She is expected to admire the male displays but not to enter into them; she cheers from the sidelines. Shows of competence on her part are treated as extraordinary and complimented just because they are unexpected (and the compliments themselves can be seen as reminders of the expected rarity of such behavior). One woman reported that, when she was alone in a group of men and spoke at length on an issue, comments to her by men after the meeting often referred to her speech-making ability rather than to what she said (e.g., "You talk so fluently"), whereas comments the men made to one another were almost invariably content or issue oriented. Competent acts that were taken for granted when performed by males were often unduly fussed over when performed by saleswomen, who were considered precocious or precious at such times. Such attitudes on the part of men in a group encourage self-effacing, girlish responses on the part of solitary women (who after all may be genuinely relieved to be included) and prevent them from realizing or demonstrating their own power and competence.

D. Iron maiden.—The iron maiden is a contemporary variation of the stereotypical roles into which strong women are placed. Women who fail to fall into any of the first three roles and in fact resist overtures that would trap them in such roles (like flirtation) might consequently be responded to as though tough or dangerous. (One saleswoman developed just such a reputation in company branches throughout the country.) If a token insisted on full rights in the group, if she displayed competence in a forthright manner, or if she cut off sexual innuendos, she was typically asked, "You're not one of those women's libbers, are you?" Regardless of the answer, she was henceforth viewed with suspicion, treated with undue and exaggerated politeness (by references to women inserted into conversations, by elaborate rituals of *not* opening doors), and kept at a distance; for she was demanding treatment as an equal in a setting in which no person of her kind had previously been an equal. Women inducted into the iron maiden role are stereotyped as tougher than they are (hence the name) and trapped in a more militant stance than they might otherwise take.

Responses of Tokens to Role Entrapment

The dynamics of role entrapment tend to lead to a variety of conservative and low-risk responses on the part of tokens. The time and awkwardness involved in correcting mistaken impressions often lead them to a preference for already-established relationships, for minimizing change and stranger contact in the work situation. It is also often easier to accept stereotyped roles than to fight them, even if their acceptance means limiting a token's range of expressions or demonstrations of task competence, because acceptance offers a comfortable and certain position. The personal consequence for tokens, of course, is a certain degree of self-distortion. Athanassiades (1974), though not taking into account the effects of numerical representation, found that women, especially those with low risk-taking propensity, tended to distort upward communication more than men and argued that many observed work behaviors of women may be the result of such distortion and acceptance of organizational images. Submissiveness, frivolity, or other attributes may be feigned by people who feel these are prescribed for them by the dominant organizational culture. This suggests that accurate conclusions about work attitudes and behavior cannot be reached by studying people in the token position, since there may always be an element of compensation or distortion involved. Thus many studies of professional and managerial women should be reexamined in order to remove the effects of numbers from the effects of sex roles.

Implications

This paper has developed a framework for understanding the social perceptions and interaction dynamics that center on tokens, using the example of women in an industrial sales force dominated numerically by men. Visibility generates performance pressures, polarization generates group-boundary heightening, and assimilation generates role entrapment. All of the phenomena associated with tokens are exaggerated ones: the token stands out vividly, group culture is dramatized, boundaries become highlighted, and token roles are larger-than-life caricatures.

The concepts identified here are also applicable to other kinds of tokens who face similar interaction contexts. Hughes's (1944, 1946, 1958) discussions of the problems encountered by blacks in white male work groups are highly congruent with the framework presented here. Taylor and Fiske's (1976) laboratory research demonstrates the perceptual phenomena mentioned above in the black-white context. Segal (1962) also provides confirming evidence that, when men are tokens in a group of women, the same concepts apply. He studied a hospital in which 22 out of 101 nurses were men. He found that male nurses were isolates in the hospital social structure, not because the men disassociated themselves from their women peers but because the women felt the men were out of place and should not be nurses. Male and female nurses had the same objective rank, but people of both sexes felt that the men's subjective status was a lower one. The women placed the men in stereotypical positions, expecting them to do the jobs the women found distasteful or considered men's work. During a personal interview, a male nursing student reported that he thought he would enjoy being the only man in a group of women until he found that he engendered a great deal of hostility and that he was teased every time he failed to live up to the manly image, for example, if he was vague or subjective in speech. And "token men" working in child-care centers were found to play minor roles, become social isolates, and bear special burdens in interaction, which they handled like the saleswomen, by defining themselves as "exceptional" men (Seifert 1974). Similarly, a blind informant indicated to me that, when he was the only blind person among sighted people, he often felt conspicuous and more attended to than he liked. This in turn created pressure for him to work harder in order to prove himself. In the solo situation, he was never sure that he was getting the same treatment as other members of the group (first, fellow students; later, fellow members of an academic institution), and he suspected that people tended to protect him. When he was the only one of his kind, as opposed to situations in which other blind people were present, sighted people felt free to grab his arm and pull him along and were more likely to apologize for references to visual matters, reinforcing his sense of being different and cast in the role of someone more helpless than he in fact perceived himself to be.

If the token's master status is higher than that of the situational dominants, some of the content of the interaction may change while the dynamics remain the same. A high-status token, for example, might find that the difference-reminding interruptions involve deference and opinion seeking rather than patronizing apology; a high-status token might be allowed to dominate formal colleague discussion while still being excluded from informal, expressive occasions. Such a token might be trapped in roles that distort competence in a favorable rather than an unfavorable direction; but distortion is involved nonetheless. Further research can uncover appropriate modifications of the framework which will allow its complete extension to cases in the category just discussed.

The analysis undertaken here also suggests the importance of intermediate-level structural and social psychological variables in affecting male-female interaction and the roles of women in work groups and organizations. Some phenomena that have been labeled sex related but have not been replicated under all circumstances might be responses to tokenism, that is, reflections of responses to situational pressures rather than to sex differences. "Fear of success" might be more fruitfully viewed as the fear of visibility of members of minority groups in token statuses. The modesty and lack of self-aggrandizement characteristic of

some professional and managerial women might be accounted for in similar ways, as situational responses rather than sex-linked traits. The prejudice of some women against others might be placed in the context of majority-culture loyalty tests. The unwillingness of some professional and managerial women to take certain risks involving a change in relationships might be explained as a reasonable response to the length of time it may take a token to establish competence-based working relationships and to the ever-present threat of mistaken identity in new relationships.

The examination of numerical effects leads to the additional question of tipping points: how many of a category are enough to change a person's status from token to full group member? When does a group move from skewed to tilted to balanced? Quantitative analyses are called for in order to provide precise documentation of the points at which interaction shifts because enough people of the "other kind" have become members of a group. This is especially relevant to research on school desegregation and its effects or changing neighborhood composition as well as occupational segregation by sex. Howe and Widick (1949, pp. 211–212) found that industrial plants with a small proportion of blacks in their work force had racial clashes, whereas those plants in which blacks constituted a large proportion had good race relations.

Exact tipping points should be investigated. Observations from the present study make it clear that even in small groups two of a kind are not enough. Data were collected in several situations in which two women rather than one were found among male peers but still constituted less than 20% of the group. Despite Asch's (1960) laboratory finding that one potential ally is enough to reduce the power of the majority to secure conformity, in the two-token situation in organizations dominants were nearly always able to defeat an alliance between two women by setting up invidious comparisons. By the exaggeration of traits in both cases, one woman was identified as a success, the other as a failure. The one given the positive label felt relieved to be accepted and praised. She recognized that alliance with the identified failure would jeopardize her acceptance. The consequence in one sales office was that the identified success stayed away from the other woman, did not give her any help with her performance, and withheld criticism she had heard that might have been useful. The second woman soon left the organization. In another case, dominants defeated an alliance, paradoxically by trying to promote it. Two women in a training group of 12 were treated as though they were an automatic pair, and other group members felt that they were relieved of responsibility for interacting with or supporting the women. The women reacted to this forced pairing by trying to create differences between themselves and becoming extremely competitive. Thus structural circumstances and pressures from the majority can produce what appear to be prejudicial responses of women to each other. Yet these responses are best seen as the effects of limited numbers. Two (or less than 20% in any particular situation) is not always a large enough number to overcome the problems of tokenism and develop supportive alliances, unless the tokens are highly identified with their own social category.

Tokens appear to operate under a number of handicaps in work settings. Their possible social isolation may exclude them from situations in which important learning about a task is taking place and may also prevent them from being in a position to look good in the organization. Performance pressures make it more dangerous for tokens to fumble and thus give them less room for error. Responding to their position, they often either underachieve or overachieve, and they are likely to accept distorting roles which permit them to disclose only limited parts of themselves. For all these reasons, in situations like industrial sales in which informal interaction provides a key to success tokens are not very likely to do well compared with members of the majority category, at least while in the token position.

These consequences of token status also indicate that tokens may undergo a great deal of personal stress and may need to expend extra energy to maintain a satisfactory relationship in the work situation. This fact is reflected in their common statements that they must work twice as hard as dominants or spend more time resolving problematic interactions. They face partially conflicting and often completely contradictory expectations. Such a situation has been found to be a source of mental stress for people with inconsistent statuses and in some cases to reinforce punitive self-images. In addition, turning against others of one's kind may be intimately connected with self-hatred. Finally, tokens must inhibit some forms of self-expression and often are unable to join the group in its characteristic form of tension release. They may be asked to side with the group in its assaults-through-humor but often cannot easily join the group in its play. They potentially face the stresses of social isolation and self-distortion.[5]

Thus social-policy formulations might consider the effects of proportions in understanding the sources of behavior, causes of stress, and possibilities for change. The analysis of tokenism suggests, for example, that merely adding a few women at a time to an organization is likely to give rise to the consequences of token status. Despite the contemporary controversy over affirmative action quotas (Glazer 1976), numbers do appear to be important in shaping outcomes for disadvantaged individuals. Women (or members of any other underrepresented category) need to be added to total group or organization membership in sufficient proportion to counteract the effects of tokenism. Even if tokens do well, they do so at a cost, overcoming social handicaps, expending extra effort, and facing stresses not present for members of the numerically dominant group. The dynamics of tokenism also operate in

---

[5]The argument that tokens face more personal stress than majority group members can be supported by studies of the psychosocial difficulties confronting people with inconsistent statuses. Among the stresses identified in the literature on class and race are unsatisfactory social relationships, unstable self-images, frustration over rewards, and social ambiguity

(Hughes 1944, 1958; Lenski 1956; Fenchel, Monderer, and Hartley 1951; Jackson 1962). Token women must also inhibit self-expression and self-disclosure, as the examples in this paper and the discussion below indicate; yet Jourard (1964) considers the ability to self-disclose a requisite for psychological well-being.

such a way as to perpetuate the system that keeps members of the token's category in short supply; the presence of a few tokens does not necessarily pave the way for others—in many cases, it has the opposite effect.

Investigation of the effects of proportions on group life and social interaction appears to be fruitful both for social psychological theory and for understanding male-female interaction. It is a step toward identifying the structural and situational variables that intervene between global cultural definitions of social type and individual responses—that shape the context for face-to-face interactions among different kinds of people. Relative as well as absolute numbers can be important for social life and social relations.

REFERENCES

Aries, Elizabeth. 1973. "Interaction Patterns and Themes of Male, Female, and Mixed Groups." Ph.D. dissertation, Harvard University.

Asch, Solomon E. 1960. "Effects of Group Pressure upon the Modification and Distortion of Judgments." pp. 189–200 in *Group Dynamics*, edited by Dorwin Cartwright and Alvin Zander. 2nd ed. Evanston, Ill.: Row, Peterson.

Athanassiades, John C. 1974. "An Investigation of Some Communication Patterns of Female Subordinates in Hierarchical Organizations." *Human Relations* 27 (March): 195–209.

Coser, Rose Laub. 1960. "Laughter among Colleagues: A Study of the Social Functions of Humor among the Staff of a Mental Hospital." *Psychiatry* 23 (February): 81–95.

Cussler, Margaret. 1958. *The Woman Executive*. New York: Harcourt Brace.

Epstein, Cynthia Fuchs. 1970. *Woman's Place: Options and Limits on Professional Careers*. Berkeley: University of California Press.

Fenchel, G. H., J. H. Monderer, and E. L. Hartley. 1951. "Subjective Status and the Equilibrium Hypothesis." *Journal of Abnormal and Social Psychology* 46 (October): 476–79.

Ferber, Marianne Abeles, and Joan Althaus Huber. 1975. "Sex of Student and Instructor: A Study of Student Bias." *American Journal* of *Sociology 80* (January): 949–63.

Glazer, Nathan. 1976. *Affirmative Discrimination*. New York: Basic.

Greenbaum, Marcia. 1971. "Adding 'Kenntnis' to 'Kirche, Kuche, und Kinder.'" *Issues in Industrial Society* 2 (2): 61–68.

Hennig, Margaret. 1970. "Career Development for Women Executives." Ph.D. dissertation, Harvard University.

Howe, Irving, and B. J. Widick. 1949. *The UAW and Walter Reuther*. New York: Random House.

Hughes, Everett C. 1944. "Dilemmas and Contradictions of Status." American Journal of Sociology 50 (March): 353–59.

———. 1946. "Race Relations in Industry." pp. 107–22 in *Industry and Society*, edited by W. F. Whyte. New York: McGraw-Hill.

———. 1958. *Men and Their Work*. Glencoe, Ill.: Free Press.

Jackson, Elton F. 1962. "Status Inconsistency and Symptoms of Stress." *American Sociological Review* 27 (August): 469–80.

Jourard, Sidney M. 1964. *The Transparent Self: Self-Disclosure and Well-Being*. Princeton, N.J.: Van Nostrand.

Kanter, Rosabeth Moss. 1972. *Commitment and Community*. Cambridge, Mass.: Harvard University Press.

———. 1975. "Women and the Structure of Organizations: Explorations in Theory and Behavior." pp. 34–74 in *Another Voice: Feminist Perspectives on Social Life and Social Science*, edited by M. Millman and R. M. Kanter. New York: Doubleday Anchor.

———. 1976a. "The Impact of Hierarchical Structures on the Work Behavior of Women and Men." *Social Problems* 23 (April): 415–30.

———. 1976b. "Interpreting the Results of a Social Experiment." *Science* 192 (May 14): 662–63.

———. 1976c. "The Policy Issues: Presentation VI." *Signs: Journal of Women in Culture and Society* 1 (Spring, part 2): 282–91.

———. 1976d. "Women and Organizations: Sex Roles, Group Dynamics, and Change Strategies." In *Beyond Sex Roles*, edited by A. Sargent. St. Paul: West.

———. In press. *Men and Women of the Corporation*. New York: Basic.

Laws, Judith Long. 1975. "The Psychology of Tokenism: An Analysis." *Sex Roles* 1 (March): 51–67.

Lenski, Gerhard. 1956. "Social Participation and the Crystallization of Status." *American Sociological Review* 21 (August): 458–64.

Levine, Adeline, and Janice Crumrine. 1975. "Women and the Fear of Success: A Problem in Replication." *American Journal of Sociology* 80 (January): 964–74.

Lorber, Judith. 1975. "Trust, Loyalty, and the Place of Women in the Informal Organization of Work." Paper presented at the annual meeting of the American Sociological Association, San Francisco.

Lynch, Edith M. 1973. *The Executive Suite: Feminine Style*. New York: AMACOM.

Megaree, Edwin I. 1969. "Influence of Sex Roles on the Manifestation of Leadership." *Journal of Applied Psychology* 53 (October): 377–82.

O'Farrell, Brigid. 1973. "Affirmative Action and Skilled Craft Work." Xeroxed. Center for Research on Women, Wellesley College.

Rieff, Philip, ed. 1963. *Freud: Sexuality and the Psychology of Love*. New York: Collier.

Sarason, Seymour B. 1973. "Jewishness, Blackness, and the Nature-Nurture Controversy." *American Psychologist* 28 (November): 961–71.

Segal, Bernard E. 1962. "Male Nurses: A Case Study in Status Contradiction and Prestige Loss." *Social Forces* 41 (October): 31–38.

Seifert, Kelvin. 1973. "Some Problems of Men in Child Care Center Work." pp. 69–73 in *Men and Masculinity*, edited by Joseph H. Pleck and Jack Sawyer. Englewood Cliffs, N.J.: Prentice-Hall, 1974.

Simmel, Georg. 1950. *The Sociology of Georg Simmel*. Translated by Kurt H. Wolff. Glencoe, Ill.: Free Press.

Strodtbeck, Fred L., Rita M. James, and Charles Hawkins. 1957. "Social Status in Jury Deliberations." American Sociological Review 22 (December): 713–19.

Strodtbeck, Fred L., and Richard D. Mann. 1956. "Sex Role Differentiation in Jury Deliberations." *Sociometry* 19 (March): 3–11.

Strong, Bryan. 1973. "Toward a History of the Experiential Family: Sex and Incest in the Nineteenth Century Family." *Journal of Marriage and the Family* 35 (August): 457–66.

Taylor, Shelley E. 1975. "The Token in a Small Group." Xeroxed. Harvard University Department of Psychology.

Taylor, Shelley E., and Susan T. Fiske. 1976. "The Token in the Small Group: Research Findings and Theoretical Implications." In *Psychology and Politics: Collected Papers*, edited by J. Sweeney. New Haven, Conn.: Yale University Press.

Tiger, Lionel. 1969. *Men in Groups*. New York: Random House.

Tiger, Lionel, and Joseph Shepher. 1975. *Women in the Kibbutz*. New York: Harcourt Brace Jovanovich.

U.S. Council of Economic Advisers. 1973. *Annual Report of the Council of Economic Advisers*. Washington, D.C.: Government Printing Office.

Wolman, Carol, and Hal Frank. 1975. "The Solo Woman in a Professional Peer Group." *American Journal of Orthopsychiatry* 45 (January): 164–71.

Zaleznick, Abraham, C. R. Christensen, and F. J. Roethlisberger. 1958. *The Motivation, Productivity, and Satisfaction of Workers: A Prediction Study*. Boston: Harvard Business School Division of Research.

Effects of Crew Composition on Crew Performance: Does the Whole Equal the Sum of Its Parts?

Aharon Tziner* and Dov Eden**

The composition of three-man military crews was varied experimentally by assigning members according to crew composition in terms of all possible combinations of levels of ability and motivation. The crews performed real military tasks in a military field setting, and unit commanders ranked the effectiveness of their performance at the end of 2 months of military activity (208 crews in all). It was found that both ability and motivation had an additive effect on crew performance. In addition, crew composition effects were found for ability but not for motivation. Most significant was the fact that the performance of uniformly high-ability crews far exceeded the levels expected on the basis of individual crew members' ability, whereas the performance of uniformly low-ability crews fell considerably below the expected level. It was concluded that when crews perform highly interdependent tasks, performance is also likely to be affected in a nonadditive manner by crew composition. The implications of the findings for crew formation are discussed.

Although many studies of group performance have been conducted, we still know very little about how group composition affects performance in tasks demanding a high level of interdependence, such as those performed by tank crews. Such groups are distinguished by the fact that the tasks they undertake require the coordination of all crew members, each of whom is performing a separate

*Faculty of Social Sciences, Tel Aviv University, Ramat Aviv, Israel.

**Faculty of Management, Tel Aviv University, Ramat Aviv, Israel.

The authors are deeply indebted to Morton B. Brown for his invaluable help in experimental design and data analysis.

Requests for reprints should be addressed to Aharon Tziner, Department of Labor Studies, Faculty of Social Sciences, Tel Aviv University, Ramat Aviv, 69 978, Israel.

and distinct role. The successful outcome of the performance depends on synchronization of the activities of all the crew members (Jones, 1974).

The reason that there is so little evidence about the relationship between group composition and group performance for this type of task could be due to the fact that most research into group performance has concentrated on unstructured collaborative task organizations (e.g., Goldman, 1971; Hoffman, 1979; Johnson & Torcivia, 1967). Only in the last few years have studies also been published on groups performing structured cooperative types of tasks similar to those of tank crews (Hewett, O'Brien, & Hornik, 1974; Kabanoff & O'Brien, 1979; O'Brien, 1968).

Clearly, it is easier for a researcher to devise collaborative rather than cooperative tasks to be performed by groups studied under laboratory settings. However, in real-life situations, tasks often require more interdependence among group members than that required in such collaborative tasks. For an accurate distinction between collaborative and cooperative task type, refer to Shiflett, 1979.

Although, as we mentioned above, task organization has already received some attention in group performance literature, to the best of our knowledge little investigation has been undertaken in the area of a cooperative task organization such as that of a three-man military crew, in which the coordination is required of all members, each of whom plays a distinct but interdependent role. In addition, there is little mention in the literature of the impact of a priori and systematic manipulations of real-life group structures (e.g., three-man military crews), in terms of members' ability and motivation, on group performance.

For this reason, the major purpose of this present experiment was to ascertain how tank crew composition, in terms of various combinations of ability and motivation levels, affects crew performance. We chose these three-man military crews because they were groups engaged in performing real tasks demanding a high level of interdependence among the members. Crew composition was varied according to members' level of ability and motivation, using as our guide a number of reviews that have

shown that ability and, to some extent, motivation, are positively related to group productivity (Hill, 1982; Steers & Porter, 1979). However, as pointed out by O'Brien and Owens (1969), the specific ways the different combinations of ability and motivation affect such group productivity have yet to be satisfactorily investigated.

A conclusion from findings reviewed and summarized by Hill (1982) and Shaw (1976) on group ability composition/group performance, in mainly collaborative, and to a much smaller extent in cooperative tasks, suggests that members' ability combines simply in an additive manner. Each member contributes to group production in direct proportion to his or her ability, irrespective of ability levels of the other members; the higher the ability level of each member, the better the group performance (Bouchard, 1972; Johnson & Torcivia, 1967). Applying this alternative interpretative approach to the present experiment, we might expect that the higher the levels of ability and motivation of crew members, the better the performance effectiveness. In the analysis of crew performance effectiveness, treating the ability and motivation of each crew member as separate independent variables, the additive effects corroborating the above hypothesis would be manifested in significant main effects and nonsignificant interactions.

However, other research results indicate that group performance exceeds what could have been expected assuming additivity (Rohrbaugh, 1981); in particular when tasks are more complex, groups might perform better (or worse) than would be predicted on the basis of the ability levels of individual members (Egerbladh, 1976; Goldman, 1971; Laughlin & Branch, 1972). Laughlin and Johnson (1966) suggested that this effect, when positive, could be explained in terms of pooling unique resources to create a single group product better than expected. When facing a complex task, presumably each group member has to contribute some unique ability relevant to a particular facet of the task. In such a case members have much to gain from each other.

Contrary research results have also shown that some combinations of ability would result in the inhibition of group product (Steiner, 1972). Secord and Backman (1974) reasoned that it is a well-known fact that annoyance and anger are experienced when one's partner is markedly inferior. Thus, we might speculate that group performance would be less than expected on the basis of members' level of ability. In short, in both cases the function relating member ability levels to group performance would involve nonadditive effects. Significant interactions would be found to indicate that there are combinations of ability more (or less) productive than expected, giving evidence that group composition affects group performance.

Applying this alternative conceptual approach in the present experiment, we may hypothesize that some combinations of ability and/or motivation would yield crew performance effectiveness higher (or lower) than anticipated on the basis of simple aggregation of ability and/or motivation levels of crew members. Statistically, in addition to the significant main effects (i.e., ability and motivation of each crew member) interactive terms would also contribute significantly to the variation in crew performance effectiveness.

Present Experiment

The present experiment was intended to ascertain whether ability and motivation of crew members combine additively or interactively only, or perhaps in both ways, to affect crew performance.

Some distinctive features of this study are notable. First, the above study question was examined in a natural organizational setting—that of active military crews performing authentic tasks. Second, the tasks required high interdependence of crew members and could only be accomplished if each member carried out his duty simultaneously with the others and if they all synchronized their activities. Third, all possible combinations of both ability and motivation levels of crew members were deliberately generated; only later were their performance effectiveness data compiled, rather than measuring on a post hoc basis both individual

attributes and crew performance, as in a previous study, which also focused in general terms on the above question (Jones, 1974). For this reason, our experimental design is a sound basis for causal interpretation.

Method

Employing a field experimental design, we manipulated crew composition by systematically assigning soldiers to three-man crews (i.e., tank crews) on the basis of predetermined combinations of high and low ability and motivation. No other interventions were made in this natural field setting. The dependent variable, the effectiveness of crew performance, was assessed by commanders of crew units as part of the natural situation.

Subjects

The candidate pool for the present experiment consisted of male soldiers whose mean age was 19, ranging between 18 and 20. These men were assigned to tank crews to perform regular military field activities. The activities were divided among the members of these crews, with each member performing the task for which he had previously received specialized training. The specific roles were designated as mover, loader, and operator. No member could perform the entire task by himself; task performance required the coordination of all three members, and crew effectiveness depended on the synchronization of their activities. The 224 crews in the present experiment were formed in a manner that systematically manipulated crew composition.

Crew Composition

Dichotomizing ability and motivation at the median for each of the three members in the crew, there were $2^6 = 64$ different ways to assign the subjects to three-man crews. Each of these 64 combinations of ability and motivation was intended to represent a distinct type of crew composition. For instance, one of the combinations included an operator and a mover high (H) in ability and low (L) in motivation with a loader low (L) in ability and high (H) in motivation, thus yielding a crew composition of the type denoted HL HL LH.

Experiment Design

All 64 crew types had to be ranked by the same rater, the unit commander, for performance effectiveness, in order to obtain just one replication of performance effectiveness for each crew composition type. In the present experiment, however, each unit commander—a commissioned male officer—could only be asked to rank the eight crews with which he was familiar. Therefore, an experimental design was needed that would allow an unbiased assignment of the 64 crew types to the different raters; we used the 2^{K-P} fractional factorial design (John, 1971) to overcome this obstacle.

K, which represents the number of factors, here equals 6 (ability and motivation of each of the three crew members). Further, P denotes the value such that when 2 is raised by it (as a power) the highest number of crew types each rater can rank is obtained. Here P equals 3.

It should be noted that $2^3 = 8$ was the number of crews each unit commander ranked in the present experiment. It should also be recalled that by the 2^{6-3} design, a special case of 2^{K-P} fractional factorial design, the rater effect is rendered negligible.

Sample size was determined in an effort to ensure the minimal number of crews of the same composition type sufficient for statistical analyses to detect significant effects, if these exist. Therefore, at least three crews of each type were produced. Altogether 224 crews were formed and placed in the military organizational setting where this experiment took place.

Finally, it should be noted that they were divided into four waves: the first, the second, and the fourth each contained all 64 different crew types, whereas the third contained only 32, due to organizational constraints. Further details describing the present design and its derivation are available in Brown, Eden, and Tziner (1979).

Measures

Ability. We employed an existing measure used to estimate general aptitude of the subjects, which has already been described in detail elsewhere (Amir, Kovarsky, & Sharan, 1970; Tziner & Dolan, 1983). It is a composite score derived from an actuarial combination of (a) an overall intelligence score obtained by a version of Raven's Matrix and an Otis-type verbal test; (b) level of formal education; (c) estimated proficiency in Hebrew; and (d) a score derived from a semistructural interview designed to assess ability to adapt to army life.

Each of the four components in the overall composite have been extensively validated against a wide range of criteria in unpublished validation research carried out in the Israel Defense Forces. Only the composite score, which we used to measure ability, has consistently shown a satisfactory and stable level of predictive validity ($r \approx .40$). This is comparable with other ability measures reported in the literature (e.g., Ghiselli, 1973). For this reason, the composite score is the only measure currently used and preserved in existing personnel records, as Reeb (1976) has already noted.

Motivation.[1] Each subject answered four questions specifically designed for the present experiment. These were closed-ended items that assessed the extent of his motivation to perform duties in the military setting where this experiment took place. The four items were combined into a single measure whose internal consistency reliability as estimated by Cronbach's coefficient alpha was .86. These four items were included as part of a much longer questionnaire routinely administered to soldiers in units such as these to assess attitudes and morale.

---

[1] Security constraints prevent us from providing in detail the descriptive statistics (e.g., *M, SD*) of ability and motivation measures; however, it is worth noting that no stringent restriction in range or severe skewness of distributions was found.

In addition, we have not as yet been allowed to report the questions that were asked in the motivation measure; but it should be noted that this measure has proved reasonably valid in past unpublished examinations in the army.

Crew performance effectiveness. No standard objective measures of performance were available. Therefore, we used subjective performance rankings made by the unit commander to whom the crews reported. Each commander ranked eight different types of crews subordinated to him for 2 months of intensive activity. In this military setting this is considered a reasonable period for the commander to draw reliable conclusions about a crew's performance. He accorded the best, in terms of performance effectiveness, the rank 8, the second 7, and so on down to 1 for the worst. No ties were allowed, with each of the eight ranks being assigned to only one crew. In order to obtain an estimate of the reliability of these rankings, in 15 sets of eight teams the deputy of each commander, also a commissioned officer, was also asked to rank the same crews independently. We were limited to 15 sets due to organization constraints. Kendall's coefficient of concordance for the amount of agreement between the two raters ranged between $W = .78$ to $.86$, with a median of .82.

The extent of agreement on the performance effectiveness measure employed here has been considered reasonably reliable (Jones, 1981). However, in the analysis we relied on the unit commander only, because in this setting he both establishes the standards for crew performance and monitors it accordingly. We used rankings rather than ratings in order to preclude leniency bias and restriction of range. Also, ranking produces equal means and variances in the performance scores of all commanders, precluding distortions in analysis that might have resulted had rating scales been used (Bernardin & Beatty, 1984).

Finally, the raters (unit commanders and deputies) were not informed of the ability and motivation composition of crews subordinated to them in order to avoid expectancy effects (Eden & Shani, 1982). In order to preclude or reduce contamination of the performance rankings by commanders' perceptions of crew members' ability and motivation, as well as other extraneous variables, they were instructed to base their general performance rankings on concrete actions of the crews that indicate their performance effectiveness, such as accuracy of fire, time lapse between sighting and firing on target, and level of equipment maintenance. We scheduled the rankings for a stage in the life of the units during which it is customary to collect such information from field commanders. Thus, the assessment of performance could not have aroused the suspicion or awareness of the commanders to the fact that a crew composition experiment was under way. The soldiers similarly had no knowledge of how they had been assigned to crews, or that an experiment was being conducted.

Results

Analyses were based on only 208 of the initial 224 crews, due to unforeseen circumstances such as sickness or organization problems. This study investigated whether crew performance effectiveness is determined only by the ability and motivation of crew members, or whether, in addition, it is a function of the interaction between different levels of ability and/or motivation for each of the positions in the crew (e.g., Operator's Ability × Loader's Ability).

To examine this issue, a regression analysis was employed.[2] Apart from the six individual factors (i.e., ability and motivation of members in three crew positions), cross-product (hyperbolic) terms were allowed to represent only two- and three-way interactions of the individual factors (individual factors henceforth designated main effects). According to Kerlinger and Pedhazur (1973), as well as Jones (1974), the possibility that higher order interactive terms might be significant is, in practice, remote and virtually without precedent in behavior research.

---

[2] A mathematical model of analysis of variance was developed to analyze the results of each wave where the balanced structure was completely retained (Brown et al., 1979). However, as it was not retained we used a regression analysis procedure, which may also be considered adequate for extracting the information from our data needed to answer the question posed by the current experiment.

TABLE 3.1. Regression of Crew Performance Effectiveness on Significant Predictors in Waves 1 through 4

Predictor	r	R	beta	F
Mover's motivation	.34*	.34	.32	26.95*
Operator's motivation	.26*	.41	.18	8.34*
Operator's ability × Loader's ability	.15*	.43	−.42	21.09*
Operator's ability	.12*	.46	.33	17.68*
Wave 3	.00	.48	.25	14.08*
Loader's ability	−.02	.51	.34	12.09*
Mover's ability	.23*	.53	.16	6.26*
Operator's ability × Loader's ability × Mover's ability	−.03	.55	−.18	5.47*

Note: n = 208 crews.
*p < .05.

Finally, the four waves were also indexed in the regression analysis by dummy variables and allowed free entrance to account for deviations from the original balanced design in each wave, which stemmed from some of the original crews having been broken up during the experiment. The regression results are presented in Table 3.1.

Five of the six main effects were positive significant predictors of crew performance effectiveness. Only the loader's motivation failed to predict effectiveness significantly, either as a main effect or in interaction with any other predictor. The first two variables entered into the regression equation were the mover's motivation and the operator's motivation, which together explained $R^2 = (.41)^2 = 16\%$ of the variance in effectiveness, which is just over half of the variance explained by the eight significant predictors.

Also, Table 3.1 includes two significant interactions. Of the 15 two-way interaction terms we entered into the analysis as potential predictors, only the interaction between operator's ability and loader's ability attained statistical significance. This is clear evidence of a crew composition effect, because it means that the contribution of one crew member's ability to crew performance depends on another member's ability. Furthermore, this significant interaction cannot be merely main effects in disguise, because the main effects of both constituent variables were also entered as significant predictors. The interaction explains performance

TABLE 3.2. Mean Crew Performance Effectiveness by Operator's Ability and Loader's Ability

	Loader's ability				
	Low		High		
Operator's ability	M	n	M	n	Total
High	4.5 (4.5)	54	5.7 (4.9)	51	5.1
Low	3.5 (3.8)	51	3.8 (4.1)	52	3.6
	4.0		4.7		4.4

Note: Main cell entries are actual mean crew performance effectiveness ranks. Numbers in parentheses are mean crew performance effectiveness ranks expected on the basis of the marginals.

variance beyond these main effects. The means in Table 3.2 reveal the nature of this interaction. First, note that the marginal difference (1.5) between the mean performance effectiveness ranking of crews with high- and low-ability operators is about twice as large as the difference (0.7) between crews with high- and low-ability loaders. This is consistent with the zero-order correlations of these predictors with effectiveness as displayed in Column 1 of Table 3.1 ($r = .12$, $p < .05$ and $r = −.02$, ns, respectively). An inspection of the four cell entries reveals that the greatest deviation of actual from expected effectiveness can be seen in the difference of nearly a whole rank earned by the high–high combination. The operator's ability is the most important of the two factors in the interaction. Given a low-ability operator, the loader's ability does not make a great deal of difference (3.5 vs. 3.8). But a high-ability operator contributes a whole rank to mean performance effectiveness, even when loader's ability is low. Similarly, a low-ability loader detracts less from a high-ability operator (4.5 vs. 5.7) than a low-ability operator detracts from a high-ability loader (3.8 vs. 5.7). Low operator ability is such an obstacle to crew effectiveness that even high-loader ability cannot overcome it. Practically speaking, a high-ability loader is "wasted" when matched with a low-ability operator.

In addition, a three-way interaction between the ability levels of all three positions was significant, as shown in the last row of Table 3.2. The meaning of the significant three-way interaction can be learned by careful inspection of the actual means

TABLE 3.3. Mean Crew Performance Effectiveness by Ability of Three Positions

	Mover's ability								
	Low				High				
	Loader's ability				Loader's ability				
	Low		High		Low		High		
Operator's ability	M	n	M	n	M	n	M	n	Average
High	4.2 (4.2)	25	5.2 (4.7)	23	4.8 (4.7)	29	6.1 (5.2)	28	5.1
Low	3.0 (3.6)	26	3.5 (3.8)	26	4.0 (4.1)	25	4.2 (4.3)	26	3.6
	3.6		4.3		4.4		5.2		4.4

Note: Main cell entries are actual mean crew performance effectiveness ranks. Numbers in parentheses are mean crew performance effectiveness ranks expected on the basis of the marginals.

in Table 3.3. The interaction derives from the fact that, for two of the three positions, a high-ability individual contributed more to crew performance when both of the other two positions were manned by high-ability comrades than when neither, or only one, of the two remaining positions was manned by a high-ability crew mate. For example, the operator's ability contributed 1.9 ranks to crew performance effectiveness when the other two men were of high ability (6.1−4.2) but added an average of only 1.25 ranks when only one other crew mate had high ability (average of 4.8−4.0 and 5.2−3.5), and improved performance effectiveness by only 1.2 ranks when teamed up with two low-ability colleagues (4.2−3.0). The same pattern can be discerned for the loader, whose high ability boosts crew performance effectiveness by 1.3 (6.1−4.8) ranks when the other two are of high ability but by only a half rank (3.5−3.0) when the others are both of low ability. The exception is the mover, whose ability appears to contribute only between about a half a rank to a rank across the board (4.8−4.2; 4.0−3.0; 4.2−3.5; 6.1−5.2). In the crews studied, an individual's ability tended to contribute most to his crew's performance effectiveness when all of his crew mates also had high ability. If both the others were not of high ability, then his contribution was the same, regardless of whether only one or both of the others were of low ability.

Finally, it is worth noting that of the dummy variables representing the four waves, only that of Wave 3 achieved a significant beta weight. This positive weight shows that the crews in this wave were ranked on average as more effective than those in the other waves. This is reasonable, because this was an unbalanced wave that contained 32 crews, of 64 possible ones, typified by higher potential in terms of members' ability and motivation. Hence, as might have been expected, their performance was, on average, ranked higher. However, entry of Wave 3 dummy variable into the regression ensured statistical removal of the effects of deviance from a balanced design that occurred in this wave. The fact that only one of the waves' dummy variables entered the regression, though all were free to enter, indicates that deviations from balanced design in other waves were negligible.

Discussion

The strongest finding in the present experiment is that individual levels of ability and motivation have strong main effects on crew performance effectiveness, even when the crew task is such that it requires coordination between members who are simultaneously performing separate roles. The ability of all three position holders and motivation of two proved to be significant predictors of crew rank. All in all the present results confirm, as expected, that group performance is a function of individual crew members' levels of ability and motivation. In this respect the present experiment produced results highly consistent with those found elsewhere in regard to collaborative type of tasks (Nevin, Johnson, & Johnson, 1982; Rohrbaugh, 1981). In many ways our findings also reaffirm the trend shown in an earlier study of O'Brien and Owens (1969, in their first experiment): For tasks where coordination is high, group productivity is likely to relate positively to the summed abilities of all group members. The present experiment does provide, however, more information than the previous one because it systematically varied ability and motivation in order to investigate how different compositions affect crew performance. Furthermore, our data are more conducive to generalizability than those of O'Brien and Owens (1969) because they were obtained from real-life crews, which accomplished tasks requiring a larger measure of interdependence and coordination among group members. Hence, it lends substantial support to the additive approach, viewing group performance as strictly affected by summation of members' task-relevant resources.

However, significant interaction effects of ability, but not of motivation, were also obtained with multiple regression, thus demonstrating the existence of some group-composition effects. Each member's ability influenced crew performance effectiveness differently depending on the ability levels of the other two members. A high-ability member appears to achieve more in combination with other uniformly high-ability members than in combination with low-ability members. Furthermore, uniformly high-ability crews impressively surpassed performance effectiveness anticipated on the basis of members' ability.

Similar results have been reported by other researchers, albeit in a laboratory setting (Egerbladh, 1976). However, such findings are relatively scarce and have usually been revealed in tasks that to some extent make interdependence demands on group members as in the case of this study. This is probably largely attributable to the nature of group tasks. When tasks are complex and require synchronization of crew members' individual activities, it seems likely that teaming high-ability members not only ensures superior performance in each position but also enhances the accomplishment of group performance more than expected, because of the unique contribution made by each crew member.

The above argument enjoys some support in Porter, Lawler, and Hackman (1975) as well as in Steers and Porter (1979) review works.

Our results also showed that replacing one member of a crew composed of three persons of high ability by a low-ability individual diminishes crew performance effectiveness disproportionately and appears detrimental to the contribution of the remaining high-ability members. Although uniformly low-ability crews were ranked lower in effectiveness than "expected," replacing one member with a high-ability individual would boost effectiveness by about the same amount as replacing a low-ability member in a crew having a high-low-low ability composition, and in both such cases of replacement the boost to effectiveness would be less than could be gained by turning a high-high-low crew into a crew of high-high-high ability composition.

Suppose one were to form eight three-man teams from a pool of 24 individuals of known ability; of the many possible combinations, our experimental results suggest that the most productive solution would be to allocate six highs and all 12 lows to six teams of high-low-low ability and to assign the six remaining highs to two teams of high-high-high ability. This avoids the disproportionately low productivity of the low-low-low ability combination, while leaving some of the highs for high-high-high ability teams where they are most productive. This way of allocating ability probably runs counter to the commonsense notion of "spreading the talent around" in order to improve overall effectiveness (Jones, 1974; Nevin et al., 1982). Our results show that talent is used more effectively when concentrated than when spread around. In this regard, we wish to refer to an interesting point in our findings: Uniform low-ability teams proved to be ranked less effective than expected. How could such a finding be accounted for, particularly as it contradicts evidence that has emerged from past investigations? These investigations indicated that uniform low-ability groups either equal or exceed performance expected on the basis of group composition (Goldman, 1971; Laughlin & Johnson, 1966).

It is plausible that when low-ability members are teamed to carry out highly interdependent roles generated by the group task structure, in a real setting where organizational policy allocates rewards according to group performance (as in the present case), each member of the team has much to lose from being grouped together with other low-ability members. Mutual annoyance consequently experienced would presumably yield interpersonal conflicts, which would subsequently reduce performance below the expected level. Some support for this argument is found in Senn's (1971) article.

Composition effects were found for ability but not for motivation. Motivation contributed only additively to crew performance effectiveness, the impact of one person's motivation on crew performance being in no way dependent on the motivation of the others. Different members' levels of motivation do not interact as their abilities do. Thus, how people perform together is determined in part by their similarity in ability, but not at all by their similarity of motivation. This finding confirms a similar result already reported by Bouchard (1972) referring to collaborative tasks.

Also conspicuously absent were any interactions between ability and motivation that could have been anticipated relying on the dictum that performance = Ability × Motivation, suggested by Vroom (1960). It is possible that the Ability × Motivation interaction needs to be tested only with individual performance as the dependent variable and that the interaction gets somehow dissipated when individual efforts are combined into group output as in the present experiment. However, it is also possible that Vroom's longstanding dictum, though plausible, convincing, and widely quoted, is a poor explanation of *actual* behavior. The measures employed in the present experiment were demonstrably reliable and valid and detected both main and interaction effects. Therefore, Ability × Motivation interactions would have been detected had there been any. This is in fact consistent with Campbell and Pritchard's conclusion (1976), following their review of the literature, that the attempts to account for additional variance in performance by some multiplicative combination of motivational and ability variables have been unsuccessful.

Alternatively, it is also possible that the Ability × Motivation interaction is not linear, but much more complex and therefore undetectable by the present analysis. The issue thus awaits theoretical elaboration and adequate testing. In the meantime, caution should be shown in conclusions regarding how and whether ability and motivation interact.

Considered as a whole, the findings suggest that at least in respect to ability, crew composition may affect crew performance in a nonadditive manner. Though crew composition effects were relatively few, this is not sufficient to completely refute nonadditive effects. Rather, we are inclined to accept that the small number of interactive terms found significant was a result of a fundamental weakness of regression models. Dawes and Corrigan (1974) have demonstrated the astonishing power of simple first-order linear models to fit highly nonlinear (i.e., interactive) processes. This effect, labelled "main effect approximation," has been argued to be a serious obstacle to research in several areas. In the present experiment, the implications of the "main effect approximation" may be direct and unfortunate: Even if important interactions existed in data concerning crew composition effects in terms of ability and motivation, we were unlikely to detect them or to assess their magnitude correctly. With so many statistical cards stacked against them, the two significant interactions that emerged in the present experiment can be interpreted as solid evidence that crew members' ability and/or motivation may combine in a nonadditive manner to determine crew performance with respect to tasks of the type used in the current study. The generalizability of the present findings might be severely constrained by the specificity of the particular situation in which our experiment was conducted. It is likely that nonadditive effects occur in many complex group task performance situations. However, the particular type of interaction, that is, whose ability facilitates whom most, will differ from group task to group task, contingent on the unique characteristics of the particular task.

However, further research is needed in order to determine the extent to which the present findings would replicate and also to examine the generalizability of the present results to measures of specific task motivation and ability, and to groups of other sizes in natural organizational settings.

REFERENCES

Amir, Y., Kovarsky, Y., & Sharan, S. (1970). Peer nominations as a predictor of multistage promotions in a ramified organization. *Journal of Applied Psychology, 54,* 462–469.

Bernardin, J. H., & Beatty, R. (1984). *Performance appraisal in organizations.* Boston: Kent-Wadsworth.

Bouchard, T. J., Jr. (1972). Training, motivation, and personality as determinants of the effectiveness of brainstorming groups and individuals. *Journal of Applied Psychology, 56,* 418–421.

Brown, M. B., Eden, D., & Tziner, A. (1979, August). *Fractional factorial designs when each judge can rank a subset of the alternatives.* Paper presented at the American Statistical Association Annual Convention, New York.

Campbell, J. P., & Pritchard, R. D. (1976). Motivation theory in industrial and organizational psychology. In M. D. Dunnette (Ed.), *Handbook of industrial and organizational psychology* (pp. 84–95). Chicago: Rand McNally.

Dawes, R. M., & Corrigan, P. (1974). Linear models in decision making. *Psychological Bulletin, 81,* 95–106.

Eden, D., & Shani, A. B. (1982). Pygmalion goes to boot camp: Expectancy, leadership, and trainee performance. *Journal of Applied Psychology, 67,* 194–199.

Egerbladh, T. (1976). The function of group size and ability level on solving a multidimensional complementary task. *Journal of Personality and Social Psychology, 34,* 805–808.

Ghiselli, E. E. (1973). The validity of aptitude tests in personnel selection. *Personnel Psychology, 26,* 461–478.

Goldman, M. (1971). Group performance related to size and initial ability of group members. *Psychological Reports, 28,* 551–557.

Hewett, T. T., O'Brien, G. E., & Hornik, J. (1974). The effects of work organization, leadership style, and member compatibility upon the productivity of small groups working on a manipulative task. *Organizational Behavior and Human Performance, 11,* 283–301.

Hill, G. W. (1982). Group versus individual performance: Are $N + 1$ heads better than one? *Psychological Bulletin, 91,* 517–539.

Hoffman, L. R. (1979). *The group problem solving process: Studies of a valence model.* New York: Praeger.

John, P. W. M. (1971). *Statistical designs and analysis of experiments.* New York: Macmillan.

Johnson, H. H., & Torcivia, J. M. (1967). Group and individual performance on a single task as a function of distribution of individual performance. *Journal of Experimental Social Psychology, 3,* 266–273.

Jones, A. (1981). Inter-rater reliability in the assessment of group exercises at a U.K. assessment center. *Journal of Occupational Psychology, 54,* 79–86.

Jones, M. B. (1974). Regressing groups on individual effectiveness. *Organizational Behavior and Human Performance, 11,* 426–451.

Kabanoff, B., & O'Brien, G. E. (1979). Cooperation task structure and the relationship of leaders and member ability to group performance. *Journal of Applied Psychology, 64,* 526–532.

Kerlinger, F. N., & Pedhazur, E. J. (1973). *Multiple regression in behavioral research.* New York: Holt, Rinehart & Winston.

Laughlin, P. R., & Branch, L. G. (1972). Individual versus tetradic performance on complementary tasks as a function of initial ability level. *Organizational Behavior and Human Performance, 8,* 201–216.

Laughlin, P. R., & Johnson, H. H. (1966). Group and individual performance on a complementary task as a function of initial level. *Journal of Experimental Social Psychology, 2,* 407–414.

Nevin, A., Johnson, D. W., & Johnson, R. (1982). Effects of group and individual contingencies on academic performance and social relations of special needs students. *The Journal of Social Psychology, 116,* 41–55.

O'Brien, G. (1968). The measurement of cooperation. *Organizational Behavior and Human Performance, 3,* 427–439.

O'Brien, G. E., & Owens, A. G. (1969). Effects of organizational structure on correlations between members' abilities and group productivity. *Journal of Applied Psychology, 53,* 525–530.

Porter, L. W., Lawler, E. E., & Hackman, J. R. (1975). *Behavior in organizations.* New York: McGraw Hill.

Reeb, M. (1976). Differential test validity for ethnic groups in the Israeli Army and the effects of educational level. *Journal of Applied Psychology, 61,* 253–261.

Rohrbaugh, J. (1981). Improving the quality of group judgement: Social judgment analysis and the nominal group technique. *Organizational Behavior and Human Performance, 28,* 272–288.

Secord, P. F., & Backman, C. W. (1974). *Social psychology* (2nd ed.) New York: McGraw-Hill.

Senn, D. J. (1971). Attraction as a function of similarity–dissimilarity in task performance. *Journal of Personality and Social Psychology, 18,* 120–123.

Shaw, M. E. (1976). *Group dynamics: The psychology of small group behavior.* New York: McGraw-Hill.

Shiflett, S. (1979). Toward a general model of small group productivity. *Psychological Bulletin, 86,* 67–79.

Steers, R. M., & Porter, L. M. (1979). *Motivation and work behavior* (2nd ed.). New York: McGraw-Hill.

Steiner, I. D. (1972). *Group process and productivity.* New York: Academic Press.

Tziner, A., & Dolan, S. (1983). *Identifying female officer potential: An exploration in predictors' payoff.* Unpublished manuscript, Tel Aviv University, Israel.

Vroom, V. H. (1960). *Some personality determinants of the effects of participation.* Englewood Cliffs, NJ: Prentice-Hall.

Received May 27, 1983
Revision received April 5, 1984 ■

PART 2

Group Structure

The interactions among group members are seldom random. Instead, they tend to follow regular patterns. These patterns of interaction reflect the structure of the group (see Cartwright & Zander, 1968; Scott & Scott, 1979). Every group has some structure, although the particular patterns of interaction among group members may vary considerably from one group to another. Research has shown that many aspects of group structure can arise very quickly, within a few minutes after members meet for the first time. (Note that structure can also be imposed immediately on a group by outsiders.) And once it arises, group structure is usually slow to change, even if the composition of a group changes over time. This stability is due in part to the social pressure exerted within the group on members whose behavior strays from the regular patterns. People who behave "properly" are rewarded, and those who behave "improperly" are punished, so improper behavior that might lead to structural changes is rare. But there are more subtle sources of stability as well (Bem, 1972; Felson, 1993). For example, people may come to see themselves as other members of the group see them, or attribute their behavior to internal causes (e.g., personality characteristics) rather than to external ones (e.g., external authorities or social pressure). In either case, people may see no reason to change their behavior (which seems "natural" to them) and might in fact resist such change.

Group structure can take several forms. Much of the research in this area focuses on status systems, roles, norms, and cohesion. *Status* involves patterns of influence in a group (Ridgeway & Walker, 1995). Status differences are often apparent in both the verbal and nonverbal behavior of group members. At a verbal level, people with higher status speak more often and more loudly, are more likely to criticize, command, and interrupt others, and are spoken to more often. And at the nonverbal level, people with higher status are more likely to stand erect, maintain eye contact, and be physically intrusive. *Norms* involve expectations about how everyone in a group should behave (Feldman, 1984). A group of teenage friends, for example, may have norms about how its members should dress, what music they should listen to, and how much they should drink at parties. *Roles* are similar to norms, in that they also involve expectations about the behavior of group members (Belbin, 2004), but roles usually apply to just one person (or a few people), rather than to everyone. Leaders, scapegoats, and newcomers are all common roles in groups. A newcomer, for example, is generally expected by oldtimers to be anxious, passive, dependent, and conforming. Finally, *cohesion* (Hogg, 1992) is a cultural element that is familiar to most people, but difficult to define (Mudrack, 1989). At an intuitive level, cohesion involves the strength and resilience of a group. A cohesive group can thus overcome obstacles and resist disruption because its members like one another, believe in similar things, and are committed to their group.

Other aspects of group structure that have been identified and studied include the networks of friendship and communication among group members and the emotional climates within groups.

Research on *social networks* often explores the relationships that bind a group's members to outsiders, including people who belong to other groups (Putnam & Stohl, 1996). But researchers have also studied the social networks within groups. For example, Krackhardt (1990) studied the real and perceived friendship and advice networks within a small entrepreneurial firm. He found that workers with more accurate views of the advice network seemed more powerful to their coworkers, above and beyond their actual job status. And several researchers (see Kelly & Barsade, 2001) have recently become interested in the *emotional climates* of groups, which are believed to affect many aspects of group behavior. For example, George (1990) studied groups of retail salespeople and found that within each group, people tended to experience similar moods, so that each group had its own emotional climate. Moreover, that climate affected several behaviors among workers, including their helpfulness to customers (and to one another) and absenteeism. Workers were less helpful in groups with negative emotional climates and less likely to miss work in groups with positive emotional climates.

Finally, groups also develop *cultures* that encompass many structural elements. A review of ethnographic research on work groups convinced Levine and Moreland (1991), for example, that every work group develops its own, distinct culture. Culture consists of socially shared knowledge and a set of related customs. Cultural knowledge can focus on the group, its members, or the work that they perform. Workers often seem to agree, for example, about how well their group is performing, who likes or dislikes whom, and which aspects of their work are most interesting. Customs embody the knowledge that workers share and thus serve (often in subtle ways) to communicate and validate that knowledge. Routines, accounts, jargon, rituals, and symbols are all examples of customs. Routines are the daily practices (e.g., coffee breaks at the same time every morning) in which group members engage; accounts are stories that group members regularly tell about the group and one another; jargon is the words and phrases that mean something special to group members, but not to outsiders; rituals are special ceremonies that mark important events in the life of the group, such as the loss of a member; and symbols are objects (e.g., costumes, flags) that mean something important to the group's members.

What is the purpose of group structure? There is convincing evidence that people dislike uncertainty, and structure obviously reduces uncertainty about what might occur in a group. There is also potential for conflict in every group, and although conflict can sometimes benefit groups, it is usually painful for group members. As a result, efforts to control conflict are made by most groups. Such efforts include the prevention of group conflict, and group structure may be helpful in that regard as well. When members of a group agree about how they are supposed to behave, they are less likely to behave any differently, thus preventing at least some of the conflicts that might otherwise occur. In groups with stronger status systems, for example, members know more about who has power over whom, and so conflicts over power should occur

less often. Similarly, there should be fewer conflicts about how to behave in particular situations (e.g., dealing with outsiders) in groups that have stronger norms.

REFERENCES

Belbin, M. (2004). *Management teams: Why they succeed or fail* (2nd ed.). Oxford: Elsevier.

Bem, D. J. (1972). Self-perception theory. In L. Berkowitz (Ed.), *Advances in experimental social psychology* (Vol. 6, pp. 1–62). New York: Academic Press.

Cartwright, D., & Zander, A. (1968). The structural properties of groups. In D. Cartwright & A. Zander (Eds.), *Group dynamics: Research and theory* (3rd ed., pp. 485–502). New York: Harper & Row.

Feldman, D. C. (1984). The development and enforcement of group norms. *Academy of Management Journal, 9,* 47–53.

Felson, R. B. (1993). The (somewhat) social self: How others affect self-appraisal. In J. M. Suls (Ed.), *The self in social perspective: Psychological perspectives on the self* (Vol. 4, pp. 1–26). Hillsdale, NJ: Lawrence Erlbaum Associates, Inc.

George, J. M. (1990). Personality, affect, and behavior in groups. *Journal of Applied Psychology, 75,* 107–116.

Hogg, M. A. (1992). *The social psychology of group cohesiveness: From attraction to social identity.* New York: New York University Press.

Kelly, J. R., & Barsade, S. G. (2001). Mood and emotions in small groups and work teams. *Organizational Behavior and Human Decision Processes, 86,* 99–130.

Krackhardt, D. (1990). Assessing the political landscape: Structure, cognition, and power in organizations. *Administrative Science Quarterly, 35,* 342–369.

Levine, J. M., & Moreland, R. L. (1991) Culture and socialization in work groups. In L. B. Resnick, J. M. Levine, & S. D. Teasdale (Eds.), *Perspectives on socially shared cognition* (pp. 257–279). Washington, DC: American Psychological Association.

Mudrack, P. E. (1989). Defining group cohesiveness: A legacy of confusion? *Small Group Behavior, 20,* 37–49.

Putnam, L. L., & Stohl, C. (1996). Bona fide groups: An alternative perspective for communication and small group decision making. In R. Y. Hirokawa & M. S. Poole (Eds.), *Communication and group decision making* (2nd ed., pp. 147–178). Thousand Oaks, CA: Sage.

Ridgeway, C. L., & Walker, H. A. (1995). Status structures. In K. S. Cook, G. A. Fine, & J. S. House (Eds.), *Sociological perspectives on social psychology* (pp. 281–310). Boston: Allyn & Bacon.

Scott, W. A., & Scott, R. (1979). Structural properties of groups. *Australian Journal of Psychology, 31,* 89–100.

Readings

The first paper in this set, by Driskell and Mullen (1990), describes a meta-analysis of several studies on the relationships among status characteristics, expectation states, and behavior in groups. Meta-analysis is a statistical method for reviewing the results from several studies, so that general trends can be identified and measured. For a long time, research reviews in psychology were *narrative* in nature—reviewers simply described verbally (and often in detail) a set of research reports for their readers. These summaries were generally qualitative rather than quantitative; at most, a reviewer might count how often a particular finding was reported. In the 1970s, however, psychologists began to use an alternative method for reviewing research, namely *meta-analysis*. Meta-analysis allows reviewers to produce more precise, quantitative summaries of research results. Imagine a phenomenon that has been studied by many researchers. Each researcher observes the behavior of many participants and then analyzes that behavior statistically to test certain hypotheses. A meta-analysis also involves statistical tests, but at a higher level (as the term "meta" implies). The raw data for meta-analyses are the results from statistical tests performed by the researchers, rather than the behaviors of the individual participants in their studies. This allows more precise conclusions to be drawn. Instead of simply counting how often a phenomenon occurs, for example, reviewers who perform meta-analyses can measure exactly how strong a phenomenon is and whether it is significant (occurs more often than would be expected by chance). They can also explore whether the strength of the phenomenon varies with

particular characteristics of the research covered by their meta-analyses. These might include the kinds of participants who were studied, the settings in which their behavior was observed, the ways in which major variables were operationalized, and so on.

Driskell and Mullen reviewed research related to expectation states theory, which offers an explanation for how status systems arise in groups. According to that theory, group members award status to one another on the basis of both specific and diffuse status characteristics. Specific status characteristics are aspects of a group's members that are clearly relevant to its success. In most work groups, for example, education and prior experience would be specific status characteristics. Workers with more education or work experience would thus be given higher status. And that status would probably be deserved, because such workers are more likely than others to help a work group succeed. However, status can also be awarded on the basis of diffuse status characteristics. Diffuse status characteristics are aspects of a group's members that are viewed in positive or negative ways, whether they are actually relevant to the group's success or not. Sex and physical attractiveness, for example, are diffuse status characteristics in many work groups. Male workers, or more attractive workers of either sex, are thus given higher status, even if that is undeserved. Because diffuse status characteristics are easier for group members to assess, they are usually used first in the development of status systems, and if mistakes are made, then they are corrected later on through the use of specific status characteristics. According to expectation states theory, status characteristics (specific and diffuse) lead to expectation states—beliefs about the worthiness of each group member. These expectation states, in turn, shape behavior within the group. If expectations about a person are positive, then he or she is treated well by other group members. The person is given more opportunities to lead the group, for example, and others react more positively to any leadership efforts made by him or her.

Driskell and Mullen reviewed the results from several studies, each of which examined the effects of status characteristics on expectation states and behavior and the effects of expectation states on behavior. They also explored whether any of these effects were related to how powerful the status characteristics were (according to a set of impartial judges who evaluated the studies independently). The main results from the meta-analysis confirmed the theory—when status characteristics were more positive, expectation states were more favorable and behavior was more deferential. Moreover, favorable expectations also led to more deferential behavior. All of these effects were significant. But *how* do status characteristics change behavior? The theory claims that such changes are *mediated* by changes in expectation states. The effects of status characteristics on behavior are thus indirect—unless status characteristics first change expectation states, they cannot change behavior. This is an important issue because expectation states are much less important in other theories about how status systems arise within groups. Several other results from the meta-analysis were consistent with the theory's mediation claim. First, the effects of status characteristics on expectation states were stronger than the effects of status characteristics on behavior. Second, the effects of status characteristics on behavior were no longer significant when differences in expectation states were taken into account

statistically (as if expectation states were the same for everyone in a group, regardless of their status characteristics). Finally, when status characteristics were more powerful, they had significantly stronger effects on expectation states, but not on behavior.

The second paper, by Prentice, Miller, and Lightdale (1994), is relevant to cohesion in groups. Group cohesion is intriguing. Although many people have an intuitive sense of what cohesion means, there has been much confusion and disagreement among psychologists about what cohesion is and how it should be measured. For many years, cohesion was studied in terms of interpersonal attraction. A cohesive group was thus one whose members all liked one another. More recently, however, cohesion has been studied from a *social identity* perspective. Unlike personal identity, which reflects those aspects of the self that make a person different from others, social identity reflects those aspects of the self that involve group memberships, which link people together.

Social identity is a critical concept in two theories that have become quite important for understanding group behavior. *Social identity theory*, which was originally developed to explain intergroup relations, focuses on the relationships among social categorization, social identity, and social comparison. Social categorization is a way of perceiving both the self and others that emphasizes their group memberships, rather than their individual qualities. When people are perceived in this way, social identity becomes more salient. Everyone wants a positive social identity (just as they want a positive personal identity). In other words, they want to belong to the best group(s). Social comparison is used to decide which groups are best—people compare their own groups to relevant outgroups on whatever dimensions are salient at a given moment. Social identity theory suggests that conflict between groups occurs (in part) because they seek more favorable results from such comparisons, thereby improving the social identities of their members. *Self-categorization theory*, a later development, is more cognitive in nature, and the motivational focus of this theory is uncertainty reduction, rather than self-esteem. According to the theory, people often try to simplify the world around them by categorizing things, including themselves and other people. Categorization of people can occur at several levels—they can be viewed as individuals, or as members of small groups, large organizations, nations, and so on. Group phenomena occur when several people (whether they are in direct contact or not) categorize themselves as members of the same group and behave accordingly. An important byproduct of this categorization process is the creation of a *group prototype*, or shared image of the type of person who embodies whatever qualities make the group distinctive. That prototype, according to the theory, is important in both intergroup *and* intragroup relations. In particular, it can play a role in group cohesion.

Self-categorization theory claims that interpersonal attraction is not the only basis for cohesion. There is another kind of cohesion, one that reflects how well the members of a group match its prototoype. Liking among group members may thus reflect how similar they are to the group's prototype, rather than any other characteristics that they possess. Thus, a group can be cohesive even when its members do not especially like one another, so long as they identify strongly with the group and

regard one another as good exemplars of it. A political protest group, for example, may contain a diverse set of people who would not otherwise choose to spend much time together, except that they are all concerned about the same issue and thus admire those who work to support the group's positions on that issue.

This approach to cohesion can be seen in the work of Prentice and her colleagues (1994), who surveyed the members of various college student groups. Their goal was to distinguish between common-identity groups, where social identity is the basis for group cohesion, and common-bond groups, where group cohesion is based on interpersonal attraction. Two studies were carried out. The first one involved eating clubs (groups of students who purchase and eat their meals at special dining halls), some of which were more selective than others. Joining the selective clubs involved a recruitment process in which interpersonal relations between new and old members were very important. But such relations were almost irrelevant in the non-selective clubs, which students joined through a lottery process. The two sets of clubs can thus be classified as common-bond and common-identity groups, respectively. In the second study, other students at the same college were asked to list campus groups to which they belonged. These groups were then classified by the researchers as common-bond or common-identity in nature. In both studies, group members completed questionnaires that measured attachment to the group versus its members and evaluations of other group members. Both studies tested the same two hypotheses. First, group attachment was expected to be stronger than member attachment in common-identity groups, but the reverse was expected in common-bond groups.

Second, group attachment was expected to depend more on member attachment, and on evaluations of other group members, in the common-bond groups than in the common-identity groups. Although the evidence for these hypotheses was not always strong, they were generally supported by the two studies.

These results show that the nature of cohesion can vary across groups. That could have interesting implications for many other aspects of group life. Internal conflicts, for example, may be less threatening to common-identity than to common-bond groups, because the latter groups depend on positive relations among their members and thus might not survive if conflict is severe. Stronger methods for handling conflict may thus develop and be applied more quickly in common-bond groups. Leadership could also differ in common-identity and common-bond groups. The leaders of common-identity groups are probably people whose personal qualities match the group prototype best, whereas in common-bond groups, the leaders are probably people whose relationships with other members are strongest. These and other issues, such as how the two kinds of group cohesion might relate to one another in the same group, are worth exploring.

The final paper in this set, by Zurcher (1970), is a case study that focuses on roles and norms in a small group of friends who played poker together on a regular basis. This is another example of qualitative research. The poker group met twice a month, always at a member's home, from early evening until midnight. Every session began with an informal discussion period, followed by several hours of poker, and ended with a modest meal (provided by the host). All of the group's members were men with similar backgrounds and interests. Zurcher joined the group himself and remained in it for one year. During that time, he observed and participated in all of the poker sessions, and at the end of the year, he interviewed each member about the group.

Zurcher identified many norms in this group. For example, no one who was not a group member was allowed to observe the group, and distractions or interruptions (e.g., playing the television or radio, answering the telephone) were not tolerated. And while the group was playing poker, everyone was expected to focus on the game. No eating or drinking was permitted (although everyone smoked pipes or cigars), nor could group members talk about anything but the game. And, of course, there were lots of "rules" about how poker should be played, not just the formal rules that any poker player would know, but also informal rules about "proper" betting, bluffing, and so on.

As time passed, the group occasionally lost members, and so attempts were made to replace them. Group members considered their friends and acquaintances and then invited some of them to play, but only on a provisional basis. Such visits were, in other words, "tryouts" for the group. The prospective members were observed carefully, and if they behaved in ways that violated group norms, then subtle signals of disapproval, such as raised eyebrows or throat clearing, were sent. Ostracism was also used occasionally—people simply ignored prospective members, as if they were not there. Other qualities of prospective members were also evaluated, such as how "nice" they were, their skill at playing poker, and how well they tolerated teasing (which was common in the group). At the end of the night, after a prospective member left for home, he was discussed by the group and a decision was made about inviting him back. Only a few of the prospective members received such invitations, and not all of them went on to become full members of the group.

Zurcher argued that groups such as these are really separate "worlds" whose main purpose is to satisfy needs that are difficult or impossible to meet in everyday life, when people are at work or with their families. Playing poker, for example, lets people compete fiercely with others; display some unusual skills (e.g., shuffling cards, betting); experience exciting events, including the sudden gain or loss of money; and lie to others (bluff) without being blamed (and in fact earning praise) for it. Because life within the poker-playing group was so different from the normal world, Zurcher speculated that the informal discussions before the games, and the meals afterward, may have served as compression and decompression periods (respectively) that helped group members to move from one world to the other. He also suggested that other kinds of leisure groups serve the same general purpose, namely allowing people to meet needs that would otherwise go unmet in their everyday lives.

Discussion Questions

1. Is the structure of a group related to its composition? For example, how do you think the structure (e.g., status systems, norms, cohesion) of male groups differs from that of female groups?
2. Have you ever had lower status in a group than you deserved? Why? What could a person in that situation to do gain status? What did you do? Did it work?
3. When people are asked about the structure of their group, they often have difficulty answering, and sometimes they deny that their group is structured at all or that their behavior is influenced by its structure. Why?
4. Think about the friendship network and the communication network in a small group to which you belong. Are they the same? How does someone's position within those networks relate to his or her status in the group?
5. Over time, people often internalize the roles that they play within groups. Why does that happen? Describe some of the positive and negative effects of role internalization.

Suggested Readings

George, J. M. (1990). Personality, affect, and behavior in groups. *Journal of Applied Psychology, 75*, 107–116.

Gersick, C. J. G., & Hackman, R. L. (1990). Habitual routines in task-performing groups. *Organizational Behavior & Human Decision Processes, 47*, 65–97.

Humphrey, R. (1985). How work roles influence perception: Structural-cognitive processes and organizational behavior. *American Sociological Review, 50*, 242–252.

Krackhardt, D., & Porter, L. W. (1986). The snowball effect: Turnover embedded in communication networks. *Journal of Applied Psychology, 71*, 50–55.

Ridgeway, C., & Diekema, D. (1989). Dominance and collective hierarchy formation in male and female task groups. *American Sociological Review, 54*, 79–93.

Status, Expectations, and Behavior: A Meta-Analytic Review and Test of the Theory

James E. Driskell and Brian Mullen

Status characteristics and expectation states theory is concerned with the processes whereby status differentials activate performance expectations and with the effect of these expectations on behavior. The relative contributions of status and expectations to behavior have not been clearly established in previous primary-level studies. Moreover, researchers working within alternative perspectives on interaction inequality have argued that expectations are a superfluous epiphenomenon of behavior. A meta-analytic integration was therefore conducted on previous research that has examined the status $\rightarrow$ expectations $\rightarrow$ behavior pattern of effects. Consistent with the formulations of the theory, the results indicate that status exerts its effects on behavior indirectly, through the effects of status on expectations and the effect of expectations on behavior.

Research, as well as casual observation, reveals that status gradients quickly emerge in initially unstructured task groups. Some group members attain a superordinate position in terms of power and prestige; they talk more, have their ideas more readily accepted by others, and receive more votes as "group leader" (e.g., Mullen, Salas, & Driskell, 1990). The theory of status characteristics and expectation states (Berger & Conner, 1969; Berger, Wagner, & Zelditch, 1985; Berger, Fisek, Norman, & Zelditch, 1977; Webster & Driskell, 1978) offers one perspective for analyzing the

NOTE: The authors would like to express their appreciation to Wendy Wood and to four anonymous reviewers for helpful comments on an earlier draft. Address correspondence to James E. Driskell, Florida Maxima Corporation, Winter Park, FL 32792, or to Brian Mullen, Department of Psychology, Syracuse University, NY 13210.

development of such differentiation within small, task-oriented groups. In short, the theory argues that certain members of these groups are treated unequally because unequal performance expectations are held for them. This article reports the results of a meta-analytic examination of this central assumption of the theory.

The basic assumption of the theory is that within task groups whose members are differentiated by some valued characteristic (e.g., race, sex, age, ability) individuals form stable conceptions of one another's performance capabilities which are consistent with the distribution of that valued characteristic. These performance expectations, or expectation states, determine the power and prestige structure of the group, including opportunities to perform, deference, and the exercise of influence. Status characteristics serve as cues to performance capability because they are culturally evaluated (e.g., it is considered preferable in our culture to be White, male, and professional) and carry performance connotations (e.g., Whites, males, and professionals are thought to do better at most tasks). The external evaluation of a status characteristic is imported into the group and forms the basis for the assignment of performance expectations.

Thus, the theory posits the following process:

status characteristics → performance
expectations → interaction inequality

External characteristics that differentiate group members lead to the formation of differential performance expectations, which, in turn, determine the observable inequalities in group interaction.

Evidence for the Theory

The three bivariate relations implied by the foregoing discussion have received differing amounts of research attention. The effects of status on behavior have been well documented in a wide range of laboratory and applied settings (Cohen, 1982; Driskell, 1982; Lockheed & Hall, 1976; Meeker & Weitzel-O'Neill, 1977; Webster & Driskell, 1978; Wood & Karten, 1986). Although the effect of status

on expectations is generally assumed (and, in fact, is a central tenet of the theory), it is rarely demonstrated (notable exceptions are Webster & Driskell, 1978; Wood & Karten, 1986; Zeller & Warnecke, 1973). Finally, few studies have explicitly reported the effect of expectations on behavior, although again the theory assumes that expectations determine behavior (again, notable exceptions are Driskell, 1986; Wood & Karten, 1986).

It must be recognized that there are two ways in which the fundamental assumptions of status characteristics and expectation states theory have not been fully and explicitly examined in the previous primary-level studies. First, relatively few studies have collected data on all three of the bivariate relations defined by the theory (status-behavior, status-expectations, and expectations-behavior), and not all of these studies have reported the specific tests for all three bivariate relations. Second, and perhaps even more important, the primary-level studies that have examined these bivariate relations have generally not examined whether the specific patterning of these three bivariate relations fits the requirements of the theory. Note that the theory does not merely suggest that the three variables of status, expectations, and behavior will be correlated with one another. Status characteristics and expectation states theory postulates that status will exert its effects on behavior *through* its effects on expectations. This postulate translates into two specific patterns of results. At the simplest level, it suggests that the effects of status on behavior will be weaker than the effects of status on expectations and the effects of expectations on behavior. At a more complex level, it suggests that partialing out the effects of expectations will reduce the magnitude of the status-behavior effect to triviality, whereas the magnitude of the expectations-behavior effect will remain considerable even after partialing out the effects of status. Although these specific patterns are assumed by status characteristics and expectation states theory and implied in the discussion sections of articles published within this domain, a narrative reading of this literature does not convey whether or to what extent these specific patterns are substantiated in the evidence collected to date.

Alternative Perspectives

Several alternative positions have been forwarded regarding the relations among status, expectations, and behavior described above. Despite the plausibility of the status characteristics and expectation states theory, its assumptions have not been unquestioningly accepted. For example, Molm (1985) has persuasively argued that the theory assumes that the status-expectations effect and the expectations-behavior effect should correspond, but that this correspondence is seldom substantiated. Mazur (1985; Mazur et al., 1980; Rosa & Mazur, 1979) has developed a biologically oriented dominance approach to status and behavior which suggests that expectations should not be the primary causal determinant of behavior. Nemeth (1988) has even pointed out that the fundamental link between status and behavior might be subject to exception, insofar as low-status group members might sometimes be expected to exert more influence in groups.

More forcefully, Lee and Ofshe's (1981, 1983) two-process theory has argued that behavior is determined directly by status and is followed by cognitive activity designed to understand that behavior. This is in direct contradiction to the patterns involving status, expectations, and behavior formulated by status characteristics and expectation states theory. For example,

> The initial idea that occupational, or race, or gender, or age, or class status leads to guesses about intelligence and hence to placing bets about who is correct was at least simple and understandable, albeit wrong. It seems that the program has become an amorphous mass of absorbed notions capable of incorporating anything into its formlessness as it smiles and burps down the road towards the confusion from whence it came. (Lee & Ofshe, 1983, p. 65)

This clearly portrays a perspective on the relations of status, expectations, and behavior that differs from the formulations of status characteristics and expectation states theory. Mazur's dominance approach and Lee and Ofshe's two-process theory represent perspectives in which expectations are little more than a superfluous epiphenomenon of behavior. This translates into two specific patterns

of results. At the simplest level, it suggests that the effects of status on behavior will be *stronger* than the effects of status on expectations and the effects of expectations on behavior. And at a more complex level, it suggests that partialing out the effects of status will reduce the magnitude of the expectations-behavior effect to triviality, whereas the magnitude of the status-behavior effect will remain considerable even after partialing out the effects of expectations.

In one of the most even-handed contributions to this debate, Sherman (1983) noted that the key issue raised by this dispute is whether expectations direct behavior (as per status characteristics and expectation states theory) or whether behavior occurs in direct response to situational factors and is coincidental with cognitive activity designed to understand the behavior (as per the dominance approach, or the two-process theory, cited above). According to Sherman, the issue is far from settled. Thus, one purpose of this meta-analytic integration is to determine whether and to what extent the results of previous research support the formulations of status characteristics and expectation states theory.

Effects of the Strength of the Status Differentials

Implicit in most discussions of status characteristics and expectation states theory (e.g., Berger et al., 1977; Webster & Driskell, 1978) is the assumption that status differentials fall along a gradient or continuum (rather than a simple dichotomy of "low status/high status"). For example, the status difference between college students who perform differently on a task-relevant pretest (Driskell, 1982) may be weaker than that between military personnel who differ in rank (enlisted vs. officers; Driskell, 1986).

An intriguing derivation of the theory can be generated from the notion of a continuum of status differential strength. If the direct effect of status is on expectations (as per status characteristics and expectation states theory), then the strength of the status differential should predict the magnitude of the status-expectation effect. Alternatively, if the direct effect of status is on behavior (as per the alternative perspectives considered in the previous section), then the strength of the status differential should predict the magnitude of the status-behavior effect. Thus, a second purpose of this meta-analytic integration is to determine the extent to which the various relations among status, expectations, and behavior are moderated by the strength of the status differentials.

Procedure

In accord with the procedures specified in Mullen (1990), Mullen and Rosenthal (1985), and Rosenthal (1980, 1984), studies were located using a comprehensive computer search of relevant databases, the "ancestry" approach (locating previous studies mentioned in reference lists of already-located studies), the "descendency" approach (locating subsequent studies that mentioned already-located studies, using the *Social Sciences Citation Index*), and the "invisible college" approach (discussion with colleagues publishing in this research domain).

Studies were selected for inclusion in this meta-analysis if they met the following criteria: (a) Each study had to manipulate some aspect of status of the group members (e.g., race, sex, ability scores, educational level, military rank), (b) Each study had to measure some facet of the group members' expectations and some type of observable task behavior, (c) Each study had to report (or allow for the retrieval of) a statistical test of the effects of status on expectations, the effects of status on behavior, and the relation between expectations and behavior. When appropriate, the authors of the original publications were contacted and supplementary analyses were requested. Seven sets of hypothesis tests, derived from six separate publications, met these selection criteria. The simple bivariate relations among status, expectations, and behavior were used to derive the partial correlations between status and behavior (partialing out the effects of expectations) and the partial correlations between expectations and behavior (partialing out the effects of status). The articles included in this

meta-analytic database and the relevant statistical information are presented in Table 4.1.

In addition, each study was evaluated for the strength of the manipulation of the status differentials. Specifically, six judges (four graduate students in social psychology and two faculty members in social psychology) evaluated the strength of each manipulated status differential condition, with no reference to study outcome or authorship, on a 9-point scale (where 1 = no difference between the two manipulated status differential conditions and 9 = large difference between the two manipulated status differential conditions). Thus, a high-strength status manipulation would be one in which the judges perceived a considerable difference between the status represented in the high-status condition and the status represented in the low-status condition. A low-strength status manipulation would be one in which the judges perceived very little difference between the high-status condition and the low-status condition. The mean interjudge reliability was $\bar{r} = .740$, $p = .0116$; the Spearman-Brown effective reliability based on six judges was $R = .945$. Thus, judges exhibited an adequate amount of agreement in gauging the strength of the status manipulations used in these studies. The mean strength of the manipulations of the status differentials, collapsed across judges, is also presented in Table 4.1.

These hypothesis tests were subjected to the following meta-analytic procedures: combination of significance levels and effect sizes, diffuse comparisons of significance levels and effect sizes, and focused comparisons of significance levels and effect sizes. Formulas and computational procedures are provided elsewhere (see Mullen, 1990; Mullen & Rosenthal, 1985; Rosenthal, 1980, 1984).

Results

Table 4.2 presents the results of the meta-analytic weighted combinations of significance levels and effect sizes (where study outcomes are weighted by sample sizes). These meta-analytic combinations reveal that status is a significant and strong

TABLE 4.1. Studies included in the Meta-Analysis

Study	Effect[a]	Test	N (df)	r	p	SSM[b]	Status Dimension	Behavior Measure
Zeller & Warnecke (1973)	S-E	r = .548	160 (158)	.548	1.0E-13	5.0	Educational attainment	Allocation of responsibility
	S-B	r = .222	160 (158)	.222	.0024			
	E-B	r = .62	160 (158)	.620	2.8E-17			
	E-B.S	r = .611	160 (157)	.611	1.01E-16			
	S-B.E	r = −.179	160 (157)	−.179	.988			
Webster & Driskell (1978)	S-E	U = 13.5	42 (20,22)	.780	1.1E-7	8.5	Race and pretest scores	Influence
	S-B	Z = 3.82	42 (20,22)	.589	6.6E-5			
	E-B	r = .602	42 (40)	.602	1.0E-5			
	E-B.S	r = .270	42 (39)	.270	.0437			
	S-B.E	r = .225	42 (39)	.225	.0788			
Driskell (1982)	S-E	U = 81.5	40 (20,20)	.507	.00068	4.8	Pretest scores	Influence
	S-B	p = .021	40 (—)	.322	.021			
	E-B	r = .417	40 (38)	.417	.0037			
	E-B.S	r = .311	40 (37)	.311	.0271			
	S-B.E	r = .141	40 (37)	.141	.1963			
Webster (1982)	S-E	U = 28.5	40 (20,20)	.733	1.8E-6	4.8	Pretest scores	Influence
	S-B	U = 139.5	40 (20,20)	.260	.05			
	E-B	r = .382	40 (38)	.382	.0075			
	E-B.S	r = .292	40 (37)	.292	.0359			
	S-B.E	r = −.032	40 (37)	−.032	.5762			
Wood & Karten (1986)	S-E	F = 6.89	68 (1,32)	.421	.0066	3.3	Gender	Proportion of task behavior
	S-B	F = 14.09	68 (1,32)	.553	.00035			
	E-B	r = .240	68 (123)	.240	.0035			
	E-B.S	r = .010	68 (31)	.010	.4780			
	S-B.E	r = .513	68 (31)	.513	.0011			
Wood & Karten (1986)	S-E	F = 9.57	68 (1,32)	.480	.0021	4.8	Pretest scores	Proportion of task behavior
	S-B	F = 4.27	68 (1,32)	.343	.0235			
	E-B	r = .240	68 (123)	.240	.0035			
	E-B.S	r = .091	68 (31)	.091	.3064			
	S-B.E	r = .268	68 (31)	.268	.0662			
Driskell (1986)	S-E	U = 53.5	39 (19,20)	.606	6.3E-5	3.5	Military rank	Influence
	S-B	U = 94	40 (19,21)	.452	.0021			
	E-B	r = .600	39 (37)	.600	2.7E-5			
	E-B.S	r = .460	39 (36)	.460	.0018			
	S-B.E	r = .138	39 (36)	.138	.2038			

[a] S = status; E = expectations; B = behavior.
[b] SSM = strength of status manipulation.

TABLE 4.2. Results of Meta-Analytic Combinations and Comparisons

	S-E	S-B	E-B	E-B.S	S-B.E
Combinations					
Significance					
Z	11.45	6.08	11.32	8.56	0.33
p	4.98E-25	7.77E-10	1.13E-24	9.53E-17	.3709
Effect size					
Fisher's Z	0.65	0.38	0.52	0.39	0.10
$\bar{r}$	.57	.36	.48	.37	.10
$\bar{r}^2$	.32	.13	.23	.14	.01
$\bar{d}$	1.39	0.78	1.10	0.79	0.21
Diffuse comparisons					
Significance					
$\chi^2(6)$	20.53	3.88	29.93	48.19	16.27
p	.0010	.6924	.000005	6.21E-11	.0124
Effect size					
$\chi^2(6)$	13.37	12.00	19.35	32.70	29.95
p	.0375	.0619	.0018	9.45E-7	.000005

predictor of expectations, status is a significant and moderate predictor of behavior, and expectations are a significant and strong predictor of behavior.

Particularly informative are the results of the meta-analytic combinations for the two partial correlations derived for each study. Partialing out the effects of status did produce a significant ($Z = 2.310, p = .0105$) reduction in the magnitude of the relation between expectations and behaviors (from $\bar{r} = .48$ to $\bar{r} = .37$). However, even when the effects of status are partialed out, expectations are still a moderate predictor of behavior (accounting for 14% of the variability in behavior). Alternatively, partialing out the effects of expectations produced an even more significant ($Z = 3.409$, $p = .0003$) reduction in the magnitude of the relation between status and behavior (from $\bar{r} = .36$ to $\bar{r} = .10$). When effects of expectations are partialed out, status becomes a trivially weak predictor of behavior (accounting for 1% of the variability in behavior). Finally, it should be noted that the magnitude of effect for the relation between expectations and behavior after partialing out the effect of status ($\bar{r} = .37$) was significantly larger ($Z = 1.766$, $p = .0387$) than the magnitude of effect for the relation between status and behavior after partialing out the effect of expectations ($\bar{r} = .10$).

These data argue strongly on behalf of the formulations of status characteristics and expectation

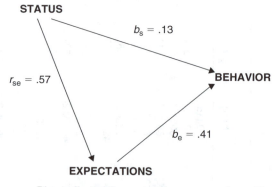

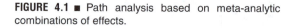

Direct effect of STATUS on BEHAVIOR: $b_s = .13$
Indirect effect of STATUS on BEHAVIOR: $b_e r_{se} = .23$
Direct effect of EXPECTATIONS on BEHAVIOR: $b_e = .41$

FIGURE 4.1 ■ Path analysis based on meta-analytic combinations of effects.

states theory: Status seems to influence expectations, expectations seem to influence behavior, and there seems to be little direct influence of status on behavior, beyond that which can be attributed to the effect of status on expectations.

One way of illustrating this pattern is with the path analysis diagram in Figure 4.1. This path analysis is obtained from the meta-analytically derived mean rs presented in Table 4.2. Figure 4.1 shows that the direct effect of status on behavior is considerably smaller than the direct effect of

TABLE 4.3. Effects of Strength of Status Manipulation

	S-E	S-B	E-B	E-B.S	S-B.E
Correlation	.724	.287	.420	.065	−.164
Focused comparisons					
Significance					
Z	2.390	0.703	0.893	0.341	0.404
p	.0084	.2409	.1858	.3667	.3432
Effect size					
Z	2.525	0.791	1.397	0.242	0.612
p	.0058	.2145	.0812	.4042	.2703

expectations on behavior and that the real contribution of status in this model is to the determination of expectations.[1]

Regarding the effects of the strength of the manipulation of the status differentials, Table 4.3 presents the correlations between Fisher's Z for effect size and the strength of status, and the corresponding meta-analytic focused comparisons, for each of the relationships considered above. These results reveal that the strong effect of status on expectations becomes even stronger with stronger manipulations of status. The moderate effect of status on behavior is not affected by the strength of the status manipulation. And the strong effect of expectations on behavior becomes somewhat stronger with stronger status manipulations. Thus, the status-expectations effect, which represents the direct effect of status, is exaggerated by stronger manipulations of status; and the status-behavior effect, which represents the indirect effect of status, is not influenced by the strength of the status manipulation.

The tendency for the expectations-behavior effect to get somewhat stronger with stronger manipulations of status might be considered at least partially inconsistent with the theory: Once status has exerted its effects on expectations, one might expect the strength of the manipulation of status differentials to be unable to exert any effect on behavior. Fortunately, examination of the prediction of the partial correlations by the strength of the status manipulation clarifies this picture. The trivially small effects of status on behavior after partialing out the effects of expectations are not affected

by the strength of the status manipulation. More important, the moderate effects of expectations on behavior after partialing out the effects of status are not at all affected by the strength of the status manipulation. Thus, converging on the pattern portrayed in Figure 4.1, the effects of status on behavior seem to be largely indirect, through the effect of status on expectations.

Discussion

The results of these analyses can be summarized as follows: Status is a strong predictor of expectations; status is a moderate predictor of behavior; and expectations are a strong predictor of behavior. When the effects of expectations are partialed out, the status-behavior effect is reduced to triviality; however, when the effects of status are partialed out, the expectation-behavior effect is still of moderate magnitude. In addition, the strength of the status differential manipulation seems to predict those effects, and *only* those effects (specifically, the status-expectations effect), that should be influenced by the strength of the status manipulation if the formulations of status characteristics and expectation states theory are accurate.

These results are not apparent from a narrative reading of the literature on status characteristics and expectation states theory. Few studies have examined the three bivariate relations postulated by the theory. Few (if any) of the studies that did measure changes in expectations and behavior as a function of status have reported comparisons of the relative magnitudes of the status-behavior effects, the status-expectations effects, and the expectations-behavior effects. Similarly, few (if any) of the studies partialed the effects of status out of the expectations-behavior relations or partialed the effects of expectations out of the status-behavior relations (as required by the specifications of status characteristics and expectation states theory).

Proponents of the theory (e.g., Berger et al., 1977) generally assume that the patterns revealed by the present integration do in fact occur, whereas critics of the theory (e.g., Lee & Ofshe, 1981, 1983) generally assume that the patterns revealed by the present integration do not in fact occur. The fact remains that either assumption might have been confirmed in the present analyses. Rather than reiterating one assumption or the other, the present efforts have put these two sets of assumptions to the test, using evidence that lay hidden in several previous primary-level studies. The results do lend support to the core assumptions of status characteristics and expectation states theory. Moreover, the results contradict the position, represented by biologically oriented dominance approaches and the two-process theory, that expectations are superfluous epiphenomena.[2]

A few cautionary notes are in order. These analyses are based on the results of seven sets of hypothesis tests, representing the responses of approximately 450 subjects. Relatively speaking, this constitutes a relatively small meta-analytic database. By ways of comparison, Mullen, Salas, and Driskell's (1989) recent meta-analytic integration of the leadership-participation effect was based on the results of 33 hypothesis tests, representing the responses of over 3,600 subjects. It is perfectly legitimate to apply meta-analytic techniques to the integration of small research domains, provided that special care is taken to conduct an exhaustive search of the domain in order to include all relevant, retrievable hypothesis tests (see Mullen, 1990; Rosenthal, 1984, for discussion). An exhaustive search and the retrieval of all relevant hypothesis tests do indeed characterize the present efforts. Nonetheless, the relatively small size of a meta-analytic database sometimes precludes the pursuit of additional, theoretically interesting issues.

For example, alternative methods of operationalizing status differentials were used in the studies integrated in these analyses (including differences in such attributes as race, gender, military rank, educational attainment, and pretest scores). Indeed, the highly reliable discriminations that judges made among the various status differential manipulations indicated that there were noticeable differences across studies in the operationalization of the core variable of "status." Even finer-grained analyses of the effects associated with different operationalizations of status (perhaps using blocking, partitioning, casement displays, and complex model testing, as described at length in Mullen, 1990) would be illuminating. The fact that these types of analyses cannot be performed on the present, relatively small, meta-analytic database does not detract from the importance of the patterns reported above as a step toward resolving the contentious (and sometimes intemperate) debate between the proponents and the critics of status characteristics and expectation states theory.

As always, patterns revealed at the meta-analytic level should be confirmed at the primary level of analysis, where possible spurious influences can be controlled. In a practical vein, the results of these analyses may help to guide and inform future research on the relations among status, expectations, and behavior. Researchers wishing to study the effects of status on behavior should be prepared to incorporate measurements of expectations into their designs, in order to confirm, extend, and add to the literature examining the status → expectations → behavior effects. In addition, the present analyses revealed reliable judgments of the strength of manipulations of status differentials. These results suggest that future efforts be devoted to more precise treatments of the components of, and contributions to, the effects of the strength of status on the status → expectations → behavior relationship.

NOTES

1. Note that these analyses employ the common strategy of weighting study outcomes by sample sizes, so that studies based on larger samples are allowed to contribute proportionately more to the meta-analytic summaries (as

described in Mullen, 1990; Mullen & Rosenthal, 1985; Rosenthal, 1980, 1984, and as illustrated in Mullen, Copper, & Driskell, 1990; Mullen & Hu, 1988, 1989; Mullen & Johnson, in press; Mullen, Salas, & Driskell, 1989). However, it should be noted that the unweighted analyses replicate the patterns presented in Table 4.2 (status-expectation $\bar{r} = .60$, $p = 1.59\text{E-}26$; status-behavior $\bar{r} = .40$, $p = 1.10\text{E-}12$; expectation-behavior $\bar{r} = .46$, $p = 4.80\text{E-}22$; status-behavior. expectations $\bar{r} = .16$, $p = .0176$; expectations-behavior. Status $\bar{r} = .31$, $p = 4.81\text{E-}11$). The path analysis derived from these unweighted combinations replicates the pattern depicted in Figure 4.1 ($r_{SE} = .60$; $b_S = .19$; $b_E r_{SE} = .21$; $b_E = .34$). Thus, the patterns reported above cannot be attributed to an invidious contribution of studies with larger sample sizes when using the common weighted analysis strategy.

2. The two-process theory might argue that expectations might influence behavior when subjects cannot interact, whereas expectations are actually an epiphenomenon in settings where nonverbal, behavioral interaction can take place. However, this qualification cannot reconcile the two-process theory with the present results, insofar as most of the included hypothesis tests did involve subjects with some modicum of exposure to the nonverbal and behavioral cues of a real human being.

REFERENCES

Berger, J., & Conner, T. L. (1969). Performance expectations and behavior in small groups. *Acta Sociologica, 12*, 186–197.

Berger, J., Fisek, M. H., Norman, R. Z., & Zelditch, M. (1977). *Status characteristics and social interaction.* New York: Elsevier.

Berger, J., Wagner, D. G., & Zelditch, M. (1985). Expectation states theory: Review and assessment. In J. Berger & M. Zelditch (Eds.), *Status, rewards, and influence* (pp. 1–72). San Francisco: Jossey-Bass.

Cohen, E. G. (1982). Expectation states and interracial interaction in school settings. *Annual Review of Sociology, 8*, 209–235.

Driskell, J. E. (1982). Personal characteristics and performance expectations. *Social Psychology Quarterly, 45*, 229–237.

Driskell, J. E. (1986, August). *Group performance under stress.* Paper presented at the annual meeting of the American Psychological Association, Washington, DC.

Lee, M., & Ofshe, R. (1981). The impact of behavioral style and status characteristics on social influence: A test of two competing theories. *Social Psychology Quarterly, 44*, 73–82.

Lee, M., & Ofshe, R. (1983). What are we to make of all of this: A reply to Berger and Zelditch. *Social Psychology Quarterly, 46*, 63–65.

Lockheed, M. E., & Hall, K. P. (1976). Conceptualizing sex as a status characteristic: Applications to leadership training strategies. *Journal of Social Issues, 32*, 111–124.

Mazur, A. (1985). A biosocial model of status in face-to-face primate groups. *Social Forces, 64*, 377–402.

Mazur, A., Rosa, E., Faupel, M., Heller, J., Leen, R., & Thurman, B. (1980). Physiological aspects of communication via mutual gaze. *American Journal of Sociology, 86*, 50–74.

Meeker, B. F., & Weitzel-O'Neill, P. A. (1977). Sex roles and interpersonal behavior in task oriented groups. *American Sociological Review, 42*, 92–105.

Molm, L. D. (1985). Gender and power use: An experimental analysis of behavior and perceptions. *Social Psychology Quarterly, 48*, 285–300.

Mullen, B. (1990). *Advanced BASIC meta-analysis.* Hillsdale, NJ: Lawrence Erlbaum.

Mullen, B., Copper, C., & Driskell, J. E. (1990). Jaywalking as a function of model behavior. *Personality and Social Psychology Bulletin, 16*, 320–330.

Mullen, B., & Hu, L. (1988). Social projection as a function of cognitive mechanisms: Two meta-analytic integrations. *British Journal of Social Psychology, 27*, 333–356.

Mullen B., & Hu, L. (1989). Perceptions of ingroup and outgroup variability: A meta-analytic integration. *Basic and Applied Social Psychology, 10*, 233–252.

Mullen B., & Johnson, C. (in press). Distinctiveness-based illusory correlation and stereotyping: A meta-analytic integration. *British Journal of Social Psychology.*

Mullen, B., & Rosenthal, R. (1985). *BASIC meta-analysis.* Hillsdale, NJ: Lawrence Erlbaum.

Mullen B., Salas, E., & Driskell, J. E. (1989). Salience, motivation, and artifact as contributions to the relation between participation rate and leadership. *Journal of Experimental Social Psychology, 25*, 545–559.

Nemeth, C. J. (1988). Style without status expectations: The special contributions of minorities. In M. Webster & M. Foschi (Eds.), *Status generalization: New theory and research* (pp. 281–290). Stanford, CA: Stanford University Press.

Rosa, E., & Mazur, A. (1979). Incipient status in groups. *Social Forces, 58*, 18–37.

Rosenthal, R. (Ed.). (1980). *Quantitative assessment of research domains.* San Francisco: Jossey-Bass.

Rosenthal, R. (1984). *Meta-analytic procedures for social research.* Beverly Hills, CA: Sage.

Sherman, S. J. (1983). Expectation-based and automatic behavior: A comment on Lee and Ofshe, and Berger and Zelditch. *Social Psychology Quarterly, 46*, 66–70.

Webster, M. (1982). Unpublished data, Stanford University.

Webster, M., & Driskell, J. E. (1978). Status generalization: A review and some new data. *American Sociological Review, 43*, 220–236.

Wood, W., & Karten, S. J. (1986). Sex differences in interaction style as a product of perceived sex differences in competence. *Journal of Personality and Social Psychology, 50*, 341–347.

Zeller, R. A., & Warnecke, R. B. (1973). The utility of constructs as intervening variables in the interpretation of experimental results. *Sociological Methods and Research, 2*, 85–110.

Asymmetries in Attachments to Groups and to Their Members: Distinguishing Between Common-Identity and Common-Bond Groups

Deborah A. Prentice, Dale T. Miller, and Jenifer R. Lightdale

Two studies sought to validate the distinction between common-identity groups, which are based on direct attachments to the group identity, and common-bond groups, which are based on attachments among group members. Study 1 focused on members of selective and nonselective university eating clubs. Study 2 focused on members of a diverse sample of campus groups. Both studies revealed asymmetries in group and member attachments: Individuals in common-identity groups were more attached to their group than to its members, whereas individuals in common-bond groups were as attached to the members as to the group (or more so). Study 2 also demonstrated that attachment to the group was more strongly related to various evaluations of individual group members in common-bond than in common-identity groups. The authors discuss the implications of these results for the development of groups over time and speculate on how the dynamics of the two types of groups might differ.

Describing the difference between Jonathan Swift and Alexander Pope, Samuel Johnson observed that the former loved men but hated mankind whereas the latter loved mankind but hated men. Dr. Johnson's observation, in addition to its insight into the animuses of two literary luminaries, contains a provocative idea about the mental representation of groups: People's feelings

NOTE: Preparation of this article was facilitated by National Institute of Mental Health Grant MH44069 to Dale T. Miller. We would like to thank Jessica Haile and Carolyn Oates for assistance with data collection and analysis and Dominic Abrams and Assaad Azzi for their helpful comments on an earlier draft. Correspondence concerning this article should be addressed to Deborah A. Prentice or Dale T. Miller, Department of Psychology, Princeton University, Green Hall, Princeton, NJ 08544-1010.

toward a group (mankind) may be distinct from their feelings toward the members of that group (men). In addition, this observation suggests the hypothesis that individuals with a stronger attachment to their group than to its members can be meaningfully and qualitatively distinguished from individuals with stronger attachments to the members of their group than to the group itself. Intuitive as this prediction might have seemed to Dr. Johnson, it has only recently begun to receive empirical and theoretical attention from social psychologists.

This lack of interest in the relation between attachments to groups and to their members is most likely due to the fact that these two types of attachment have been viewed instead as competing bases for groups. For most of this century, social psychology has been dominated by an individualistic conception of the group, by which groups are simply the sum of their individual parts. The manifesto of the individualist position was provided by Floyd Allport (1924) in his classic, *Social Psychology*. Allport began his text by dismissing the group as a meaningful unit of analysis, stating, "If we take care of the individual, psychologically speaking, the groups will take care of themselves" (p. 9). Forty years later, Allport's commitment to the individualist position had not diminished: "When the group dynamicist speaks of the 'attraction of the group for the individual' does he not mean just the attraction of the individuals for one another? If individuals are all drawn toward one another, are they not ipso facto drawn to the group?" (1962, pp. 23–24). Thus, for Allport and for successors to the individualist position, any question of the relation between attachment to the group and attachment to the individual group members is meaningless. There can be no greater or lesser attachment to the group than to the individual members, because the group has no representation or reality distinct from that of its members. Humankind consists solely of the men and women who make it up, no more and no less.

In the last two decades (i.e., 1970s/80s), social identity theorists have mounted a serious challenge to the individualistic conception of groups (e.g., Hogg & Abrams, 1989; Tajfel, 1981; Turner, Hogg,

Oakes, Reicher, & Wetherell, 1987). The heart of their attack rests on the findings of a fascinating series of studies on the minimal conditions necessary for group formation (e.g., Billig & Tajfel, 1973; Locksley, Ortiz, & Hepburn, 1980; Turner, Sachdev, & Hogg, 1983). These studies revealed that providing individuals with even the most minimal of shared identities—ones based on trivial criteria (e.g., preferring one artist over another) or explicitly random criteria (e.g., a coin toss)—was sufficient to generate in-group attachment and out-group discrimination. The ethnocentric biases in perception, evaluation, and memory demonstrated in these experiments could not have stemmed from attachment to individual group members: Subjects did not know, nor did they have any contact with, the other members of their group.

In recent years, these two very different conceptions of groups have typically been seen as providing competing accounts of group formation and cohesion (see Hogg, 1993; Moreland, 1987; Turner et al., 1987, for reviews). Individualists, who focus primarily on member attachment, do not need and, in the extreme case, do not even believe in direct attachment to the group itself. Social identity theorists, in contrast, do not need attachments between group members in order to claim the existence of a group. Recognition of this divergence in perspectives has led researchers to propose that direct attachment to the group (what we will call *group attachment*) and attachment to group members (what we will call *member attachment*) are two separate dimensions of group definition and cohesion (see Carron & Chelladurai, 1981; Hogg & Hardie, 1991; Karasawa, 1991; and Piper, Marrache, Lacroix, Richardsen, & Jones, 1983, for related distinctions). The majority of these researchers have tended to emphasize the importance of the former relative to the latter (e.g., Hogg & Hardie, 1991; Piper et al., 1983), although others have argued for a consideration of their interplay (e.g., Moreland, 1987).

In our research, we consider the relation between these two dimensions of attachment to be a defining property of groups. We distinguish between *common-bond groups*, which are based primarily on attachments among group members, and *common-identity groups*, which are based primarily on direct attachments to the group identity (see Jennings, 1947, for a related distinction). Common-bond groups are the groups to which Allport referred, in which attachment to the group is largely isomorphic with attachment to fellow group members. In these groups, the strength of group attachment depends critically on the extent to which one knows, likes, and feels similar to other members of the group, as well as the extent to which the group as a whole is seen as homogeneous (see, e.g., Festinger, Schachter, & Back, 1950; Lott & Lott, 1965; Lott, 1961; Newcomb, 1961, 1968). In common-bond groups, member attachment is primary, and group attachment follows from it; therefore, group attachment should never be stronger than member attachment and should be highly correlated with any and all evaluations of individual group members. Common-identity groups, in contrast, are more similar to Tajfel's minimal groups, in which attachment to the group is largely independent of attachment to fellow group members. In these groups, the strength of group attachment depends first and foremost on one's commitment to the identity of the group. Common-identity groups should be characterized by group attachment that is considerably stronger than member attachment and that is relatively independent of evaluations of individual group members.[1]

The two studies reported in this article sought to validate this distinction between common-bond and common-identity groups. In both, we surveyed members of real-world groups that we had reason to believe, on the basis of their dynamics or functions, would exemplify the distinction. Our aim was not to develop a theory of why groups vary in the types of attachment they foster or of the conditions under which the two types of groups are likely to develop; these efforts, in our view, would be premature (although we do comment on these issues in the General Discussion). Instead, we simply sought to demonstrate that the distinction between common-bond and common-identity groups is meaningful and to explore some of the characteristics of these two types of groups. We began with the hypothesis that members of common-bond

and common-identity groups would show asymmetries in their attachments to their group versus to their fellow group members, with relatively stronger group attachment in common-identity groups and relatively stronger member attachment in common-bond groups. We also predicted stronger relations of group attachment to member attachment and to other evaluations of individual group members in common-bond than in common-identity groups.

Study 1

In looking for groups that might qualify as common-bond and common-identity groups, we first considered the eating clubs at Princeton University. The Princeton eating clubs are a set of 12 independently run, nonprofit institutions that are unique to Princeton University. These clubs have provided three meals a day for third- and fourth-year students, and parties on weekends for the whole student body, for the past century. First- and second-year students at Princeton are not permitted to join the eating clubs, and the university both provides and mandates a meal contract that accommodates these students. The situation for third- and fourth-year students is quite different. Despite the de jure separation of the clubs from the university, the university acknowledges the de facto link by providing neither a dining system nor a dining hall for these students: They are expected to join, and, indeed, over 85% do join, an eating club.

The eating clubs are divided into nonselective and selective clubs. Seven of the clubs maintain their membership with a lottery system by which students in the spring of their second year sign into the club of their choice. These are the nonselective, or "sign-in," clubs. The remaining five clubs select their members from a pool of students who elect to "bicker," or interview, at the clubs of their choice. For these "bicker clubs," members are selected during a 2½-day bicker process that takes place once a year.

With respect to their facilities and their role in campus life, the bicker and sign-in clubs are very similar. The club life of their members is also similar: Although members do not reside in their clubs, most of their social life revolves around the club and occurs in the company of their fellow club members. Despite these common features, the group dynamics of the two types of clubs strike us as markedly different (an impression shared by the student body). In particular, bicker clubs appear to conform much more to traditional, individualist assumptions about what makes for a cohesive group: Bicker clubs are seen as more homogeneous, more insular, and, indeed, more close-knit than sign-in clubs. Sign-in clubs are seen as collections of diverse individuals whose attachment to the club is much less dependent on their similarity or attraction to their fellow club members. In short, sign-in clubs appear to be common-identity groups, whereas bicker clubs appear to be common-bond groups.

The purpose of Study 1 was to examine these impressions further. Specifically, we wished to test the hypothesis that bicker and sign-in clubs differ not just in the strength of their in-group attachments but also in the nature of those attachments. We expected to find asymmetries in attachments to the club versus club members, such that members of bicker clubs would show levels of attachment to fellow club members that equaled or exceeded their attachment to the club itself, and members of sign-in clubs would show lower levels of attachment to the members than to the club. We also expected club attachment to correlate more strongly with member attachment and with interpersonal similarity for members of bicker clubs than for members of sign-in clubs.

Method

Subjects. A total of 176 undergraduates (77 women, 99 men) in their third year at Princeton participated in this study. They were approached during meal-time at their eating clubs and were asked to fill out a brief questionnaire. Data were collected at two bicker clubs and two sign-in clubs, with sample sizes ranging from 42 to 47 students at each club.

Procedure. Subjects complete a questionnaire that included items designed to measure their attachment to the club, their attachment to other club members, and their similarity to other club members. The first

two of these constructs were assessed with items adapted from Karasawa (1991), whose distinction between identification with the group member-ship and identification with other group members mapped nicely onto our own. The questions con-cerning club attachment were as follows:

1. How important is belonging to your eating club to you?
2. How accurate would it be to describe you as a typical member of your club?
3. How often do you acknowledge the fact that you are a member of your club?
4. How good would you feel if you were described as a typical member of your club?
5. How often do you mention your club when you first meet someone?
6. To what extent do you feel attachment to your club?

Subjects responded to each item by circling a number on an appropriately labeled 9-point scale; higher numbers always corresponded to more positive responses. Each subject's responses to these six items were averaged to form a single index of club attachment ($\alpha = .85$).

Member attachment was assessed with the following three items:

1. How close do you feel to the other members of your eating club?
2. How many members of your club have influenced your thoughts and behaviors?
3. How many of your friends come from your club?

Subjects again responded to each item by circling a number on an appropriately labeled 9-point scale; higher numbers always corresponded to more positive responses. Each subject's responses to these three items were averaged to form a single index of member attachment ($\alpha = .80$).

In addition, the questionnaire included a single item to measure perceived similarity:

1. How similar are you to the other members of your club?

Subjects indicated their similarity to other club members on a 9-point scale (1 = *not at all similar*, 9 = *very similar*).

Results and Discussion

To confirm the distinction between club and member attachment, we conducted a factor analysis of the nine items used to assess these constructs. Much to our surprise, this factor analysis yielded only one factor. Separate factor analyses within bicker and sign-in clubs revealed the reason for this unexpected outcome: The analyses yielded two factors (as predicted) in the sign-in clubs and only one factor in the bicker clubs. This result was completely consistent with our theoretical analysis, but it did raise some question about whether we could treat club and member attachment as separate constructs across both types of clubs. We resolved to proceed with the analyses as planned; the results should be interpreted in light of the fact that club and member attachment were not factorially distinct in the bicker clubs.

We hypothesized that bicker and sign-in clubs would differ qualitatively in the nature of their ingroup attachment. Specifically, we expected to find asymmetries in attachments to clubs versus club members, such that bicker club members would show greater attachment to club members than to the club and sign-in club members would show greater attachment to the club than to the members. Means and standard deviations for the indexes of club and member attachment are presented in Table 5.1. An initial analysis revealed no significant gender differences, and so we collapsed across male and female respondents. A 2 (Club Type) × 2 (Attachment Type) analysis of variance (ANOVA), with clubs nested within club type, yielded the predicted Club Type × Attachment Type interaction; with subjects as random, $F(1, 172) = 4.39$, $p < .05$; with clubs as random, $F(1, 2) = 433.01$, $p < .005$. Bicker club members expressed greater attachment to club members than to the club itself; with subjects as random, $F(1, 172) = 3.61$, $p < .06$; with clubs as random, $F(1, 2) = 356.57$, $p < .005$. Sign-in club members showed the reverse pattern of club and member attachment; with subjects as random, $F(1, 172) = 1.10, p > .10$; with clubs as random, $F(1, 2) = 98.69$, $p < .01$. The subject analysis also revealed a significant main effect of club type—with subjects as random, $F(1, 172) = 11.79, p > .001$; with clubs as random,

TABLE 5.1. Means and Standard Deviations for Measures of Club Attachment and Member Attachment for Members of Bicker and Sign-in Clubs, Study 1

Club		Club attachment	Member attachment
Bicker club #1	M	5.51	5.76
	SD	1.47	1.56
Bicker club #2	M	6.56	6.76
	SD	1.54	1.42
Combined bicker clubs	M	6.03	6.26
	SD	1.58	1.56
Sign-in club #1	M	5.49	5.36
	SD	1.35	1.42
Sign-in club #2	M	5.51	5.39
	SD	1.38	1.64
Combined sign-in clubs	M	5.50	5.38
	SD	1.37	1.52

Note: Indexes of attachment could range from 1 to 9; higher numbers indicate greater attachment.

$F(1, 2) = 2.01$, $p > .10$—indicating that bicker club members showed higher levels of attachment than sign-in club members across both indexes.

To explore further the difference in attachment patterns for members of bicker and sign-in clubs, we examined the relation of club attachment to member attachment and to perceived similarity. We reasoned that if club attachment in bicker clubs derives from bonds between club members, then it should depend heavily on the strength of member attachment and on perceived similarity to other club members. Club attachment in sign-in clubs, however, should be more independent of member attachment and perceived similarity. We therefore expected higher correlations of club attachment with member attachment and with perceived similarity in bicker clubs than in sign-in clubs. We conducted two regression analyses, one predicting club attachment from club type, member attachment, and their interaction and the other predicting club attachment from club type, perceived similarity, and their interaction. The interaction terms tested our hypotheses. The correlations between club attachment and member attachment were .74 in bicker clubs and .73 in sign-in clubs; the correlations between club attachment and perceived similarity were .62 in bicker clubs and .57 in sign-in clubs. Although both these differences were in the right direction, the regressions indicated that neither was significant, both $Fs(1, 172) < 1.70, ps > .20$.

One final set of analyses provided a further test of the utility of the patterns of club and member attachment for distinguishing between the two types of clubs. We performed two discriminant analyses, using responses on the attachment questions to predict club membership and club-type membership. If the differential patterns of club and member attachment in bicker and sign-in clubs constitute evidence of a qualitative difference between the two types of groups, then it should be possible to classify individuals as members of bicker or sign-in clubs on the basis of their responses to the nine attachment questions. Separate discriminant analyses were conducted to test this logic, one to classify individuals as members of one of the four specific clubs and the other to classify them as members of either a bicker or a sign-in club. These analyses used equal prior probabilities. The results indicated that group membership could be predicted quite well from a linear combination of responses to the attachment questions: 52% of subjects were classified into the appropriate eating club (chance level being 25%), and 66% were classified into the appropriate club type (chance level being 50%). Considered individually, six of the nine attachment questions were significant predictors of club type.

Taken together, the results of Study 1 support a qualitative distinction in the in-group attachment of bicker and sign-in clubs but provide less clear-cut evidence of the nature of that distinction. The observed asymmetries in attachments to the club and to club members, as well as the utility of the attachment measures for predicting club membership, suggest that bicker and sign-in clubs are indeed characterized by different types of in-group attachment. Our initial assumption that this difference is captured by the distinction between common-bond groups and common-identity groups received mixed support: The patterns of club and member attachment in the two types of clubs were consistent with our predictions, but the correlational evidence was not. Nevertheless, the enormous degree of similarity in the structure and function of the two types of clubs no doubt militated against our finding any club differences. Consequently, in

light of the generally promising evidence for our proposed distinction, we conducted a second study to explore it further.

Study 2

In Study 2, we again surveyed members of campus groups about their attachment to their group and to their fellow group members, but this time we sampled across a much broader range of groups, including sports teams, residential units, performing arts groups, and social clubs. We categorized groups as common bond or common identity a priori on the basis of their primary function: Groups that serve to build friendships were considered common-bond groups; groups that are organized around a common interest or activity were considered common-identity groups. We again predicted asymmetries in group and member attachment across the two types of groups and differences in the relation of group attachment to member attachment and to perceived similarity. In addition, we included measures of perceived value homogeneity, perceived value similarity, and knowledge of group members, which were also hypothesized to differ in their relation to group attachment in the two types of groups.

The purposes of this study were twofold: First, we sought stronger evidence for the distinction between common-bond and common-identity groups than was obtained in Study 1. Second, we sought to generalize the results of our first study beyond the eating clubs. Although the bicker and sign-in clubs are similar in most respects, the nature of their in-group attachment is not the only feature that distinguishes between them. In particular, one of the primary differences between the two types of clubs is how members join them: Bicker clubs involve an extended and rigorous interview process after which new members are selected by the group; sign-in clubs are nonselective and require no effort to join. As a result, bicker club members know one another well when they enter the group, whereas sign-in club members are relative strangers. These differences alone could account for the pattern of results that we observed (see Aronson & Mills, 1959; Gerard & Matthewson, 1966). Hence, an additional purpose of Study 2 was to extend our exploration of group and member attachment beyond groups that differ in selectivity.

Method

Subjects. A total of 270 undergraduates voluntarily attended a mass testing session, in which they participated in this and other short studies for pay. The sample contained 167 women and 103 men, with approximately even distribution of women and men across the first- through fourth-year classes.

Procedure. Subjects completed a questionnaire very similar to that used in Study 1. They were first asked to think of a group or organization of which they considered themselves a member and to name that group. Then they were asked the same nine attachment questions and the perceived similarity question that were used in Study 1 with respect to the group they listed (i.e., "How important is belonging to this group to you?," etc.).

After completing the attachment and similarity questions, subjects were asked to rate the importance of each of the following values in their own lives: social justice, accepting my position in life, choosing own goals, humbleness, protecting the environment, honoring parents and elders, preserving my public image, an exciting life, social recognition, freedom, enjoying life, loyalty, daring, true friendship, sense of belonging, independence, equality, family security, a varied life, social order, and self-discipline. Subjects rated each value on a 9-point scale (1 = *not at all important*; 9 = *of supreme importance*). These values were taken from Triandis, McCusker, and Hui (1990), who found that they distinguished between people with an individualist orientation and people with a collectivist orientation. We were not interested here in individual subjects' endorsement of the values per se; instead, we simply wished to use the values as a domain for judgments of group homogeneity and similarity.

Finally, subjects were asked three additional questions about their group:

1. How much do members of this group agree on the importance of the values listed?

2. How similar are their values to yours?
3. How well do you know the members of this group?

Subjects responded to each question on an appropriately labeled 9-point scale; higher numbers indicated more agreement, more similarity, and more knowledge, respectively.

Results and Discussion

Subjects identified a diverse set of groups to which they belonged, as listed in Table 5.2. For 230 of the 270 subjects, the group they identified was classified as either a common-bond group or a common-identity group. Common-bond groups were residential units and social clubs, including fraternities, sororities, and eating clubs. Common-identity groups were performing arts groups (e.g., dance troupes, drama clubs, film societies), music groups, media groups (e.g., newspaper staffs, yearbook staff), and sports teams. We did not classify groups defined by social category membership (e.g., religious groups, ethnic groups, women's groups) or off-campus groups (primarily military groups and service organizations), because we

TABLE 5.2. Groups Identified by Subjects in Study 2

Type of group	Number of subjects
Common-bond groups	98
Resident assistant	37
Social groups (fraternities, sororities, eating clubs)	61
Common-identity groups	132
Performing arts groups	9
Music groups	22
Media groups (newspaper and magazine staffs, yearbook staff)	16
Sports teams	85
Unclassified	35
Groups defined by social category membership (ethnic groups, religious groups, women's groups)	17
Off-campus groups (service organizations, military groups)	11
Unidentifiable	7
No group listed	5

wanted to restrict consideration to group allegiances that students had formed since coming to Princeton. In addition, 7 subjects listed groups that we could not identify, and 5 failed to list any group at all.

In light of the results of our first study, we conducted a separate factor analysis of the nine attachment items within each type of group. Results paralleled those of Study 1: The analyses yielded two factors in common-identity groups and only one factor in common-bond groups. This result was theoretically encouraging but empirically problematic. Again, we resolved to treat group and member attachment as separate constructs and averaged subjects' responses to the relevant questions, as in Study 1; these indexes were highly reliable ($\alpha = .84$ for group attachment and .84 for member attachment). It is important, however, to bear in mind that group attachment and member attachment were not factorially distinct in common-bond groups.

We hypothesized that members of common-bond and common-identity groups would show asymmetries in attachments to their groups versus their fellow group members. Means and standard deviations for the two indexes are presented in Table 5.3. A 2 (Subject Gender) × 2 (Group Type) × 2 (Attachment Type) ANOVA yielded the predicted Group Type × Attachment Type interaction, $F(1, 225) = 56.47, p < .0001$.[2] Members of common-identity groups were more attached to their group than to their fellow group members, $F(1, 225) = 129.89, p < .0001$, whereas members of common-bond groups did not differ in these two types of attachment, $F < 1$. The analysis also revealed main effects of gender, $F(1, 225) = 4.03, p < .05$, and of attachment type, $F(1, 225) = 48.59, p < .0001$, as well as interactions of gender with group type, $F(1, 225) = 7.16, p < .01$, and with attachment type, $F(1, 225) = 6.80, p < .01$. These additional effects indicated that men expressed stronger attachment of both types in common-identity groups and women in common-bond groups and that, across groups, women expressed more group attachment than member attachment relative to men. But the predicted interaction of group type and attachment type held across both male and female respondents; for the

TABLE 5.3. Means and Standard Deviations for Measures of Group Attachment and Member Attachment for Members of Common-Bond Groups and Common-Identity Groups, Study 2

Type of group		Group attachment	Member attachment
Common-bond groups			
Women (*n* = 65)	M	6.01	5.96
	SD	1.62	1.65
Men (*n* = 33)	M	4.85	5.00
	SD	1.96	1.97
Total	M	5.62	5.64
	SD	1.81	1.81
Common-identity groups			
Women (*n* = 73)	M	6.34	4.67
	SD	1.37	2.14
Men (*n* = 58)	M	6.12	5.19
	SD	1.48	1.96
Total	M	6.25	4.92
	SD	1.42	2.08

Note: Indexes of attachment could range from 1 to 9; higher numbers indicate greater attachment.

Gender × Group Type × Attachment Type interaction, $F(1, 225) = 2.32, p > .10$.

In addition to differences in the relative levels of group and member attachment in the two types of groups, we again predicted that group attachment would show a stronger relation to member attachment and to perceived similarity in common-bond than in common-identity groups. We expected similar group differences in the relation of group attachment to perceived value homogeneity, perceived value similarity, and knowledge of group members.[3] Correlations of group attachment with these measures are shown in Table 5.4. We conducted separate regression analyses to predict group attachment from each of these five measures, group type, and the interaction of the measure with group type (i.e., one analysis regressed group attachment on member attachment, group type, and the interaction of member attachment and group type; another analysis regressed group attachment on perceived similarity, group type, and the interaction of similarity and group type; and so on). The interaction terms tested for group differences in the relation of group attachment to each measure. In all cases, these interactions were significant: For

TABLE 5.4. Correlates of Group Attachment in Common-Bond Groups and Common-Identity Groups, Study 2

Predictor of group attachment	Common-bond groups	Common-identity groups
Member attachment	.82	.70
Perceived similarity	.64	.59
Perceived value homogeneity	.49	.30
Perceived value similarity	.63	.38
Knowledge of group members	.56	.47

member attachment, $F(1, 226) = 22.62, p < .0001$; for perceived similarity, $F(1, 226) = 6.78, p < .01$; for value homogeneity, $F(1, 224) = 4.99, p < .05$; for value similarity, $F(1, 224) = 11.25, p < .001$; for knowledge of group members, $F(1, 226) = 9.70, p < .005$. Thus, attachment to the group was more strongly related to all evaluations of individual group members in common-bond than in common-identity groups.

Finally, we performed a discriminant analysis to predict membership in common-bond or common-identity groups from responses to the attachment questions. Our assumption, as in Study 1, was that if common-bond and common-identity groups differ qualitatively in the nature of their in-group attachment, then it should be possible to discriminate between them on the basis of members' responses to the group and member attachment measures. A discriminant analysis was conducted, using equal prior probabilities, to classify individuals as members of one of these two types of groups on the basis of a linear combination of their responses to the nine attachment questions. The results indicated that 77% of subjects were correctly classified into a common-bond or a common-identity group (chance level being 50%). Considered individually, seven of the nine attachment questions were significant predictors of group type. These results again support the validity of our proposed distinction.

General Discussion

The finding that some real-world groups appear to be based on direct attachment to the group and others on attachments to fellow group members is significant in a number of respects. First, and most obviously, this finding provides a way of reconciling competing conceptions of the group. In our surveys of members of real-world groups, we found some support for the individualist assumptions that member attachment is dominant and that the group and its members are largely isomorphic (Allport, 1924, 1962; Lott & Lott, 1965; Lott, 1961). However, we also found support for the social identity theory assumptions that group attachment is dominant and that the group and its members are functionally independent (see Turner et al., 1987). Thus, rather than competing accounts for group formation and cohesion, these perspectives might instead be viewed as describing two separable processes in the development and maintenance of groups, either of which might dominate under a given set of circumstances (see Hogg & Abrams, 1989).

Second, and following from this first point, the present research supports the view that group dynamics depend critically on how individual members cognitively represent the group (Turner et al., 1987). Our findings, particularly for members of common-identity groups, add to the growing evidence that individuals can have separate representations of their groups and of the members of those groups. This cognitive perspective on the nature of in-group attachment marks a recent shift from the learning perspective that characterizes the individualist approach (see Turner et al., 1987). Whereas the learning view holds that interpersonal bonds, based on mutual need satisfaction, combine piecemeal to determine overall liking for the group, recent studies (e.g., Miller & Felicio, 1990) suggest that one can also evaluate a category or group directly, with no reference to individuals. As researchers continue to explore the group-level and individual-level processes underlying in-group attachment and other group phenomena, we expect the contributions of these two contrasting perspectives to become increasingly integrated (see Moreland, 1987).

Finally, the present studies do more than just add to the accumulating evidence for the independence of group and member attachment: They suggest that a consideration of the relation of these two types of attachment can provide a meaningful scheme for categorizing groups. Some groups cohere because of the members' attachment to the group itself, and others cohere because of the members' attachment to one another. The relative levels of these two types of attachment and their dependence on each other may provide more insight into the group and its dynamics than a consideration of each type of attachment in isolation. Thus, for example, a simple quantitative characterization of the difference between group and member attachment in the bicker and sign-in clubs investigated in Study 1 would fail to capture the psychological distinctiveness of the two groups, just as a quantitative characterization of the difference between Pope and Swift would fail to capture the psychological distinctiveness of these two individuals. Pope did not simply like mankind more than did Swift, and Swift men more than did Pope; the two writers differed in their relative liking for these two social representations.

Common-Bond and Common-Identity Groups

We have argued for a qualitative distinction between common-bond and common-identity groups.[4] The significance of this distinction rests, in part, on its ability to shed light on observed group differences. In this section, we will examine the implications of the distinction for understanding several of the ways in which groups differ.

First, consider the rules of fairness that operate within groups. Some groups operate on the principle of equity, whereby each individual is entitled to rewards in proportion to his or her contributions to the group. Other groups operate on the principle of equality, whereby each individual is entitled to an equal share of the rewards. Justice researchers have many theories to account for these group differences (see Lerner & Lerner, 1981). We would suggest that what is considered fair in a group depends on whether it is a common-bond or a common-identity group. Common-identity groups, in which members share an attachment to the group, should operate on the principle of equality; common-bond groups, in which attachment is an aggregate of individual bonds, should operate on the

principle of equity. Support for this conjecture comes from Lerner (1974). He found that when children were defined as a "team," they tended to distribute rewards equally to fellow team members, whereas when they were defined as "coworkers," they tended to distribute rewards to other coworkers in proportion to their contributions. We would expect common-identity groups to function like teams and common-bond groups to function like coworkers, regardless of their quantitative levels of cohesion.[5]

A second property that varies across groups is their longevity. Again, the distinction between common-bond and common-identity groups may account for why some groups last longer than others. Because attachment in common-bond groups is determined by relations between individuals, the existence of the group depends critically on the individual members and how they relate to each other. Attachment in common-identity groups is more independent of the current roster of group members. We would therefore expect common-identity groups to show greater continuity over time and greater stability in the face of changes in membership. Consistent with this analysis, observations of real-world groups implicate attachment to a collective goal or identity as an important factor in sustaining a group. For example, social movement researchers have noted that participants must have a common identity that constitutes a significant portion of their social existence to sustain collective action (see Blumer, 1953; Scott, 1990; Turner & Killian, 1957). Similarly, studies of utopian communities have revealed that enduring communities tend to have strong group identities and to discourage intimate dyadic relations that could threaten allegiance to the group (Kanter, 1972). It is important to note, however, that these communities do not survive on group attachment alone: When commitment to the concerns of the collective weakens interpersonal bonds, the communities often fail.

Finally, groups differ in their reactions to conflict. Some groups rally in the face of internal discord or external threat; other groups disintegrate at the first sign of trouble. We would argue that which of these courses a group follows depends, in part, on whether it is a common-bond or a common-identity group. In cases of internal conflict, common-identity groups should fare much better than common-bond groups, because common-identity groups do not depend on, nor do they necessarily require, interpersonal harmony. Common-bond groups are unlikely to withstand internal discord, as it threatens the basis for their existence. In cases of external conflict, the predictions are less clear. One interesting possibility is that an external threat may serve to give the group a common cause and thus may transform common-bond groups, temporarily or permanently, into common-identity groups (see Coser, 1956). Indeed, although researchers of intergroup conflict have tended to adopt an individualist perspective, we would suggest that conflict increases in-group attachment not only by strengthening bonds between individuals but also by strengthening bonds to the group (see also Turner et al., 1987).

Group and Member Attachment Over Time

Although the present research examined the nature of in-group attachment by assessing groups at only one point in time, in the real world, the processes through which groups develop and change take place over weeks, months, or even years. It is therefore useful to speculate on the implications of our findings for the more dynamic aspects of in-group attachment. In line with the distinction between common-bond and common-identity groups, one can distinguish between accounts of group development that are bottom-up and top-down in focus. Bottom-up accounts suggest that group attachment is an emergent feature of attachment to group members: Once there are sufficient interpersonal bonds among a collection of individuals, they will become a group. Top-down accounts suggest that group attachment originates in social categorization and leads to, rather than follows from, interpersonal bonds (see also Miller & Felicio, 1990). In recent years, research has tended to favor the top-down over the bottom-up accounts. In particular, as we have noted, researchers in the social identity tradition have shown that social categorization alone, in the absence of interpersonal attachment, is

sufficient to promote in-group attachment (see Turner et al., 1987, for a review). Some researchers have gone further to argue that social categorization is a *necessary* condition for group formation (Hogg & Turner, 1985a, 1985b), but the empirical basis for this claim is not yet well established.

Although laboratory evidence for the importance of social categorization in group formation is quite strong, its role in the formation of real-world groups is less clear-cut. In the common-bond groups examined in the present studies, for example, the attachment experienced by group members did not seem to derive from attachment to the group. We would therefore argue that social categorization may not always precede individual attachment; instead, collections of individuals who have strong attachments to one another may be motivated to identify categories they share in order to give themselves a common identity. In this case, the category is an effect of their interpersonal attachment, rather than a cause of it. As an example, one of us attended a conference in which Henri Tajfel and Robert Zajonc were presenting. As Tajfel introduced Zajonc, he made reference to the fact that they were both members of a very select group: individuals having the letter combination *aj* in their last names. From Tajfel's work, we know that such a designation would meet the minimal requirements for a group identity. But surely the identification of this shared category reflected a bond that was already present. We have here a case of a group in search of an identity. This identity did not create the bond between Tajfel and Zajonc; it merely codified it.

Groups that exist at the level of member attachment may nevertheless have a social identity. Take, as an example, groups of people who call a radio station to request a song. These groups frequently identify themselves with category labels: "the guys in Ivy 222" or "the mechanics at Al's garage" or "the gang at Sam's Bar and Grill." But, in fact, these individuals request songs together not because of their attachment to their category but because of their attachment to one another. The group identity they have created simply formalizes their status as a friendship group. They may be categorized as the guys in Ivy 222 or the gang at Sam's by others and by themselves, but their attachment to this group derives entirely from their interpersonal bonds. Not all coworkers or roommates will request songs together; only those with close interpersonal attachments will consider themselves a meaningful group.

The present results certainly do not prove that groups can exist without a collective identity, and there may, in fact, be a number of group functions that require one (collective action, for example). But the results for common-bond groups do suggest that a collective identity need not be the driving force behind a group and may be an effect, rather than a cause, of the interpersonal bonds between group members. Consequently, we would simply suggest that common-bond groups deserve the status of real groups and are worthy of study. They surely will not function like groups with strong identities, but this fact alone should not disqualify them as groups, nor should it mark them as less-developed groups. Instead, it should motivate their investigation. Defining the group so as to exclude those based on interpersonal bonds will not alter the fact that individuals identify such collections of people as groups and define themselves as members of those groups.

NOTES

1. We should note that self-categorization theory would make similar predictions about attachment in these two types of groups (see Turner, Oakes, Haslam, & McGarty, this issue [of *PSPB*]). It would suggest that, in common-identity groups, group identity is salient, and therefore intergroup comparisons, in which distinctions are made between rather than within groups, are relevant. In common-bond groups, by contrast, group identity is not salient, and therefore intragroup comparisons, based on distinctions among group members, are relevant. We have no quarrel with this account for the processes involved; we simply wish to make the argument that these processes produce qualitatively different types of groups.

2. In Study 2, analyses were carried out at the individual level rather than at the group level, because subjects came from many different groups and it was not possible to ascertain common-group membership.

3. Although we were not interested in subjects' own endorsement of the values, we did analyze for group differences in their personal value orientations. An initial factor analysis of the value ratings, using a varimax rotation and specifying two factors, divided the values into the following categories: Individualistic values were choosing own goals, preserving my public image, an exciting life, social recognition, freedom, enjoying life, daring, independence, and a varied life ($\alpha = .70$). Collectivistic values were social justice, accepting my position in life, humbleness, protecting the environment, honoring parents and elders, loyalty, true friendship, sense of belonging, equality, family security, social order, and self-discipline ($\alpha = .68$). (This division is largely, though not completely, consistent with that suggested by Triandis, McCusker, and Hui, 1990.) ANOVAs indicated no group differences in endorsement of either individualistic or collectivistic values, both $Fs(1, 224) < 2.00$, $ps > .10$.

4. In the real world, these two types of groups mark opposite poles of a continuum, but for simplicity, we will treat the distinction as dichotomous.

5. Of course, common-identity groups may also be more likely than common-bond groups to have role differentiation within the group, which will militate against the equal distribution of resources.

REFERENCES

Allport, F. H. (1924). *Social psychology*. Boston: Houghton Mifflin.

Allport, F. H. (1962). A structuronomic conception of behavior: Individual and collective. *Journal of Abnormal and Social Psychology, 64,* 3–30.

Aronson, E., & Mills, J. (1959). The effect of severity of initiation on liking for a group. *Journal of Abnormal and Social Psychology, 59,* 177–181.

Billig, M. G., & Tajfel, H. (1973). Social categorization and similarity in intergroup behavior. *European Journal of Social Psychology, 3,* 27–52.

Blurner, H. (1953). Collective behavior. In A. Lee (Ed.), *Principles of sociology* (pp. 167–222). New York: Barnes & Noble.

Carron, A. V., & Chelladurai, P. (1981). The dynamics of group cohesion in sports. *Journal of Sport Psychology, 3,* 123–139.

Coser, L. (1956). *The functions of social conflict*. New York: Free Press.

Festinger, L., Schachter, S., & Back, K. (1950). *Social pressures in informal groups*. New York: Harper & Row.

Gerard, H., & Matthewson, G. (1966). The effects of severity of initiation on liking for a group: A replication. *Journal of Experimental Social Psychology, 2,* 278–287.

Hogg, M. A. (1993). Group cohesiveness: A critical review and some new directions. In W. Stroebe & M. Hewstone (Eds), *European review of social psychology* (Vol. 4, pp. 85–112). Chichester, England: Wiley.

Hogg, M. A., & Abrams, D. (1989). *Social psychology: A social identity perspective*. London: Methuen.

Hogg, M. A., & Hardie, E. A. (1991). Social attraction, personal attraction, and self-categorization: A field study. *Personality and Social Psychology Bulletin, 17,* 175–180.

Hogg, M. A., & Turner, J. C. (1985a). Interpersonal attraction, social identification and psychological group formation. *European Journal of Social Psychology, 15,* 51–66.

Hogg, M. A., & Turner, J. C. (1985b). When liking begets solidarity: An experiment on the role of interpersonal attraction in psychological group formation. *British Journal of Social Psychology, 24*, 267–281.

Jennings, H. H. (1947). Sociometric differentiation of the psychegroup and the sociogroup. *Sociometry, 10*, 71–79.

Kanter, R. (1972). *Commitment and community: Communes and utopias in sociological perspective.* Cambridge, MA: Harvard University Press.

Karasawa, M. (1991). Toward an assessment of social identity: The structure of group identification and its effects on in-group evaluations. *British Journal of Social Psychology, 30*, 293–307.

Lerner, M. (1974). The justice motive: "Equity" and "parity" among children. *Journal of Personality and Social Psychology, 29*, 539–550.

Lerner, M., & Lerner, S. (1981). *The justice motive in social behavior.* New York: Plenum.

Locksley, A., Ortiz, V., & Hepburn, C. (1980). Social categorization and discriminatory behavior: Extinguishing the minimal intergroup discrimination effect. *Journal of Personality and Social Psychology, 39*, 773–783.

Lott, A. J., & Lott, B. E. (1965). Group cohesiveness as interpersonal attraction: A review of relationships with antecedent and consequent variables. *Psychological Bulletin, 64*, 259–309.

Lott, B. E. (1961). Group cohesiveness: A learning phenomenon. *Journal of Social Psychology, 55*, 275–286.

Miller, C., & Felicio, D. (1990). Person-positivity bias: Are individuals liked better than groups? *Journal of Experimental Social Psychology, 26*, 408–420.

Moreland, R. L. (1987). The formation of small groups. *Review of Personality and Social Psychology, 8*, 80–110.

Newcomb, T. (1961). *The acquaintance process.* New York: Holt.

Newcomb, T. (1968). Interpersonal balance. In R. Abelson, E. Aronson, W. McGuire, T. Newcomb, M. Rosenberg, & P. Tannenbaum (Eds), *Theories of cognitive consistency: A sourcebook.* Chicago: Rand McNally.

Piper, W. E., Marrache, M., Lacroix, R., Richardsen, A. M., & Jones, B. D. (1983). Cohesion as a basic bond in groups. *Human Relations, 36*, 93–108.

Scott, A. (1990). *Ideology and the new social movements.* London: Unwin Hyman.

Tajfel, H. (1981). *Human groups and social categories.* Cambridge: Cambridge University Press.

Triandis, H. C., McCusker, C., & Hui, C. H. (1990). Multimethod probes of individualism and collectivism. *Journal of Personality and Social Psychology, 59*, 1006–1020.

Turner, J. C., Hogg, M. A., Oakes, P. J., Reicher, S. D., & Wetherell, M. S. (1987). *Rediscovering the social group: A self-categorization theory.* Oxford: Basil Blackwell.

Turner, J. C., Sachdev, I., & Hogg, M. A. (1983). Social categorization, interpersonal attraction, and group formation. *British Journal of Social Psychology, 22*, 227–239.

Turner, R., & Killian, L. (1957). *Collective behavior.* Englewood Cliffs, NJ: Prentice-Hall.

The "Friendly" Poker Game: A Study of an Ephemeral Role

Louis A. Zurcher, Jr.*

Twice monthly for one year the author attended the "friendly" poker games of a group which had played twice monthly for more than ten years. Players' role expectations are discussed, as are formal and informal group-maintaining norm systems, criteria for selecting and socializing a "new man," and the process of leaving the group. Personal interactions before, during, and after the poker game are sketched, emphasizing the social-psychological benefits. The "friendly game" is seen to present each player with an "ephemeral role" which affords satisfactions limited or impossible in the social world "outside."

Games, forms of play with consensually validated sets of rules, assist in the socialization and personality formation of the individual. The structure and dynamics of various games often reflect specific traits, values, expectations, and kinds of social control within a given culture. For adults, games may maintain existing societal forms, or resolve perceived conflicts and threats in the social world (cf. Caillois, 1961; Erikson, 1950; Huizinga, 1955; Piaget, 1951; Robbins, 1955; Strauss, 1956; Sutton-Smith and Roberts, 1963).

Card playing apparently continues to be a favorite American game. Though recent statistics are not available, an American Institute of Public Opinion poll (1948), with a national sample, revealed that *56* percent of the respondents played cards either regularly or occasionally, and *19* percent preferred poker. There have been several studies of gamblers, gambling, and gaming behavior (cf. Bergler, 1957;

* University of Texas at Austin.

The author expresses his appreciation to William Key, William Bruce Cameron, Erving Goffman and James Henslin, and to Frank Bean, Ivan Belknap, Richard Curtis, Russell Curtis, Robert Cushing, Dale McLemore, and Susan Lee Zurcher for their helpful comments. For the opportunity to have known and interacted with the poker group members, and for the insights they generously offered during interviews, the author is profoundly grateful.

Herman, 1967a; Edwards, 1955), but few studies which seek to determine the social-psychological functions of card playing (cf. Crespi, 1956), and fewer such studies of poker playing (cf. Lukacs, 1963; Martinez and LaFranci, 1969) despite the fact that poker and many of its terms are prominent in our culture. There is no previous study, to the author's knowledge, of the "friendly game" of poker, that regularly scheduled game "among the boys" held alternately in one of their houses for relatively low stakes.

The participants of the friendly game are not gamblers in the social-problem sense of the word. Their game is not part of a commercial enterprise, yet they are drawn together regularly, take their participation seriously, and usually thoroughly enjoy themselves. What social-psychological functions does the friendly game serve for the participants? What is its attraction? What aspects of society-at-large are reflected in its dynamics?

The structure and some of the social-psychological functions of a friendly game were observed by a participant, yielding an analytical ethnography of the poker group and highlighting the theoretical concept "ephemeral role." An ephemeral role is a temporary or ancillary position-related behavior pattern *chosen* by the enactor to satisfy social-psychological needs incompletely satisfied by the more dominant and lasting roles he regularly must enact in everyday life positions.[1]

Procedure

For twelve months the author attended the twice-monthly friendly game of a long-established poker group. He was a "complete participator" in Gold's (1958) classification. That is, he played and the other players did not know they were being observed. No notes were taken during the game, nor were any recording devices used. Though such techniques would have enhanced reliability, they may have disrupted the game. The author did,

however, outline his observations immediately following adjournment of the session, and dictated a narrative based on the outline within eight hours.

Recreation, and not detached research was the primary reason for the author's joining the friendly game. However, after the first session he felt that the social dynamics of the game and the manifest benefits of participation for the players were important to record and analyze.

The day after his last game (the day before his departure to a job in another state), the author conducted semistructured individual interviews with all of the regular players concerning their reasons for playing, criteria for selecting new players, socialization processes, group rituals, and group argot.

The Players

The seven "core" players who attended almost every game during the period of observation were all college educated, married, professional men: a lawyer, a college coach, a high school coach, an engineer, a sociologist, a social-psychologist (the author), and an insurance broker. Four had been playing poker together for over ten years, and two others for over five years. They ranged in ages from early thirties to late forties, and all were in the middle, salaried, socioeconomic bracket. Four had been reared and educated in the midwestern city (population *125,000*) where the game took place, and where all of the players presently resided. When the friendly game first formed, the players had been associated with a small local college. Three of the current players still were employed by the college, each in a separate department. A second common characteristic of the founding members and four of the current members was experience in coaching scholastic athletic teams.

Since three core players, because of job transfers or time conflicts, were going to leave the group, members were actively recruiting "new men." Those new men invited during the course of the observation included, after the author: an accountant, a rancher, a sports writer, a high school teacher,

---

[1] For an earlier definition and example of the concept, see Zurcher (1968).

and a purchasing agent. The author had been brought into the group by the sociologist, who was a co-worker at a local psychiatric research facility.

The Setting and Structure of the Game

The games were held twice monthly, between *7:30* p.m. and *12:00* p.m. on Monday nights, in rotation at each of the core player's homes. One of the players hosted the game in a den; the others in dining rooms, kitchens, or spare rooms. Three had purchased commercially produced, green felt covered, poker tables; the others used whatever large table was available. The playing table was surrounded by smaller tables containing ashtrays, and bowls of chips and pretzels. Hot coffee and soft drinks were available throughout the game, but no alcoholic beverages were allowed during the game. Then, after the completion of the "last deal around the table," which started at *12:00* p.m., the hosting player was responsible for a meal of hors d'oeuvres, sandwiches, and desserts.

The evening's leisure was divided into three major components: (1) the informal discussion while waiting for all the players to arrive and the poker chips to be distributed; (2) the game itself; (3) the meal following the game. During the game it was understood that there were to be no "outside" interruptions. There were no radios or television sets playing, no wives serving beverages, no children looking over shoulders. The atmosphere was quite relaxed and the dress casual (although on occasion a member arrived in suit and tie following a business meeting). There was no apparent seating preference around the table except that if there was an empty chair, it generally would be next to a new man.

At the beginning of the game each player purchased *$3.00* worth of chips (blue, *25* cents; red, *10* cents; white, *5* cents). One had the option to buy additional chips at any time, although frequently cash was introduced in place of chips. The host player was responsible for being the banker, and also for dragging a dime or so out of each pot to defray the cost of the post-game meal. The betting limit was established at *25* cents, with a three-raise limit. Drawing "light" (borrowing money) from the pot or purchasing chips by check was tolerated.

The general rules of poker were closely followed, but the games played under "dealer's choice" were more varied than in a commercial poker setting. Use of the joker or naming of wild cards was forbidden. Often the "draw" and "stud" games were dealt with the stipulation that the high hand split with the low hand, or the high hand split with the low spade. Rarely, low ball (where low hand wins) was played. Each player seemed to have one or two favorite games which he dealt regularly and which were called "his" games.

Becoming a Member: Selection and Role Socialization

The criteria by which a new man was judged for membership revealed much about the group dynamics and functions. The core players, when being interviewed by the author, reflected about these criteria:

> A fellow coming into the game almost must feel like he's walking into a closed group, because we've been playing together for quite a while. I guess some newcomers leave the game sometimes feeling "will they ever ask me back again" or "I don't want to play with that bunch of thieves again." Sometimes we have fellows join us who we decide we don't want to come back. In particular, we don't like people who slow up the game, or bad players who get wiped out. They have to be capable of playing with the other players, or we don't want them.

> In our game the group is the thing. We invite people in who we think are nice persons, and who we can be friends with. That's the important thing. But he has to be more than a nice person. He has to be able to play poker with the rest of us. It's no fun to sandbag a sucker! So to get invited to sit in regularly, we've got to like the person, and he's got to know what he's doing so that he adds to the game and doesn't subtract from it. The group has to be kept in balance. One dud can throw the whole thing out of focus. Another thing, too. In our group, he has to be able to take a lot of teasing, and maybe give out some too. We have a good time teasing each other.

The new man therefore had to be friendly and experienced enough to learn, compete, and to maintain the pace and stability of the game.

Lukacs (1963:58) has observed that "there are a thousand unwritten rules in poker, and continuous social standards and codes of behavior." The new man, as a prerequisite to invitation was expected to know the basic rules and etiquette of poker. He was to be socialized, however, in accordance with the group's idiosyncratic expectations. He was to learn the local rules of the game, the style and tempo of play, and the patterned interactions. In other words, he was not going to be taught how to play poker, but how to be a member of this poker group.

Many of the socialization messages were verbal instructions from the core members, particularly with regard to betting rules, games allowed, quitting time, and borrowing money. Other socialization messages were more subtle, though no less forceful. The player who slowed the pace of the game might hear the drum of fingers on the green felt or an annoyed clearing of the throat. The player who talked too lengthily about a topic unessential to the game might be reminded that it was his deal, or his turn to bet.

The new man would be strongly reinforced for behavior that conformed to the group's expectations by verbal compliment, camaraderie, or a simple but effective "now you've got it!" One new man, for example, unwittingly disrupted the group's unwritten strategy, that of killing large raises from a strong hand by exhausting the three-raise limit with nickel bets. Three of the core players immediately made pleasant comments about the "lack of insurance" in that particular hand. They did not directly admonish the new man for not having enacted his part of the "insurance." When on a later occasion he did carry out the strategy, he was immediately reinforced by a hearty, "good play!" from two core players.

At no point during the entire period of observation did any of the core players show overt anger at a new man's violation of group expectations. They did on a few occasions invoke what appeared to be their most severe sanction, an absence of response cutting the errant player momentarily from group interaction. When, for example, a new man challenged a dealing core player's choice of game, the dealer dealt and the rest continued to play their cards as if the new man had not said a word. On another occasion, when a new man angrily threw down his cards in disgust, two of the core players quietly gathered them up, handed them to the dealer, and there was otherwise a total absence of response.[2] If someone suggested a game be played which was not in the group's repertoire, he would be met with a lack of enthusiasm that was more crushing than any verbal negation could have been.

One of the core players commented about the "silent communication that takes place" within the group:

> We've been playing together for so long that we can read each other's expressions for the opinions that we have about something. If one of the fellows who's new or who is just sitting in for the night does something out of line, there's a quick and silent communication that takes place, and almost simultaneously we know what to do about it. We tease him or we give him instruction or something.

Sometimes the core players united in humorously expressed sanctions of a player's behavior. One new player had committed the cardinal sin of criticizing the play of core members. He had also lectured on the "right way to play poker." As if on cue, a core player deliberately checked his bet and, when the bet came around to him again, laughingly announced he was going to raise (an act which actually was forbidden by the group, as the bettor knew). The new man exploded:

> You can't do that! You can't check and then raise! What kind of a game is this! Where did you learn to play poker!

A second core member with straight face replied,

> We always do that! We do some strange things in our group!

A third added,

> Yes, sometimes we allow ourselves to take back our discards if we think they can improve our hand.

---

[2] See Goffman (1956) for a description of emotionally "flooding out" from group interaction.

A fourth added,

> Well, but we have to match the pot first!

Shortly thereafter, when the man won his first pot, a core member again with straight face asked for 25 percent of the pot to put into the kitty, since "it is a custom that you always donate one-fourth of your first pot in this game." The new man, who was not asked to return, was effectively excluded from the group interaction, even though he was present for the remainder of the evening.

One core player told how novices were covertly appraised:

> It's hard to put your finger on it, but there's a secret evaluation of a new player during the game. You know, we look at each other, and seem to be able to come to a conclusion about whether or not we want him to come back and play with us again, even before the game is over. Sometimes we talk about the player after the game, or during the week if we see each other before the next game. But most of the time we know even before that.

Of six new men, including the author, invited to "sit in for a night" three were asked to return. Each of these had manifested during their first night, behavior which corresponded to group expectations and which was openly reinforced. In two cases, the new men at the end of the session were welcomed to "our group" and told where the game would be held two weeks hence. The third man was informed by telephone after some of the core members had "talked it over," and agreed to invite him back. When core members felt unsure about inviting a new man back, or when they were certain that they did not want to invite him back, there was no post-game discussion of the next meeting.

A new man who was being accepted could be observed increasingly identifying himself as a member. During the early hours of the game he would ask questions about specific rules that "you fellows have." In the later hours he might phrase his questions differently, asking what "we" do in certain situations.

The core players clearly seemed to enjoy instructing a new man, overtly and covertly, about their expectations. In fact, his receptivity to those socialization messages was a key criterion for acceptance. A core player expressed how he felt about the socialization process:

> I think there is a certain enjoyment in teaching the rules of our game to people that can learn them. It's a kind of pride. Maybe it's a simple pride, but it's still a matter of pride to be able to show other people how to play in our game, when you know all the rules, but they don't.

Once accepted as a core member the individual retained that status even if circumstances precluded his regular participation. This was clearly illustrated when three core members terminated regular attendance. The author was present when the first member announced he was being transferred to a job in another state. The players were eating their post-game meal, when he said:

> I may as well tell you fellows this before you find out from somewhere else. I won't be able to play anymore because I got orders to go to Wisconsin. I hate to tell you this, because I hate to leave my contacts here with all my friends, and especially I hate to leave the poker club.

The group was silent for several seconds, and a few players stopped eating. Finally, one said, sadly, "That's too bad." Several inquiries were made about the specifics of his transfer, and players commented that he would be missed. One added that "the gang won't be the same without you." They talked briefly about the "breaking up of the group," and discussed the importance of starting to recruit new men for permanent positions. As they left, they warmly said goodbye to the departing member, and several of them earnestly asked him to "get in touch" whenever he visited the city. "Remember," encouraged one, "there will always be a chair open for you in the game." The offer of "an open chair" was similarly made to two core members who subsequently had to terminate regular attendance; one of them has played while in town at the time of a scheduled session.

A returning core member was not immune from socialization, however. During the author's participation one returned to "sit in for a night" after an absence of two years. Throughout the evening he inadvertently violated some of the group norms. He started to bet beyond the limit, and he began to deal a game not in the repertoire. One of the core members smilingly reminded him of the norms, and said, "You've been away so long you've forgotten our standing rules." The visitor was gently being resocialized.

Benefits of Membership: Satisfactions From the Ephemeral Role

Participation in the friendly game seemed to provide the individual with several rewarding social-psychological experiences, including opportunities for: scripted competition; self- and situation control; event brokerage; normative deception and aggression; micro-institutionalizing; and retrospective conquest.

Scripted Competition: "Knocking Heads"

The criteria for acceptance as a core member included one's ability to "hold his own" in the game. He was not to be "easy" or a "pigeon," but rather should be able to "put up a fight" and maintain the "balance" of the play. The new man was expected to be a competitor, to have "guts" and not be a "feather merchant."

Zola (1964) has pointed out that the importance and relevance of competition to gambling varies with the social context in which it occurs. Competition among the players seemed to be a carefully scripted and central dynamic in the friendly game. Competition involved money, but more importantly accomplishments of skill, daring, and bluffing, as two core players indicated:

> We cut each other's throats while the game is going on. We forget about it after the game, but it's that very competitive part of the game that I enjoy so much. Maybe it's a carry-over from my sports days, but I just like to compete. There aren't many places anymore where I can really get eye to eye with someone and 'knock heads.' A hand starts and you try to get other players to drop out. Then there's just two or three of you left, and you really start putting the pressure on. You can really slug it out, but it's only a game, and you forget about it when you leave the table.

> It's sort of like when you were a kid, and you were testing yourself all the time. Poker is like the good old days; you get a chance to test yourself.

Several other observers have reported that competition in gambling, whether against others or "the system," provides individuals with opportunities to demonstrate self-reliance, independence, and decision-making abilities which for some reason or other are unavailable to them in their major life roles (cf. Herman, 1967b; Bloch, 1951; Crespi, 1956; Goffman, 1967). All of the core players were employed in bureaucracies. It may have been that their jobs made impossible the kind of competition, the kind of "testing" that they desired—particularly in the case of those members who had histories of athletic competition. Within the friendly game they could carefully and normatively script for themselves satisfactory and safe competitive experiences.

Self- and Situation Control: "Showing Skill"

Each of the players was expected to possess considerable skill in dealing, betting, playing his hand, and bluffing. A player who noticeably showed skill was pleased with his accomplishment, whether or not he won the hand. Core members rewarded his demonstration of skill with compliments and verbal recounting ("instant replay") of the action.

Skill was closely related to competition, as illustrated by the following:

> I like to keep a mental file about the way people play. I like to think about how a person acts when he has something, and how I might act myself when I have something, and try and change that periodically. I think about how someone played a hand last time, and then try to figure out what he has by the way he's playing this time. You decide how to play your hand by the way you see others playing. That's the real skill in the game.

> It's a beautiful thing to see a guy play a hand of poker well. It's better, of course, if you are the one who's doing it, but it's still nice to watch somebody else make a good bet, play his cards right, and then win. I don't like to lose, but if I've got to lose, I'd much rather lose to someone who's

showing some skill in the game than to somebody who just steps into it.

Crespi (1956) pointed out that "skill players of necessity play frequently and by preference with others who are also highly skilled," and that they "seek to demonstrate their mastery of the necessary skills and, if possible, their skill superiority." Zola (1964:255) concurred when he observed in the horse parlor that "the handicapper gains and retains prestige not because of monetary profits or preponderance of winners, but because he demonstrates some techniques of skill enabling him to select winners or at least come close."

Skill, as it appeared in the friendly game, seemed also to be related closely to control over other players, over self (e.g., "poker face;" resisting temptations to bet or draw cards impulsively), and to a large extent over luck. Lukacs (1963:57) considered "the uniqueness of poker to consist of its being a game of chance where the element of chance itself is subordinated to psychological factors, and where it is not so much fate as human beings who decide." Zola (1964:260) extrapolated this interpretation to gambling in general, and felt that it "occasionally allows bettors to beat the system through rational means, and thus permits them to demonstrate to themselves and their associates that they can exercise control, and for a brief moment that they can control their fate … (it) denies the vagaries of life and gives men a chance to regulate it." Skill in this sense indeed has a rational character, but also seems to have a kind of magical quality.

Event Brokerage: "Feeling the Action"

The poker group did not tolerate disruption of the "pace" of the game. Some players commented about the rapid series of "thrills" that were strung together in a night's playing—the thrill of the "chance" and the "risk." Gambling, according to Bloch (1951:217–218), allows the player to "escape from the routine and boredom of modern industrial life in which the sense of creation and instinctive workmanship has been lost. Taking a chance destroys routine and hence is pleasurable." Bergler (1957:117) wrote of the "mysterious tension" that

is "one of the pivotal factors in deciphering the psychology of gambling … This tension is a mixture, part pleasurable, part painful. It is comparable to no other known sensation."

Goffman (1967:155, 185) saw gambling as being most thrilling when it requires "intense and sustained exercising of relevant capacity," and when, as "action," "squaring off, determination, disclosure and settlement occur over a period of long enough time to be contained within a continuous stretch of attention and experience." Each hand of poker met the criteria for "action" and the requirement for "intensive and sustained exercising of relevant capacities" (skill and competitiveness). Central to this process was the opportunity for the player to make decisions concerning his participation in the play, decisions which were perceived to influence the outcome of his "action." Herman (1967b:101) wrote that the function of money, in the context of the gambling institution, is primarily to reify the decision-making process, establishing "the fact of a decisive act" and "verifying the involvement of the bettor in the action."

Both Goffman and Herman, in their discussions of "action" and "decision-making," referred to commercial gambling establishments. However, these factors, particularly as they relate to the stimulation of players and their experiencing of "thrill," were clearly manifested in the friendly game. A core member explained, when the author first joined, "We don't eat sandwiches and things like that during the game, and we don't shoot the bull, because it causes a break in the action." Another remarked, "It's like a new game every hand. There's a new dealer, you get a new set of cards, and it's a whole new ball game. You get your new cards dealt to you and you've got to think all over again what you are going to do with this hand." Each player was a broker of events potentially thrilling to himself and his colleagues.

Normative Deception and Aggression: "You're a Liar!"

To "bluff" in poker is to attempt by a pattern of betting, physical cues, and playing the cards to deceive other players about the quality of your hand. In poker the bluff is

> not only occasional but constant, not secondary
> but primary. Like certain other games of chance,
> poker is played not primarily with cards but with
> money; unlike other games the money stakes in
> poker represent not only our idea of the value of
> cards, but our idea of what the other player's idea
> of the value of cards might be (Lukacs, 1963:57).

Goffman (1961:38–39) observed that, "assessing a possible bluff is a formal part of the game of poker, the player being advised to examine his opponents' minor and presumably uncalculated expressive behavior."

Bluffing is related to the dynamics of competition, skill, decision-making, and action. Each player attempts to "fake out" the others. By giving the appearance that the cards randomly dealt to him are really something other than what they appear to be, he tries symbolically to control fate. With each succeeding hand the player must decide whether to try to "run one by" or to "play them straight."

Shortly after the author joined the group, he was shown a cartoon sketch of the players that one had drawn. The drawing caricatured the core members at play. They were addressing one another, and strikingly every comment referred to self, others, or the whole group "lying." In the friendly game, to "lie" or "speed" meant to bluff, and the performance of this act, successful or not, brought great pleasure to all, as indicated by the following interview responses:

> I really enjoy slipping one by the other guys …
> Putting one over on them—that's *really* a great
> feeling. I get a kick out of that.

> I like the teasing that goes on in the game. You can
> say things there to people that you couldn't say else-
> where. I tell one of the other players he's a damned
> liar, for example, and he might take offense at that
> under other circumstances. But here it's almost a
> form of endearment. You'll say something to the rest
> like "nobody here is telling the truth. Everybody is
> a phony." Well, some of the guys may hit you on the
> head with something if you said that anywhere else.

To be called a "liar" or to be accused of speeding was a compliment, a sign that one could engage in the intense personal interaction that bluffing stimulated. The game, and particularly the bluff established the kind of "focused gathering" that Goffman (1961:17–18) described as providing "a heightened and mutual relevance of acts; an eye to eye ecological huddle" quite generative of a gratifying "we rationale."

Core members often discussed their ability to catch one another "speeding," and the cues that would give fellow players away:

> When he puts a big stack of chips on his cards like
> that, I know he's bluffing. … When he puffs his
> pipe like that, he's trying to speed. … He's got
> that funny look in his eye. … When he says, "I
> don't know why I'm doing this" or "I must be stu-
> pid to stay in this," you better look out!

Lukacs (1963:57) commented, "Since the important thing to poker is not the cards but the betting, not the value of the player's hands but the player's psychology, as one gets to know the habits, the quirks, the tendencies, the strengths, the weaknesses of the other players, the play becomes increasingly interesting."

To be caught speeding and then teased as a liar seemed to be a *rite de passage* for a new man. On his first night, a new player was caught attempting to bluff and lost to a better hand. The men burst into laughter, and a core player loudly commented, "Now you're a member of this thieving group! You've been caught lying! Trying to speed, huh? Now you're one of us!" The new man was asked to return for subsequent sessions.[3]

On the other hand, not to have the capacity or inclination to bluff, or to be considered "honest," was flatly an insult. A new man in exasperation asked during his first and only night why it was that everyone dropped out whenever he initiated a bet or a raise. A core player shook his head and responded, "because you are too honest." This was said unsmilingly, and was based upon the new man's tendency to bet only when he had cards to validate the size of his bet. He was not inclined to bluff or lie. He was *too* predictable. One didn't have to read subtle cues or study the pattern of his

---

[3] The "liar" in the poker group seems honorifically similar to the "handicapper" in horse playing (cf. Zola, 1964:255).

play in order to approximate whether or not he was speeding or "for real." Potentially, he was a "pigeon" who would destroy the group "action."

Ironically, a player had to be caught bluffing if others were to know that he was a "speeder." Once caught and appropriately teased, he established his potential for speeding and further stimulated the intense personal interaction, competition, and opportunity for cue-reading skill that generated from the bluff. In essence, the speeder contributed to the uncertainty in the game and to cognitive imbalance for the players. The resolution of this uncertainty and cognitive imbalance seemed to be pleasurable and thus rewarding.

When a core player was caught in a particularly gross bluff, there were comments from others about historically memorable "lies," and the former culprit, if present, was again teased for his attempt. Usually someone would add, "Well, that's a time we caught him. Nobody knows how many times his lying is successful!" The uncalled winner does not have to show his hand in poker, so players are never really certain when he was bluffing. A common poker strategy used occasionally in the group is deliberately to be caught bluffing so that on subsequent occasions the relation between betting and hand strength is less clear.

The lie can also be interpreted as an opportunity to engage safely in behavior which might be considered "deviant" according to norms outside the friendly game.[4] "Honesty" became a negative attribute and "dishonesty" became a positive attribute. A fellow player could be called a liar and he would laugh. To have called him such in public would probably have invited anger. Within the game, delimited aggression and deception were normative and functional.

Micro-Institutionalizing: "Almost a Law"

Ritual, magic, and tradition, complexly interrelated, have often been described as central components in human play. That component complex is present in poker, and was dramatically apparent in

the friendly game. In addition to the more explicit rules governing play discussed above, there were instances of at least implicit "rules of irrelevance." According to Goffman (1961:19–21), rules of irrelevance are an important aspect of focused interactions. They strengthen idiosyncratic norms and the cohesion and "separateness" by declaring irrelevant certain characteristics of the participants or setting which may have considerable saliency in the world "outside."

In the friendly game, even though a player's occupational status may have had some influence in his being invited that status became irrelevant. The author was, for example, asked by a new man what his occupation was. Before he could answer, a core player laughingly but nonetheless forcefully exclaimed, "Right now he's a poker player, and it's his deal!"

Although all the core players were married, family roles were also deemed irrelevant. One might talk about family problems or items of mutual interest in the "socializing" before the game began or during the meal after the game but certainly not in the game. The mere presence of wives or children was prohibited, and even the thought of allowing wives to play was, as one core player summarized it, "horrible!" Another commented, "My son would like to come and watch us, but I won't let him. It's kind of an invasion of privacy, and you don't want *people* to be butting in at times like that."

During the game virtually all topics of conversation not appropriate to the action were deemed irrelevant. "My wife asked me what we talk about when we play cards," observed a core player. "I tell her we don't talk about anything, we play cards. She can't understand that, because they gossip when they play bridge. But they aren't really playing a game then." On one occasion a core player worriedly interjected, "My God, how about this war in Viet Nam!" The others were silent for a few seconds, then one answered, "Whose deal is it?" The player who had commented about the war continued his statements, and quickly was interrupted by another who somewhat sternly though not angrily advised, "I didn't come here to hear you give a speech. I came here to play poker. I could give a speech myself you know." "Who will

---

[4]For a relevant treatment of group norms for deviance, see Erikson (1962).

sell me some chips," inquired another, and the game continued.

Along with the accepted and expected verbal interactions of teasing and "game talk," the players enjoyed, indeed institutionalized, a core member's occasional references to the sagacity of his grandfather as a poker player. Whenever he was facing a particularly difficult decision, he would lean back in his chair, puff on a cigar (all but one of the players smoked either pipes or cigars during the game), and reflectively comment, "Well, my grandfather used to say," (for example) "never throw good money after bad." Often other players would make similar statements when they were faced with problem situations. The "grandfather" quotes had reference to betting, bluffing, soundness of decision, or competition. The content of the messages might accurately be described, as suggested by an interviewee, as "a poker player's Poor Richard's Almanac." The quotes seemed to be an important mechanism for bringing into the friendly game, as a lesson of a wise, "pioneer" man, considerations of the Protestant Ethic. The advice of grandfather was often cited to new men, thus serving a socialization function.

The verbal rituals, rules of irrelevance, and various behavioral taboos seemed to support valued group dynamics. The no-alcohol rule, for example, was adopted early in the group's history when an inebriated player had disrupted the pace. Similarly, the no-eating rule was inaugurated when players were observed to drop cards, or get them sticky. A number of specific games or methods of playing split-pot games were outlawed because they had in the past caused anger among players.

Although the players stressed the use of skill, particularly as a manifestation of control over fate, they also invoked what Malinowski (1948:38, 88) called "practical magic," primarily in an attempt to control the flow of cards or to change their luck. They would, for example, talk to the deck, urging it to give them good cards; rap the table with their knuckles just before receiving a card; slowly "squeeze out" a hand dealt to them, particularly after having drawn another card or cards, in order to "change the spots"; make a "fancy cut" as a luck changer; bet a hand "on the come" or "like

you had them," as a means of guaranteeing getting the card or cards desired; deal a different game in order to "cool off" or "heat up" the deck; get up and stretch, or get a cup of coffee, in order to "change the way the money is flowing on the table"; stack their chips in a "lucky" way. On one occasion a player reached over and disordered another's chips, laughingly saying, "That should change your luck! You're winning too much!"[5]

The most striking example of magical behavior within the friendly game was the clearly understood and always followed rule that a player must bet fifteen cents, no more and no less, on the first face-up ace he received in a hand. It was agreed that if one did not follow this rule he would "insult the ace" and would inevitably lose. No one seemed to know where the "rule" originated, but all followed it and made a point of instructing new men to do likewise. Three members specifically referred to the fifteen-cent rule when interviewed about "specific rules." "I don't know why we do that," commented one, "but that's our precious ritual. I do remember one time I forgot to bet in that way, and by God I lost!" The second member thought betting fifteen cents on the ace was "a funny rule, but still a rule." The third man referred to the fifteen-cent bet as "almost a law. It's stupid, I guess, but it makes the game more fun." In this case, the magic served not only the function of insuring against possible loss but also as another contributor to group cohesion. It may have been a "stupid" law, but it was "our" law.

The meal following the game might be considered a ritual feast. The strict poker rules and interactions were loosened, and the players discussed various topics deemed inappropriate during the game itself.

Retrospective Conquest: "If I Had Only …"

In the friendly game, winners necessitate losers. Unlike forms of betting games in which the participants play against the "house," not every player in poker can win.

---

[5] For a fascinating discussion of such behavior among craps shooters, see Henslin (1967).

The most a member could win or lose was approximately *$30.00*. Generally, there was one "big winner," one "big loser," and the rest were distributed in between. One core player was a "big winner" more often than the others, but not enough to disrupt the balance of the group. There was no consistent "big loser." All of the members were in approximately the same income bracket, and thus winning or losing *$30.00* had a similar impact upon them. Goffman (1961:69) pointed out that if betting is low relative to the financial capacities of the players, interest may be lacking in the game and they may not take it seriously. If conversely players feel that betting is too high then interest may be "strangled" by concern for the money they could lose. The core members understood the impact of someone who "couldn't afford to lose" or "didn't care about losing." In their view the former "makes you feel guilty if you win," and the latter "is no challenge, because if he's not really losing anything, you're not really winning anything." It was important that the financial conditions of the players be such that they maintained the dynamic equilibrium of the group.

The players knew that someone had to lose and inevitably at times it would be themselves. All agreed it was better to win than lose, but losing was not a disgrace so long as one did so through no lack of skill. For the member who had "played well" but nonetheless ended up a loser at the end of the evening the group offered and accepted several rationalizations, most commonly sympathizing about a plague of "second-best hands." This meant that the loser had played his cards well, "knocked heads" to the very end, and then come up with a slightly inferior hand. In essence, the cards were being blamed for his loss. It was no fault of his, because he "played well." When a player of this quality lost, luck was the culprit. But, when he won, it was by virtue of his skill; luck had nothing to do with it.

The core members looked with disfavor upon anyone who won by luck alone. A skillful player might invest some money early in a hand, but should not consistently "ride the hand out" hoping subsequently to be dealt some good cards. He should assess the odds, appraise through observation of cues and actions the quality of others' hands, and if evidence warranted he should decide to drop out and take his temporary loss.

Those who had lost a hand were often seen to "relive" the play. They would utter such statements as: "I figured that you …"; "If I hadn't thrown away those …"; "All I needed was another spade and …"; "I thought you had three of a kind because you were betting …" Zola (1964:256) observed this phenomenon, which he called "the hedge," in the horse parlor, and described it as a means of maintaining some status even when losing. The loser would give a series of reasons why he lost, and how he wouldn't have if he had done some minor thing differently.

Goffman (1967:247) pointed out instances where in competitive interactions "both parties can emerge with honor and good character affirmed." This opportunity was clearly provided in the friendly game for those players who would "knock heads." There was potential in that situation for a "good winner" and one or more "good losers."

If a core player clearly had made a blunder, he would be teased by the others. Often the blunderer, in defense, would narrate a blunder historical for the group, whether made by himself or some other player. "Remember the time when Joe bet like crazy on his low hand because he thought the game was high-low split, and it was a high hand take all!" Considerable detail would be shared about the nature of the epic mistake. The current blunderer effectively would have anchored his own current error on a point somewhere less gross than a historical one. The core players appreciated and were comforted by the fact that all of them made mistakes. As one interviewee pointed out, "Nobody likes to play poker against a machine."

The player who had lost despite his skill might choose some other form of rationalization. He might consider the evening to have been "cheap entertainment," or "the cost of some lessons in poker." He might indicate that it was "his turn to lose tonight," or he had "let the host win." Nobody ever really complained about losing (although frustration was expressed concerning "second-best hands"). "I have more fun *losing* in this group," commented a core member, "than I do *winning* at roulette, or something like that."

The amount of money won or lost was discussed only in the most off-hand manner. Specific figures were seldom mentioned, only estimates given, and then only sporadically and without pattern by different players. A core member reflected,

> At the end of the evening the game is over. Who cares how much you win or lose on one evening because each of us wins or loses, and it balances it out. It's each hand during the game that counts, and whether you win or lose that hand. The overall thing doesn't mean as much.

The money, out of the context of group interaction, seemed unimportant.

Conclusions: The Ephemeral Role

The core members perceived themselves to be in a "different world" when they were playing. The friendly game, with its idiosyncratic roles, norms, rituals and rules of irrelevance, maintained clearly established boundaries. New men were selected carefully, and anyone or anything that disrupted the group dynamics or reduced the satisfactions experienced was eliminated or avoided. The players testified to their awareness that the poker group was "separate" from their other, broader, day-to-day social relationships:

> I look forward every other Monday to getting away from it all. I can do that when I'm playing poker with the guys. I forget about my job, and other problems that I have, and I can just sort of get lost in the game.

> It's a chance to get away from our wives and families. Every man needs a chance to get away from that once in awhile.

> When that first card hits the table, it's like we're on an island, you know, all to ourselves. Nobody bothers us. You're your own man! I miss it whenever we have to cancel a game for some reason or another.

In this sense, the friendly game seemed, as did Zola's (1964:248–249) horse parlor, to allow the players to effect "disassociation from ordinary utilitarian activities."

Goffman (1961:36, 67–68) described a "gaming encounter" as having social participants deeply involved in a focused interaction, and as such has "a metaphorical membrane around it." When the core players had all arrived, they formed the metaphorical membrane, and the friendly game became "a little cosmos of its own" (Riezler, 1941:505). Within the group boundaries, each member enacted the "ephemeral role" of core member, providing him the opportunity for scripted competition, self- and other-control, event brokerage, normative deception and aggression, microinstitutionalizing, and retrospective conquest. More specifically it provided him with the following opportunities for satisfaction: to share in the establishing and/or maintaining of a personally relevant group structure and interaction pattern; to compete vigorously but safely with equals; to bluff, tease, or otherwise "one-up" equals; to demonstrate and be admired for skill in betting and playing; to become deeply involved in intense but controlled personal interaction; to read, analyze, and utilize cues emitted from other players; to control and become immersed in action, including a series of thrills and the exhilaration of "pace;" to enjoy the fellowship of a chosen and mutually developed primary group; to exert control over self, others and luck or fate; to capture or relive some of the competencies and freedoms of youth; to reaffirm one's masculinity; to enjoy legitimized deviancy; to implement, in rapid succession, a great number of significant decisions; to declare as irrelevant, norms and roles which society-at-large deems mandatory in favor of idiosyncratic group norms and roles; and to escape the routine and "ordinary" social dynamics of everyday life.

The core member appeared to enter and leave the metaphorical membrane and ephemeral role through two buffer zones structured into the friendly game. The first buffer zone was the pre-game socializing period during which players waited and discussed various topics until all had arrived. The transition from everyday social interaction to the contrived interaction in the game, the "easing" into the ephemeral role, was facilitated by this short delay. Players who had arrived late and thus missed the socializing period were heard to comment, for example, "give me a second to shift gears," or "let me put on my poker hat."

The other buffer zone, the meal after the game, served a similar function. The players then were behaving as members of any other group sitting down to have a snack together. The topics of conversation were unrestricted, and only rarely and briefly were any comments made concerning the game itself. During that period of the evening, the players were being "eased back" into their day-to-day complex of social roles.

Those who could not make the transition into the ephemeral role were disruptive to the group. This happened on only two occasions observed by the author. The first occasion involved a new man whose home had some months before been destroyed by a severe tornado. Shortly before the game had begun a tornado watch had been announced for the area; the sky was heavy with clouds and the wind was noticeably increasing. The new man kept looking over his shoulder and out of the window, rose several times to walk to the front porch and look up at the sky, and twice dropped out of the game to phone his wife. A core player commented, in an uncriticizing manner, "Your mind is wandering, isn't it." The distracted man commented that since he was "so nervous" it might be a "good idea" for him to go home. The group quickly agreed with him, and he left. A minute or so later a core player announced, "Okay, let's settle down and play some poker," and the game went on.

In the second incident, a core player seemed to be distracted throughout the game. He told short jokes, talked about "irrelevant" topics, and generally slowed down the pace. "What the hell's the matter with you!" inquired another, "Why are you so talkative tonight?" The reasons for his behavior were not clear until later, during the meal, when he announced that he was being moved to another area and would no longer be able to participate. He apparently had found it difficult to enact fully the ephemeral role, since he realized he would no longer be part of the friendly game. His distraction by the world "out there" had distracted the other players. As Goffman (1957) observed, in a gaming encounter "the perception that one participant is not spontaneously involved in the mutual activity can weaken for others their own involvement in the encounter and their own belief in the reality of the world it describes."

Core member of the friendly game is only one example of an ephemeral role. Other examples might include such diverse behavioral patterns as LSD "tripper," encounter "grouper," adulterer, volunteer work crew member (Zurcher, 1968), vacationer, weekend fisherman, or whatever is intense and intermittent and defined in contrast to one's day-to-day social world. Hopefully, we may see more systematic and comparative studies showing why people choose to develop or enact specific ephemeral roles, the satisfactions they gain, and the relation between ephemeral roles and major "life" roles.

REFERENCES

American Institute of Public Opinion. 1948 "The Quarter's Polls." *Public Opinion Quarterly* 12(Spring): 146–176.

Bergler, E. 1957 *The Psychology of Gambling.* New York: Hill & Wang.

Bloch, H. A. 1951 "The Sociology of Gambling." *American Journal of Sociology* 57(November): 215–221.

Caillois, R. 1961 *Man, Play and Games.* New York: Free Press of Glencoe.

Crespi, I. 1956 "The Social Significance of Card Playing as a Leisure Time Activity." *American Sociological Review* 21(December): 717–721.

Edwards, W. 1955 "The Prediction of Decisions Among Bets." *Journal of Experimental Psychology* 50(September): 201–214.

Erikson, E. 1950 *Childhood and Society.* New York: Norton.

Erikson, K. 1962 "Notes on the Sociology of Deviance." *Social Problems* 9(Spring): 307–314.

Goffman, E. 1956 "Embarrassment and Social Organization." *American Journal of Sociology* 62(November): 264–271.

——, 1957 "Alienation from Interaction." *Human Relations* 10(February): 47–60.

——, 1961 *Encounters: Two Studies in the Sociology of Interaction.* Indianapolis: Bobbs-Merrill.

——, 1967 *Interaction Ritual.* Chicago: Aldine.

Gold, R. 1958 "Roles in Sociological Field Observation." *Social Forces* 36(March): 217–223.

Henslin, J. M. 1967 "Craps and Magic." *American Journal of Sociology* 73(November): 316–330.

Herman, R. D. (ed.) 1967a *Gambling.* New York: Harper & Row.

——, 1967b "Gambling as Work: A Sociological Study of the Race Track." pp. 87–104 in R. D. Herman (ed.), *Gambling.* New York: Harper & Row.

Huizinga, J. 1955 *Homo Ludens, The Play Element in Culture.* Boston: Beacon Press.

Lukacs, J. 1963 "Poker and American Character." *Horizon* 5(November): 56–62.

Malinowski, B. 1948 *Magic, Science and Religion.* New York: Doubleday.

Martinez, T. M., and R. LaFranci. 1969 "Why People Play Poker." *Transaction* 6(July–August): 30–35, 52.

Piaget, J. 1951 *Play, Dreams and Imitations in Childhood.* New York: Norton.

Riezler, K. 1941 "Play and Seriousness." *The Journal of Philosophy* 38(September): 505–517.

Robbins, F. G. 1955 *The Sociology of Play, Recreation and Leisure Time.* Dubuque, Iowa: Brown.

Strauss, A. 1956 *The Social Psychology of George Herbert Mead.* Chicago: University of Chicago Press.

Sutton-Smith, B., and J. M. Roberts. 1963 "Game Involvement in Adults." *Journal of Social Psychology* 60(First Half): 15–30.

Zola, I. K. 1964 "Observations on Gambling in a Lower Class Setting." pp. 247–260 in H. Becker (ed.), *The Other Side.* New York: Free Press.

Zurcher, L. A. 1968 "Social Psychological Functions of Ephemeral Roles." *Human Organization* 27(Winter): 281–297.

PART 3

Conflict in Groups

It is hard to imagine a group that does not experience at least some conflict, and in many groups conflict plays a central role in how members relate to one another (Levine & Thompson, 1996; Pruitt, 1998). Conflict arises from group members' beliefs that they are pursuing incompatible goals, so that one person's ability to achieve his or her goals interferes with the ability of others to achieve their goals. Conflict can occur over many issues, including access to scarce resources (e.g., money, space) and people's opinions and behaviors. In many cases, conflict has negative consequences for the group. These include hostility among members, reduced effort on joint tasks, and, in extreme cases, dissolution of the group. Most of the research on conflict has focused on its negative effects, trying to understand when and why they occur and suggesting strategies for reducing the damage that they cause. But conflict is not always harmful, and in some cases it can be beneficial. For example, disagreement about the best solution for a problem can cause group members to rethink their views and lay the groundwork for innovation. Thus, rather than trying to eliminate all conflict, groups should try to regulate it (and sometimes even encourage it).

Some researchers have investigated how group members resolve conflicts regarding the allocation of scarce resources. Although people in such situations are sometimes motivated only to compete, more often their behavior is based on a mixture of cooperative and competitive motivation. In recent years, particular attention has been devoted to an interesting class of mixed-motive situations called *social dilemmas* (Schroeder, 1995).

These situations pit short-term individual welfare against long-term group welfare, with the group often losing out. In one kind of social dilemma, called collective traps, behavior that is *rewarding* for individual members produces negative group (and individual) outcomes when *exhibited* by enough members. For example, fishermen sometimes harvest so many fish during a season that the population is unable to replenish itself, resulting in a serious loss of income the next season for everyone. In another kind of social dilemma, called collective fences, behavior that is *costly* for individual members produces negative group (and individual) outcomes when *avoided* by enough people. For example, viewers of public television sometimes fail to donate money to their local station, because they can watch the programs for free. This creates financial problems for the station that may translate into reduced program options for everyone. Because social dilemmas are so common in everyday life and group members often respond to them by seeking to maximize their short-term individual welfare, researchers have searched for ways to increase the likelihood that members will cooperate rather than compete (Kerr & Park, 2001). Evidence indicates, for example, that cooperation increases when group members view their contributions as critical, when they can communicate with one another, and when the group has a system for punishing people who refuse to cooperate.

Group members are interdependent regarding information and opinions, as well as more tangible outcomes. This occurs, in part, because of a powerful need to believe that one's beliefs about the world are valid. Often that need can only be satisfied by agreement with others who share one's group membership (Abrams & Hogg, 1990; Festinger, 1950). Disagreement among group members about information and opinions is thus is a source of conflict, which in turn motivates efforts to reduce or eliminate the disagreement. In studying the impact of disagreement on group behavior, most researchers have focused on cases in which two factions exist and one is larger than the other (a majority and a minority). Two general methods for reducing majority-minority conflict can be identified. The first is social influence. This can involve members of both factions moving toward one another's position (compromise), minority members moving toward the majority position (conformity), or majority members moving toward the minority position (innovation). The second method is redefinition of group boundaries. This can involve majority and/or minority members rejecting the other faction, voluntarily leaving the group, or adding new members who agree with their position.

Most of the research on majority-minority conflict has focused on unilateral influence (either conformity or innovation) rather than bilateral influence (compromise). In an early study of conformity, Asch (1956) exposed a lone participant to several peers who unanimously disagreed with his judgment regarding the lengths of lines. Although control participants who responded alone hardly ever made any errors, experimental participants responding in the presence of an erroneous majority conformed about a third of the time. In an early study of innovation, Moscovici, Lage, and Naffrechoux (1969) exposed several participants to two peers who disagreed with group consensus on color judgments. When the two-person minority consistently give the same erroneous response, participants were more likely to give that response themselves than were control participants who responded alone. Moreover, when participants later made color judgments on their own, those who had seen the consistent two-person minority behaved as though their perception of color had actually changed as a result of their experience. Many later studies have confirmed that both majorities and minorities can influence members of the other faction, at least under certain conditions. The mechanisms underlying these two kinds of influence remain controversial, however. A major issue is whether majority and minority influence involve a single psychological process or two processes (Martin & Hewstone, 2001). One two-process theory (Nemeth, 1986) claims that majorities produce a narrow focus on their message, whereas minorities produce a broader focus on new information and alternative positions. For this reason, people exposed to majority dissent engage in convergent thinking, which leads to uncreative problem solutions, whereas people exposed to minority dissent engage in divergent thinking, which leads to creative solutions.

Given that group members desire agreement, it would not be surprising if they responded negatively to people who refuse to conform to group consensus. This phenomenon has been observed repeatedly in studies of group reactions to opinion deviance (Levine, 1989). Among the variables that influence how groups respond to deviates are the extremity and content of the deviate's position, the degree to which the deviate interferes with the attainment of group goals, the deviate's perceived responsibility for his or her behavior, the deviate's status in the group, and the group's openness to alternative perspectives. In recent years, work on reactions to opinion deviance has also begun to focus on the intergroup context in which the deviance occurs. Much of this work involves the "black sheep effect"—unlikeable ingroup members are evaluated more negatively (and likeable ingroup members more positively) than similar outgroup members (Marques & Paez, 1994). For example, a Democrat who deviates from the party line on an issue will be evaluated more negatively by fellow Democrats than a Republican who takes the same position. This reaction may reflect an effort to maintain positive group identity by rejecting members who threaten that identity.

Group members often vary in their ability to influence the process and outcome of conflict resolution. This can be attributed to differences in power, defined as the capacity to influence other people (French & Raven, 1959). In a well-known analysis, French and Raven (1959; Raven, 1965) identified several kinds of power, which differ in the conditions they require and the effects they produce. These are reward, coercive, legitimate, referent, expert, and informational power. For example, reward and coercive power require surveillance by the power source and produce public but not private influence. In contrast, informational power does not require surveillance and produces private as well as public influence. Several researchers have studied the consequences of possessing high versus low power (e.g., Keltner, Gruenfeld, & Anderson, 2003).

Evidence suggests that high power is associated with positive emotion, attention to rewards, and socially inappropriate behavior, whereas low power is associated with negative emotion, attention to threats, and inhibited social behavior.

REFERENCES

Abrams, D., & Hogg, M. A. (1990). Social identification, self-categorization and social influence. In W. Stroebe & M. Hewstone (Eds.), *European review of social psychology* (Vol. 1, pp. 195–228). Chichester, England: Wiley.

Asch, S. E. (1956). Studies of independence and submission to group pressure: I. A minority of one against a unanimous majority. *Psychological Monographs, 70*, No. 9 (Whole No. 417).

Festinger, L. (1950). Informal social communication. *Psychological Review, 57*, 271–282.

French, J. R. P., & Raven, B. (1959). The bases of social power. In D. Cartwright (Ed.), *Studies in social power* (pp. 150–167). Ann Arbor, MI: University of Michigan Press.

Keltner, D., Gruenfeld, D. H., & Anderson, C. (2003). Power, approach, and inhibition. *Psychological Review, 110*, 265–284.

Kerr, N. L., & Park, E. S. (2001). Group performance in collaborative and social dilemma tasks: Progress and prospects. In M. A. Hogg & R. S. Tindale (Eds.), *Blackwell handbook of social psychology: Group processes* (pp. 107–138). Malden, MA: Blackwell.

Levine, J. M. (1989). Reaction to opinion deviance in small groups. In P. B. Paulus (Ed.), *Psychology of group influence* (2nd ed., pp. 187–231). Hillsdale, NJ: Lawrence Erlbaum Associates, Inc.

Levine, J. M., & Thompson, L. (1996). Conflict in groups. In E. T. Higgins & A. W. Kruglanski (Eds.), *Social psychology: Handbook of basic principles* (pp. 745–776). New York: Guilford.

Marques, J. M., & Paez, D. (1994). The "Black Sheep Effect": Social categorization, rejection of ingroup deviates, and perception of group variability. In W. Stroebe & M. Hewstone (Eds.), *European review of social psychology* (Vol. 5, pp. 37–68). Chichester, England: Wiley.

Martin, R., & Hewstone, M. (2001). Conformity and independence in groups: Majorities and minorities. In M. A. Hogg & R. S. Tindale (Eds.), *Blackwell handbook of social psychology: Group processes* (pp. 209–234). Malden, MA: Blackwell.

Moscovici, S., Lage, E., & Naffrechoux, M. (1969). Influence of a consistent minority on the responses of a majority in a color perception task. *Sociometry, 32*, 365–380.

Nemeth, C. J. (1986). Differential contributions of majority and minority influence. *Psychological Review, 93*, 23–32.

Pruitt, D. G. (1998). Social conflict. In D. T. Gilbert, S. T. Fiske, & G. Lindzey (Eds.), *The handbook of social psychology* (4th ed., Vol. 2, pp. 470–503). Boston, MA: McGraw-Hill.

Raven, B. H. (1965). Social influence and power. In I. D. Steiner & M. Fishbein (Eds.), *Current studies in social psychology* (pp. 371–382). New York: Holt, Rinehart, & Winston.

Schroeder, D. A. (Ed.) (1995). *Social dilemmas: Perspectives on individuals and groups*. Westport, CT: Praeger.

Readings

In the first paper in this section, Kramer and Brewer (1984) studied behavior in collective traps, where the continued availability of a common resource is endangered by selfish behavior on the part of individual group members. They were especially interested in how the belief that they share a common (superordinate) group identity affects people's willingness to behave cooperatively. Kramer and Brewer predicted that people who share a common identity will assume that other group members will reciprocate any unselfish behavior on their part, and so they will behave cooperatively in a social dilemma. Moreover, the researchers reasoned that the impact of a common identity will increase as the conflict between the individual's interests and the group's interests intensifies (e.g., when the common resource becomes depleted). Kramer and Brewer thus predicted that group identification will have little impact on cooperation when a common resource is maintained at an adequate level. But as the resource becomes depleted, people who identify with the group will behave more cooperatively than those who do not.

To test their ideas, Kramer and Brewer conducted three laboratory experiments using similar experimental paradigms. In all cases, six-person groups were created, composed of three real participants and three bogus participants (allegedly located at another location). All interactions among participants occurred over a computer network. The participants' task was to withdraw points (worth money) from a shared pool, with instructions to accumulate as many points as they could *and* make the pool last as long as possible. After participants withdrew points on each trial, the pool was replenished at a rate that guaranteed its continued existence only if participants used restraint on subsequent trials. Feedback was given indicating that the pool either dropped steadily across trials (depletion condition—Experiments 1–3) or did not (sustained-use condition—Experiments 2–3). In all cases, the three real participants in each group were told that (a) all six people were members of a single superordinate group (e.g., residents of Santa Barbara) or (b) three people were members of one subordinate group (e.g., young people), and the other three were members of a different subordinate group (e.g., old people). The major dependent variable was the number of points that participants withdrew from the pool over the series of trials.

Similar results were obtained in the three experiments. When *subordinate* group identity was salient, participants withdrew more points (showed less restraint) as the pool approached depletion. In contrast, when *superordinate* group identity was salient, participants withdrew fewer points (showed more restraint) as depletion approached. Participants in the subordinate and superordinate identity conditions behaved similarly when the pool level was sustained. The consistency of results across the three experiments is impressive, given that Kramer and Brewer used different manipulations of social identity in each case.

The second paper, by Gruenfeld (1995), describes an archival study of majority and minority influence, focusing on the "integrative complexity" of U.S. Supreme court opinions. Integrative complexity has two components—*differentiation* (recognition that an issue has multiple dimensions) and *integration* (recognition of the relations among different dimensions). As noted earlier, minority targets exposed to majority sources often engage in convergent thinking, which focuses on the validity of the majority's position, whereas majority targets exposed to minority sources engage in divergent thinking, which involves considering multiple perspectives and generating novel alternatives. Because integrative complexity is a form of divergent thinking, membership in a majority should thus be associated with more integrative complexity than membership in a minority (or a unanimous group).

To test her predictions, Gruenfeld compared the integrative complexity of (a) minority and majority opinions written by Supreme Court justices in nonunanimous cases and (b) majority opinions written by justices in unanimous and nonunanimous cases. These comparisons were made in three studies, using verbatim records of opinions written from 1953 through 1990. The results supported Gruenfeld's hypotheses. In Study 1, the opinions of both liberal and conservative justices showed more integrative complexity when they were written on behalf of the majority rather than the minority. In Study 2, nonunanimous majority opinions were more integratively complex than either minority opinions or unanimous opinions. And in Study 3, both liberal and conservative opinions were higher in integrative complexity during eras when the Court's dominant ideology was consistent with that opinion (i.e., when the opinion reflected a "majority" viewpoint). Taken as a whole, Gruenfeld's research makes a strong case for the relationship between justices' majority/minority status and their level of integrative complexity. Her findings thus cast doubt on an earlier explanation of integrative complexity based solely on ideology, namely that political liberals are more cognitively complex than are conservatives.

The third paper, by Marques, Abrams, and Serodio (2001), describes three experiments on how people respond to ingroup and outgroup members who violate or uphold generic norms (which apply to all groups). The researchers hypothesized that people (a) react more negatively to ingroup than to outgroup deviates, because the former (but not the latter) undermine the ingroup's claim to uphold generic norms, and (b) reject ingroup deviates more strongly when group support for generic norms is unclear, because that lack of clarity also undermines the group's claim to uphold these norms.

In the first experiment, participants who supported a generic norm of their university (that new students should be hazed) were told that members of their ingroup (psychology students) or an outgroup (law students) either supported (validated) or opposed (undermined) the norm. Participants then were asked to evaluate two students, one who supported hazing and one who opposed it. When the norm was undermined, but not when it was validated, participants responded (a) more *negatively* to ingroup deviates than to outgroup deviates and (b) more *positively* to ingroup conformers than to outgroup conformers.

Apparently, group members are especially threatened by deviance and especially reassured by conformity when a generic norm is undermined. The second and third experiments provided additional evidence for this conclusion. Marques and his colleagues suggested that people want to associate their group with generic norms in order to show that it reflects the views of most people and thus deserves to have authority and power.

In the final paper in this section, Kipnis (1972) explored the old adage that "power corrupts." By corruption, people usually mean the exploitation of others, the maximization of personal gain, or the tendency to seek power as an end in itself. Kipnis focused on a different consequence of power, namely powerholders' views of themselves and the people under them.

To investigate the impact of power on self- and other-perceptions, Kipnis conducted a laboratory experiment in which participants worked as managers in a simulated industrial setting. Their job was to manage four workers, allegedly located in another building, by sending messages to them and reviewing reports of their performance. In fact, there were no workers, and their "performance" was controlled by the experimenter. Some of the participants were given several types of power to influence the workers' behavior, including pay increases and job transfers. Other participants were not given these powers and had to rely only on their legitimate power as appointed leaders and their personal power of persuasion. All participants received exactly the same reports describing the workers' performance. Nevertheless, Kipnis found that access to special powers increased participants' efforts to influence the workers' behavior. Access to these powers also caused participants to devalue the workers' behavior, to view their own powers as the cause of that behavior, and to maintain psychological distance from the workers. Contrary to predictions, the exercise of power did not increase participants' self-esteem. As Kipnis noted, a different pattern of results might have occurred if workers had actively resisted participants' efforts to control their behavior. In that case, participants might have restructured their views of workers, for example by seeing them as stronger and more capable.

Discussion Questions

1. Think about a group that you belong to and the kinds of conflict that occur there. Which conflicts are most harmful to the group? Are any helpful?
2. If you were designing ways to increase cooperation in a social dilemma, what techniques would you consider, besides those already discussed?
3. People holding a minority position in a group often move to the majority position. Such conformity is often criticized as harmful, but when might it be beneficial for (a) the conformer and (b) the group as a whole?
4. When there is conflict between two members of a group and it cannot be resolved, one person may recruit other group members to form a coalition. How do members decide whether to join such a coalition?
5. People who have high power in a group often look down on those with low power. What about low-power people? When do they respect those with higher power, and when do they resent them? When do they feel good about themselves for taking orders, and when do they not?

Suggested Readings

De Dreu, C. K. W., & Weingart, L. R. (2003). Task versus relationship conflict, team perform-ance, and team member satisfaction: A meta-analysis. *Journal of Applied Psychology*, *88*, 741–749.

Levine, J. M. (1989). Reaction to opinion deviance in small groups. In P. B. Paulus (Ed.), *Psychology of group influence* (2nd ed., pp. 187–231). Hillsdale, NJ: Erlbaum.

Marques, J. M., Yzerbyt, V. Y., & Leyens, J.-P. (1988). The "Black Sheep Effect": Extremity of judgments towards ingroup members as a function of group identification. *European Journal of Social Psychology*, *18*, 1–16.

Nemeth, C. J., & Nemeth-Brown, B. (2003). Better than individuals? The potential bene-fits of dissent and diversity for group creativity. In P. B. Paulus & B. A. Nijstad (Eds.), *Group creativity: Innovation through collaboration* (pp. 63–84). New York: Oxford University Press.

Samuelson, C. D., Messick, D. M., Rutte, C. G., & Wilke, H. (1984). Individual and struc-tural solutions to resource dilemmas in two cultures. *Journal of Personality and Social Psychology*, *47*, 94–104.

Effects of Group Identity on Resource Use in a Simulated Commons Dilemma

Roderick M. Kramer and Marilynn B. Brewer

In a review of research on in-group categorization and group identity, Brewer (1979) proposed that cooperative solutions to social dilemmas, such as Hardin's (1968) "tragedy of the commons," may be achieved by exploiting the positive consequences arising from a common social-group identity. Three laboratory experiments were conducted to assess the effects of making salient either a superordinate (collective) or subordinate (differentiating) group identity in heterogeneous groups. In the first two experiments, naturally occurring social categories were used as a basis for group differentiation. In the third, the level of social-group identity was manipulated by varying the common fate of the group members. It was predicted that individual restraint would be most likely when a superordinate group identity was made salient and under conditions in which feedback indicated that the common resource was being depleted. Results from all three experiments provide support for this general hypothesis, indicating that cooperative responding is enhanced even when the basis for superordinate group identity is minimal.

In the last few decades, shortages of both manu-factured and natural resources have become increasingly frequent and severe. Dwindling fossil fuel deposits, electrical brownouts, depleted fresh water reserves, and the unavailability of clean, breathable air are all symptomatic of less than optimal use of scarce public resources. Each of these scarcities represents an example of

This research was supported in part by National Institute of Aging Grant AGO1503 and in part by funds from a University of California faculty research grant.

The authors would like to thank Richard Parker and Layton Lui for their assistance with computer programming.

Requests for reprints should be sent to Marilynn B. Brewer, Department of Psychology, University of California, Los Angeles, California 90024.

Hardin's (1968) "tragedy of the commons," a specific form of social interdependence in which the long-run consequence of self-interested individual choice is disaster.

In the absence of quick technological solutions, resource scarcities place the individual user in a dilemma between individual and collective rationality. The individual may be motivated to act in the collective interest by exercising personal restraint. Unilateral restraint, however, is ineffective. As Kelley and Grzelak (1972) noted, these interdependent situations are characterized by a fundamental asymmetry wherein the collectivity as a whole has a strong effect on the individual, but the individual's decision has relatively little effect on the collective. Thus, in the absence of assurance that others are behaving in the collective interest, self-interest dictates against personal restraint.

In a review of recent research in this area, Messick and Brewer (1983) identified two types of nontechnical solutions to such social dilemmas. One type involves structural solutions that come about through coordinated, organized group action. These include the political solutions based upon "mutual coercion mutually agreed upon" that Hardin (1968) emphasized in his analysis of the dilemma. The use of regulatory agencies and other forms of external control represents one type of socially approved coercion designed to constrain individual choices in the collective interest. Other solutions rely on individual preferences and social motives, maximizing those factors that influence individuals to include collective interests in their personal decision making. The present research focuses on the latter type of solution, seeking to identify conditions under which individuals will voluntarily restrain their use of a public resource in the absence of external constraint or coercion.

In his recent and thoughtful review of commons dilemma research, Edney (1980) noted the conspicuous absence of empirical research that explores the relationship between constructive social bonds or group ties and cooperative decision making in commons dilemma situations. Messick and Brewer (1983) discussed a number of reasons why a sense of membership in a common group or social category may enhance an individual's willingness to exercise personal restraint in the interests of collective welfare. One arises from processes associated with in-group favoritism. Both field studies of ethnocentrism (e.g., Brewer & Campbell, 1976) and laboratory studies of in-group bias (Brewer, 1979) indicate that members of a social group tend to perceive other members of their own group in generally favorable terms, particularly as being trustworthy, honest, and cooperative, a bias that emerges even when the basis for group identification is minimal and transient. Such attributions may induce a willingness to exercise individual restraint, because other members of the group are expected to reciprocate. In one experiment involving a six-person simulated commons dilemma, Messick, Wilke, Brewer, Kramer, Zemke, and Lui (1983) found that individual expectations of reciprocity predicted cooperative response to a resource crisis. When a common resource pool was being depleted, those who believed that others would reciprocate restraint reduced their own use to preserve the pool, whereas those whose expectations of reciprocity were low tended to increase the amount they took as the resource became scarce.

Even apart from evaluative biases and expectations associated with in-group favoritism, however, cooperative tendencies may be enhanced by the cognitive consequences of mere unit formation alone (Campbell, 1958). In a theoretical analysis of the relationship between in-group formation and social identification, Brewer (1979) proposed that one effect of group identification may be that individuals attach greater weight to collective outcomes than they do to individual outcomes alone. Inclusion within a common social boundary reduces social distance among group members, making it less likely that individuals will make sharp distinctions between their own and others' welfare. As a result, outcomes for other group members, or for the group as a whole, come to be perceived as one's own. Indeed, there is evidence that feedback regarding total group outcomes can have more impact on the individual than does feedback on his or her performance (e.g., Zander & Armstrong, 1972).

Subordinate and Superordinate Group Identity

Social-group boundaries are typically somewhat fluid or elastic, corresponding to the fact that in most societies, individuals have multiple social identities and multiple category memberships. One may, for example, simultaneously be a member of a scientific community, a member of a political party, and a citizen of a municipality facing a severe resource shortage. The boundaries of these social categories may be overlapping or hierarchically ordered, and which category boundaries are salient will vary across time and situations.

The potential benefits of group identification for solving collective-choice dilemmas require that the salient group boundary correspond fairly closely to access to the common resource. The shared resource, and associated interdependence, must, in effect, form the basis for a superordinate group identity, which encompasses all of the individuals in the commons. If subordinate boundaries or distinctions that differentiate members of a commons into identifiable subgroups are made salient, processes of in-group bias and intergroup competition may undermine collective interests. In a recent study by Komorita and Lapworth (1982), it was found that the creation of subgroup units in an N-person prisoner's dilemma game introduced an element of intergroup competition (out-group bias) that decreased the proportion of cooperative choices.

The series of studies reported here was designed to assess the differential effects of superordinate and subordinate category salience on subjects' responses to a common-resource crisis. Our general hypothesis was that individual restraint in such a crisis will be most evident when a superordinate group identity is made salient. It was predicted that, as a resource crisis continues over time, individuals with a superordinate identity will show increasing restraint in an effort to preserve the resource for the collective. On the other hand, when a subordinate or differentiating group identity is salient, individual restraint is less likely to occur, and individual choices will reflect protection of self-interests, especially as the resource crisis grows more acute. Our primary prediction, then, involved an interaction between level of group identification and status of the resource pool. If the resource is being sustained at an adequate level, there will be no essential conflict between individual and group interests, so level of group identification should have little or no effect on individual choice behavior. As the resource becomes depleted, however, the individual users should alter their choices in the direction of either greater self-interest or greater collective interest, and it is at this point that the effects of group identity should be most evident.

The general paradigm followed in each experiment is illustrated in Figure 7.1. In each experiment, instructions are varied to manipulate the relative salience of one or the other of two existing social boundaries in a small heterogeneous group. Each subject belongs to both a subordinate group and a superordinate group, with shared access to a common resource pool. The manipulations were intended to either emphasize or de-emphasize the differentiation of the total group into two subordinate subgroups. It was assumed that individual social identification conforms to category salience, so that we could investigate the effects of

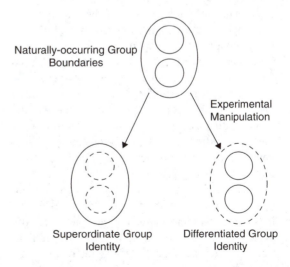

Naturally-occurring Group Boundaries

Experimental Manipulation

Superordinate Group Identity

Differentiated Group Identity

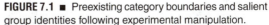

FIGURE 7.1 ■ Preexisting category boundaries and salient group identities following experimental manipulation.

identification with the superordinate social unit on behavior in a commons-dilemma setting.

Overview of Method

The three experiments conducted shared a number of procedures. For convenience, these common features will be described first, before the details of the individual experiments are discussed.

Task Instructions

Each experiment involved a six-person group, composed of three "real" subjects and three "bogus" group members who were presumably participating in the experiment from a remote location. On arrival at the laboratory, the three actual subjects were told that they would be participating in a study of how small groups use limited shared resources and that the study was being conducted simultaneously in two locations linked by an interactive computer system. The two locations provided the basis for a natural differentiation into two subgroups, the nature of which was varied from experiment to experiment.

Several steps were taken to make the interaction with a remote facility as convincing as possible. At the beginning of the experimental session, the experimenter demonstrated how the linkup would occur, using a master control terminal. Instructions were conspicuously displayed near the terminal, specifying how to send messages to the remote facility as well as computer operations necessary for the six-terminal linkage. As he demonstrated the system, the experimenter sent a message to the other facility, asking them to indicate their operating status. After a brief delay, a response message appeared on the control terminal screen indicating that the remote system was up, that the other three subjects were present, and that they were ready for linkup at their own individual terminals. Subjects were generally intrigued with the system and, with one exception, gave no indication that they suspected that the interaction was not real.

After being given these orienting instructions, each subject was seated in an individual booth, separated by partitions, in front of a computer terminal connected to a PDP 11/34 central processor. From that point on, all instructions and information were delivered via the terminal. Subjects were identified by color codes, with color names associated with the location of terminals in the two facilities.

The task that subjects were given was patterned after the replenishable-resource task developed by Messick et al. (1983). The first part of the instructions explained the nature of the commons dilemma, stressing the interdependence of the group members and the fact that the resource pool in the experiment was replenishable. Subjects were told that they had two goals: (a) to accumulate as many points as possible during the course of the experiment and (b) to make the resource last as long as possible, in order to maximize the length of time over which points could be collected. Using a recent regional water shortage as an example, subjects were made aware of the parallels between the experimental task and real-world settings (i.e., that use of the resource entails choosing between "taking all that one can or wants at the moment—at the risk of using up the resource—or taking a little on many occasions, with the possibility of getting more in the end because the pool is able to replenish itself").

Following this general introduction, subjects were given more specific instructions about the experimental task. Subjects were told that they would share, as a group, a resource pool initially containing 300 points. On each trial, subjects could collect or "harvest" 0–10 points. Subjects were told that after all group members had selected the number of points to withdraw for that trial, the computer would subtract this total from the existing pool size, multiply the remaining amount by a variable replenishment rate of about 1.1, and then present subjects with the new pool size, subject to the constraint that the maximum pool size was 300. Subjects were told that they could continue to take points from the pool for as long as the resource was sustained.

Subjects were given several practice trials to ensure their familiarity with the task requirements. Before beginning the actual experiment, subjects responded to a brief series of questions designed to assess their understanding of the task.

At the start of each trial, subjects were asked how many points they wished to withdraw from the pool. The computer terminals were synchronized so that each group member had to make a choice before the computer would display the feedback for the next trial. After each group member had selected a number of points to withdraw for that trial, the computer paused for a few seconds, as if to calculate the new pool size, and then displayed the feedback for the next trial.

Feedback Procedures

Subjects were led to believe that they were interacting with the five other persons in their group in determining the outcome of each trial in the resource task. In actuality, however, each subject received bogus feedback about the behavior of other group members, and only the feedback about their own choices was veridical. The variable-replenishment-rate aspect of the task prevented subjects from discovering that their own choices were not actually influencing the pool size directly. (Replenished pool size was calculated by assuming that subjects took an average of five points per trial.)

The feedback that subjects were given specified the number of points taken from the pool on each trial by each of the five other group members, identified by color. Although the information about amount taken by any one group member varied from trial to trial, the feedback was prearranged such that, in addition to feedback about his or her own behavior, each subject received information that two of the other group members (one from each subgroup) had taken a relatively large amount from the resource pool, two (one from each subgroup) had taken relatively small amounts, and one had taken a moderate amount.

Our primary interest was in conditions in which information about the total taken from the pool on each trial exceeded the replenishment rate, so that the pool size was steadily depleted across trials. To sustain the pool, each group member would have to take about five points or fewer per trial. Under depletion-feedback conditions, subjects received information that the total take of the other group members on each trial averaged between 6 and 8 points per person. Consequently, over the course of 12 trials, the pool level dropped steadily from 300 to 26 points. All three experiments included this depletion-feedback condition. In addition, in two of the experiments this was compared with a condition in which feedback about total take was such that the pool size was sustained at a relatively steady level across trials. In this condition, information about the pattern of behaviors of the other group members was the same as it was in the depletion condition, but the average amount taken was 5 points or fewer per person per trial.

Dependent Measures

The primary dependent measure in all three experiments was the number of points subjects chose to take (or harvest) from the common resource pool across trials. In addition to this behavioral measure, subjects were asked to respond to a number of questions regarding their perceptions of the experiment and the behavior of group members at the end of the series of trials. These questions included estimates of the total amount taken from the resource pool across all trials by themselves and by each of the other group members, as well as ratings of their own and other group members' selfishness, cooperativeness, and trustworthiness. These measures were included to determine the veridicality of subjects' memory for the behavior of the other group members and to determine whether their memory and evaluation of others were affected by level of group identification.

Experiment 1

In the first experiment subjects were told that the study was being conducted jointly by the University of Santa Barbara (UCSB) and the "Santa Barbara Consortium on Environmental Research (SBCER)" and that the remote facility was located downtown at SBCER headquarters. The three participants at the downtown facility were identified as elderly residents of the Santa Barbara community. Category salience was manipulated during the task instructions delivered via computer terminal. In the superordinate-group-identity condition, subjects were told that the researchers were interested in "how the behavior of residents of a small community like Santa Barbara would compare to residents of other areas." This instruction was intended to make salient a community identity shared by all six participants. Subjects in the differentiated subordinate-group-identity condition, on the other hand, were told that the researchers were interested in "how the behavior of young people compares to the behavior of elderly persons," an instruction intended to make salient the differentiation of participants into age-based subgroups.

Method

Subjects

Subjects were 22 male and 36 female undergraduate students from UCSB, who participated either to fulfill a course requirement or for base pay of $2.50. Three actual subjects were recruited for each experimental session. Within a session, subjects were randomly assigned to either the superordinate or subordinate group identity condition.

Procedure

After subjects had been introduced to the computer facility and seated in separate booths, the experiment was completely computer controlled. To reinforce the instructional manipulations, subjects were asked to start by typing in their color name, age, and the location of their terminal (UCSB or SBCER). Summary feedback was then displayed so that subjects were reminded of the age distribution of the six-person group and made aware of the color names associated with the UCSB and SBCER subgroups.

During the task instructions, subjects were informed that each point they took from the resource pool would be worth 5¢, which they would receive in addition to subject credit or the base pay for which they had been recruited to participate.

Once the trials began, subjects in both conditions received feedback indicating that the total harvest of the group members on each trial was depleting the resource pool steadily and rapidly, reducing it from

300 points to 26 points across 12 trials. Feedback about individual group members' behavior was constructed so that the average take of the other five participants was 7 points per trial; the total points accumulated across 12 trials ranged from 94 for the two high users to 74 for the two low users. At the end of the 12th trial, the experimenter announced that the pool size had dropped to a level too low to continue, so the first part of the experiment was over. At this point, subjects were asked to estimate the total number of points they and the other group members had accumulated during the 12 trials and to make ratings of themselves and the other group members on 7-point scales of selfishness, cooperativeness, and trustworthiness.

Upon completion of this second part of the experiment, subjects were debriefed by the experimenter, who explained that the feedback provided about other group members' choices had been predetermined. Subjects were paid an additional $3 for their participation, which corresponded to the amount they would have earned if they had taken five points per trial, the optimal amount required to sustain the resource pool.

Results

Resource use

Because subjects' decisions about how much of the resource pool to take on each trial were actually made independently of each other, the individual subject was treated as the unit of analysis for purposes of statistical analyses. Harvest choices for each subject were summed across adjacent trials, to form six trial blocks. A $2 \times 2 \times 6$ (Group Identity $\times$ Subject Sex $\times$ Trial Blocks) analysis of variance (ANOVA) with repeated measures was performed on the choice data. The main effect for group identity, $F(1, 54) = 6.48, p < .02$, and the Group Identity $\times$ Subject Sex interaction, $F(1, 54) = 9.88, p < .003$, were both significant. As is evident in Figure 7.2, the choices of female subjects remained fairly constant across trials, regardless of group-identity condition (mean take $= 6.7$ points per trial). Male subjects' choices, on the other hand, differed as a function of the group-identity condition: males in the

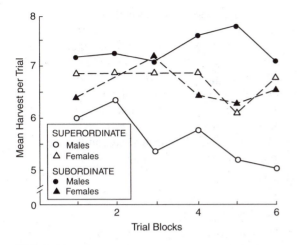

FIGURE 7.2 ■ Resource use across trial blocks as a function of group identity and sex: Experiment 1.

superordinate condition took fewer points per trial overall ($M = 5.6$) than did males in the subordinate condition ($M = 7.3$). A separate 2×6 (Group Identity × Trials) ANOVA with repeated measures, using choice data for the male subjects only, revealed that the Group Identity × Trials interaction was significant, $F(5, 100) = 2.50$, $p < .03$. Consistent with the general hypothesis, when subgroup identity was made salient, male subjects increased their take across trials as the resource pool approached depletion, whereas males for whom a superordinate identity was salient decreased their take in response to resource depletion.

Perceptions of own behavior

A 2×2 (Group Identity × Sex of Subject) ANOVA of subjects' estimates of their own total take from the resource pool revealed a marginal group-identity effect, $F(1, 46) = 2.51$, $p < .12$. A comparison of actual takes ($M = 81.7$) and estimated takes ($M = 65.1$) indicated that subjects in both experimental conditions tended to underestimate their own pool use somewhat but that variations in estimates were fairly veridical. On the average, subjects in the superordinate condition estimated (correctly) that they had taken fewer total points ($M = 59.6$) than did subjects in the subordinate condition

($M = 69.6$). Subjects in the former condition also rated themselves as less selfish than did those in the latter condition, $F(1, 54) = 7.90$, $p < .007$. Significant group-identity effects were not found on the two other self-rating measures, however.

Perceptions of other group members' behavior

Subjects' estimates of the total amount of points taken by the other group members were also analyzed. These analyses were limited to the perceptions of the two group members who had been consistently portrayed as taking high amounts per trial (high users) and the two other group members who had taken relatively few points per trial (low users). Results of a $2 \times 2 \times 2$ (Group Identity × Sex of Subject × Use Feedback) ANOVA with repeated measures revealed a significant main effect of the feedback provided about others' choices, $F(1, 43) = 42.79$, $p < .0001$. On the average, subjects correctly estimated that high users had taken more points ($M = 83.1$) than low users had ($M = 71.3$). High users were also rated as significantly more selfish than low users, $F(1, 54) = 128.63$, $p < .0001$. Overall, subjects' estimates of others' use of points were fairly veridical, particularly considering the degree of variability in the trial-by-trial feedback they had been given. There was no evidence that accuracy of subjects' memory or evaluation of others' behavior was affected by the level of group identity.

Discussion

In general, the behavior of male subjects in the resource task was affected by different levels of group identification, as had been predicted. Across trials, as the depletion of the resource pool became apparent, males in the two conditions diverged in their decisions as to how much to take from the pool on each trial. Those for whom superordinate group boundaries had been made salient reduced their personal take, as if to help sustain the resource. Those for whom differentiated sub-group identity was salient, on the other hand, increased their take from the pool across trials until it was almost entirely depleted.

Female subjects in the present experiment showed no such responsiveness to group-identity conditions. On the average, females took somewhat more than the optimal five points per trial and did not vary significantly in that behavior as a function of group identity or pool depletion. One possible explanation for this sex difference is that male subjects were more responsive to the group-level competition implicit in the instructional manipulation. In the superordinate condition, males may have thought of their six-person group as a "team" in competition with other such groups and were thus more concerned with maximizing total points for the group as a whole rather than for themselves individually. In the subordinate condition, on the other hand, the implicit competition was between subgroups within the experiment, which led to a concern for getting as much of the resource as possible for their own group, in comparison with the out-group, before the pool was depleted. Females may have been less responsive to this situational competitiveness and responded more in terms of personal norms or self-interest. An alternative possibility is that the sex interaction reflects a differential response by subjects to the basis of subgroup differentiation itself (i.e., young vs. elderly persons), and males were more responsive to this categorization variable than were females.

An interesting finding was that the differences in behavior that were obtained across group-identity conditions were not associated with any consistent differences in perceptions or evaluations of fellow group members. In general, memory of own and others' behavior corresponded closely to the actual behavior (or behavior feedback provided) and did not vary as a function of group condition. Thus, whatever effects on choice behavior were obtained resulted directly from the salience of group boundaries and were not apparently mediated by differential perceptions of group members.

Experiment 2

Because of the possibility that the sex interaction obtained in the first experiment was related to the particular subgroup composition employed, and not the group-identity manipulation per se, a second experiment was conducted that essentially replicated the features of the first experiment but varied the basis for intragroup differentiation. In this experiment, the three real subjects in each session, who were all students enrolled in an introductory psychology course, were told that the other three group members were economics majors who were participating from a computer facility located in another building on campus.

Method

Subjects

The subjects were 29 male and 19 female students, who participated in partial fulfillment of course requirements. Data from one subject were excluded from the data analysis when it was learned during debriefing that he was a computer science major, was intimately familiar with the operation of the PDP system, and suspected that false feedback had been used.

Procedure

After the interactive nature of the computer system had been explained to the three subjects in each session, the experimental manipulation of group identity was introduced. Subjects in the superordinate-group-identity condition were told that the experiment was concerned with how the resource utilization behavior of university students compared with that of other groups. Subjects in the differentiated subordinate-group-identity condition were told that the research was concerned with how the behavior of students in psychology classes would compare with that of students in economics courses.

After being given these instructions, subjects were seated in individual booths, and all further instructions were provided via computer terminal. Following several practice trials and pretrial questions, subjects were given 24 trials in which to take points from the resource pool. As in the previous experiment, subjects were informed that each point would be worth 5¢. After the first 12 trials (Phase 1), the experiment was interrupted, and subjects responded to a series of questions regarding their perceptions and evaluations of their own and other group members' behavior. The experiment was then resumed for another 12 trials (Phase 2), followed by a post trial questionnaire. At the close of the session, subjects were debriefed and paid $3 for their participation.

Feedback that subjects received about the use of the resource pool across the 24 trials was varied. In the depletion condition, subjects received feedback during the first 12 trials (Phase 1) indicating that the pool was being sustained at a high level (close to 290 points) and was thus in no danger of depletion. In Phase 2 trials (13–24), subjects received feedback that the resource pool was being steadily depleted (overused), dropping from 290 points to 26 points by the end of the last trial.

In the sustained-use condition, subjects received feedback that the group as a whole was taking moderate amounts from the resource pool during Phase 1, so that the pool dropped slowly from 300 to 155 points. During Phase 2, group use leveled off, and the pool was maintained steadily at around 160 points for the remainder of the trials.

Based upon the general hypothesis, and the results of Experiment 1, it was predicted that individual restraint would be evident under conditions in which resource depletion occurred (Phase 2 of

the depletion condition) and that the degree of restraint manifested would vary over time, depending on the level of group identity made salient. No such divergence in restraint was expected when the resource was being sustained at a steady level (Phase 2 of the sustained-use condition).

Results

Resource use

A preliminary ANOVA of subjects' harvest from the resource pool across trials revealed no main effect or interactions involving subject sex, so data were collapsed across sex for all further analyses. For purposes of overall analysis, a $2 \times 2 \times 12$ (Group Identity $\times$ Feedback $\times$ Trial Blocks) ANOVA with repeated measures was performed. There were no main effects for group identity or feedback. There was, however, a main effect for trials, $F(11, 273) = 4.53$, $p < .001$, and a Trials $\times$ Feedback interaction, $F(11, 473) = 2.74$, $p < .002$. The three-way interaction, however, was not significant, $F(11, 473) = 1.32$, $p > .10$, when taken across all 24 trials. These results are depicted in Figure 7.3.

Because the hypothesis predicted that differences in individual restraint as a function of group identity would be evident only under resource depletion

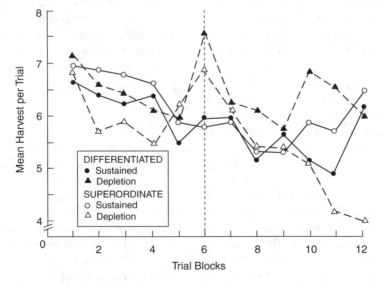

DIFFERENTIATED
● Sustained
▲ Depletion
SUPERORDINATE
○ Sustained
△ Depletion

FIGURE 7.3 ■ Resource use across trial blocks as a function of group identity and feedback condition: Experiment 2.

conditions, a separate $2 \times 2 \times 6$ (Group Identity $\times$ Feedback $\times$ Trial Blocks) ANOVA with repeated measures was performed using the harvest data from the Phase 2 trials only. The three-way interaction was significant, $F(5, 215) = 2.36, p < .05$. The nature of this interaction is consistent with the hypothesis (see Figure 7.3). In the sustained-use condition, there was virtually no difference between the average take per trial of subjects in the superordinate condition ($M = 5.8$) and that of subjects in the differentiated condition ($M = 5.5$). Furthermore, subjects in both conditions increased their take in the final trials, as it became evident to them that the resource pool was being sustained and that they could, consequently, take more without immediately endangering the resource.

In the depletion condition, the picture that emerges is quite different. Although subjects in both conditions initially (Trial Block 7) had nearly identical takes (trial means of 6.1 and 6.4 for the superordinate and differentiated groups, respectively), the size of their takes for the remaining trials clearly diverged, so that, by the final trial block, subjects in the superordinate condition were taking an average of about 4.0 points per trial, whereas those in the subordinate condition were taking 6.0.

Perceptions of own and others' behavior

Subjects' estimates of their own total take at the end of each trial phase did not vary significantly as a function of group identity or feedback condition, although subjects in the superordinate–depletion condition did drop their actual take in the last trials of Phase 2. The variance of own-take estimates in Phase 2 was extremely high (estimates ranged from 12 to 250 total points), which suggests that some subjects misunderstood instructions for this measure and made estimates of total take across all 24 trials.

Perceived mean total take of the two high users and two low users across both phases were analyzed using a $2 \times 2 \times 2$ (Group Identity $\times$ Feedback $\times$ Use) ANOVA with repeated measures. A highly significant main effect for use was obtained, $F(1, 43) = 73.95, p < .001$, which demonstrates that subjects again accurately perceived that the high users in their group had accumulated more

points than the low users had, regardless of group-identity condition. There was also a Use $\times$ Feedback interaction, $F(1, 43) = 7.17, p < .01$, such that the high users were perceived as taking more in the depletion condition than they did in the sustained-use condition, whereas the low users were perceived as taking less in the depletion condition than they did in the sustained-use condition. Both sets of estimates corresponded in general to the actual feedback provided.

Ratings of other group members' selfishness, cooperativeness, and trustworthiness were also analyzed using $2 \times 2 \times 2$ ANOVAs. With respect to the selfishness ratings, there was a feedback main effect, $F(1, 43) = 7.90, p < .001$; a use main effect, $F(1, 43) = 90.03, p < .001$; and a Use $\times$ Feedback interaction, $F(1, 43) = 13.45, p < .001$. Others were perceived to be more selfish in the depletion condition than they were in the sustained-use condition, and the high users were perceived as much more selfish than the low users were in depletion conditions (Ms of 6.2 and 3.0, respectively), whereas the differences in their ratings were less extreme under sustained-use conditions (Ms of 4.7 and 3.3, respectively). The main effects for use and the Use $\times$ Feedback interaction with respect to the trustworthiness ratings were similar. Analysis of the cooperation ratings revealed a significant feedback effect: others in the sustained-use condition were perceived as more cooperative than those in the depletion condition. Overall, these evaluations corresponded closely to the feedback provided about others' behavior and were not affected by level of group identity.

Discussion

In the second series of 12 trials, subjects in the superordinate-group-identity condition responded to pool depletion by restraining their personal take of the common resource, as was predicted by the general hypothesis. In fact, subjects in this condition dropped their own mean take to as low as four points per trial, although the feedback they were receiving indicated that the average take for the group as a whole was increasing. When subgroup identity was made salient, however, subjects responded to depletion competitively, by increasing their average take across trials, and this was equally true for males and females. By contrast, no such difference between groups was evident when pool level was sustained across trials. The absence of a sex interaction suggests that the differential response of males and females noted in Experiment 1 was not a generalized difference between males and females in their responsiveness to different levels of group identification.

Experiment 3

In Experiments 1 and 2, social-group identity was manipulated in terms of category distinctions, using naturally existing categories (i.e., age and student status). In Experiment 3, level of group identification was manipulated by varying "common fate" (Campbell, 1958) so that it corresponded to either the six-person or three-person unit. In this experiment, the three real subjects in each session were told that the remaining three subjects were other undergraduate students participating from a facility located nearby in the campus computer center. Thus, no preexisting categorical distinctions differentiated participants in the two subgroups.

Method
Subjects

The subjects were 40 male and 26 female students from an introductory psychology class, who participated for course credit.

Procedure

After being given a preliminary introduction to the nature of the experiment, subjects were told that, in addition to course credit for their participation, they would be paid for each point they collected during the experiment. Determining the amount they would be paid provided the opportunity for introducing the common fate manipulation. It was explained to subjects that the monetary value of the points in different experimental sessions would be either 1¢ or 5¢, depending on the results of a lottery. In the superordinate-group-identity condition,

the fate of all six participants in the session was determined by a single lottery. The experimenter selected one of the subjects to draw a slip of paper from a large bowl containing 100 slips, half of which subjects thought were marked "1" and half "5" (in actuality, all slips were marked "5"). After the subject had drawn the slip, the experimenter announced the result and then ostensibly contacted the remote facility by telephone to inform the three subjects there what the outcome was.

In the differentiated subordinate-group-identity condition, the fate of the three students in the psychology department facility was made independent of the fate of the three in the remote facility through the use of two separate lotteries. The experimenter had one of the three subjects draw a slip from the bowl and announced the result (always 5¢), stressing that this determined the value of points for the three of them. It was then explained that a similar lottery was being held by an experimenter at the computer center facility to determine whether the points would be worth 1¢ or 5¢ for the three participants there. The experimenter then called the remote facility and announced that the results of the second lottery had also been 5¢ per point. Thus, the outcome from the lotteries was the same as that for the common fate condition.

After subjects were seated in their separate booths, all procedures, instructions, and feedback conditions (across two 12-trial periods) were the same as those used in Experiment 2. At the end of the experiment, subjects were debriefed and paid $3.

Results
Resource use

As was the case in Experiment 2, preliminary ANOVAS revealed no main effects or interactions involving subject sex, so sex was dropped as a variable for further analyses. A $2 \times 2 \times 12$ (Group Identity $\times$ Feedback $\times$ Trial Blocks) ANOVA with repeated measures replicated the trials main effect, $F(11, 550) = 6.65$, $p < .001$, and the Trials $\times$ Feedback interaction, $F(11, 550) = 3.26$, $p < .002$, obtained in Experiment 2. The group

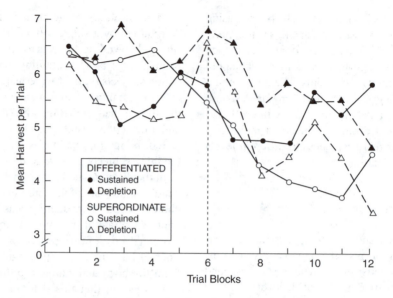

FIGURE 7.4 ■ Resource use across trial blocks as a function of group identity and feedback condition: Experiment 3.

identity main effect was not significant, $F(1, 50) = 1.42$, $p > .10$, but the three-way interaction between group identity, feedback, and trial blocks was significant, $F(11, 550) = 1.97, p < .03$. These results are depicted in Figure 7.4.

As in Experiment 2, because restraint was expected to be most evident under the depletion conditions of Phase 2, a separate $2 \times 2 \times 6$ (Group Identity $\times$ Feedback $\times$ Trial Blocks) ANOVA was performed using the harvest data from Phase 2 only. The three-way interaction was again significant, $F(5, 285) = 2.36$, $p < .05$, and replicated that obtained in Experiment 2, although the divergence is less marked in Experiment 3 because subjects in both group conditions reduced their harvests somewhat (see Figure 7.4).

Perceptions of own and others' behavior

A 2×2 ANOVA of subjects' estimates of their own total take across the 24 trials revealed a Group Identity $\times$ Feedback interaction, $F(1, 62) = 4.49$, $p < .04$. Comparison of these estimates with subjects' actual behavior shows that they were generally veridical, although subjects in the subordinate condition did tend to underestimate their total take

under sustained-use conditions. Consistent with their behavior, subjects in the superordinate condition rated themselves as less selfish than subjects in the subordinate condition, $F(1, 60) = 4.20, p < .05$.

Estimates of the total take of the other group members revealed a use main effect and a significant Use $\times$ Feedback interaction that was similar to that obtained in Experiment 2 and showed that estimates conformed to feedback provided about others' behavior. Ratings of others' selfishness revealed a comparable use main effect and a Use $\times$ Feedback interaction. In general, the high users in the group were perceived as being significantly more selfish than the low users, and the extremity of the ratings differed depending on whether the pool had been depleted or sustained. Again, this finding is consistent with that obtained in Experiment 2. Ratings of others' trustworthiness and cooperativeness were in line with these ratings as well. With respect to ratings of others' trustworthiness, however, there was also a main effect for group identity, $F(1, 62) = 5.30, p < .03$. Subjects in the superordinate condition rated others in their group as being relatively more trustworthy ($M = 4.18$) than did subjects in the differentiated condition ($M = 3.7$).

Discussion

The results of Experiment 3 strengthen the generalizability of group-identity effects in a commons-dilemma situation. The induction of group identity through manipulation of common fate differs in a number of ways from the instructional manipulations used in Experiments 1 and 2. First, the common fate manipulation avoids any preexisting group stereotypes that may have influenced subjects' expectations about their fellow group members in Experiments 1 and 2. It also contains no implicit intergroup competition, because no mention of group comparisons are made in the common fate instructions. This latter feature may account for the fact that subjects in the differentiated subordinate-group-identity condition in Experiment 3 showed less tendency to increase their personal take from the resource pool as the pool became depleted than did subjects in this condition in Experiments 1 and 2. In Experiment 3, subjects in all conditions showed some tendency to reduce their own take in response to Phase 2 depletion, although subjects in the superordinate condition showed significantly more personal restraint over the 12 trials.

General Discussion

The results of all three experiments provide convergent validity for the hypothesis that level of group identity affects individual decision making in response to depletion of a shared resource. In general, individuals in heterogeneous groups were found to be more likely to exercise personal restraint in their use of an endangered common resource when a superordinate group identity, corresponding to access to the resource, was made salient. Across three experiments, in no case did the mean take per trial block of individuals in differentiated subordinate-group-identity conditions reach the optimal level required to sustain the resource pool. When a superordinate group boundary was salient, however, mean individual takes reached or fell below this optimal level in all three experiments under depletion conditions.

Differences between superordinate and subordinate conditions were consistently most evident when the common resource pool was being depleted (i.e., when the group as a whole had been taking too much on each trial for the pool to replenish itself). It is precisely under such conditions that the individual decision maker is faced with the greatest conflict between self-interest and collective welfare. On the one hand, the history of overuse of the resource creates normative pressures that promote high use. On the other hand, it is overuse by the rest of the group that makes deviance in the direction of personal restraint most necessary for the collective good. Our experiments suggest that awareness of common group identity can help individuals resolve this conflict in favor of group welfare.

Although these experiments demonstrate an effect of group identity on resource use under a number of conditions, they provide relatively little insight into the mechanisms that mediate this effect. In two of the experiments, individuals in the superordinate condition rated themselves as less selfish than did individuals in the subordinate condition. Thus, individuals in the superordinate-group-identity conditions seem to have been consciously aware of their decision to exercise personal restraint and to feel that this was the right thing to do even though they were also aware that the other group members were not necessarily doing the same. The results of all of these studies suggest that individuals with a sense of collective identity may be willing to act to compensate for the selfish behavior of others in their groups. In this respect, it is important to note that in these groups, only some of the other participants were conspicuously selfish. Thus, it is possible that individuals with a superordinate identity are willing to compensate for the selfish and destructive acts of others as long as they are not alone in so doing.

With the exception of the trustworthiness ratings in Experiment 3, perceptions and evaluations of other group members were not apparently influenced by the boundary manipulations. Thus, it does not appear as if the group-identity effects obtained in these experiments can be explained in terms of a simple positive group bias, as might be suggested by an in-group favoritism hypothesis. On the other hand, it is possible that one consequence of unit formation is a heightened sense of responsibility toward the social unit and concern with collective outcomes themselves, quite apart from strong concomitant evaluative and attributional effects.

Certainly, in these experiments, the consistent finding that estimates and evaluations of others' behavior were veridical suggests that the use feedback provided was highly salient to individuals as a basis for judging their fellow participants. In nearly every instance, subjects' estimates of others' total take and their subsequent evaluations of others' selfishness, cooperativeness, and trustworthiness conformed to feedback about actual behavior, regardless of group-identity condition. Given the nature of the interaction in this task, such a finding is not altogether surprising. The group-identity manipulations were introduced early in the beginning of each session and consisted entirely of a few sentences describing the experimenter's interest in studying how a particular social group would behave in a decision-making task. For the remainder of the experimental session, subjects were given detailed information about the state of the resource and the individual decisions of each of the group members. Thus, feedback about the behavior may have represented for subjects an obvious criterion to use in making their posttrials evaluations.

That behavioral effects for the group-identity manipulation were consistently obtained in these experiments, even when the basis for superordinate group identification was so seemingly trivial, suggests that such effects may translate into cooperation in settings in which the basis of group identity is of greater intrinsic significance to the individuals. In real-world resource dilemmas, common access to a valued resource is sometimes correlated with group boundaries, which do have more psychological meaning to individuals (e.g., citizens in a small town confronting a shortage of coal during a hard winter). In such cases, a preexisting sense of community may be exploited during times when it is crucial that individuals forgo their own immediate gain in the collective interest. The results of these experiments thus provide some basis for optimism about the potential for personal restraint in resource use even in the absence of coercive constraints over other group members.

The results also raise some interesting questions about the adaptiveness of different levels of group identity in human society. Throughout history, the unit of identification has gradually expanded beyond the small, proximal group to encompass larger and larger social units in response to changing levels of interdependency. As interdependence reaches global levels, it will be of interest to determine whether there are inherent limits on individuals' ability to adopt correspondingly high levels of social identification.

REFERENCES

Brewer, M. B. (1979). In-group bias in the minimal intergroup situation: A cognitive-motivational analysis. *Psychological Bulletin, 86*, 307–324.

Brewer, M. B., & Campbell, D. T. (1976). *Ethnocentrism and intergroup attitudes: East African evidence*. New York: Halstead Press.

Campbell, D. T. (1958). Common fate, similarity, and other indices of the status of aggregates of persons as social entities. *Behavioral Science, 3*, 14–25.

Edney, J. J. (1980). The commons problem: Alternative perspectives. *American Psychologist, 35*, 131–150.

Hardin, G. J. (1968). The tragedy of the commons. *Science, 162*, 1243–1248.

Kelley, H. H., & Grzelak, J. (1972). Conflict between individualized and common interest in an n-person relationship. *Journal of Personality and Social Psychology, 21*, 190–197.

Komorita, S. S., & Lapworth, C. W. (1982). Cooperative choice among individuals versus groups in an N-person dilemma situation. *Journal of Personality and Social Psychology, 42*, 487–496.

Messick, D. M., & Brewer, M. B. (1983). Solving social dilemmas: A review. In L. Wheeler & P. Shaver (Eds.), *Review of personality and social psychology* (Vol. 4, pp. 11–44). Beverly Hills, CA: Sage.

Messick, D. M., Wilke, H., Brewer, M. B., Kramer, R. M., Zemke, P., & Lui, L. (1983). Individual adaptations and structural change as solutions to social dilemmas. *Journal of Personality and Social Psychology, 44*, 294–309.

Zander, A., & Armstrong, W. (1972). Working for group pride in a slipper factory. *Journal of Applied Social Psychology, 2*, 293–307.

Received August 8, 1983
Revision received September 6, 1983 ■

Status, Ideology, and Integrative Complexity on the U.S. Supreme Court: Rethinking the Politics of Political Decision Making

Deborah H. Gruenfeld

Prior studies of integrative complexity indicate that political conservatives tend to interpret policy issues in less complex ways than do liberals and moderates. However, ideological preference in that work was systematically confounded with decision makers' status in the groups to which they belonged. The study reported here varied both factors independently in a content analysis of Supreme Court opinions. In contrast to previous conclusions, results supported a *status-contingency* model, which predicts higher levels of complexity among members of majority factions than among members of either minority factions or unanimous groups independently of the ideological content of their views.

The outcomes of political decision making have been the subject of substantial psychological inquiry. Much of this inquiry has been focused on the characteristics of individual decision makers, including their personality structures (Gibson, 1981; M. G. Hermann, 1977; Winter, 1973), expertise (Judd & Krosnick, 1989), attitudes (Converse, 1964; Sears & McConahay, 1970; Segal & Spaeth,

This research was supported in part by a grant from the National Science Foundation (# DIR-9113599) to the Mershon Center Research Training Group on the Role of Cognition in Collective Political Decision Making at Ohio State University. The group provided considerable intellectual support as well.

This article is based on my doctoral dissertation. I am grateful for the sage advice of my thesis committee at the University of Illinois in Champaign-Urbana: Robert S. Wyer, Jr. (Chair), Joseph McGrath, Peter Carnevale, Ulf Bockenholt, Janet Sniezek, and Lawrence Baum at The Ohio State University. I also thank Stephen Campbell, Larry Gail, Micki Hallam, Bethany Hengsbach, Perikles F. Konstantinides, and Joan Alster for assistance with coding data management, and Max Bazerman, Margaret Neale, and two anonymous reviewers for helpful comments on a draft of this article.

Correspondence concerning this article should be addressed to Deborah H. Gruenfeld, J. L. Kellogg Graduate School of Management, Northwestern University, 2001 Sheridan Road, Evanston, Illinois 60208.

1993), ideological orientation (Adorno, Frenkel-Brunswick, Levinson, & Sanford, 1950; Tetlock, 1983), and cognitive style (Rokeach, 1956; Sidanius, 1978; Tetlock, 1991b). These factors have been used to understand both the choice and justification of public policy outcomes.

One important variable in this domain has been conceptual or integrative complexity (Schroder, Driver, & Streufert, 1967; Streufert & Streufert, 1978; Suedfeld, 1983, 1992; for reviews see Tetlock, 1991a, 1991b). Complexity measures are generally used to assess the conceptual organization of decision-relevant information and are derived from individuals' verbal rationales for their preferences. Specifically, integrative complexity is characterized by two components of cognitive style: *differentiation*, which refers to recognition of multiple perspectives on, or dimensions of, an issue; and *integration*, which refers to recognition of conceptual relations among differentiated dimensions. Individuals at the low end of the complexity continuum tend to rely on rigid, evaluative rules in interpreting events and to make decisions on the basis of only a few salient items of information. Individuals at the high end tend to interpret events in multidimensional terms and to base their decisions on evidence from multiple perspectives. Research on political decision making has linked differences in integrative complexity to ideological orientation (Stone, 1980; Tetlock, 1983, 1984, 1986; Wilson, 1973), consistency of voting behavior (Tetlock, Bernzweig, & Gallant, 1985), and decision quality (for reviews, see Suedfeld, 1992; Tetlock, 1992), among other factors at the individual level of analysis.

However, many political decisions are made in groups. Although the effects of group process on policy outcomes are widely noted (Allison, 1971; Gruenfeld, McGrath, Beasley, & Kaarbo, 1993; Hermann, 1993; Janis, 1982; Staub, 1991), they have not been the subject of nearly as much systematic investigation. The subjects in many of the integrative complexity studies noted above were members of governmental decision-making bodies (cf. Tetlock, 1979, 1983, 1984; Tetlock, Hannum, & Micheletti, 1984; Tetlock et al., 1985), but the effects of group membership on policy makers'

behaviors were rarely a theoretical focus (but see Tetlock, 1979; Tetlock et al., 1984). Instead, previous work has emphasized how ideological preferences are related to styles of reasoning. As a result, the impact of group interaction on integrative complexity, and on the individual factors to which it has been linked, is not well understood.

In fact, research on social influence provides copious evidence that group dynamics affect the ways in which decisions are both privately made (Kruglanski & Mackie, 1990) and publicly expressed (Davis, 1973; Levine & Russo, 1987). A major determinant of such effects is the group member's status. For example, targets of majority influence (i.e., members with minority status) tend to comply in public (Latané & Wolf, 1981; Tanford & Penrod, 1984) but do not necessarily change their private views (Moscovici & Lage, 1976). In contrast, targets of minority influence (i.e., members with majority status) do not usually conform in public but may be privately swayed toward the minority position (Moscovici, Lage, & Neffrechoux, 1969; Mugny, 1982).

In addition to such changes in preference, group members' styles of reasoning can also be affected by their status. For example, it is now well established that majority members think *divergently* in response to minority influence by considering multiple perspectives and generating new alternatives to the problems they face (Nemeth, 1992). In contrast, minority members respond to majority influence with *convergent* thinking, which involves a unidimensional focus on the validity of the majority position (Nemeth, 1986). As a result of these differences, groups with a vocal deviant perform better on problems requiring creativity than do unanimous groups, which lack the necessary stimulant to engage in divergent thought (Nemeth & Kwan, 1987).

To the extent that divergent thinking involves recognition of new perspectives on a problem, majority members of groups with dissenters might also be expected to exhibit greater integrative complexity than (a) minority members or (b) members of unanimous groups. In fact, this prediction is supported by the results of several of the integrative complexity studies referenced above (Tetlock,

1979, 1983, 1984; Tetlock et al., 1984; Tetlock et al., 1985), although it was rarely predicted. With one exception (Tetlock et al., 1984), status differences were not controlled or examined directly in previous research. However, they did covary systematically with the individual-level factors on which predictions about complexity differences were based. Specifically, in several independent studies, higher levels of integrative complexity were exhibited by policy makers with majority status than by those in the minority (Gruenfeld, 1992). Indirect evidence bearing on complexity levels in unanimous groups was obtained in a study of groupthink (Tetlock, 1979). Statements by participants in foreign policy decision groups characterized by groupthink (i.e., premature unanimity) were lower in integrative complexity than those of participants in non-groupthink decisions.

These results provide empirical grounds for a "status-contingency" model of integrative complexity in decision groups. However, a single, coherent theoretical explanation for this pattern has not been explicated or tested. Furthermore, prior work on styles of reasoning in majorities, minorities, and unanimous groups has been focused primarily on differences in cognitive processes. Yet the data in prior complexity research has been derived largely from the content of public statements, including political speeches and published government documents. It is possible therefore that the differences observed are rhetorical, rather than cognitive, in nature (Tetlock et al., 1984).

In addition, as noted above, prior studies of integrative complexity in political groups have been focused on the effects of ideological orientation (e.g., liberal vs. conservative). Although status factors were operant in these contexts, which included the U.S. Congress (Tetlock, 1983; Tetlock et al., 1984), U.S. Supreme Court (Tetlock et al., 1985), and British House of Commons (Tetlock, 1984), their effects were neither predicted nor controlled (but see Tetlock et al., 1984). Hence, the relations of political ideology, member status, and integrative complexity in political decision groups remain largely unexplored. The research reported here examines these factors, and their interactions, in the context of U.S. Supreme Court decision making.

Theoretical Considerations

Ideology-Contingency Model

A prior study of integrative complexity in Supreme Court decision making showed that opinions authored by politically liberal and moderate justices were characterized by greater integrative complexity than opinions authored by political conservatives (Tetlock et al., 1985). This result replicated a robust finding linking liberal and moderate political orientation with complex cognitive style (Tetlock, 1983, 1984; Tetlock et al., 1984).

Theoretically, the finding was attributed to the rigidity-of-the-right hypothesis, which asserts that conservatism involves a rigid, dichotomous, and value-laden style of interpretation that develops as a means for restoring order to a chaotic and threatening world (Adorno et al., 1950). Hence, conservative attitudes are associated with a simplistic cognitive style (Tetlock, 1983). It is also consistent with the value-pluralism hypothesis (Tetlock, 1986), which links integrative complexity in political contexts to preferences for individual freedom and social equality. This hypothesis predicts that democratic socialists (e.g., American liberals), who value both freedom and equality, will exhibit greater integrative complexity than (a) conservative capitalists (e.g., American conservatives), who value freedom over equality, (b) communists, who value equality over freedom, or (c) fascists, who value neither.

Both of these explanations attribute the complexity expressed by Supreme Court justices to their individual values and beliefs. However, an alternative interpretation involving the effects of group membership is also plausible. Liberal and conservative Supreme Court justices are members of ideological factions on the Supreme Court (Baum, 1989a, 1989b; Segal & Spaeth, 1993), which endow them with differing degrees of influence. Justices in the majority have greater control over group decision outcomes than do justices in the minority. According to the logic underlying the rigidity-of-the-right hypothesis, this may affect their styles of reasoning. For example, justices in the minority on a given decision may respond to their lack of potency with reductions in integrative complexity. Hence, the complexity of Supreme Court opinions might reflect justices' psychological reactions to membership in an ideological faction, and the status that entails, as well as reflecting the ideological content of their views per se.

As noted above, although both ideological and group-based factors were operant in previous research, they could not be empirically disentangled. In fact, ideological preference and member status were consistently confounded, such that liberal and moderate political views are held by members of the majority, and conservative or extreme political views are held by the minority (Gruenfeld, 1992). Studies of the U.S. Senate showed that although liberals were greater than conservatives in both the overall level of complexity (Tetlock, 1983) and the flexibility of cognitive style, both groups exhibited more complex decision-making styles during sessions of Congress in which they held the majority than during periods when the opposing group was dominant (Tetlock et al., 1984).

A study comparing the complexity levels of extreme socialists, moderate socialists, moderate conservatives, and extreme conservatives in the British House of Commons obtained a similar result: Socialists showed greater complexity than conservatives, but only among political moderates. The complexity expressed by extreme socialists did not differ from that of extreme conservatives, although both were significantly lower in complexity than were politically moderate members. Furthermore, in this study, integrative complexity increased as a function of the number of members of each parliamentary faction. Specifically, there were 12 extreme conservatives, 12 extreme socialists, 24 moderate conservatives, and 41 moderate socialists in the group at the time the analysis was done. Correspondingly, complexity increased linearly with faction size.

The results of the Supreme Court study mentioned earlier (Tetlock et al., 1985) are consistent with this pattern and are especially relevant to the study reported here. The opinions of liberal and moderate Supreme Court justices were higher in complexity than those of conservatives, but the authors of majority opinions also exhibited greater

complexity than the authors of minority opinions, regardless of the ideological content of the views espoused. In addition, only 6 of the justices in the time period analyzed could be characterized as conservative, as compared with 9 who were classified as liberals and 10 who were classified as moderates. Hence, although the data supported the ideology-contingency hypotheses they were designed to test, which predicted that liberals would exhibit greater complexity than conservatives, they supported a status-contingency alternative as well: Majority members showed greater complexity than did minority members.

During the period from which the data were drawn (1946–1978), the Supreme Court was generally dominated by liberals and moderates. It is interesting to note that this ideological balance in favor of liberals and moderates does not exist today. That is, since the mid 1980s, the Court has been dominated by ideological conservatives (Segal & Spaeth, 1993). According to the status-contingency perspective, an analysis of liberal, moderate, and conservative opinions written during the current, conservatively dominated era on the court should produce results that are incompatible with the rigidity-of-the-right and value-pluralism hypotheses. That is, opinions expressing conservative views, which are currently held by the majority on the Court, should be characterized by higher integrative complexity levels than those expressing liberal views, which have been held in recent times by a shrinking minority. Tetlock et al. (1985) anticipated this possibility, but it could not be evaluated in their study.

Status-Contingency Model

The effects of majority, minority, and unanimity status on integrative complexity can be explained by means of two theoretical paths. The first path, derived from research on divergent thinking (Nemeth, 1986), suggests that status differences in decision groups affect members' cognitive processes. From this view, expressions of integrative complexity in public statements might reflect the structure of private thoughts underlying them. However, such differences might also be explained according to more strategic psychological mechanisms. That is, policy makers might construct their public statements to serve specific influence objectives in ways that reflect their communication strategies (cf. Tetlock, 1981; Tetlock et al., 1984). To the extent that these strategies vary as a function of member status, public expressions of integrative complexity by majority, minority, and unanimous group members might not correspond to the complexity that characterizes their private cognitions. Each of these alternatives will be discussed in turn.

Cognitive processes. As noted earlier, majority members apparently respond to minority influence with increased cognitive flexibility in the form of divergent thinking (Nemeth, 1986). In this view, the process of explaining away the minority position often requires reconceptualizing the problem as a whole and leads the majority to identify dimensions of the issue that were not obvious beforehand. This occurs because majority members are stimulated by minority influence to reconsider their own position, but, believing that the minority alternative is incorrect, search for new alternatives (Nemeth & Wachtler, 1983). As a result, they may recognize aspects of the problem that were not detected previously because they lacked pertinence to the majority frame (Nemeth, 1986).

These cognitive processes lead to the implementation of multiple strategies and the detection of novel solutions, in problem-solving groups where minority influence occurs (Nemeth, 1985; Nemeth & Kwan, 1987). Such groups generally outperform unanimous groups, which lack the minority stimulant for divergent thinking, on problem-solving tasks (Nemeth, 1986; but see Nemeth, Mosier, & Chiles, 1991).

Theoretically, divergent thinking should lead majority members to experience an increase in integrative complexity. Specifically, the process of generating and considering alternative viewpoints, and recognizing multiple dimensions of a stimulus, corresponds to cognitive differentiation (Suedfeld, Tetlock, & Streufert, 1992). To the extent that divergent thinking involves specifying the relations among alternative perspectives, dimensions, or both,

it should also be associated with cognitive integration. This might be expected to occur when, for example, minority influence induces a validation process (Moscovici, 1980) through which majority members use an explicit rule or an overarching conceptual framework to explain the relations between the positions proposed and the issue itself.

In contrast, minority members respond to pressure from the majority by thinking convergently, which involves a unidimensional focus on the majority position (Nemeth & Wachtler, 1983). This occurs because minority members assume the majority is correct and are eager to avoid rejection. They are therefore motivated to conform as quickly as possible, and they turn their attention toward thoughts that will facilitate this process (Nemeth, 1986). (See Gibbons, 1990; Liebling & Shaver, 1973; Lord & Saenz, 1985, for accounts that attribute cognitive constraint in minority members to heightened self-awareness.) These convergent thought processes should correspond with relatively low integrative complexity among minority members. Specifically, unidimensional reasoning corresponds to a lack of differentiation (Suedfeld et al., 1992). Without differentiation, integration cannot occur.

These considerations indicate that majority status in a decision group should be associated with greater integrative complexity than either minority status or membership in a unanimous group, because of the different cognitive processes operating in each of these group contexts. Membership in a majority, where dissent exists, should be associated with divergent thinking and greater integrative complexity than membership in either a unanimous group, in which divergent thinking is unlikely to occur, or a minority, in which convergent thinking is likely to dominate.

Communication strategies. As noted earlier, expressions of integrative complexity in public statements need not reflect private comprehension alone. Indeed, strategic adjustments in integrative complexity have been observed in many studies (for reviews see Tetlock, 1991a; Suedfeld et al., 1992). For example, an increase in the integrative complexity of speeches by U.S. presidents after they were elected was attributed to impression-management strategies rather than to learning (Tetlock, 1981). Similarly, Tetlock et al. (1984) argued that majority members of the U.S. Senate, who control the group's policy outcomes, would feel more accountable for the consequences of the policy adopted than minority members, who presumably favored an alternative. As a result, majority members would engage in relatively complex reasoning to demonstrate their understanding of the policy's limitations to its beneficiaries. In contrast, minority members might respond to their relative lack of accountability by taking strong, unqualified stands in opposition to the majority. This prediction was generally supported.

The impact of such accountability pressures has also been observed in laboratory experiments (Tetlock, 1991a). Subjects in these studies shifted their public positions toward those of the audience to whom they felt accountable (Tetlock & Kim, 1987), as long as they were not constrained by prior commitments (Tetlock, Skitka, & Boettger, 1989). When the views of the audience were known, this involved presenting unidimensional support for the favored position; hence involving relatively low integrative complexity. When the views of the audience were unknown, however, subjects apparently attempted to present arguments that would appeal to multiple constituencies, and hence, they showed higher integrative complexity (Tetlock et al., 1989). In a third accountability condition, subjects who felt committed to a position expressed earlier engaged in defense bolstering, which involved unidimensional support of the committed-to position. Hence, prior commitment was also associated with relatively low complexity.

These conditions correspond to the influence environments typically faced by minority, majority, and unanimous group members. Minority members experience pressure to conform in public when faced with pressure from a majority whose views are known (Asch, 1956; Latané & Wolf, 1981). They assume the majority view is correct and therefore respond by generating reasons to consider accepting it (Nemeth, 1986). Furthermore, unwavering commitment to the minority position has been identified as a critical minority influence tactic

(Moscovici et al., 1969; Mugny, 1982). Hence, regardless of whether minority members experience accountability pressures or view the issue with high complexity in private, it apparently would behoove them to present their views by communicating in a low-complexity style (Moscovici, 1985).

In contrast, majority members, when faced with a vocal minority, encounter evidence that multiple constituencies exist. To have influence in such an environment, majority members may publicly acknowledge the validity of positions that they do not believe are correct in hopes that it will make a positive impression on as many constituents as possible (Tetlock et al., 1984). Defensive bolstering, on the other hand, is most likely to characterize public reasoning by unanimous group members, who, in the absence of opposing parties to placate, are likely to focus on reaffirming the consensus they have already established (Janis, 1982).

These considerations suggest that majority members are more likely to use high integrative complexity as an influence tactic than are minorities, for whom oppositional, low-integrative-complexity tactics should be more effective (Moscovici, 1985). For members of unanimous groups, however, neither of these strategies seems sensible. When there are no alternatives to oppose or consider, attempts to justify a unanimous decision are likely to consist of bolstering, that is, reaffirming the validity of already accepted arguments (Tetlock et al., 1989). This strategy also leads to low integrative complexity. Hence, the public statements of majorities might be characterized by higher levels of integrative complexity than those of minorities or members of unanimous groups, regardless of the complexity of the cognitions underlying their private beliefs.

Role of affective intensity. Both the cognitive and communication-based effects of status on integrative complexity involve affective intensity. That is, cognitive reactions to majority and minority influence are thought to be mediated by stress and arousal (Nemeth, 1986, 1992). Specifically, convergent thinking by minorities occurs as a consequence of the high stress associated with the pressure to conform (Nemeth & Wachtler, 1983). This affective state is associated with conceptual concreteness, restricted attentional focus, and an inability to go beyond the information given (Easterbrook, 1959; Zajonc, 1965). In contrast, minority influence induces enough arousal to stimulate reconsideration of the issue, but not enough to restrict the range of plausible alternatives (Nemeth & Wachtler, 1983). Such moderate stress levels are thought to be optimal for problem solving (Nemeth, 1986).

Differences in stress and arousal have also been shown to affect the capacity for integratively complex reasoning (Schroder et al., 1967; Streufert & Streufert, 1978), in a function resembling the Yerkes–Dodson law (Yerkes & Dodson, 1908). Complex cognitive activity is most likely to occur when patterns of information in the environment are moderately complex, when changes occur at a moderate rate, or when rewards are uncertain, because these conditions induce moderate levels of arousal. However, integrative complexity is inhibited when environments are either too challenging or too simple because of the affective reactions they induce (Schroder et al., 1967).

These conditions can be related to the different influence environments faced by majority, minority, and unanimous group members. Minority status is associated with high stress, in response to the highly punitive and disorienting patterns of information enacted through majority influence (Asch, 1956). Such conditions should inhibit minority members' abilities to engage in integratively complex reasoning (Schroder et al., 1967). Majority members, when they face minority dissent, perceive equivocality in the information environment, yet they face a reasonable probability of a successful outcome. This combination of forces induces moderate stress, stimulates a search for further information, and is associated with increases in integrative complexity (Schroder et al., 1967). Unanimous group members face a task environment that is neither complex nor uncertain and is therefore unlikely to induce even moderate arousal levels. Hence, unanimous group members may lack the motivation required to engage in complex reasoning (Schroder et al., 1967).

These considerations can be summarized in the form of three propositions. First, affective intensity and faction size are negatively correlated, such that minority members experience greater affective intensity than majority members, who experience greater affective intensity than unanimous group members. Second, the relation between affective intensity and integrative complexity is curvilinear, such that moderate affective intensity will lead to greater integrative complexity than either high affective intensity or low affective intensity. Third, and consequently, majority members, who experience moderate affective intensity, should exhibit greater complexity than either minority members, whose affective intensity levels are too high, or unanimous group members, whose affective intensity levels are too low, to facilitate complex thought processes.

To the extent that these processes are operating, members of these groups may express their stress levels in the affective intensity of their communication (Hermann, Hermann, & Hutchins, 1982). That is, the high stress experienced by minority members might be expressed inadvertently in the form of strong affect and emotion when they present their views. Majority members should express arousal levels that are moderate by comparison. In contrast, the lack of arousal experienced by unanimous group members may be reflected in relatively flat or uninspired presentations of their views.

Affective intensity may also play a role in the implementation of communication strategies, however. For example, expressing strong emotion may be a useful tactic for the minority to convey urgency and commitment (Habeeb, 1988), whereas majority members may attempt to tone down their affective responses in a debate to appear flexible and accommodating to a determined minority that appears volatile or easily provoked. As for unanimous group members, discussions in which all members agree are inherently less emotional than those in which conflict occurs. Thus, it seems unlikely that public statements by unanimous group members who face no external threat would be emotional in tone. Hence, if public statements made by minority, majority, and unanimous group members differ in their affective intensity, this could be attributed to their respective influence tactics.

Summary

These considerations suggest that public statements by majority members should be characterized by greater integrative complexity than those of members of either minorities or unanimous groups. Furthermore, minority members should express greater affective intensity than majority members, who in turn should express greater affective intensity than members of unanimous groups. These status contingencies can be attributed to either (a) inadvertent cognitive responses to others' influence attempts or (b) strategic use of communication styles in attempting to influence others. These alternatives are not considered mutually exclusive.

The research reviewed also contains considerable evidence that the integrative complexity expressed by members of political decision-making groups is affected by both individual-level and group-level factors. Studies that focus on ideological preferences indicate that political liberals and moderates tend to show greater complexity, and greater flexibility, than conservatives or extremists. When the effects of group membership are examined systematically, a comparably consistent pattern is revealed: Majority members tend to show greater complexity than minority members or members of unanimous groups.

Study Overview

In the archival analysis of U.S. Supreme Court opinions conducted here, these two variables were manipulated independently. Three experiments compared the integrative complexity of (a) minority and majority Supreme Court opinions that were written in the case of nonunanimous decisions and (b) majority opinions written on behalf of unanimous versus nonunanimous decisions. For each of these comparisons, half of the decisions had liberal political outcomes and half had conservative political outcomes. This allowed the relative merits of the ideology-contingency and status-contingency perspectives to be evaluated.

Experiment 1 compared majority and minority opinions written by the 8 most liberal and 8 most conservative justices, who were classified according to their voting records. It replicates Tetlock et al.'s (1985) study, with the addition of data from a conservatively dominated era (1986–1990) and the systematic sampling of majority and minority opinions (they treated opinion status as a random variable). In this study, ideological preference was operationalized as a trait (i.e., a long-term dispositional characteristic of the author), and status was operationalized as a state (i.e., associated solely with a single decision outcome).

Experiment 2 introduced a new factor, unanimous-group membership, that was not examined in prior research. Hence, comparisons involved unanimous majority opinions, nonunanimous majority opinions, and minority opinions, written in the case of liberal and conservative decisions (the author's general ideological orientation was a random variable). Here, both ideology and status were defined on the basis of a single decision outcome; hence, both were operationalized as states. Thus, the relative effects of trait-versus-state-defined ideological orientation can be tested by comparing the results of Experiments 1 and 2.

Experiment 3 was a comparison of liberal and conservative opinions written during liberally and conservatively dominated eras on the Court. Thus, the status variable was trait-defined (i.e., continued membership in a general ideological faction over time), whereas the ideology variable was state-defined. A comparison of the effects of member status in Experiments 2 and 3 provided information about the relative impacts of trait-versus-state-defined status.

Method Overview

Sampling

The data for this study are the verbatim records of judicial opinions authored by justices of the U.S. Supreme Court. Sampling was performed using the *U.S. Supreme Court Judicial Data Base* compiled by Spaeth (1991) and colleagues, which contains data on all cases decided by the U.S. Supreme Court from 1953 through 1990. Each case was assigned a value for the year it was decided (1953–1990), the vote distribution (9–0 to 5–4), the case content (e.g., civil liberties, judicial power, or economic activities), the ideological direction of the decision (liberal vs. conservative), the author of the opinion, the status of the opinion (e.g., majority vs. dissenting), and the reference book citation.

The decisions were arrayed chronologically. The data were divided into four time periods of equal length: (a) 1953–1961, (b) 1962–1971, (c) 1972–1981, and (d) 1982–1990. Cases were sampled systematically from these time periods to fulfill the following criteria.

Decisions made by a full (9-member) body, with a majority of 7 and a minority of 2, were selected whenever possible. When this requirement could not be met, 6-person majorities and 3-person minorities were allowed. Only opinions for which a sole justice was the primary author were allowed. This was the case for both majority opinions of the Court and dissenting opinions. Coauthored opinions, separate opinions expressing regular concurrence (agreement with the Court's opinion as well as its disposition), special concurrence (agreement with the Court's disposition but not its opinion), judgments of the Court (occurring when less than a majority of the participating justices agree on the language that a majority opinion should contain), dissent from a denial or dismissal of certiorari, dissent from summary affirmation of an appeal, and jurisdictional dissent (disagreement with the Court's assertion of jurisdiction without addressing the merits or without providing the parties' oral argument) were not included.

Coding

Each opinion was divided into thirds of equal length. The middle paragraph of each third was excerpted and coded in isolation. This eliminated the potential confounding effects of differences in the construction of formal Court documents. That is, authors of the official Court (majority) opinion are generally required to provide a comprehensive review of the background and precedent that is relevant to the case at hand and to highlight all of the nuances that exist. In contrast, authors of dissenting (minority) opinions are free to address any single aspect of the majority view that they wish, without providing a thorough discussion of previous rulings that are relevant. Because of this difference, majority opinions viewed in their entirety might very well exhibit greater integrative complexity than dissenting opinions on these grounds alone. However, it is hard to imagine on a priori grounds how differences in document complexity would be manifested at the paragraph level. Scores assigned to each of the three paragraphs were averaged for the purposes of analysis.

Integrative complexity. Each paragraph sampled from the database was scored for integrative complexity (see Tetlock & Hannum, 1983, for detailed coding instructions). As noted earlier, integrative complexity coding entails an assessment of the extent to which two structural dimensions are present in the text: differentiation and integration.

Evidence of differentiation consists of references to more than one dimension of a problem or more than one perspective on an issue. Low differentiation is reflected by a tendency to focus on only one theme in the analysis (e.g., abortion is murder). Higher levels of differentiation include the recognition that problems have multiple dimensions and that there are reasonable arguments on both sides of a controversy (e.g., abortion deprives a child of life, but bringing an unwanted child into the world is not always a better alternative). When differentiated elements are compared, contrasted, or otherwise linked conceptually, evidence of integration is inferred. Low integration is characterized by descriptions of differentiated aspects as operating in isolation, whereas higher integration entails descriptions of differentiated aspects as operating in simple interactions or multiple contingent patterns.

Integrative complexity scores range from 1 to 7. The following examples of actual Supreme Court opinions illustrate the different levels. Scores of 1 are assigned when there is no evidence of differentiation or of integration. For example,

> There should be no doubt that this large-scale, systematic, continuous solicitation and exploitation

of the Illinois consumer market is a sufficient "nexus" to require Bellas Hess to collect from Illinois customers and to remit the use tax, especially when coupled with the use of the credit resources of residents of Illinois, dependent as that mechanism is upon the State's banking and credit institutions.

Scores of 3 are assigned when differentiation exists but there are no signs of integration. The individual recognizes alternative points of view but does not perceive relationships among them. For example:

> The State admittedly has a legitimate interest in the welfare of a child born out of wedlock who is receiving public assistance, as well as in securing support for the child from those legally responsible. In addition, it shares the interest of the child and the defendant in an accurate and just determination of paternity. Nevertheless, the State also has financial concerns; it wishes to have the paternity actions in which it is involved proceed as economically as possible and, hence, seeks to avoid the expense of blood grouping tests.

Scores of 5 are assigned when differentiation exists and an explicit rule has been used to compare differentiated dimensions. For example:

> I certainly agree that state public school authorities in the discharge of their responsibilities are not wholly exempt from the requirements of the 14th Amendment respecting the freedoms of expression and association. At the same time I … believe that … school officials should be accorded the widest authority in maintaining discipline and good order in their institutions. To translate that proposition into a workable constitutional rule, I would, in cases like this, cast upon those complaining the burden of showing that a particular school measure was motivated by other than school concerns—for example, the desire to prohibit the expression of an unpopular point of view, while permitting expression of the dominant opinion.

Scores of 7 are used when a complex rule or set of rules has been used to describe the relations among differentiated alternatives. This typically involves acknowledgment of complex value trade-offs or of complex conceptual links between different ways

of looking at the world. No scores of 7 were assigned to the data from this Supreme Court study.

Scores of 2, 4, and 6 represent transition points between adjacent levels. They are assigned when there is evidence of implicit differentiation (information seeking or qualification to an absolute rule) or implicit integration (hints of recognition of interactions and trade-offs). Text that is merely descriptive and shows no signs of interpretation is designated unscorable by integrative complexity coding rules (Tetlock & Hannum, 1983). When unscorable paragraphs were encountered during sampling, they were replaced by the next scorable paragraph.

Integrative complexity coding was performed by two trained raters who were blind to the hypotheses being tested. Interrater reliability was assessed using Kendall's (W) coefficient of concordance. The mean level of agreement was .87. Most disagreements pertained to the assignment of scores above 4, which occurred infrequently. Discrepancies were resolved by an expert rater who was aware of the nature of the hypotheses and independent variables but was blind to the conditions under which the coded material had been generated.

Affective intensity. Rating of affective intensity were also assigned to the paragraphs sampled. These data were collected to explore the possibility that differences in integrative complexity might be accompanied by differences in affective intensity, as suggested by considerations raised earlier (e.g., Nemeth, 1986; Streufert & Streufert, 1978; Zajonc, 1965). The procedures used by Hermann et al. (1982) for coding the affective tone of political figures' public statements were adapted for this purpose. In that work, *affect* is defined as having both direction (positive vs. negative) and intensity (weak vs. strong). During training, however, coders agreed that it was nearly impossible to assess the direction of affect expressed in the content of legal opinions. Therefore, the system was modified to exclude this aspect of the measure. Coders judged the intensity of affect expressed in each paragraph by noting use of verb modifiers, italics, and punctuation. They assigned ratings using the following scale: *no affective intensity* (1): "no use of strong verb modifiers, italics or punctuation to indicate feeling intensity"; *mild affective intensity* (2): "occasional use of strong verb modifiers, or italics, or punctuation to indicate feeling intensity"; *moderate affective intensity* (3): "regular use of strong verb modifiers, or italics, or punctuation to indicate feeling intensity"; *strong affective intensity* (4): "regular use of strong verb modifiers in combination with italics and or punctuation to indicate feeling intensity"; and *extreme affective intensity* (5): "excessive use of strong verb modifiers in combination with italics and or punctuation to indicate feeling intensity." Coding was performed by one trained rater who was blind to the conditions under which the opinions were written. A second rater coded a random sample of 12 opinions for the purposes of computing inter-rater reliability. The level of agreement was moderate (Kendall's $W = .84$). Discrepancies were resolved using the procedure described above.

Paragraph length. The number of printed lines subsumed by each paragraph was counted and recorded.

Statistical Analyses

Analyses were performed at the group level. Specifically, majority and minority status were treated as within-subjects factors for comparisons within justices (in Experiment 1) and within nonunanimous groups (in Experiment 2). For comparisons of unanimous groups with majorities and minorities in nonunanimous groups, member status was treated as a between-subjects variable.

Experiment 1

The ideology-contingency perspective proposed and supported in Tetlock et al.'s (1985) Supreme Court study predicts that liberal justices will exhibit higher integrative complexity than conservative justices, regardless of the status (majority vs. minority) of the opinion they author. This perspective makes no predictions about levels of affective

intensity, and there is no theoretical reason that liberal and conservative justices should differ in this regard. On the basis of status-contingency considerations, both liberal and conservative justices should exhibit greater integrative complexity when writing on behalf of the majority than when writing on behalf of the minority. Furthermore, their minority opinions should be characterized by greater affective intensity than their majority opinions.

Method

To sample justices for this study, I computed and rank ordered the percentages of opinions authored on behalf of liberal and conservative decisions by each of the 25 justices included in the database. On the basis of this ranking, the 8 most liberal and 8 most conservative justices were selected. For each justice, 8 cases for which the justice had authored the majority opinion and 8 cases for which the justice had authored a minority opinion were drawn using the following procedure.

Table 8.1 lists the 16 justices selected and the majority and minority opinions they authored that were sampled for content analysis by year, status, issue, and title (in the Case column). An equal number of cases pertaining to civil liberties and economic activities were selected within majority and minority opinions from each time period (see Tetlock et al., 1985, for data pertaining to this distinction). Beginning with the first year of each justice's term, the cases were searched sequentially until one majority and one minority opinion of the same issue type were identified. Then, beginning with the last year of the term, the cases were searched in reverse order until one majority and one minority opinion of the other issue type were identified. There was no relation between paragraph length and integrative complexity ($r = -.14$, $p > .10$), decision ideology, or opinion status ($Fs < 1.0$).

Results and Discussion

Two majority and two minority opinions authored by each of the 8 most liberal and 8 most conservative justices during the period from 1953 to 1990 were selected (see Table 8.1) and coded as

TABLE 8.1. Supreme Court Data Sample for Justice-Defined Analysis

Justices	Year	Status	Issue	Case
Liberal				
Black (1953–1971)	56	M	EA	Schulz v. Penn R. Co.
	58	m	EA	NLRB v. United Steelworkers
	69	M	CL	R.A. Orozco v. S. of Texas
	71	m	CL	California v. J.R. Byers
Marshall (1967–1990)	70	M	EA	NLRB v. Raytheon Co.
	72	m	EA	Central Hardware Co. v. NLRB
	88	M	CL	T.B. Amadeo v. Walter Cont.
	88	m	CL	A.L. Lockhart v. Nelson
Warren (1953–1969)	60	M	CL	U.S. v. Hougham
	58	m	CL	NLRB v. United Steelworkers
	67	M	EA	Alexander Tcherepnin v. J.E. Knight
	66	m	EA	U.S. v. T.F. Johnson
Goldberg (1962–1965)	63	M	CL	R.L. Haynes v. State of Washington
	64	m	CL	U.S. v. R.R. Barnett et al.
	65	M	EA	NLRB v. Metropolitan Life Ins. Co.
	63	m	EA	B'hood of Loco. Eng's v. L & N RR Co.
Fortas (1966–1969)	67	M	EA	Wyandote Trans. Co. et al. v. U.S.
	67	m	EA	Nat'l Bellas Hess, Inc. v. IL Dep't. Rev.
	68	M	CL	S. Epperson et al. v. State of Arkansas
	68	m	CL	S. Ginsberg v. State of New York
Stevens (1976–1990)	78	M	CL	L.A. Dep't of Water . . . v. Manhart et al.
	78	m	CL	Flagg Bros. Inc. et al. v. S.H. Brooks et al.
	90	M	EA	Texaco Inc. v. Hasbrouch, Rick's Texaco
	90	m	EA	Atlantic Richfield Co. v. USA Petroleum
Douglas (1954–1975)	56	M	CL	Rea v. U.S.
	57	m	CL	S. Achilli v. USA
	73	M	EA	USU Pharmaceutical v. C.W. Weinberger
	73	m	EA	Kern C'ty Land Co. v. Occid'l Petroleum
Brennan (1957–1990)	59	M	EA	"SS Monrosa" v. Carbon Block Export
	59	m	EA	The Vessel M/V "Tungus" v. O. Skovgaard
	88	M	CL	R. Riley v. NFOB of N.C., Inc.
	88	m	CL	R. Frisby, et al. v. Schultz and Braun
Conservative				
Harlan (1955–1971)	57	M	EA	West Point Grocery Co. v. Opelika
	58	m	EA	Kernan v. American Dredging Co.
	69	M	CL	Adickes v. Kress & Co.
	69	m	CL	Tinker v. Des Moines Comm. Sch'l.
Frankfurter (1953–1962)	54	M	CL	Wajder v. U.S.
	57	m	CL	Green v. U.S.
	60	M	EA	Clay v. Sun Insurance Office
	60	m	EA	Braniff Airways v. Nebraska Board
Whittaker (1957–1961)	60	M	EA	Fed. Power Comm. v. Tuscarora, Ind.
	60	m	EA	Federal Trade Com. v. Henry Broch
	61	M	CL	Wilson v. Schnettler
	61	m	CL	Deutch v. U.S.
Burton (1953–1958)	54	M	CL	U.S. v. Guy W. Capps., Inc.
	55	m	CL	Boston Metals v. Winding Gulf
	57	M	EA	U.S. v. Turley
	57	m	EA	Moore v. Michigan

(Continued)

TABLE 8.1. (*Continued*)

Justices	Year	Status	Issue	Case
Burger (1970–1986)	71	M	CL	*Gordon v. Lance*
	72	m	CL	*Dunn v. Brumstein*
	84	M	EA	*U.S. v. Varig Airlines*
	82	m	EA	*Harlow v. Fitzgerald*
Powell (1972–1987)	74	M	CL	*U.S. v. Calandra*
	74	m	CL	*U.S. v. Giordano*
	85	M	EA	*Pattern Makers League v. NLRB*
	87	m	EA	*Fall River Dyeing & . . . v. NLRB*
Rehnquist (1972–1994)	73	M	CL	*Gustafson v. Florida*
	74	m	CL	*Blackledge v. Perry*
	89	M	EA	*Allegheny Pitt v. Webster County*
	90	m	EA	*Reves v. Ernst & Young*
O'Connor (1982–)	89	M	EA	*Sec. of Interior v. California*
	89	m	EA	*Dixson v. U.S.*
	88	M	CL	*JETT v. Dallas Ind. Sch'l District*
	88	m	CL	*Metro Broadcasting v. FCC*

Note: M = majority; m = minority; EA = economic activities; CL = civil liberties.

described previously. Complexity was expected to be greater in opinions (a) written by liberal justices rather than conservative justices and (b) representing the views of the majority rather than in those representing the views of a minority.

Integrative complexity. Integrative complexity levels expressed by each justice are shown in Table 8.2 as a function of justice ideology and opinion status. The predicted effects of status are evident. Individual justices expressed significantly lower levels of integrative complexity when writing minority opinions ($M = 1.34$) than when writing majority opinions ($M = 2.05$), $F(1, 14) = 22.14$, $p < .0001$. Contrary to Tetlock et al.'s (1985) finding, liberal and conservative justices did not differ in overall integrative complexity ($M = 1.64$ and 1.76 for liberal and conservative justices, respectively; $F < 1.0$), nor was the effect of opinion status contingent on justice ideology, $F(1, 14) = 1.10, p > .10$.

Affective intensity. Mean levels of affective intensity in majority and minority opinions written by

TABLE 8.2. Integrative Complexity Levels Expressed in Majority and Minority Opinions Written by Liberal and Conservative Supreme Court Justices

Justice	Mean integrative complexity	
	Majority opinion	**Minority opinion**
Liberal		
Black	2.00	1.00
Marshall	2.25	1.66
Warren	3.17	1.33
Goldberg	2.25	1.00
Fortas	1.50	1.00
Stevens	1.83	1.17
Douglas	1.50	1.17
Brennan	2.08	1.33
M	2.07	1.21
Conservative		
Harlan	1.50	2.00
Frankfurter	2.50	1.83
Whittaker	1.83	1.00
Burton	1.92	1.00
Burger	2.50	1.17
Powell	1.83	1.33
Rehnquist	1.50	2.00
O'Connor	2.65	1.50
M	2.03	1.48

TABLE 8.3. Affective Intensity Expressed in Majority and Minority Opinions Written by Liberal and Conservative Supreme Court Justices

Justice	Mean affective intensity	
	Majority opinion	Minority opinion
Liberal		
Black	1.17	2.67
Marshall	1.00	1.33
Warren	1.17	1.17
Goldberg	1.17	1.83
Fortas	1.17	1.50
Stevens	1.00	1.00
Douglas	1.33	1.33
Brennan	1.00	1.00
M	1.13	1.48
Conservative		
Harlan	1.00	2.00
Frankfurter	1.67	1.83
Whittaker	1.67	1.00
Burton	1.00	1.00
Burger	1.00	1.17
Powell	1.00	1.33
Rehnquist	1.00	2.00
O'Connor	1.00	1.50
M	1.17	1.42

liberal and conservative justices are shown in Table 8.3. As expected, both liberal and conservative justices expressed significantly greater affective intensity in the minority opinions they authored ($M = 1.45$) than in their majority opinions ($M = 1.15$), $F(1, 14) = 5.99$, $p < .03$. There was no overall difference between liberal and conservative justices in their expressions of affective intensity ($M = 1.31$ and 1.30, respectively; $F < 1.0$), nor was the interaction of ideology and opinion status reliable ($F < 1.0$).

Summary. The effects of member status on complexity levels are consistent with predictions. That is, majorities were expected to exhibit greater integrative complexity than minorities because of their differences in accountability (Tetlock et al., 1984), communication strategies (Moscovici, 1985), and cognitive flexibility (Nemeth, 1986). This result was obtained. Consistent with this explanation, affective intensity was greater in minority than majority opinions. However, the complexity "advantage" of majority members is thought to be contingent on

the presence of a vocal minority. Because all of the cases sampled for this experiment involved nonunanimous decisions, this prediction cannot be tested here. It is addressed in Experiment 2.

Contrary to expectations based on prior research, the opinions of liberal and conservative justices did not differ from one another, nor did they interact with the effects of status on integrative complexity. As noted earlier, this outcome may reflect the shifting balance of ideological preferences on the Court. That is, if liberal justices exhibited greater complexity in earlier work because they held a majority on the Court during the period from which the data were drawn, the inclusion of data from the more recent conservatively dominated period, in which complexity should be greater among conservatives, might obscure any overall effect of ideology. Evidence bearing on this possibility is presented in Experiment 3.

Experiment 2

This analysis differed from the previous one in two ways. First, it compared majority opinions written in the case of nonunanimous groups with those written when the group was unanimous. Nonunanimous majority opinions were expected to show evidence of greater cognitive flexibility (i.e., integrative complexity) than either minority opinions or unanimous opinions (Nemeth & Kwan, 1987; Schroder et al., 1967). Second, Experiment 2 examined the effects of state-based ideology (i.e., based on a specific decision outcome) as opposed to trait-based ideology (i.e., based on justices' overriding political orientations). Justice ideology was treated as a random variable. Opinions written in the case of liberal outcomes were expected to show greater complexity than those written in the case of conservative outcomes.

Method

Thirty-two cases (eight unanimous liberal, eight nonunanimous liberal, eight unanimous conservative, and eight nonunanimous conservative) were selected using the procedures described above. Eight legal issues were included and were evenly distributed across cells of the design. For this sample, liberal and conservative decision outcomes were used as a basis for selection. Criteria used for designating liberal and conservative decision outcomes are defined by the policy areas included in the Supreme Court Judicial Data base: criminal procedure, civil rights, First Amendment, privacy, due process, unions, economic activity, judicial power, federalism, and federal taxation. Decisions are coded using rules provided in Spaeth (1991) for designating liberal outcomes (conservative outcomes are defined as the opposite). As described in Segal and Spaeth (1993, p. 243):

> Liberal outcomes include: support of persons accused or convicted of crime, or those denied a jury trial, support of those alleging violation of their civil rights, or support of those alleging deprivation of First Amendment freedoms. With regard to privacy, a liberal vote supports females in matters of abortion, and disclosure in actions concerning freedom of information except for student and employment records. With regard to due process, a liberal position opposes government action, where deprivation of due process is alleged except in takings clause cases where conservatives oppose the governmental actions. A liberal vote supports labor unions except where the union is alleged to violate the antitrust laws; in these cases, a liberal vote supports a competition. In economic activity, the liberal position opposes business, the employer, and arbitration, while supporting competition, liability, indigents, small businesses vis-a-vis big ones, debtors, bankrupts, consumers, the environment, and accountability. In judicial power, a "liberal"—more accurately, a judicial activist as opposed to judicial restraintist—supports the exercise of judicial power, including review of administrative agency action. In federalism, a liberal vote supports national supremacy—that is, is pro-national and anti-state. In federal taxation, the liberal position supports the United States and opposes the taxpayer.

One liberal and one conservative decision that were similar in all other respects were sampled from the last year (1990) of the last database decade. The next pair was selected from the year immediately prior. This sampling was repeated for each of the remaining three decades. Using this method, two pairs of cases matched on the relevant variables were selected from each decade

on the first pass. A second pass was made, starting with the most recent year not already sampled, to complete the selection process.

Table 8.4 presents a summary of these cases in terms of their ideological outcome (liberal vs. conservative); the year they were decided; the distribution outcome (unanimous vs. nonunanimous); issue content; chief justice: Warren, Burger, or Rehnquist; and case. These 48 opinions were coded using the procedure described above. There was no relationship between paragraph length and decision ideology (liberal vs. conservative), opinion status (minority vs. majority vs. unanimity) or integrative complexity ($Fs < 1.0$ and $r = -.04$, respectively).

Results and Discussion

The data in Table 8.4 were analyzed in three subanalyses, corresponding to the three between-status comparisons. Minority opinions were compared with the nonunanimous majority opinions to which they refer using a mixed-model analysis of variance (ANOVA) with one within-subject factor (majority vs. minority status) and one between-subject factor (liberal vs. conservative ideology). Comparisons involving unanimous majority opinions used a 2 (status) × 2 (ideology) between-subjects ANOVA. In addition to the predictions tested in Experiment 1, Experiment 2 evaluated the hypothesis that majority opinions written on behalf of unanimous decisions would be lower in integrative complexity than majority opinions written in the case of nonunanimous decisions.

Integrative complexity. Data bearing on this issue are shown in Table 8.5. Consistent with expectations, majority opinions written on behalf of nonunanimous decisions had higher levels of integrative complexity ($M = 2.35$) than opinions written in the case of unanimous decisions ($M = 1.18$), $F(1, 31) = 19.00, p < .0001$. Nonunanimous majority opinions were also significantly more complex ($M = 2.35$) than minority opinions ($M = 1.19$), $F(1, 14) = 18.61, p < .001$. This replicates the result obtained in Experiment 1. The integrative complexity levels exhibited in unanimous opinions ($M = 1.18$) and minority opinions ($M = 1.19$) did not differ significantly from one another ($F < 1.0$). Again, contrary to prior research, liberal

TABLE 8.4. Supreme Court Data Sample for Outcome-Defined Analysis

Year	Vote	Issue	Chief	Case
Liberal, unanimous cases				
90	9-0	JP	R	Sullivan v. Finkelstein*
89	9-0	CP	R	Brower v. County of Inyo*
81	9-0	CR	B	Little v. Streater
79	8-0	DP	B	F.O. Addington v. State of Texas
71	7-0	EA	B	O'Keefe v. Aerojet-General Ship.*
69	9-0	FA	W	Stanely v. Georgia*
61	9-0	FT	W	Turnbow v. Comm'r. of Int. Rev.*
59	9-0	U	W	NLRB v. Fant Milling Co.
Liberal, nonunanimous cases				
90	7-2	JP	R	Maislin Ind's. v. Primary Steel*
88	6-2	CP	R	Coy v. Iowa*
81	7-2	CR	B	McDaniel v. Sanchez
79	6-3	DP	B	Vaughn v. Vermilion Corp.
71	5-2	EA	B	U.S. v. Falstaff Brewing Corp.*
69	7-2	FA	W	Tinker v. Des Moines Comm. Sc'l Dist.*
60	7-2	FT	W	U.S. v. Hougham
59	7-2	U	W	Mitchell v. Lublin, McGaughty & Assoc.
Conservative, unanimous cases				
89	9-0	JP	R	Lewis v. Bank Corp.*
88	9-0	CP	B	Michigan v. Chesternat*
79	9-0	CR	B	S.E. Community College v. F.B. Davis
79	9-0	DP	B	U.S. v. Bodcaw Co.
70	7-0	EA	B	United States v. ICC*
68	8-0	FA	W	Clark v. Gabriel*
61	9-0	FT	W	U.S. v. Consolidated Edison*
57	8-0	U	W	NLRB v. Truck Driver's Union
Conservative, nonunanimous cases				
89	7-2	JP	R	Hallstrom v. Tillamook County*
87	7-2	CP	R	Colorado v. Bertine*
79	7-2	CR	B	Personnel Admin. of Mass. v. Feeney
78	6-3	DP	B	Penn Central Transport v. NY City
72	6-2	EA	B	Laird v. Nelms
68	7-2	FA	W	Cameron v. Johnson*
60	7-2	FT	W	U.S. v. Durham Lumber Co.
58	7-2	U	W	NLRB v. United Steelworkers

Note: JP = judicial power; CP = criminal procedure; CR = civil rights; DP = due process; EA = economic activity; FA = First Amendment; FT = federal taxation; U = unions; R = Rehnquist; B = Burger; W = Warren.
* These cases denote data from Experiment 3.

and conservative opinions did not differ significantly in their integrative complexity levels, $F(1, 14) = 1.83$, $p > .10$, for within-group comparisons, and $Fs < 1.0$ for between-group comparisons.

Affective intensity. The literature on status differences suggested that low levels of integrative complexity exhibited in minority opinions should be accompanied by greater affective intensity than the high integrative complexity exhibited in majority opinions written on behalf of nonunanimous decisions. These, in turn, should show greater affective intensity than the opinions written on behalf of unanimous decisions.

Data bearing on this proposition are presented in Table 8.5. As expected, minority opinions contained significantly greater affective intensity

TABLE 8.5. Mean Integrative Complexity and Expressed Affective Intensity as a Function of Opinion Status, Group Distribution, and Outcome Ideology

Variable	Opinion status		
	Unanimity	Majority	Minority
Integrative complexity			
Liberal	1.12	2.04	1.25
Conservative	1.23	2.67	1.12
M	1.18	2.35	1.19
Affective intensity			
Liberal	1.17	1.13	1.63
Conservative	1.04	1.04	1.54
M	1.10	1.08	1.58

($M = 1.58$) than majority opinions ($M = 1.08$), $F(1, 14) = 8.40$, $p < .01$, or opinions written for unanimous decisions ($M = 1.10$), $F(1, 31) = 8.32$, $p < .007$. Contrary to expectations, however, majority opinions written on behalf of unanimous and nonunanimous decisions did not differ from one another ($F < 1.0$). None of these effects were contingent on the ideological outcome of the decision (all $Fs < 1.0$).

Summary. These results replicate those obtained in Experiment 1. Majority opinions exhibited greater integrative complexity than minority opinions. However, these data suggest that the effect of majority status depends on the pattern of endorsement underlying the majority opinion. Specifically, unanimous majority opinions do not differ significantly from minority opinions in their complexity levels. Nonunanimous majority opinions were more complex than both. These findings are consistent with Nemeth's (1986) explanations for the effects of minority influence in groups. However, they would not have been predicted on the basis of accountability theory alone. Again, no effects of ideology were observed. Hence, neither trait-defined ideology nor state-defined ideology is directly related to integrative complexity levels in the data examined here. Experiment 3 examined the possibility of an indirect relation, moderated by status effects.

Experiment 3

Experiment 1 compared the effects of trait-based ideological orientation (i.e., justices' long-term voting patterns) with state-based status (i.e., agreement with the outcome of a specific decision). Experiment 2 compared the effects of state-based ideological orientation (i.e., the content of the views expressed in a single opinion) and state-based status (as in Experiment 1). In Experiment 3, comparisons involved trait-based status (i.e., membership in a general ideological majority or minority over time) and state-based ideology (as in Experiment 2).

This final analysis assessed whether majority and minority status defined in this more general way would have the same effects on integrative complexity levels as case-based majority and minority status. If this is the case, the relation between the integrative complexity and ideological orientation of Supreme Court opinions should be contingent on the dominant ideological orientation of the Court at the time the opinion was written. That is, liberal opinions should be associated with higher levels of integrative complexity than conservative opinions during an era in which the Court contains a liberal majority. During an era in which a conservative majority exists on the Court, the integrative complexity of liberal (now minority-status) opinions should be lower than that of conservative opinions.

Method

Cases from Experiment 2 were examined to determine the most liberal and most conservative eras on the Court represented by those decisions. According to Supreme Court decision-trend analysts (Baum, 1989a, 1989b; Segal & Spaeth, 1993), the most liberal period within the 1953–1990 time frame began in 1961 and continued until approximately 1972, at which time a strong conservative majority was established (Segal & Spaeth, 1989). By this time the percentage of liberal decisions dropped below 50% (to 46.3%) and has risen to that level only once since (in 1974; Segal & Spaeth, 1989). Relative to the liberal Warren Court (1953–1969), which produced 63% liberal decision outcomes, the conservative Rehnquist Court (1986–1994) produced only 45% liberal decisions. This is particularly true with regard to civil liberties cases (i.e., those pertaining to criminal procedure, civil rights, First Amendment, due process, and privacy). On these issues, the percentage of liberal outcomes rarely exceeds the mid-30s, and falls below 20% for at least one member of that group in criminal procedure, First Amendment, and privacy (Segal & Spaeth, 1993, pp. 244–245).

In total, 6 liberal opinions and 6 conservative opinions authored during the liberal era (1961–1972) were included in the between-cases data set. Collapsing over opinion status, those opinions were grouped to compose the liberal-era sample. Because the Rehnquist Court is generally considered more conservative than the Burger or Warren Courts (Baum, 1989a) and has grown more conservative over time (Segal & Spaeth, 1993), the conservative-era sample was constructed by selecting the 6 most recently authored liberal opinions and the 6 most recently authored conservative opinions. These 12 cases were decided between 1987 and 1990. Hence, a total of 24 cases were included in the era-driven analysis (see cases denoted by an asterisk in Table 8.3).

Results and Discussion

Cases selected for the outcome-driven analysis that fell within the most liberally dominated era (1961–1972) and the most conservatively dominated era (1987–1990) on the U.S. Supreme Court during the 1953–1990 period (see Table 8.3) were analyzed to examine the relations between political ideology and majority status over time. Because these cases were selected from the outcome-defined sample alone, the small number of opinions falling within these time periods made performing separate between- and within-group analyses impractical. Instead, the scores of minority opinions, majority opinions, and those written on behalf of unanimous decisions were averaged and analyzed together as a function of the ideological orientation of their content and the ideological orientation of the majority on the Court at the time the opinions were written.

Integrative complexity. Mean levels of integrative complexity for liberal and conservative opinions written during liberal and conservative eras are shown in Table 8.6. The effects of minority, nonunanimous majority, and unanimous majority status on integrative complexity that were obtained in Experiment 2 are evident in this test as well. Across both eras, majority opinions written on behalf of nonunanimous decisions were higher in integrative complexity ($M = 2.19$) than either minority opinions ($M = 1.14$) or majority opinions written on behalf of unanimous decisions ($M = 1.13$), $F(2, 23) = 22.29, p < .0001$.

In addition, over and above this case-defined status effect, the integrative complexity of opinions that were ideologically consistent with the general ideology of the Court ($M = 1.70$) was greater than that of opinions in which the views expressed were inconsistent with the Court's ideology ($M = 1.23$). Using the "inappropriate" statistical procedure described above, this result was marginally significant, $F(1, 23) = 3.69, p < .07$. However, this pattern of differences is evident for all three status conditions. Specifically, integrative complexity was higher when the views expressed were ideologically consistent than when they were ideologically inconsistent, regardless of whether the opinion expressed was that of a unanimous majority

TABLE 8.6. Mean Integrative Complexity as a Function of Opinion Ideology, Era Ideology, and Opinion Status

	Era ideology			
	Liberal (1961–1971)		Conservative (1987–1990)	
Opinion ideology	M	n	M	n
Liberal				
Unanimous	1.00	3	1.17	2
Majority	2.67	2	1.84	2
Minority	1.33	1	1.00	2
M	1.53	6	1.39	6
Conservative				
Unanimous	1.00	3	1.50	2
Majority	1.33	1	2.50	2
Minority	1.17	2	1.17	2
M	1.06	6	1.87	6

TABLE 8.7. Mean Affective Intensity Expressed as a Function of Opinion Ideology, Era Ideology, and Opinion Status

	Era ideology			
	Liberal (1961–1971)		Conservative (1987–1990)	
Opinion ideology	*M*	*n*	*M*	*n*
Liberal				
Unanimous	1.33	3	1.00	2
Majority	1.00	2	1.00	2
Minority	1.83	1	2.33	2
M	1.38	6	1.44	6
Conservative				
Unanimous	1.11	3	1.00	2
Majority	1.00	1	1.00	2
Minority	2.00	2	1.33	2
M	1.39	6	1.23	6

(1.25 vs. 1.09), $F(1, 9) < 1.0$, *ns*, a nonunanimous majority (2.59 vs. 1.59), $F(1, 6) = 6.16$, $p < .09$, or a minority (1.25 vs. 1.09), $F(1, 6) = 1.20$, *ns*.

Affective intensity. The affective intensity levels expressed in liberal and conservative opinions written during liberal and conservative eras are presented in Table 8.7. As observed previously, minority opinions written during both eras exhibited greater affective intensity ($M = 1.95$) than either majority opinions written on behalf of nonunanimous opinions ($M = 1.00$) or opinions written on behalf of unanimous groups ($M = 1.13$), regardless of their ideological content, $F(1, 23) = 21.98$, $p < .0001$. Expressions of affect were also somewhat greater during times when opinion ideology was inconsistent with the ideology held by the majority on the Court ($M = 1.42$) than when opinion and era ideology were consistent ($M = 1.23$), although that difference was not statistically significant ($F < 1.0$). The effects of opinion ideology and time on affective intensity were also not significant ($Fs < 1.0$).

General Discussion

This study was designed to disentangle the effects of two factors that had been confounded in previous

integrative complexity research. Robust differences between the complexity levels of political liberals, moderates, conservatives, and extremists had been identified and attributed to the general values and beliefs underlying those ideological preferences (Tetlock, 1983, 1984, 1986). However, in each of those studies, ideological preference was systematically confounded with policy makers' status in the decision-making groups to which they belonged, such that liberals and moderates, who exhibited relatively high complexity levels, were also members of a general ideological majority, whereas conservatives and extremists, who exhibited significantly lower complexity, belonged to a general ideological minority. Because the research was generally conducted to distinguish among various ideology-contingency hypotheses, the findings were attributed to individuals' ideological preferences in spite of this confounding.

The research reported here challenges this interpretation. Whereas the ideology-contingency hypotheses (e.g., rigidity of the right and value pluralism) predicted that conservative members of the U.S. Supreme Court would be less complex than liberal members, independently of their status in the group, the status-contingency hypothesis predicted that minority opinions, and those written on behalf of unanimous decisions, would be less complex than majority ones, regardless of the ideology they espoused. This prediction was clearly supported. The findings showed that opinion status was a stronger predictor of integrative complexity in Supreme Court opinions than either (a) justices' predominant ideological orientations or (b) the ideological nature of the views they espoused in the context of a given case.

In fact, the only apparent effect of ideology occurred in the context of the era-drive analysis, where it was used to operationalize status. There, the relation between expressions of political ideology and integrative complexity depended on the ideological climate on the Court at the time the opinions were written. That is, liberal opinions were higher in integrative complexity when liberals held a majority on the Court, but conservative opinions were higher in integrative complexity when the Court was dominated by conservatives.

This may explain why the ideology effect identified by Tetlock et al. (1985) in their Supreme Court study was not replicated here. Specifically, the data from that study were drawn from a time (1946–1978) in which the Court was dominated by liberals. Hence, the finding that opinions written by members of a general ideological majority on the Court (i.e., liberals and moderates) were higher in integrative complexity than those written by political "outcasts" (i.e., conservatives) is not inconsistent with the status-contingency model. In fact, that finding was replicated here. However, during the conservative era sampled, conservative opinions, which had majority status, were higher in integrative complexity than liberal opinions, which had minority status. Therefore, when the data from these two periods are analyzed together, no effects of ideology emerge. These latter effects are predicted by the status-contingency hypotheses, but cannot be accounted for by the ideology-contingency hypotheses described earlier.

The finding that majority opinions written on behalf of nonunanimous Supreme Court decisions were higher in integrative complexity than minority opinions is also consistent with the accountability explanation advanced to explain majority and minority differences in the U.S. senate (Tetlock et al., 1984). However, in Experiment 2, nonunanimous majority opinions were also higher in complexity than opinions written when the Court was unanimous, although both groups were equally accountable for the outcomes they endorsed. In addition, minority opinions and unanimous opinions were equally low in integrative complexity. These differences cannot be explained on the basis of accountability to external constituents alone.

In short, the status-contingency perspective developed in this article is consistent with earlier findings. However, in contrast to previous conceptions, it predicted the results obtained. The model suggests that the integrative complexity expressed by members of political decision-making groups reflects not their political views, but rather, the pressures and strategies associated with attempting to wield influence from positions of relative status.

The model posits that membership in a minority, majority, or unanimous group, and the status it entails, can affect the integrative complexity of members' decision rationales at several critical points. When individuals are first exposed to a decision task, they typically develop a preference for the solution and a rationale for that preference based on their personal perceptions of the issue. They may bring this preference with them to the group decision context, and it may be the strongest determinant of their final position.

When interaction ensues, however, group members are confronted with evidence about the extent to which their colleagues share that preference. This status recognition process involves two considerations. The first is the degree to which one is similar to the majority of group members and hence is likely to be accepted or rejected. The second is the degree to which one's point of view is likely to prevail. These perceptions are likely to be accompanied by varying degrees of stress, excitement, uncertainty, and frustration about the task, as well as different influence strategies. Hence, member status may be the strongest determinant of a group member's final position. The data reported here suggest that the contingences associated with member status are a stronger determinant of complexity differences than those associated with ideological orientation in the Supreme Court context investigated.

Alternative Interpretations

Despite the strong support obtained in the experiments reported here, a number of the model's aspects require further specification. As noted earlier, Tetlock et al. (1985) speculated that the ideology effect they reported in their Supreme Court study "might not generalize to an historical era in which conservatives dominated the national political scene" (p. 1235). They provided three potential reasons.

One is similar to the status-contingency argument presented here. Specifically, the authors suggested that low integrative complexity might be a typical reaction of political movements that fear an erosion of their power base and their influence in society at large (see also Tetlock et al., 1984).

A second proposed possibility was that parties interested in upholding precedent would reduce cases to a simple legal issue that can readily be covered by existing legal rules, whereas those interested in overturning precedent would depict cases as presenting bodies of fact that are so complex that they could not have been anticipated by previous law and thus require new legal rules. A third possibility referred to earlier research (Tetlock et al., 1984) that attributed complexity differences among senators in the majority and minority to their different political roles. Policy making, it was argued, required greater integrative complexity than policy opposing. These alternatives are all consistent with the data reported, but their relative merits cannot be evaluated here.

These alternatives raise a fourth alternative that is of critical importance to interpretation of these findings, as well as previous results of integrative complexity research. It concerns the extent to which the integrative complexity expressed in public statements reflects strategic communication, rather than actual comprehension, about policy issues. While the effects of different communication objectives on complexity have been demonstrated (Tetlock, 1981; Tetlock et al., 1984; Tetlock et al., 1989), the psychological locus of those effects cannot be conclusively demonstrated here.

In fact, a consideration of this possibility suggests an explanation for the affective intensity data reported. That is, in addition to higher integrative complexity, the authors of nonunanimous majority opinions were expected to express greater affective intensity than the authors of unanimous opinions. Contrary to expectations, however, unanimous and nonunanimous opinions did not differ in their affective intensity levels, although minority opinions were characterized by higher levels than both.

It is possible that at the time Supreme Court justices are working on an opinion, they are more concerned with designing an influential message than with the process or outcome of decision making itself. Hence, regardless of the extent to which the decision task itself was stressful or arousing, authors of unanimous, majority, and minority opinions might be differentially inclined to use expressions of affect as a communication tactic. As noted earlier, minority members might use affective intensity to convey urgency, commitment, and inflexibility. In contrast, majority members might avoid expressing affective intensity to convey flexibility and a willingness to make concessions. If this were the case, the effects of member status on affective intensity during the decision task might be overshadowed by adjustments in expressions of that affect after the decision task for the purposes of creating a persuasive rationale. This possibility should be evaluated in future research.

Furthermore, it is not possible to evaluate which of the many psychological mechanisms discussed in the social influence and integrative complexity literatures is responsible for group members' opinion-writing behaviors. The following questions, among others, remain unaddressed: Does member status exert its effects on the ability, or the motivation to engage in complex reasoning? Are these effects a consequence of accountability to constituents, or control over decision outcomes? To whom do members of decision groups feel accountable: their constituents or their fellow members? Do status differences lead to complexity differences, as suggested here, or do people with differing complexity levels systematically choose different social roles? These issues need to be resolved for the status-contingency perspective to make a useful contribution to research in relevant domains.

Generalizability of Findings

In addition to the qualifications raised above, it is not possible to assess whether the results of this study can be considered generalizable to group-decision contexts other than the U.S. Supreme Court. As noted earlier, it is possible that the integrative complexity differences between majority, minority, and unanimity Supreme Court opinions reflect differences in the content requirements of each of these types of legal documents, rather than psychological characteristics of the authors per se. It is hoped that the sampling procedures used here controlled for some of these effects. However, the fact that integrative complexity levels were higher in opinions written on behalf of nonunanimous cases than in those written on behalf of unanimous opinions might simply reflect the fact that cases on which all nine members of the Supreme Court can agree are less complex to begin with than cases that are more controversial. Differences in case complexity were not controlled or measured in the study reported here. Attempts to replicate these findings, controlling for differences in case complexity and using data from less formal documents, would be informative.

Implications for Group Decision Making

To the extent that this research reflects real differences in the reasoning styles of minority, majority, and unanimous group members, it suggests several prescriptions for effective group decision making. Specifically, for tasks in which integrative complexity leads to better performance (see Gruenfeld & Hollingshead, 1993; Tetlock, 1992), groups with diverse membership should outperform groups whose members are homogeneous in their beliefs and perspectives. However, these findings also suggest that the conceptual gains of majority members may be offset by the absence of such gains for deviant members. To the extent that this is the case, minority members may learn less from their participation in group decision activity than they might have under conditions in which they were endowed with majority status.

REFERENCES

Adorno, T., Frenkel-Brunswik, E., Levinson, D., & Sanford, N. (1950). *The authoritarian personality.* New York: Harper.

Allison, G. T. (1971). *Essence of decision: Explaining the Cuban missile crisis.* Glenview, IL: Scott, Foresman & Co.

Asch, S. (1956). Studies of independence and conformity. *Psychological Monographs, 70* (9, Whole No. 416).

Baum, L. (1989a). Comparing the policy positions of Supreme Court justices from different periods. *Western Political Quarterly, 42*(4), 509–521.

Baum, L. (1989b). *The Supreme Court* (3rd ed.). Washington, DC: CQ Press.

Converse, P. E. (1964). The nature of belief systems in mass publics. In D. E. Apter (Ed.), *Ideology and discontent* (pp. 206–261). New York: Free Press.

Davis, J. H. (1973). Group decision and social interaction: A theory of social decision schemes. *Psychological Review, 80,* 97–125.

Easterbrook, J. A. (1959). The effect of emotion on cue utilization and the organization of behavior. *Psychological Review, 66,* 183–201.

Gibbons, F. X. (1990). Self-attention and behavior: A review and theoretical update. *Advances in Experimental Social Psychology, 23,* 249–303.

Gibson, J. L. (1981). Personality and elite political behavior: The influence of self-esteem on judicial decision-making. *Journal of Politics, 43,* 194–125.

Gruenfeld, D. H. (1992). *A "status-contingency" model of cognition and communication in decision making groups.* Paper presented at the 15th Annual Meeting of the International Society of Political Psychology, San Francisco.

Gruenfeld, D. H., & Hollingshead, A. B. (1993). Sociocognition in work groups: The evolution of group integrative complexity and its relation to task performance. *Small Group Research, 24,* 383–405.

Gruenfeld, D. H., McGrath, J. E., Beasley, R., & Kaarbo, J. (1993, September). *A conceptual framework for analysis of group processes in political decision making.* Paper presented at the annual meeting of the American Political Science Association, Washington, DC.

Habeeb, W. M. (1988). *Power and tactics in international negotiation: How weak nations bargain with strong nations.* Baltimore: Johns Hopkins University Press.

Hermann, C. F. (1993). Avoiding pathologies in foreign policy decision groups. In D. Caldwell & T. McKeown (Eds.), *Diplomacy, force, and leadership: Essays in honor of Alexander George* (pp. 179–207). Boulder, CO: Westview Press.

Hermann, M. G. (1977). *The psychological examination of political leaders.* New York: Free Press.

Hermann, M. G., Hermann, C. F., & Hutchins, G. L. (1982). Affect. In P. Callahan, L. P. Brady, & M. G. Hermann (Eds.), *Describing foreign policy behavior* (pp. 207–222). Beverly Hills, CA: Sage.

Janis, I. (1982). *Groupthink* (2nd. ed., rev.). Boston: Houghton Mifflin.

Judd, C. M., & Krosnick, J. A. (1989). The structural bases of consistency among political attitudes: Effects of political expertise and attitude importance. In A. R. Pratkanis, S. J. Breckler, & A. G. Greenwald (Eds.), *Attitude structure and function* (pp. 99–128). Hillsdale, NJ: Erlbaum.

Kruglanski, A. W., & Mackie, D. M. (1990). Majority and minority influence: A judgmental process analysis. In W. Stroebe & M. Hewstone (Eds.), *European review of social psychology,* (Vol. 1, pp. 229–261). London: Wiley.

Latané, B., & Wolf, S. (1981). The social impact of majorities and minorities. *Psychological Review, 88,* 438–453.

Levine, J. M., & Russo, E. M. (1987). Majority and minority influence. In C. Hendrick (Ed.), *Review of personality and social psychology* (Vol. 3, pp. 13–54). Beverly Hills, CA: Sage.

Liebling, B. A., & Shaver, P. (1973). Evaluation self-awareness and task performance. *Journal of Experimental Social Psychology, 9,* 297–306.

Lord, R. G., & Saenz, D. S. (1985). Memory deficits and memory surfeits: Differential cognitive consequences of tokenism for tokens and observers. *Journal of Personality and Social Psychology, 49*, 918–926.

Moscovici, S. (1980). Toward a theory of conversion behavior. In L. Berkowitz (Ed.), *Advances in experimental social psychology*, (Vol. 13, pp. 209–239). New York: Academic Press.

Moscovici, S. (1985). Social influence and conformity. In G. Lindzey & E. Aronson (Eds.), *The handbook of social psychology* (3rd ed., Vol. 2, pp. 347–412). New York: Random House.

Moscovici, S., & Lage, E. (1976). Studies in social influence, 3: Majority versus minority influence in a group. *European Journal of Social Psychology, 6*, 149–174.

Moscovici, S., Lage, E., & Naffrechoux, M. (1969). Influence of a consistent minority on the responses of a majority in a color perception task. *Sociometry, 32*, 365–380.

Mugny, G. (1982). *The power of minorities*. New York: Academic Press.

Nemeth, C. J. (1985). Dissent, group process and creativity: The contribution of minority influence. In E. Lawler (Ed.), *Advances in group processes* (Vol. 2, pp. 57–75). Greenwich, CT: JAI Press.

Nemeth, C. J. (1986). Differential contributions of majority and minority influence. *Psychological Review, 93*, 23–32.

Nemeth, C. J. (1992). Minority dissent as a stimulant to group performance. In S. Worchel, W. Wood, & J. A. Simpson (Eds.), *Group process and productivity* (pp. 95–111). Newbury Park, CA: Sage.

Nemeth, C. J., & Kwan, J. L. (1987). Minority influence, divergent thinking and detection of correct solutions. *Journal of Applied Social Psychology, 17*, 786–797.

Nemeth, C. J., Mosier, K., & Chiles, C. (1991). When convergent thought improves performance: Majority versus minority influence. *Personality and Social Psychology Bulletin, 18*, 139–144.

Nemeth, C. J., & Wachtler, J. (1983). Creative problem solving as a result of majority vs. minority influence. *European Journal of Social Psychology, 13*, 45–55.

Rokeach, M. (1956). Political and religious dogmatism: An alternative to the authoritarian personality. *Psychological Monographs, 70* (18, Whole No. 425).

Schroder, H. M., Driver, M. J., & Streufert, S. (1967). *Human information processing*. New York: Holt, Rinehart & Winston.

Sears, D. O., & McConahay, J. B. (1970). Racial socialization, comparison levels, and the Watts riot. *Journal of Social Issues, 26*, 121–140.

Segal, J. A., & Spaeth, H. J. (1989). Decisional trends on the Warren and Burger Courts: Results from the Supreme Court Data Base Project. *Judicature, 73*, 103–107.

Segal, J. A., & Spaeth, H. J. (1993). *The Supreme Court and the attitudinal model*. Cambridge, England: Cambridge University Press.

Sidanius, J. (1978). Intolerance of ambiguity and socio-politico ideology: A multidimensional analysis. *European Journal of Social Psychology, 8*, 215–235.

Spaeth, H. J. (1991). *United States Supreme Court judicial database. 1953–1989 terms.* Inter-university Consortium for Political and Social Research (ICPSR 9422). Second ICPSR release, September, 1991.

Staub, A. B. (1991). *Individual differences in integrative complexity: A group influence hypothesis.* Unpublished undergraduate honors thesis, Harvard College.

Stone, W. F. (1980). The myth of left-wing authoritarianism. *Political Psychology, 2*, 3–20.

Streufert, S., & Streufert, S. (1978). *Behavior in the complex environment.* Washington, DC: Winston.

Suedfeld, P. (1983). Authoritarian leadership: A cognitive-interactionist view. In J. Held (Ed.), *The cult of power: Dictators in the twentieth century* (pp. 1–23). New York: Columbia University Press.

Suedfeld, P. (1992). Cognitive managers and their critics. *Political Psychology, 13*, 435–453.

Suedfeld, P., Tetlock, P. E., & Streufert, S. (1992). Conceptual/integrative complexity. In C. P. Smith (Ed.), *Motivation and personality: Handbook of thematic content analysis* (pp. 393–400). Cambridge, England: Cambridge University Press.

Tanford, S., & Penrod, S. (1984). Social influence model: A formal integration of research on majority and minority influence processes. *Psychological Bulletin, 95*, 189–225.

Tetlock, P. E. (1979). Identifying victims of groupthink from the public statements of decision makers. *Journal of Personality and Social Psychology, 37*, 1314–1324.

Tetlock, P. E. (1981). Pre- to post-election shifts in presidential rhetoric: Impression management or cognitive adjustment? *Journal of Personality and Social Psychology, 41*, 207–212.

Tetlock, P. E. (1983). Cognitive style and political ideology. *Journal of Personality and Social Psychology, 45*, 118–126.

Tetlock, P. E. (1984). Cognitive style and political belief systems on the British House of Commons. *Journal of Personality and Social Psychology, 46*, 365–375.

Tetlock, P. E. (1986). A value pluralism model of ideological reasoning. *Journal of Personality and Social Psychology, 50*, 819–827.

Tetlock, P. E. (1991a). *An integratively complex look at integrative complexity.* Paper presented at the 99th Annual Convention of the American Psychological Association, San Francisco.

Tetlock, P. E. (1991b). An alternative metaphor in the study of judgment and choice: People as politicians. *Theory and psychology, 1*, 451–477.

Tetlock, P. E. (1992). Good judgment in international politics: Three psychological perspectives. *Political Psychology, 13*, 517–540.

Tetlock, P. E., Bernzweig, J., & Gallant, J. L. (1985). Supreme Court decision making: Cognitive style as a predictor of ideological consistency of voting. *Journal of Personality and Social Psychology, 48*, 1127–1239.

Tetlock, P. E., & Hannum, K. (1983). *Integrative complexity coding manual.* Unpublished manuscript, University of California, Berkeley.

Tetlock, P. E., Hannum, K. A., & Micheletti, P. M. (1984). Stability and change in the complexity of senatorial debate: Testing the cognitive versus rhetorical style hypotheses. *Journal of Personality and Social Psychology, 46*, 979–990.

Tetlock, P. E., & Kim, J. I. (1987). Accountability and judgment processes in a personality prediction task. *Journal of Personality and Social Psychology, 52,* 700–709.

Tetlock, P. E., Skitka, L., & Boettger, R. (1989). Social and cognitive strategies of coping with accountability: Conformity, complexity, and bolstering. *Journal of Personality and Social Psychology, 57,* 632–641.

Yerkes, R. M., & Dodson, J. D. (1908). The relation of strength of stimulus to rapidity of habit-formation. *Journal of Comparative Neurological Psychology, 18,* 459–482.

Wilson, G. D. (1973). *The psychology of conservatism.* New York: Academic Press.

Winter, D. G. (1973). *The power motive.* New York: Free Press.

Zajonc, R. B. (1965). Social facilitation. *Science, 149,* 269–274.

Received December 28, 1993
Revision received April 27, 1994
Accepted April 30, 1994 ■

Being Better by Being Right: Subjective Group Dynamics and Derogation of In-Group Deviants When Generic Norms are Undermined

José M. Marques, Dominic Abrams, and Rui G. Serôdio

The authors predicted that derogation of group deviants depends on the extent to which in-group norms or values are validated or undermined in a social context. In Experiment 1 participants were less tolerant and derogated in-group deviants more when other in-group members opposed the norm. In Experiment 2 participants derogated in-group deviants more than out-group deviants and than noncategorized individuals, but only when normative in-group members lacked uniformity. In Experiment 3 participants derogated in-group deviants more when there was uncertainty about in-group superiority. These results are consistent with previous research on the black sheep effect (J. M. Marques, V. Y. Yzerbyt, & J.-P. Leyens, 1988) and with the model of subjective group dynamics (D. Abrams, J. M. Marques, N. J. Bown, & M. Henson, 2000; J. M. Marques, D. Abrams, D. Paez, & C. Martinez-Taboada, 1998).

José M. Marques and Rui G. Serôdio, Faculty of Psychology and Educational Sciences, University of Porto, Porto, Portugal; Dominic Abrams, Department of Psychology, University of Kent, Canterbury, England.

This research is part of project PRAXIS XXI/P/PSI/13192/98, which is funded by the Portuguese Foundation for Science and Technology.

Correspondence concerning this article should be addressed to José M. Marques or Rui G. Serôdio, Faculdade de Psicologia e de Ciências da Educação, Universidade do Porto, Rua do Campo Alegre, 1055, P-4156-004 Porto, Portugal; or to Dominic Abrams, Department of Psychology, University of Kent, Canterbury CT2 7NP, England. Electronic mail may be sent to marques@psi.up.pt, rserodio@psi.up.pt, or d.abrams@ukc.ac.uk.

The social–psychological study of group processes evolved mainly from two longstanding traditions, the small group approach (e.g., Cartwright & Zander, 1968; Forsyth, 1990; Shaw, 1976) and the social identification approach, including social identity theory (Tajfel, 1978) and self-categorization theory (Turner, Hogg, Oakes, Reicher, & Wetherell, 1987). However, the two approaches differ both in their scope and in their assumptions about the functions and the processes involved in group members' perceptions of their groups and of other members. The small group approach focuses on *dynamic* groups (Wilder & Simon, 1998)—that is, groups whose membership relies on interpersonal similarity, interdependence, and face-to-face interaction (cf. Lott & Lott, 1965; Shaw, 1976). Research driven by this approach has explored in detail the functions and antecedents of hostile reactions of members of small groups to deviants, but it typically has neglected the broader context of intergroup relations in which these reactions take place. In turn, the social identification approach has traditionally focused on *categorical*, as opposed to dynamic, groups (Wilder & Simon, 1998). Social identity research has centered on intergroup relations and typically neglected how social categories deal with emerging deviance.

There is evidence that large groups deal with deviants in a way analogous to that of small, or face-to-face, groups, and that this process is built into their relations with other groups and their respective normative systems. This is the case in examples such as the Puritan "moral crusades" (Erikson, 1966), lynch mobs (Inverarity, 1976), and witch-hunting (Ben-Yehuda, 1980). As a case in point, Rokeach, Toch, and Rottman (1960) found a significant correlation between the amount of perceived threat to the Roman Catholic Church and the amount of punishment prescribed to violators in more than 140 canons between the 4th and 16th centuries. In addition, in his analysis of "mechanical" solidarity, sociologist Emile Durkheim (Durkheim, 1960) argued that punishment of deviants emerges mainly when there is the need to reinforce individuals' sense of cohesion and commitment to society's norms. The present work aims to integrate that research into the more general scope of our recent model of *subjective group dynamics*

(Abrams et al., 2000; Marques, Abrams, Paez, & Hogg, 2001; Marques et al., 1998; Marques & Paez, 1994; Marques, Paez, & Abrams, 1998).

One foundation of the small group approach is Festinger's (1950) influential idea that individuals selectively affiliate with similar others both to avoid uncertainty about relevant matters of opinion and to achieve goals that they could not accomplish in isolation. Specifically, conformity to group norms upholds members' beliefs on the correctness of their opinions on relevant issues and confirms their positive expectations both about themselves and about other members (e.g., Boyanowsky & Allen, 1973; Burnstein & Vinokur, 1975; Insko, Drenan, Solomon, Smith, & Wade, 1983; Kelley & Volkart, 1962). In turn, lack of conformity disrupts modal members' subjective validity of opinions on relevant issues and can undermine prospects of collective goal achievement. As a result, modal members engage in normative attempts to make deviants conform (Deutsch & Gerard, 1955; Levine & Thompson, 1996; Turner, 1991). Despite these attempts, deviants may persist in their disagreement or lack of solidarity with group goals. In this case, members express hostility toward deviants, redefine the deviants' status in the group, and, ultimately, ostracize them (e.g., Cota, Evans, Dion, Kilik, & Stewart-Longman, 1995; Festinger, Schachter, & Back, 1950; Jones & DeCharms, 1957; Schachter, 1961; cf. also Levine, 1989).

According to the social identity approach, group membership depends on the specification of a set of characteristics commonly held by all group members that differentiate them from contrasting categories (cf. Prentice, Miller, & Lightdale, 1994). A primary goal for group members is to bolster a positive and distinctive social identity. Individuals cognitively maximize the ratio of intergroup to intragroup differences, assimilate themselves to an in-group prototype, and develop in-group-favoring attitudes (cf. Brewer, 1979; Hogg & Abrams, 1988; Tajfel, 1978; Tajfel & Turner, 1979; Turner et al., 1987). Recent research within the social identification framework suggests that these processes may explain a large set of small group phenomena that had formerly been attributed to sheer interpersonal similarity and interdependence (cf. Hogg, 1992, 1996). For example, attraction to the in-group prototype, rather than actual interpersonal similarity or interdependence with others, can mediate individuals' expectancies about in-group members' beliefs and behavior as well as individuals' own judgments and behavior (e.g., Abrams, Wetherell, Cochrane, Hogg, & Turner, 1990; Hogg & Hains, 1996; Hogg, Hardie, & Reynolds, 1995; Jetten, Spears, & Manstead, 1996; cf. also Hogg, 1992; Turner, 1991).

Self-categorization theory proposes that the basic motivation underlying social categorization is to generate cognitive clarity in social stimulus settings (e.g., Oakes, Haslam, & Turner, 1994). Consequently, individuals expect *normative fit* between the members' and their respective groups' prototypical characteristics (Oakes, Haslam, & Turner, 1994). Greater normative fit should allow individuals to focus on intergroup differences as a means of upholding a clear-cut, prototypical description of the groups and to subjectively validate expectancies for their characteristics and behavior. In contrast, lower normative fit should decrease the cognitive clarity and subjective certainty of intergroup differences. As a result, perceivers should switch to alternative categorizations that better account for the stimulus setting (Oakes et al., 1994).

However, in many, perhaps most, situations it is not feasible to recategorize in-group deviants as outgroup members or to switch to alternative dimensions of categorization. Moreover, group members may be highly motivated to sustain positive distinctiveness for their salient in-group. Under these circumstances, an in-group deviant may pose a significant threat both to in-group distinctiveness and to the positivity of the in-group. Thus, a deviant group member should attract negative evaluation and should cause attempts among the other group members to reinforce in-group consensus and, hence, the subjective value of their social identity.

Recently, we proposed a model of subjective group dynamics to account for the processes through which intragroup differentiation allows individuals to sustain the subjective validity of positive intergroup differentiation (Abrams et al., 2000; Marques, Abrams, Paez, & Martinez-Taboada, 1998; cf. also Marques & Paez, 1994; Marques, Paez, & Abrams, 1998). We proposed that people differentiate between groups in terms of descriptive

norms (e.g., whether members meet particular criteria for category membership, such as gender), but they also differentiate within categories in terms of prescriptive norms. Our previous studies examined situations in which in-group and outgroup prescriptive norms were opposed. Consistent with subjective group dynamics, we found that participants judged the in-group as a whole more favorably than they judged the out-group as a whole. In other words, they favored in-groups that were defined in descriptive terms. More important, upgrading of normative in-group members and derogation of deviant in-group members increased when a prescriptive in-group norm was salient and when participants were accountable to normative in-group members (Abrams et al., 2000; Marques, Abrams, et al., 1998). Together, these results support two ideas. First, individuals may engage in positive intergroup differentiation and, at the same time, differentiate among normative and deviant in-group members within groups. Second, intra-group differentiation within both in-groups and out-groups seems to be influenced by the implications of prescriptive norm deviance for the validity of in-group values. Individuals only derogate deviant in-group members if those members undermine the prescriptive norm of the in-group as a whole. Conversely, individuals upgrade deviant out-group members only when those members help to validate the prescriptive norm of the in-group. These conclusions are broadly consistent with a social identity theory account of group behavior, which proposes that individuals seek both positive distinctiveness and legitimacy for their group's position when in-group and out-group norms are opposed (e.g., Tajfel, 1978).

Many norms are group specific (e.g., Muslims should follow the Koran, Christians should follow the Bible, Jews should follow the Torah). However, other norms are generic in that they apply equally to all groups and to their members, regardless of their group membership. For example, one ought to wear the *kippah* at the Shabbat whether one is Jewish or not, and one should not wear shoes in a Mosque whether one is Muslim or not. These norms thus do not function as criterion attributes for defining group membership, as is the case of other norms. They correspond more to societal norms (e.g., Cialdini & Trost, 1998) because they involve generic values and standards of conduct. An interesting prediction that is consistent with our subjective group dynamics perspective is that the way that individuals judge others who uphold or breach generic norms may also be affected by the group membership of the target. In-group members who deviate from a generic norm create uncertainty about the legitimacy of positive social identity because they reduce the fit between the in-group and the superordinate (societal) group. These in-group deviants should therefore be derogated more than similar out-group members because these out-group members actually contribute positively to in-group distinctiveness by reducing out-group fit to the superordinate category. In turn, in-group members who uphold the norm validate such positivity and are positively evaluated, as compared with similar out-group members.

Previous research on the so-called black sheep effect (e.g., Marques, 1990; Marques & Paez, 1994; Marques et al., 1988) supports the preceding idea. This research indicates that in-group and out-group deviants are judged differently even when they are deviating in terms of a generic norm. We interpret these findings as showing that individuals attribute positive value for the in-group, as compared with the out-group. Therefore, they expect in-group members to display socially desirable characteristics and behavior and perceive socially undesirable in-group members as deviating from the group prototype. In the context of an intergroup comparison, in-group deviance contributes negatively to the overall value assigned and desired for the in-group (Marques et al., 1988). Indeed, individuals may upgrade likable in-group members and derogate unlikable in-group members, as compared with similar out-group members, while simultaneously judging the in-group more favorably than the out-group as a whole (e.g., Marques, Robalo, & Rocha, 1992, Experiment 2; Marques & Yzerbyt, 1988, Experiments 1 and 2). In addition, this black sheep effect emerges when the likability dimension is key to positive intergroup differentiation (Marques, 1990; Marques et al., 1988) and when participants strongly identify with the in-group (Branscombe, Wann, Noel, & Coleman,

1993). Other evidence suggests indirectly that individuals are more likely to conform to others when there is a concern both to emit a valid opinion and to be positively evaluated by others (cf. Insko et al., 1983; Insko, Smith, Alicke, Wade, & Taylor, 1985). Together with evidence from the black sheep effect, this supports the idea that attraction to the in-group may lead individuals to attempt to contribute to establishing in-group consensus on the group's positiveness.

The preceding evidence is consistent with the basic assumptions of the social identification framework, namely that judgments of in-group and out-group members depend on a basic motivation to affirm a positive value for the in-group, as compared with the out-group. However, these studies manipulated the attractiveness of the deviant group members directly rather than through manipulation of norm-related behavior, and therefore it remains to be demonstrated that phenomena such as the black sheep effect are in fact determined by a focus on generic prescriptive norms.

The goal of the present research is to test the idea that group members are especially sensitive to deviance from generic prescriptive norms when the in-group's claim to be embracing those norms is undermined. We see the role of generic prescriptive norms as particularly important for establishing the legitimacy of the in-group's claim to being correct in its views. The battle to represent generic prescriptive norms is commonly observed in political debate, where representatives of opposing parties may try to lay claim to the center ground, Middle England, or the views of the American people. By establishing that the in-group represents the majority or consensual view in society, it is also possible to claim that the in-group has the legitimate right to authority and power. For this reason, when an in-group member departs from the generic norm, it becomes important to react effectively to reestablish group consensus.

Overview and Hypotheses

Our recent research examined reactions to deviants when in-group and out-group prescriptive norms were opposed (e.g., Abrams et al., 2000; Marques, Abrams et al., 1998). In contrast, the present studies examine prescriptive norms that are generic and held to be widely shared, socially desirable views (cf. Cialdini, Kallgren, & Reno, 1991). We examine three factors that contextualize judgments of deviant group members. These factors are the disagreement with valued in-group standards by salient in-group members, the lack of in-group consensus, and insecure social identity. In addition, we examine the idea that individuals derogate deviants not because these deviants are interpersonally different from themselves but because they are viewed as in-group members who undermine the in-group's embodiment of generic prescriptive norms.

We assume that when individuals observe deviance in terms of these prescriptive generic norms, they respond differentially depending on whether in-group support for the norm is undermined. If members of the in-group appear to vary from a generic prescriptive norm, this potentially undermines the perceived legitimacy of the positive value assigned to the in-group. Individuals should be more motivated to restore in-group than out-group consensus in line with the prescriptive generic norm by derogating an in-group deviant more negatively than an out-group deviant. Moreover, if in-group support for the generic norm is unclear, an in-group deviant who opposes that norm has a greater potential to undermine the in-group's embodiment of that norm. In this case, the deviant should be evaluated more negatively, and group members should be more concerned with encouraging the deviant to conform. In contrast, an out-group deviant is irrelevant because intergroup boundaries prevent the out-group deviant from having any impact on the in-group's legitimacy derived from endorsement of the prescriptive norm. In summary, group members are more motivated to ensure that the generic norm is associated with the in-group than to ensure that it is supported by the out-group.

Experiment 1

In Experiment 1, psychology and law students examined answers purportedly given by 50 other

psychology (in-group) or law (out-group) students to a previous survey about student initiation practices. Depending on group opinion condition, target group members appeared either to give clear support for initiation (norm validating condition) or to give a clear challenge to initiation (norm undermining condition). Participants indicated the most pronorm and least pronorm position they would accept about student initiation along a proinitiation–anti-initiation continuum. Then participants evaluated targets who had adopted each of these positions and expressed their willingness to try to persuade these targets to change their opinions about student initiation. We expected participants to express greater endorsement of the in-group norm when confronted by responses endorsing in-group or out-group positions, particularly in the in-group condition and in the norm undermining condition. This would be indicated by a higher threshold of rejection, as given by the least pronorm position participants found acceptable, stronger derogation of in-group deviants relative to out-group deviants, and upgrading of normative in-group members, as compared with normative out-group members.

Pilot Study

We asked 13 law students (6 men and 7 women) and 13 psychology students (6 men and 7 women) to state which of seven statements was their personal opinion on the issue of student initiation practices. We chose law and psychology students because the two departments exist in the same university building; they share some facilities but are, consensually, out-groups to each other. We chose the initiation social desirability dimension because it is part of the student culture in the university and is widely supported by the large majority of students in these two departments. The seven statements were listed from lowest to highest support for initiation, as follows.

Initiation is: 1. "Unnecessary, I definitely disagree with it, and it should be forbidden"; 2. "Very useless, I disagree with it, and it should be discouraged"; 3. "Useless, I tend to disagree with it, and one should be critical about it"; 4. "Neither useful nor useless, and I neither agree nor disagree with it"; 5. "Useful, I tend to agree with it, and I think it should be regarded favorably"; 6. "Very useful, I agree with it, and I think it should be encouraged"; and 7. "Necessary, I strongly agree with it, and I think it should be mandatory."

All participants except 1 male psychology student and 1 female law student, who both endorsed Statement 5, endorsed Statement 6, indicating a clear and strong norm in favor of initiation practices.

Method

Participants and design. In the main experiment 40 female and 18 male ($N = 58$) law and psychology undergraduates, ranging in age from 19 to 23 years old, volunteered to participate. There were between 12 and 16 participants in each condition. Gender, age, and course and year of studies were similarly distributed across conditions. The design was a 2 (group: in-group vs. out-group) × 2 (group opinion: norm validating vs. norm undermining) × 2 (member: normative vs. deviant) structure. Target group and group opinion were between-subjects factors, and member was a within-subject factor.

Procedure. The experiment was conducted by questionnaire. An interviewer approached lone participants in public places in the faculty building and asked them whether they wished to answer a questionnaire on student initiation practices. When the participants agreed, the interviewer handed the questionnaire to them. On the first page, participants read information about the purported goal of the study:

> As you know, student initiation practices have recently caused some debate, and are, at the same time, one of the most important aspects of student life, inside and outside the University. In the first phase of this study, we asked a sample of 50 Psychology (vs. Law) students to indicate, which of the 7 sentences written on the next page, they agreed [with] the most. With the present questionnaire, we intend to validate the results obtained in that phase.

On the second page, depending on the between-subjects group opinion condition, participants were shown a distribution of responses from in-group or out-group members. This distribution either validated (norm validating condition) or undermined (norm undermining condition) the generic norm. In the norm validating condition, the frequencies of responses for the seven assertions were, respectively, 2, 3, 4, 6, 17, 16, and 2. This distribution was reversed in the norm undermining condition. Participants were fully debriefed on the deceptions involved in the experimental procedure when the study was completed.

Before the pattern manipulation, participants indicated their opinion about student initiation using three 7-point bipolar scales. All scales began with the statement, "In your opinion, student initiation is . . . ", followed by a bipolar statement: very negative–very positive, very useless–very useful, and should be forbidden–should be mandatory, respectively. Participants were also asked to indicate to what extent they agreed with student initiation ($1 = $ *fully disagree*; $7 = $ *fully agree*). We averaged these four responses to create an agreement score (Cronbach's $\alpha = .80$). Participants were also asked to estimate the consensus about student initiation by writing down the percentage of target faculty students that were proinitiation.

Participants then indicated which of the seven positions they personally agreed with most (their personal opinion) and the position on the continuum with which they would clearly disagree (e.g., every statement from Statement 4 and below). We labeled this measure the *rejection threshold*. Next, participants were asked to use a series of bipolar 7-point scales to evaluate group members who adopted their personal opinion and their rejection threshold. These positions are subjectively normative and deviant, respectively. Participants evaluated each target in turn in response to the following statement: "Your opinion about the students of the [target group] Faculty who adopted this position is . . ." The bipolar response options were as follows: very unfavorable–very favorable, bad classmates–good classmates, lack a lot of solidarity–show a lot of solidarity, and contribute nothing to student cohesion–contribute very much to student cohesion. We averaged these measures to create a *normative member attractiveness* score and a *deviant member attractiveness* score (Cronbach's α = .84 and .78, respectively). Two final questions asked participants whether they considered that the normative and the deviant members conveyed a good image of the target group (*image conveyed by normative member* and *image conveyed by deviant member*): "In your opinion the image conveyed by the students of the [target group] Faculty who adopted your personal opinion [rejection threshold] position about their Faculty in general is . . ." Response options ranged from 1 (*very bad*) to 7 (*very good*).

Results

There were no significant effects involving participants' school, highest $F(1, 50) = 2.20$, *ns*. We thus disregarded this variable and used the described 2×2 between-subjects design.

Agreement with initiation. To check for agreement with initiation, we submitted the agreement score to a Group × Group Opinion analysis of variance (ANOVA) that yielded no significant effects, all $Fs(1, 54) < 1$. All participants favored student initiation ($M = 5.49$), as shown by the significant difference between this score and the scale midpoint, $t(57) = 16.21, p < .001$.

A Group × Group Opinion ANOVA with perceived consensus estimates (proinitiation, anti-initiation) as a within-subject factor indicated that participants considered that a higher proportion of individuals would have a proinitiation position ($M = 64.98\%$) than an anti-initiation position ($M = 26.48\%$), $F(1, 54) = 62.40, p < .001$. All other effects were nonsignificant (all $Fs < 1.60$). The proinitiation percentage was also significantly different from 50%, $t(57) = 5.39, p < .001$. These results validate the choice of student initiation as a relevant normative dimension to test our hypotheses. Participants agreed with, and expected more others to agree than to disagree with, student initiation.

TABLE 9.1. Participants' Rejection Threshold as a Function of Group Members' Opinions and Group Membership (Experiment 1)

Group and statistic	Group members' opinions	
	Norm validating	Norm undermining
In-group		
M	1.44	4.00
SD	1.50	3.13
Out-group		
M	1.86	2.38
SD	2.18	2.42

Note: Ratings were made on a scale ranging from 1 (*most anti-initiation position*) to 7 (*most proinitiation position*).

Personal opinion and rejection threshold. As expected, the position participants agreed with most did not vary across conditions, all $Fs(1, 57) < 1.00$, and in line with the pilot study, there was strong agreement with initiation (overall $M = 5.71$).

More important, according to our hypothesis, participants should adopt a higher rejection threshold in the in-group, norm undermining condition than in all others. To test this hypothesis, we ran a contrast analysis on the rejection threshold by assigning values to the in-group/validating (-1), in-group/undermining (3), out-group/validating (-1), and out-group/undermining (-1) conditions. This analysis supported our hypothesis, $t(54) = 2.80, p < .01$. As shown in Table 9.1, rejection thresholds were significantly less counter normative in the in-group/undermining condition ($M = 4.00$) than in the in-group/validating, out-group/undermining, and out-group/validating conditions (respectively, $M = 1.44$, $M = 2.38$, and $M = 1.86$).[1]

Normative and deviant member attractiveness. To control for possible effects of personal opinion and rejection threshold on evaluations of group

---

[1] To examine the possibility that there were significant differences among the three conditions made equal in our contrasts, we first checked for differences among the two out-group conditions by assigning values to the in-group/validating (0), in-group/undermining (0), out-group/validating (1), and out-group/undermining (-1) conditions. This analysis revealed no significant difference, $t(54) < 1$. We also compared the in-group/validating condition with the out-group condition as a whole ($M = 2.13$) by assigning values to the in-group/validating condition (-1), the in-group/undermining condition (0), and the out-group condition as a whole (1) Again, the analysis revealed no significant difference, $t(55) < 1$.

members, we entered these scores as covariates in all analyses involving evaluations of normative and deviant members. We predicted that participants would upgrade the normative in-group members and derogate the deviant in-group members, as compared with the out-group counterparts, more strongly in the norm undermining than in the norm validating condition. To test this hypothesis, we examined evaluations of in-group or out-group members who adopted participants' personal opinion and rejection threshold, respectively. We submitted these evaluations to a Group × Group Opinion × Member ANOVA with member as a within-subject factor and personal opinion and rejection threshold as covariates.

We found significant effects of member, $F(1, 53) = 30.51$, $p < .001$, Group × Member, $F(1, 53) = 5.11$, $p < .03$, and Group × Group Opinion × Member, $F(1, 53) = 7.62$, $p < .01$; remaining $Fs(1 < 53) < 1.81$, ns. The significant Group × Group Opinion × Member effect supported our hypothesis. In the norm validating condition, we found no significant Group × Member effect, $F(1, 54) < 1$. However, in the norm undermining condition, the Group × Member effect was significant, $F(1, 54) = 12.52$, $p = .01$. As illustrated in Figure 9.1, in line with our predictions, in this condition participants upgraded normative

in-group members ($M = 5.58$) relative to normative out-group members ($M = 4.77$), $F(1, 54) = 6.83$, $p < .02$. In contrast, they derogated deviant in-group members ($M = 2.72$) relative to deviant out-group members ($M = 3.56$), $F(1, 54) = 4.87$, $p = .03$. It is interesting to note that this occurred even though deviant in-group members in the norm undermining condition were objectively less deviant (i.e., more normative) than deviants in all other conditions.

Image conveyed by normative and deviant members. We ran a Group × Group Opinion × Image ANOVA with image conveyed by the normative and deviant members as a within-subject factor and personal opinion and rejection threshold as covariates. The results were consistent with those of the previous analysis. We found significant effects of Member, $F(1, 53) = 15.48$, $p < .001$, Group × Member, $F(1, 53) = 7.15$, $p < .01$, and Group × Group Opinion × Member, $F(1, 53) = 10.25$, $p < .01$.

In parallel with the results on members' attractiveness, in the norm validating condition we found no significant Group × Member effect, $F(1, 54) < 1$. However, in the norm undermining condition, the Group × Member effect was highly significant, $F(1, 54) = 16.95$, $p < .001$. In this

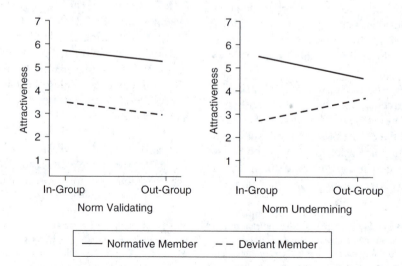

FIGURE 9.1 ■ Attractiveness of normative and deviant members as a function of response pattern and group membership (Experiment 1).

condition, participants considered that the normative in-group members conveyed a better image of the in-group ($M = 5.75$) than the normative out-group members conveyed of the out-group ($M = 4.69$), $F(1, 54) = 9.30, p < .01$. In contrast, participants considered that the deviant in-group members conveyed a worse image of their group ($M = 2.83$) than the equivalent out-group members conveyed of their respective group ($M = 3.88$), $F(1, 54) = 3.69, p = .06$.

Discussion

Our results reveal that perceivers are more favorable toward others who support rather than deviate from generic prescriptive norms. We expected that the validity of the in-group's norms and values should be particularly important for group members. Consistent with this idea, perceivers reacted more strongly to deviant in-group members when the norm was being undermined than when it was not, whereas they did not react differently to out-group deviants as a function of whether the norm was being undermined. Specifically, when salient in-group members undermined the subjective validity of the norm, participants reinforced it by adopting a higher threshold of rejection and by derogating deviant in-group members more strongly. However, deviant in-group members in a norm-validating context and deviant out-group members whose deviance was, by definition, less relevant to the validity of the in-group norm were not subjected to such strong derogation.

We interpret these effects as reflecting group members' motivation to ensure that in-group norms are valid. It follows that reactions to deviant group members could be moderated by other contextual variables that could influence the extent to which those members undermine the norm. Under conditions in which the norm is more secure, we expect that group members would be less strongly motivated to derogate a deviant in-group member or to revalidate the norm. Specifically, we believe that when nondeviant in-group members are highly consensual, the norm is relatively secure. Therefore, although an individual group member may be deviant, that member may not necessarily affect

the clarity of the prescriptive norm and should be less likely to be judged harshly. In contrast, when nondeviant in-group members are less uniform, the presence of a deviant member becomes more undermining, and this should prompt additional efforts to validate the norm. Moreover, this effect should appear more strongly when group membership is salient (in an intragroup setting) relative to a purely interpersonal setting.

Experiment 2

To examine these ideas, in Experiment 2 we asked participants to respond to two ostensibly unrelated tasks: a bogus imagination test and questions on an ethical continuum. In a second session, participants received false feedback about their performance and the performance of other target individuals on the test and their responses to the continuum. In the intragroup condition, we categorized participants as having one of two opposed types of imagination and asked them to judge either two in-group or two out-group members. In the interpersonal condition, we simply pointed out that the target individuals' imagination was either similar or different from the participants' own but made no mention of imagination types, and participants judged two noncategorized individuals. The feedback indicated that most target individuals adopted norm validating positions on the continuum (normative targets). The normative set of target individuals was either highly consensual (high uniformity condition) or somewhat dispersed (low uniformity condition). One target individual (deviant target) adopted a norm undermining position. Participants then evaluated 1 normative and 1 deviant individual and expressed how willing they were to influence these individuals to change their positions on the continuum. We expected participants to evaluate the normative target more positively and the deviant target more negatively when the targets were presented as in-group members than when they were presented as out-group members or simply as individuals. However, we expected this result to emerge especially strongly in the in-group/low uniformity condition. We also predicted that participants would be more willing to influence deviant individuals to change their opinion in this condition.

Method

Participants. Sixty-eight female and 30 male undergraduates ($N = 93$), with ages ranging from 18 to 23 years old ($M = 21.81$), volunteered to participate in the experiment. The number of participants varied between 10 and 13 per condition. Gender and age were similarly distributed across conditions.

Design. The design was a 2 (context: interpersonal vs. intragroup) × 2 (stimulus-set similarity: in-group vs. out-group or similar vs. different set of persons) × 2 (uniformity: high uniformity vs. low uniformity) × 2 (target: normative vs. deviant individual) structure. Context, stimulus set, and uniformity were between-subjects factors, and target was a within-subject factor.

Procedure. The experiment was conducted in two sessions. In the first session, we informed participants that the study was designed to "examine the relationship between the psychological profile of people in terms of their imagination characteristics and their ethical values." The experimenter than handed each participant a bogus Creative Imagination Test that consisted of a series of questions purportedly aiming to evaluate people's imagination characteristics. After completing the imagination test, participants received a Condensed Ethical-Value Survey. It was made clear to participants that this survey was unrelated to the imagination test. The Ethical-Value Survey consisted of a list of seven statements that pilot work had established as representing equal interval steps on a liberal–conservative continuum. Participants were asked to indicate which statement in the continuum best represented their opinion. The statements were organized in a manner similar to that used in Experiment 1, ranging from the most anti-norm to the most pronorm position, but in the present study the opinion issue concerned homosexuals. On the basis of our pilot work, we expected that almost all participants would adopt a pronorm position, specifically that "homosexual people, like everyone else, are entitled to choose their own sexual life" (Position 6). On the opposite end of the continuum was a set of increasingly counter normative positions about homosexuals. At the end of the session, participants enclosed their response sheets in a folder, on which they wrote a personal code.

One week later, participants returned for a "validation session" in which they received the folder containing their responses to the imagination test, information about their imagination characteristics, and information about responses to the Condensed Ethical-Value Survey. Depending on the context manipulation, we either categorized participants in groups according to their type of imagination, highlighting the existence of differences between the two types (the intragroup condition), or we simply explained that varying characteristics exist across people but made no reference whatsoever to imagination types (the interpersonal condition).

We began by providing participants with feedback about their own standing on the Creative Imagination Test and the Condensed Ethical-Value Survey. Participants in the intragroup condition were informed,

> You belong to the pictorial [experiential] type. Pictorials' imagination ensues from their grasp of the external world, their values, and expectations. These features distinguish between pictorial and experiential persons. For experientials [pictorials], the external factors articulate with the self-concept to convey a general view of the world.

We counterbalanced this information across participants to avoid a confound between categorization and descriptions of the attributes of category members. Participants in the interpersonal condition were informed that

> Imagination is a very personal issue. In your personal case, your imagination ensues from your grasp of the external world, your values, and expectations. These features differ from person to person. For other persons, the external factors articulate with the self-concept to convey a general view of the world.

This information was also counterbalanced across participants.

Participants then received feedback about the responses of five other individuals (the stimulus set) in the first phase of the study on the creative imagination measures and on the Condensed Ethical-Value Survey. First, the information indicated that the five individuals were indistinguishable from one another in terms of their imagination type. Depending on the stimulus-set condition, all five were classified either as similar or as dissimilar to the participant in their imagination characteristics. In the interpersonal condition, they were described simply as five individuals. In the intragroup condition, they were described as people who were in the same or a different imagination type.

Second, we gave specific feedback about the ethical value judgments made by each individual in the stimulus set. This feedback indicated that four individuals (normative members) adopted the norm validating position (Position 6) on the value continuum and that one individual (deviant member) adopted a norm undermining position (Position 2). In the high uniformity condition, all normative members adopted the same position, the same one that the participants themselves adopted (Position 6). In the low uniformity condition, two normative members adopted this position and two adopted the two neighboring positions. The experimenter then invited participants to collaborate as judges in the validation of the results of the first phase of the study. First, they answered a series of questions designed to measure group attraction. They then read (bogus) photocopies of response sheets on the Condensed Ethical-Value Survey, ostensibly showing the responses of five other participants. Participants were fully debriefed at the end of the experiment.

After being informed about their imagination characteristics (interpersonal condition) or that they belonged to a type of imagination (intragroup condition), and before being presented with the target stimulus set, participants answered two questions measuring *stimulus-set attraction*: "How much do you like belonging to the pictorial [experiential] type of imagination/having these imagination characteristics?" and "How much would you like to belong to the [alternative] type of imagination/hold different characteristics?"

Participants then judged the normative target individual and the deviant target individual on four traits—nice, loyal, honest, and generous—using a scale ranging from 1 (*not at all*) to 7 (*very much*). We averaged these judgments to form a normative target score and a deviant target score (Cronbach's α = .84, and .52, respectively). Next, participants read, "In the third session, we will ask you to discuss this matter with the two persons you evaluated. How willing would you be to attempt to convince this person to change their opinion?" They answered this question for each target using a scale ranging from 1 (*not at all*) to 7 (*very much*). We labeled these scores willingness to influence normative target and willingness to influence deviant target, respectively.

Participants were also asked to judge the target stimulus set as a whole on the same series of four traits as those used for evaluations of the stimulus set (i. e., stimulus-set attractiveness) using a scale ranging from 1 (*not at all*) to 7 (*very much*). The traits were as follows: nice, loyal, honest, and generous. We pooled these judgments to form a stimulus score (Cronbach's α = .82). Finally, as a measure of self-to-stimulus-set similarity, participants were asked to judge how similar they thought they were to the five individuals as a whole, on a scale ranging from 1 (*very different from them*) to 7 (*very similar to them*).

Results

Stimulus-set attraction. We analyzed the stimulus-set attraction items using a Context × Stimulus Set ANOVA, with stimulus-set attraction as a within-subject factor. The significant effect of stimulus-set attraction shows that participants were more attracted to stimulus sets that were similar to them or to an in-group (M = 5.35) than to stimulus sets that were different from them or similar to an out-group (M = 3.15), $F(1, 91)$ = 116.40, $p <$ .001; highest remaining $F(1, 91)$ = 1.64, *ns*.

Target attractiveness. We analyzed the target attractiveness ratings using a Context (interpersonal vs. intragroup) × Stimulus Set (similar to participant/in-group vs. different from participant/out-group) ×

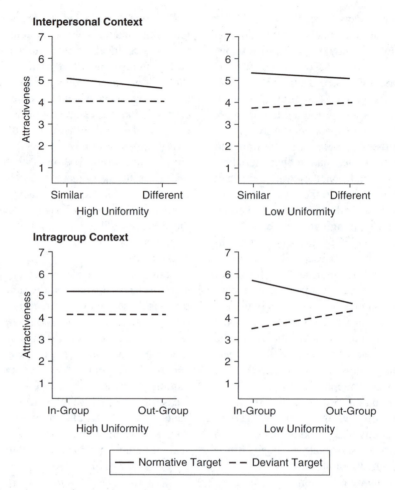

FIGURE 9.2 ■ Attractiveness of normative and deviant targets as a function of context, uniformity, and stimulus set (Experiment 2).

Uniformity (high vs. low) × Target (normative vs. deviant) ANOVA with target as a within-subject factor. There were significant effects of target, $F(1, 85) \times 107.36$, $p < .001$, Stimulus Set × Target, $F(1, 85) = 11.58$, $p < .01$, and Stimulus Set × Uniformity × Target, $F(1, 85) = 5.12$, $p < .05$. More important and in support of our predictions, we found a significant Context × Stimulus Set × Uniformity × Target interaction, $F(1, 85) = 5.54$, $p = .02$; highest remaining $F(1, 85) = 2.31$, *ns*. We decomposed this interaction within the interpersonal and intra-group conditions. There was no significant Stimulus Set ×

Uniformity × Target interaction in the interpersonal condition, $F(1, 86) < 1$, but this interaction was significant in the intragroup condition, $F(1, 86) = 10.95, p = .001$. Within the intragroup condition we examined the Stimulus Set × Target interaction within the high and low uniformity conditions. In the high uniformity condition the Stimulus Set × Target interaction was not significant, $F(1, 90) < 1$. However, in the low uniformity condition the Stimulus Set × Target interaction was significant, $F(1, 90) = 19.98$, $p < .001$. As illustrated in Figure 9.2 and in line with our predictions, participants judged the normative in-group

TABLE 9.2. Means and Standard Deviations of Attractiveness Ratings of Normative and Deviant Targets as a Function of Context, Uniformity, and Stimulus Set (Experiment 2)

Target and statistic	Context			
	Interpersonal		Intragroup	
	Similar	Different	In-group	Out-group
High uniformity				
Normative				
M	5.02	4.66	5.13	5.17
SD	0.97	0.52	0.81	0.87
Deviant				
M	4.06	4.16	4.08	4.12
SD	0.31	0.36	0.62	0.56
Low uniformity				
Normative				
M	5.20	5.00	5.73	4.62
SD	1.08	0.89	0.81	0.51
Deviant				
M	3.83	4.05	3.55	4.31
SD	0.68	0.71	0.55	0.62

Note: Ratings were made on a scale ranging from 1 (*nonattractive*) to 7 (*attractive*).

target more favorably than the normative out-group target, $F(1, 90) = 10.08$, $p = .002$, and the deviant in-group target more unfavorably than the deviant out-group target, $F(1, 90) = 10.03$, $p = .002$ (see also Table 9.2).[2]

Willingness to influence normative and deviant targets. A Context × Stimulus Set × Uniformity × Target ANOVA on willingness to influence the normative individual and the deviant individual as a within-subject factor yielded significant main effects of target, $F(1, 85) = 273.25$, $p < .001$, and stimulus set, $F(1, 85) = 4.60$, $p < .05$. In support of our predictions, we also found a significant effect of Context × Stimulus Set × Uniformity × Target, $F(1, 85) = 3.97$, $p = .05$; highest remaining $F(1, 85) = 2.67$, *ns*.

By decomposing this interaction, we found no significant Stimulus × Uniformity × Target interaction in the interpersonal condition, $F(1, 86) < 1$. However, this interaction was significant in the intragroup condition, $F(1, 86) = 4.29$, $p = .04$. In parallel with the target attractiveness results, the Stimulus Set × Target interaction was not significant in the intragroup/high uniformity condition, $F(1, 90) < 1$. However, this interaction was significant in the intragroup/low uniformity condition, $F(1, 90) = 7.44$, $p = .008$. In this condition, participants' willingness to influence the normative in-group and out-group members did not differ significantly, $F(1, 90) = 1.59$, *ns*. However, participants were more willing to exert influence on the deviant in-group member than on the deviant out-group member, $F(1, 90) = 7.77$, $p = .006$. These results are consistent with our predictions (see Table 9.3).[3]

Stimulus attractiveness and self-to-stimulus-set similarity. The Context × Stimulus Set × Uniformity ANOVAs on stimulus attractiveness and on self-stimulus similarity both yielded only a significant effect of stimulus set, $F(1, 85) = 29.08$, $p < .001$, and $F(1, 85) = 93.59$, $p < .001$, respectively. Participants were more attracted to in-group or similar individuals ($M = 4.89$) than to out-group or different persons ($M = 4.20$) and considered themselves to be more similar to the former ($M = 4.78$) than to the latter ($M = 2.17$). The remaining effects were not significant, highest $F(1, 85) = 3.72$, *ns*.

Discussion

Together, the results of the present experiment indicate that evaluations of norm validating and norm undermining targets are a function of the targets' group membership and that any influence

---

[2] We also checked for effects within each uniformity condition. Within the low uniformity condition, we found significant effects of Stimulus Set × Target, $F(1, 86) = 14.16$, $p < .001$, and, more important, Context × Stimulus Set × Target, $F(1, 86) = 5.49$, $p = .02$; all remaining $Fs(1, 90) < 1$. In the high uniformity condition we found no significant effects, highest $F(1, 90) = 1.29$, *ns*.

[3] For willingness scores, we checked for effects within each uniformity condition. In the low uniformity condition, we found a marginally significant context effect, $F(1, 86) = 3.06$, $p = .08$, and, more important, a significant Context × Stimulus Set × Target interaction, $F(1, 86) = 6.31$, $p < .02$; highest remaining $F(1, 86) = 2.33$, *ns*. In the high uniformity condition we found no significant effects, highest $F(1, 86) = 2.48$, *ns*.

TABLE 9.3. Means and Standard Deviations of Willingness to Influence Normative and Deviant Targets as a Function of Context, Uniformity, and Stimulus Set (Experiment 2)

Target and statistic	Context			
	Interpersonal		Intragroup	
	Similar	Different	In-group	Out-group
High uniformity				
Normative				
M	2.15	1.64	2.00	1.62
SD	1.34	1.03	1.78	1.33
Deviant				
M	6.15	5.55	5.69	5.64
SD	1.14	1.97	1.75	1.20
Low uniformity				
Normative				
M	2.10	1.20	1.80	2.46
SD	1.66	0.42	1.32	1.56
Deviant				
M	5.30	5.22	5.90	4.31
SD	1.77	0.92	1.20	1.55

Note: Ratings were made on a scale ranging from 1 (*not willing*) to 7 (*willing*).

of interpersonal similarity between participants and targets on judgments can only be considered in the broader context of social categorization. These results thus match findings of classical research on small group processes. However, traditional research in small group dynamics assumes that derogation of group deviants depends on their interpersonal differences with majority members (e.g., Shaw, 1976). Our data indicate that individuals also derogate in-group deviants precisely because they see the deviants as in-group members and that this derogation occurs mainly when other in-group members show lack of uniformity. Moreover, evaluative derogation of these deviants arises in conjunction with greater willingness to persuade them to conform. This suggests that the motivation for derogation is actually part of an inclusive rather than an exclusive reaction. When group uniformity is low and group membership is salient, perceivers react negatively to in-group deviants and are motivated to persuade them to change their behavior. These results suggest that judgments of people who deviate from prescriptive norms ensue from group members' motivation to reinforce the legitimacy of the in-group's positive image, not by redefining in-group boundaries but rather by generating internal conformity to valued in-group standards.

Experiment 3

Our goal in Experiments 1 and 2 was to demonstrate that participants derogate deviant in-group members as a response to intragroup constraints, namely, when those deviant in-group members jeopardize the subjective validity of prescriptive norms that provide legitimacy for the in-group. In Experiment 3, we wanted to discover whether similar reactions emerge in the presence of validating and undermining factors external to the group. The procedure was similar to that of Experiment 2, but instead of manipulating the interpersonal versus intragroup context or normative members' uniformity, we manipulated the security of the validity of the in-group's position. Participants learned either that the in-group's ethical level was definitely superior to the out-group's (secure identity condition) or that there was a lot of uncertainty about which group was better (insecure identity condition). Participants then rated how positively normative and deviant members contributed to their group's image, evaluated the target members, and stated their willingness to persuade the targets to change their opinion. In line with the previous experiments, we expected participants in the insecure identity condition to judge normative and deviant in-group members to convey, respectively, a better and a worse image of their group than normative and deviant out-group members. We also expected them to, respectively, upgrade normative and derogate deviant in-group members, as compared with their out-group equivalents, and to be more motivated to exert persuasive pressures on deviant in-group members than on deviant out-group members.

Method

Participants. Fifty-eight female 2nd-year psychology students, aged 18 to 34 years old (*M* = 20.11), volunteered to participate in the experiment.

These students had no prior courses in social psychology.

Design. The design of the experiment was a 2 (group: in-group vs. out-group) × 2 (context: secure identity vs. insecure identity) × 2 (member: normative vs. deviant) structure. Group and context were between-subjects factors, and member was a within-subject factor. Participants were assigned randomly to condition.

Procedure. The "cover story" was the same as that of Experiment 2, with some exceptions. In the second session of the experiment, participants received their personal results and answered a series of questions tapping social identification and the manipulation checks. While ostensibly disclosing the study's goals to participants, the experimenter then informed them, "The study is designed to reveal which type of imagination is superior to the other in terms of ethical values." In the secure identity condition, the experimenter proceeded to inform participants that "the results in Session 1 were entirely clear and left no doubt about the ethical superiority of one type of imagination over the other" and that "the purpose of Session 2 is to confirm this result." In the insecure identity condition, the experimenter explained, "The results in Session 1 were totally ambiguous and did not allow the researchers to decide which type of imagination was superior to the other" and told the participants, "The purpose of Session 2 is to clarify the data we have so far." In both conditions, the experimenter showed an obscure data listing to participants as a justification for this claim. The experimenter then handed participants a folder containing their responses to the imagination test and the ethical survey as well as information about the perception category to which they belonged. All participants belonged to the same category, which was the superior one in the secure identity condition.

Participants were then given a new booklet, including bogus photocopies of the responses to the liberal–conservative continuum (as in Experiment 2) given by two target individuals who were ostensibly participants in the first session. These individuals were described either as in-group members or as out-group members. One target (normative member) adopted a norm validating position. This was, in fact, Statement 6, which was the one endorsed by almost all participants in Experiment 2. The other target (deviant member) adopted a norm undermining position (Statement 2). Participants were fully debriefed at the end of the experiment.

After being informed that they belonged to a particular type of perception and before they viewed information about the target members, participants answered the following four questions tapping group attraction, using a scale ranging from 1 (*not at all*) to 7 (*very much*): "How much do you like belonging to the Pictorial/Experiential type of imagination?" "How much do you feel that you belong to the Pictorial/Experiential type of imagination?" "How much do you identify with your Imagination Type?" and "How much do you like your Imagination Type?" We averaged these responses to create a group attraction score (Cronbach's $\alpha = .88$).

After completing these group attraction items and after the group and member manipulations, participants judged the normative and the deviant members on the following five bipolar dimensions to tap member attractiveness: "What is your opinion about this person?" ($1 = negative$; $7 = positive$), "In your opinion, this person is . . ." ($1 = unlikable$; $7 = likable$), "In your opinion, this is a . . ." ($1 = bad\ person$; $7 = good\ person$), "In your opinion, this person is a . . ." ($1 = bad\ colleague$; $7 = good\ colleague$), and "In your opinion, this person is . . ." ($1 = insensitive$; $7 = sensitive$). We pooled these judgments for each target to a create a normative member attractiveness score and a deviant member attractiveness score (Cronbach's $\alpha = .75$ and $.86$, respectively).

Participants were then asked what kind of image the target members conveyed of their group: "In your opinion, the image this person conveys about their Imagination Type is . . ." ($1 = very\ bad$; $7 = very\ good$). Finally, participants reported their willingness to influence the deviant member to adopt a more norm validating position: "In the third session, we will ask you to discuss ethical values with this person. How willing would you be to attempt to convince this person to change their opinion?" (1 = *not at all*; 7 = *very much*).

Results

Group attraction. Although group attraction measures were actually collected before the group and context manipulations, we submitted the group attraction score to an ANOVA with these two factors. As we expected, there were no significant effects, highest $F(1, 54) = 2.30$, *ns*. When we compared the mean of this score with the midpoint of the scale, we found that the difference was highly significant ($M = 5.34$), $t(57) = 11.75$, $p < .001$. Participants felt positive about their in-group, confirming that the group membership manipulation was meaningful and successful.

Member attractiveness. A Context × Group × Member ANOVA on normative and deviant member scores yielded significant effects of member, $F(1, 54) = 520.11$, $p < .001$, context, $F(1, 54) = 3.96$, $p = .05$, and Group 3 Member, $F(1, 54) = 4.12$, $p = .05$. More important and in support of our predictions, there was a significant effect of Context × Group × Member, $F(1, 54) = 4.49$, $p < .05$; highest remaining $Fs(1, 54) = 1.75$, *ns*. In the secure identity condition the Group × Member interaction was not significant, $F(1, 55) < 1$. However, in the insecure identity condition the same interaction was significant, $F(1, 55) = 8.24$, $p = .006$. As predicted, in this condition participants judged the normative in-group member more favorably than the normative out-group member, $F(1, 55) = 5.65$, $p = .02$, and derogated the deviant in-group member, as compared with the deviant out-group member, $F(1, 55) = 5.02$, $p = .03$ (see Table 9.4).

Image conveyed by the normative and deviant members. A Context × Group × Member ANOVA yielded significant effects of group, $F(1, 54) = 5.09$, $p < .05$, member, $F(1, 54) = 313.43$, $p < .001$, and Group × Member, $F(1, 54) = 4.99$, $p = .05$. These effects were qualified by a significant Context × Group × Member effect, $F(1, 54) = 10.13$, $p = .002$. Consistent with the results

TABLE 9.4. Means and Standard Deviations of Attractiveness Ratings of Normative and Deviant Members as a Function of Intergroup Context and Group Membership (Experiment 3)

| | Context | | | |
| | Secure identity | | Insecure identity | |
Member type and statistic	In-group	Out-group	In-group	Out-group
Normative				
M	5.97	5.73	6.56	5.97
SD	0.57	0.83	0.42	0.59
Deviant				
M	2.72	2.45	2.29	2.96
SD	0.95	0.79	0.51	0.87

Note: Ratings were made on a scale ranging from 1 (*nonattractive*) to 7 (*attractive*).

obtained in Experiment 1 and in parallel with results for target attractiveness, in the secure identity condition we found no significant Group × Member effect, $F(1, 55) < 1$. However, in the insecure identity condition the Group × Member effect was highly significant, $F(1, 55) = 13.79$, $p < .001$. In support of our hypothesis, in this condition participants considered that the normative in-group member conveyed a better image of the in-group ($M = 6.71$) than the normative out-group member conveyed of the out-group ($M = 5.28$), $F(1, 55) = 14.53$, $p < .001$. Conversely, participants considered the deviant in-group member to convey a worse image of the in-group ($M = 1.50$) than the deviant out-group member conveyed of the out-group ($M = 2.36$), $F(1, 55) = 4.53$, $p = .04$.

Willingness to influence the deviant member. A Context × Group ANOVA revealed a significant two-way interaction, $F(1, 54) = 6.66$, $p = .01$, highest remaining $F(1, 54) = 1.84$, *ns*. In the secure identity condition, participants were equally willing to exert influence on the deviant in-group member ($M = 5.60$) as on the deviant out-group member ($M = 6.00$), $F(1, 55) < 1$. However, in the insecure identity condition, participants were significantly more willing to influence the deviant in-group member ($M = 6.79$) than the deviant out-group member ($M = 5.50$), $F(1, 55) = 7.47$, $p < .01$. This result is consistent with those of Experiment 2 and supports our hypothesis.

General Discussion

The present results support our hypotheses and are consistent with the idea that intergroup and intragroup differentiation processes may function together as a means of sustaining individuals' sense of the subjective validity of in-group norms. Experiments 1 and 2 suggested that one factor underlying upgrading of normative in-group members and derogation of deviant in-group members is other members' lack of support of the norms that legitimate the in-group's positive image. Our results suggest that in these situations individuals are motivated to find ways to ensure that in-group deviants adhere to valued in-group norms in a way analogous to that observed in face-to-face groups. Specifically, when the in-group norm is in doubt or undermined, group members make sharper distinctions between normative and deviant members and seek to restore consensual support for the prescriptive norm. In addition, Experiment 2 shows that normative and deviant individuals are more upgraded or more derogated, respectively, when they are defined in intragroup rather than interpersonal terms. Experiment 3, in turn, shows that deviant in-group members are derogated more and normative in-group members are upgraded more when the image of their group as a whole is at stake. Experiments 2 and 3 together indicate that individuals are motivated to try to persuade deviant in-group, but not deviant out-group, members to change their opinion, suggesting that their reaction to in-group deviants is part of an inclusive rather than an exclusive attitude toward in-group deviants (cf. Levine & Thompson, 1996).

Our results are consistent with the operation of subjective group dynamics. Specifically, our model of subjective group dynamics establishes a parallel between reactions to deviants in face-to-face small groups and evaluations of normative and deviant in-group category members, as compared with out-group members in categorical groups. Our model was developed within the broad framework of the social identification approach, which takes as a starting point the cognitive differentiation between social categories (Hogg & Abrams, 1988; Tajfel & Turner, 1979). However, the subjective group dynamics model explicitly focuses on the function of norms as a basis for the perceived validity and legitimacy of the in-group's, and hence the perceiver's, perspective on social phenomena.

The basic idea is that perceptual intergroup differentiation is accompanied by intragroup differentiation that focuses on norms that legitimate individuals' beliefs about positive in-group distinctiveness (Abrams et al., 2000; Marques, Abrams, et al., 1998). These norms anchor judgments of what individuals believe ought to be consistent with in-group membership (cf. Cialdini et al., 1991; Cialdini & Trost, 1998). This process applies to situations such as those typically examined by research on the social identity framework, in which there is perceptual interchangeability between the self and the in-group prototype. Often, in such situations, individuals cannot or do not wish to recategorize deviants as members of another group (e.g., when groups are defined by race, ethnicity, or gender, or when group solidarity is a highly valued group norm). In derogating in-group deviants, normative members may not be simply expressing dislike for these deviants, but, more important, they may be attempting to sustain the correctness of their beliefs about the in-group's superiority and, by the same token, their sense of self-worth both by enchancing their social self-concept and by gaining approval from normative in-group members (cf. also Insko et al., 1983, 1985; Marques, Abrams, et al., 1998).

The present studies extend our analysis by considering how intergroup contexts affect reactions to deviance in terms of widespread or generic prescriptive norms. Unlike situations in which in-group and out-group norms are opposed, generic norms are shared, and thus if subjective group dynamics merely entailed a cognitive generalization of small group processes, we should have found that both in-group and out-group deviants were derogated. Instead, consistent with the idea that in-group validity is at stake, participants were primarily concerned with establishing in-group uniformity in support of generic norms and were less concerned when out-group members deviated from those norms.

Our findings also are consistent with the idea that intergroup differentiation increases individuals' focus on the implications of prescriptive norms for intragroup relations. This was the case when salient in-group members disrupted a valued norm (Experiment 1), when normative in-group members lacked consensus in support of the normative position (Experiment 2), and when the group's image was threatened by a potentially superior out-group (Experiment 3). Our data support the subjective group dynamics prediction that derogation of in-group deviants may be part of a response that aims to sustain a positive image of the in-group. First, by derogating their deviants, in-group members are able to assert their own endorsement of the in-group norm and in-group identity (cf. Marques, Abrams, et al., 1998, Experiment 2). Second, by expressing willingness to persuade these deviants to adopt the normative in-group position, in-group members reveal their motivation to restore the sense that the norm is valid.

The preceding idea is consistent with other research showing that individuals perceptually increase in-group homogeneity when the in-group is threatened, either by a dominated or minority status (Ellemers, Spears, & Doosje, 1997; Lorenzi-Cioldi, Eagly, & Stewart, 1995; Simon & Hamilton, 1994) or by a malevolent out-group (Rothberger, 1997) or external negative beliefs (Iwoo, 1963; Lee & Ottati, 1995). In addition, when group goals involve important values, when there is a high degree of similarity between group members, or when the group must reach consensus quickly, in-group deviance appears particularly aversive for modal members (e.g., Berkowitz & Howard, 1959; Earle, 1986; Festinger & Thibaut, 1951; Goethals & Nelson, 1973; Janis, 1982; Schachter, Ellerston, McBride, & Gregory, 1951; Wiggins, Dill, & Schwartz, 1965). Taken together, this evidence suggests that attempts to reinforce in-group consensus, both in terms of the cognitive bolstering of in-group homogeneity and in terms of normative reactions to deviants, serves to reinforce the subjective validity of in-group norms and social identity. Moreover, when considering prescriptive generic norms, group members are more concerned with ensuring that these norms

are associated with their own group than with others, thereby laying claim to greater legitimacy in the social order.

REFERENCES

Abrams, D., Marques, J. M., Bown, N. J., & Henson, M. (2000). Pro-norm and anti-norm deviance. *Journal of Personality and Social Psychology, 78*, 906–912.

Abrams, D., Wetherell, M., Cochrane, S., Hogg, M. A., & Turner, J. C. (1990). Knowing what to think by knowing who you are: Self-categorization and the nature of norm formation, conformity and group polarization. *British Journal of Social Psychology, 29*, 97–119.

Ben-Yehuda, N. (1980). The European witch craze of the 14th to the 17th centuries: A sociologist's perspective. *American Journal of Sociology, 85*, 1–31.

Berkowitz, L., & Howard, R. (1959). Reaction to opinion deviates as affected by affiliation need and group member interdependence. *Sociometry, 22*, 81–91.

Boyanowsky, E., & Allen, V. (1973). In-group norms and self-identity as determinants of discriminatory behavior. *Journal of Personality and Social Psychology, 25*, 408–418.

Branscombe, N. R., Wann, D. L., Noel, J. G., & Coleman, J. (1993). In-group or out-group extremity: Importance of the threatened social identity. *Personality and Social Psychology Bulletin, 19*, 381–388.

Brewer, M. B. (1979). Ingroup bias in the minimal intergroup situation: A cognitive–motivational analysis. *Psychological Bulletin, 86*, 307–324.

Burnstein, E., & Vinokur, A. (1975). What a person thinks upon learning he has chosen differently from others: Nice evidence for the persuasive arguments explanation of choice shifts. *Journal of Experimental Social Psychology, 11*, 412–426.

Cartwright, D., & Zander, A. (1968). *Group dynamics.* London: Tavistock.

Cialdini, R. B., Kallgren, C. A., & Reno, R. R. (1991). A focus theory of normative conduct: A theoretical refinement and reevaluation of the role of norms in human behavior. In L. Berkowitz (Ed.), *Advances in experimental social psychology* (Vol. 24, pp. 201–234). San Diego, CA: Academic Press.

Cialdini, R. B., & Trost, M. R. (1998). Social influence: Norms, conformity, and compliance. In D. T. Gilbert, S. T. Fiske, & G. Lindzey (Eds.), *The handbook of social psychology* (Vol. 2, pp. 151–192). Boston: McGraw-Hill.

Cota, A. A., Evans, C. R., Dion, K. L., Kilik, L., & Stewart-Longman, R. (1995). The structure of group cohesion. *Personality and Social Psychology Bulletin, 21*, 572–580.

Deutsch, M., & Gerard, H. B. (1955). A study of normative and informational influences upon individual judgment. *Journal of Abnormal and Social Psychology, 51*, 629–636.

Durkheim, E. (1960). *The division of labor in society.* Glencoe, IL: Free Press.

Earle, W. B. (1986). The social context of social comparison: Reality versus reassurance. *Personality and Social Psychology Bulletin, 12*, 159–168.

Ellemers, N., Spears, R., & Doosje, B. (1997). Sticking together or falling apart: In-group identification as a psychological determinant of group commitment versus individual mobility. *Journal of Personality and Social Psychology, 72*, 617–626.

Erikson, K. (1966). *Wayward Puritans*. New York: Wiley.

Festinger, L. (1950). Informal social communication. *Psychological Review, 57*, 271–282.

Festinger, L., Schachter, S., & Back, K. (1950). *Social pressures in informal groups: A study of human factors in housing*. New York: Harper & Row.

Festinger, L., & Thibaut, J. (1951). Interpersonal communications in small groups. *Journal of Abnormal and Social Psychology, 46*, 92–100.

Forsyth, D. R. (1990). *Group dynamic*. Pacific Grove, CA: Brookes/Cole.

Goethals, G. R., & Nelson, R. E. (1973). Similarity in the influence process: The belief–value distinction. *Journal of Personality and Social Psychology, 25*, 117–122.

Hogg, M. A. (1992). *The social psychology of group cohesiveness: From attraction to social identity*. Hemel Hempstead: Harvester Wheatsheaf.

Hogg, M. A. (1996). Intragroup processes, group structure and group identity. In W. P. Robinson (Ed.), *Developing the legacy of Henri Tajfel* (pp. 65–93). Bodmin, England: Butterworth Heinemann.

Hogg, M. A., & Abrams, D. (1988). *Social identifications: A social psychology of intergroup relations*. New York: Routledge, Chapman & Hall.

Hogg, M. A., & Hains, S. C. (1996). Intergroup relations and group solidarity: Effects of group identification and social beliefs on depersonalized attraction. *Journal of Personality and Social Psychology, 70*, 295–309.

Hogg, M. A., Hardie, E. A., & Reynolds, K. J. (1995). Prototypical similarity, self-categorization, and depersonalized attraction: A perspective on group cohesiveness. *European Journal of Social Psychology, 25*, 159–177.

Insko, C. A., Drenan, S., Solomon, M. R., Smith, R., & Wade, T. (1983). Conformity as a function of the consistency of positive self-evaluation with being liked and being right. *Journal of Experimental Social Psychology, 19*, 341–358.

Insko, C. A., Smith, R. H., Alicke, M. D., Wade, J., & Taylor, S. (1985). Conformity and group size: The concern with being right and the concern with being liked. *Personality and Social Psychology Bulletin, 11*, 41–50.

Inverarity, J. (1976). Populism and lynching in Louisiana 1889–1896: A test of Erikson's theory of the relationship between boundary crises and repressive justice. *American Sociological Review, 41*, 262–280.

Iwoo, S. (1963). Internal versus external criticism of group standards. *Sociometry, 26*, 410–421.

Janis, I. L. (1982). *Groupthink: Psychological studies of policy-decisions and fiascoes* (2nd ed.). Boston: Houghton-Mifflin.

Jetten, J., Spears, R., & Manstead, A. S. R. (1996). Intergroup norms and intergroup discrimination: Distinctive self-categorization and social identity. *Journal of Personality and Social Psychology, 71*, 1222–1233.

Jones, E. E., & DeCharms, R. (1957). Changes in social perception as a function of the personal relevance of behavior. *Sociometry, 20*, 175–185.

Kelley, E. E., & Volkart, E. H. (1962). The resistance to change of group anchored attitudes. *American Sociological Review, 17*, 453–465.

Lee, Y. T., & Ottati, V. (1995). Perceived in-group homogeneity as a function of group membership salience and stereotype threat. *Personality and Social Psychology Bulletin, 21*, 610–619.

Levine, J. M. (1989). Reaction to opinion deviance in small groups. In P. B. Paulus (Ed.), *Psychology of group influence* (2nd ed., pp. 187–231). Hillsdale, NJ: Erlbaum.

Levine, J. M., & Thompson, L. (1996). Conflict in groups. In E. T. Higgins & A. W. Kruglanski (Eds.), *Social psychology: Handbook of basic principles* (pp. 745–776). New York: Guilford Press.

Lorenzi-Cioldi, F., Eagly, A. H., & Stewart, L. (1995). Homogeneity of gender groups in memory. *Journal of Experimental Social Psychology, 31*, 193–217.

Lott, A. J., & Lott, B. E. (1965). Group cohesiveness as interpersonal attraction. *Psychological Bulletin, 64*, 259–309.

Marques, J. M. (1990). The black sheep effect: Out-group homogeneity in social comparison settings. In D. Abrams & M. A. Hogg (Eds.), *Social identity theory: Constructive and critical advances* (pp. 131–151). London: Harvester Wheatsheaf.

Marques, J. M., Abrams, D., Paez, D., & Hogg, M. A. (2001). Social categorization, social identification, and rejection of deviant group members. In M. A. Hogg & R. S. Tindale (Eds.), *Blackwell handbook of social psychology (Vol. 3): Group processes* (pp. 400–424). Oxford, England: Blackwell.

Marques, J. M., Abrams, D., Paez, D., & Martinez-Taboada, C. (1998). The role of categorization and in-group norms in judgments of groups and their members. *Journal of Personality and Social Psychology, 75*, 976–988.

Marques, J. M., & Paez, D. (1994). The black sheep effect: Social categorisation, rejection of ingroup deviates, and perception of group variability. In W. Stroebe & M. Hewstone (Eds.), *European review of social psychology* (Vol. 5, pp. 37–68). Chichester, England: Wiley.

Marques, J., Paez, D., & Abrams, D. (1998). Social identity and intragroup differentiation as subjective social control. In S. Worchel, J. F. Morales, D. Paez, & J.-C. Deschamps (Eds.), *Social identity: International perspectives* (pp. 124–141). New York: Sage.

Marques, J. M., Robalo, E. M., & Rocha, S. A. (1992). Ingroup bias and the black sheep effect: Assessing the impact of cognitive–motivational and informational antecedents of judgemental extremity towards ingroup members. *European Journal of Social Psychology, 22*, 331–352.

Marques, J. M., & Yzerbyt, V. Y. (1988). The black sheep effect: Judgemental extremity towards ingroup members in inter- and intra-group situations. *European Journal of Social Psychology, 18,* 287–292.

Marques, J. M., Yzerbyt, V. Y., & Leyens, J.-P. (1988). The black sheep effect: Judgmental extremity towards ingroup members as a function of group identification. *European Journal of Social Psychology, 18,* 1–16.

Oakes, P. J., Haslam, S. A., & Turner, J. C. (1994). *Stereotyping and social reality.* Oxford, England: Blackwell.

Prentice, D. A., Miller, D. T., & Lightdale, J. R. (1994). Asymmetries in attachments to groups and their members: Distinguishing between common-identity and common-bond groups. *Personality and Social Psychology Bulletin, 20,* 484–493.

Rokeach, M., Toch, H. H., & Rottman, T. (1960). The effect of threat on the dogmatization of Catholicism. In M. Rockeach (Ed.), *The open and closed mind: Investigations into the nature of belief systems and personality systems* (pp. 376–388). New York: Basic Books.

Rothberger, H. (1997). External intergroup threat as an antecedent to perceptions of in-group and out-group homogeneity. *Journal of Personality and Social Psychology, 73,* 1206–1212.

Schachter, S. (1961). Deviation, rejection and communication. *Journal of Abnormal and Social Psychology, 46,* 190–207.

Schachter, S., Ellerston, N., McBride, D., & Gregory, D. (1951). An experimental study of cohesiveness and productivity. *Human Relations, 4,* 229–238.

Shaw, M. E. (1976). *Group dynamics: The psychology of small group behavior* (2nd ed.). New York: McGraw-Hill.

Simon, B., & Hamilton, D. L. (1994). Self-stereotyping and social context: The effects of relative ingroup size and ingroup status. *Journal of Personality and Social Psychology, 66,* 699–711.

Tajfel, H. (1978). *Differentiation between social groups: Studies in the social psychology of intergroup relations.* London: Academic Press.

Tajfel, H., & Turner, J. C. (1979). An integrative theory of intergroup conflict. In W. Austin & S. Worchel (Eds.), *The social psychology of intergroup relations* (pp. 33–47). Monterey, CA: Brooks/Cole.

Turner, J. C. (1991). *Social influence.* Milton Keynes, England: Open University Press.

Turner, J. C., Hogg, M. A., Oakes, P. J., Reicher, S. D., & Wetherell, M. (1987). *Rediscovering the social group: A self-categorization theory.* Oxford, England: Blackwell.

Wiggins, J. A., Dill, F., & Schwartz, R. D. (1965). On "status liability." *Sociometry, 28,* 197–209.

Wilder, D., & Simon, A. F. (1998). Categorical and dynamic groups: Implications for social perception and intergroup behavior. In C. Sedikides, J. Schopler, & C. A. Insko (Eds.), *Intergroup cognition and intergroup behavior* (pp. 27–44). Mahwah, NJ: Erlbaum.

Received December 29, 2000
Revision received February 8, 2001
Accepted February 13, 2001 ■

Does Power Corrupt?[1]

David Kipnis[2]

How control of institutional powers influenced self-esteem and esteem for others was experimentally examined in a simulated organizational setting. It was found that the control of power caused subjects to (*a*) increase their attempts to influence the behavior of the less powerful, (*b*) devalue the worth of the performance of the less powerful, (*c*) attribute the cause of the less powerful's efforts to power controlled by themselves, rather than to the less powerful's motivations to do well, (*d*) view the less powerful as objects of manipulation, and (*e*) express a preference for the maintenance of psychological distance from the less powerful. No support was found for the prediction that the control of power would elevate self-esteem. The findings are discussed in terms of recent writings concerned with the disruptive influences of inequities in power.

There has been very little research in psychology concerned with how the control of power may influence the power holder's views of both himself and the less powerful. Much of the writing in political science and philosophy, however, contain pertinent and suggestive information related to this question. This information indicates that persons who control economic and political power are viewed with mixed emotions. On the one hand, there is admiration for their ability to amass great power and admiration at times for the ways in which this great power is used to influence society.

On the other hand, there is profound suspicion that these power holders, no matter what their original motives, will use their resources to exploit others and to further enrich themselves. This suspicion of the corrupting influence of power has been voiced by political scientists for many centuries. There is fear that power, once consolidated, becomes used for despotic ends. Indeed Hobbes, in *Leviathan* (1968), maintained that men formed societies as a means of limiting the exploitative consequence of the unequal division of power. The system of checks and balances and the separation of powers between

[1] This research was supported by a small grant from the Trustees Fund of Temple University.

[2] My thanks to Mitchel Anderman, who actively assisted in all phases of the study from planning to data analysis. Requests for reprints should be sent to David Kipnis, Department of Psychology, Temple University, Philadelphia, Pennsylvania 19122.

the executive, legislative, and judicial departments contained in the American Constitution are based on the same fears of the consequence of excessive power. Underlying these fears is the assumption that human nature is mean and self-serving. For instance, in one of the The Federalist papers written by James Madison, it is stated that all men are "ambitious," "vindictive," and "rapacious," whose access to power had to be limited.

While earlier writers were in fair agreement about the consequences of the control of power, the writings of modern social scientists reflect ambivalent feelings. In fact, these writers reveal a remarkable divergence of opinions concerning the possible corrupting influence of power. Cartwright and Zander (1968), for instance, suggest that the burdens and responsibilities of power may produce compassionate, rather than exploitive, behavior in the power holder. Adolph Berle (1967) has also suggested that the control of power may produce similar beneficial changes, at least in some individuals. From this view, one might say that power ennobles the individual by broadening and deepening his understanding of himself and others.

Lasswell (e.g., Rogow & Lasswell, 1963) adopted a more neutral stand and maintained that the control of power neither leads to corruption or to ennoblement. Rather, the connection between power and corruption depends on various combinations of individual ego needs and the type of social organization of which the individual is a member. Based on a variety of studies of political leaders, Lasswell has concluded that the kind of deprivations experienced by these politicians as children determine how they will use power as adults. Thus, some politicians, because of economic deprivations, use their offices to enrich themselves and their families. Other politicians use their offices to obtain admiration and love from others by granting favors in return for flattery. These latter politicians are deprived of affection as children. Finally, Lasswell also specifically considered organizational context, in that he sees some political organizations, which by reason of their traditions, reputations, and leadership, such as state legislatures, as encouraging corrupt behaviors, while other institutions, such as the Supreme Court, as discouraging corrupt behavior.

There are other social scientists who flatly state that the very control of power induces individuals to act in an inequitable and exploitive manner toward the less powerful (Haroutunian, 1949; Sampson, 1965; Sorokin & Lundin, 1959). The well-known observation of Lord Acton that "power tends to corrupt and absolute power corrupts absolutely" clearly reflects this point of view. These latter theorists view the corrupting influence of power in one of two ways. The first refers to the belief that those who hold power tend to value it above all other values, and restlessly pursue additional power throughout their lives. The corruption refers here to the fact that power becomes an end in itself and replaces more Christian values of love, charity, compassion, and the like.[3]

The second meaning of corruption refers to behavior in office that is motivated by a desire for personal gain. Power is corrupting in this context because it provides the power holder with maximum temptation and the opportunity to line his pocket. Power in this second usage is only a means to an end, rather than an end in itself.

Corruption can also refer to the way in which the control of power changes the power holder's self-perceptions and his perceptions of others. Sorokin and Lundin (1959), in a review of the behavior and attributes of individuals controlling political and economic power, suggested that power holders develop an exalted and vain view of their own worth which inhibits compassion for others. Interestingly enough, power holders frequently believe themselves exempt from common morality. This view has come down through history in several forms. Machiavelli, for instance, argued that it is necessary for a prince to learn how not to be good. A recent study of business executives (cited in Sorokin & Lundin, 1959) similarly found them leading a double life with reference to morality—having one set of moral values for the office and a

[3] This view may be placed in the context of modern learning theory by assuming that the control of institutional power allows the individual to gratify appetitive needs more readily. This is because control of power allows the individual to allot to himself more of those things that do indeed provide satisfaction. Because of these need reduction properties inherent in the control of power, it follows that individuals should learn to value it.

second for the home. Sorokin believes that the very possession of vast power tends to demoralize the power holder.

These changes in self-regard appear to occur for several reasons that are of concern to psychologists. First, the power holder finds that he is able to influence others because of the power he controls. Such compliance may lead the power holder to believe that his ideas and views are superior to other persons. Second, the power holder tends to be the recipient of flattery and well-wishes from the less powerful. This flattery may also contribute to the idea that he is something special. Finally, it may be that the control of resources demands that the individual adopt a morality consistent with the kinds of power he controls. For instance, Galbraith (1967) has said that managers in large corporations are practically forced to make decisions which minimize risks to corporate investments, despite the fact that these decisions violate laws and the general welfare of the public. Thus, the morality that develops is designed to protect and extend corporate power and resources. Berle (1967) has also noted that the control of institutional power frequently obliges the power holder to ignore conventional morality. In essence, this view suggests that to understand the behavior of officeholders, one must examine the kinds of powers they control and the involvement of the individual in his office, rather than examining personal beliefs and attributes.

Corruption also refers to the fact that the power holder is seen as devaluing the worth of the less powerful and acting to increase social distance from them. The literature suggests several reasons for this. First of all, the power holder may believe that the behavior of the less powerful is not completely autonomous, but is, in part, caused by the power holder's suggestions and orders. As a result, the less powerful are not given full credit for their own performances. In essence, the locus of control is seen to reside in the power holder who attributes causality for change to himself. Raven and Kruglanski (1970) have proposed a similar explanation to this view in a recent review article. Second, as Fiedler (1967) has noted, it is easier to influence others if psychological distance is maintained and emotional involvement is kept to a minimum. This

is especially true if the power holder believes it likely that he will order the less powerful to carry out behaviors that are distasteful. To the extent that the power holder feels sympathy for the position of the less powerful, he may not want to issue these orders.

Because of these tendencies to devalue others and to maintain psychological distance, most writers believe that the control of power precludes the possibility of harmonious interpersonal relations. According to Sampson, inequity in power inevitably produces dominance, manipulation, and precludes the possibility of truly loving relations. He further states that it is impossible for any human relationship to avoid distortion to the extent that power enters into it. "At a minimum," according to Sampson (1965), "the deference and compliance shown by the less powerful is seen by the latter as a sign of weakness, if not servility [p. 233]." Studies of conflict resolution (Deutsch, 1969; Deutsch & Krauss, 1960; Swingle, 1970; Tedeschi, 1970) also reveal that the introduction of either unilateral or bilateral power of a coercive kind into the bargaining process markedly reduces chances that conflicts can be amiably negotiated. Furthermore, these latter studies suggest that once coercion and threats are introduced into the process of negotiation, psychological reactance (Brehm, 1966) and resistance to influence (Raven & Kruglanski, 1970) tend to be evoked within the target of influence.

The present study is one of a series of field (Kipnis & Cosentino, 1969; Kipnis & Lane, 1962) and laboratory (Goodstadt & Kipnis, 1970; Kipnis & Vanderveer, 1971) studies that have examined how power holders use the resources they control and what influences this usage. In this study, it is proposed to study how the control of power influences self-perception and the perceptions of others. Based on what has been said above, it is predicted that the control of delegated power will elevate an individual's self-esteem, lower the power holder's esteem for the less powerful, and influence the power holder to maintain greater psychological distance from the less powerful. Thus, the corrupting influence of power in the last sense that this term was used, is being investigated, that is, in terms of providing false feedback to the individual concerning his own worth and in terms of disrupting interpersonal harmony.

Method

The procedure was similar to the previous laboratory studies. Twenty-eight university juniors and seniors majoring in business were recruited to act as the manager in an industrial simulation experiment. At the laboratory, the subjects were informed they would supervise four Temple Technical High School students who were located in an adjacent building. This high school is located on campus and is for young adults. As an explanation for the separation of workers and managers, the subjects were told that in previous weeks, when both had been in the same room, personality clashes between managers and workers had interfered with the simulation of the business. Hence, we were attempting to minimize this factor by separating the groups. The subjects were told that they would not meet their workers. Actually, the workers were nonexistent, and their output was preprogrammed. The subjects were told they would be paid $2 and that the workers would receive a base rate of $1. In an attempt to increase motivation and interest, the subjects were also told that this industrial simulation had been shown to be a good test of executive ability. They were further told that their job was to operate the company at a profitable level by maintaining the efficiency of the workers.

Tasks

There were two products sold by the company and presumably produced by the workers: coded letters and crossed-out letters. The subjects were instructed that all of the workers would begin on the coding task, actually a digit-symbol substitution task. The crossing-out task served as a possible alternative duty for the workers. The subjects were informed that this second task made less money for the company and was also more boring for the workers.

Every 3 minutes the preprogrammed output from workers was carried in from the other room by an assistant. The subjects were told that the assistant's job was to give initial instructions to the workers in the other building, keep them supplied with raw materials, and bring the completed products to the subjects. Each worker's output was identified by his number (1, 2, 3, 4). The subjects tallied the output and recorded it on a summary sheet under each worker's number. They were told that standard production for the coding task was 85 coded letters per 3-minute period. They were also told that the more each worker completed beyond that point, the more money the company made, since labor costs were the main determinant of profits. The standard for the crossing-out task was 65. There were six trials of 3 minutes each; the subjects were not informed of this in advance.

A one-way communication device, consisting of a light signal for contacting a specific worker and a microphone, allowed the subjects to speak with their workers. The subjects were told that they could speak to only one worker at a time, who would put on a set of earphones on receiving a light signal. All of the subjects' conversations were recorded on tape. The trial in which the conversation took place and the worker spoken to was also noted by the experimenter. The subjects were told that workers could communicate with them by sending notes along with their work output. Actually, in this study, the only communication from the workers was at the end of the third work trial, when Worker 3 asked if he could smoke. Social influence was defined as the frequency with which subjects contacted their workers.

Experimental Conditions

The experimental manipulation of the study was very simple. Fourteen of the subjects were delegated a range of institutional powers with which to influence their workers, if they so chose. The remaining 14 subjects were not given control of these powers. The procedure was as follows: All subjects listened to tape-recorded instructions which described the business and their roles. Toward the end of the recording, half of the subjects were told that as managers they were authorized to use any of the following means in doing their job: They consisted of promising or actually awarding 10¢ pay increases per trial, threatening to transfer or actually transferring workers to another job (Cartwright, 1965, has called this the exercise of power through ecological control), giving workers additional instruction, threatening or actually deducting 10¢ per trial from a worker's pay, and threatening or actually firing a worker. In addition, a sign was posted in front of these subjects listing these options.

For the 14 subjects in the no-power condition, the portion of the taped instructions which described the above powers and the posted sign were omitted. As a result, the subjects in this condition could only rely on two bases of power when attempting to influence their workers—their legitimate power as appointed leader and their personal powers of persuasion.

At the conclusion of the study, all of the subjects were asked to complete a questionnaire that asked them to evaluate their workers' performances, their own performance, and the arrangement of the study. The specific questions asked will be given when presenting the appropriate results.

Performance of the Four Workers

In the present study, the production of all four workers exceeded minimum company standards and tended to rise erratically but steadily by one or two units per trial. Thus, from the subject's point of view, he was directing a group of workers who were making money for the company.

Experimental Manipulation Check

On the postexperimental questionnaire, the subjects were asked to rate on an 11-point scale whether they had enough authority. Using a median split on the distribution of responses, 64% of the subjects with power and 36% of the subjects without power were classified as stating they had enough authority ($\chi^2 = 2.2$, $df = 1$, ns). Perhaps if the subjects had encountered resistance from one of their workers, as was done in prior experiments, the subjects without power might have been more concerned about the amount of authority they held and the differences in response might have been

significant. There were also nonsignificant differences in the subjects' initial levels of self-confidence concerning their ability to act as managers, such that the subjects given power felt less confident. That is, after receiving instructions on their roles that included information on powers they controlled, the subjects rated their self-confidence to act as manager on an 11-point scale. Using a median split on these ratings, 64% of the subjects in the no-power condition and 36% of the subjects in the power condition were classified as being confident ($\chi^2 = 2.2$, $df = 1$, ns).

Results

The first question examined was whether the subjects with power attempted to influence their workers more frequently than those without power. While perhaps the answer to this question may appear obvious in the present context, it does not necessarily follow that the control of delegated power is perfectly correlated with attempts to exert influence. Mott (1970), for example, in discussing issues in the study of community power, has suggested that the amount of power possessed by community leaders is at best only a weak indicator of whether they will actually attempt to influence others. Further, it could be argued that merely appointing a person as a leader is sufficient to induce him to influence others, and that the possession of delegated powers is redundant. This could be especially true in the present study since all workers were performing at a satisfactory level and were improving.

Table 10.1 shows the average number of times that the subjects contacted their workers over the six trials, as a function of power. An analysis of variance of these data yielded a main effect for power ($F = 5.43$, $df = 1/26$, $p < .05$), indicating that the subjects with power attempted to influence their workers more frequently than those without power. While the interaction between trials and power was not significant ($F = 2.57$, $df = 2/52$), it can be seen in Table 10.1 that the difference in amount of influence attempted by those with and without power was steadily widening. In short, the

TABLE 10.1. Mean Frequency of Influence Attempts

Subjects	Blocks of trials			
	1–2	3–4	5–6	Total
With power	2.1	4.0	8.2	14.3
Without power	1.1	2.3	3.6	7.0

control of delegated power encouraged the exertion of influence. As can be imagined, the communications of those without power were limited to their persuasive powers (i.e., praising performance, goal setting, urging workers to try harder). Of interest was that very few subjects with power relied on personal persuasion. Out of 198 separate influence attempts made by the subjects with power, only 32 (16%) relied solely on persuasion. The remainder all included reliance on their delegated powers (i.e., promises of raises, threats of deductions, arranging of contests for money, etc.). These findings, then, support and extend Deutsch's belief (Deutsch, 1969; Deutsch & Krauss, 1960) that the availability of a punishing response encourages the use of such a response. The present study suggests that other bases of power, in addition to coercion, also tempt the power holder.

Control of Power and Self-Esteem

Four items on the postexperimental questionnaire asked the subjects to rate their own performances on four 11-point scales covering the (a) quality of their work, (b) their competence as manager, (c) their ability to make money for the company, and (d) their ability to make workers carry out their orders. In no instance did subjects with power evaluate themselves as more capable than those without power. It is possible that the lack of support for the prediction that control of power would raise self-esteem was due to the fact that the subjects received no flattering feedback from the less powerful and also received no direct feedback that their orders, in fact, changed the behavior of subordinates. As was discussed in the introduction, both of these conditions may be necessary for changes in self-regard.

Evaluation of Subordinates

The subjects were asked to evaluate each worker on four questions, each scaled from 1 to 11, covering (a) worker's ability; (b) worker's overall worth to the company; (c) willingness to rehire the worker for a second experiment; and (d) recommendation that the worker be promoted to manager in a future experiment. Because of the high intercorrelation between ratings, they were summed and then combined over all four workers to provide an overall appraisal of the workers by the subjects. Using a median split in the resulting distribution, it was found that, as predicted, the subjects with power devalued the worth of their workers. Seventy-two percent of the subjects without power and 28% of the subjects with power were classified as giving above median appraisal of their workers ($\chi^2 = 5.14$, $df = 1$, $p < .05$). Of interest was that in the power condition there was a negative correlation of $-.36$ ($p < .20$) between evaluation of worker's ability and frequency of influence during the first two work periods. This suggests that the more those with power attempted to influence their workers, the less they thought of their work. The corresponding correlation in the no-power condition was .21.

Psychological Distance

The subjects' preference for psychological distance from their workers was measured in two ways on the postexperimental questionnaire. First, the subjects used an 11-point scale to answer the following question: "Now that the work is over, would you like to meet the workers and talk with them while sharing a coke or cup of coffee?" As predicted, the subjects without power expressed a significantly greater willingness to meet socially with their workers than did those with power. Based on a median split (not exact because of skewed distributions), 79% of the subjects in the no-power condition and 35% of the subjects in the power condition expressed a preference to met socially with their workers ($\chi^2 = 5.25$, $df = 1$, $p < .05$).

Perhaps more revealing of the way in which the control of power influenced psychological distance was found in the responses to a second open-ended question. The subjects were asked: "What personal skills and abilities do you believe it takes to be successful as a manager in this study?" It was originally expected that the subjects without power would deny that any special skills were needed, while the subjects with power would elaborate all kinds of special skills as being important. This kind of a result would have supported the belief that the control of power induces individuals to overestimate the worth of their inputs into a given situation. In fact, five subjects without power and one subject with power wrote in that no special skills were needed. However, among the remaining subjects who described the kinds of skills needed, those with power appeared to stress skills that involved manipulating workers as a means of raising production, while those without power appeared to stress skills relating to keeping the worker happy. To test this impression, each subject's written comments were typed on a card. Four faculty members[4] were asked to rate each card, assigning a score from 1 to 10, on the extent to which the skills described showed concern for the worker as an individual as compared with concern for the worker as an object of manipulation. A low score reflected a concern for the worker as an individual. Although working independently, the four raters were in high agreement with each other. An analysis of variance analogue of the Spearman-Brown formula yielded a reliability of .86 for these ratings.

Sample comments rated as high on manipulative intent (combined scores of 21 or more) were: "You have to know how to influence the men to do more and do it better." "You have to know how to motivate the workers, even when they may not want to be." "You need quick judgment in order to answer questions: ability to determine how well the workers are working and if they are up to standard."

Sample comments rated as expressing concern for the worker as a person (combined scores of 20 or less) were: "You must have control, but not to the point where you would dominate the worker. You must also have gentleness so you won't offend the worker." "An easygoing, level-headed approach

---
[4] Thanks are due to Russell Eisenman, Phillip Hineline, Ralph Rosnow, and Rose Zacks.

TABLE 10.2. Subjects' Perceptions of Skills Needed to be a Success

Item	Subjects	
	With power	Without power
Manipulative abilities stressed (ratings of 21 or more)	10	3
Concern for workers stressed (ratings of 20 or less)	2	6
No special abilities needed	1	5
Total N	13	14

Note: —One subject in the power condition did not answer this question.

which praises the workers for their success and informs them when they have erred. A friendly participative approach I feel is important." "Ability to show confidence in the worker, encouragement, and allow them freedom to perform their jobs in their own way."

Table 10.2 shows the distribution of these ratings, trichotomized into those who expressed high manipulative intent, low manipulative intent, and those who stated that no skills were necessary. One subject in the power condition did not answer this question. It may be seen that 10 out of 13 subjects in the power condition and 3 out of 14 in the no-power condition felt that an important skill needed to be a success as a manager in the study was the ability to manipulate others. Both a chi-square test using all subjects and a chi-square test using only the subjects who directly answered the question (12 subjects in the power condition and 9 in the no-power condition) indicated that the subjects in the power condition expressed significantly more manipulative attitudes and showed less concern for their workers as individuals than the subjects in the no-power condition ($p < .05$).

Locus of Control

It was proposed that one possible reason as to why those with power should devalue the less powerful was the belief that these latter individuals' behavior was caused by the power holder's orders and influence. Thus, the less powerful person was not his own master. Hence, he was not given full credit for his performance. To test this proposal, the subjects were asked what motivated their workers: "To what extent do you believe each of the following influenced the amount of work done by your workers?" There were three alternatives: the workers own motivations to do well; your orders, instructions, and guidance; the workers desire to obtain their pay. Each of these three alternatives was rated using an 11-point scale, with a rating of 1 indicating no influence at all. This procedure allowed the subjects to indicate not only which of these three sources of motivation they considered most important, but also the relative importance of each.

Using median splits for each distribution of ratings, and chi-square for evaluating significance, it was found that 72% of the subjects without power and 28% of the subjects with power were classified as attributing the workers' efforts to the worker's own motivation to do well ($\chi^2 = 6.54$, $df = 1$, $p < .05$). Contrarily, more subjects with power than those without power attributed their workers' efforts to a desire to obtain their pay ($\chi^2 = 5.64$, $df = 1$, $p < .05$). There was no difference by experimental conditions in the extent to which the subjects attributed workers' efforts to the subject's own personal orders and guidance. Nine subjects in the power condition and one subject in the no-power condition rated the workers' desire for pay as the most important reason for the workers' efforts. Clearly then, the subjects with power viewed their workers as being controlled by the subject's power, that is, the subject's control of pay raises. The subjects with no power viewed their workers as free agents, whose efforts originated in the workers' own motivations to achieve.

This latter finding is perhaps another reason why the subjects with power did not evaluate their own performances more favorably than the subjects without power. Apparently the former subjects made a distinction between their own personal influence and the influence of the power they controlled. That is, those with power appeared to be saying: "I personally may not be overly effective, but the money I control makes those guys work hard." It is possible that over time this distinction becomes blurred. That is, as a person becomes more used to the control of power, he may be more likely to attribute its

consequences to himself, rather than viewing them as external forces that he controls. Data from a previous field study (Kipnis & Cosentino, 1969) revealed that appointed leaders go through a process of learning to use delegated powers.

Discussion

The findings are consistent with the views of Sampson (1965) and Sorokin and Lundin (1959) that inequity in power is disruptive of harmonious social relations and drastically limits the possibilities that the power holder can maintain close and friendly relations with the less powerful. First of all, power increases the likelihood that the individual will attempt to influence and manipulate others. Second, the control of power appears to facilitate the development of a cognitive and perceptual system which serves to justify the use of power. That is, the subjects with power thought less of their subordinates' performance, viewed them as objects of manipulation, and expressed the desire to maintain social distance from them. Interestingly enough, the more the subjects with power attempted to influence their workers, the less they wanted to meet them socially. The correlation between total amount of influence attempted and willingness to share a coke was $-.30$ (*ns*) in the power condition. A similar correlation in the no-power condition was .19. Within the power condition, this correlation rose to $-.51$ ($p < .06$) when the measure of influence was the number of pay raises awarded. In other words, the more the subjects dispensed pay raises, the less they were inclined to seek out the social company of their workers.

It is suggested that the control of power triggers a train of events, which, in theory at least, goes like this: (*a*) With the control of power goes increased temptations to influence others' behavior. (*b*) As actual influence attempts increase, there arises the belief that the behavior of others is not self-controlled, but is caused by the power holder,[5]

---

[5] The correlation between frequency of influence attempts and attributing the amount of work done by the workers to "my orders, instructions, and guidance" was .65 (p < .05) in the power condition and .39 in the no-power condition.

(*c*) hence, a devaluation of their performance. In addition, with increased influence attempts, forces are generated within the more powerful to (*d*) increase psychological distance from the less powerful and view them as objects of manipulation. The reason for this latter set of events is not completely clear. Perhaps as B. F. Skinner points out, Western man balks at information which sets limits on his conception of himself as an agent of free will. By extension, we may also desire to avoid those persons who appear not to be in control of their own behavior, and at some level feel contemptuous of them.

In any case, it is suggested that meaning, fact, and feelings become interpreted within the context of existing power relationships. Perhaps at a fundamental level it is necessary to invoke the concept of reciprocity, as described by Gouldner (1960) to explain this. By that, it is meant that because of a basic inequity in what the more powerful put into the situation and get out of it, as compared to the less powerful, it is necessary for the more powerful to restore cognitive balance by viewing the less powerful as less worthy, less interesting, and deserving of their fate.

The findings on the relation between control of resources and frequency of influence also suggests a link between two alternate views of power. The first view describes power in terms of the control of resources, which provide the power holder with the potential to influence others (e.g., Cartwright, 1965). Whether or not he will use these powers is another issue. The second view of power places greater emphasis on the exercise of power—as a process of forcing or persuading others to carry out some behavior they would otherwise not do (Bachrach, 1963; Dahl, 1957; Goldhammer & Shils, 1939). Those who view the exercise of power as a manifestation of personality also stress the manipulative aspects of interpersonal relations. For example, McClelland (1969) defines need for power as "concern about having influence over others [p. 143]." Yet clearly there is a difference between power defined as a dimension of social interaction, where the emphasis is on dominance and the manipulation of others, and power defined as the control of resources. The present study suggests a functional relationship between these two

definitions, in that the control of resources, in fact, tempts the power holder to manipulate others.

As a final point, it should be noted that the present study was concerned with a situation in which the power holder encountered no resistance to his influence. Relations between the more and less powerful were relatively stable. In a sense, the power holder incurred no "opportunity costs," to use Harsanyi's (1962) term. It is believed that the findings of this study would not extend to situations where the power holder's influence was being actively resisted. Counter resistance that appears successful forces those in power to restructure their views of the needs and capabilities of the less powerful. Protests by women, blacks, and students, among others, are present day instances of this process of restructuring more powerful individual's views of the less powerful.

REFERENCES

Bachrach, P. Decisions and non-decisions: An analytic framework. *American Political Science Review*, 1963, *57*, 632–642.

Berle, A. A. *Power*. New York: Harcourt, Brace & World, 1967.

Brehm, J. W. *A theory of psychological reactance*. New York: Academic Press, 1966.

Cartwright, D. Influence, leadership and control. In J. G. March (Ed.), *Handbook of organizations*. Chicago: Rand McNally, 1965.

Cartwright, D., & Zander, A. *Group dynamics*. (3rd ed.) New York: Harper, 1968.

Dahl, R. A. The concept of power. *Behavioral Science*, 1957, *2*, 201–215.

Deutsch, M. Conflicts: Productive and destructive. *Journal of Social Issues*, 1969, *25*, 7–42.

Deutsch, M., & Krauss, R. M. The effect of threat upon interpersonal bargaining. *Journal of Abnormal and Social Psychology*, 1960, *61*, 181–189.

Fiedler, R. E. *A theory of leadership effectiveness*. New York: McGraw-Hill, 1967.

Galbraith, J. K. *The new industrial state*. Boston: Houghton Mifflin, 1967.

Goldhammer, H., & Shils, E. Types of power and status. *American Journal of Sociology*, 1939, *54*, 2–5.

Goodstadt, B., & Kipnis, D. Situational influences on the use of power. *Journal of Applied Psychology*, 1970, *54*, 201–207.

Gouldner, A. W. The norm of reciprocity: A preliminary statement. *American Sociological Review*, 1960, *25*, 161–179.

Haroutunian, J. *Lust for power*. New York: Scribner, 1949.

Harsanyi, J. C. Measurement of social power, opportunity costs, and the theory of two-person bargaining games. *Behavioral Science*, 1962, *7*, 67–79.

Hobbes, T. *Leviathan*. Middlesex, England: Penguin Books, 1968.

Kipnis, D., & Cosentino, J. Use of leadership powers in industry. *Journal of Applied Psychology*, 1969, *53*, 460–466.

Kipnis, D., & Lane, W. Self-confidence and leadership. *Journal of Applied Psychology*, 1962, *46*, 291–295.

Kipnis, D., & Vanderveer, R. Ingratiation and the use of power. *Journal of Personality and Social Psychology*, 1971, *17*, 280–286.

McClelland, D. C. The two faces of power. *Journal of International Affairs*, 1969, *24*, 141–154.

Mott, P. E. Power, authority, and influence. In M. Aiken & P. E. Mott (Eds.), *The structure of community power*. New York: Random House, 1970.

Raven, B. H., & Kruglanski, A. W. Conflict and power. In Paul Swingle (Ed.), *The structure of conflict*. New York: Academic Press, 1970.

Rogow, A. A., & Lasswell, H. D. *Power, corruption and rectitude*. Englewood Cliffs, N.J.: Prentice-Hall, 1963.

Sampson, R. V. *Equality and power*. London: Heinemann, 1965.

Sorokin, P. A., & Lundin, W. A. Power and morality: *Who shall guard the guardians?* Boston: Sargent, 1959.

Swingle, P. G. Dangerous games. In Paul Swingle (Ed.), *The structure of conflict*. New York: Academic Press, 1970.

Tedeschi, J. T. Threats and promises. In Paul Swingle (Ed.), *The structure of conflict*. New York: Academic Press, 1970.

Received July 26, 1971 ■

PART 4

Group Performance

Theory and research on conflict emphasize the competitive side of group life and the strategies that members use to reconcile divergent interests and opinions. But group life involves more than competition—members also cooperate to achieve common goals. These goals, and the belief that they can only be attained through cooperative efforts, are often what lead people to join groups in the first place and keep them there despite the inevitable conflicts that arise.

In this section, we focus on group performance, defined as the process and outcome of members' efforts to create a joint product in which they all have a stake. The organizations on which society depends (e.g., business, military, religious) are composed of many groups, whose performance strongly influences organizational effectiveness. For this reason, there is widespread interest in the processes underlying group performance and the factors that cause some groups to succeed and others to fail. This interest has stimulated a great deal of theoretical and empirical work on group performance. Three major lines of research are discussed in this section, namely how group members make collective decisions, how groups motivate their members to work hard and coordinate their actions, and how leaders organize and direct group activities and thereby influence group performance.

PART 4A

Decision Making

One of the most important activities that groups perform is making decisions. Groups seek consensus on such diverse issues as whether a criminal defendant is guilty or innocent, a particular advertising campaign will sell a new brand of toothpaste, additional resources should be devoted to recruiting minority college students, and so on. Although decision making is a cooperative activity, in that group members want to reach agreement on an issue, it can involve elements of competition as well. This might happen, for example, if members have different views about the issue and a history of conflict regarding it.

Most organizations entrust their critical decisions to small groups, rather than individuals. Why? One reason is the belief that groups make better decisions than do individuals, because groups have more problem-relevant expertise and group discussion allows members to pool that expertise. Another reason is the assumption that group decisions are fairer because the biases of different members cancel out one another. Finally, a third reason is the belief that decisions reached collectively elicit more support and thus are easier to implement. As we shall see, however, the trust placed in groups as decision makers is often misplaced.

Group decision making has been analyzed from several theoretical perspectives (Stasser & Dietz-Uhler, 2001). Two of the most important are the social combination approach and the social influence approach. The *social combination* approach focuses on the relationship between the initial preferences of group members and the group's final decision. Researchers have identified several simple rules, called "social decision schemes," that can predict a group's final decision from the initial distribution of its members' preferences (Laughlin & Ellis, 1986). For example, the "majority wins" rule is generally used on judgmental tasks, which lack demonstrably correct answers, such as whether Klee or Kandinsky is the better artist. In contrast, other decision rules are generally used on intellective tasks, which do have such answers. When the correct answer is obvious once someone points it out, the dominant group decision rule is "truth wins," where the group adopts a correct solution if it is advocated by even a single member. When the correct answer is not obvious, the dominant decision rule is "truth-supported wins," where the group adopts the correct answer only if it is advocated by at least two members.

The *social influence* approach focuses on the motives that underlie group members' willingness to go along with others' views. Much of the work based on this approach involves Deutsch and Gerard's (1955) distinction between normative and informational influence. Normative influence occurs when people seek rewards that others control and assume that others are more likely to reward agreement than disagreement. Informational influence occurs when people seek an accurate view of reality and assume that others know more than they do. According to Kaplan (1987), normative influence tends to occur when issues are judgmental, the goal is group harmony, and responses are public. In contrast, informational influence tends to occur when issues are intellective, the goal is group accuracy, and responses are private.

Although groups are often asked to make decisions, the evidence shows that both the process and outcome of group decision making are often flawed. One problem stems from the fact that group members seldom begin a discussion with exactly the same information. Although some information relevant to the decision is shared by everyone, other information is unshared, in the sense that only one member or a few members know it. This would not be a problem if the unshared information came out during discussion. However, many studies show that group members spend most of their time discussing shared information. When unshared information is critical for making the correct decision, the failure to discuss it is obviously problematic (Stasser, 1999). However, the bias toward discussing shared information is not inevitable. Groups are more likely to discuss unshared information, for example, when members are aware of their own and others' expertise, the task has a demonstrably correct answer, and the group discussion lasts for some time (Larson, Foster-Fishman, & Keys, 1994).

Problems associated with the failure to exchange information were also considered by Janis (1982) in his influential analysis of *groupthink*, a syndrome that often leads to poor group decisions. According to Janis, several factors can lead to groupthink, including external threats, overly directive leaders, and high group cohesiveness. The symptoms of groupthink include pressure on dissenters, feelings of invulnerability, and belief in the group's inherent morality. Groupthink, in turn, has negative consequences for decision making, including failure to assess the risks of the preferred solution, restricted consideration of alternative solutions, and inadequate contingency plans. Janis analyzed several historical cases of groupthink, such as the decision to launch the ill-fated Bay of Pigs invasion. In the years since Janis offered his analysis, groupthink has been used to explain many highly publicized group decisions (e.g., the Challenger space shuttle disaster), and several studies have tested portions of the theory. The evidence to date is mixed, however, and so Janis's theory is controversial.

One alleged outcome of groupthink is the tendency for groups to engage in risky courses of action that are not warranted by the relevant evidence. Early research indicated that groups often reach riskier decisions than their members advocated prior to discussion, a phenomenon called the "risky shift." Later evidence, however, indicated that groups sometimes shift toward caution rather than risk and that opinion shifts can occur on issues where risk/caution is irrelevant. These findings led theorists to conclude that the risky shift is a special case of *group polarization*, which occurs when people with similar views engage in group discussion. As a result of that discussion, group members' opinions become more extreme in whatever direction the members were initially leaning (Moscovici & Zavalloni, 1969). Several explanations have been offered for group polarization, but the two most popular are *persuasive arguments* (informational influence) and *social comparison* (normative influence). According to persuasive arguments theory, polarization occurs because group members hear new and persuasive arguments favoring their initial position during their discussion, which causes them to shift further in the direction they were already leaning (Burnstein & Sentis, 1981). There are several versions of social comparison theory, but one of them argues that polarization occurs because group members discover that others hold more extreme positions

than their own during their discussion, which causes them to adopt a more extreme position in order to feel superior to those persons (Isenberg, 1986). Both of these explanations can account for some of the data on group polarization, but neither can account for all of the data. In recent years, additional explanations of polarization have been offered, including conformity to the assumed norms of one's ingroup (Mackie, 1986) and the adoption of attitudes that are repeatedly expressed during group discussion (Brauer, Judd, & Gliner, 1995).

Finally, when a poor decision has been made, groups (like individuals) often fall prey to *entrapment*, or the escalation of commitment to a losing course of action. Rather than ending an unwise project, for example, a group may allocate more and more resources, hoping that it will eventually succeed. Evidence indicates that entrapment is stronger in groups than in individuals (Seibert & Goltz, 2001) and that group entrapment is more likely when members identify more strongly with their group (Dietz-Uhler, 1996).

Because group decision making is often faulty, several techniques have been developed to help groups make better decisions. One of the most popular is "brainstorming," which seeks to increase group creativity by encouraging members to generate as many ideas as possible, without regard to their quality. Unfortunately, brainstorming is not very effective. Nominal groups, composed of individuals working alone, generally perform better than interacting groups (Diehl & Stroebe, 1987). Several explanations have been offered for the (non)productivity of brainstorming groups. One is production blocking, which occurs because members cannot all speak at once and sometimes forget their ideas while waiting for an opening in the discussion. A second is free riding, which occurs because members feel that their contributions are not identifiable or necessary for group success. And a third is evaluation apprehension, which occurs because members fear that others will evaluate their contributions negatively. Given that brainstorming is generally ineffective, why is it so popular? One answer is that people in brainstorming groups enjoy their experience because they believe they are more effective than they really are (Paulus, Dzindolet, Poletes, & Camacho, 1993). And brainstorming may serve other purposes in groups besides the generation of ideas (Sutton & Hargadon, 1996). In spite of its shortcomings, brainstorming continues to be studied, in part because it provides an interesting context for exploring the cognitive consequences of group membership (Nijstad, Diehl, & Stroebe, 2003).

REFERENCES

Abrams, D., & Hogg, M. A. (1990). Social identification, self-categorization and social influence. In W. Stroebe & M. Hewstone (Eds.), *European review of social psychology* (Vol. 1, pp. 195–228). Chichester: England: Wiley.

Brauer, M., Judd, C. M., & Gliner, M. D. (1995). The effects of repeated expressions on attitude polarization during group discussions. *Journal of Personality and Social Psychology, 68*, 1014–1029.

Deutsch, M., & Gerard, H. B. (1955). A study of normative and informational social influences upon individual judgment. *Journal of Abnormal and Social Psychology, 51*, 629–636.

Diehl, M., & Stroebe, W. (1987). Productivity loss in brainstorming groups: Toward the solution of a riddle. *Journal of Personality and Social Psychology, 53*, 497–509.

Dietz-Uhler, B. (1996). The escalation of commitment in political decision-making groups: A social identity approach. *European Journal of Social Psychology, 26*, 611–629.

Isenberg, D. J. (1986). Group polarization: A critical review and meta-analysis. *Journal of Personality and Social Psychology, 50*, 1141–1151.

Janis, I. L. (1982). *Groupthink: Psychological studies of policy decisions and fiascoes* (2nd ed.). Boston: Houghton Mifflin.

Kaplan, M. F. (1987). The influencing process in group decision making. In C. Hendrick (Ed.), *Review of personality and social psychology* (Vol. 8, pp. 189–212). Newbury Park, CA: Sage.

Larson, J. R., Foster-Fishman, P. G., & Keys, C. B. (1994). Discussion of shared and unshared information in decision-making groups. *Journal of Personality and Social Psychology, 67*, 446–461.

Laughlin, P. R., & Ellis, A. L. (1986). Demonstrability and social combination processes on mathematical intellective tasks. *Journal of Experimental Social Psychology, 22*, 177–189.

Mackie, D. M. (1986). Social identification effects in group polarization. *Journal of Personality and Social Psychology, 50*, 720–728.

Moscovici, S., & Zavalloni, M. (1969). The group as a polarizer of attitudes. *Journal of Personality and Social Psychology, 12*, 125–135.

Nijstad, B. A., Diehl, M., & Stroebe, W. (2003). Cognitive stimulation and interference in idea-generating groups. In P. B. Paulus & B. A. Nijstad (Eds.), *Group creativity: Innovation through collaboration* (pp. 137–159). Oxford, UK: Oxford University Press.

Paulus, P. B., Dzindolet, M. T., Poletes, G., & Camacho, L. M. (1993). Perception of performance in group brainstorming: The illusion of group productivity. *Personality and Social Psychology Bulletin, 19*, 78–89.

Seibert, S. E., & Goltz, S. M. (2001). Comparison of allocations by individuals and interacting groups in an escalation of commitment situation. *Journal of Applied Social Psychology, 31*, 134–156.

Stasser, G. (1999). The uncertain role of unshared information in collective choice. In L. L. Thompson, J. M. Levine, & D. M. Messick (Eds.), *Shared cognition in organizations: The management of knowledge* (pp. 49–70). Mahwah, NJ: Lawrence Erlbaum Associates, Inc.

Stasser, G., & Dietz-Uhler, B. (2001). Collective choice, judgment, and problem solving. In M. A. Hogg & R. S. Tindale (Eds.), *Blackwell handbook of social psychology: Group processes* (pp. 31–55). Malden, MA: Blackwell.

Sutton, R. I., & Hargadon, A. (1996). Brainstorming groups in context: Effectiveness in a product design firm. *Administrative Science Quarterly, 41*, 685–718.

Readings

The first paper in this section, by Laughlin and Shippy (1983), describes research on how groups make decisions on tasks that mimic the scientific process. On these "collective induction" tasks, group members observe patterns or regularities in a set of data, develop hypotheses to account for what they see, and then test their hypotheses through further observation or experimentation. These tests, in turn, affect the plausibility of the hypotheses under consideration. All hypotheses are either consistent with the evidence (plausible) or inconsistent with it (nonplausible). Collective induction tasks thus have both intellective and judgmental characteristics. They are intellective in the sense that nonplausible hypotheses can be shown to be wrong (inconsistent with the evidence). They are judgmental in the sense that a correct hypothesis cannot be shown to be the only one that is right (more consistent with the evidence than other plausible hypotheses).

Laughlin and Shippy conducted a laboratory experiment to see whether cooperative groups merely choose correct hypotheses proposed by one or more of their members, or can agree on correct hypotheses that no member proposed. They used a task that allowed people to generate and test hypotheses about a rule (e.g., "multiples of 3") for partitioning decks of playing cards. Groups of four or five people, or individuals working alone, were shown an examplar of the rule (e.g., the 9 of hearts for the rule mentioned above) and asked to figure out the rule in as few trials as possible. For each trial, participants went through a series of steps that involved proposing and testing hypotheses about the rule until a correct hypothesis was proposed or time was up. Laughlin and Shippy found that both four-person and five-person groups reached solutions faster than did individuals and produced a higher proportion of plausible hypotheses. Moreover, both kinds of groups were very successful in adopting correct hypotheses proposed by at least one of their members, but rarely adopted such hypotheses if none of their members proposed them. On collective induction tasks, then, groups are much better at

recognizing the right answer if someone suggests it than at generating this answer if no one suggests it.

In the second paper in this section, Kerr (1981) investigated the sequential processes that lead to decisions in groups. Kerr's approach goes beyond the traditional goal of social combination analysis, namely describing the relationship between members' initial preferences and the group's final decision. Instead, Kerr's social transition scheme (STS) model focuses on the successive changes that occur in members' preferences during interaction. Stated differently, the model "charts the group's road to agreement" by estimating or predicting the likelihood of transitions between different distributions of members' preferences. In this paper, Kerr's primary goal was to test two assumptions of his model—path-independence (that the group's current state, but not how it got there, determines where it goes next) and stationarity (that the length of the group's deliberation does not affect how it moves toward consensus). Secondary goals were to examine how time limits on deliberation, group experience, and group sex composition influence the group decision-making process.

In this experiment, six-person groups were instructed to act as mock juries deliberating armed-robbery cases. Some groups were told to continue deliberating until they reached unanimous decisions (unlimited time), whereas other groups were given a maximum of 10 minutes to reach such decisions (limited time). As they deliberated, group members continuously updated their personal verdict preferences by pressing buttons on a response panel. In these six-person juries, there were five possible distributions of individual member preferences at the beginning of deliberation (ranging from 5 guilty/1 not guilty to 1 guilty /5 not guilty). Kerr found that majorities (particularly large ones) had strong drawing power and that the closer the group was to consensus (the larger the majority), the faster the next shift occurred. He also found that although group experience sped up movement under some conditions, neither time limits nor group sex composition had much effect on the decision process. And Kerr failed to confirm either the path independence or the stationarity assumption. That is, how the group got to its current state *did* determine where it went next, and the length of the group's deliberation *did* affect how it moved toward consensus. In regard to path (in)dependence, Kerr found a momentum effect, such that groups were likely to continue moving in the direction they had just moved.

The third paper, by Stasser and Titus (1985), describes research on information sharing during group discussion. The researchers were interested in situations where individual members initially possess partial and biased information that would allow the group to reach an unbiased decision if the information were fully discussed. They argued that group members often fail to pool all their information, because their discussions are dominated by information that they initially share and that supports their initial preferences. Stasser and Titus thus predicted that when the information members initially share is biased toward the wrong answer, group discussion will strengthen this bias by increasing members' endorsement of that answer. They also hypothesized that discussion will be more likely to counter an initial bias when group members have information that causes them to disagree, rather than agree, about the right answer. This is

because disagreement should encourage more thorough information exchange in the group as members struggle to convince one another that their positions are correct.

In this laboratory experiment, four-person groups were asked to decide which of three hypothetical candidates was best suited to become president of the student body. Information provided about the candidates was constructed so that Candidate A was the best choice, in that he had better attributes than did Candidates B and C. In one condition (shared), all four participants read all of the information about each candidate. In the two remaining conditions (unshared), participants read only partial information about each candidate, and this information biased them against Candidate A. But if all of the participants in these conditions discussed everything they knew, then the group as a whole would have information leading it to favor Candidate A. In one of the unshared conditions (consensus), information was distributed to favor Candidate B. In the other unshared condition (conflict), information was distributed to create ambiguity about whether Candidate B or Candidate C was better. The results confirmed Stasser and Titus's first hypothesis. Group discussion strengthened the bias in favor of shared information, even though full discussion of unshared information could have eliminated that bias. In fact, the percentage of groups choosing the best candidate (A) was dramatically lower in the unshared (18%) than in the shared (83%) condition. However, discussion was not more likely to counter an initial bias when group members had information that produced initial disagreement (conflict) rather than agreement (consensus).

In the fourth paper, Turner, Pratkanis, Probasco, and Leve (1992) focused on the phenomenon of groupthink, which is often viewed as the cause of poor group decision making. They argued that Janis's theory has not been adequately evaluated in prior experiments, in part because key antecedents of groupthink were not adequately manipulated. Seeking to do a better job of testing the theory, Turner and her colleagues used improved manipulations of group cohesion (in terms of social identity) and group threat (in terms of lowered self-esteem), and they examined the combined effects of cohesion and threat on groupthink.

In an initial laboratory experiment, three-person groups made decisions about how to deal with poor group productivity caused by the inadequate performance of one worker. Two independent variables were manipulated—group threat (high, low), based on the belief that poor group performance would be made public, and group cohesion (high, low), based on the belief that group members shared a common social identity. Consistent with Janis's model of groupthink, some of the worst decision making occurred in the high-threat, high-cohesion condition. In a later experiment, Turner and her colleagues investigated how social identity maintenance affected group performance under conditions that foster groupthink. Their major hypothesis was that groups with an excuse for poor performance would do better than groups without such an excuse, because the former groups would feel less constrained to protect their self image and thus would engage in fewer "self-handicapping" strategies (e.g., low effort) that harm performance. An experiment using distracting music as an excuse for poor performance confirmed this

prediction. High-cohesion, high-threat groups with distraction performed better than did high-cohesion, high-threat groups without distraction.

Finally, in the fifth paper, Brauer, Judd, and Gliner (1995) investigated group polarization. As noted earlier, this phenomenon has traditionally been explained in terms of informational and normative influence. Brauer and his colleagues tested a new explanation based on research showing that repeatedly expressing an attitude causes that attitude to become more extreme. This presumably occurs because people who repeatedly express an attitude focus more attention on features of the attitude target that are consistent with their overall evaluation of it. Extrapolating this logic to group polarization, Brauer and his colleagues predicted that repeated expression of attitudes during group discussion may produce polarization, independently of informational and normative influence.

To test their hypothesis, the researchers conducted two experiments. In the first, four-person groups discussed several issues that members initially agreed on (e.g., reductions in the military budget). The researchers independently manipulated the number of times that group members (a) presented their own opinions and (b) heard others present theirs. This was accomplished by having members meet in pairs and controlling the frequency with which they either spoke or listened to one another on each issue. Comparisons between participants' final responses on issues they discussed and issues they did not discuss revealed that discussion produced polarization. This polarization was influenced by both expressing opinions and hearing opinions. The effects of hearing opinions depended on the number of people heard from, rather than the number of opinions heard. Moreover, the repeated expression of opinions was especially likely to produce polarization when group members picked up and repeated each other's arguments.

In the second experiment, Brauer and his colleagues used a more natural group discussion format in which the frequency of expressing and hearing opinions was measured, rather than manipulated. Three-person groups discussed several issues on which members initially agreed. In each group, one person was privately asked to (a) repeat arguments made by the other two group members or (b) refrain from repeating these arguments. This manipulation was included to test the hypothesis, derived from the results of the first experiment, that polarization would be greater when group members' arguments were picked up by others. The results indicated that polarization was influenced by expressing, but not by hearing, opinions. Moreover, as predicted, groups in which one member repeated others' arguments polarized more than did groups in which this did not occur. Taken as a whole, these two experiments provide evidence that the repeated expression of opinions plays a potentially important role in group polarization.

Discussion Questions

1. Although groups seem to have a hard time developing good ideas when no member offers one, there may be times when groups come up with valuable ideas that no member suggests. When might this happen?
2. Momentum effects, in which groups keep moving toward whatever decision they are heading, may help explain why groups find it hard to rethink their views when they encounter information that they are wrong. If you were advising groups about how to make better decisions, how would you suggest they avoid momentum effects?
3. There are several reasons why groups are biased toward discussing information that members initially share. What are they?
4. Groupthink is a more popular explanation for poor group decision making than it probably deserves to be on the basis of scientific evidence. Why do people find the theory so appealing?
5. Have you ever been in a group that experienced polarization following discussion? What factors seemed to produce that polarization? Were you aware it was happening during the discussion? If not, did it dawn on you later?

Suggested Readings

Kameda, T., Ohtsubo, Y., & Takezawa, M. (1997). Centrality in socio-cognitive network and social influence: An illustration in a group decision-making context. *Journal of Personality and Social Psychology, 73*, 296–309.

Isenberg, D. J. (1986). Group polarization: A critical review and meta-analysis. *Journal of Personality and Social Psychology, 50*, 1141–1151.

Larson, J. R., Foster-Fishman, P. G., & Keys, C. B. (1994). Discussion of shared and unshared information in decision-making groups. *Journal of Personality and Social Psychology*, *67*, 446–461.

Nijstad, B. A., Stroebe, W., & Lodewijkx, H. F. M. (2002) Cognitive stimulation and interference in groups: Exposure effects in an idea generation task. *Journal of Experimental Social Psychology*, *38*, 535–544.

Wittenbaum, G. M., Hubbell, A. P., & Zuckerman, C. (1999). Mutual enhancement: Toward an understanding of collective preference for shared information. *Journal of Personality and Social Psychology*, *77*, 967–978.

R E A D I N G   1 1

Collective Induction

Patrick R. Laughlin and Thomas A. Shippy

Is a cooperative group able to induce a general principle that none of the group members could have induced alone, or does the group merely adopt an induction proposed by one or more group members? Individuals, four-person groups, and five-person groups attempted to induce a general rule that partitioned a deck of standard playing cards into exemplars and nonexemplars. Both four-person and five-person groups required fewer trials to solution than individuals, and both had a higher proportion of plausible hypotheses than individuals. A social combination analysis indicated that both four-person and five-person groups were remarkably successful at recognizing and adopting correct inductions if they had been proposed by individual group members: If proposed by one member, correct inductions were recognized either on the trial on which they were proposed or on a subsequent trial; if proposed by two or more members, correct inductions were almost always recognized on the trial on which they were proposed. In contrast, collective induction in the strong sense of a correct group induction that none of the group members had proposed as an individual induction was extremely rare.

Induction is a circular process. Some regularity is perceived in some domain, and a generalization is postulated to account for the regularity. Consideration of the generalization suggests predictions. The predictions are then tested by observation and experiment, conceptual or actual. If the results of observation and experiment confirm the predictions, the proposed induction becomes more plausible. If the results disconfirm the predictions, the proposed induction is revised or rejected. As a body of relevant evidence emerges, new inductions are proposed, new predictions formulated, new observations and experiments suggested, and the process is repeated.

When such induction occurs for a single individual, the same person proposes the generalization, formulates predictions, and tests the predictions by observation and experiment. When the process

We thank Joan M. Barth, William R. Emmons, Dorothy E. Evans, and David S. Ragsdale for assistance as experimenters.

Requests for reprints should be sent to Patrick R. Laughlin, Department of Psychology, 603 East Daniel Street, University of Illinois, Champaign, Illinois 61820.

occurs for cooperative groups, various combinations of different persons may propose the generalization, formulate the predictions, and test the predictions by observation and experiment. We may call the process for cooperative groups *collective induction*. The fundamental issue in collective induction may be posed as follows: Is a cooperative group able to induce a general principle that none of the group members could have induced alone, or does the group merely adopt an induction proposed by one or more group members?

To address this issue, the following experiment compared the induction of individuals and the collective induction of four-person groups and five-person groups. The task required the induction of a rule that partitioned a deck of 52 standard playing cards into exemplars and nonexemplars. Instructions indicated that the rule could be based on any characteristics of the cards, such as numerical value, logical connectives, suit and color, alternation, and so forth. Each card was assigned the corresponding numerical value, with aces as 1, deuces as 2, up to the kings as 13. Examples of the very large number of possible rules included "multiples of three," "black or even," and "two odd-numbered cards alternate with one even-numbered card." The problem began from a known exemplar. The group members then each wrote a private hypothesis (proposed induction) on their own hypothesis sheet. Next, they discussed the problem until they reached a consensus on a collective group hypothesis, which a member wrote on a group hypothesis sheet. The group members then discussed until they reached consensus on the choice of a card play, which may be considered an experiment to test predictions from the proposed induction. The experimenter classified the card as an exemplar or nonexemplar of the rule, and then checked the group hypothesis. A correct hypothesis solved the problem, whereas an incorrect hypothesis required a new cycle of individual hypotheses, group hypothesis, and group card play (trial). As successive exemplars and/or nonexemplars were played a progressive layout of evidence developed. Because the individual hypotheses and the group hypothesis were known within each trial, it was possible to conduct a social combination analysis of

the processes by which the group maps varying distributions of individual hypotheses into a group response and thus to address the fundamental issue in collective induction.

Method

The subjects were 300 college students at the University of Illinois at Urbana-Champaign who were fulfilling required experimental participation in introductory psychology courses. There were 30 four-person groups, 30 five-person groups, and 30 individuals, with subjects randomly assigned to these three experimental conditions in a between-groups design.

A rule was defined as any basis of partitioning decks of 52 standard bridge playing cards (no jokers) into exemplars and nonexemplars. Each card was assigned the corresponding numerical value, with aces as 1, deuces as 2 ..., tens as 10, jacks as 11, queens as 12, kings as 13. Any characteristics of the cards could be the basis of the rule, such as color, number, suit, logical connectives (conjunction, disjunction, etc.), alternation, or any combination of these. Pilot work was conducted to determine 10 rules of a wide range of difficulty, given an experimental session of 1 hour. These 10 rules were (1) multiples of 3, (2) two odd and one even alternate, (3) two even and one odd alternate, (4) multiples of 4, (5) three odd and one even alternate, (6) red and even, or black and odd, (7) two black and one red alternate, (8) black and even, or red and odd, (9) two red and one black alternate, and (10) alternate cards are greater than and less than the previous card. These 10 rules were used in five sets of two rules, Rules 1 and 2, Rules 3 and 4, ..., Rules 9 and 10. There were six replications of each of these five sets of two rules within each of the individual, four-person group, and five-person group experimental conditions.

The instructions explained the nature of the task and the procedure, indicating that the rule could be based on any characteristics of the cards such as numerical value, color, suit, logical connectives, alternation, or any combination of these. Examples of each type of rule were given. The problems began with a known positive exemplar of the rule, for example, the 9 of hearts for Rule 1, multiples of 3. The objective was to induce the rule in as few trials as possible. A trial consisted of the following five stages. First, each individual group member wrote an individual hypothesis (proposed induction) on an individual hypothesis sheet. Second, the group members discussed until they reached a consensus on a group hypothesis, which a randomly designated group recorder wrote on a group hypothesis sheet. Third, the group members discussed until they reached a consensus on a play of any one of the cards, which was shown to the experimenter. Fourth, the experimenter classified this card as either an exemplar or a nonexemplar. An exemplar was placed to the right of the known initial exemplar on the table, and a nonexemplar was placed below the known initial exemplar. Fifth, the experimenter checked the group hypothesis. If the group hypothesis was correct, the problem was solved; if the group hypothesis was incorrect, a new cycle of the five stages followed, consisting of a second cycle of individual hypotheses, group hypothesis, play of a card, feedback on the status of the card, and check of the group hypothesis as correct or incorrect. This cycle continued until a correct group hypothesis was reached or the problem was terminated at the end of the experimental hour. As many decks of cards as desired were available, so that a given card could be played more than once. In the individual condition, Stage 2 (group hypothesis) was of course omitted, and there was no discussion of the card play in Stage 3. All other aspects were identical for the individual and the two group conditions. If sufficient time remained after solution of the first problem, the second problem in that set was attempted.

Each successive exemplar was placed to the right of the previous exemplar, and each nonexemplar was placed below the previous card (exemplar or nonexemplar). Thus, a progressive layout of exemplars and nonexemplars emerged, with exemplars on a horizontal line from left to right and nonexemplars placed vertically downwards from the point of the last exemplar, indicating the order of play. Each group member had a list of individual hypotheses, and could inspect any other individual list or the list of group hypotheses. In other words, a complete record of all individual and group hypotheses, and all exemplars and nonexemplars in the order of play, was available throughout the experiment.

This procedure required each group member to write one and only one hypothesis on the individual hypothesis sheet on each trial. Although the individual may have considered many hypotheses, the single hypothesis was to be the most probable. Discussion was completely free, so that an individual might or might not propose the hypothesis on that trial. Similarly, one and only one group hypothesis was recorded on each trial, so that the group hypothesis would correspond to anywhere from none of the individual hypotheses to all of the individual hypotheses on the trial.

Results

Overall Performance

The individuals solved 24 of the possible 60 problems, the four-person groups solved 30 problems, and the five-person groups solved 36. The mean number of trials to solution on the first problem was 15.23 for individuals, 8.73 for four-person groups, and 8.53 for five-person groups (an additional trial was added for nonsolved problems), with respective standard deviations of 9.51, 3.98, and 4.09. Analysis of variance indicated a significant effect of group size, $F(2, 87) = 10.62, p < .001$, and Newman-Keuls comparisons indicated more trials for individuals than either four-person groups or five-person groups (both $p < .001$), who did not differ reliably from each other. The same pattern emerged on Problem 2, which was attempted by 14 individuals, 14 four-person groups, and 19 five-person groups, with respective means of 14.29, 7.86, and 8.21, and standard deviations of 5.03, 3.37, and 3.41. The main effect of group size was significant, $F(2, 44) = 12.25, p < .001$, and Kramer comparisons for unequal numbers of replications indicated more trials for individuals than for each of four-person and five-person groups, who did not differ reliably from each other.

Induction leads to plausible or implausible, rather than correct or incorrect, hypotheses. Each hypothesis was analyzed as plausible or implausible relative to all cards played to that time. For example, the hypothesis "diamonds" would be implausible if either a nondiamond were an exemplar or a diamond were a nonexemplar. The proportion of plausible hypotheses was determined by dividing the number of plausible hypotheses by the number of trials on the problem. Means for the first problem were .83 for individuals, .97 for four-person groups, and .94 for five-person groups, with respective standard deviations of .21, .07, and .14. Means on the second problem were .72, .92, and .98, respectively, with standard deviations of .27, .14, and .05. Analyses of variance on arcsin transformations of these proportions indicated significant effects of group size on both problems, $F(2, 87) = 10.45$, $p < .001$; $F(2, 44) = 11.57$, $p < .001$. Post hoc comparisons indicated higher proportions for both four-person groups and five-person groups than for individuals on both problems (all $ps < .01$ or .001), whereas four-person and five-person groups did not differ from each other.

In summary, both four-person groups and five-person groups performed better than individuals but did not differ reliably from each other. This superiority of group over individual performance is consistent with a large amount of previous research (see Davis, 1969; Davis, Laughlin, & Komorita, 1976; Hackman & Morris, 1975; Hill, 1982; Kelley & Thibaut, 1969; Lorge, Fox, Davitz, & Brenner, 1958; McGrath, in press; McGrath & Kravitz, 1982; and Steiner, 1972, for reviews).

Social Combination Analyses

Four-person groups. In the four-person groups four, three, two, or one of the group members may have proposed the correct answer (C) as individuals on that trial, and four, three, two, or one of them may have proposed a given incorrect hypothesis (I). Using subscripts to denote the number of group members who had proposed a given hypothesis as individuals, there are 12 possible distributions of group members on a given trial: C_4, C_3I_1, C_2I_2, $C_2I_1I_1$, C_1I_3, $C_1I_2I_1$, $C_1I_1I_1I_1$, I_4, I_3I_1, I_2I_2, $I_2I_1I_1$,

TABLE 11.1. Frequencies of Six Types of Group Responses for 12 Possible Distributions of Members of Four-Person Groups

Distribution	C	I_4	I_3	I_2	I_1	I_0	Σ
C_4	5	–	–	–	–	0	5
C_3I_1	4	–	–	–	0	0	4
C_2I_2	0	–	–	0	–	0	0
$C_2I_1I_1$	3	–	–	–	1	0	4
C_1I_3	0	–	2	–	–	0	2
$C_1I_2I_1$	4	–	–	5	0	2	11
$C_1I_1I_1I_1$	8	–	–	–	4	1	13
I_4	0	24	–	–	–	0	24
I_3I_1	1	–	43	–	7	2	53
I_2I_2	0	–	–	10	–	0	10
$I_2I_1I_1$	2	–	–	62	25	12	101
$I_1I_1I_1I_1$	3	–	–	–	96	30	129
Σ	30	24	45	77	133	47	356

Note: C = correct, I = incorrect. Subscripts indicate the number of group members who proposed a hypothesis as individuals on that trial. Dashes (–) indicate impossible group responses for a given distribution. Frequencies of 0 indicate possible group responses that did not occur. Frequencies sum over 30 first problems and 14 second problems.

and $I_1I_1I_1I_1$. The group response may be C, I_4, I_3, I_2, I_1, or I_0 (an incorrect group response not proposed by any individual on that trial). The frequencies of each of the six possible group responses for each of the 12 possible distributions of group members are given in Table 11.1. (Table 11.1 sums over both 30 first problems and 14 second problems.) As indicated in Table 11.1, the group response was always correct for the five cases when four members were correct and the four cases when three members were correct, as well as in three of the four $C_2I_1I_1$ distributions, for a total probability of $12/13 = .92$ when two or more members were correct. Given a single correct member, the group was correct with a probability of $0/2 = .00$ in the C_1I_3 distribution, where the incorrect majority prevailed; correct with a probability of $4/11 = .36$ in the $C_1I_2I_1$ distribution; and correct with a probability of $8/13 = .62$ in the $C_1I_1I_1I_1$ distribution where the correct member did not face either an incorrect majority or plurality. Thus, a single correct individual prevailed with an overall probability of $12/26 = .46$ on that trial. All of these groups eventually solved the problem on a subsequent trial. Thus, the four-person groups were remarkably successful in recognizing and adopting a correct hypothesis; if proposed by one member, correct inductions were recognized either on the trial on which they were proposed or on a subsequent trial, and if proposed by two or more members, correct inductions were almost always recognized on the trial on which they were proposed.

In marked contrast, the overall probability of a correct response in the five distributions where no individual proposed the correct answer was $6/317 = .02$. Three of these six correct collective inductions occurred in the $I_1I_1I_1I_1$ distribution, whereas the other four distributions generally followed either a majority process (I_4 and I_3I_1) or a plurality process ($I_2I_1I_1$), with an equiprobability process for I_2I_2. Thus, collective induction in the strong sense of a correct group hypothesis that none of the group members had proposed as an individual was extremely rare.

These previous analyses have considered the single correct response versus all other incorrect responses, which may be plausible or implausible. On each trial four of the individual hypotheses may be plausible and none implausible (4–0), three plausible and one implausible (3–1) . . ., or none plausible and four implausible (0–4). The group hypothesis for each of these five distributions may be plausible or implausible. The proportions of plausible group hypotheses for the five distributions were $230/230 = 1.00$ for 4–0; $65/68 = .96$ for 3–1; $38/39 = .97$ for 2–2; $4/11 = .36$ for 1–3; and $2/4 = .50$ for 0–4. Thus, the group hypothesis was virtually certain to be plausible if at least two members had proposed plausible hypotheses (whether correct or incorrect), indicating an error-checking process.

The data of Table 11.1 are the frequencies of possible group responses for possible member distributions, aggregated over all trials. As such, they do not indicate sequential transitions from a given distribution on trial t to a given distribution on trial $t + 1$. Because of the relatively small frequencies on trial t for a given distribution (row sums of Table 11.1), full analysis of the 12×12 matrix of transition probabilities (such as those of Godwin &

Restle, 1974; Kerr, 1981, 1982; or Stasser & Davis, 1981) would not be meaningful. However, Table 11.1 indicates a relatively large frequency of 129 for the $I_1I_1I_1I_1$ distribution on trial t. Three of the group responses for this distribution were correct, and seven were the final group response for groups that failed to solve the problem. For the remaining 119 cases the transition probability to a distribution with at least one correct individual hypothesis was .09, and all of these groups eventually solved the problem. There was a transition probability of .50 to another $I_1I_1I_1I_1$ distribution, indicating that groups with no agreement tended to continue proposing new individual hypotheses. This individualistic behavior is collectively rational, as such groups had a greater probability of eventually including a correct individual hypothesis (and hence solving the problem) than groups in which more than one member agreed on an incorrect individual hypothesis.

Five-person groups. The frequencies of each of the seven types of possible group responses for each of the 19 possible distributions of group members are given in Table 11.2. As indicated in Table 11.2, the group was correct for the four cases where a strong majority (C_5 or C_4I_1) favored the correct response, eight of the nine cases where a weak ($C_3I_1I_1$) majority favored the correct response, and seven of the eight cases where two members were correct; the overall probability was $19/21 = .90$ of a correct group response when at least two members were correct. Given a single correct member, the overall probability of a correct group response on that trial was $13/37 = .35$. All but three of these groups solved the problem on a subsequent trial.

In marked contrast, the overall probability of a correct group response in the seven distributions where no individual proposed the correct answer was $4/341 = .01$. Moreover, all four of these correct collective inductions occurred in the $I_1I_1I_1I_1I_1$ distribution, the single distribution where two or more group members did not favor the same incorrect response. In these distributions there was a probability of $50/117 = .43$ that the group would propose a new hypothesis not proposed by any group member, and four of these were correct. The

TABLE 11.2. Frequencies of Seven Types of Group Responses for 19 Possible Distributions of Members of Five-Person Groups

Distribution	Type of group response							
	C	I_5	I_4	I_3	I_2	I_1	I_0	Σ
C_5	2	–	–	–	–	–	0	2
C_4I_1	2	–	–	–	–	0	0	2
C_3I_2	0	–	–	–	0	–	0	0
$C_3I_1I_1$	8	–	–	–	–	0	1	9
C_2I_3	0	–	–	0	0	–	0	0
$C_2I_2I_1$	1	–	–	–	0	0	0	1
$C_2I_1I_1I_1$	6	–	–	–	–	0	1	7
C_1I_4	1	–	0	–	–	–	0	1
$C_1I_3I_1$	0	–	–	1	–	0	0	1
$C_1I_2I_2$	0	–	–	–	1	–	0	1
$C_1I_2I_1I_1$	3	–	–	–	6	1	2	12
$C_1I_1I_1I_1I_1$	9	–	–	–	–	8	5	22
I_5	0	16	–	–	–	–	0	16
I_4I_1	0	–	29	–	–	1	0	30
I_3I_2	0	–	–	8	5	–	2	15
$I_3I_1I_1$	0	–	–	49	–	10	4	63
$I_2I_2I_1$	0	–	–	–	26	3	2	31
$I_2I_1I_1I_1$	0	–	–	–	39	17	13	69
$I_1I_1I_1I_1I_1$	4	–	–	–	–	67	46	117
Σ	36	16	29	58	77	107	76	399

Note: See Table 11.1 for abbreviations. Frequencies sum over 30 first problems and 19 second problems.

other distributions followed majority or plurality processes. Thus, as with the four-person groups, collective induction in the strong sense of a correct group hypothesis that none of the group members had proposed as an individual was extremely rare.

The proportions of plausible group responses for the six possible distributions of plausible and implausible hypotheses were 222/224 = .99 for 5–0; 96/98 = .98 for 4–1; 37/38 = .97 for 3–2; and 28/33 = .85 for 2–3, again indicating an error-checking process for groups with at least two members who proposed plausible hypotheses. (The frequencies of the 1–4 and 0–5 distributions were too small for reliable conclusions.)

As indicated in Table 11.2, there was a relatively large frequency of 117 cases for the $I_1I_1I_1I_1I_1$ distribution on trial *t*. Four of the group responses for this distribution were correct, and five responses were the final distribution for groups who failed to solve the problem. For the remaining 108 cases the transition probability to a distribution with at least one correct individual hypothesis was .10, and all but three of these groups eventually solved the problem. There was a transition probability of .52 to another $I_1I_1I_1I_1I_1$ distribution, again indicating, as in four-person groups, that groups with no agreement tended to continue proposing new individual hypotheses. Again, this individualistic behavior is collectively rational.

Discussion

These results are remarkably orderly. Both four-person groups and five-person groups were remarkably successful at recognizing and adopting a correct group response if it was proposed by at least one group member. Two or more correct individuals were virtually certain to prevail on the trial on which they proposed the correct response. One correct individual had a probability of .46 of prevailing on the trial when he or she proposed the correct response in four-person groups, and a probability of .35 of prevailing on such a trial in five-person groups. All of these incorrect group responses were plausible, and all of the four-person groups and all but three of the five-person groups eventually solved the problem on a subsequent trial. In marked contrast, the overall probability of a correct group response in the distributions where no individual proposed the correct hypothesis was .02 for four-person groups and .01 for five-person groups. Thus, collective induction in the strong sense of a correct group induction that none of the group members had proposed as an individual induction was extremely rare. Moreover, it was most likely in the distributions where no two or more members favored the same incorrect response. In these distributions the group was likely to propose a hypothesis none of the members had proposed as an individual (with a probability of .26 in four-person groups and .43 in five-person groups), and a few of these were correct. Finally, groups with no agreement tended to continue proposing new individual hypotheses on the subsequent trial. This apparently individualistic behavior is collectively rational.

In a review of social combination models, Laughlin (1980) has proposed a group-task continuum anchored by intellective and judgmental tasks. An intellective task involves a demonstrably correct solution within some conceptual system, whereas a judgmental task involves group consensus on some nondemonstrably correct behavioral, ethical, or aesthetic judgment. There is strong evidence that cooperative groups follow fundamentally different social combination processes on intellective and judgmental tasks. On intellective tasks, such as English vocabulary (Laughlin, Kerr, Davis, Halff, & Marciniak, 1975), verbal analogies (Laughlin & Adamopoulos, 1980, 1982), and general achievement items (Laughlin, Kerr, Munch, & Haggarty, 1976), the basic social combination process is truth-supported wins: two correct members are necessary and sufficient for a correct group response. On judgmental tasks, such as mock jury decisions (see Davis, 1980, and Davis, Bray, & Holt, 1977, for extensive reviews) and attitudinal judgments (e.g., Kerr, Davis, Meek, & Rissman, 1975), the basic social combination process is majority wins: a majority (typically two thirds) of the group members determines the group response. All of this previous research with intellective tasks has involved a single demonstrably correct solution and all of this previous research with judgmental tasks has involved a set of nondemonstrably correct solutions. The inductive task of the present experiment involved a set of plausible solutions (one of which was arbitrarily correct) and a set of implausible solutions. If at least two group members proposed the correct solution, a truth-supported wins process occurred, consistent with previous research with intellective tasks. In these groups the correct answer may be demonstrated to match the set of exemplars and nonexemplars, and hence to be at least as plausible as any other plausible hypothesis, although not uniquely correct. Another proposed hypothesis may be demonstrated to be implausible from a single failure to match either the set of exemplars or the set of nonexemplars. Thus, the correct answer is demonstrably preferable to a rival implausible hypothesis, and as demonstrable as a rival plausible hypothesis. A similar process occurred, but to a lesser extent, in the groups where only a single

person proposed the correct answer. Finally, a strong majority process occurred in groups in which no member proposed the correct answer and a majority proposed a given incorrect answer, consistent with previous research on judgmental tasks.

The task in the present experiment models the circular process of generalization, prediction, and experiment in extraexperimental induction, but there are two basic differences. First, one of the set of plausible inductions was arbitrarily defined as "correct." Extraexperimental induction is plausible or implausible, rather than correct or incorrect. The paradox of experimental study of induction is that some criterion of correctness must be imposed in order to terminate the experiment. Extraexperimental induction, in contrast, never terminates. Second, the experimenter indicated whether proposed inductions were correct or incorrect. There is no such omniscient experimenter to inform us whether our extraexperimental inductions are correct or incorrect. As all analogies, the task in the present experiment is a simplification of a more complex reality. However, the simplification led to some remarkably orderly results. Indeed, consideration of the regularity may suggest a generalization to the reader. Consideration of the generalization may suggest predictions. The predictions may then be tested by observation and experiment, conceptual or actual. Induction is a circular process.

REFERENCES

Davis, J. H. *Group performance*. Reading, Mass.: Addison-Wesley, 1969.

Davis, J. H. Group decision and procedural justice. In M. Fishbein (Ed.), *Progress in social psychology*. Hillsdale, N.J.: Erlbaum, 1980.

Davis, J. H., Bray, R. M., & Holt, R. W. The empirical study of decision processes injuries: A critical review. In J. Tapp & F. Levine (Eds.), *Law, justice, and the individual in society: Psychological and legal issues*. New York: Holt, Rinehart & Winston, 1977.

Davis, J. H., Laughlin, P. R., & Komorita, S. S. The social psychology of small groups: Cooperative and mixed-motive interaction. *Annual Review of Psychology*, 1976, *27*, 501–541.

Godwin, W., & Restle, F. The road to agreement: Subgroup pressures in small group consensus processes. *Journal of Personality and Social Psychology*, 1974, *30*, 500–509.

Hackman, J. R., & Morris, C. G. Group tasks, group interaction process, and group performance effectiveness: A review and proposed integration. In L. Berkowitz (Ed.), *Advances in experimental social psychology* (Vol. 8). New York: Academic Press, 1975.

Hill, G. W. Group versus individual performance: Are *N* + 1 heads better than one? *Psychological Bulletin*, 1982, *91*, 517–539.

Kelley, H. H., & Thibaut, J. W. Group problem solving. In G. Lindzey & E. Aronson (Eds.), *The handbook of social psychology* (Vol. 4). Reading, Mass.: Addison-Wesley, 1969.

Kerr, N. L. Social transition schemes: Charting the group's road to agreement. *Journal of Personality and Social Psychology*, 1981, *41*, 684–702.

Kerr, N. L. Social transition schemes: Model, method, and applications. In H. Brandstätter, J. H. Davis, & G. Stocker-Kreichgauer (Eds.), *Group decision making*. London: Academic Press, 1982.

Kerr, N. L., Davis, J. H., Meek, D., & Rissman, A. K. Group position as a function of member attitudes: Choice shift effects from the perspective of social decision scheme theory. *Journal of Personality and Social Psychology*, 1975, *31*, 574–593.

Laughlin, P. R. Social combination processes of cooperative problem-solving groups on verbal intellective tasks. In M. Fishbein (Ed.), *Progress in social psychology*. Hillsdale, N.J.: Erlbaum, 1980.

Laughlin, P. R., & Adamopoulos, J. Social combination processes and individual learning for six-person cooperative groups on an intellective task. *Journal of Personality and Social Psychology*, 1980, *38*, 941–947.

Laughlin, P. R., & Adamopoulos, J. Social decision schemes on intellective tasks. In H. Brandstätter, J. H. Davis, & G. Stocker-Kreichgauer (Eds.), *Group decision making*. London: Academic Press, 1982.

Laughlin, P. R., Kerr, N. L., Davis, J. H., Halff, H. M., & Marciniak, K. A. Group size, member ability, and social decision schemes on an intellective task. *Journal of Personality and Social Psychology*, 1975, *31*, 522–535.

Laughlin, P. R., Kerr, N. L., Munch, M. M., & Haggarty, C. A. Social decision schemes of the same four-person groups on two different intellective tasks. *Journal of Personality and Social Psychology*, 1976, *33*, 80–88.

Lorge, I., Fox., D., Davitz, J., & Brenner, M. A survey of studies contrasting the quality of group performance and individual performance, 1920–1957. *Psychological Bulletin*, 1958, *55*, 337–372.

McGrath, J. E. *Groups: Interaction and performance*. Englewood Cliffs, N.J.: Prentice-Hall, in press.

McGrath, J. E., & Kravitz, D. A. Group research. *Annual Review of Psychology*, 1982, *33*, 195–230.

Stasser, G., & Davis, J. H. Group decision making and social influence: A social interaction sequence model. *Psychological Review*, 1981, *88*, 523–551.

Steiner, I. D. *Group process and productivity*. New York: Academic Press, 1972.

Received July 12, 1982
Revision received November 16, 1982 ■

Social Transition Schemes: Charting the Group's Road to Agreement

Norbert L. Kerr

A stochastic model of the group decision-making process, the social transition scheme model, is outlined. Two key assumptions of the model are identified: the path-independence assumption holds that where the group goes next depends on its current state but not on how it reached that state; the stationarity assumption holds that the likelihood of any particular movement toward consensus does not depend on how long the group has been deliberating. The deliberations of mock juries were analyzed to see whether the process was path independent and stationary. In addition, the effects of group experience, member sex, and deliberation time limits on the decision-making process were examined. The process was found to be path dependent and nonstationary. The path dependence reflected a momentum effect: Groups tended to continue in the direction in which they had just moved. However, incorrectly assuming path independence and stationarity had relatively little effect on the predictive accuracy of the model. Group experience was found to speed up movement when the group was sharply divided. Member sex and time limitations had no effect on the decision process. The relevance of the latter result for simulation research on juries is discussed.

Two features characterize most previous research on small-group decision making. First, relatively little of this research has directly observed and analyzed the group decision-making process itself.

Second, nearly all existing process-oriented research has used at its unit of analysis one or another aspect of the group's verbal communication—its content, temporal flow, patterning, and so on (e.g., Bales,

This research was supported by National Institute of Mental Health Grant MH29919-01. Thanks go to John Hunter and Shelby Haberman for suggestions on the data analysis and to James H. Davis, Reid Hastie, and Steven Penrod for their comments on an earlier draft.

Requests for reprints should be sent to Norbert L. Kerr, Department of Psychology, Michigan State University, East Lansing, Michigan 48824.

1950; Fisher, 1970; Leavitt, 1951; Schachter, 1951; Stephan & Mishler, 1952; Vinokur & Burnstein, 1974). This paper reports a study of small-group decision making that departs from both of these research traditions. This study systematically examines the internal dynamics of decision-making groups using a unit of analysis other than verbal behavior, namely, the distribution of member preferences across decision alternatives.

A large body of research employing Davis's (1973) social decision scheme (SDS) model has demonstrated that simple stochastic functions, termed *social decision schemes*, can reliably relate the initial distribution of member preferences to a group's ultimate decision (see Davis, 1980, for a comprehensive review). For example, some variation on a majority-wins scheme has been shown to do a remarkably good job of predicting group decisions for attitudinal issues (Kerr, Davis, Meek, & Rissman, 1975), duplex bets (Davis, Kerr, Sussman, & Rissman, 1974), and jury verdicts (e.g., Davis, Kerr, Atkin, Holt, & Meek, 1975; Kerr et al., 1976; Kerr, Nerenz, & Herrick, 1979). Since the distribution of preferences appears to be highly predictive of the group's product, it seems a promising unit of analysis for the decision-making process as well.

Such an analysis was undertaken here using the social transition scheme (STS) model, which is an extension of the SDS model. Detailed descriptions of the STS model have been provided elsewhere (Kerr, in press-b; Stasser, Kerr, & Davis, 1980). For present purposes, a simple example will suffice to demonstrate how the SDS product model may be extended to create the STS process model. Consider a 12-person jury that must decide whether a criminal defendant is guilty or not guilty. There are 13 possible ways that the 12 jurors might be distributed across the two decision alternatives at the outset of jury deliberation: 12 guilty (G)–0 not guilty (NG), 11G–1NG, ..., 0G–12NG. In general, for an r-person group choosing among n decision alternatives, there are $m = (n + r - 1)/r$ unique ways of distributing members across alternatives. For each of the possible initial distributions, the objective of the SDS model would be to either estimate or predict (depending on one's research strategy) the probability of the group choosing each alternative. The full set of initial-split to final-decision transition probabilities is summarized in an $m \times n$ stochastic matrix, D.

By way of contrast, the STS model focuses not on the group's final decision but, rather, on the successive changes in group members' positions throughout the group decision-making process. Whereas the SDS model would attempt to specify, for example, the likelihood that a jury beginning with an even 6G–6NG split would ultimately arrive at a guilty or not-guilty verdict, the STS model attempts to specify the likelihood of the jury shifting from the group "state" 6G–6NG to 7G–5NG, 5G–7NG, and so on. In the simplest form of this model, these state-to-state transition probabilities can be summarized in a single $m \times m$ transition matrix, T, the ith row of which specifies the probabilities of transition from the ith state to each of the m states.

The goal of the STS model is, in terms of Godwin and Restle's (1974) metaphor, to chart the group's "road to agreement." One can think about each of the nonunanimous group states as "forks" in the road to agreement. For example, a jury with an even 6G–6NG split can shift toward agreement on conviction, (6G–6NG) → (7G–5NG), shift toward agreement on acquittal, (6G–6NG) → (5G–7NG), or remain where it is. The STS model provides a means of looking for patterns in a group's movement down the road to agreement. For example, by which of the many possible paths do groups usually travel? How quickly do groups move down the various possible paths? How do group, task, and member characteristics affect the routes that groups take?

Conceptual Distinctions

Before taking up the substantive questions to be addressed here with the STS model, we should draw two conceptual distinctions. First, the very notion of process implies the observation of behavioral change. There are at least two potentially useful ways one might break up the flow of group behavior in applying the STS model, and they define two general classes of models. In STS *shift* models, one takes a change in member preference as an event but one ignores all failures to change. In essence, with shift models one is only concerned with which path the group takes down the road to agreement but is unconcerned with how rapidly it takes that path. Formally, the diagonal elements of a shift model's T are either 0 (for states that do not satisfy the operative decision criterion or rule, e.g., unanimity for most juries), or 1 (for states that do). By contrast, with an STS *rate* model, one continually reassesses a group's state at regular time intervals. Rate models are concerned not only with the paths groups take down the road to agreement but with their speed of movement as well. Hence, for rate models, generally $0 < t_{ii} < 1$.

The second conceptual distinction is between the two general research strategies that can govern model application (Kerr, Stasser, & Davis, 1979). With a *model-testing* strategy one begins with one or more theories of the group decision-making process, translates each distinct theory into a specific transition scheme (i.e., T), and then empirically tests the absolute or relative accuracy of each such T. Each theory specifies how heavily the various routes to agreement should be traveled, and a poor theory may be identified by carefully monitoring the "traffic." (See Godwin & Restle, 1974, for an illustration of this strategy with STS shift models.) The emphasis in the model-testing strategy is on prediction and theory testing. With a *model-fitting* strategy one does not fix the value of the model parameters (i.e., t_{ij}) theoretically but, rather, tries to estimate them directly from one's data, perhaps contrasting parameter estimates across conditions of special interest. The estimated STS matrix, $\hat{T}$, represents the model's descriptive summary of the process. One observes the traffic on the road to agreement with an eye to charting regular patterns and noting how the traffic depends on such factors as decision task, group composition, and the like. (See Davis, Stasser, Spitzer, & Holt, 1976, for an illustration of this strategy with STS rate models.) The emphasis in the model-fitting strategy is on description and theory building.

Path Independence and Stationarity

In terms of these conceptual distinctions, the present study represents a model-fitting application of both shift and rate models. Rather than construct and test theoretical models of the group decision-making process, we empirically tested two important assumptions that have routinely—and often only implicitly—been made by those employing a model-testing strategy (e.g., Godwin & Restle, 1974; Stasser & Davis, 1977): the assumptions of path independence and stationarity. *Stationarity* means that group decision-making process does not change over time; that is, the likelihood of a particular transition is constant throughout the course of group decision making. *Path independence* means that the likelihood of a group shifting into a particular state is independent of all previous states of the group except the one it is now in; in other words, where our group is going depends only on where it is right now but not on how we got here. It is hardly surprising that most STS modelers have made the stationarity and path-independence assumptions. Clearly, STS models that need not be concerned with the passage of time or a group's history will be considerably less complex than models that must somehow incorporate these factors. Under these assumptions, the STS model becomes a simple Markov chain and the SDS and STS models may be explicitly and very simply related (see Kerr, in press-b). But the investigation of these issues represents more than preliminary steps to the construction of parsimonious predictive models. The issues of stationarity and path independence represent fundamental psychological questions about the nature of small-group interaction: How does it vary over time, and how does the history of the group alter its future course? It is hardly surprising, therefore, that the same issues have been explored by other small-group investigators, although from quite different perspectives.

Several investigators (Bales & Strodtbeck, 1951; Bennis & Shepard, 1956; Fisher, 1970; Scheidel & Crowell, 1964; Tuckman, 1965) have concluded, from analyses of verbal communication during group decision making, that groups usually pass sequentially through several qualitatively different stages or phases as they work for consensus. Although the several phase models that have been suggested differ from one another in emphasis, the basic distinctions between phases are fairly similar for all of them. The group first must define the problem and allow the members to become oriented to the demands of the task and the conditions of the group. If there is no initial consensus, a period of more open exchange of views and conflict follows. Members of the group now tend to take sides and become committed, defending their positions and attacking those of nonallies. Eventually, the group will move into a period of conflict resolution in which a mutually acceptable decision begins to emerge. Group members converge in their positions and mutually support one another, attempting to heal the wounds of conflict and establish group solidarity and commitment to the final decision. This work clearly suggests that the group decision-making process is not stationary. In terms of STS rate models, it suggests that there is relatively little and relatively slow movement down the road to agreement during the early portions (orientation and conflict phases) of group interaction but much more rapid movement during the latter (conflict resolution and reconciliation) phases of the process. Such phase models have no obvious implications for the stationarity of STS shift models, however.

There is considerably less theory or research that addresses the path-independence issue than addresses the stationarity issue. If one can view movement toward an opposing faction during group discussion as a concession, then the bargaining research on reciprocation of concessions (e.g., Komorita & Brenner, 1968) clearly argues against path independence. Path independence would also be violated if the movement toward consensus tended to build momentum. Unfortunately, we know of few data that address these speculations (cf. Levine, Sroka, & Snyder, 1977). There appear to be several plausible possibilities: (a) Path independence may strictly and generally hold true. (b) It may be that path independence is violated only for a few extreme instances of defection from majorities or of recalcitrance. (c) There may be so much uniformity in the paths that groups take to agreement that the path-independence issue is irrelevant; that is, nearly every group may have arrived at its current fork in the road to agreement by the same path. Godwin and Restle's (1974) and Davis et al.'s (1976) data tend to support the latter possibility.

Time Limits, Group Experience, and Sex of Members

Besides examining the path-independence and stationarity assumptions, we examined the effect of three variables on the group decision-making process. The first variable was the amount of time available for group discussion. We were curious to see whether minorities yielded more readily to majorities when the amount of time available to the group to reach its decision was limited. The second variable was the amount of experience a group had in its decision task. At the minimum, one would expect groups to travel down the road to agreement faster as they become more accustomed to working together. If the futility of opposing strong majorities (consistently demonstrated by SDS research) becomes more apparent to group members as their experience with the process increases, one would also expect a shift-model representation of the process to vary with group experience. The third variable examined was the sex of the group members. Interaction process analyses (Bales, 1950) of decision-making groups has consistently indicated that females are relatively less likely to voice opinions and relatively more likely to voice support for others' opinions than are males (Piliavin & Martin, 1978; Strodtbeck & Mann, 1956). Also, most conformity and attitude change research that has looked for sex effects finds that females are more likely to yield to social pressure than are males, although this may well depend on task features (Eagly, 1978; Sistrunk & McDavid, 1971). Using the STS analyses, we wanted to see whether movement toward agreement on the more popular position was more certain and more rapid in female groups than in male groups.

The decision task used in this study was that of a jury. The reasons for this choice of task are worth considering briefly. Because our mock juries had only two decision alternatives (guilty or not guilty) the number of possible group "states" (i.e., distributions of preferences) was relatively small, making application of the model feasible and greatly simplifying the description and interpretation of the process data. It was also of interest to compare the results of the sizable literature applying the SDS model to jury decision making with an STS analysis. Also, there has recently been great interest and activity in modeling the decision-making process of juries (Penrod & Hastie, 1979). Several recently proposed models either are in the form of STS models (Klevorick & Rothschild, 1979; Stasser & Davis, 1977) or include an STS-type stage (Penrod & Hastie, 1980). All of these models assume path independence except for Penrod and Hastie's DICE model, which assumes that after having changed verdict preference, a juror becomes less likely to change preference again. And, except for Stasser and Davis's model, all of the models assume stationarity. Direct empirical evidence testing these theoretical assumptions is badly needed.

Finally, most jury research has consisted of extremely artificial simulations (Bray & Kerr, in press). Widespread concern for the ecological validity of jury simulation research has stimulated work examining the effect of the most common artificialities on jury verdicts (Weiten & Diamond, 1979). For example, research has examined the common use of students instead of community members as jurors (e.g., Bray, Struckman-Johnson, Osborne, McFarlane, & Scott, 1978; Simon & Mahan, 1971); brief, written case summaries instead of live trials (e.g., Bermant, McGuire, McKinley, & Salo, 1974); and hypothetical decisions instead of verdicts having important consequences for a defendant (e.g., Kerr, Nerenz, & Herrick, 1979). One factor that has not yet been examined is the limitation of deliberation time for mock juries (or, for that matter, any other decision-making group). While the deliberation time of actual juries is not limitless, it is rarely as short as (and never restricted to) the intervals typical of research using simulated juries. The design of this experiment permits an examination of this issue. It seems probable that mock juries with severe time limits would hang more often. A much more interesting question is whether such limits would materially affect the jury decision-making process.

Summary

To summarize, the primary objectives of this study were to examine the group decision-making process

for violations of path independence and stationarity. Secondary objectives were to examine the process for the effects of group experience, sex of members, and the imposition of time limits.

Method

Subjects and Design

The subjects were 282 (156 male, 126 female) undergraduate students who participated in partial fulfillment of a course requirement. Approximately 15 subjects of the same sex were scheduled for each experimental session. The first 12 subjects to arrive were tested in 2 6-person groups; if fewer than 12 subjects arrived, only 1 6-person group was tested. In all, 47 groups (26 male, 21 female) were tested. Because of an experimenter's error, an incorrect procedure was followed for 4 male groups. The data for these groups were not included in the present analyses, leaving a final sample of 258 subjects (132 males, 126 females) in 43 6-person groups (22 male, 21 female).

There was a single between-groups experimental manipulation: deliberation time limit. All groups performed as mock juries. In the unlimited condition, groups were to continue deliberation until they reached a unanimous verdict and were not permitted to declare themselves hopelessly deadlocked unless they had deliberated the case for at least 30 minutes.[1] In the limited condition, groups were given a maximum of 10 minutes to reach a unanimous verdict and were declared hung if they were unable to do so. There were 22 unlimited groups (12 male, 10 female) and 21 limited groups (10 male, 11 female).

Stimuli and Apparatus

The groups considered a set of nine one-page summaries of armed-robbery cases. Of course, if the evidence strongly favored either the prosecution or

---

[1] This provision was not followed for the four male groups that were dropped from the sample. They were unlimited groups that were allowed by the experimenter to declare themselves hung even though they had not yet deliberated a full 30 minutes.

the defense, there would be little or no disagreement in the group and, hence, nothing for the group to decide. Therefore, these cases were developed through pilot work and previous research (Kerr, in press-b) to produce roughly equal numbers of convictions and acquittals in individual predeliberation verdicts. Each case summary consisted of two paragraphs, one summarizing the evidence for the prosecution and the other summarizing the evidence for the defense.[2] Immediately before the start of deliberation, each group member received a folder containing all nine cases. On a cover sheet there was a summary of the instructions typically provided by the judge to juries considering armed-robbery cases (e.g., a legal definition of armed robbery, a reminder of the presumption of innocence, a definition of the reasonable-doubt concept). The order of cases in the folder was randomized separately for each group.

Subjects indicated their predeliberation verdicts and any change in verdict preference during group deliberation by pressing one of two buttons (for guilty and not guilty) on a response panel. Each subject had one panel, and the mock jury foreman had a second panel to indicate the group's verdict. The buttons on the response panel were interlocking; when a button was pressed it lit up as the light for the last response was extinguished. Hence, group members could always check their last response with a glance at their respective panels. When a subject made a response, the response and the time it was made were automatically encoded and stored in the memory of a microcomputer.

Subjects were seated around a large rectangular table. Each group member was identified by a letter (A through F). The person sitting in Position F was arbitrarily designated foreman. Low wooden partitions separated the seating positions. They permitted group members to see and talk to one another without obstruction but prevented observation of one another's response panels. This arrangement made it possible for subjects to make changes in verdict preference either unobtrusively and privately (e.g., by keeping one's hand on the table by the response panel) or publicly (e.g., by making quick or obtrusive movements to the response panel). Our goal in arranging the apparatus in this way was to disrupt the usual flow of group decision making as little as possible while still accurately monitoring each shift in position as it occurred.[3]

Procedure

Subjects were greeted and told that the study was concerned with how jurors arrive at a verdict. They were to take on the role of a jury and deliberate several armed-robbery cases tried in the local courts within the preceding 2 years.

The use of the response panels and the procedure to be followed were then described. When subjects began reading a case summary, they were to press a "begin reading" button on their panels. The purpose of this step was twofold: to clear the panels and to help separate encoded data for different cases. After reading the case summary, subjects were to individually and privately consider the evidence of the case and to personally decide how they would vote if they were on the actual jury that tried the case. After indicating their verdict preference on the response panel, they were to quietly wait until every member of the group finished reading the case and recorded a verdict. When the foreman (arbitrarily the person in Seat F) saw that everyone in the group had finished, he or she was to press a button on the jury's panel to signal the start of group deliberation.

The manipulation of deliberation time limit was introduced at this point. Members of unlimited groups were told that "although we would like you to finish as many of the cases as you possibly can today, there is no time limit on your deliberations of any case; you should continue to deliberate

---

[2] Copies of these case summaries may be obtained from the author on request.

[3] In a recent methodological study (Kerr, in press-b) we found that with only minor exceptions the use of an even more obtrusive monitoring procedure (polling the members of the group at 1-minute intervals) did not generally affect mock juries' verdicts, the length of deliberation, or subjects' perceptions of deliberations. (There were trends for polled groups to hang less and to reach their verdicts more rapidly than the unpolled control groups; see Stasser, Kerr, & Bray, in press, for an explanation of these trends.) It seems probable that the monitoring technique used in the present study is even less reactive.

on each case until you reach a unanimous verdict." The group was not to enter a response of "hung" on the jury's panel and proceed to the next case without first checking with the experimenter. They were not explicitly instructed on the necessity of deliberating for 30 minutes before being allowed to hang. Members of limited groups were told that they would have a maximum of 10 minutes to deliberate each case. The foreman was to note the time at which deliberations began on a digital clock visible to all members of the group. The group was to keep track of the time. In addition, the experimenter would signal them after 10 minutes had elapsed. If they were unable to agree unanimously on a verdict within the time limit, the foreman could enter a verdict of hung and the group could proceed to the next case.

Subjects were warned that unanimity at the start of jury deliberations was rare and, therefore, that most unanimous verdicts reflected changes in jurors' positions as a result of deliberation. Jurors were to indicate any change in position when it occurred by pressing the appropriate button on their response panel. The focus of this research was not on the effects of group discussion on members' personal opinions, unlike most research on risky shift or group polarization (e.g., Myers & Lamm, 1976) but on the process of group decision making itself. This is why we purposely avoided characterizing such changes as private acceptance of the new verdict. Less restrictively, these were described as indicating a willingness to support the new verdict alternative in pursuance of a group decision (i.e., "As deliberation goes along, if you decide you can support a different verdict, indicate this by changing your verdict on your juror box").

The foreman was told to take an oral poll of the jury whenever necessary to check the group's progress toward a unanimous verdict. If the group reached a unanimous verdict, the foreman was to record it on the jury's panel and the group was to proceed to the next case. Groups were instructed to consider the cases in the order in which they were contained in their folders. Again, this order was randomly determined for each group. After giving the foreman a sheet that summarized the procedure and after answering all questions, the experimenter gave subjects their case folders, told

them to read the cover sheet carefully, and then instructed them to begin reading the first case.

The groups were isolated during their deliberations, although they were told that they would be tape-recorded. All communication with the experimenter was conducted over an intercom system. If an unlimited group called the experimenter to say that they were hopelessly deadlocked and if 30 minutes had not elapsed, the group was told to continue deliberation and attempt to reach agreement. If such a deadlock report occurred after 30 or more minutes had elapsed, the group was allowed to halt deliberations and proceed to the next case. The experimenter signaled limited groups over the intercom if 10 minutes had elapsed without the submission of a group verdict. When a group had completed all nine cases or the 2-hour session length expired, groups were debriefed, thanked, and excused.

Results

The basic plan of the analyses was to compare the direction and speed of movements taken by groups down the road to agreement under several conditions of interest (e.g., comparing groups with different histories to test path independence, or comparing groups with and without time limits). For each such contrast, the analysis of the shift-model data, which describes only the direction of movement, is presented first. (These "shift" data should not be confused with choice shifts, i.e., differences in average member preference before vs. after discussion.) This is followed by the analysis of the rate data, which describes the speed of movement.

Overall Analyses

We begin with a description of the shift and rate data for the entire sample. This is done (a) to provide a general description of the groups' decision-making processes in terms of the STS model and (b) to present the notation, presentational format, and statistical assumptions used in all subsequent analyses.

Shift data. The task and the manner in which the shift data were collected make them fairly simple to summarize. Since there were only two decision alternatives available to the mock jurors, there were relatively few distinguishable distributions of preferences. For a six-person mock jury, there were seven such "states." Two of these states (7G–0NG, 0G–7NG) were end or "absorbing" states from which further movement should not have occurred (and did not occur). The remaining five states are listed in the left-most column of Table 12.1. The assessment of the timing of shifts was sufficiently precise to preclude simultaneous shifts by two or more members of the group.[4] Since only one member could shift at a time, this meant that groups could shift only into adjacent states. For example, a group with a 3G–3NG split could only shift to either a 4G–2NG split or a 2G–4NG split. Since there are only two directions of movement possible, toward fewer or more votes for a guilty verdict, only two columns are needed to present the shift data. The observed frequency of shifts for the entire data set is presented in the left panel of Table 12.1. (One would convert these, row by row, into relative frequencies to estimate the overall shift T, but the raw frequencies are more informative in the present context.)

The rows of this 5×2 matrix are the five possible states of the group from which movement can occur, and the columns are the two possible directions of movement. Consider, for example, the first row of the table. There were 89 instances in which a member of a group with a 5G–1NG[5] split was observed to change his or her vote. In 12 of these 89 instances, the shift reduced the number of guilty votes (i.e., was a shift from 5–1 to 4–2), whereas in the other 77 instances, the shift increased the number of guilty votes (i.e., was a shift from 5–1 to 6–0).

Two patterns are immediately evident in these data. The first is the strong drawing power of a majority. Group members were more likely to join a majority than to defect from one (one can confidently [$p < .01$] reject the null hypothesis of a uniform shift distribution for the 5–1, 2–4, and 1–5 rows but not for the 4–2 row), and this drawing power increases with the size of the majority (size of majority and shift distribution are significantly associated both when the majority favors conviction, $\chi^2 = 23.1$, $p < .001$, and when it favors acquittal, $\chi^2 = 4.32$, $p < .05$).[6]

The second clear pattern is that the table is asymmetric: Advocates of acquittal were more likely to win converts than were advocates of conviction. This can be seen most clearly when there is no majority in the group, that is, when there is a shift from a 3–3 split. Group members were about three

---

[4] Of course, simultaneous shifts by two or more group members are not precluded in principle. Because of equipment limitations, we could resolve the timing of shifts to an accuracy of approximately .01 second; responses made closer together than this would have been ordered by the microprocessor in an essentially random manner. Fortunately, none of the observed shifts occurred so closely together, just as previous research would have suggested (Davis et al., 1976).

[5] Henceforth, when speaking of an *a–b* split, we assume that *a* is the number favoring a guilty verdict and *b* is the number favoring a not-guilty verdict.

[6] In all of the statistical tests reported in the text, the unit of analysis was a shift by a group member. Statistically, this means that we have assumed that the shifts were independent events. Of course, since each group considered several cases, it was not uncommon for the same kind of shift to be made more than once by a single group, either on different cases or (infrequently) on the same case. The primary reason for making this assumption was that parameter estimation and statistical inference would have effectively been impossible for several of the questions of interest had we followed the standard practice of using the group as the unit of analysis. For example, in attempting to address the question of path independence, we could have included in the analysis only groups that took both possible paths at a fork in the road to agreement. But as we soon will show, since certain paths are almost never taken, there were always few and sometimes no groups that could have been included in such analyses. Besides hard necessity, one can justify making this assumption on other grounds. First, it has been standard practice in research of this type. Statistical analyses of all previous applications of STS-type models made this assumption either explicitly or implicitly (cf. Davis et al., 1976; Godwin & Restle, 1974). Second, the observed shifts are not logically or functionally dependent; each is a distinct and unique event. Third, the test bias that would result from the most likely type of dependence (i.e., positive autocorrelations between responses within a group) is a conservative bias (i.e., $\alpha_{\text{true}} < .05$). Finally, where possible, we repeated the analyses reported in the test using the average group response as the replicate. The patterns of these results were the same as the patterns presented in the text, although sometimes tests could not be performed at all and the extremely small sample sizes that we often wound up with meant that some effects were not significant in these analyses.

TABLE 12.1. Overall Shift Frequencies and Mean Times to Shift

ith state[a]	Shift to (i + 1) state[b]		Mean tts[c]	n[d]
	G↓	G↑		
5–1	12	77	160.0	87
4–2	43	52	251.4	93
3–3	80	27	290.7	104
2–4	126	10	155.9	128
1–5	143	2	84.0	134

[a] For the ith state column, the first value signifies the number of votes for a guilty verdict and the second value signifies the number of votes for a not-guilty verdict.
[b] The G↓ signifies a shift that reduced the number of votes for a guilty verdict, whereas the G↑ signifies a shift that increased the number of votes for a guilty verdict.
[c] Time to shift (measured in seconds).
[d] The number of cases on which the mean time to shift was calculated was sometimes less than the number of shifts because the microprocessor clock was not working for three groups.

times as likely to shift toward the faction favoring acquittal than to shift toward the faction favoring conviction.[7] When the majority favored acquittal, these two patterns reinforced each other, making the drawing power of such majorities very strong. When the majority favored conviction, these two tendencies opposed each other, thus attenuating the drawing power of such majorities. These two patterns, which we hereinafter term the *majority* and *asymmetry* effects, have been repeatedly

---

[7] Such asymmetries have also been reported for other types of decision tasks. For example, Vinokur (1969) showed that for choice-dilemma items which consistently produce risky shifts, the average postdiscussion shift was toward risk, even when the groups began discussion with symmetric preference distributions. Asymmetries in shift Ts may thus serve to signal when a "social value" (Brown, 1965) is attached to advocacy of a particular point of view.

The explanation of the asymmetry effect in jury decision making is an interesting substantive issue in its own right. It may reflect a strong leniency norm among the college student subjects who typically serve as mock jurors (Cvetkovick & Baumgardner, 1973), a greater perceived cost of convicting an innocent defendant in jury—as opposed to juror—decision making (cf. Kerr, 1978), or the greater apparent ease of raising a single reasonable doubt than of refuting all reasonable doubts (Nemeth, 1977). See Stasser et al. (in press) for a discussion of these issues.

observed in previous jury research (cf. Davis, 1980; Kalven & Zeisel, 1966; Stasser et al., in press).[8]

Rate data. One way to describe the rate at which groups move along the road to agreement is to estimate the diagonal elements of a T matrix, that is, the probability that the group will remain in its current state per unit time. In this paper, however, we use a different although closely related statistic: the mean time to shift (*tts*) out of a state.[9] The whole-sample *tts* means (in seconds) are presented in the right portion of Table 12.1. The *tts* varied significantly across states, $F(4, 541) = 10.74$, $p < .001$. These data tend to parallel the shift data. The closer the group was to consensus (i.e., the larger the majority), the more quickly the next shift occurred. Generally, the more certain the direction of shift, the faster the shift. However, shifts seemed to occur a bit more slowly in the evenly split juries than this rule would suggest.

Path Independence

Shift data. The whole-sample shift data clearly show that the direction in which a group is likely to move on the road to agreement depends strongly on where it currently stands. The question we now address is, Does it also depend on how the group got to where it now stands? For any given current state (i.e., split) of a jury, it has, at most, three possible immediate shift histories: It may always have been in its current state (i.e., it may have started deliberation in that state); the last shift could have been one that increased the number of guilty

---

[8] In order to check the possibility that these effects were case specific, we undertook additional overall shift analyses that included stimulus case as a factor in the contingency table analyses. The magnitude of the majority effect was not significantly different across cases. Although cases did differ significantly in the strength of the asymmetry effect, these differences were of degree, not of kind; asymmetry was evident for every case.

[9] Besides being a more readily interpreted statistic than t_{ii}, the *tts* statistic is not as sensitive to the effects of outliers. That is, t_{ii} is directly proportional to the total time spent by all groups in the ith state. This means that even when almost all groups shift quickly out of that state, one could obtain a very large t_{ii} value because of an occasional deadlocked group.

votes; or the last shift could have been one that decreased the number of guilty votes. Path independence requires that the probabilities of further movement in each direction not vary across these histories.

To examine this issue, we cast the shift data in a three-dimensional contingency table (see Table 12.2), with the dimension's *previous shift* (i.e., shift from the $i - 1$th state), *current state* (i.e., the ith state), and *next shift* (i.e., shift to the $i + 1$th state). Thus, for example, there were 44 instances of the sequence $(4-2) \rightarrow (5-1) \rightarrow (6-0)$, 18 instances where the first shift of the group was a $(3-3) \rightarrow (4-2)$ shift, and so on. These frequencies were analyzed by log-linear techniques for incomplete, multidimensional contingency tables (see Bishop, Fienberg, & Holland, 1975, Chap. 5). There are two effects relevant to the path-independence issue. The first is the association between the previous shift and the next shift, which is analogous to a main effect of prior history on future movement of the group. The significance of this effect signifies that movement toward or away from conviction differs with prior history, but this effect is constant across the possible current states of the group. The second relevant effect is the three-way association among previous shift, current state, and the next shift. This is analogous to an interaction effect of current state and prior history on the future movement of the group. The significance of this effect signifies that prior history does have an effect on the direction of the next shift, and the effect varies with the current state of the group.

We tested these effects by likelihood ratio statistics, denoted G^2 which are asymptotically distributed as χ^2. The "main effect" of history was highly significant, $G^2(2) = 19.12$, $p < .001$. As the data in Table 12.2 show, there was a kind of "momentum" effect at work. Groups whose last shift increased the number of guilty votes were more likely to continue movement in that direction than were groups with no shift history. Conversely, groups whose last shift decreased the number of guilty votes were more likely to continue movement in that direction than were groups with no shift history. The only glaring exception to this pattern

TABLE 12.2. Path-Independence Analyses: Shift Frequencies

	Shift from ($i - 1$)th state						
	$G\uparrow$		$G\downarrow$		Start		
	Shift to $i + 1$th state						
ith state	$G\downarrow$	$G\uparrow$	$G\downarrow$	$G\uparrow$	$G\downarrow$	$G\uparrow$	τ
5–1	3	44	–	–	9	33	.088
4–2	11	11	7	1	25	40	.075
3–3	3	5	*35*	4	42	18	.105
2–4	1	1	*66*	2	59	7	.061
1–5	–	–	*117*	2	26	0	.003

Note: For the ith state column, the first value signifies the number of votes for a guilty verdict and the second value signifies the number of votes for a not-guilty verdict. Shift frequencies are italicized for those groups in which at least one shift has occurred and which have taken the most typical path to their current state. The $G\downarrow$ signifies a shift that reduced the number of votes for a guilty verdict, whereas the $G\uparrow$ signifies a shift that increased the number of votes for a guilty verdict.

occurred for the 4–2 current split: The sequence $(3-3) \rightarrow (4-2) \rightarrow (3-3)$ occurred more frequently than the overall main effect pattern would suggest. However, the test of the "interaction effect" of prior and current state did not achieve statistical significance, $G^2(6) = 11.00$, $p < .09$.

Thus, the group decision-making process for these groups was not path independent. However, some other patterns should also be noted in these data. First, almost all groups traveled down the same road to agreement. Stated another way, almost every group with some shift history had the same shift history. This is not surprising in the 5–1 and 1–5 states, since groups are unlikely to shift out of states of unanimous agreement. But this was also true for the other states. Almost all groups with a 2–4 split either always had that split (i.e., began deliberation with it) or previously had a 3–3 split; in only 2 of 136 2–4 splits did the group get there by the $(5-1) \rightarrow (2-4)$ route. Similarly, but less strikingly because of the asymmetry effect, almost all groups with a 4–2 split either always had such a split or previously had a 3–3 split; in only 8 of 95 4–2 splits did the group get there by the $(5-1) \rightarrow (4-2)$ route. These data again reflect just how rare it is for a group member to defect from a faction with a strong majority. The asymmetry effect underlies the typical history of groups with an even 3–3 split. Usually they either had begun deliberation with an even split or had come to one by the (4–2) → (3–3) path; in only 8 of 110 3–3 splits did the group get there by the (2–4) → (3–3) route.

Clearly, some paths to agreement are almost never taken. This raises the question of whether the violation of path independence is caused by these very unusual and perhaps disruptive shifts. To answer this question, we contrasted groups with no prior shift history with those with the most typical shift history (the italicized distributions in Table 12.2). Again, we applied log-linear model analyses. Contrary to the notion that it was the unusual shift (e.g. defections from large majorities) that altered the group decision-making process, the interaction of prior shift and current state on next shift was significant, $G^2(4) = 12.94$, $p < .02$.[10] The majority and asymmetry effects tended to be accentuated in groups with the normative shift history relative to those with no shift history. These two tendencies came into most direct conflict where there was only a weak majority for conviction (i.e., the 4–2 split). The asymmetry effect seems to have predominated here.

The preceding analyses demonstrate that the violation of path independence is reliable and is not solely attributable to certain unusual, potentially disruptive shifts. However, it is also important to note that the violation of path independence is not particularly strong. We used the τ statistic (Bishop et al., 1975, pp. 389–392) to estimate the strength of association between the prior history of groups and their next shift. We chose this statistic because it can be directly interpreted as a measure of percentage of variation accounted for by the prior history factor, much like an ω^2 statistic for analyses of variance. The τ statistics resulting from row-by-row analyses are presented in Table 12.2. Generally, the proportion of variance in the next shift accounted for by the group's prior history was quite low. The strongest effect is in the 3–3 row, for which $\tau = .105$. The τ statistic over the full table

was .082. This means that one would decrease the proportion of incorrect predictions of groups' next shift by only 8.2% by taking into account the groups' immediately prior shift history instead of ignoring it. Hence, an STS model that assumed path independence (i.e., a Markov chain model), while not being strictly correct, would predict these mock juries' shift data almost as well as a model that did not assume path independence.

Rate data. We performed several least squares analyses of variance on the *tts* scores. Unlike the analysis of the shift data, the empty cells in Table 12.2 prevented a fully crossed 3 (Prior Shift) × 5 (Current State) factorial analysis. We restricted the first analysis to the three middle rows, which produced no significant effects involving the prior history factor. When we compared the speed of shifting for groups without a previous shift with the speed of all those with a previous shift in a 2 (Prior Shift: none vs. some) × 5 (Current State) analysis of variance (ANOVA), we obtained a significant main effect of prior history, $F(1, 536) = 11.18, p < .001$. Groups with a previous shift were faster to shift than those without a previous shift ($M = 128.1$ and 246.1 seconds, respectively). This effect did not vary with current state, $F < 1$.

Stationarity

Shift data. The primary difficulty in testing for stationarity was determining how best to divide the groups' deliberations for purposes of comparison. We have already described one approach: by contrasting groups with and without previous shifts. Another way of thinking about this question is in terms of real time. However, choosing one or more cutoff points in real time (e.g., every 3 minutes) might result in confounding the stationarity contrast with one between groups that finished quickly and those that did not (and, perhaps, between limited with unlimited groups).

---

[10] The test of the "main effect" of prior history was not meaningful here, since the "normal" prior history varied across current states. It is worth noting that this test (i.e., the significant "interaction" effect) also examined stationarity, in a sense.

Since the progress of the process for a shift model is marked by shifts, by comparing groups with no shifts with (nearly all) those with some shifts, we tested the shift stationarity of the process.

TABLE 12.3. Stationarity Analyses on Shift Frequencies

	Time of shift				
	Early		Late		
*i*th state	$G\downarrow$	$G\uparrow$	$G\downarrow$	$G\uparrow$	τ
5–1	5	2	7	73	.24
4–2	18	14	23	38	.03
3–3	29	10	48	17	3×10^{-5}
2–4	16	6	102	4	.12
1–5	4	1	128	1	.09

Note: For the *i*th state column, the first value signifies the number of votes for a guilty verdict and the second value signifies the number of votes for a not-guilty verdict. Early-shift data are based on shifts occurring prior to the midpoint of each group's deliberation. Late-shift data are based on shifts occurring after the midpoint of each group's deliberation. The $G\downarrow$ signifies a shift that reduced the number of votes for a guilty verdict, whereas the $G\uparrow$ signifies a shift that increased the number of votes for a guilty verdict.

We chose instead to compare the shifts occurring during the first half of every group's deliberation with the shifts that occurred during the second half. These data are presented in Table 12.3. As with the tests of path independence, there were two effects to be tested: a "main effect" of timing (early vs. late in deliberation) on the direction of shift and an "interaction effect" of timing and the group's current state. The former effect was not significant, $G^2(1) = .68$, but the latter effect was highly significant, $G^2(4) = 30.6$, $p < .001$. The majority effect was stronger during the second half than during the first half of group deliberation. When no majority existed (3–3 splits), the asymmetry effect was also stronger during the second half of deliberation.

The preceding tests of the stationarity assumption were not altogether independent of the tests of path independence. This was so because the longer the deliberation process, the more likely it was that the group had already shifted. Since the effect of the passage of time seemed to be similiar to the effect of having previously shifted, we undertook another analysis. We broke down the shift data in Table 12.3 into the group's first shift versus its later shifts. If the violation of stationarity was attributable to the path dependence of the group decision-making process, we would not expect stationarity to be violated for the first shift made by the group. A test of this hypothesis was not significant,

$G^2(4) = 2.11$; the nonstationarity effect held equally for first and later shifts. Apparently the violation of stationarity involved something more than the violation of path independence.

Although the stationarity assumption was violated, the strength of the effect was generally not great. The τ statistics for row-by-row tests of the stationarity assumption are presented in Table 12.3. Again, they tend to be fairly small. The τ statistic for the entire table was .07. Thus, ignoring the nonstationarity of the group decision-making process would reduce the predicted variance of shifts by only about 7%.

Rate data. When the *tts* scores were analyzed in a 2 (Timing: early vs. late) × 5 (Current State) least squares analysis of variance, timing produced a significant ($p < .02$) main effect: Shifts were made more rapidly during the first half of deliberation. However, this result was artifactual. Shifts that occurred during the first half of deliberation could have a maximum time equal to half of the deliberation. But shifts that occurred during the second half could have been preceded by the entire length of deliberation. When we repeated the analysis with the restriction that the last and current shift had to occur within the same half of the group's deliberation, there were no significant effects involving timing.

Time Limits

Product data. Before the effects of imposing a time limit on the shift and rate process data are examined, it is of interest to see whether such limits affected group decisions. The group verdict data, broken down by case, are presented in Table 12.4. Log-linear model analysis indicated that time limits and verdicts were significantly associated. $G^2(2) = 29.4$. The data suggest that the principal effect of limiting deliberation time was to increase the likelihood that the jury would hang. Indeed, when hung juries were dropped from the analysis of Table 12.4, the time limit factor was no longer associated with jury verdicts. But do these product differences stem from differences in the process through which groups with and without a deadline

TABLE 12.4. Time Limits and Jury Verdicts

	Limited			Unlimited		
Case	G	NG	H	G	NG	H
1	7	6	7	6	11	2
2	7	9	4	7	8	3
3	2	11	8	0	14	0
4	2	12	6	4	11	1
5	4	12	5	7	7	1
6	8	4	9	5	9	1
7	6	6	9	8	5	1
8	1	12	7	4	11	2
9	9	3	7	9	6	3

Note: G = guilty, NG = not guilty, H = hung.

TABLE 12.5. The Effect of Time Limit on Shift Frequencies

	Limited		Unlimited	
*i*th state	$G\downarrow$	$G\uparrow$	$G\downarrow$	$G\uparrow$
5–1	7	36	5	41
4–2	16	24	27	28
3–3	33	12	47	15
2–4	53	5	73	5
1–5	66	0	77	2

Note: For the *i*th state column, the first value signifies the number of votes for a guilty verdict and the second value signifies the number of votes for a non-guilty verdict. The $G\downarrow$ signifies a shift that reduced the number of votes for a guilty verdict, whereas the $G\uparrow$ signifies a shift that increased the number of votes for a guilty verdict.

work toward consensus, as many critics of mock jury research have feared?

Shift data. The shift data for the limited and unlimited groups are presented in Table 12.5. Inspection of these data indicates that the imposition of time limits had little effect on the groups' path to consensus. This was confirmed statistically by the log-linear model analyses. There was no significant main effect of time limits on the direction of shift, $G^2(1) = .12$, nor did time limits affect direction of shift differentially across current states, $G^2(4) = 3.99$. In light of these results, we computed no τ statistics.

Rate data. When we analyzed *tts* scores in a 2 (Time Limits: limited vs. unlimited) × 5 (Current State) least squares analysis of variance, time limits produced a significant main effect on speed of shifting, $F(1, 536) = 5.73$, $p < .02$. The intershift interval was longer on the average for groups that were not limited in their deliberations. However, this did not necessarily imply that members of limited groups hurried to meet the deadline. It might just reflect the fact that whenever a limited group reached an impasse, the time limit might have run out without another shift occurring, whereas an unlimited group might eventually have been able to make further progress. These hard-won, time-consuming shifts would inflate the unlimited groups' mean *tts* scores. One way of eliminating this artifact would be to analyze only shifts that occurred before 10 minutes of deliberation had elapsed. If

limited groups rushed to meet the time limit, there should still have been a time limit main effect for this data subset. This was not the case. There were no significant main or interaction effects involving time limits when we restricted analysis to the same period for both conditions. Hence, the rate data closely paralleled the shift data; neither analysis indicated any effect of imposing a time limit on the speed with which or direction in which groups moved along the road to agreement.

Group Experience

Shift data. We tallied the shift frequencies separately for cases in which the group was relatively inexperienced at working together (i.e., the first four cases considered) and those in which they were relatively experienced at working together (the fifth and later cases). These data are presented in Table 12.6. Log-linear analyses were done. The amount of experience in the group was not associated with the direction of shifts: $G^2(1) = .03$ for the main effect of experience and $G^2(4) = 3.4$ for the Experience × Current State interaction effect.

Rate data. The *tts* scores were analyzed in a 2 (Experience) × 5 (Current State) least squares analysis of variance. The experience main effect was significant, $F(1, 536) = 6.94$, $p < .01$, and the interaction effect was also significant, $F(4, 536) = 3.12$, $p < .02$. The mean *tts* scores are given in Table 12.6 and indicate that the experienced groups were quicker to shift, particularly

TABLE 12.6. The Effect of Group Experience on Shift Frequencies and Rate Data

	Shift frequencies				Time to shift			
	Low exp.		High exp.		Low exp.		High exp.	
*i*th state	G↓	G↑	G↓	G↑	M (in sec.)	n[a]	M (in sec.)	n[a]
5–1	6	41	6	36	171.9	45	147.2	42
4–2	22	28	21	24	251.8	49	251.0	44
3–3	45	13	35	14	394.1	55	174.6	49
2–4	70	6	56	4	180.2	72	124.7	56
1–5	72	2	71	0	85.5	70	82.3	64

Note: Exp. = experience. For the *i*th state column, the first value signifies the number of votes for a guilty verdict and the second value signifies the number of votes for a not-guilty verdict. The G↓ signifies a shift that reduced the number of votes for a guilty verdict, whereas the G↑ signifies a shift that increased the number of votes for a guilty verdict.
[a] Sample size.

for the even 3–3 split. We examined one possible artifactual explanation. Some unlimited groups took so long discussing the first few cases that they were not able to consider all nine cases. Thus, the slower groups may have been under-represented in the experienced-group sample. However, when the analysis was restricted to limited groups only, we obtained the same significant pattern of results. Even though the direction of movement did not seem to change with experience, experience seemed to hasten movement, particularly when the group was sharply divided.

Sex of Group Members

Shift data. The shift frequency data are presented in Table 12.7. Log-linear analyses resulted in no significant associations involving group member sex and next shift: $G^2(1) = .24$ for sex main effect and $G^2(4) = 3.49$ for Sex × Current State interaction.

Rate data. The analysis of variance of the *tts* scores produced no significant effects involving member sex.

Predicting the Group Product

The path-independence analyses suggested that there was a kind of momentum effect in the group decision process: movement in one direction signaled a greater likelihood of further movement in that direction. Hence, the first shift made in a group may be particularly informative about the group's eventual decision (Hawkins, 1960). This suggested

TABLE 12.7. The Effect of Sex on Shift Frequencies

	Males		Females	
*i*th state	G↓	G↑	G↓	G↑
5–1	6	36	6	41
4–2	27	26	16	26
3–3	45	14	35	13
2–4	58	7	68	3
1–5	68	1	75	1

Note: For the *i*th state column, the first value signifies the number of votes for a guilty verdict and the second value signifies the number of votes for a not-guilty verdict. The G↓ signifies a shift that reduced the number of votes for a guilty verdict, whereas the G↑ signifies a shift that increased the number of votes for a guilty verdict.

a rather simple predictive rule: The group will choose that alternative toward which the first shift in opinion in the group occurs. We compared the predictive accuracy of this rule with that of a simple majority rule (i.e., the group will choose that alternative initially favored by a majority of its members). This comparison is of particular interest because much of the SDS research suggests that one need not look at the group decision-making process to predict its product reasonably well; simple rules (e.g., majority wins) often relate initial member preferences with the group's final decision. If a "first shift" rule exceeded the predictive accuracy of such decision schemes, it would strengthen the argument for more process-oriented analyses.

The results of this model comparison are given in Table 12.8. Generally, the first-shift model was

TABLE 12.8. Comparison of Majority-Wins and First-Shift-Wins Model

Variable	Majority wins	First shift wins
Total number of guilty, not-guilty, and hung juries	297	297
Number of juries for which the model makes no predictions	76	37
Number of juries for which the model makes a prediction	221	260
Total number of guilty and not-guilty verdicts for which the model makes a prediction	177	221
Number of jury verdicts correctly predicted	151	212
Number of jury verdicts incorrectly predicted	70	48

superior. Both models were unable to make predictions for certain groups—when no majority existed or when no shift occurred (although the latter cases were, by definition, hung juries and were, in this circular sense, predictable). In the present sample there were fewer such indeterminate cases for the first-shift rule. However, this simply reflects the large number of groups with initially even splits, a consequence of our choice of cases. Among the cases for which the models could make a prediction, the first-shift model was superior (81% vs. 68%

[11] Of course, if the group's first shift was (5–1) → (6–0) or (1–5) → (0–6), by definition the group decision would be in the direction of the first shift. The superiority of the first-shift rule was not, however, the result of this degenerate case. When all groups beginning with 5–1 or 1–5 splits were dropped from the above analysis, the first-shift rule predicted 78% (150/192) correct of those cases for which it could make a prediction versus 61% (91/149) for the majority-wins rule. Excluding hung juries, again the first-shift rule was superior (95% vs. 80%).

Although it was not directly relevant to the group-process questions posed in this paper, another pattern in these data might be noted. As in a previous study (Kerr, in press-b), we observed that subjects who started group deliberation as members of a minority faction for one case were significantly more likely than majority-faction members to choose the opposite predeliberation verdict on the following case. Minority-faction members switched predeliberation verdicts in 268 of 455 instances, or 59% of the time, compared with 47% (540/1,140) of majority-faction jurors. This "minority reversal" (Kerr, in press-a) effect has interesting implications for the effects of prior juror experience on juror behavior.

correct). If we exclude hung juries, the accuracy of both models is very high, but again, knowledge of the first shift is more informative than knowledge of the initial majority (96% vs. 85% correctly predicted).[11]

Discussion

The primary objectives of this paper were to test the path-independence and stationarity assumptions: Does the next step of a group's journey down the road to agreement depend on the path it has already traveled and on how long it has been traveling? The answer to both questions appears to be a qualified yes. The qualification is that the *speed* with which the group continues on its journey is not dependent on the path the group has taken or on how long it has been traveling. We should note, however, that the tests on which these conclusions were based may have been somewhat conservatively biased[12] and were sometimes based on few observations.

Although the rate at which groups moved seemed to be stationary and path independent, the process governing the choice of route did not. The path dependence of the process took the form of a momentum effect.[13] A group was relatively more likely to continue in the same direction in which it had last moved than to reverse its direction. This effect partially explains why a group's first shift is so strongly related to its final decision: If movement builds momentum, indications of early movement should be particularly informative (cf. Hawkins, 1960). Demonstrating this momentum effect poses

[12] See Footnote 6.

[13] The term *momentum* is used differently here than it has been elsewhere by researchers employing STS-like models (Klevorick & Rothschild, 1979; Penrod & Hastie, 1980). Others have used the term to refer to an increase in the drawing power of majorities as they increase in size. In physics, of course, momentum is a quantity directly proportional to the velocity of an object and which requires the application of some external force to be altered. Since previous researchers have not been directly concerned with the way in which the drawing powers of a majority depend on the group's "velocity" (i.e., its direction and speed of movement), their use of the term is less appropriate than the present use.

several interesting questions. One unresolved issue is whether the momentum effect reflects a genuine sensitivity of group members to movement by the group. The momentum effect could be a kind of "bandwagon effect" in which less strongly committed group members await some evidence of progress by one of the opposing factions before "climbing aboard." Or, once a group member has taken the difficult step of changing his or her position, he or she, or the others in the group, may consider it difficult for him/her to backslide, and thus conclude that if progress is to be made at all it must be made in the direction begun. The assumptions of Penrod and Hastie's (1980) computer model of jury decision making and Hawkins's (1960) data are consistent with the latter possibility; for example, Hawkins reported that his mock jurors almost never switched votes more than once.

On the other hand, the momentum effect may be a spurious one. Someone in the group may make a particularly persuasive argument which convinces several opponents to ultimately shift allegiance. To check out the latter possibility, apparent motion and discussion content must be independently manipulated. Assuming for the moment that the momentum effect is not spurious, an interesting strategic possibility is raised: Rather than support one's preferred position from the outset, it may be a better strategy under certain conditions to begin group discussion supporting a position other than one's genuine preference and then to shift to the preferred position early in group discussion. For example, suppose you were one of three members of a six-person jury who felt that the defendant was guilty, with the other three jurors voting not guilty. Our data suggest that if your group began deliberation with an even 3–3 split, the probability of the first shift going in your preferred direction, that is, of a (3–3) → (4–2) shift, is only .30. However, if you began deliberation supporting acquittal and were the first person to shift— in support of conviction—our data indicate that the probability of the desired shift would be .625. Again, experimental research is needed to test this notion.

The groups' decision-making process was nonstationary in two senses. When we compared groups that had never before shifted with those that had shifted in the usual direction, we found that the latter displayed majority and asymmetry effects more strongly. This first type of nonstationarity is closely related to the path-dependence effect. But in addition, when we compared groups that shifted during the first half of their deliberation period with those that shifted in the second half, again the latter exhibited stronger majority and asymmetry effects. Furthermore, this second type of nonstationarity is not just a restatement of the first type: The effect was just as strong for the first shift as it was for later shifts. It may be that the longer the group deliberates without someone defecting from the majority, the more resigned the minority members become to the necessity of shifting in order to arrive at a decision. Or perhaps the longer the discussion continues, the greater the cumulative weight of arguments for the majority position becomes (Hawkins, 1962), producing genuine persuasion, or at least grounds for minority members to justify their capitulation. The strengthening of the asymmetry effect has an obvious interpretation: The longer the discussion time, the more time for airing different arguments against conviction and the better the chance that one of those doubts about the defendant's guilt will strike a "guilty" voter as a reasonable one.

Thus, path independence and stationarity appear to be reliably violated in theoretically interesting and interpretable ways. But from the perspective of those who want to build models of the group decision-making process, an equally important finding may be that these effects, although significant, are rather weak. Generally, one who had chosen to ignore the nonstationarity and path dependence of the process would have done very nearly as well in predicting these shift data as one who had not ignored them. Of course, STS-like models that incorporate path dependence and nonstationarity are necessarily much more complex than models that do not. In light of the current results, it seems defensible to conclude that the predictive gain of incorporating nonstationarity and path dependence is not worthwhile, at least for models of jury decision making.

Such a conclusion is encouraging for the jury decision-making models of Penrod and Hastie (1980) and Klevorick and Rothschild (1979), since they assume stationarity and/or path independence. However, some features of our data contradict other

TABLE 12.9. Observed and Theoretical Ts

	Observed T		Theoretical Ts			
			Klevoric & Rothschild (1979)		Penrod & Hastie (1980)	
*i*th state	G↓	G↑	G↓	G↑	G↓	G↑
5–1	.13	.86	.17	.83	.20	.80
4–2	.45	.55	.33	.67	.45	.55
3–3	.75	.25	.50	.50	.50	.50
2–4	.92	.07	.67	.33	.55	.45
1–5	.99	.01	.83	.17	.80	.20

Note: For the *i*th state column, the first value signifies the number of votes for a guilty verdict and the second value signifies the number of votes for a not-guilty verdict. The G↓ signifies a shift that reduced the number of votes for a guilty verdict, whereas the G↑ signifies a shift that increased the number of votes for a guilty verdict.

key assumptions of these models. For example, Klevorick and Rothschild assume that the distribution of time to shift is constant across current states. The rate data of the current study indicate that as the size of a majority grew, not only did the direction of shift become more certain but the mean time to shift became shorter. The overall shift, $\hat{T}$, for jury decision making derived from our data (presented in the left panel of Table 12.9) also differs sharply with the shift T matrices suggested by these two models. Klevorick and Rothschild's model assumes that the probability that a group member will shift into a faction is equal to the proportion of jurors in that faction. The resultant shift, T, is presented in Table 12.9. Penrod and Hastie's model is based on a function that relates faction size with the probability that a juror will remain in that faction per unit time.[14] This function was arrived at by applying their model to several older data sets and systematically evaluating

alternative functions by Monte Carlo techniques. The resultant shift T for six-person juries is also presented in Table 12.9.

Comparison of the theoretical Ts of the models and the T estimated from our data shows that neither model mirrors the observed shift data. The models do not do badly when there is a strong majority for conviction, but as the number of jurors favoring conviction decreases, they do less and less well. A key difficulty for both models is that their theoretical assumptions require symmetric T matrices, whereas our shift data evidence a strong asymmetry effect. All of the SDS mock jury studies in which decision schemes were directly estimated (e.g., Davis, Kerr, Stasser, Meek, & Holt, 1977; Kerr et al., 1976) reported the asymmetry effect, and Davis et al.'s (1976) $\hat{T}$s were markedly asymmetric. (Stasser et al., in press, review the evidence for the asymmetry effect, discuss its external validity, and examine possible explanations for it.)

Secondary objectives of this study were to examine the effect of a group variable (the amount of experience at the task), a group member variable (sex of members), and a task variable (time limits) on the group decision-making process. These factors had very little effect. The amount of experience at the task did not affect the path the groups took to agreement, but sometimes was related to the speed with which they traveled down the path. Among the most sharply divided groups (i.e., those with a 3–3 split), a deadlock-breaking shift tended to occur sooner when the group was relatively more experienced at working together. Sex of group members had no effect on either the shift or the rate data. These results contribute to the research evidence that females are not generally more influenceable than males are (Eagly, 1978; Nemeth, 1977; Sistrunk & McDavid, 1971).[15]

The effects of imposing time limits is of both general theoretical interest and of special methodological importance for jury simulation research. Not surprisingly, the mock juries whose deliberation was limited to a maximum of 10 minutes per

---

[14] For the six-person jury, Penrod and Hastie (1980; corrected in an erratum in *Psychological Review*, 1980, 87, 476) assume that p (the probability that a member of an *s*-person faction will remain in that faction from time t to $t + 1$) is given by the function

$$p = [.5 + (.5|1 - 2s/n|^{2.5})]^{1/s}$$

for $s > 3$ and

$$p = [.5 - (.5|1 - 2s/n|^{2.5})]^{1/s}$$

for $s < 3$.

---

[15] These results also contradict the suggestion made by Penrod and Hastie (1980) that the asymmetry effect is stronger among females.

case were significantly less likely to reach unanimous verdicts than those whose time was effectively unlimited. However, the STS analysis produced no evidence of process differences between these conditions. One might argue that the case summaries were so brief that groups would not need more than 10 minutes to thoroughly discuss each case. But if this were so, one would also expect that unlimited groups that did reach a verdict would need no more time than the limited groups. In fact, they took significantly more time. The most reasonable interpretation of the full pattern of results is that the same process described both types of groups but that this process was halted after 10 minutes for the limited groups. One must also note that there was really no pressure on the limited groups to reach a decision in the available time. Some bargaining research (e.g., Komorita & Barnes, 1969) has shown that time pressures increase the rate of concessions and the frequency of agreement. Similarly, it may be that a decision deadline with attendant penalties for failure to reach agreement would affect the decision-making process. Although this possibility is an interesting theoretical question, it is not of much concern for jury decision making, since real juries are not pressured to meet a time deadline (although they are strongly encouraged to come to agreement, if possible). Altogether, our results offer encouragement to jury simulation researchers in that limits on deliberation time, which must generally be imposed as a practical matter, may not alter the process juries use to reach agreement.

In conclusion, the present application of the STS model demonstrates its utility for the study of the group decision-making process. The observed violations of the simplifying path independence and stationarity assumptions, besides being interesting phenomena for study in their own right, were not so serious as to preclude the development of simple process (and, hence, product) models. The STS model can also be a useful analytic tool. The analysis of shift and rate data holds much promise as an alternative/adjunct to communication-focused analysis. The STS model's basic unit of analysis, the internal distribution of preferences, may be obtained simply (particularly in comparison with

standard analyses like the interaction process analysis and nonreactively; Kerr, in press-b) and lends itself naturally to the study of many variables of relevance to small-group research besides those examined here (e.g., group size, position extremity, interfaction distance, etc.). The STS model should be a useful tool in future efforts to accurately chart the group's road to agreement.

REFERENCES

Bales, R. F. *Interaction process analysis.* Reading, Mass.: Addison-Wesley, 1950.

Bales, R. R., & Strodtbeck, F. L. Phases in group problem solving. *Journal of Abnormal and Social Psychology*, 1951, *46*, 485–495.

Bennis, W. G., & Shepard, H. A. A theory of group development. *Human Relations*, 1956, *9*, 415–437.

Bermant, G., McGuire, M., McKinley, W., & Salo, C. The logic of simulation in jury research. *Criminal Justice and Behavior*, 1974, *1*, 225–233.

Bishop, Y., Fienberg, S. E., & Holland, P. W. *Discrete multivariate analyses: Theory and practice.* Cambridge, Mass.: MIT Press, 1975.

Bray, R. M., & Kerr, N. L. Methodological considerations in the study of the psychology of the courtroom. In N. Kerr & R. Bray (Eds.), *The psychology of the courtroom.* New York: Academic Press, in press.

Bray, R. M., Struckman-Johnson, C., Osborne, M., McFarlane, J., & Scott, J. The effects of defendant status on the decisions of student and community jurors. *Social Psychology*, 1978, *41*, 256–260.

Brown, R. *Social psychology.* New York: Free Press, 1965.

Cvetkovich, G., & Baumgardner, S. Attitude polarization: The relative influence of discussion group structure and reference group norms. *Journal of Personality and Social Psychology*, 1973, *80*, 97–125.

Davis, J. H. Group decision and social interaction: A theory of social decision schemes. *Psychological Review*, 1973, *80*, 97–125.

Davis, J. H. Group decision and procedural justice. In M. Fishbein (Ed.), *Progress in social psychology.* Hillsdale, N.J.: Erlbaum, 1980.

Davis, J. H., Kerr, N. L., Atkin, R. S., Holt, R., & Meek, D. The decision processes of 6- and 12-person mock juries assigned unanimous and 2/3 majority decision rules. *Journal of Personality and Social Psychology*, 1975, *32*, 1–14.

Davis, J. H., Kerr, N. L., Stasser, G., Meek, D., & Holt, R. Victim consequences, sentence severity, and decision processes in mock juries. *Organizational Behavior and Human Performance*, 1977, *18*, 346–365.

Davis, J. H., Kerr, N., Sussman, M., & Rissman, A. K. Social decision schemes under risk. *Journal of Personality and Social Psychology*, 1974, *30*, 248–271.

Davis, J. H., Stasser, G., Spitzer, C. E., & Holt, R. W. Changes in group members' decision preferences during discussion: An illustration with mock juries. *Journal of Personality and Social Psychology*, 1976, *34*, 1177–1187.

Eagly, A. H. Sex differences in influenceability. *Psychological Bulletin*, 1978, *85*, 86–116.

Fisher, B. Decision emergence: Phases in group decision making. *Speech Monographs*, 1970, *37*, 53–66.

Godwin, W., & Restle, F. The road to agreement: Subgroup pressures in small group consensus processes. *Journal of Personality and Social Psychology*, 1974, *30*, 500–509.

Hawkins, C. H. *Interaction and coalition realignments in consensus seeking groups: A study of experimental jury deliberations.* Unpublished doctoral dissertation, University of Chicago, 1960.

Hawkins, C. H. Interaction rates of jurors aligned in factions. *American Sociological Review*, 1962, *27*, 689–691.

Kalven, H., & Zeisel, H. *The American jury*, Boston: Little, Brown, 1966.

Kerr, N. L. Severity of prescribed penalty and mock jurors' verdicts. *Journal of Personality and Social Psychology*, 1978, *36*, 1431–1442.

Kerr, N. L. Effects of prior juror experience on juror behavior. *Basic and Applied Social Psychology*, in press. (a)

Kerr, N. L. Social transition schemes: Model, method, and applications. In J. H. Davis & H. Brandstätter (Eds.), *Group decision making processes.* New York: Academic Press, in press. (b)

Kerr, N. L., Davis, J. H., Meek, D., & Rissman, A. K. Group position as a function of member attitudes: Choice shift effects from the perspective of social decision scheme theory. *Journal of Personality and Social Psychology*, 1975, *31*, 574–593.

Kerr, N. L., et al. Guilty beyond a reasonable doubt: Effect of concept definition and assigned decision rule on the judgments of mock jurors. *Journal of Personality and Social Psychology*, 1976, *34*, 282–294.

Kerr, N. L., Nerenz, D., & Herrick, D. Role playing and the study of jury behavior. *Sociological Methods and Research*, 1979, *7*, 337–355.

Kerr, N. L., Stasser, G., & Davis, J. H. Model-fitting, model-testing, and social decision schemes. *Organizational Behavior and Human Performance*, 1979, *23*, 399–410.

Klevorick, A. K., & Rothschild, M. A. Model of the jury decision process. *Journal of Legal Studies*, January 1979, pp. 141–161.

Komorita, S., & Barnes, M. Effects of pressure to reach agreement in bargaining. *Journal of Personality and Social Psychology*, 1969, *13*, 245–252.

Komorita, S., & Brenner, A. R. Bargaining and concession making under bilateral monopoly. *Journal of Personality and Social Psychology*, 1968, *9*, 15–20.

Leavitt, H. H. Some effects of certain communication patterns on group performance. *Journal of Abnormal and Social Psychology*, 1951, *46*, 38–50.

Levine, J. M., Sroka, K., & Snyder, H. Group support and reaction to stable and shifting agreement/disagreement. *Sociometry*, 1977, *40*, 214–224.

Myers, D., & Lamm, H. The group polarization phenomenon. *Psychological Bulletin*, 1976, *83*, 602–627.

Nemeth, C. Interactions between jurors as a function of majority vs. unanimity decision rules. *Journal of Applied Social Psychology*, 1977, *7*, 38–56.

Penrod, S., & Hastie, R. Models of jury decision making. A critical review. *Psychological Bulletin*, 1979, *86*, 462–492.

Penrod, S., & Hastie, R. A computer simulation of jury decision making. *Psychological Review*, 1980, *87*, 133–159.

Piliavin, J., & Martin, R. The effects of the sex composition of groups on style of social interaction. *Sex Roles*, 1978, *4*, 281–296.

Schachter, S. Deviation, rejection and communication. *Journal of Abnormal and Social Psychology*, 1951, *46*, 190–207.

Scheidel, T. M., & Crowell, L. Idea development in small discussion groups. *Quarterly Journal of Speech*, 1964, *50*, 140–145.

Simon, R. J., & Mahan, L. Quantifying burdens of proof: A view from the bench, the jury, and the classroom. *Law and Society Review*, 1971, *5*, 319–330.

Sistrunk, F., & McDavid, J. W. Sex variable in conforming behavior. *Journal of Personality and Social Psychology*, 1971, *17*, 200–207.

Stasser, G., & Davis, J. H. Opinion change during group discussion. *Personality and Social Psychology Bulletin*, 1977, *3*, 252–256.

Stasser, G., Kerr, N. L., & Bray, R. M. The social psychology of jury deliberations: Structure, process, and product. In N. Kerr & R. Bray (Eds.), *The psychology of the courtroom.* New York: Academic Press, in press.

Stasser, G., Kerr, N. L., & Davis, J. H. Influence processes in decision making groups: A modeling approach. In P. Paulus (Ed.), *Psychology of group influence.* Hillsdale, N.J.: Erlbaum, 1980.

Stephan, F. F., & Mishler, E. G. The distribution of participation in small groups: An exponential approximation. *American Sociological Review*, 1952, *17*, 598–608.

Strodtbeck, F., & Mann, R. Sex role differentiation in jury deliberations. *Sociometry*, 1956, *19*, 2–11.

Tuckman, B. W. Developmental sequence in small groups. *Psychological Bulletin*, 1965, *63*, 384–399.

Vinokur, A. Distribution of initial risk levels in group decisions involving risk. *Journal of Personality and Social Psychology*, 1969, *13*, 207–214.

Vinokur, A., & Burnstein, E. Effects of partially shared persuasive arguments on group-induced shifts: A group-problem-solving approach. *Journal of Personality and Social Psychology*, 1974, *29*, 305–315.

Weiten, W., & Diamond, S. S. A critical review of the jury simulation paradigm: The case of defendant characteristics. *Law and Human Behavior*, 1979, *3*, 71–95.

Received October 29, 1980 ■

READING 13

Pooling of Unshared Information in Group Decision Making: Biased Information Sampling During Discussion

Garold Stasser and William Titus*

Decision-making groups can potentially benefit from pooling members' information, particularly when members individually have partial and biased information but collectively can compose an unbiased characterization of the decision alternatives. The proposed biased sampling model of group discussion, however, suggests that group members often fail to effectively pool their information because discussion tends to be dominated by (a) information that members hold in common before discussion and (b) information that supports members' existent preferences. In a political caucus simulation, group members individually read candidate descriptions that contained partial information biased against the most favorable candidate and then discussed the candidates as a group. Even though groups could have produced unbiased composites of the candidates through discussion, they decided in favor of the candidate initially preferred by a plurality rather than the most favorable candidate. Group members' pre- and postdiscussion recall of candidate attributes indicated that discussion tended to perpetuate, not to correct, members' distorted pictures of the candidates.

Portions of this study were reported at the 91st annual meeting of the American Psychological Association, Anaheim, California, 1983. We thank Alison Karas, Jerry Kasai, Scott Snell, and Amelia Tynan for assisting in data collection and analysis. We also thank James Davis and Norbert Kerr for reading and commenting on an earlier draft of this article.

Requests for reprints should be sent to Garold Stasser, Department of Psychology, Miami University, Oxford, Ohio 45056.
* Briar Cliff College.

Decision-making groups must often choose from a set of specified alternatives (e.g., guilty and not guilty for a jury, a set of applicants for a selection committee), and this choice is typically preceded by discussion of the merits of each alternative. One goal of discussion is to achieve a consensus among the group's members. Another goal is to pool members' expertise and knowledge. In principle, pooling information permits a group decision that is more informed than the decisions of members acting individually. In particular, discussion can perform a corrective function when members individually have incomplete and biased information but collectively can piece together an unbiased picture of the relative merits of the decision alternatives. Notwithstanding the potential of discussion to serve such a corrective function, group discussion may often fall short of its potential. Discussion is rarely a systematic and balanced exploration of the relevant issues. On the contrary, it is often thematic and consensus confirming; that is, discussion tends to focus on particular issues and to support an existing or emergent consensus (cf. Fisher, 1980). Such patterns may counter effective pooling of information and may perpetuate biases that members bring to the group.

In this article, we explore the dynamics of discussion within the framework of an information sampling model. This model highlights the role of the pregroup information distribution, a summary of which group members are exposed to what information before discussion. The distribution of information among group members may give rise to several types of bias. Informational bias occurs when individual group members are given partial sets of information that do not reflect the balance of available supporting arguments for the various decision alternatives. Such biased sets of information may, in turn, result in preferential bias: individual members' preferring alternatives at the onset of discussion that they would not prefer if they had complete information. Finally, the sampling model suggests that the pregroup biases in information and preference may act to bias the content of subsequent discussion. Thus the content of discussion tends to reflect but not to correct biases introduced by the distribution of information over group members before discussion.

Pregroup Information Distributions

For many topics of group discussion and decision, we can think of a set of relevant information and arguments (cf. Burnstein & Vinokur, 1977). Members are usually aware of some subset of these arguments before the group convenes and, on the basis of this subset, have a tentative preference for one of the alternatives. During group discussion, members exchange arguments and reevaluate their initial preferences. The information and arguments that members collectively bring to the group guide the emergence of a consensus in two ways. On the one hand, such information shapes the initial preferences of the group members; these initial preferences define the degree of consensus that exists at the onset of discussion. On the other hand, the content of discussion is drawn from the existing pool of information and arguments, and the balance of arguments favoring one position relative to another partly determines which preferences are likely to be strengthened or changed during the course of discussion.

It is important to consider not only how much supporting information exists for each alternative but also how this information is distributed across a group's members before their discussion. In the extreme, there are two kinds of pregroup information distributions: *shared* information is familiar to all group members, whereas *unshared* information is held by only one of the group's members. (Of course, there are degrees between these two extremes in that an argument or fact may be shared by several but not all members; for our purposes, we shall only consider these two extreme cases.) Burnstein and Vinokur (1977) made a similar distinction in their persuasive arguments theory of group polarization. We will use an example suggested by their analysis to illustrate the distinction between shared and unshared information distributions.

Consider a simple case in which a three-person group must decide between two alternatives, A and B. Suppose that there exist seven items of information favoring A (denoted as a_1, a_2, ..., a_6, and a_7) and four items of information favoring B (denoted as b_1, b_2, b_3, and b_4). For ease of discussion, we assume that these 11 items of information

TABLE 13.1. Some Possible Pregroup Distributions of Seven Pro-A (a_i) and Four Pro-B (b_i) Items of Information Over Three Group Members

	Group member		
Item position	X	Y	Z
Case 1: All information shared			
Pro-A	$a_1, a_2, a_3, a_4, a_5, a_6, a_7$	$a_1, a_2, a_3, a_4, a_5, a_6, a_7$	$a_1, a_2, a_3, a_4, a_5, a_6, a_7$
Pro-B	b_1, b_2, b_3, b_4	b_1, b_2, b_3, b_4	b_1, b_2, b_3, b_4
Case 2: Unbiased distribution			
Pro-A			
Shared	a_1	a_1	a_1
Unshared	a_2, a_3	a_4, a_5	a_6, a_7
Pro-B			
Shared	b_1	b_1	b_1
Unshared	b_2	b_3	b_4
Case 3: Mildly biased distribution			
Pro-A			
Shared	a_1, a_2, a_3, a_4	a_1, a_2, a_3, a_4	a_1, a_2, a_3, a_4
Unshared	a_5	a_6	a_7
Pro-B[a]	b_1, b_2, b_3, b_4	b_1, b_2, b_3, b_4	b_1, b_2, b_3, b_4
Case 4: Severely biased distribution			
Pro-A			
Shared	a_1	a_1	a_1
Unshared	a_2, a_3	a_4, a_5	a_6, a_7
Pro-B[a]	b_1, b_2, b_3, b_4	b_1, b_2, b_3, b_4	b_1, b_2, b_3, b_4

[a] All shared.

are equally convincing. In Table 13.1 we present four ways in which this information could be distributed across the group members before discussion. In Case 1, all information is shared; that is, every member is aware of the seven pro-A and four pro-B pieces of information. In this case, we would expect that each member would prefer A before discussion and thus an initial unanimous consensus would occur. Group discussion would serve primarily to reassure the members that they were aware of all the critical information. This reassurance might increase members' confidence in their preferences, but discussion would provide little impetus for modifying initial preferences.

In Case 2, some information about both A and B is unshared. We refer to this case as an unbiased distribution of unshared information because each individual possesses a ratio of pro-A to pro-B that is nearly identical to the ratio in the total information pool. Members bring three pro-A and two pro-B items to the group and, if information exchange is exhaustive, would leave the group

with seven pro-A and four pro-B items. Thus members should prefer A both before and after group discussion.

In Case 3, three of the pro-A items of information (viz., a_5, a_6, and a_7) are unshared, but all of the pro-B information is shared. Each group member still has more pro-A than pro-B information; however, from each member's perspective, the advantage to A appears proportionately less than if they were aware of all of the available information. Thus members would be likely to bring a relatively weak preference for A to the group's discussion, but discussion could strengthen these initial preferences because each member could inform the others of a pro-A argument of which they were previously unaware. As suggested by Burnstein and Vinokur (1977), pregroup distributions of information similar to those in Cases 2 and 3 would probably result in group polarization (cf. Myers & Lamm, 1976); that is, group discussion should enhance the initial predispositions of the members to select A.

Case 4 in Table 13.1 is a more extreme version of Case 3. In this version, only one pro-A item of information (viz., a_1) is shared and the other six are unshared; thus group members should tend to prefer B rather than A at the onset of discussion because they each possess only three pro-A pieces of information. When pregroup distributions of information are sufficiently biased to shift pregroup preferences in this way, we refer to them as *severely* biased (as opposed to mildly biased distributions that tend to weaken but not change initial preferences). An extension of the logic of Burnstein and Vinokur's (1977) persuasive arguments theory suggests that group discussion could counter this initial bias in favor of B. By exchanging information, each group member can gain several items of new pro-A information but no new pro-B information. Ideally, even a group having a pregroup distribution of information severely biased against A could conclude discussion favoring A.

Thus in all cases presented in Table 13.1, exhaustive information exchange could result in members' preferring A after discussion and in the group's choosing A as its decision. Nonetheless, Case 4 presents the most challenging situation. In this case, for the group to eventually choose the best alternative (best in terms of the total available information[1]), the initial preferences of the members must be changed, whereas in the other cases a group would choose the best alternative by simply acting on the initial predispositions of the members. As a result, group discussion is critical to effective decision making when pregroup distributions of information are severely biased against the best alternative.

Case 4 also illustrates a situation in which a group's decision should be better than the decisions of individuals acting alone. A potential advantage of group versus individual decision making is that groups can pool information and thus make a more informed decision. In practice, groups are often composed of members who are believed to have unshared information (e.g., experts or representatives of special-interest populations). This strategy would have the greatest potential benefit when the total information pool favors one alternative but individuals have information that is severely biased in favor of another alternative. However, the following biased sampling model of group discussion suggests that this potential advantage of group decision making may often be unrealized.

Biased Sampling Model of Group Discussion

The biased sampling model identifies several sources of bias in unstructured, face-to-face discussion when a group is confronted with a consensus requirement. Moreover, we are concerned primarily with decision tasks for which there is no commonly accepted system of logic that would lead to an unambiguously correct decision. In Laughlin's (1980) terms, we are restricting our attention to *judgmental* rather than *intellective* decision tasks. For such tasks, according to the model, the content of discussion is biased in two ways. First, discussion is biased in favor of shared information: An item of information is more likely to enter discussion if it is shared rather than unshared. Second, discussion is biased in favor of the current preferences of group members: An item of information is more likely to enter discussion if it favors rather than opposes the existent preferences of group members.

According to the biased sampling model, group members rarely exhaust their store of information during discussion but sample a subset of the information to contribute to discussion. At the level of the individual member, sampling is biased by the member's current preference. Preference consistent

---

[1] In this article, we use term *best* in a very restricted way. The *best* alternative, in our sense, is the alternative that is supported by the preponderance of the information that is collectively available to the group. We do not mean that this alternative is correct. Indeed, criteria of correctness are usually undefined or unavailable for the kinds of decision tasks that we are considering

(viz., judgmental tasks; cf. Laughlin, 1980). Furthermore, we recognize that in practice the information that is collectively available to a particular group may be incomplete, and thus the best alternative, relative to the informational resources of that group, may not be the best alternative in view of a more complete set of information.

information is more salient and thus more likely to be recalled during discussion (cf. Fishbein & Ajzen, 1975). Furthermore, the contribution of recalled information to discussion is probably governed by a norm of advocacy: a social expectation that group members will actively advocate their preferred alternative during debate. At the level of the group, sampling is biased by the number of members who are cognizant of a given piece of information. The more members there are who have been exposed to an item of information, the more likely it is that at least one of them will recall and mention it. If sampling of the content of discussion is biased in these ways, then it is also the case that the amount of discussion favoring an alternative depends on the number of members who prefer that alternative.

Regarding the severely biased pregroup information distribution that is illustrated by Case 4 in Table 13.1, the biased sampling model predicts that group discussion will be biased in favor of alternative B even though there exists more information, in total, favoring A over B. This bias in discussion is expected for two reasons. First, group members will tend to prefer B initially and, as a result, will be predisposed to argue in favor of B. Second, shared information favors B even though the total set of information favors A. In summary, Case 4 illustrates a situation in which the collective decision of a group could be better (i.e., more consistent with the implications of all the available information) than the decision of any member acting alone. However, the biased sampling model suggests that groups will often fail to realize their potential, especially when pregroup distributions are biased sufficiently to shift initial preferences away from the best alternative, as in Case 4.

The role of initial consensus in determining the outcome of group discussion and decision is emphasized by the biased sampling model. This emphasis is not new in the group decision-making literature (cf. Davis, 1973; Stasser, Kerr, & Davis, 1980) but deserves some elaboration in the context of our study. In terms of the initial consensus, Case 4 illustrates the worst of all possible cases: Group members possess sets of information that are not only biased against the best alternative but

are also consistently biased in favor of another alternative. Thus we expect an initial consensus that favors an alternative other than the best one. Limiting our example to two alternatives precluded illustrating another possibility. If more than two decision alternatives exist, it is possible for pregroup distributions of information to be biased against the best alternative but not consistently, across members, biased in favor of another alternative. In other words, none of the group members may support the best alternative but, at the same time, they may not agree on any one of the remaining alternatives. Such a lack of an initial consensus may avoid discussion that uniformly supports one alternative and promote more extensive and exhaustive sampling of the total available information. In this way, initial disagreement or conflict may actually encourage more effective information exchange. Others have noted the apparent value of conflict in group decision making (e.g., Fisher, 1980; Janis, 1972).

We designed our study to examine two implications of the biased sampling model of group discussion. First, when pregroup distributions of information are severely biased against one alternative, group discussion tends to enhance rather than erode this initial bias. Second, "discussion is more likely to counter an initial bias when there is disagreement that is due to conflicting patterns of information across group members than when pregroup information is consistently biased in favor of one alternative." We examined these predictions by comparing the distributions of pregroup preferences with the distributions of group decisions and postgroup individual preferences.

Method

Overview

University students read descriptions of three hypothetical candidates for student body president and then met in 4-person groups to decide which candidate was best suited for the position. The profile of Candidate A contained more positive and fewer neutral attributes than the profiles of Candidates

B and C. The valences (positive, neutral, or negative) of profile attributes were determined via pre-experimental ratings. Thus Candidate A was the best candidate in the sense that his profile contained more of the consensually valued attributes of a student body president. We defined three experimental conditions according to how the information about the candidates was distributed over the 4 group members before discussion. In the *shared* condition, participants read descriptions that contained all of the profile information about each candidate. Two unshared conditions were used; in both, a participant was given only partial information about each candidate. However, the distribution of information across a group's members was designed so that a group, collectively, had all of the information and potentially could recreate the complete candidate profiles during discussion. In the *unshared/consensus* condition, positive information about A and negative information about B were unshared (i.e., given to only one member) before discussion in order to bias initial preferences against A and for B. In the *unshared/conflict* condition, the same strategy for distributing positive information about A was used; however, negative information about both B and C was unshared with the intent of shifting pregroup preferences away from A but, at the same time, avoiding a strong initial consensus for either B or C.

Subjects

Miami University students participated in order to partly fulfill a research experience requirement of introductory psychology courses. Assignment to experimental conditions and to decision-making groups within conditions was random. There were 72 subjects in the shared and unshared/conflict conditions and 84 in the unshared/consensus condition.

Materials

The candidate profiles contained 16 items of information about each of the three candidates. This information consisted of biographical data (e.g., extracurricular activities and hobbies, academic classification and major, grade point average) and positions on local and university issues such as dorm policies (e.g., visitation hours, dorm assignments), academic policies (e.g., class evaluations, course scheduling), and student social life (e.g., program board activities, local drinking ordinances). On the basis of an independent sample's pre-experimental ratings of candidate characteristics and policy statements, we constructed the profiles to include a specific number of positive, negative, and neutral items of information. Positive items are those that were rated, on the average, as both desirable and important attributes for a candidate by pretest participants, whereas negative items were rated as both moderately undesirable and important. (In order to avoid unrealistic profiles, extremely undesirable attributes were not used.) Neutral items either were judged unimportant or received neutral desirability ratings. The profile for Candidate A contained eight positive, four neutral, and four negative items, whereas the profiles for Candidates B and C contained four positive, eight neutral, and four negative items.

The descriptions that were read by participants before group discussion were based on the overall profiles and included a summary of biographical information followed by interview excerpts stating the candidate's position on various local issues. In Table 13.2 we summarize the ways in which

TABLE 13.2. Number of Items of Information About Each Candidate Received by Group Members Before Discussion

Condition and information valence	Candidate		
	A	B	C
Shared			
Positive	8	4	4
Neutral	4	8	8
Negative	4	4	4
Unshared/consensus			
Positive	2	4	1
Neutral	4	5	8
Negative	4	1	1
Unshared/conflict			
Positive	2	4 [4]	4 [4]
Neutral	4	6 [4]	4 [6]
Negative	4	0 [2]	2 [0]

Note: In the unshared/conflict condition, 2 members of a 4-person group received configurations of information about Candidates B and C given by the numbers without brackets, whereas the other 2 members received configurations given by the numbers in brackets.

positive, neutral, and negative items were distributed in the descriptions read by a group's members. In order to be consistent with our earlier definition, shared information was included in all of the descriptions, whereas unshared information appeared in only one of the members' descriptions.

The scheme for distributing information in the shared condition is straightforward because all information was shared. Every group member received identical descriptions containing all of the information in each candidate profile. In the unshared conditions, only eight items of information about each candidate were shared. For the eight unshared items, the description read by the first group member contained two of the unshared items, the description read by the second member contained another two of the unshared items, and so forth. In other words, each member read a description that contained one fourth of the unshared information. This method of distributing unshared information ensured that every item of information was contained in at least one of the descriptions read by a group's members.

The actual items of information to be unshared were selected to bias individual members' pregroup preferences in the unshared conditions. In the unshared/consensus condition, a given description of Candidate A contained only two of the eight positive items but all four of the negative items. In contrast, a given description of candidate B contained all four of B's positive attributes but only one of his negative attributes. The descriptions of candidate C remained relatively balanced because both positive and negative items about C were unshared. Thus each group member in this condition read descriptions that were biased against A and in favor of B.

A similar effect was obtained in the unshared/conflict condition except that 2 members of a 4-person group read descriptions that were biased in favor of Candidate B over Candidate C (non-bracketed configurations in Table 13.2) and the other 2 members read descriptions that were biased in favor of Candidate C over Candidate B (bracketed configurations in Table 13.2). The intent was to split pregroup support between B and C.

We emphasize that even though the descriptions read by participants were biased in the unshared

conditions, the total pool of information received by a group's members still favored Candidate A. For example, if each member of a group were to mention his or her two items of positive information about A during discussion, then all the members of the group would be informed of all eight pro-A items.

Procedures

The procedures for all experimental conditions were identical except for the aforementioned differences in the descriptions that were read by participants before group discussion. Participants met in a classroom at the beginning of an experimental session and were seated at random in locations that determined their experimental condition and discussion group assignment. Exceptions to random assignment were made in order to obtain the maximum number of 4-person groups, given the number of participants attending any one session. Participants remaining after the maximum number of groups were formed were given a different experimental task, and their data are excluded from this report.

Preliminary instructions stated that the research was concerned with group decision making and briefly described the role of a caucus in political elections. Participants were told that they would be reading descriptions of three hypothetical candidates for student body president and then meeting as a "political caucus" to decide which candidate was best suited for the position. We noted that members of a real political caucus rarely have identical information about candidates and, therefore, the information given to each member before discussion might not be entirely identical to the information received by their fellow group members. Thus in this study, participants in all conditions were alerted to the possibility that the descriptions might not be complete and their fellow group members might have information of which they were unaware.

Participants studied the candidate descriptions and then indicated their initial preferences on a private questionnaire. After collection of the candidate descriptions, participants completed a free recall task by listing as much information as they could remember about each candidate. Our intent for this task was to assess the salient information that participants retained before group discussion.

Participants then adjourned to nearby "caucus" rooms to, as a group, discuss the candidates and decide which one was the best candidate for student body president. After reaching a decision, group members privately completed a final questionnaire. In addition to assessing their postdiscussion preferences, this questionnaire repeated the free recall task.

Results

Pre- and Postgroup Individual Preferences

The distributions of pregroup preferences, given in Table 13.3, are significantly different among the experimental conditions, $\chi^2(4, N = 228) = 51.44, p < .001$. In the shared condition, Candidate A was the popular choice as expected. By comparison, Candidate A was significantly less popular in the unshared conditions, $\chi^2(1, N = 228) = 51.63$, $p < .001$, and Candidate B was more popular, $\chi^2(1, N = 228) = 27.95, p < .001$. Thus the method of distributing unshared information had the intended effect of reducing pregroup support for A and increasing support for B. Furthermore, Candidate C was more popular in the unshared/ conflict condition than in the unshared/consensus condition, $\chi^2(1, N = 156) = 7.91, p < .005$. In summary, pregroup support shifted from A to B in the unshared/consensus condition, whereas in the unshared/conflict condition, both B and C gained support at the expense of A.

One can assess the effects of group discussion on individual preferences by comparing pregroup with postgroup preference distributions. The biased sampling model suggests that candidates having the predominance of support before discussion will maintain or even gain support during discussion. This expectation follows because the content of discussion is presumed to reflect the initial allegiances of group members. If, however, groups do effectively pool members' information, group discussion should substantially increase support for Candidate A in the unshared conditions.

The distributions of postgroup preferences, given in Table 13.3, are consistent with the biased sampling model predictions. The differences among the experimental conditions observed in the pregroup preferences are enhanced rather than mitigated in the postgroup preferences. For example, in the shared condition, the proportion of participants preferring A increased from .67 to .85, and in the unshared/consensus condition the proportion preferring B increased from .61 to .75. Overall, the distributions of postgroup preferences are significantly different, $\chi^2(4, N = 227) = 122.00, p < .001$. Again, A was chosen more frequently in the shared condition than in the unshared conditions, $\chi^2(1, N = 227) = 89.51, p < .001$, and B was chosen more frequently in the unshared conditions than in the shared conditions, $\chi^2(1, N = 227) = 51.17, p < .001$. Finally, C was more popular in the unshared/conflict condition than in the unshared/consensus condition, $\chi^2(1, N = 155) = 24.17, p < .001$.

In sum, the patterns of differences obtained for pregroup preferences tend to be exaggerated in the postgroup data. Our expectation was that conflicting patterns of pregroup information would increase the likelihood of discussion shifting preferences toward A when information was unshared; this expectation was not supported. The postgroup

TABLE 13.3. Relative Frequencies of Pregroup and Postgroup Preferences and Group Decisions

	Candidate			
Condition	A	B	C	n
Pregroup preferences				
Shared info.	.67	.17	.17	72
Unshared info./consensus	.25	.61	.14	84
Unshared info./conflict	.21	.46	.33	72
Postgroup preferences				
Shared info.	.85	.11	.04	72
Unshared info./consensus	.20	.75	.05	83[a]
Unshared info./conflict	.17	.47	.36	72
Group decisions				
Shared info.	.83	.11	.06	18
Unshared info./consensus	.24	.71	.05	21
Unshared info./conflict	.12	.53	.35	17[b]

[a] One participant failed to report a postgroup preference.
[b] One group failed to reach a decision.

support for A is not significantly different between the unshared/consensus and unshared/conflict conditions.

Group Decisions

The distributions of group decisions in Table 13.3 parallel closely the distributions of postgroup preferences. Overall, the distributions of decisions are significantly different among the experimental conditions, $\chi^2(4, N = 56) = 28.81$, $p < .001$. In the shared condition, 83% of the 18 groups chose Candidate A whereas only 18% of the 38 groups in the unshared conditions chose A, $\chi^2(1, N = 56) = 21.59$, $p < .001$. Candidate B was chosen more often in both of the unshared conditions than in the shared condition, $\chi^2(1, N = 56) = 13.31$, $p < .001$, and Candidate C was chosen more often in the unshared/conflict condition than in the unshared/consensus condition, $\chi^2(1, N = 38) = 5.83$, $p < .025$. Again, there was no support for the notion that conflicting patterns of pregroup information would increase the likelihood that sentiment would shift toward Candidate A during discussion when pro-A information was unshared. In fact, groups in the unshared/conflict condition tended to choose A less frequently than did groups in the unshared/consensus condition; however, this difference is not significant.

Davis (1973) suggested that group process can be represented as a rule (social decision scheme) relating the group decisions to the configuration of members' preferences at the onset of discussion. In Table 13.4, we represent the initial preference

configuration of a group by (r_1, r_2, r_3), whereby r_i is the number of members in a fraction such that $r_1 > r_2 > r_3$, and $r_1 + r_2 + r_3 = r$, group size. In the present case, $r = 4$, and the possible initial configurations of preference are as follows: $(4, 0, 0) =$ initial unanimity; $(3, 1, 0) =$ initial majority; $(2, 1, 1) =$ initial plurality; and $(2, 2, 0) =$ initial nonplurality. In Table 13.4, the decision of a group is classified as the candidate initially supported by the largest faction (plurality supported), by a minority faction (minority supported), or by no members of the group (unsupported). Note that for some initial configurations, one of the classifications for decisions does not exist. In particular, the distinction between plurality supported and minority supported does not exist for the $(2, 2, 0)$ case. Thus for the $(2, 2, 0)$ configuration, decisions are simply tabulated as unsupported or plurality supported.

Candidates with initial unanimity or majority support won with one exception: the unsupported candidate chosen by a group with an initial $(3, 1, 0)$ configuration. Candidates with only plurality support in the $(2, 1, 1)$ configuration won very frequently (81%) over the minority-supported candidates. Given the nonplurality configuration $(2, 2, 0)$, one of the two supported candidates always won over the unsupported candidate. Thus a "plurality-supported wins" rule accounts for most of the group decisions; that is, a candidate with at least a plurality of initial support was likely to be the group's decision. Such a process suggests that discussion rarely erodes even a minimal consensus. This finding is consistent with Laughlin and Earley's (1982) conclusion that groups deciding issues of judgment or social preference seem to follow a majority rules process. However, the dominance of the initial plurality in our groups is particularly noteworthy because the distributions of unshared information provided ample opportunity for discussion to counter the initial consensus in the unshared conditions.

Furthermore, it is worth noting that the seven groups that chose Candidate A in the unshared conditions were, by chance, assigned at least two members who favored A at the onset of discussion. Thus it was not the lack of a consensus for B or C that resulted in groups' discovering the

TABLE 13.4. Group Decisions as a Function of Initial Support Within the Group

Initial consensus	Supported		Unsupported
	By plurality	By minority	
(4, 0, 0)	6	–	0
(3, 1, 0)	24	0	1
(2, 1, 1)	13	3	–
(2, 2, 0)	9	–	0

Note: Dashes indicate outcomes that are not defined for an initial consensus configuration.

merits of A (the intended effect in the unshared/conflict condition); rather, it was the presence of at least two members who supported A.

Information Recall

Even though group discussion may often fail to correct the bias in information that members bring to the group, the biased sampling model suggests that the content of discussion is nonetheless instrumental in producing shifts of preference. The point is that shifts of preference occur in the direction of the initial consensus because members tend to recall and contribute arguments and facts that support their existent preferences. The content of discussion serves not only to give members new information but also to change the salience of old information. If shifts of preference and the emergence of a group decision are dependent on the content of discussion, there should be a concomitant increase in the salience of information that supports the winning candidate from pre- to postdiscussion. Thus information that supports the winning candidate should be more likely to be recalled after than before discussion.

The numbers of positive and negative items recalled before and after discussion were tabulated separately for the winning and losing candidates. Because Candidate A had more positive attributes than B and C, and because there was always more total information about the two losing candidates than about the one winning candidate, we analyzed the percentage of information recalled rather than the absolute frequency. Also, because of a possible dependency of postdiscussion recall among a group's members, we averaged the recall scores of the four members of each group and conducted an analysis of variance (ANOVA), using these group means (following a method of analysis suggested by Myers, DiCecco, & Lorch, 1981).

Figure 13.1 contains the average pre- and postdiscussion recall of positive and negative information about the winning and losing candidates for each experimental condition. Although we are primarily interested in the changes of recall from pre- to postdiscussion, it is important to note that the prediscussion recall of positive attributes of the winning candidate is noticeably higher in the unshared conditions than in the shared condition. This inflated recall reflects the biasedness of the sets of information given to members before discussion in the unshared conditions; that is, the percentage of unshared information recalled before discussion in the unshared conditions is necessarily low because each member received only one fourth of the unshared information. The winning candidate in these conditions was typically (except for the few groups who chose A) the one for whom members were given all of the positive information before discussion. Unshared information, in these conditions, was typically (a) negative information about the winning candidate and (b) positive and negative information about one or both of the losing candidates. Thus if group discussion had corrected the bias introduced by the patterns of shared and unshared information in the unshared conditions, this disproportionate recall of positive-winning information should have been reduced in postdiscussion recall. However, visual inspection of Figures 13.1c and 13.1e suggests that this bias in recall increased from pre- to postdiscussion.

A $3 \times 2 \times 2$ (Experimental Condition × Winning vs. Losing Candidate × Positive vs. Negative Valence × Prediscussion vs. Postdiscussion) ANOVA of the recall scores was conducted. Two three-way interactions are of primary interest: the Condition × Candidate × Time interaction, $F(1, 53) = 5.43$, $p < .01$, and the Candidate × Information Valence × Time interaction, $F(1, 53) = 8.98$, $p < .01$. Post hoc analyses suggested that both of these three-way interactions are due primarily to three simple main effects of time. In the shared condition there is a significant decrease in the recall of negative information about the winning candidate, $F(1, 53) = 12.05$, $p < .01$ (see Figure 13.1a). In contrast, there is a significant increase in the recall of positive information about the winning candidate in both the unshared/consensus and the unshared/conflict conditions, $F(1, 53) = 16.38$, $p < .01$, and $F(1, 53) = 8.43$, $p < .01$, respectively (see Figures 13.1c and 13.1e). All other simple main effects of time are not significant.

Thus the results for the unshared conditions support the predictions of the biased sampling model. Effective information exchange during discussion should have resulted in a substantial

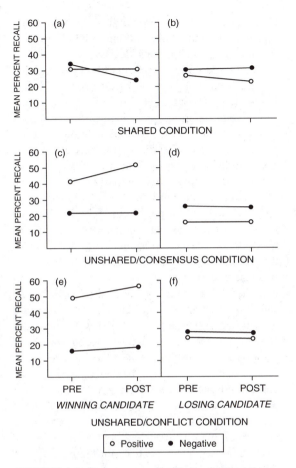

FIGURE 13.1 ■ Mean percentage of pre- and postdiscussion recall of positive and negative information about the winning and losing candidate for each of the experimental conditions.

gain of negative information about the winning candidate in these conditions because group members could give each other new information that opposed the winning candidate. Clearly, discussion did not serve this corrective function but tended to increase the salience of information supporting the winning candidate even though members of most groups had been exposed to this information before discussion.

The results for the shared condition are somewhat more puzzling although they are not necessarily inconsistent with the biased sampling model. It seems that when group members had received all of the information before discussion, the discussion maintained the salience of information favoring

the initially preferred (and ultimately winning) candidate, whereas information opposing this candidate was less likely to be recalled after discussion. One interpretation of this finding is that giving members all of the information before discussion resulted in information overload. Discussion then served to reduce this overload by focusing on information that supported the initially popular candidate and ignoring other information. The net effect of this focus, coupled with information overload, would be to reduce the recall of nonsupporting information.

Discussion

Several theoretical perspectives emphasize the role of information exchange in guiding the emergence of a consensus and modifying members' preferences during group discussion (e.g., Anderson & Graesser, 1976; Hoffman & Maier, 1964; Kaplan, 1977; Stasser & Davis, 1981). Burnstein and Vinokur's (1977) persuasive arguments theory suggests that shifts of preference are due to the number of persuasive and unique arguments that are introduced into discussion. Unique arguments are considered particularly instrumental in producing preference shifts. Viewed in this way, information that is unshared before discussion should be more likely than shared information to affect members' preferences during discussion. However, Burnstein and Vinokur (1977) are primarily concerned with the group polarization phenomenon, and in their analysis they assumed that the preponderance of unshared arguments tends to favor the initially most popular position for tasks used in this research tradition. They thus concluded that unique arguments exchanged during discussion tend to bolster the initially popular sentiment within a group.

We are primarily concerned with a situation in which the balance of unshared information opposes the initially most popular position. In this case, according to the biased sampling model, the unshared information will tend to be omitted from discussion and, therefore, will have little effect on members' preferences during group discussion. Our results confirm this notion. Group decisions and postgroup preferences reflected the initial preferences of group members even when the exchange of unshared information should have resulted in substantial shifts of opinion. Furthermore, discussion did not increase the recall of unshared information. On the contrary, discussion tended to increase the recall of information that supported the initially most popular (and ultimately winning) candidate even though this information was primarily shared before discussion.

The unshared conditions in this study simulated a situation in which the quality of the group's decision was potentially better than the quality of its members' pregroup choices. The pregroup choices were based on biased sets of information, but if members had effectively exchanged information during discussion, the collective choice would have been based on less biased information.

Extending Steiner's (1972) process-loss model of group productivity, Shiflett (1979) proposed a general model that analyzes group performance in terms of resources, transformers, and outputs. *Resources* include knowledge and abilities that are relevant to performing a task. *Transformers* are variables that mediate the ways in which member resources are combined or weighted to yield the group *output* (e.g., a solution to a problem, a judgment, or a decision). For our decision-making groups, the information in the candidate profiles can be viewed as resources, and the collective choice of the best-qualified candidate as the group output. Transformers would include variables that affect the likelihood that information is introduced into discussion and thus is reflected in a group's decision. Shiflett (1979) also distinguished unique resources (resources held by one member) from redundant resources (resources held by all members). In our case, unique resources are items of information unshared before discussion, and shared information constitutes redundant resources. We suggest that one criterion of group productivity in a judgmental task could be the extent to which unique resources are considered in a group's final judgment. Viewed in this way, the decisions of groups in the shared conditions are a standard against which to judge the decisions of groups in the unshared conditions. If unique and redundant informational resources were weighted equally, there should be no difference in the distributions of group decisions between the shared and unshared conditions. However, our results suggest that unique or unshared information had little impact on groups' decisions.

The biased sampling model of group discussion identifies several possible mechanisms that may result in commonly held information receiving more weight than uniquely held information in a group's decision. One possibility follows directly from Shiflett's (1979) distinction between unique and redundant resources: The more members there are who are exposed to an item of information, the more likely it is that at least one of them will recall and mention it during discussion. In Shiflett's (1979) words, "The fact that two or more individuals possess the same resource does not increase the total set of available resources but does increase the probability of that resource being used" (p. 72). Furthermore, according to the biased sampling model, members' initial preferences are a transformer variable in Shiflett's formulation. Initial preferences may mediate the contribution of information to discussion in either of two ways. First, members' recall may be biased because preference-consistent information is more salient than preference-inconsistent information. Second, members may tend to advocate or defend their initial preference and thus bias their contributions to discussion even if their recall is not biased. In sum, initial preferences may act as transformer variables by introducing selective recall or selective contribution of information during discussion.

In many contexts, a desirable goal may be to increase the weight of uniquely held information in the determination of a group's judgment. One suspects that unshared information may often be just as important, or even more important, than commonly held information in arriving at a collective choice. For example, if a group is composed of members who have differing areas of expertise, consideration of unshared information may be very critical to the quality of the group's final decision. Similarly, groups whose members represent disparate points of view or special-interest populations may err by focusing on their shared perspectives and thereby negating any advantage that accrues from multiple sources of diverse input. Our results suggest that unstructured discussion in the face of a consensus requirement may often fail as a means of combining unique informational resources. Ironically, our analysis also suggests that this failure to consider unique information is most likely when the unique information counters the prevailing sentiment in the group and could change its final decision.

REFERENCES

Anderson, N. H., & Graesser, C. (1976). An information integration analysis of attitude change in group discussion. *Journal of Personality and Social Psychology, 34*, 210–222.

Burnstein, E., & Vinokur, A. (1977). Persuasive argumentation and social comparison as determinants of attitude polarization. *Journal of Experimental Social Psychology, 13*, 315–332.

Davis, J. H. (1973). Group decisions and social interaction: A theory of social decision schemes. *Psychological Review, 80*, 97–125.

Fishbein, M., & Ajzen, I. (1975). *Belief, attitude, intention and behavior: An introduction to theory and research*. Reading, MA: Addison-Wesley.

Fisher, B. A. (1980). *Small group decision making: Communication and the group process* (2nd ed.). New York: McGraw-Hill.

Hoffman, L. R., & Maier, N. R. F. (1964). Valence in the adoption of solutions by problem-solving groups: Concept, method, and results. *Journal of Abnormal and Social Psychology, 69*, 264–271.

Janis, I. L. (1972). *Victims of groupthink*. Boston: Houghton Mifflin.

Kaplan, M. F. (1977). Discussion polarization effects in a modified jury paradigm: Informational influences. *Sociometry, 40*, 261–271.

Laughlin, P. R. (1980). Social combination processes of cooperative problem-solving groups on verbal intellective tasks. In M. Fishbein (Ed.), *Progress in social psychology* (Vol. 1, pp. 127–155). Hillsdale, NJ: Erlbaum.

Laughlin, P. R., & Earley, P. C. (1982). Social combination models, persuasive arguments theory, social comparison theory, and choice shift. *Journal of Personality and Social Psychology, 42*, 273–280.

Myers, D. G., & Lamm, H. (1976). The group polarization phenomenon. *Psychological Bulletin, 83*, 602–627.

Myers, J. L., DiCecco, J. V., & Lorch, R. F., Jr. (1981). Group dynamics and individual performances: Pseudogroup and quasi-*F* analyses. *Journal of Personality and Social Psychology, 40*, 86–98.

Shiflett, S. C. (1979). Toward a general model of small group productivity. *Psychological Bulletin, 86*, 67–79.

Stasser, G., & Davis, J. H. (1981). Group decision making and social influence: A social interaction sequence model. *Psychological Review, 88*, 523–551.

Stasser, G., Kerr, N. L., & Davis, J. H. (1980). Influence processes in decision-making groups. A modeling approach. In P. Paulus (Ed.), *Psychology of group influence* (pp. 431–477). Hillsdale, NJ: Erlbaum.

Steiner, I. D. (1972). *Group process and productivity*. New York: Academic Press.

Received February 1, 1984
Revision received July 6, 1984 ■

Threat, Cohesion, and Group Effectiveness: Testing a Social Identity Maintenance Perspective on Groupthink

Marlene E. Turner, Anthony R. Pratkanis,
Preston Probasco, and Craig Leve

Although Janis's concept of groupthink is influential, experimental investigations have provided only weak support for the theory. Experiment 1 produced the poor decision quality associated with groupthink by manipulating group cohesion (using group labels) and threat to group members' self-esteem. Self-reports of some groupthink and defective decision-making symptoms were independently, but not interactively, affected by cohesion and threat. Experiment 2 confirmed the success of the cohesion manipulation. Experiment 3 replicated the poor-quality decision making observed in Experiment 1 and provided support for a social identity maintenance perspective on groupthink: Groups who operated under groupthink conditions but who were given an excuse for potential poor performance produced significantly higher quality decisions than groups who worked under groupthink conditions alone. The results are used to interpret the groupthink phenomenon as a collective effort directed at warding off potentially negative views of the group.

Portions of this research were presented at 1989 Midwestern Psychological Association meetings.

We thank Arthur Aron, Anthony G. Greenwald, David Myers, Thomas Pettigrew, Gerald Salancik, Heather Smith, Jeffrey Stone, John C. Turner, and the anonymous reviewers for their helpful comments on a previous version of this article. We are also grateful to Nakiye Boyacigillar, Forest Jourdan, Alan Kawamoto, Michael Lee, and Kaye Schoonhoven for assistance with subject recruitment. Carrie Fried, Sharon R. Hertle, Tracy Muckleroy, and Allan Roberts provided assistance in data collection.

Correspondence concerning this article should be addressed to Marlene E. Turner, Department of Organization and Management, San Jose State University, San Jose, California 95192, or to Anthony R. Pratkanis, Board of Psychology, University of California, Santa Cruz, California 95064.

Janis (1972, 1982, 1989) defined *groupthink* as the extreme concurrence sought by decision-making groups. Groupthink is most likely to occur when a group experiences antecedent conditions such as high cohesion, insulation from experts, limited methodological search and appraisal procedures, directive leadership, and high stress combined with low self-esteem and little hope of finding a better solution than that favored by the leader or influential group members. Such conditions lead to symptoms of groupthink such as illusions of invulnerability, collective rationalization, belief in the inherent morality of the group, stereotypes of outgroups, pressure on dissenters, self-censorship, illusions of unanimity, and self-appointed mind-guards. Groupthink is hypothesized to result in poor quality decisions and defective decision-making symptoms such as incomplete survey of alternatives and objectives, failure to examine risks of preferred solution, failure to reappraise initially rejected alternatives, poor information search, selective bias in processing information at hand, and failure to develop contingency plans.

Janis's concept of groupthink has been an influential one, frequently appearing in social psychology (Aronson, 1988; Deaux & Wrightsman, 1988; Myers, 1987; Raven & Rubin, 1976) and management (Steers, 1990) textbooks. The appeal of the concept is evidenced by the ease with which it can be applied to numerous group decisions such as Nazi Germany's decision to invade the Soviet Union in 1941, Israel's lack of preparedness for the October 1973 war, Ford Motor Company's decision to market the Edsel, Grunenthal Chemie's decision to market the drug thalidomide (Raven & Rubin, 1976), governmental decisions regarding earthquake retrofitting before the Loma Prieta earthquake (M. E. Turner & Pratkanis, 1991), the National Aeronautics and Space Administration's and Morton Thiokol's decision to launch the Challenger space shuttle (Aronson, 1988), the decision by top executives of the Buffalo Mining Company to continue to dump slag into the Buffalo River (Wheeler & Janis, 1980), the Carter Administration's decision to use military measures to rescue Iranian hostages (Ridgeway, 1983; Smith, 1984), the check-kiting scheme at E. F. Hutton (Moorhead & Griffin, 1989), and the potential for groupthink to occur in various work situations (Manz & Sims, 1982; Moorhead & Montanari, 1986). Nevertheless, the empirical evidence in support of groupthink has been, at best, mixed. Case and content analyses of naturalistic group decision making have sometimes obtained some support for the concept, whereas experimental investigations have obtained inconsistent results.

Case Studies of Groupthink

Janis (1972, 1982) first developed the concept of groupthink through qualitative analyses of defective decision making in the cases of the appeasement of Nazi Germany, Pearl Harbor, the Bay of Pigs, the North Korean invasion, the escalation of the Vietnam War, and the Watergate cover-up. Janis compared the decision-making processes involved in these fiascoes with those that resulted in more effective decision making such as the Cuban Missile Crisis and the Marshall Plan.

Tetlock (1979) conducted a more quantitative test of Janis's hypotheses by performing a content analysis of archival records of public statements made by key decision makers involved in the groupthink (North Korean invasion, Bay of Pigs, and Vietnam War escalation) and nongroupthink decisions (Marshall Plan and Cuban Missile Crisis) identified by Janis (1972). Results of this analysis suggested that decision makers in groupthink situations had more simplistic perceptions of policy issues and made more positive references to the United States and its allies. However, these decision makers did not engage in more out-group stereotyping. (See Tetlock, Peterson, McGuire, Chang, & Feld, 1992, for additional confirmation.)

In a study of the decision to launch the Challenger space shuttle, Esser and Lindoerfer (1989) analyzed 88 statements referring to groupthink processes in the *Report of the Presidential Commission on the Space Shuttle Challenger Accident*. They found little evidence for the antecedent conditions of group cohesion (defined as mutual attraction to members), lack of impartial leadership, and homogeneity of members' backgrounds, but they did find some evidence that the team faced a highly stressful situation. Evidence was obtained for groupthink symptoms of illusion of invulnerability, rationalization, illusion of unanimity, pressure on dissenters, mindguards, and biased information processing. Evidence for other groupthink symptoms was inconclusive.

Hensley and Griffin (1986) found evidence for groupthink in the 1977 decision by the Kent State University board of trustees to build a gymnasium on the site of the shooting of students by the Ohio National Guard. The highly controversial decision was made by an isolated, highly cohesive group of trustees in a stressful situation. The board exhibited a wide range of groupthink symptoms (invulnerability, rationalization, stereotyping of enemies, etc.) and defective decision-making processes (incomplete survey of alternatives and objectives, poor information search, etc.).

Raven's (1974) analysis of groupthink in the Nixon White House during the Watergate era suggested that Janis's antecedent condition of cohesion required reformulation. Raven proposed that cohesion in this instance depended not so much on the presence of an esprit de corps but rather the desire to maintain group membership at all costs. According to Raven, the Nixon White House demonstrated such groupthink symptoms as illusion of superior morality, illusion of invulnerability, illusion of unanimity, and mindguards (see Janis, 1982, for another discussion of the Watergate cover-up). However, the members of the White House team did not form a closely knit group with high esprit de corps, nor did they exhibit a high degree of mutual attraction and admiration for each other. According to Raven, groupthink stemmed from the low political self-esteem of Nixon's subordinates (none of whom had ever been elected to a political office) and the fact that "despite their personal antagonisms, all of them wanted with all their hearts and souls to be in that group and to be central to that group" (p. 310).

In sum, these lines of research provide some support for the groupthink theory. However, it is clear that inconsistent evidence regarding the conceptualization and consequences of cohesion, as well as the prevalence of groupthink and defective decision-making symptoms, does exist.

The use of historical materials is useful for "hypothesis construction" (Janis, 1982, p. ix). However, Janis (1982; see also Moorhead, 1982) suggested that controlled, experimental research is needed to identify cause-and-effect relations among groupthink antecedent conditions and processes. Experimental research on groupthink has sought to provide such development.

Experimental Research on Groupthink

Six experimental studies have attempted to manipulate multiple antecedent conditions of groupthink while assessing groupthink symptoms and group-decision effectiveness. These studies reported only limited evidence for groupthink symptoms and no evidence for decrements in group-decision effectiveness in groupthink treatments.

Three studies have examined the effects of cohesion and leadership style on groupthink processes. Flowers (1977) trained appointed leaders of 4-person groups to be either participative or directive. Groups composed of either friends (high cohesion) or strangers (low cohesion) proposed solutions to a case involving an elite high school faced with several crises (e.g., financial problems, senile teachers, influx of students of lower socioeconomic status, and a possible teacher strike). Supporting the groupthink hypothesis, groups with directive leaders proposed fewer solutions, shared less case information, and used fewer case facts before and after reaching decisions. But, in contradiction with the groupthink hypothesis, cohesion did not affect these processes. Agreement with the group decision and freedom to express opinions were not affected by leadership style or cohesion.

Using a similar design, Leana (1985) gave groups composed of either strangers (low cohesion) or students who had worked together in class for 15 weeks (high cohesion) 20 min to solve a case involving a hypothetical business crisis (i.e., selecting which of five employees should be laid off). Leaders of these groups were instructed to be either participative or directive. Groups with directive leaders proposed and discussed fewer solutions than did participative groups. Contrary to prediction, high-cohesion groups shared more information than low-cohesion groups. Evaluation of solution riskiness was unaffected by cohesion or leadership.

Finally, Fodor and Smith (1982) asked 5-person groups led by an appointed leader who had either a high or low need for power to solve a business case. Groups were either told they had the possibility to win a reward if they had the best performance (high-cohesion treatment) or were not given an opportunity to win a reward (low-cohesion treatment). Groups with low-power leaders discussed more facts, considered more options, and demonstrated greater moral concern. However, group cohesion did not influence any dependent measures.

Research investigating the effects of cohesion and decision procedures also provides mixed support for the groupthink theory. Courtwright (1978) asked high-cohesion groups (told they had similar attitudes and that they should do well on the task) and low-cohesion groups (told they had incompatible attitudes and not to worry about the task) to recommend the best method for recruiting university students. Groups were either (a) instructed to air competing ideas, (b) instructed to strive for cooperation and examine few ideas, or (c) given no instructions. As predicted, high-cohesion groups told to limit their discussion made fewer statements of disagreement than all other groups. However, the number, creativity, quality, feasibility, significance, and competence of solutions were unaffected by cohesion and decision processes.

Along similar lines, Callaway and Esser (1984) found that decision quality on the Horse Trader and Lost at Sea tasks was unaffected by cohesion (manipulated using false feedback concerning the likelihood of the group being compatible or incompatible) or decision procedure guidelines (instructions that stressed full consideration of alternatives or no instructions). Other groupthink processes such as statements of disagreements, confidence in the group solution, and agreement with the group solution also were unaffected by manipulated variables (although an internal analysis using perceived cohesion measures provided some evidence for groupthink). In a second study, Callaway, Marriott, and Esser (1985) again found that decision quality on the Lost at Sea task was unaffected by decision procedures (as defined above) used by highly cohesive groups (formed on personality compatibility) composed of high- or low-dominance members.

Taken together, these results provide, at best, partial support for the groupthink theory. Not surprisingly, procedures designed to limit group discussion (e.g., directive leadership and instructions emphasizing the importance of avoiding disagreement) tend to produce fewer solutions, less sharing of information, and fewer statements of disagreement. In contrast to these results, cohesion generally has failed to affect any groupthink processes or indicators. (Note that cohesion has been manipulated in a variety of ways, conforming in varying degrees to traditional concepts of cohesion; see Point 3 below.) Finally, research has failed to demonstrate that antecedent conditions theoretically associated with groupthink actually impair decision quality (see also Park, 1990, for a methodological critique).

Toward the Reconciliation of Conflicting Results

The equivocal support for groupthink processes leads to the predicament of the disconfirmation dilemma (Greenwald & Ronis, 1981): Is the groupthink theory invalid or is it being tested improperly or is it a little of both? Longley and Pruitt (1980) have criticized Janis's theory on a number of counts including the lack of a clear specification of the meaning of cohesion and an inadequate delineation of the causal links between antecedent conditions and groupthink symptoms. In the same vein, Steiner (1982), in noting the limited empirical support for cohesion, questioned Janis's causal ordering, suggesting that cohesion may be a consequence rather than an antecedent of groupthink. Steiner also observed that groupthink and defective decision-making symptoms can be obtained in a variety of situations not consistent with Janis's antecedent conditions. Finally, McCauley (1989) suggested that groupthink fails to adequately address the distinction between compliance and internalization. However, at least four concerns about the experimental research on groupthink that may account for the null or contradictory results can be raised.

First, the failure to link groupthink antecedent conditions with defective decision making may be partially attributable to the insensitivity of many decision-making tasks used to detect groupthink effects. Although the theory is vague in the specification of links among antecedents, symptoms, and decision effectiveness, it is at least necessary to use tasks on which solution quality ranges from very poor to very good—a range that may be lacking in many tasks used in previous research.

Second, research has been focused on a limited subset of antecedent conditions, namely, cohesion and methods for limiting group discussion. Direct manipulation of other antecedents possibly may be necessary for groupthink to occur.

Third, the procedures used to operationalize and control for the antecedent conditions may not fully capture the original meanings or intentions specified by the theory. For example, the operationalizations of stress and cohesion appear less consistent with Janis's original specifications (again perhaps due to the ambiguity of conceptualization, as noted by Longley & Pruitt, 1980). Consistent with traditional definitions of threat as potential harm or loss (Lazarus & Folkman, 1984), Janis (1982, p. 301) defined threat as the potential lowering of self-esteem and as the fear of failure or defeat. However, stress or threat, as an antecedent variable, primarily has been controlled by using tasks involving some form of crisis. Although these are ecologically valid sources of stress (i.e., they have mundane realism), they present few personal consequences for subjects and thus lack experimental realism (Aronson & Carlsmith, 1968).

Cohesion has been manipulated by forming groups on the basis of friendship (Flowers, 1977), previous classroom work together (Leana, 1985), and personality or attitude compatibility (Callaway & Esser, 1984; Callaway et al., 1985; Courtwright, 1978). These manipulations may not map closely onto Janis's definition of cohesion as the desire for the rewards of remaining in a pleasant group atmosphere or in a prestigious group. They also may not incorporate the implicit assumption made by the theory that groups identify themselves as a group. A self-categorization and social identity perspective suggests that the perception of others as group members rather than as unique persons may be a precondition for group cohesion (Tajfel, 1981; J. C. Turner, 1981, 1982; J. C. Turner, Hogg, Oakes, Reicher, & Wetherell, 1987). Note

that the groups studied by Janis appear to conform to this precondition.

Finally, only a selected range of groupthink and defective decision-making symptoms have been investigated. Group information search, survey of objectives, development of contingency plans, and rationalization have been largely untested. Given the equivocal support for the theory, examinations of broader ranges of groupthink indicators particularly are needed for specifying the theoretical links between antecedent conditions and groupthink symptoms.

The following experiment examined the effects of two antecedent conditions of groupthink, threat and cohesion, on group decision quality. Using a design approach (Greenwald, Pratkanis, Leippe, & Baumgardner, 1986), we attempted to maximize the possibility of obtaining groupthink in an experiment that (a) used a group discussion task with a broader range of solution quality, (b) examined the effects of a threat that incorporated personal consequences, (c) used a self-categorization and social identity perspective to develop a cohesion manipulation, and (d) examined a wider range of groupthink symptoms, including members' perceptions of decision processes.

Predictions

Given that previous work has not orthogonally manipulated threat and cohesion, it is essential to specify their possible effects on group performance and symptoms of groupthink and defective decision making. The groupthink theory, however, is equivocal with respect to delineating the causal relations among antecedents and consequences (Longley & Pruitt, 1980). Three possible interpretations can be raised. We will discuss each of these as they apply first to decision quality and then to self-reports of groupthink and defective decision-making symptoms.

Decision Quality

One perspective can be called the *strict* interpretation of groupthink. According to this interpretation, poor quality decision making should occur only in the high-threat, high-cohesion treatment because this is the only treatment with all groupthink antecedents present (Janis, 1982). Another perspective might be termed an *additive* interpretation: Each additional antecedent should result in increasingly poorer decision making. Thus, groups in the high-cohesion, high-threat condition should perform poorest, groups in the low-cohesion, low-threat cell the best, with the other two treatments at an intermediate level. However, little support exists for either the strict or additive interpretations: No published study documented impaired decision quality under the combined presence of the particular antecedents examined.

A third, *liberal* interpretation suggests that performance will depend on the unique situational properties invoked in each cell. The groupthink theory is not clear about the specific effects on decision quality when either cohesion or threat is high. However, prior research provides some guidance. Decision quality actually may be enhanced when cohesion alone is high. Apparently, cohesive groups are better at attaining their goals than are noncohesive groups (Shaw & Shaw, 1962). Thus, cohesive groups that have the goal of increased productivity will be more productive than both noncohesive groups with the same goal and cohesive groups that do not subscribe to such a goal (Seashore, 1954; Shaw & Shaw, 1962). In laboratory situations such as the one we are constructing, these goals (when not affected by other conditions such as preexisting organizational factors) tend to favor higher productivity (Festinger, Back, Schachter, Kelley, & Thibaut, 1952; McGrath, 1984). The type of threat used in the study, by itself, should also produce higher quality decisions. This may occur because the threat induces greater motivation to perform effectively (e.g., Kruglanski & Freund, 1983). Prior research has provided little empirical evidence about how decision quality will be affected when both cohesion and threat are high. According to the groupthink hypothesis, decision quality will, of course, be impaired. Little evidence likewise exists regarding group performance quality under conditions of low cohesion and low threat. In the absence of the enhancing effects of either threat or cohesion, we might expect these groups to achieve lower levels of performance quality. Although not deriving

his idea directly from the groupthink theory, Janis (1982), in discussing what might happen under these conditions, suggested that decision quality is likely to suffer because such groups may adopt a win–lose or bargaining approach to problem resolution that may result in defective decisions. Note that this is opposite to what would be predicted by either the strict or the additive interpretation of groupthink. It is, however, consistent with Janis's further theorizing on conditions not specifically treated by the groupthink theory and with Steiner's (1982) points regarding the multiple routes to poor quality decision making.

Self-Reports of Groupthink and Defective Decision-Making Symptoms

We can also apply each of these interpretations to self-reports of symptoms of groupthink and defective decision making. According to the strict interpretation, groupthink and defective decision-making symptoms should occur only in the groupthink cell—the high-cohesion, high-threat cell. According to an additive interpretation, groupthink and defective decision-making symptoms should become increasingly more pronounced with the presence of each additional antecedent. Thus, groups in the high-cohesion, high-threat condition should report the most apparent symptoms, groups in the low-cohesion, low-threat cell the least apparent symptoms, with the other treatments at an intermediate level. But, little empirical support for these interpretations exists: More pronounced symptoms have not been found under combinations of various antecedents in any experiment.

The liberal perspective suggests that self-reports of symptoms would again depend on the unique situational properties associated with each antecedent. For example, research indicates that cohesion may lead to more risky decisions (Thompson & Carsrud, 1976) as well as greater social influence, agreement, and conformity (Festinger, Schachter, & Back, 1950). Threat may increase rationalization about the decision (Janis & Mann, 1977), denial (Lazarus & Folkman, 1984), premature closure (Janis, 1982; Janis & Mann, 1977), and decreased participation in group decision processes (Hall & Mansfield, 1971). In addition, if our analysis of the experimental research on groupthink is correct, procedures limiting group discussion may reduce information-processing activities. Conversely, in the absence of such procedures, information-processing activities should be unaffected. However, little empirical evidence exists regarding the impacts of the presence of both cohesion and threat on group-think and defective decision-making symptoms.

Finally, one other point regarding the impact of antecedents on self-reports of symptoms is worth noting. If, as Janis (1982) suggested, one outcome of groupthink is a mutual effort among members of the group to maintain emotional equanimity, one must question whether self-reports of groupthink symptoms will, in fact, conform to theoretical pre-dictions. Group members may not admit or even recognize that they have engaged in faulty decision processes. For example, in analyzing the decision to escalate the Vietnam war, Janis (1982) noted that groups may pressure a dissenter to limit objections to issues that do not threaten to shake the group's confidence in the rightness of their judgments. The doubter's presentation of opposing viewpoints (that actually do little to threaten the group) permits members to think that their group tolerates dissent. Such a group would report it actually tolerated dis-sent and encouraged evaluation of the group deci-sion even though it did not. We might see similar outcomes regarding other groupthink symptoms.

Clearly, multiple theoretical predictions can be delineated. As Janis noted (1982), "until we have a good theory—one that is well supported by con-trolled experiments and systematic correlational research, as well as by case studies—we must recog-nize that any prescriptions we draw up are specula-tive inferences based on what little we know, or think we know, about when and why groupthink occurs" (p. 259). The following research was undertaken with the goal of shedding light on these processes.

Experiment 1

Method

Sample and design

One hundred eighty undergraduate students par-ticipated in 3-person groups as part of a class assignment. Subject to schedule constraints, groups were randomly assigned to each condition of a 2 (cohesion: low vs. high) $\times$ 2 (threat: low vs. high) between-subjects design.[1]

Procedures

On arriving, subjects were randomly assigned seats in groups of 3. They received a brief overview of the study and informed consent materials along with the appropriate threat and cohesion manipu-lations. Groups then read and discussed Maier's (1952) Parasol Subassembly Case. On completing a write-up of the solution, group members noti-fied the experimenter that they had reached a solution. Each subject then completed a postex-perimental questionnaire assessing perceptions of group processes. Finally, subjects were fully debriefed.

Group discussion task

Groups were told they were staff analysts assem-bled to solve a problem. The Parasol Subassembly problem (Maier, 1952) describes a group of assem-bly workers producing automobile instrument pan-els whose group productivity has fallen below standard. Problems centered on an aging worker with limited abilities named Joe, whose work frequently piled up. The materials also included information concerning company procedures and environmental conditions that made some solutions (i.e., hire additional workers) difficult or impossi-ble to implement. Solution quality was determined using a 7-point coding scheme developed by Maier.

This task has two advantages for investigating groupthink. First, solution quality can range from solutions that violate case information (e.g., hire additional workers when none were available) to solutions that were adequate but somewhat incom-plete (e.g., promote Joe) to solutions of high qual-ity (e.g., rotate the workers on an hourly basis so that pileups do not occur). (These solutions would

---

[1] Because of scheduling and room constraints, each class was randomly assigned to three of the four experimental condi-tions. Within each class, subjects were randomly assigned to groups, and groups were randomly assigned to one of the con-ditions running simultaneously.

be coded as 1, 4, and 7, respectively, using Maier's, 1952, coding scheme.) The range of problem solutions map onto the range of decision quality for groups experiencing groupthink (see Steiner, 1982, for a discussion of this task and its relationship to groupthink). For example, groupthink processes of incomplete survey of alternatives, poor information search, selective information processing, and acceptance of a dominant solution would result in a low-quality decision. On the other hand, Maier reported that groups who fully consider and evaluate solution alternatives (i.e., groups not exhibiting groupthink symptoms) achieve solutions at the higher end of the quality scale. A second advantage of the parasol task is that groups tend to converge on a dominant solution of somewhat below average quality (i.e., removing the nonproductive worker from the station, which would be coded as a 3). This convergence is particularly likely to occur in groups that are not encouraged to explore additional alternatives. We used this dominant solution to supplant Janis's requirement of the advocation of a single solution.

Independent variables

Threat. Consistent with previous research, threat was manipulated by varying the degree of potential loss. High-threat groups were told their discussion was to be videotaped and that tapes of groups not exhibiting functional processes would be used for training in classes held both on campus and in corporations. Specifically they were told,

> As you can see, we will be videotaping your session. We are doing this because we are planning to use these tapes for training both in classes here on campus and in classes held for corporations. We are particularly interested in groups that do not exhibit functional group processes. The task we are using is particularly good for this purpose because it shows that even people who think they are good at decision making actually may not be that good. What this means is that for these campus and corporate training sessions, we will only be using tapes of groups that have dysfunctional group processes.

A videocamera was prominently displayed and was apparently operating to film each group in the high-threat condition. In contrast, subjects assigned to the low-threat treatment were told the study was in the pilot stage. In specific, they were told, "The situation that you'll be working on is a pilot case that's never been used before." No videocameras were present in the low-threat treatment.

Cohesion. Group members assigned to the high-cohesion treatment were given name tags bearing separate group identities (e.g., Barracuda and Rattler) and wore their group names throughout the experiment. In addition, high-cohesion groups spent 5 min at the beginning of the study discussing and listing the similarities and commonalities among group members. In contrast, low-cohesion groups were not given group identities or name tags. These groups spent 5 min discussing and listing their dissimilarities and differences.

Dependent variables

Group performance. We used two measures of group effectiveness: Performance quality and performance speed. The primary measure of group performance was the quality of the solution each group developed. Solution quality was determined using Maier's (1952) coding scheme. Two independent coders rated each solution (interrater reliability = .85). Disagreements were resolved by negotiation. Performance speed was measured in minutes to solution.

Self-reports of groupthink symptoms. To assess perceptions of various symptoms of groupthink, subjects rated (on 7-point Likert scales) their (a) confidence in group solution (a measure of invulnerability), (b) annoyance at members raising viewpoints conflicting with group decision (pressure on dissenters), (c) discomfort at raising points others would find disagreeable (self-censorship), and (d) evaluation of other members' agreement with the group decision (unanimity). Rationalization was measured by asking subjects to list their thoughts about the group solution and to rate each thought as positive, negative, or neutral. Stereotyping of outgroups and the belief in the inherent morality of the group were not measured because they were not aspects of our experimental situation.

The presence of mindguards may be inferred through the existence of limitations on expressions of opinions.

Self-reports of defective decision-making symptoms. Each subject was asked to (a) list the solution objectives considered (survey of objectives), (b) list all the solution alternatives the group considered (evaluation of multiple alternatives), (c) rate (on a 7-point Likert scale of agreement) the riskiness of the solution (evaluation of solution risk), (d) list other types of information they would have liked (limited information search), (e) list the case facts they could remember (biased information processing), and (f) list the contingency plans the group formulated (development of contingency plans). Both the solution alternative and the contingency plan measures were coded using the same scheme used for solution quality.

Table 14.1 presents the intercorrelations among the groupthink and defective decision-making measures. Most correlations were generally quite low, indicating that groupthink and defective decision-making symptoms seem to tap separate facets of the groupthink effect.

Manipulation checks

So that we could assess perceptions of threat, subjects rated (on 7-point Likert scales) the degree of

apprehension, tension, and stress they experienced. These measures were combined to form a threat scale ($\alpha = .70$). A cohesion index was formed by combining two questions assessing subjects' perceptions of the cohesiveness of their group ("My group was cohesive") and liking for their group members ("I liked my group members," scale $\alpha = .68$). Because it was not intercorrelated with the previous two questions, an item measuring subjects' desire to work with the group again was analyzed separately.

Results
Group performance

Analysis of group-solution quality revealed a significant Cohesion × Threat interaction, $F(1, 56) = 9.49, p < .01$. This interaction is depicted in Figure 14.1. As post hoc Tukey tests confirm, groups in the high-threat, high-cohesion treatment ($M = 2.39$) and groups in the low-threat, low-cohesion treatment ($M = 2.32$) formulated poorer quality solutions than groups in the high-threat, low-cohesion treatment ($M = 3.87$; $ps < .05$). Groups in the low-threat, high-cohesion treatment ($M = 3.4$) also produced higher quality decisions than groups in the high-threat, high-cohesion and low-threat, low-cohesion cells, although the comparisons did not reach significance (all $ps > .05$). The poorer quality

TABLE 14.1. Intercorrelations Among Symptoms of Groupthink and Defective Decision Making for Experiment 1

Symptoms	1	2	3	4	5	6	7	8	9	10	11
Groupthink											
1. Invulnerability	—										
2. Self-censorship	−.13	—									
3. Rationalization	.33	−.13	—								
4. Unanimity	.58	.20	.31	—							
5. Pressure on dissenters	−.21	.35	−.43	−.51	—						
Defective Decision Making											
6. Failure to examine risks	−.51	.29	−.39	−.42	.41	—					
7. Failure to reappraise alternatives	−.22	.18	−.32	−.23	.12	.15	—				
8. Omission in survey of objectives	−.18	−.08	.35	.13	−.12	−.19	.23	—			
9. Omission in survey of alternatives	−.18	−.20	−.01	−.06	−.08	.18	−.11	.12	—		
10. Information processing bias	.24	−.08	.46	.18	−.12	−.39	−.27	.39	−.16	—	
11. Poor information search	−.09	−.26	.009	−.12	.05	.11	−.11	.24	.27	.35	—
12. Contingency plans	.08	.04	.15	.13	−.12	−.30	.18	.30	.02	.15	.06

Note: Correlations greater than .36 are significant at the .01 level.

solutions of high-cohesion, high-threat groups is, of course, an example of the defective decision making associated with groupthink.[2] Analysis of the time-to-solution measure revealed no significant differences among experimental conditions (all $ps > .10$).

Self-reports of symptoms of groupthink

Table 14.2 summarizes the results of separate two-way analyses of variance (ANOVAs) on measures of groupthink symptoms for Experiments 1 and 3. As column 3 indicates, cohesion and threat

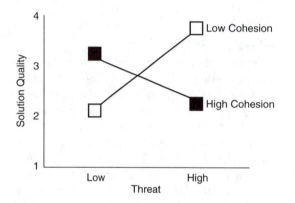

FIGURE 14.1 ■ Mean decision quality for Experiment 1 as a function of threat and cohesion.

independently affected groupthink symptoms. Cohesion apparently contributed to the illusion of invulnerability, with high-cohesion subjects reporting greater confidence in their solution accuracy than low-cohesion subjects, $F(1, 56) = 2.91$, $p < .07$. Cohesion seemed to decrease self-censorship: High-cohesion subjects said they were more comfortable about raising dissenting points than low-cohesion subjects, $F(1, 56) = 5.88$, $p < .01$. This contrasts with previous groupthink research that has generally failed to find a strong relationship of any type between cohesion and self-censorship.

Threat appeared to contribute to rationalization about the group decision and pressure on dissenters. High-threat subjects generated more positive thoughts about the group solution than did low-threat subjects, $F(1, 56) = 6.28$, $p < .01$, and reported they were somewhat less annoyed when members raised issues conflicting with the solution than were low-threat subjects, $F(1, 56) = 2.7$, $p < .09$.

Self-reports of symptoms of defective decision making

The third column of Table 14.3 summarizes results of separate two-way ANOVAs on measures of

TABLE 14.2. Summary of Analyses on Groupthink Symptoms in Experiments 1 and 3

Groupthink symptoms	Measure	Experiment 1 results	Experiment 3 results[a]
Illusion of invulnerability	Confidence in solution	High cohesion = 5.86 Low cohesion = 5.46	No effects
Self-censorship	Discomfort at raising dissenting points	High cohesion = 1.64 Low cohesion = 1.99	No effects
Rationalization	Number of positive thoughts listed about group solution	High threat = 3.80 Low threat = 2.97	No effects
Illusion of unanimity	Agreement with group solution	No effects	No effects
Pressure on dissenters	Annoyance with dissenters	High threat = 1.68 Low threat = 2.07	No effects

[a] Experiment 3 did not manipulate cohesion and thus does not serve as a test of the replicability of Experiment 1 cohesion effects.

---

[2] One potential alternative explanation for our pattern of results regarding group decision quality centers on the hypothesized inverted-U relationship between the arousal associated with threat and performance. We rejected this interpretation for two reasons. First, recent reviews of the literature provide little support for this relationship (cf. Lazarus & Folkman, 1984). Second, for the interpretation to be plausible, the pattern of decision-quality findings should match the pattern of reported tension and apprehension findings. These patterns are not similar. For example, subjects in the low-threat, high-cohesion treatment had superior performance yet reported lower levels of apprehension and tension. In addition, we also conducted an internal analysis using perceptual indices of threat that did not confirm this interpretation.

defective decision-making symptoms. Inspection of the table reveals that cohesion and threat independently affected separate defective decision-making symptoms. High-cohesion subjects assessed their solutions as less risky than did low-cohesion subjects, $F(1, 56) = 11.83, p < .001$. High-threat subjects reported they were somewhat less likely to stop searching for a solution once an acceptable alternative was found than were low-threat subjects, $F(1, 56) = 3.2, p < .07$.

Experimental treatments did not affect the number of case facts correctly recalled (all $ps > .10$), the number of case facts inaccurately recalled (all $ps > .10$), the number of items of additional information that were requested (all $ps > .15$), the average number of solution objectives (all $ps > .15$), and the average number of solution alternatives that group members listed (all $ps > .15$). Only 40 of 60 groups indicated they formulated contingency plans. Analysis of the quality of solution alternatives that subjects reported they discussed but ultimately rejected revealed a marginally significant Threat × Cohesion interaction, $F(1, 56) = 2.89, p < .09$. Post hoc comparisons revealed that high-threat, high-cohesion

treatment subjects produced significantly higher quality rejected alternatives $(M = 2.93)$ than did low-threat, high-cohesion subjects $(M = 2.02, p < .05)$. Other comparisons did not reach significance: Subjects in the low-cohesion, low-threat treatment $(M = 2.58)$ and the low-cohesion, high-threat condition $(M = 2.43)$ had similar solution alternatives of intermediate quality.

Manipulation checks

Analysis of the threat index revealed a significant Threat × Cohesion interaction, $F(1, 56) = 6.69, p < .01$. Post hoc comparisons indicated that high-threat, high-cohesion subjects $(M = 2.47)$ reported significantly greater threat than high-threat, low-cohesion subjects $(M = 1.99)$ and low-threat, high-cohesion subjects $(M = 2.01)$ reported. Low-threat, low-cohesion subjects $(M = 2.38)$ did not differ in threat assessments from subjects in the other three conditions. These multiple influences and the failure to observe a main effect for threat on threat assessments are consistent with research demonstrating the vagaries of producing

TABLE 14.3. Summary of Analyses of Defective Decision-Making Symptoms in Experiments 1 and 3

Defective decision-making symptoms	Measure	Experiment 1 results	Experiment 3 results[a]
Failure to examine risks of preferred solution	Perceived risk of solution	Low cohesion = 3.02 High cohesion = 2.20	No effects
Failure to reappraise initially rejected alternatives	Perceptions of failure to reappraise once an acceptable solution was obtained	Low threat = 4.69 High threat = 3.55	Low threat = 4.85 High threat = 4.07 High threat, distraction = 4.16
Omission in survey of objectives	Number of solution objectives reported	No effects	No effects
Omission in survey of alternatives	Number of solution alternatives reported	No effects	No effects
Selective bias in processing information at hand	Number of correct and incorrect case facts recalled	No effects	No effects
Poor information search	Number of additional items of information requested	No effects	No effects
Failure to develop contingency plans	Number of contingency plans reported	No effects	No effects

[a] Experiment 3 did not manipulate cohesion and thus does not serve as a test of the replicability of Experiment 1 cohesion effects.

perceptual confirmations of threat manipulations (see Lazarus & Folkman, 1984, for a review).

Analysis of the cohesion index revealed only a main effect of threat, $F(1, 56) = 3.92$, $p < .05$: High-threat subjects reported greater cohesion ($M = 6.08$) than did low-threat subjects ($M = 5.71$). This finding is consistent with some research showing that threat may, under certain conditions, be associated with heightened group cohesion (e.g., Dion, 1979). Desire to work with the group was unaffected by experimental treatments. However, cohesion had no effect on the perceptual measures. Although this is unexpected, it is consistent with both groupthink and group dynamics research (e.g., Back, 1951; Courtwright, 1978; Leana, 1985).

Discussion

Comparison of our results with previous research

The results of this study provide preliminary evidence for the defective decision making theoretically associated with groupthink. Group solution quality was poorer in the high-threat, high-cohesion and the low-threat, low-cohesion treatments than in the high-threat, low-cohesion treatment. Decision quality was also higher in the high-threat, low-cohesion and the low-threat, high-cohesion conditions (although this latter comparison did not attain conventional levels of significance). Thus, our findings demonstrate the hypothesized link between the antecedent conditions of cohesion and threat and ineffective group performance—a link not previously established in existing experimental research.

Our results replicated previous research demonstrating that threat and cohesion each may independently enhance decision quality. The poorer quality decisions observed in the low-threat, low-cohesion condition confirm Janis's ancillary theorizing about groups working under these conditions. He suggested that noncohesive groups working under nonthreatening circumstances should produce poor quality decisions because they adopt a win–lose bargaining strategy for reaching decisions. This poor quality decision making is also consistent with Steiner's (1982) points regarding groupthink as but one of many routes to defective

decision making. Although the decision processes of noncohesive groups working under nonthreatening conditions should certainly provide interesting topics for future research, these groups are not examined further in this article because we are primarily concerned with the processes of groups operating under the presence rather than the absence of groupthink conditions.

Although the lower quality decisions associated with groupthink were obtained, not all of the expected intervening conditions suggested by the theory were present. Failing to support either the strict or additive interpretation of groupthink, the symptoms of groupthink and of defective decision making were *not* most readily apparent in the groupthink treatment—that is, the high-threat, high-cohesion cell. Rather, cohesion and threat independently affected some symptoms of groupthink and defective decision making. Moreover, information-gathering strategies were unaffected by the antecedent conditions examined in this study. Thus, as we had expected, it is possible that some explicit mechanism for constraining group discussion (e.g., instructions favoring limited solution evaluation or participation) may be required to produce these symptoms.

The failure to support the strict or even the additive interpretations of groupthink is quite consistent with previous research. For example, Flowers (1977) found that (a) directive leadership resulted in fewer solutions, less sharing of case information, and less use of case facts; (b) cohesion failed to affect any of these measures; and (c) measures of freedom to express opinions and agreement with the group decision were affected by neither leadership nor cohesion. Other inconsistencies are reported by Fodor and Smith (1982), Courtwright (1978), Esser and Lindoerfer (1989), Leana (1985), and Callaway and Esser (1984). In none of these studies were the groupthink symptoms most pronounced in the groupthink conditions—that is, in the conditions in which all manipulated antecedents were present. Thus, our results, in conjunction with previous research, suggest that a global, strict interpretation of groupthink is unwarranted. These results do point to a more liberal interpretation of groupthink in which specific antecedents are associated with unique situational properties that affect symptoms and decision making in more complex ways.

Groupthink as social identity maintenance

Our overall pattern of data reinforces Janis's view of groupthink as a process in which group members attempt to maintain a shared, positive view of the functioning of the group (Janis, 1982) or as social identity maintenance. Groupthink can be viewed as a process by which group members attempt to maintain a shared positive view of the functioning of the group in the face of threat. This perspective highlights three important aspects of groupthink identified in the original case studies (but somewhat ignored in subsequent research). First, as a precondition to cohesion, members should categorize themselves as a group. This categorization has several important consequences. J. C. Turner (1981) suggested that groups given a social identity have a tendency to seek positive distinctiveness for the in-group and to exhibit a motivational bias for positive self-esteem. Thus, members tend to develop a positive image of the group and, importantly, are motivated to protect that image.

A second condition a social identity maintenance perspective highlights is that the group should experience a collective threat. Furthermore, this threat should involve an attack on the positive image of the group. The shared categorization induced by social identity provides a basis on which the collective threat can operate. The third factor underscored by a social identity perspective is that members may use a variety of tactics to protect the group image. Groups can exhibit a variety of groupthink processes and indicators as members attempt to maintain a positive image of the group. There are, in fact, interesting parallels between the symptoms of groupthink and the tactics of social identity maintenance or enhancement. For example, the groupthink symptom of stereotyping of outgroups bears a distinct resemblance to the out-group discrimination that can accompany the induction of social identities.

Similarly, illusion of invulnerability and rationalization are similar, in some ways, to social identity maintenance strategies involving the selective enhancement of various group characteristics undertaken to achieve positive distinctiveness. Finally, pressures toward uniformity and self-censorship induced by groupthink can be compared with the process of referent informational influence (whereby group members form and subscribe to norms of their shared categorization) that may accompany social identities (J. C. Turner, 1982).

Two concerns, however, can be raised about our first experiment. The first pertains to the effectiveness of our manipulations: Did we truly induce cohesion and threat? Recall that our perceptual manipulation checks did not correspond to the respective cohesion or threat conditions. The second involves the replicability of our findings: Did we really produce groupthink? Can the defective decision making be replicated? The following two studies were conducted to address these questions. The next experiment further tests our induction of cohesion and provides evidence for the success of this manipulation (in contrast to the manipulation check results obtained in Experiment 1). The third experiment is a partial replication and an extension of the first study. It replicates the first experiment by examining the decision-making effectiveness of cohesive groups operating under threatening and nonthreatening circumstances. (Again, we are primarily interested in the presence rather than the absence of groupthink antecedents and will not examine the decision effectiveness of groups working under conditions of low cohesion and low threat.) The third experiment also extends the first study by providing evidence for our perspective of groupthink as a collective effort directed at maintaining a positive identity in the face of a shared threat. To that end, we investigated the decision effectiveness of cohesive groups working under threat who are given a potential excuse for their poor performance. Additionally, this final study provides further evidence regarding the success of our threat induction (in contrast to the manipulation check results obtained in Experiment 1).

Experiment 2

Because of the failure to obtain perceptions corresponding to the cohesion manipulation, the question, of course, remains: Did we really induce cohesion in the first experiment? Previous groupthink research manipulating cohesion has (a) generally failed to produce the predicted effects of cohesion and (b) frequently failed to produce perceptual verifications of cohesion manipulations. In contrast to much groupthink research, the manipulation of cohesion used in the first study produced effects consistent with previous research on group cohesion and with a liberal interpretation of the groupthink theory. However, our research also adds to the growing body of evidence attesting to the difficulty of producing perceptual assessments of cohesion that correspond to its manipulation.

There are two possible explanations for why subjects' perceptions of group cohesion did not differ in accord with our empirical results. First, we may not have induced cohesion at all. Two factors argue against this. First, our findings replicate previous research that has documented consistent consequences of cohesion. Second, research using the self-categorization and social identity perspective has demonstrated that induction of social identities and group categorization may foster cohesion. Categorization can generate intragroup attraction or social cohesion by allowing the development of conditions traditionally conducive to the development of interpersonal attraction and also can reinforce the similarities between the individual and other group members (J. C. Turner, 1981, 1982; J. C. Turner et al., 1987; see also Hogg & Abrams, 1988).

A second explanation for the inconsistency between perceptual measures and empirical consequences of cohesion in the first study pertains to the nature of the perceptual measures used. It is possible that the measures we used were not sensitive enough to capture meaningful differences in our subjects' perceptions of the cohesion manipulation. In particular, it is possible that the inclusion of items that more clearly and directly examine subjects' opinions of how their groups operated will produce perceptions corresponding to the manipulation. Thus, the use of more standard cohesion scales might demonstrate the effectiveness of our manipulations. The following experiment was conducted to test this possibility.

Method
Sample and design

Seventy-two college students participated in groups of 3. Groups were randomly assigned to a two-group (cohesion: low vs. high) between-subjects design.

Procedures and independent variable

On arriving, subjects were randomly assigned seats in groups of 3. Subjects were told the study was part of a larger research project and that the purpose was to test some discussion materials. After receiving informed consent materials, subjects were given the appropriate cohesion manipulation. These manipulations were identical to those used in the first study. Subjects then completed a postexperimental questionnaire containing the dependent variables. Ten filler items assessing subjects' perceptions of the setting (noise level, temperature, lighting, etc.) and study attributes (interest, length, etc.) were included in the questionnaire to deter subjects from guessing the true nature of the experiment.

Dependent variables

We used three separate measures of cohesion. The first scale, developed by Terborg, Castore, and DeNinno (1976), is composed of three items: "How would you describe the way you and other members of your group 'got along' on this task?" "Would you socialize with the members of your group outside of class?" and "Would you want to remain a member of this group on future projects?" ($\alpha = .81$). Scores on each item ranged from 1 to 7, with higher scores associated with more cohesion. The second cohesion scale, developed by J. C. Turner, Hogg, Turner, and Smith (1984), consists of four measures: "How much do you like the people in your group?" "How much do you want to carry on working in the group for your next task?" "How favorable are your feelings about your group?" and "How favorable are your feelings about other groups?" (reverse scaled; scale $\alpha = .89$). Scores on each item ranged from 1 to 9, with higher scores indicating more cohesion. Finally, we also included the two cohesion measures we used in the first study (scale $\alpha = .64$).

Results

Analysis of the Terborg et al. (1976) scale revealed a highly significant effect for cohesion treatment, $F(1, 22) = 11.45, p < .001$. Subjects in the high-cohesion treatment ($M = 17.59$) reported more cohesion than did subjects in the low-cohesion treatment ($M = 15.16$). Analysis of the J. C. Turner et al. (1984) scale revealed similar results. A highly significant effect for cohesion treatment, $F(1, 22) = 6.76, p < .01$, was obtained. Once again, high-cohesion treatment subjects ($M = 29.14$) indicated more cohesion than low-cohesion treatment subjects ($M = 26.5$). In contrast, analysis of the cohesion index used in the first experiment showed no significant cohesion effect ($p > .5$).

Discussion

The results of this study suggest that our manipulation of cohesion was indeed successful. Both the Terborg et al. (1976) and the J. C. Turner et al. (1984) measures differed significantly and in the predicted direction as a function of manipulated cohesion. In contrast, our measure of cohesion, despite it being similar to measures used in previous research, did not produce significant differences in subjects' perceptions of the cohesiveness of their groups. Although it is not entirely clear why the scales produced different results, one possibility is that both the Terborg et al. (1976) and the J. C. Turner et al. (1984) scales were directly tied to more specific and more clearly articulated aspects of the group, whereas the scale used in the first study was both more diffuse and less specific.

Our findings again document the complexity of producing perceptual verification of cohesion inductions. Although the measures we developed were certainly consistent with prior research on cohesion, they failed to produce perceptual differences.

But, two cohesion indices successfully used by other researchers did indeed document that subjects' perceptions confirmed our predictions. These findings also underscore the importance of the categorization aspect of group cohesion—that is, the categorization of others as members of the group rather than as unique individuals (see J. C. Turner et al., 1987). It is possible that previous cohesion inductions have paid inadequate attention to this consideration. For example, a typical manipulation asks one individual to assemble several friends for a discussion task. This manipulation does not ensure that the individuals actually categorize or come to view themselves as a group.

Finally, we note that this approach is not inconsistent with previous group dynamics conceptualizations of cohesion. The social identity aspect can be viewed as one force described in the Cartwright and Zander (1953) definition of cohesion as the resultant of all forces acting on members to remain in the group. This may suggest that, consistent with Raven's (1974) analysis, the maintenance of membership in the group may be an important determinant of cohesion, and one that may be useful in producing the effects hypothesized by the groupthink theory, particularly when members face a shared threat to the collective positive image of the group.

Experiment 3

As noted above, our overall pattern of data in Experiment 1 reinforces Janis's view of groupthink as a process in which group members attempt to maintain a shared, positive view of the functioning of the group (Janis, 1982). In other words, groupthink can be viewed as a process by which group members attempt to maintain a positive image of the group in the face of potential failure to adequately deal with a collective threat. If this interpretation of groupthink is viable, it may suggest a potential strategy for both producing and overcoming the defective decision making associated with groupthink. Under traditional groupthink antecedent conditions, the group is faced with a threat to self-esteem and experiences doubt about its capabilities to successfully perform under that threat. When this occurs, research suggests that people are likely to self-handicap (Higgins, 1990; Jones & Berglas, 1978; C. R. Snyder, 1990). Individuals who are uncertain about their competence seek to protect against potential failure by actively setting up circumstances or by claiming certain attributes or characteristics that may be blamed for poor performance (Higgins, 1990; Jones & Berglas, 1978; C. R. Snyder, 1990).

When people are faced with a threat to self-esteem, they may attempt to avoid the negative implications of failure by adopting self-handicapping strategies that ultimately result in poor performance (Frankel & Snyder, 1978; Miller, 1976; M. L. Snyder, Smoller, Strenta, & Frankel, 1981). However, providing threatened individuals with another potential explanation for their expected failure (such as poor lighting) may obviate the need to use self-handicapping as a strategy for maintaining self-esteem. As a consequence, performance should then improve. In contrast, performance should be impaired when such an excuse is not provided. M. L. Snyder et al. (1981) provided evidence supporting these predictions. They manipulated self-esteem threat by giving subjects unsolvable or solvable anagrams that purportedly measured intelligence. Subjects then worked on an additional set of anagrams with or without background music described as distracting and detrimental to performance. As predicted, performance decrements occurred when subjects initially given unsolvable anagrams worked without background music. In contrast, performance decrements were not observed when threatened subjects were given an excuse for their poor performance.

Similar predictions can be made concerning the performance of highly cohesive, threatened groups who are given an alternative excuse for their performance. Assuming that these groups strive to protect against a negative image of the group suggests that providing them with an excuse for possible poor performance (such as the distracting music used by M. L. Snyder et al., 1981) should reduce the need to justify performance. Freed of the need to engage in handicapping strategies, these groups should, in turn, formulate higher quality decisions than groups not given such an excuse. Thus, cohesive groups facing a threat and given an excuse for their potential poor performance should perform better than cohesive groups also facing a threat who are not provided with such an excuse.

How will the self-reports of groupthink and decision-making symptoms be affected by the provision of an excuse for poor performance? Previous research examining these consequences has been limited (cf. Higgins, Snyder, & Berglas, 1990). Moreover, what little research there is has produced conflicting findings. Arkin and Baumgardner (1985) argued that individuals who are uncertain or anxious about their competency and who are provided with a handicapping strategy experience more positive affect than their more certain counterparts. On the other hand, other research shows that self-evaluations of affect and achievement mood did not differ with the availability of a self-handicapping strategy (Frankel & Snyder, 1978; Leary, 1986).

Consequently, multiple predictions can be made regarding how the provision of an excuse will affect groupthink symptoms. For example, we can speculate that highly cohesive, threatened groups given an excuse such as distracting music will report less pronounced groupthink symptoms because performance is not impaired. On the other hand, it is just as possible that self-reports of groupthink symptoms will be unaffected by the provision of an excuse. This may occur because groups are unsure whether they have completely warded off a negative image.

The following experiment was designed to examine predictions drawn from the social identity maintenance view of groupthink. Our central prediction was that groups operating under groupthink conditions (that is, under conditions of threat and cohesion) who were provided with an excuse of "distracting music" for poor performance would achieve higher quality performance than groups also operating under identical groupthink conditions who were not provided with such an excuse. To provide further comparison with the previous study, we also examined the decision-making performance and groupthink symptoms of groups working under nonthreatening conditions and given group cohesion inductions. If we replicate results obtained in our first study, we should find that these groups produce higher quality decisions than do groups in the groupthink condition.

Method

Subjects, design, and procedures

One hundred twenty-three college students participated in groups of 3. Groups were randomly assigned to each condition of a three-group design: (a) low threat; (b) high threat; and (c) high threat with distraction. All groups were given the high-cohesion manipulation described in the first study. This study used the same procedures as Experiment 1, with the exception of modifications in the threat manipulation and posttask questionnaire and the addition of a distraction treatment.

Independent variables

Threat. Threat was manipulated in the same manner as in Experiment 1 with the following exceptions. First, to control for identifiability and objective self-awareness concerns, we told subjects in the high-threat treatments that their individual identities would be masked. Second, we also asked subjects to sign an additional "release form" that purportedly allowed us to show their videotapes in classes and sessions. Specifically, subjects were told,

> Because we may show your tape in certain classes and sessions, we need to get you to sign a release form. Please sign your name in the appropriate spot. This release form allows us to use your tape for these purposes. You should know that your faces will not be identifiable. We will block out your faces, although your body will still be seen.

Let me show you a picture we developed from a tape we are currently using.

At this point, the experimenter showed subjects a photograph of a group working on the discussion task. The face of each group member was masked by a large black square produced by a photographic retouching process. Finally, to ensure that groups were aware that the quality of the decision and not just the group process was of concern, we told subjects that the tapes of groups exhibiting poor processes and decisions would be used for training purposes.[3]

Distraction. As in the M. L. Snyder et al. (1981) study, subjects in the distraction treatment worked on the discussion task while background music played at a moderate volume. The music consisted of sequences drawn from various synthesizer recordings. Subjects were told,

> As you probably know, various forms of music are often played in work settings. We will be simulating that today. While you will be working and discussing, a tape of some music will be played in the background. Based upon experiences previous subjects have had, I can tell you that the music will probably be very distracting and detrimental to your performance on the group discussion task.

In actuality, results of a pretest study using 40 groups found no difference in performance on the experimental task between groups working with the background music and groups working without the background music. Pretesting also indicated that, as found by previous researchers (e.g., Frankel & Snyder, 1978), the distraction was

---

[3] A second purpose of Experiment 3 was to provide evidence on the success of our threat manipulation. Several concerns can be raised about the manipulation used in the first study. First, self-reports of threat did not match our hypotheses. Despite evidence documenting the difficulty of producing perceptual confirmation of self-threat (due to such factors as denial, simple refusal to admit threat, and so forth; cf. Lazarus & Folkman, 1984), this remains an unresolved issue. In an attempt to produce perceptual verification of the threat manipulation, we included additional perceptual measures of threat. These measures differed from those in Experiment 1 in that they were constructed to be less intrinsically threatening to subjects (e.g., by focusing on context, subjects should be less

threatened by the questions themselves and less reluctant to acknowledge threat; cf. Sudman & Bradburn, 1982). It is also possible that the actual threat manipulation itself may have induced some unintended consequences. Two especially critical repercussions may have been the unintended induction of identifiability and objective self-awareness of the individual subject. Both these processes may have affected our findings in unintended ways. We attempted to control for these concerns by taking steps to mask each individual subject's identity. (See Durval & Wicklund, 1972; Wicklund, 1975; and Williams, Harkins, & Latané, 1981, for a discussion of these issues.) We are indebted to several anonymous reviewers for raising these points.

effective only if the subjects believed the evaluators were aware of the presence of the distracting music. To that end, we also provided each group in the distraction condition with a sign that indicated that distracting music was playing. This placard was prominently displayed next to each group and was clearly visible to the videocamera. Again, similar to the M. L. Snyder et al. study, subjects in the low-distraction conditions were not provided with background music.

Dependent variables

Measures of group performance, symptoms of groupthink, and symptoms of defective decision making were identical to those used in the previous study. Two independent coders scored the group performance measures, achieving 93% agreement. Table 14.4 reports the intercorrelations among symptoms of groupthink and defective decision-making measures. As in the previous study, intercorrelations among the symptoms are generally quite low, indicating that the symptoms seem to largely tap different facets of the groupthink effect.

Manipulation checks

To assess their perceptions of our threat manipulation, subjects responded to a series of 7-point semantic differential items assessing the degree to which they were comfortable (vs. uncomfortable), secure (vs. shaky), calm (vs. tense), confident (vs. panicky), and relaxed (vs. frightened) with the setting. These items were combined into a threat index ($\alpha = .91$). To examine the effectiveness of the distraction manipulation, we asked subjects to (a) indicate whether music was playing during the session, (b) rate on a 7-point Likert-type scale the degree of distraction of background noises during the session, and (c) rate on a 7-point Likert-type scale their difficulty concentrating during the session. These latter two items were combined into a distraction index ($\alpha = .61$).

Results
Manipulation checks

Analysis of our manipulation checks revealed that our experimental procedures affected subjects' perceptions in the expected directions. Subjects clearly understood whether background music was playing: 96% of the subjects correctly indicated whether music was playing, $\chi^2(2, N = 123) = 93.49$, $p < .0001$. More important for our purposes, analysis of the distraction index revealed highly significant differences between subjects in the distraction condition and those in the nondistraction conditions, $F(2, 38) = 44.37, p < .0001$. Post hoc comparisons confirmed that subjects in the distraction

TABLE 14.4. Intercorrelations Among Symptoms of Groupthink and Defective Decision Making for Experiment 3

Symptoms	1	2	3	4	5	6	7	8	9	10	11
Groupthink											
1. Invulnerability	—										
2. Self-censorship	.03	—									
3. Rationalization	.38	−.22	—								
4. Unanimity	.49	.27	.24	—							
5. Pressure on dissenters	−.15	.24	−.17	−.11	—						
Defective Decision Making											
6. Failure to examine risks	−.10	.16	−.11	−.17	.06	—					
7. Failure to reappraise alternatives	−.06	−.26	−.05	.04	−.03	.04	—				
8. Omission in survey of objectives	.49	−.26	.45	.16	−.16	−.11	−.04	—			
9. Omission in survey of alternatives	−.18	.07	−.05	−.03	.005	.51	.24	−.15	—		
10. Information processing bias	.43	−.20	.23	.18	−.38	−.21	−.16	.62	−.21	—	
11. Poor information search	.10	−.08	−.03	−.19	−.06	−.04	−.20	.18	−.16	.27	—
12. Contingency plans	−.14	−.02	−.05	−.26	.39	.14	.13	.22	.38	−.15	−.26

Note: Correlations greater than .41 are significant at the .01 level.

condition reported they found the setting more distracting and less conducive to concentration ($M = 4.24$) than did subjects in the no-distraction conditions ($Ms = 1.84$ and 2.12 for the low-threat, no-distraction and the high-threat, no-distraction treatments, respectively). Analysis of the threat index revealed significant differences between subjects in high-threat and low-threat treatments, $F(2, 38) = 6.87$, $p < .002$. Post hoc comparisons confirmed that subjects in the high-threat ($M = 14.7$) and in the high-threat, distraction ($M = 15.4$) treatments reported greater threat than did subjects in the low-threat treatment ($M = 11.2$).

Group performance

Analysis of our group solution quality measure supported our predictions. A one-way ANOVA using a planned contrast of 1, -2, 1 for the low-threat, high-threat, and high-threat and distraction treatments, respectively, indicated that these conditions differed significantly in the quality of the solutions, $F(1, 38) = 4.50$, $p < .04$. Figure 14.2 displays the pattern of means. As predicted, high-threat groups developed lower quality solutions ($M = 2.17$) than did their counterparts in the high-threat and distraction ($M = 3.68$) and the low-threat ($M = 3.66$) treatments.

Several points about these results are worth highlighting. Replicating the first study, groups in the groupthink condition—that is, the high-threat cell—formulated poorer quality solutions than did groups in the low-threat cell. Furthermore, the findings provide evidence supporting a social identity perspective on groupthink: Groups facing the same antecedent conditions as those in the groupthink treatment but who were given an excuse for their potential poor performance developed significantly higher quality solutions than did those in the groupthink treatment. Finally, levels of performance across the two experiments are quite similar. Taken together, these results provide some converging evidence regarding the stability of our findings concerning performance quality.

Analysis of the time-to-solution measure revealed that groups in the low-threat treatment ($M = 19.65$) worked more rapidly than did groups in the high-threat ($M = 25.97$) and the high-threat, distraction ($M = 28.61$) treatments, $F(2, 38) = 4.04$, $p < .03$. This contrasts with results obtained in the first experiment in which groups in all treatments took about 30 min to complete the task.

Self-reports of symptoms of groupthink

Table 14.2 summarizes the results of a series of one-way ANOVAs on our measures of self-reports

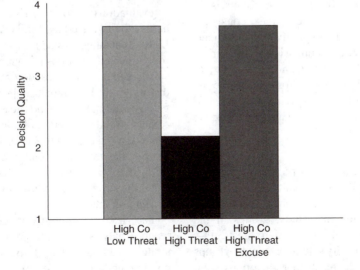

FIGURE 14.2 ■ Mean decision quality for Experiment 3 as a function of threat and distraction. (Co = Cohesion.)

of groupthink symptoms. Recall that because Experiment 3 did not manipulate cohesion, it does not provide a test of Experiment 1 cohesion results. Self-reports of illusion of invulnerability and self-censorship were unaffected by our experimental procedures. This is consistent with the first study, which found a main effect for cohesion: High-cohesive groups reported greater invulnerability and less self-censorship than did low-cohesive groups. The mean obtained in the current study ($M = 2.4$) is quite similar to that for high-cohesion subjects in the first study. In contrast to results from the first study showing that threat increased rationalization but decreased annoyance with dissenters, these measures in this study were unaffected by our manipulations ($ps > .2$).

Self-reports of symptoms of defective decision making

Self-reports of symptoms of defective decision making appear somewhat consistent with results obtained in the first study. Table 14.3 summarizes these findings. Perceived risk of the group solution was unaffected by experimental treatments ($p > .15$), although the overall mean ($M = 2.4$) was quite similar to that reported by high-cohesion subjects in the first study. As in the previous study, low-threat groups reported greater failure to reappraise initially rejected alternatives than high-threat subjects, $F(2, 38) = 2.98$, $p < .08$. Post hoc comparisons confirmed this pattern of results. Also consistent with the previous study, experimental treatments did not affect measures of omission in the survey of objectives ($p > .14$), omission in the survey of alternatives ($p > .13$) biased information processing ($p > .57$), information search ($p > .59$), and failure to develop contingency plans ($p > .32$).

Discussion

The results of this experiment provide converging evidence regarding the poor quality decision making associated with groupthink antecedent conditions. Replicating the first study, groups in the groupthink condition—that is, the high-threat cell—formulated poorer quality solutions than did groups in the low-threat cell (recall that all groups were given the high-cohesion induction). Furthermore, the findings provide evidence regarding the social identity maintenance perspective on groupthink: Groups facing the same antecedent conditions as those in the groupthink treatment but who were given an excuse for their potential poor performance developed significantly higher quality solutions than did those in the groupthink treatment. Moreover, groups facing groupthink conditions and given an excuse were capable of performing at the same level as groups working under nonthreatening conditions.

One potential alternative explanation for the performance data is that the distraction manipulation, rather than inducing self-handicapping and identity protection, might have motivated subjects to overcome the supposed obstacles they faced. This interpretation is unlikely. Prior research (as well as pretesting we conducted) suggests that this type of manipulation does in fact induce the processes hypothesized and does not, by itself, produce enhanced performance. Moreover, Kruglanski and Webster (1991) suggested that distraction (albeit a different type than what we used) motivates members to terminate, rather than overcome, the distracting situation.

Self-reports of groupthink and defective decision-making symptoms replicated previous research by their very inconsistency. Measures affected by group cohesion in our first study, such as evaluations of solution risk, were quite similar across the two studies. Similarly, in both studies, high-threat subjects said they reappraised their initially rejected solutions to a greater extent than did subjects in the low-threat conditions. In contrast to the first study, high-threat subjects exhibited neither greater rationalization nor less pressure on dissenters. We also failed to obtain more pronounced groupthink and defective decision-making symptoms in the groupthink conditions, once again replicating much previous research and failing to support either the strict or the additive interpretations of the groupthink theory.

The view of groupthink as social identity maintenance may be useful in pointing out traditional strategies that are likely to be ineffective in overcoming groupthink. For example, if groups are concerned about avoiding the presentation of a negative image, strategies such as a "second-chance" meeting are more likely to reinforce, rather than reduce, that tendency. Other strategies, such as dividing the group into competing work teams, calling in outside experts, and assigning members to the role of devil's advocate, may work only to the extent that such procedures reduce the threat to a group's image. In many cases, such procedures may actually serve to strengthen the threat and the incidence of groupthink itself.

On a more hopeful note, the view of groupthink as social-identity maintenance did identify one strategy for mitigating the adverse consequences of groupthink. The provision of an excuse for potential poor performance was capable of overcoming the lower quality decisions associated with groupthink antecedent conditions of threat and cohesion. This result may point the way to other strategies for mitigating groupthink consequences—strategies that involve divorcing the group's image from the threatening situation.

General Discussion

Taken together, our results point both to the utility of the groupthink theory and to the need to refine it. Our findings, in conjunction with previous research, underscore the need for revisions to the groupthink theory in at least three areas: (a) clarifying the nature of the antecedents of groupthink, (b) delineating the conceptualization of groupthink itself, and (c) specifying the links among antecedents and consequences of groupthink.

Clarifying Antecedent Conditions

Despite its importance in the groupthink theory, threat previously had not been directly examined as an antecedent condition. Our results lend support to Janis's delineation of threat. Consistent with Janis (1982), our threat of using videotapes for training purposes presented a direct threat to the esteem that members could derive from being part of a functional group. However, Janis (1982) also noted that other forms of threat (such as financial loss) may produce groupthink. Further research is

needed to examine the conditions under which other types of threat will result in groupthink.

Previous groupthink research manipulating cohesion has (a) generally failed to produce the predicted effects of cohesion on groupthink processes and (b) frequently failed to produce perceptual verifications of cohesion. In contrast to much groupthink research, the current manipulation of cohesion produced effects consistent with previous research on group cohesion and with a liberal interpretation of the groupthink theory. Our results also highlight the importance of the self-categorization and social-identity aspect of cohesion, that is, the categorization of others as members of the group rather than as unique individuals (cf. J. C. Turner et al., 1987).

Refining the Conceptualization of Groupthink

Results obtained in Experiments 1 and 3 reinforce the view of groupthink as a process in which group members attempt to maintain a shared, positive view of the functioning of the group in the face of a collective threat (Janis, 1982). This approach is predicated on the induction of a group social identity—an attribute characteristic of many groups in the original case studies. This identity is important in two respects. First, it ensures that members categorize and perceive themselves as a group and develop a positive view of the group they are motivated to maintain. Second, it provides the basis on which the shared threat can operate.

Specifying the Links Among Groupthink Antecedents and Consequences

Our results have several implications for the causal sequences suggested by the groupthink theory. We found little support for the strict interpretation of groupthink, that is, that consequences should only occur when all antecedents under consideration are present. Similarly, we found little support for an additive interpretation that would suggest that consequences should be most pronounced when greater numbers of antecedents are present. These findings, in conjunction with prior research that also fails to find support for the strict or additive interpretations, suggest that more careful empirical analyses of the unique situational consequences of each antecedent be undertaken. Our pattern of findings is strongly consistent with previous research supporting this more liberal interpretation of groupthink (and indeed some of the case studies in Janis, 1982, do not exhibit all the symptoms). Perhaps more fruitful than adherence to a strict interpretation that seems to lack empirical support might be research directed toward more fine-grained analyses of the links between antecedents and consequences of groupthink and toward a delineation of the groupthink process itself. The current research reinforces one interpretation (among possible others) that might be useful in facilitating this research: The view of groupthink as group members' effort to collectively reduce the potential damage from threat and to ward off negative images of the group that produces, as Janis (1982, p. 167) termed it, "the genuine sharing of illusory beliefs."

REFERENCES

Arkin, R. M., & Baumgardner, A. H. (1985). Self-handicapping. In J. H. Harvey & G. Weary (Eds.), *Attribution: Basic issues and applications* (pp. 169–202). San Diego, CA: Academic Press.

Aronson, E. (1988). *The social animal.* New York: Freeman.

Aronson, E., & Carlsmith, M. J. (1968). Experimentation in social psychology. In G. Lindzey & E. Aronson (Eds.), *Handbook of social psychology* (2nd ed., Vol. 2, pp. 1–79). Reading, MA: Addison-Wesley.

Back, K. W. (1951). Influence through social communication. *Journal of Abnormal and Social Psychology, 46,* 9–23.

Callaway, M. R., & Esser, J. K. (1984). Groupthink: Effects of cohesiveness and problem-solving procedures on group decision making. *Social Behavior and Personality, 12,* 157–164.

Callaway, M. R., Marriott, R. G., & Esser, J. K. (1985). Effects of dominance on group decision making: Toward a stress-reduction explanation of groupthink. *Journal of Personality and Social Psychology, 4,* 949–952.

Cartwright, D., & Zander, A. (1953). *Group dynamics: Research and theory.* Evanston, IL: Row, Peterson.

Courtwright, J. (1978). A laboratory investigation of groupthink. *Communication Monographs, 45,* 229–246.

Deaux, K., & Wrightsman, L. (1988). *Social psychology* (5th ed.). Pacific Grove, CA: Brooks/Cole.

Dion, K. L. (1979). Intergroup conflict and intragroup cohesiveness. In W. G. Austin & S. Worchel (Eds.), *The social psychology of intergroup relations* (pp. 211–224). Monterey, CA: Brooks/Cole.

Duval, S., & Wicklund, R. A. (1972). *A theory of objective self-awareness.* San Diego, CA: Academic Press.

Esser, J. K., & Lindoerfer, J. S. (1989). Groupthink and the space shuttle Challenger accident: Toward a quantitative case analysis. *Journal of Behavioral Decision Making, 2,* 167–177.

Festinger, L., Back, K. W., Schachter, S., Kelley, H. H., & Thibaut, J. W. (1952). *Theory and experiment in social communication.* Ann Arbor, MI: Edwards Brothers.

Festinger, L., Schachter, S., & Back, K. W. (1950). Social pressures in informal groups: A study of human factors in housing. New York: Harper.

Flowers, M. L. (1977). A laboratory test of some implications of Janis's groupthink hypothesis. *Journal of Personality and Social Psychology, 35,* 888–896.

Fodor, E. M., & Smith, T. (1982). The power motive as an influence on group decision making. *Journal of Personality and Social Psychology, 42,* 178–185.

Frankel, A., & Snyder, M. L. (1978). Poor performance following unsolvable problems: Learned helplessness or egotism? *Journal of Personality and Social Psychology, 36,* 1415–1423.

Greenwald, A. G., Pratkanis, A. R., Leippe, M. R., & Baumgardner, M. H. (1986). Under what conditions does theory obstruct research progress? *Psychological Review, 93,* 216–229.

Greenwald, A. G., & Ronis, D. L. (1981). On the conceptual disconfirmation of theories. *Personality and Social Psychology Bulletin, 7,* 131–137.

Hall, D., & Mansfield, R. (1971). Organizational and individual response to stress. *Administrative Science Quarterly, 16,* 533–547.

Hensley, T. R., & Griffin, G. W. (1986). Victims of groupthink: The Kent State University board of trustees and the 1977 gymnasium controversy. *Journal of Conflict Resolution, 30,* 497–531.

Higgins, R. L. (1990). *Self-handicapping:* Historical roots and contemporary approaches. In R. L. Higgins, C. R. Snyder, & S. Berglas (Eds.), *Self-handicapping: The paradox that isn't* (pp. 1–35). New York: Plenum Press.

Higgins, R. L., Snyder, C. R., & Berglas, S. (Eds.). (1990). *Self-handicapping: The paradox that isn't.* New York: Plenum Press.

Hogg, M. A., & Abrams, D. (1988). *Social identifications: A social psychology of intergroup relations and group processes.* New York: Routledge.

Janis, I. L. (1972). *Victims of groupthink.* Boston: Houghton Mifflin.

Janis, I. L. (1982). Groupthink: Psychological studies of policy decisions and fiascoes (2nd ed.). Boston: Houghton Mifflin.

Janis, I. L. (1989). Crucial decisions: Leadership in policy-making and crisis management. New York: Free Press.

Janis, I. L., & Mann, F. (1977). *Decision making.* New York: Free Press.

Jones, E. E., & Berglas, S. (1978). Control of attributions about the self through self-handicapping strategies. *Personality and Social Psychology Bulletin, 4*, 200–206.

Kruglanski, A., & Freund, T. (1983). The freezing and unfreezing of lay-inferences: Effects on impression primacy, ethnic stereotyping, and numerical anchoring. *Journal of Experimental Social Psychology, 19*, 448–468.

Kruglanski, A. W., & Webster, D. M. (1991). Group members' reactions to opinion deviates and conformists at varying degrees of proximity to decision deadline and of environmental noise. *Journal of Personality and Social Psychology, 61*, 212–225.

Lazarus, R., & Folkman, S. (1984). *Stress, appraisal, and coping*. New York: Springer.

Leana, C. R. (1985). A partial test of Janis' groupthink model: Effects of group cohesiveness and leader behavior on defective decision making. *Journal of Management, 11*, 5–17.

Leary, M. R. (1986). The impact of interactional impediments on social anxiety and self-presentation. *Journal of Experimental Social Psychology, 22*, 122–135.

Longley, J., & Pruitt, D. G. (1980). Groupthink: A critique of Janis's theory. In L. Wheeler (Ed.), *Review of Personality and Social Psychology* (Vol. 1, pp. 74–93). Beverly Hills, CA: Sage.

Maier, N. R. F. (1952). *Principles of human relations*. New York: Wiley.

Manz, C. C., & Sims, H. P. (1982). The potential for "groupthink" in autonomous work groups. *Human Relations, 35*, 773–784.

McCauley, C. (1989). The nature of social influence in groupthink: Compliance and internalization. *Journal of Personality and Social Psychology, 57*, 250–260.

McGrath, J. E. (1984). *Groups: interaction and performance*. Englewood Cliffs, NJ: Prentice-Hall.

Miller, R. T. (1976). Ego involvement and attribution for success and failure. *Journal of Personality and Social Psychology, 34*, 901–906.

Moorhead, G. (1982). Groupthink: Hypothesis in need of testing. *Group and Organization Studies, 7*, 492–504.

Moorhead, G., & Griffin, R. W. (1989). *Organizational Behavior* (2nd ed.). Boston: Houghton Mifflin.

Moorhead, G., & Montanari, J. R. (1986). An empirical investigation of the groupthink phenomenon. *Human Relations, 39*, 399–410.

Myers, D. G. (1987). *Social psychology* (2nd ed.). New York: McGraw-Hill.

Park, W. (1990). A review of research on groupthink. *Journal of Behavioral Decision Making, 3*, 229–245.

Raven, B. H. (1974). The Nixon group. *Journal of Social Issues, 30*, 297–320.

Raven, B. H., & Rubin, J. Z. (1976). *Social psychology: People in groups*. New York: Wiley.

Ridgeway, C. L. (1983). *The dynamics of small groups*. New York: St. Martin's Press.

Seashore, S. E. (1954). *Group cohesiveness in the industrial work group*. Ann Arbor: University of Michigan.

Shaw, M. E., & Shaw, L. M. (1962). Some effects of sociometric grouping upon learning in a second grade classroom. *Journal of Social Psychology, 57*, 453–458.

Smith, S. (1984). Groupthink and the hostage rescue mission. *British Journal of Political Science, 15*, 117–126.

Snyder, C. R. (1990). Self-handicapping processes and sequelae. In R. L. Higgins, C. R. Snyder, & S. Berglas (Eds.), *Self-handicapping: The paradox that isn't*. (pp. 107–150). New York: Plenum Press.

Snyder, M. L., Smoller, B., Strenta, A., & Frankel, A. (1981). A comparison of egotism, negativity, and learned helplessness as explanations for poor performance after unsolvable problems. *Journal of Personality and Social Psychology, 40*, 24–30.

Steers, R. M. (1990). *Introduction to organizational behavior* (4th ed.). New York: HarperCollins.

Steiner, I. D. (1982). Heuristic models of groupthink. In H. Brandstatter, J. H. Davis, & G. Stocker-Kreichgauer (Eds.), *Group decision making* (pp. 503–524). San Diego, CA: Academic Press.

Sudman, S., & Bradburn, N. M. (1982). *Asking questions: A practical guide to questionnaire design*. San Francisco: Jossey-Bass.

Tajfel, H. (1981). *Human groups and social categories*. Cambridge, England: Cambridge University Press.

Terborg, J. R., Castore, C., & DeNinno, J. A. (1976). A longitudinal field investigation of the impact of group composition on group performance and cohesion. *Journal of Personality and Social Psychology, 34*, 782–790.

Tetlock, P. E. (1979). Identifying victims of groupthink from public statements of decision makers. *Journal of Personality and Social Psychology, 37*, 1314–1324.

Tetlock, P. E., Peterson, R. S., McGuire, C., Chang, S., & Feld, P. (1992). Assessing political group dynamics: A test of the groupthink model. *Journal of Personality and Social Psychology, 63*, 403–425.

Thompson, J. E., & Carsrud, A. L. (1976). The effects of experimentally induced illusions of invulnerability and vulnerability on decisional risk taking in triads. *Journal of Social Psychology, 100*, 263–267.

Turner, J. C. (1981). The experimental social psychology of intergroup behavior. In J. C. Turner & H. Giles (Eds.), *Intergroup behavior* (pp. 66–101). Chicago: University of Chicago Press.

Turner, J. C. (1982). Towards a cognitive redefinition of the social group. In H. Tajfel (Ed.), *Social identity and intergroup relations* (pp. 15–40). Cambridge, England: Cambridge University Press.

Turner, J. C., Hogg, M. A., Oakes, P. J., Reicher, S. D., & Wetherell, M. S. (1987). *Rediscovering the social group: A self-categorization theory*. New York: Basil Blackwell.

Turner, J. C., Hogg, M. A., Turner, P. J., & Smith, P. M. (1984). Failure and defeat as determinants of group cohesiveness. *British Journal of Social Psychology, 23*, 97–111.

Turner, M. E., & Pratkanis, A. R. (1991). *Groupthink as social identity maintenance: Evidence from the field and the laboratory.* Unpublished manuscript, San Jose State University.

Wheeler, D., & Janis, I. L. (1980). A practical guide for making decisions. New York: Free Press.

Wicklund, R. A. (1975). Objective self-awareness. In L. Berkowitz (Ed.), *Advances in experimental social psychology* (Vol. 8, pp. 233–275). San Diego, CA: Academic Press.

Williams, K., Harkins, S., & Latané, B. (1981). Identifiability as a deterrent to social loafing: Two cheering experiments. *Journal of Personality and Social Psychology, 40,* 303–311.

Received September 11, 1991
Revision received June 1, 1992
Accepted June 4, 1992 ■

The Effects of Repeated Expressions on Attitude Polarization During Group Discussions

Markus Brauer, Charles M. Judd, and Melissa D. Gliner

Classic explanations of the "group polarization phenomenon" emphasize interpersonal processes such as informational influence and social comparison (Myers & Lamm, 1976). Based on earlier research, we hypothesized that at least part of the polarization observed during group discussion might be due to repeated attitude expression. Two studies provide support for this hypothesis. In Study 1, we manipulated how often each group member talked about an issue and how often he or she heard other group members talk about the issue. We found that repeated expression produced a reliable shift in extremity. A detailed coding of the groups' discussions showed that the effect of repeated expression on attitude polarization was enhanced in groups where the group members repeated each other's arguments and used them in their own line of reasoning. Study 2 tested for this effect experimentally. The results showed that the effect of repeated expression was augmented in groups where subjects were instructed to use each other's arguments compared to groups where instructions were given to avoid such repetitions. Taken together, these studies show that repeated expression accounts for at least part of the attitude polarization observed in the typical studies on group polarization and that this effect is augmented by social interaction, i.e., it occurs particularly in an environment where group members repeat and validate each other's ideas.

Markus Brauer, Fachgruppe Psychologie, Universität Konstanz, Germany; Charles M. Judd, Department of Psychology, University of Colorado, Boulder; Melissa D. Gliner, Department of Psychology, University of California, Santa Cruz.

This research is based on a doctoral dissertation submitted by Markus Brauer to the University of Colorado and supported by a National Institute of Mental Health Grant (R01 MH45049).

We thank Lewis O. Harvey, Reid Hastie, Bernadette Park, and Walter Stone for their helpful suggestions and comments.

Correspondence concerning this article should be addressed to Markus Brauer, Universität Konstanz, Fachgruppe Psychologie, Postfach 5560, D39, 78434 Konstanz, Germany, or to Charles M. Judd, Department of Psychology, University of Colorado, Boulder, Colorado 80309-0345.

The notion of attitude strength has enjoyed considerable interest among social psychologists recently. Petty and Krosnick (in press) argue that attitude strength is a multidimensional concept that expresses itself in multiple ways such as attitude importance, attitude accessibility, and attitude extremity (see also Krosnick, Boninger, Chuang, Berent, & Carnot, 1993). The aspect of attitude strength that is of interest for our purposes is attitude extremity. This construct has been shown to have powerful effects on behavior, memory, and judgment. Extreme attitudes are more consistent with behaviors (Fazio & Zanna, 1978; Petersen & Dutton, 1975) and are more resistant to persuasion than moderate attitudes (Ewing, 1942; Osgood & Tannenbaum, 1955; Sarat & Vidmar, 1976). Individuals with extreme attitudes tend to remember congruent information to a greater extent than less extreme individuals (Roberts, 1984). Finally, extreme attitudes seem to be associated with judgments that a larger proportion of others share one's own point of view (Allison & Messick, 1988; Crano, Gorenflo, & Shackelford, 1988).

There has been a long-standing tradition in social psychology to examine the interpersonal factors that lead to attitude extremity, such as the *group polarization phenomenon* (Myers & Arenson, 1972; Myers & Lamm, 1976) and polarization due to intergroup conflict (Abelson, in press; Sherif, Harvey, White, Hood, & Sherif, 1961). Group polarization refers to the fact that an individual's attitude toward a given issue tends to polarize during a group discussion with other people who hold a similar opinion on that issue (Myers, 1978; Myers & Lamm, 1976). For example, Moscovici and Zavalloni (1969) observed that French students' initially positive attitudes toward DeGaulle and negative attitudes toward Americans were strengthened through discussion. In a study conducted by Myers and Bishop (1970), a discussion with others having similar racial attitudes increased the gap between high- and low-prejudice groups. Polarization due to intergroup conflict describes the well-known finding that group members' attitudes toward the out-group become more extreme when the two groups are placed in a situation of competition or conflict (Bettelheim & Janowitz, 1949; Levine &

Campbell, 1972). For example, in the famous Robbers Cave Experiment (Sherif et al., 1961), the boys' attitudes toward the other group became more extreme when the experimenters introduced conflict in the form of a series of athletic events.

Other research on attitude extremity has focused on more cognitive or intrapersonal factors related to attitude polarization. It has been found, for example, that being repeatedly exposed to an attitude object can lead to attitude polarization in the absence of any new stimuli from the environment (Brickman, Redfield, Harrison, & Crandall, 1972; Perlman & Oskamp, 1971). Similarly, Tesser and his colleagues have shown that extended thought devoted to an attitude object leads to a more extreme evaluation of that object (Tesser, 1978; Tesser & Leone, 1977). Our own research has demonstrated that repeated attitude expression also causes attitudes to become more extreme. In a study by Downing, Judd, and Brauer (1992), participants were asked to state their attitudes toward a number of political issues with varying frequency. The results showed a reliable linear trend of frequency such that the more often an issue was responded to, the greater the polarization of participants' attitudes toward this issue during the experiment. As argued elsewhere (Judd & Brauer, in press), it seems as if repeated exposure to the attitude object, extended thought about one's evaluation of the object, and repeated attitude expression may all involve the same cognitive processes (consistent with the explanation originally offered by Tesser, 1978). All three processes cause the individual to focus increasingly on features of the attitude object that are consistent with his or her overall evaluation and to gradually disregard features that are inconsistent with the overall evaluation. As a result, the underlying attribute dimensions become more evaluatively consistent, leading, in turn, to attitude polarization.

Based on our earlier results showing that repeated expression results in polarization (Downing et al., 1992), it seemed plausible that repeated attitude expression might also play a role in the attitude polarization observed in group discussion (Myers & Arenson, 1972). The original studies in this area involved discussion about choice dilemmas (Stoner,

1961), where group members advise an imaginary person who is deciding between two alternatives. In general, one of the alternatives is risky but has a very desirable outcome whereas the other alternative is safe but has only a moderately positive outcome. Stoner (1961) found that individuals were considerably riskier after the group discussion than before. It was Myers and Arenson (1972) who showed that group discussions do not always cause a shift toward the risky alternative but do produce an increase in extremity in the direction of the original inclination. In other words, the phenomenon was not risky shift but rather group polarization. Since then, more than 200 studies have shown in a variety of laboratory and field settings that group discussion polarizes individuals' attitudes toward a given issue as long as all group members have the same original inclination (Brown, 1986; Isenberg, 1986; Myers, 1973; Myers & Lamm, 1976).

Two primary explanations have been suggested for the group polarization effect (Isenberg, 1986; Myers & Lamm, 1976). According to the *persuasive arguments* explanation, there exists a pool of arguments for each issue, favoring extremes at either end. Each person who considers the issue will have knowledge of a sample of the pool of arguments, which will determine his or her initial attitude. During the group discussion, individual arguments are expressed and become fully shared. Because participants are more likely to express arguments that favor their initial attitude, a large pool of arguments favoring the groups' initial inclination will be shared among all group members. Each individual participant learns new arguments in favor of his or her initial viewpoint and, as a result, attitude polarization occurs (Burnstein & Vinokur, 1977). Support for this interpretation comes from several studies in which participants were exposed to new arguments without knowing the other group members' attitudes (Burnstein & Vinokur, 1973; Vinokur & Burnstein, 1974). Other research has shown that the valence and number of the arguments are good predictors of the size of the mean shift in extremity (Bishop & Myers, 1974).

The second explanation for the group polarization phenomenon is a *social comparison* or normative explanation. According to this explanation, individual group members polarize when they realize that others share their opinions to a greater extent than they had thought (Myers & Lamm, 1976). Many of us have the desire to be perceived as more favorable than what we perceive to be the average tendency (Fromkin, 1970). As Roger Brown (1974) pointed out, "to be virtuous . . . is to be different from the mean—in the right direction and to the right degree" (p. 469). When all members of an interacting group engage in the same social comparison process, the result is an average shift in the direction of the predominant attitude. Experimental research has shown that mere exposure to central tendency or to the distribution of responses is sufficient to produce attitude polarization even if no discussion between group members takes place (Baron & Roper, 1976; Myers, 1978).

Both explanations have accumulated at this point abundant supportive evidence and accordingly are generally given credence in the literature. Notice that both explanations, as commonly interpreted, focus on interpersonal processes, that is, they imply that polarization results from what we hear from other group members—their arguments or their normative positions. However, participants not only listen to other people during a typical group discussion; they also state their opinion and are likely to defend it multiple times. According to our earlier results (Downing et al., 1992), repeated attitude expression alone should lead to attitude polarization, independently of the effect due to persuasive arguments from others or due to social comparison processes. This led us to the hypothesis that not all of the attitude polarization observed during a group discussion is due to interpersonal influence, but that at least part of it can be attributed to interpersonal processes such as repeated attitude expression and thoughts about one's evaluation of the attitude object. We argue that the contribution of these processes has so far been underestimated because the traditional experimental procedure does not allow one to separate the effects of intrapersonal and interpersonal processes on attitude polarization. This is because in typical groups, issues that are discussed involve both hearing from others and speaking to others. If we were to compare participants' extremity on the discussed issue versus an issue that was not discussed, it would be impossible to determine whether the polarization is due to interpersonal processes (hearing arguments and normative positions from others) or to intrapersonal processes (saying one's own position and arguments repeatedly).

We conducted a study in which we unconfounded these two processes. We assessed the effects of hearing other people's point of view and the effects of repeated attitude expression on the extremity of attitudes. Participants met in groups of four and were instructed to discuss five issues that they all generally agreed on. The issues were national political issues such as a nationally funded health care system or reductions in the military budget. To examine the influence of interpersonal and intrapersonal processes on attitude polarization, we independently manipulated the number of times group members stated their own point of view and the number of times they heard other group members state their point of view. To accomplish this, participants in the groups met in dyads throughout the experiment and told the other person in their dyad their opinion toward a given issue. Who said what to whom was determined by a fixed schedule, which was designed so that the number of attitude expressions toward an issue was, on average, independent of the number of times the participant heard someone else talk about this issue. At the end of the experiment, participants indicated their attitudes on all issues. We predicted that both repeated attitude expression and repeated exposure to other people's attitudes would lead to greater extremity on the final attitude ratings.

Study 1

Method

Participants. Participants were undergraduate students at the University of Colorado who participated in partial fulfillment of an introductory psychology course requirement. Because we wanted to form groups of four individuals who all generally agreed on at least five issues, we always scheduled more participants for a session than we

TABLE 15.1. Percentage of Groups That Discussed Each Stimulus Issue in Study 1 and Study 2

Stimulus issues	Study 1	Study 2
Federally funded national health care system	43	55
Laws that guarantee the rights of gays and lesbians	29	36
Legalization of marijuana	31	39
Increases in federally guaranteed student loan programs	83	91
Increased taxes in order to reduce the federal deficit	37	23
Further reductions in the military budget	46	41
Closing down many of the nuclear power plants that currently are used to generate electricity	23	23
Decreasing logging operations in National Forests	69	50
Statutes to assure animal rights	49	59
Federal programs to create jobs for inner-city youth	91	84

actually needed. Based on participants' responses on an initial attitude questionnaire, we selected a group of four participants who participated in the actual experiment. The other participants were dismissed and did not participate in the study. In total, 204 participants came to the laboratory but only 140 participants participated in the study. These 140 participants constituted 35 independent groups of four participants each.

Design. Participants in a group talked about six issues. Of the 10 issues on the initial questionnaire (the issues are identified in Table 15.1), 6 were selected such that participants had generally similar viewpoints on 5 issues (designated Issues 1 to 5) and dissimilar viewpoints on a sixth issue (designated Issue 6). The sixth issue was included because pretest participants realized very quickly that they generally agreed on all the issues and tended not to take the experiment very seriously. In any group, each participant participated in 15 dyadic encounters, 5 with each of the other three group members. During each encounter, the participant stated his or her opinion toward a given issue to the other group member in the dyad and listened to the other group

TABLE 15.2. Encounter Schedule for Study 1

	Dyad 1				Dyad 2			
Encounter	Participant	Issue	Participant	Issue	Participant	Issue	Participant	Issue
1	A	1	B	3	C	5	D	6
2	B	3	C	2	D	5	A	2
3	C	2	A	2	D	4	B	4
4	C	4	D	6	A	1	B	3
5	B	3	C	2	C	5	A	1
6	C	3	A	2	B	4	D	5
7	D	1	C	5	A	4	B	1
8	D	2	A	6	C	2	B	1
9	A	3	C	6	B	5	D	4
10	B	3	A	1	C	6	D	5
11	C	5	B	6	D	1	A	3
12	B	4	D	5	A	1	C	2
13	A	1	B	6	D	4	C	5
14	D	5	A	6	C	2	B	3
15	B	4	D	4	A	2	C	3

member who stated his or her opinion toward an issue. Across all participants within a given group, there were thus 60 attitude statements where one person was the speaker and one person the listener.

In addition to issue, two factors were manipulated within each group: the frequency with which attitudes were stated on an issue by a participant and the frequency with which a participant heard another person state his or her attitude on an issue. Frequency of attitude expression varied between 0 and 6, such that participants expressed their own point of view toward a given issue either 0, 1, 2, 4, or 6 times. Likewise, frequency of hearing or exposure varied between 0 and 5. A schedule was designed such that frequency of attitude expression and frequency of hearing other people's opinions were relatively independent of each other across encounters. The exact schedule for all encounters is given in Table 15.2. This table indicates for each of the 15 encounters which participants were put in each dyad and which issue each participant talked about and heard about from the other participant in the dyad. (The designation of Dyad 1 and Dyad 2 in the table is arbitrary.)

This schedule of encounters can be summarized in two tables that reflect the two important manipulations: one that lists the number of times each participant stated his or her opinion toward the six

TABLE 15.3. Summary of the Exchanges During the Group Discussion in Study 1

	Issues					
Participants	1	2	3	4	5	6
Number of times each issue was said						
A	6	4	2	1	0	2
B	2	0	6	4	1	2
C	0	6	2	1	4	2
D	2	1	0	4	6	2
Number of times each issue was heard (from 1 or more participants)						
A	2	3	5	0	3	2
B	4	4	0	4	3	0
C	3	3	4	1	1	3
D	1	1	1	5	4	3
Number of people from whom each issue was heard						
A	2	2	2	0	1	2
B	1	1	0	2	2	0
C	3	1	2	1	1	2
D	1	1	1	2	2	2

issues across the 15 encounters (the top panel of Table 15.3), and one that lists the number of times each participant heard someone else state his or her opinion toward the six issues across the 15 encounters (the middle panel of Table 15.3). Note that across participants in a group, issue was unconfounded with frequency of saying and hearing, such that each of the five agreement issues was talked about equally often. This does not mean, however, that across groups issues were talked about equally often. Naturally there were some issues where participants were more often in initial agreement (e.g., inner city youth) than others (e.g., nuclear power plants). Such issues tended to be included in the set of discussed issues more frequently across groups. (The frequencies with which issues were discussed are also given in Table 15.1.) But again, the important point is that frequency of expression and frequency of exposure were manipulated within each group and these manipulations were unconfounded with issue and participant.

The third panel in Table 15.3 presents the number of different people from whom each participant heard an opinion on each issue across the 15 encounters. It is unclear whether social influence— be it normative or informational—predicts polarization as a function of the number of different attitude expressions one hears or the number of different people one hears from. Accordingly we kept track of this latter variable as well.

Our fairly complicated dyadic design was used to ensure that frequency of attitude expression and frequency of hearing other people's viewpoints were relatively independent of each other. This was indeed the case: the correlation between the top panel and the middle panel of Table 15.3 is .06, calculated across participants and issues (excluding the disagreement Issue 6, which was not used in the analyses). Similarly, the correlation between the top panel and the bottom panel of Table 15.3 is .04. As expected, the correlation between the second and third panels is fairly high, $r = .66$, because hearing an issue more frequently meant one was likely to hear it from multiple others.

Procedure. Between four and six participants were scheduled at any one time. When participants arrived at the laboratory they were asked to fill out a questionnaire where they indicated their attitudes toward 10 different issues (given in Table 15.1). These ratings were done on 9-point scales with the endpoints labeled *strongly favor* and *strongly oppose*. Participants were asked to wait in an

adjacent room while their responses from the questionnaire were entered into a computer. A computer program then generated a group of four participants who all generally agreed on five issues (labeled Issues 1 to 5) and disagreed on a sixth one (Issue 6). Participants were said to agree when their ratings were on the same side of the 9-point rating scale, that is, when all ratings were ≥ 5 or ≤ 5. When participants agreed on six or more issues, the computer program listed the five issues containing the fewest number of neutral responses (i.e., ratings of 5). All other participants were dismissed and did not participate in the study.

The remaining four participants were told that our research was concerned with how people discussed political issues. More specifically, we were interested in how people formed impressions of other people's point of views. The experimenter told participants that they would be asked to discuss some of the issues they had just seen on the questionnaire. She explained that one problem with group discussions was that some people always talked more than others. In order to avoid this problem, the discussion in this study would take a somewhat special format. Each of the participants would be paired with one other member of the group and they would have 1 min to exchange their points of view on a particular issue with the other person. After that, they would be paired with another group member and again they would have a minute to state their opinions, and so on. For each exchange with another person, each participant would receive a little paper slip indicating which issue he or she should talk about. The experimenter made it clear that occasionally both partners in a pair would say their opinion about the same issue but that most of the time each partner would talk about a different issue. Each dyadic exchange would take exactly one minute; during the first 30 s the first person would say what he or she thought about the issue on his or her paper slip and during the last 30 s the second person would state his or her opinion toward the issue on his or her slip.

Participants were told that a prearranged schedule would determine who is paired with whom and who talks about which issue. At the beginning of each exchange, the experimenter would give them their paper slip and would send them to one of four locations, called "Location 1," "Location 2," "Location 3," and "Location 4." The experimenter pointed out that Locations 1 and 2 were in the same room and Locations 3 and 4 were in the adjacent room. Persons in Locations 1 and 3 would always talk first; after 30 s the experimenter would say "stop" and then, the persons in Locations 2 and 4 would have 30 s to state their opinion. Thus, the first two locations defined the first dyad and Locations 3 and 4 defined the second dyad. Across encounters, participants were assigned to locations in such a way that each one spoke first or second in a dyad approximately equally often. It was made clear that the exchanges should be simple one-way communications. That is, the listener should not ask questions or state his or her opinion during the 30 s allocated to the other speaker. Participants were told that they would always have the full 30 s available though they need not use it all. After the exchange, participants would be asked to give back the paper slips to the experimenter who would then give them new paper slips and send them to new locations. This process would continue until they were through the whole schedule. In total, they would meet 15 times with one other member of the group. The experimenter warned participants not to be concerned if they received the same issue more than once, or if they talked to the same person about the same issue more than once. The experimenter said that this also occurred in natural group discussions and that our goal was to replicate this process as closely as possible. Participants were told to simply tell their partner how they felt about the issue at that particular moment.

Participants were asked to put on name tags so that they would get to know each other a little better. The experimenter also informed them that they should look at their paper slip only at the last moment before talking. This was done to ensure that both partners listened to each other instead of preparing their statement in their mind. Finally, the experimenter informed participants that their statements would be taped. After the 15 encounters, participants were asked to fill out a final questionnaire which asked them to indicate one more time their attitudes toward the 10 issues. Here, the ratings

were done on 29-point rating scales. Like before, the endpoints were labeled *strongly favor* and *strongly oppose*. Following completion of this questionnaire, participants were fully debriefed and dismissed.

Results

Our first objective was to test whether our experimental procedure succeeded in inducing group polarization. Because different scales were used for the initial and the final attitude ratings, we could not determine the amount of polarization by directly comparing the pretest versus the posttest ratings of discussed issues. However, it was possible to compare participants' ratings on the discussed issues with their ratings on the issues that were not discussed. There were five discussed issues on which there was initial agreement and on which we expected polarization, and there were four not-discussed issues. We transformed the ratings on the initial and the final questionnaire into extremity scores by taking the absolute value of the difference between the scale midpoint and each of the participant's ratings. We then averaged the extremity scores of the final ratings of all participants toward the five issues that were discussed within a group and compared this value with the average of the extremity scores of the final ratings toward the four issues that were not discussed, controlling for the pretest extremities on the same issues. The analysis involved a repeated measures analysis of covariance (ANCOVA), with discussed versus not-discussed issues as the within-subject (or group) variable. The repeated measures covariate was the pretest average extremities for these same issues. Because participants in any group constitute non-independent observations, in this analysis and all others we treated the group as the unit of analysis. Accordingly, the two scores on the dependent variable of each group (and on the covariate) are averages computed across both participants and issues.

The mean posttest extremity scores were 6.02 and 4.63 for discussed and nondiscussed issues. The same extremity means, adjusted for the extremities of the pretest ratings, were 5.81 and 4.84. The

ANCOVA indicated that these two adjusted mean extremity scores were reliably different from each other, $F(1, 33) = 25.70$, $p < .001$. This indicates that discussed issues were given substantially more extreme posttest attitude ratings than nondiscussed issues, even controlling for initial differences in extremity between the two sets.[1]

Our next and primary objective was to determine whether repeated attitude expression was at least partly responsible for this polarization of attitudes. Because of dependence of observations within groups, the test of our hypotheses involved a hierarchical or multilevel analysis. First, we calculated scores for each of the 35 groups that expressed the extent to which the individual attitudes in a group polarized as a function of the frequency of a participant's expressing his or her own opinion and as a function of the frequency of a participant's hearing another's opinion. These scores estimate the effects of these independent variables at the level of the individual attitude and are unbiased by the group dependence. However, their within-group standard errors are biased because of group-induced nonindependence (Kenny & Judd, 1986). Accordingly, the second level of the analysis treated the group as the unit of analysis (thus treating it as a random variable in a hierarchical design). At this level we tested whether the mean values of these scores were reliably different from zero across groups.

The polarization scores, which were calculated in the first step, are simply within-group unstandardized regression coefficients. Two different regression models were estimated in each group. The first regressed posttest attitude extremity scores on frequency of expression and frequency of hearing, controlling for pretest extremity scores. The second regressed posttest extremity scores on frequency of expression and the number of people from whom one heard on the issue, again controlling

for pretest extremity scores. These within-group regression coefficients were estimated across the 20 observations (four participants × five issues) within each group. Separate models were calculated for the frequency of hearing and number of people heard from because these variables are highly redundant. These two within-group regressions yielded four regression coefficients for each group that are of interest. First, two coefficients (SAY1 and SAY2) indicate the magnitude of polarization per unit increase in the frequency with which participants expressed their own opinion on an issue. The first (SAY1) is from a model that controls for the frequency of hearing another participant on the issue and the second (SAY2) controls for the number of others heard from on the issue. Additionally, a regression coefficient indicates the magnitude of the polarization difference per unit increase in the frequency with which participants heard someone else express their opinion on an issue (HEAR). The final coefficient (PEOPLE) indicates the increase in polarization due to hearing one more person express his or her opinion on an issue. Both of these latter coefficients were estimated while controlling for the frequency of the participant's own expression. Because pretest extremity scores were controlled in both models, these coefficients portray polarization differences over time associated with each predictor variable.

The means and the standard deviations for these four polarization scores are given in Table 15.4. Single sample t tests were performed for each to determine whether each was, on average, reliably different from 0 across groups. As predicted, groups polarized as a function of repeated attitude expression, independent of what other variable was in the model; the mean of the SAY polarization scores was .09, $t(34) = 2.63$, $p < .02$, with HEAR included in the model, and .09, $t(34) = 2.50$, $p < .02$, with PEOPLE included in the model. This makes clear

---

[1] To the extent that there are errors of measurement in the pretest extremity scores, this analysis of covariance underadjusts for the pretest extremity differences between the discussed and undiscussed issues. However, we do not think that this potential underadjustment calls into question the conclusion that polarization occurred. First, because extremity scores were aggregated across both issues and participants within groups, the resulting averages contain substantially less random error than do the individual scores. Second, the adjusted difference in extremity between discussed and undiscussed issues is sufficiently large and reliable that we are confident that it would persist even with totally error-free pretest measures.

TABLE 15.4. Polarization Results From the Within-Group Regressions in Study 1

Results	Regression model 1		Regression model 2	
	SAY1	HEAR	SAY2	PEOPLE
M	.09	.05	.09	.21
s	.21	.26	.21	.61
t	2.63	1.22	2.50	2.02
p	<.02	ns	<.02	<.06

Note: There were 35 groups included in the analyses. The degrees of freedom for the t tests is 34.

that some of the polarization observed during the group discussion was due to the frequency of attitude expression by a participant. Somewhat surprisingly, groups did not become reliably more extreme as a function of repeated exposure to other people's viewpoints. The mean of the HEAR polarization scores was .05, $t(34) = 1.22$, ns. However, the number of different people from whom arguments were heard had a positive effect on attitude extremity. The mean PEOPLE polarization score was .21, $t(34) = 2.02$, $p = .051$, supporting the traditional explanations of group polarization, that is, that exposure to other people's viewpoints leads to attitude polarization.

It is interesting to observe that the number of different people from whom statements were heard (PEOPLE) had a greater impact on attitude extremity than the number of times an individual participant heard someone else talk about an issue (HEAR). In other words, if one hears the opinions of three different people, that causes greater attitude polarization than if one hears the same person talking about the issue three times in a row. Also, note that with a p value of .051, the polarization as a function of PEOPLE fell just short of the traditional alpha level of .05. One must realize, however, that we did not have a lot of statistical power

for this test. The number of different people from whom each participant heard about an issue only varied between 0 and 3, with all but one value lying between 0 and 2 (see Table 15.3, bottom panel).

Even though the SAY polarization scores were reliably greater than zero on average, in support of our hypothesis, there was considerable variability from group to group in the magnitude of this effect. Some groups showed a large effect of repeated expression on polarization; others showed a much smaller effect. To understand the effect in more detail, participants' statements were transcribed and coded along a number of dimensions. Because the coding was very detailed (see below) and fairly time consuming, we selected for coding the eight groups that polarized most and the eight groups that polarized least as a function of repeated attitude expression.[2] For the same reasons, only some of the statements from these groups were coded. For each participant, we looked only at the statements made on the issue which that participant talked about six times. We coded all statements made by the participant on that issue and all statements heard by that participant on that issue. For example, Participant A always talked about Issue 1 six times and heard about it two times (see Tables 15.2 and 15.3). All eight statements on this issue, whether given by Person A or the other person in A's dyadic encounters, were used in the coding analyses. This way, 32 of the 60 statements per group were coded. Statements in which the target speaker talked about his or her issue (i.e., the one he or she talked about six times) are referred to as target-speaker statements. Statements in which the target speaker heard another group member talk about the target member's issue are called guest-speaker statements.

Participants' statements during the 30-s time period allocated to each encounter were broken down into idea units. Any utterance that contained a new idea was considered a separate unit. Idea

[2]When we transcribed participants' statements we realized that there had been problems with the recording in 4 of the 16 groups that we had selected for coding. The problems we encountered were that one or more participants did not talk loud enough, the tape recorder battery was too low, or the tape recorder had been switched off accidentally. As a

result, we lost three of the four groups with the highest SAY polarization scores and one group with a fairly low SAY polarization score. These four groups were replaced by other groups so that we ended up with the 16 most extreme groups on the SAY polarization scores from which we had complete recordings.

units were initially assigned to one of three groups: position statements, arguments, and irrelevant statements. Position statements were idea units where the participant indicated his or her attitude toward the issue ("I really think logging operations in the national forests should be decreased," or "I am sort of neutral on this issue"). Arguments were idea units where the participant provided a reason for his or her attitude or suggested a new way of action ("National forests should be kept for recreational purposes," or "We should recycle more, then we don't have to chop down so many trees"). Irrelevant statements were idea units that were neither a position statement nor an argument ("I really don't know much about this issue," or "I wonder whether this tape recorder really works").

Arguments were broken down further, into the categories different arguments, repeated arguments, and integrated arguments. The goal in this further breakdown was to identify if an argument had been used in a previous encounter in that group or was new. Hence, coding was done in the order statements were made with knowledge of the codes given to previous idea units. A different argument was an argument that had not been mentioned in any encounters previously coded for the group either by the target speaker or by the other participants who talked to him or her about the issue. A repeated argument was an argument that the speaker himself or herself had mentioned before. An integrated argument was an argument that a speaker used and that had been stated previously by a different participant. Two decision criteria were used to decide whether or not an argument was the same as a previous one. According to the strict criterion, an argument was considered repeated (or integrated) only if it contained the identical wording or a very similar wording as a previous argument. According to the lenient criterion, an argument was classified as repeated (or integrated) if it referred to the same idea as a previous argument. For example, if a participant said "gays and lesbians should have the same rights as anybody else" and another participant said later on "regardless of their sexual orientation, equal people should have equal rights," then the second idea unit would be coded as a different argument according to the strict criterion and

as an integrated argument according to the lenient criterion. The lenient criterion certainly corresponds more to what we spontaneously would apply if we were asked whether or not two arguments contain the same idea. However, we were interested also in the strict criterion because we wanted to know whether it makes a difference if someone repeated himself or herself word by word or if he or she repeated the same idea using different words. As it turned out, the results involving the strict criterion were similar to those of the lenient criterion, but generally weaker. For this reason, only the analyses of the lenient criterion codes will be reported.

All coding was done by two coders who were blind to the groups' polarization scores. All transcribed statements in all groups were first judged by both coders individually, and then differences between the coders were resolved through discussion. We established the intercoder reliability using the first two groups coded. We simply counted how many decisions the two coders agreed on in doing a complete coding of these two groups. Decisions included judgments concerning where a new idea unit started, which of the categories a given idea unit belonged to, and, if it was a repeated or an integrated argument, what other argument it was identical to. Following extensive training, the two coders agreed on more than 99% of these decisions.

To summarize, each idea unit belonged to one of five categories: position statement, irrelevant statement, different argument, repeated argument, and integrated argument. The total number of idea units in each category was calculated for each group, and these sums were correlated with the groups' SAY polarization scores (actually SAY1). The resulting correlations are shown in Table 15.5.

Because of the small sample size involved, we present and interpret some of these correlations even when they do not meet the traditional level of statistical significance. First, there was a marginally reliable relationship between the number of idea units and the group's regression coefficient for SAY ($r = .44, p < .09$). In other words, groups who polarized more as a function of repeated attitude expression simply talked more than groups whose attitudes did not polarize as much. There

TABLE 15.5. Bivariate Correlations Between the Groups' Polarization Scores and the Content Variables From the Coding of Participants' Statements in Study 1

| | Polarization scores | | | |
| | SAY1 | | PEOPLE | |
Content variables	r	p	r	p
Number of thought units (all speakers)	.44	<.09	.29	ns
Number of arguments (all speakers)	.36	<.18	.10	ns
Number of position statements (all speakers)	−.07	ns	.31	ns
Number of irrelevant statements (all speakers)	.18	ns	.29	ns
Number of different arguments (all speakers)	.28	ns	.28	ns
Number of repeated arguments (all speakers)	.35	<.19	.07	ns
Number of integrated arguments (all speakers)	.62	<.01	.13	ns
Number of integrated arguments (target speaker only)	.47	<.07	−.18	ns
Number of integrated arguments (guest speaker only)	.57	<.03	.02	ns

Note: There were 16 groups included in the analysis.

was also a slight, albeit nonsignificant, tendency for them to generate more arguments, as indicated by the correlation between the SAY polarization scores and the total number of arguments ($r = .36$, $p < .18$). However, the number of position statements and the number of irrelevant statements were not related to the group's tendency to polarize as a function of repeated attitude expression.

The number of repeated arguments was only weakly related to the groups' tendency to polarize as a function of repeated attitude expression ($r = .35$, $p < .19$). More impressively, the number of integrated arguments was reliably related to the magnitude of the SAY polarization score ($r = .62$, $p < .01$). This indicates that the more group members repeated each other's arguments, the more the group tended to polarize as a function of repeated attitude expression. To examine this correlation a bit further, we broke down integrated arguments further into arguments made by a guest speaker that the target speaker subsequently integrated and arguments made by the target speaker that a guest speaker subsequently integrated. The former correlated .47 with SAY polarization; the latter correlated .57. In other words, it seems as if repeated expression has the biggest effect on attitude extremity when individuals to whom arguments are made repeat them back to the arguer.[3]

None of these coding categories correlated with the groups' PEOPLE polarization scores, that is, the group's tendency to polarize as a function of the number of different people that each participant heard talking about an issue. This is somewhat surprising. One should not forget, however, that groups were selected for coding to maximize the variability on the SAY polarization scores rather than on their PEOPLE scores. Accordingly, the absence of correlations for PEOPLE polarization probably reflects the fact that these scores were not particularly variable among the coded groups.

The correlation of SAY polarization with argument integration is exceedingly interesting because it implies that attitude expression leads to

---

[3] Because we only coded expressions for issues where participants stated their attitudes six times, it might be argued that we should correlate these coded variables not with the overall SAY polarization scores but with a measure of the extent to which participants polarized on just those issues where they expressed their opinions six times. To do this, we needed to measure polarization due to repeated expression on just these issues. Accordingly, within each group we regressed the extremity of the participants' posttest ratings on the extremity of the pretest ratings ($n = 20$) and then averaged the four residuals of the issues that were repeated six times. These four residuals express the extent to which participants polarized

more on the issues which they said six times than we would expect them to polarize based on the other issues. This average is just another way to express the amount of polarization as a function of repeatedly stating one's opinion. It is based, however, only on the issues that were repeated six times. These new polarization scores were highly correlated with the over-all SAY polarization scores ($r = .87$, $p < .0001$). Not surprisingly, they correlated in a very similar manner with the coded variables. The correlation with the number of thought units was .52 ($p < .05$), with the number of arguments .43 ($p < .10$), and with the number of integrations .62 ($p < .01$).

polarization particularly if the arguments expressed are integrated or repeated by others. Of course, this correlation could well be due to other argument characteristics that are correlated with integration. The most obvious candidate is that integrated arguments are better quality arguments, and thus the observed correlation is really due to argument quality. To examine this possibility, we recoded the attitude statements previously coded, this time giving a subjective rating of argument quality to each. These ratings were done on a 4-point scale, where 1 indicated that the participant provided no reason for his or her viewpoint and 4 indicated that the participant's statement contained a detailed justification of his or her viewpoint, including a number of intelligent arguments that revealed advanced knowledge of the subject matter. Two independent judges coded 60 attitude statements and achieved an interjudge reliability of .81. One of these two judges subsequently completed the subjective quality ratings of all other coded attitude statements. Like the other variables, a summary argument quality measure was computed for each group as the average subjective quality of all coded statements. Perhaps not surprisingly, this subjective variable was highly correlated with the number of arguments coded in our detailed content coding, $r = .93$. More importantly, the correlation between argument integration and SAY polarization remained large and reliable even when subjective argument quality was controlled, $r(13) = .54, p < .05$.

Discussion

Downing, Judd, and Brauer (1992) showed that repeated expressions of attitudes result in greater attitude extremity. Our intention in Study 1 was to determine whether this might account for some of the polarization observed during a group discussion of like-minded individuals. The data suggest that repeated attitude expression indeed constitutes a partial explanation for group polarization. Additionally, and importantly, our data also provide evidence for the role of interpersonal influence in producing group polarization, consistent with abundant prior literature. Interestingly, what seems to matter is the number of different people

one hears from on an issue rather than the number of times one hears from others on an issue. This difference could, we think, be reasonably accommodated by either the persuasive arguments or social comparison approaches to group polarization. Accordingly, our data are nondiscriminating about the nature of the interpersonal influence that is at work.

In addition to supporting our hypothesis concerning the role of repeated expression in group polarization, our data also provide unanticipated evidence concerning factors that augment this effect. The coding of the actual attitude expressions in groups that varied in the magnitude of the predicted effect suggests that repeated attitude expression gives rise to attitude polarization especially when those repeated expressions provide arguments that others pick up and repeat in turn. In essence, this puts a distinctly social cast on the repeated expression effect. As a result, the distinction that we made in the introduction between interpersonal and intrapersonal explanations for extremity shifts becomes much fuzzier. One can think of a variety of reasons why repeated expression should be particularly potent in producing polarization when others repeat one's expressed arguments and we provide such theoretical speculation in the General Discussion section below.

But first, we report an additional study on the effect. We had two goals in mind for this second study. First, we wanted to document the effect of repeated expression on group polarization in a more natural group discussion. In Study 1, participants expressed themselves only in dyads, they were told what issue to discuss when, and they engaged in an exchange of viewpoints rather than a true discussion, because they could not react to each other's statements. This structure was imposed because of our desire to manipulate expression and hearing others' points of view independently. Although our second study placed some restrictions on the group discussion in order to keep these two factors somewhat independent of each other, the group interactions in this second study resembled much more closely typical group discussions. Our independent variables, frequency of repeated expression and repeated hearing, accordingly, became measured rather than precisely manipulated factors, as explained below.

Beyond showing the robustness of our repeated expression effect in a more natural group discussion, our second goal in Study 2 was to provide experimental evidence for the hypothesis that the effect of repeated expression on attitude polarization is enhanced when participants hear other group members integrate and repeat their own arguments. To accomplish this goal, we formed groups of three individuals who discussed six different issues. One person in each group was given a special role. In half of the groups, this participant was instructed to repeat arguments made by other group members; in the other half of the groups this participant was explicitly told to refrain from repeating the arguments of other group members. The two other participants in each group were given instructions designed to avoid a complete confounding of attitude expression and hearing others' points of view, as explained below. Consistent with the results of Study 1, we expected to find attitude polarization as a function of repeated expression in all groups and, additionally, we expected this effect to be larger in groups in which one participant integrated other group members' arguments.

Study 2

Method

Participants. Participants were undergraduates at the University of Colorado who participated in partial fulfillment of an introductory psychology course requirement. As in Study 1, we formed groups of participants who all generally agreed on five target issues. For this reason, not all of the 214 participants who came to the laboratory actually participated in the study. We formed 46 groups of three participants, using a total of 138 participants.

Design. As in Study 1, because of group-induced dependence, the unit of analysis was the group, although the effect of repeated expression was estimated at the level of the individual participant. There were two within-groups independent variables and one between-groups experimental factor. Frequency of expression and frequency of hearing were the within-groups independent variables. Two group members (Participants A and B) were each made responsible for two issues, that is, it was their task to bring up their issues fairly frequently and to state their opinion on them. As a result, for each of the two group members, there were two issues that were likely to be said frequently and heard infrequently, a second set of two issues that were likely to be heard frequently and said infrequently, and a fifth issue that was likely to be said infrequently and heard infrequently. As in Study 1, a sixth issue on which participants disagreed was included to make the discussion more interesting.

The manipulation of issue responsibility by group members A and B was designed to keep frequency of expression and frequency of hearing relatively uncorrelated in these groups. To measure these independent variables, however, we recorded for each participant the frequency with which the participant actually expressed an opinion on each issue. These frequency counts were then converted to frequency of expression and frequency of hearing measures for each participant on each issue. It is these measured independent variables that were used to predict attitude polarization.

Instruction type was a between-groups experimental factor. In a randomly determined half of the groups, the third participant (Participant C) received the instruction to integrate others' arguments; in the other groups he or she was told not to integrate others' arguments.

Procedure. When participants arrived at the laboratory, they were asked to fill out a short questionnaire on which they indicated their attitudes toward 10 current political issues (same stimuli as in Study 1, see Table 15.1). The major difference from Study 1 was that participants used a 29-point rating scale for these ratings and not a 9-point rating scale. These data were entered into a computer program that formed groups of three participants (A, B, and C) who all generally agreed on five particular issues (Issues 1 to 5) and disagreed on a sixth (Issue 6), defining agreement as we did in Study 1.

All remaining participants were sent home and did not participate in the study.

Participants were told that they were participating in a study on group discussion. They would be asked to discuss six issues with each other, all of which are determined by the experimenter. The discussion should be as similar as possible to a casual discussion with friends. The only restriction was that the experimenter would ask them to change the topic of discussion relatively frequently. Every 2 min, the experimenter would ring a bell and one of the three participants would be asked to state his or her opinion on an issue that was different from the one they were discussing when the bell rang. A fixed schedule determined the order in which the individual participants were asked to change the issue at the ringing of the bell. This schedule was the same in all groups: B, A, C, A, B, A, C, B.[4]

Participants then received a paper slip with specific instructions. The instructions for the first participant (Participant A) in the integration condition were as follows:

> This is a special form of a group discussion. First, you should change the issue of discussion as often as possible. I expect you to change the issue at least once every minute, if possible even more frequently. Second, every group member has assigned roles which he or she should try to fulfill as well as possible:
>
> You are "responsible" for the issues of —— (issue 1), and —— (issue 2). This means that it is your task to bring up these issues as often as possible. You might bring up one of your issues by simply stating your opinion on this issue whenever there is a pause in the group discussion. Another occasion for you to bring up these issues is when it is your turn to change the topic after the bell rings (however, please be aware that you are supposed to *change* the topic, i.e., if the group talked about one of "your" issues when the bell rang you have to start out with the other one). I expect you to bring up each of your issues at least 5 to 8 times during the group discussion. Never change the issue when the group is talking about one of "your" issues.
>
> Also, please try to ignore the issue of —— (issue 5). This doesn't mean that you are not allowed to say your opinion on this issue, but try to talk about it as little as possible. Never start out with this issue when it is your turn to change the topic after the ringing of the bell.
>
> Please be aware that other group members may have other issues assigned to them or may be responsible for no issue at all. Under no circumstances should you reveal your role to the other group members. Please try to keep the discussion fairly natural. In other words, feel free to react to other group members' statements even if it is not one of "your" issues. Despite that, make sure that you bring up your issues as often as possible.
>
> Please take some seconds and memorize the three issues mentioned above and what you should do with each one. Try to do your best. Good luck!

The instructions for the second participant (Participant B) were identical with the only difference being that he or she was made responsible for Issues 3 and 4 instead of Issues 1 and 2. Note that the second participant was also asked to talk as little as possible about Issue 5. The instructions for Participants A and B in the no-integration condition were virtually identical. The only difference was that in the middle of the second to the last paragraph, the following two sentences were added: "Please try to avoid repeating other group members' arguments. I want to know what YOU have to say, not how well you can repeat other people's ideas."

The third participant (Participant C) received instructions which were radically different and depended to a great extent on the condition the group was in. If the group was in the integration condition then the instructions for the third participant were as follows:

> This is a special form of a group discussion. First, you should change the issue of discussion as often as possible. I expect you to change the issue at least once every minute, if possible even more frequently. Second, every group member has

---

[4] We asked participants to change the topic of discussion fairly frequently in order to avoid them talking about the sixth disagreement issue most of the time. Additionally, this procedure allowed participants to bring up their issues without directing too much attention to the fact that they changed the topic.

assigned roles which he or she should try to fulfill as well as possible:

Your task is to use as much as possible the arguments of the other two group members. You can simply repeat what they said before or rephrase it in your own words. Try to memorize what reasons the other group members used to defend their viewpoints and try to use these reasons in your own statements. To use a fictitious example, if some other group member says that roller blades should be forbidden on campus (1) because roller blades scare pedestrians, and (2) because the Student Health Center is not equipped for treating the kind of accidents that occur with roller blades, then try to memorize these two reasons and try to integrate them in your own reasoning later on. Try to keep your own input of original arguments fairly minimal. Rather, try to use the other group members' arguments when you justify your own point of view. You may find it useful to use expressions such as "As Jennifer pointed out earlier . . .", "I agree with Andy that we should . . .", or "I think Stephanie made a really good point when she said . . ." and so on. Of course, you can do this only when you agree with the person on the issue.

Please be aware that other group members may have other roles assigned to them. You can be sure, however, that the other subjects' assignments have nothing to do with using or not using the arguments of others. Under no circumstances should you reveal your role to the other group members. Please try to keep the discussion fairly natural. In other words, feel free to say your own ideas whenever you think it is appropriate. Despite that, make sure that you use other group members' arguments as often as possible. It is perfectly okay if they notice that you are integrating their arguments all the time. However, it is not okay if they realize that using other people's arguments is your assigned role. Try to do it as much as possible without appearing unnatural. It doesn't matter if they think you are not very smart because you often use other people's ideas in your own reasoning.

In some respects, your role is the hardest of the three. Try to do it as well as possible. Good luck!

If the group was in the no-integration condition, the second and the third paragraph of the instructions for the third participant read as follows (the first and the last paragraph were identical):

Your task is to react as little as possible to the arguments of the other two group members. In other words, you should come up with your own arguments and give the other group members as little feedback as possible about what you think about their arguments. Do NOT use another person's reasoning in your own argumentation. Try to memorize what reasons the other group members used to defend their viewpoints and try NOT to use these reasons in your own statements. To use a fictitious example, if some other group member says that roller blades should be forbidden on campus (1) because roller blades scare pedestrians, and (2) because the Student Health Center is not equipped for treating the kind of accidents that occur with roller blades, then try to memorize these two reasons and try NOT to mention them later on. Try to avoid expressions such as "As Jennifer pointed out . . .", "I agree with Andy that we should . . .", or "I think Stephanie made a really good point when she said . . ." and so on. Even short exclamations like "Good point!" or "I agree!" should be avoided. If you run out of ideas (which is likely to occur), feel free to repeat your own arguments, i.e., the ones you have said before.

Please be aware that other group members may have other roles assigned to them. You can be sure, however, that the other subjects' assignments have nothing to do with using or not using the arguments of others. Under no circumstances should you reveal your role to the other group members. Please try to keep the discussion fairly natural. In other words, if it is really unavoidable you can go ahead and use someone else's argument but please try to do this as little as possible. Try to use your own arguments, i.e., arguments that you alone have said and that were not mentioned by any other group member. It doesn't matter if they think you are not very responsive because you never react to other people's ideas.

Participants were seated around a table and were instructed to discuss the six issues during 16 min. They were told that the goal of the discussion was to exchange opinions on the issues, that is, to communicate one's own opinion to the other group members and to find out where the others stand on the issues. It was made clear to them that they should keep the discussion going during the whole time. Groups who succeeded in doing so would receive a bonus at the end of the study (i.e., a lollipop). Participants' statements during the discussion were recorded. The experimenter remained in the same room, rang a bell every 2 min, recorded how often each participant talked about each issue, and noted any abnormalities. At the end of the discussion, participants were asked to fill out a questionnaire where they indicated their own attitudes one more time. They were then debriefed and dismissed.

Results and Discussion

The experimenter noted spontaneously that in two of the groups, participants disagreed considerably with each other on issues where they were supposed to agree. A coder, who was blind to group number, listened to all 46 recordings and verified that indeed, there was an unusual amount of disagreement in these two groups: the participants strongly disagreed on three out of the five important issues (Issues 1 to 5). In all cases this happened because a participant, who indicated that he or she was neutral on a particular issue on the pretest questionnaire, adopted a position opposite to the other group members when he or she heard them advocating a strong viewpoint. Although these two groups were not the only instances where this happened, in no other group did the group members disagree on more than one issue.[5] Because similar attitudes toward an issue are a prerequisite for group polarization (Myers & Lamm, 1976), we decided to exclude these two groups from the analyses. One of these groups was in the integration condition, the other in the no-integration condition. This reduced the total number of groups to 44.

In order to see whether our between-groups manipulation was effective, we tested whether groups in the integration condition actually integrated more than groups in the no-integration condition. We randomly selected five groups from each

condition and transcribed all the recorded statements. Two coders, who were blind to condition, counted the number of integrated arguments in each group. Differences between coders were resolved through discussion. The intercoder reliability was established as in Study 1; the two coders agreed on 86% of the decisions. The mean number of integrations in the five groups in the no-integration condition was 6.00 ($s = 3.16$); in the integration condition the mean was 11.00 ($s = 3.39$). The difference between the two conditions is reliable, $t(8) = 2.41$, $p < .05$. Thus, looking at the discussions of only 10 groups, there is consistent evidence that participants understood and followed the instructions concerning the integration of other group members' arguments. Nevertheless, we were surprised by the relatively high number of integrated arguments in the no-integration condition. Despite the fact that we specifically instructed all three participants in these groups not to repeat each other's arguments, they had on average six integrations. Even though the difference between the two conditions is reliable, we would certainly have hoped to find more variability on this independent variable. It is noteworthy, however, to observe that in a natural group discussion, members have the tendency to use other people's arguments in their own reasoning, even if instructed not to do so.

Our next goal was to assess the reliability of the experimenter's recording of how often each participant expressed an opinion on each issue. Recall that the experimenter kept track of this during each group's discussion and that these values were used to compute the actual frequency with which each participant expressed him or herself on each issue and the actual frequency with which each participant heard others offer opinions on each issue. These actual frequencies were then used as the measured independent variables in predicting group polarization. In order to test the reliability of the experimenter's frequency counts, we used once more the 10 groups where we had fully transcribed their discussions. For each of these 10 groups, we

---

[5] There were three groups where participants disagreed on one of the five agreement issues (issues 1–5). Here, the disagreement was more a matter of how to proceed (e.g., what taxes to

increase in order to reduce the deficit) and not so much a substantial difference in viewpoints. In all other 41 groups, the three group members agreed on all five agreement issues.

coded from the transcriptions the frequency with which each participant expressed an opinion on each of the six issues. We then correlated these frequency counts with the experimenter's frequency counts that were kept during the actual experimental session. Across groups, the correlation between the two frequency counts was .98. We also calculated the same correlation within each group. The average within-group correlation was .93. We can conclude that the experimenter's assessment of the frequency with which each participant talked about the issues was quite accurate.

The last manipulation check was to verify that our instructions to Subjects A and B concerning issue responsibility had the desired effect of making the correlation between the frequency of expression and the frequency of exposure to others' opinions fairly low. Only if these two are relatively unconfounded, as they are unlikely to be in totally unstructured group discussions, can we assess their independent effects on group polarization. The average values for frequency of expression and frequency of exposure for each issue and participant, calculated across groups, are shown in Table 15.6. Underlined issues in this table are issues for which Participants A and B were responsible. The correlation between these average values, computed across participants and issues, was .10, ns. We also calculated the correlation between the frequency of expression and the frequency of exposure within each group. The average of the 44 correlations was

.08 ($s = .39$); the values ranged from $-.75$ to .76. This shows that our experimental procedure, whereby certain participants were made responsible for certain issues, succeeded in making repeated attitude expression and repeated exposure to others' viewpoints relatively orthogonal. Deleting groups with very high or very low correlations between these two independent variables did not affect the analyses performed later on, and that is why the results reported below include all 44 groups.

Turning to the main analysis, we first wished to verify overall attitude polarization. Unlike Study 1, participants in Study 2 made their pretest and posttest ratings on the same 29-point rating scale. This allowed us to test directly whether a shift in attitude extremity on the discussed issues occurred during the discussion. All ratings were transformed into extremity scores by calculating the absolute values of the difference between the scale midpoint and each of the participant's ratings. These scores were then averaged across issues and participants within each group and analyzed as a function of pretest versus posttest (within-groups) and integration condition (between-groups). This mixed-model analysis of variance revealed a reliable pretest–posttest difference, such that posttest ratings were reliably more extreme on average than pretest ratings, Pretest $M = 8.36$, Posttest $M = 8.85$, $F(1, 42) = 6.66$, $p < .02$. Neither the condition main effect nor the condition by pretest versus posttest interaction were reliable.

TABLE 15.6. Summary of the Exchanges During the Group Discussion in Study 2

Participant	Issues									
	1		2		3		4		5	
	M	SD	M	SD	M	SD	M	SD	M	SD
Mean number of times each issue was said										
A	4.2	1.4	4.1	1.9	2.5	1.6	2.2	1.6	1.0	.9
B	2.2	1.2	1.8	1.3	4.3	1.7	3.9	1.5	.8	1.0
C	1.9	1.2	2.5	1.4	2.6	1.5	2.1	1.2	1.9	1.0
Mean number of times each issue was heard (from 1 or more participants)										
A	4.1	2.1	4.4	2.1	6.9	2.7	6.0	2.1	2.7	1.5
B	6.0	2.0	6.6	2.5	5.0	2.7	4.3	2.4	2.9	1.5
C	6.4	2.0	5.9	2.6	6.8	2.8	6.1	2.6	1.8	1.4

Note: Mean values are averaged across groups. Underlined issues are issues for which Participants A and B were responsible.

To determine whether participants polarized as a function of repeated attitude expression and of repeated exposure to other group members' viewpoints, we conducted a multilevel analysis as we did in Study 1. First, we performed a regression analysis for each group where we regressed the extremity of the final attitude ratings on the number of times the participant talked about the issue, the number of times he or she heard another group member talk about the issue, and the extremity of the initial attitude ratings. Because three participants talked about five agreement issues, the n in each regression analysis was 15. These within-group regressions yielded two regression coefficients of interest: The SAY coefficient estimated the difference in polarization per one additional time of attitude expression; the HEAR coefficient estimated the difference in polarization per one additional time of exposure to someone else's position on an issue. Unlike Study 1, the frequency of expression and exposure predictor variables were measured in each group rather than being manipulated. Additionally, we did not include a predictor that represented the number of people one heard from on an issue because virtually all participants in each group talked about all issues.

Two questions are of interest concerning these coefficients. First, we wanted to know whether each was reliably different on average from zero, parallel to the analyses of Study 1. The mean SAY polarization score equaled .29 and a single-sample t test revealed that this value was reliably different from zero, $t(43) = 3.31$, p $= .002$ (see Table 15.7). The mean value for the HEAR polarization score, $-.05$, did not differ from zero, $t(43) = 0.63$, ns. Thus, replicating the results of Study 1, more frequent expressions of attitude positions resulted in greater attitude polarization in this group setting. In fact, with the more natural discussion in this study, the average magnitude of this effect was considerably larger than it was found to be in Study 1. However, there was no polarization as a function of frequency

of attitude exposure or hearing others' points of view. Perhaps this latter result is unsurprising given the results of Study 1, which showed that what seems to matter is the number of people one hears from rather than the number of actual expressions from others one hears.

The second question concerned condition differences in the magnitude of these polarization scores. As can be seen in Table 15.7, the mean SAY polarization score in the integration condition was .44, which was reliably different from zero, $t(21) = 3.78$, $p = .002$. In the no-integration condition, however, the average SAY polarization score was not reliably different from zero, $M = .14$, $t(21) = 1.14$, ns. Additionally, these two average coefficients were marginally different from each other, $F(1, 42) = 2.90, p < .10$. Given the relatively high level of argument integration that occurred in both conditions, and particularly in the no-integration condition where integration took place in spite of our instructions, we take this marginally reliable difference in the magnitude of the effect of repeated expression in the two conditions to be reasonably strong evidence in support of the role of argument integration.

An examination of the residual SAY scores from this between-condition analysis of variance revealed that one of the groups clearly qualified as an outlier. Group 42, in the integration condition, had a SAY polarization score of -1.06. With group 42 included, the mean SAY polarization score in this condition was .44 ($s = .54$); without group 42, it was .51 ($s = .44$, see Table 15.7). Thus the score of group 42 was more than three and a half standard deviations away from the mean score of all the other groups in the integration condition. Additionally, traditional outlier statistics strongly suggested that it qualified as an outlier in the between-condition analysis. The value of its Studentized Deleted Residual was -3.02 and the value of Cook's D associated with it was .17.[6] We listened to the group's recorded statements and found out that

[6]Belsley, Kuh, and Welsch (1980) suggested that observations with an RSTUDENT larger than 2 in absolute value need special attention. The suggested cut-off point for COOK'S D is $4/pn = .05$ where p is the number of parameters in the model (here: $p = 2$), and n is the number of observations used to fit the model (here: $n = 44$). Group 42 qualifies as an outlier independent of what influence diagnostic is used. The COVRATIO of group 42 is .75 (considered an outlier if $|\text{COVRATIO-1}| \geq 3\,p/n = .14$), its DFFITS is $-.64$ (suggested cut-off point: $2(p/n)^{.5} = \pm 43$).

TABLE 15.7. Polarization Results From the Within-Group Regressions in Study 2

Results	Both conditions (with outlier, $n = 44$)	Both conditions (without outlier, $n = 43$)	No integration condition ($n = 22$)	Integration condition (with outlier, $n = 22$)	Integration condition (without outlier, $n = 21$)
			SAY polarization		
M	.29	.32	.14	.44	.51
s	.58	.55	.60	.54	.44
t	3.31	3.84	1.14	3.78	5.34
p	<.002	<.001	ns	<.002	<.0001
			HEAR polarization		
M	−.05	−.04	−.02	−.08	−.06
s	.49	.50	.57	.42	.42
t	−.63	−.54	−.16	−.85	−.69
p	ns	ns	ns	ns	ns

the three group members had virtually nothing to say about any of the six issues that were suggested to them. The statement "I don't know anything about this issue" occurred at least 30 times during the 16-min group discussion. In total, the three participants did not give more than five reasons why they supported or opposed a particular issue.

One way to address the issue of this outlying group is to use a rank transformation and analyze the resulting ranks. This analysis is equivalent to conducting a nonparametric Wilcoxon Rank Sum test or a Mann Whitney U test (Judd & McClelland, 1989). Following this rank transformation, groups in the no-integration condition had a mean rank SAY polarization score of 18.8 ($s = 12.7$), whereas groups in the integration condition had a mean rank score of 26.2 ($s = 12.1$). A test of the difference in these mean ranks yielded stronger support for our argument that the average SAY polarization was larger in the integration condition, $F(1,43) = 3.84$, $p = .056$.

Even in this nonparametric test, however, Group 42 still qualified as a marginal outlier (Studentized Deleted Residual = −2.07). Therefore, we conducted an additional analysis of the unranked SAY polarization scores excluding this group. The resulting condition means are given in Table 15.7 and now the difference in the magnitude of the SAY polarization scores in the two conditions achieved traditional levels of reliability, $F(1,41) = 5.17$, $p < .05$. In sum, there was consistent support that groups in the integration condition polarized

significantly more as a function of repeated attitude expression than groups in the no-integration condition. In fact, the groups' SAY polarization scores were more than three times greater when Participant C was instructed to integrate other group members' arguments than when he or she was instructed not to do so.

The mean HEAR polarization scores did not differ from zero in either condition nor did they differ from each other. Although the integration instructions affected polarization due to repeated expression, it had no impact on polarization resulting from repeated exposure to others' expressions.

General Discussion

Two different studies were conducted to demonstrate the effects of repeated attitude expression on polarization during group discussions. In the first study we directly manipulated the frequency of attitude expression independently of the frequency of exposure to other participants' points of view. In addition to an overall polarization effect across discussed issues, the results showed that frequent attitude expression led to greater polarization. Additionally, there was reliably greater polarization when participants heard the opinions of multiple other participants on an issue. The first of these results clearly shows that repeated expression is partially responsible for polarization during a group discussion. The second is consistent with previous research on interpersonal processes responsible for group polarization, offering the significant qualification that the number of sources of attitude arguments may matter more than the actual number of attitude arguments one receives from others.

The detailed coding of discussions from some of the groups in Study 1 suggested an important and unexpected mechanism that seems to augment the polarizing effect of attitude expression in a group setting. Although on average all groups polarized as a function of repeated expression, groups where arguments stated by one participant were repeated or integrated by other participants showed a particularly large effect of repeated expression on polarization. This relationship was found even when we controlled for the overall quality of arguments offered during attitude expressions. Thus, it appears that the social dynamics involved in stating one's position and hearing others repeat it are partially responsible for the effect of attitude expression on polarization.

To test this hypothesis more directly and in a somewhat more natural group setting, we conducted a second study where we measured attitude expression and exposure rather than directly manipulating them. Additionally, we assigned groups to one of two conditions. In one, a participant in each group was explicitly told to integrate others' arguments. In the other condition, integration was discouraged. As the coding data of Study 1 led us to expect, the effect of attitude expression on polarization was substantially greater in the integration condition than in the no-integration condition. Additionally, the overall effect of attitude expression on polarization was considerably larger in these more natural group discussions than it was in the highly constrained discussions of Study 1 groups.

Our initial theoretical approach to the effect of attitude expression on group polarization relied on the distinction between interpersonal processes, such as persuasive arguments and normative positions heard from others, and intrapersonal processes such as frequent attitude expression and thought that produces attitude polarization even outside of a group setting (Downing et al., 1992; Tesser, 1978). Downing et al. (1992) clearly showed that repeated expression by itself, outside of the social context in which repeated expression took place in the present studies, has a small but consistent effect on attitude polarization. The present results are consistent with this conclusion, because groups on average in both studies showed polarization due to repeated expression. Admittedly, in the no-integration condition of the second study, the simple effect of repeated expression was not statistically reliable. Nevertheless, its magnitude in this condition is consistent with our earlier conclusion about the role of repeated expression in producing polarization outside of a social context.[7]

That said, however, it is clear from the present studies that the effect of repeated expression on attitude polarization is considerably enhanced by placing it in a social context where group members can integrate repeated arguments into their own arguments. Accordingly, this leads us to reconsider the theoretical distinction we made in the introduction between interpersonal factors responsible for group polarization and intrapersonal factors. Our work has shown that the process of polarization through attitude expression is very much a social process, being enhanced in groups where one hears others integrate one's own arguments. As a result, we believe that the polarizing effects of frequent attitude expression are likely to be particularly potent in most group settings where, we suspect, argument integration and repetition is a very frequent occurrence.

Of course, we have no direct evidence that argument repetition and integration is a frequent occurrence or potent effect in natural groups. Our groups in the first study engaged in rather unusual

---

[7] The nonsignificant simple effect for repeated expression in the no-integration condition perhaps suggests that the relative absence of integrations in this condition, compared to what participants might normally expect in group discussions, actually reduces the overall impact of repeated expressions on polarization. Although this seems a possibility, we remind the reader that the effect size in this condition is as large as the effects demonstrated for repeated expression outside of a group discussion context. Thus, its unreliability is due, we believe, to insufficient statistical power in the present case.

group discussions. Even in the second study, where an attempt was made to make the discussions more natural, the discussions were highly constrained and regulated by the experimenter. One might therefore wish that the effects of repeated expression on attitude polarization, and the augmentation of those effects through argument integration by others, could be documented in naturally occurring group discussions. Unfortunately, for reasons given earlier, we believe that this would be impossible to do because frequency of argument expression is likely to be very highly correlated with frequency of argument exposure in naturally occurring groups. Groups tend to discuss some issues and not others. And individual group members both state their own positions and hear others' positions on those issues that are discussed. They fail to do both on nondiscussed issues. Because of this confound in naturally occurring group discussions, it was necessary for us to impose some structure in the current studies in order to separate the effects of repeated expression from repeated exposure. For us, that is the nature of the scientific enterprise. In order to demonstrate the effect of a single independent variable, one necessarily isolates it or unconfounds it with the myriad of other variables with which it is correlated in the real world. Admittedly, some loss of generality results. And one struggles to regain that generality by continuing to demonstrate the effect in a less structured situation, as we have done in the second study. But ultimately, the generalization to naturally occurring discussions, where all the contributing factors are highly interwoven, must be done on theoretical rather than empirical grounds.

Although we have consistent evidence that argument integration increases the effect of repeated attitude expression on group polarization, we do not have a firm understanding of exactly why this is the case. A number of explanations seem plausible at this point and future research will be necessary to tease them apart. First, one could argue that it is simply the fact of hearing one's own argument out of someone else's mouth that drives the effect. Hearing it from another person makes the argument more vivid and more accessible in memory. As a result, the argument plays a greater role in the subsequent computation of the attitude toward the issue, and attitude polarization occurs. A second possible explanation is that one feels responsible for an argument once another group member has integrated it into his or her line of reasoning. According to this explanation, an individual participant may feel that it is because of him or her that others hold a particular opinion. Likewise, he or she may be held accountable for that argument if later on in the discussion this argument turns out to be wrong or not relevant. In other words, as soon as another group member repeats one person's arguments that person becomes more committed to it and it becomes more central in his or her representation of the issue. Finally, one may argue that one feels validated when someone else repeats one's arguments. If another person uses one's argument, the individual concludes that it must have been a really good and smart argument. In other words, other group members give feedback on the quality of arguments. As a result, people attach a special value to an argument that seems to have been picked up by others and consider it to be more important when they are asked to state their attitude on the final questionnaire. It is this last explanation that we consider the most plausible. However, all three are viable explanations and future research will be needed to tease them apart.

It is interesting to observe that Myers and Lamm (1976), in their detailed summary on the group polarization phenomenon, talked about the role of cognitive rehearsal and verbal commitment in the polarization process. According to these authors, the presentation of new arguments produces a smaller shift in extremity when it does not involve participation of the group members compared to a situation where participants actively discuss these arguments (Bishop & Myers, 1974). They write: "The subject must actively reformulate the information he has received in order for it to stimulate an internalization of attitude change" (Myers & Lamm, 1976, p. 617). Despite the fact that the authors present very little hard evidence on this issue, it is encouraging for us that they recognize the importance of rehearsal. Myers and Lamm (1976) seemed to think that the individual group member first integrates the arguments and then rehearses them. We, on the other hand, have evidence for a reverse temporal order: an individual group member repeatedly states a number of arguments (which leads to polarization) and when he or she hears that other group members integrate his or her arguments, the polarizing effect is even stronger. Note that Myers and Lamm (1976) did not assume that the cognitive rehearsal has to be overt and out loud, which makes a direct contrast of the two explanations impossible. It seems likely to us that both processes occur at the same time. Participants hear other people's arguments and rehearse them to themselves, sometimes silently and sometimes out loud, and, at the same time, they repeatedly express their own arguments and realize that other people validate some of their good arguments by integrating them.

This way of looking at our results suggests that they may be seen as a significant extension of the persuasive arguments explanation of group polarization (Burnstein & Vinokur, 1977). At its core, that explanation simply says that polarization results from persuasive arguments. The approach has uniquely concentrated on arguments that one hears from other group members and that one finds to be persuasive. But there is nothing inconsistent to say that one might find one's own arguments particularly persuasive in a group setting because of the feedback one receives about the quality of those arguments. In a group discussion, one throws out arguments for consideration. When others validate them and reinforce them, they become more convincing and attitude polarization ensues.

Although our results might well be fit within an expanded version of persuasive arguments theory, we feel that they represent a significant advancement to our understanding of group polarization. Additionally, we believe that our results point to the very potent impact of others in socially validating one's own ideas, aspirations, and opinions. People convince themselves with the aid of others and the feedback they give. This in large part, we believe, is responsible for group polarization.

REFERENCES

Abelson, R. P. (in press). Psychological mechanisms that make group controversies worse. In R. E. Petty & J. A. Krosnick

(Eds.), *Attitude Strength: Antecedents and Consequences*, Hillsdale, NJ: Erlbaum.

Allison, D. E., & Messick, D. M. (1988). The feature-positive effect, attitude strength, and the degree of perceived consensus. *Personality and Social Psychology Bulletin, 14*, 236–241.

Baron, R. S., & Roper, G. (1976). Reaffirmation of social comparison views of choice shifts: Averaging and extremity effects in an autokinetic situation. *Journal of Personality and Social Psychology, 33*, 521–530.

Belsley, D. A., Kuh, E., & Welsch, R. E. (1980). *Regression Diagnostics: Identifying Influential Data and Sources of Collinearity.* New York: Wiley.

Bettelheim, B., & Janowitz, M. (1949). Ethnic tolerance: A function of social and personal control. *American Journal of Sociology, 55*, 137–145.

Bishop, G. D., & Myers, D. G. (1974). Informational influence in group discussion. *Organizational Behavior and Human Performance, 12*, 92–104.

Brickman, P., Redfield, J., Harrison, A. A., & Crandall, R. (1972). Drive and predisposition as factors in the attitudinal effects of mere exposure. *Journal of Experimental Social Psychology, 8*, 31–44.

Brown, R. (1974). Further comment on the risky shift. *American Psychologist, 29*, 468–470.

Brown, R. (1986). *Social Psychology—The Second Edition.* New York: Free Press.

Burnstein, E., & Vinokur, A. (1973). Testing two classes of theories about group-induced shifts in individual choice. *Journal of Experimental Social Psychology, 9*, 123–137.

Burnstein, E., & Vinokur, A. (1977). Persuasive argumentation and social comparison as determinants of attitude polarization. *Journal of Experimental Social Psychology, 13*, 315–332.

Crano, W. D., Gorenflo, D. W., & Shackelford, S. L. (1988). Overjustification, assumed consensus, and attitude change: Further investigation of the incentive-aroused ambivalence hypothesis. *Journal of Personality and Social Psychology, 55*, 12–22.

Downing, J. A., Judd, C. M., & Brauer, M. (1992). Effects of repeated expressions on attitude extremity. *Journal of Personality and Social Psychology, 63*, 17–29.

Ewing, T. N. (1942). A study of certain factors involved in changes of opinion. *Journal of Social Psychology, 16*, 63–88.

Fazio, R. H., & Zanna, M. P. (1978). Attitudinal qualities relating to the strength of the attitude–behavior relationship. *Journal of Experimental Social Psychology, 14*, 398–408.

Fromkin, H. (1970). Effects of experimentally aroused feelings of undistinctiveness upon valuation of scarce and novel experiences. *Journal of Personality and Social Psychology, 16*, 521–529.

Isenberg, D. J. (1986). Group polarization: A critical review and meta-analysis. *Journal of Personality and Social Psychology, 50*, 1141–1151.

Judd, C. M., & Brauer, M. (in press). Repetition and evaluative extremity. In R. E. Petty & J. A. Krosnick (Eds.), *Attitude Strength: Antecedents and Consequences*, Hillsdale, NJ: Erlbaum.

Judd, C. M., & McClelland, G. H. (1989). *Data Analysis: A Model Comparison Approach*. San Diego: Harcourt Brace Jovanovich.

Kenny, D. A., & Judd, C. M. (1986). Consequences of violating the independence assumption in analysis of variance. *Psychological Bulletin*, 99, 422–431.

Krosnick, J. A., Boninger, D. S., Chuang, Y. C., Berent, M. K., & Carnot, C. G. (1993). Attitude strength: One construct or many related constructs? *Journal of Personality and Social Psychology*, 65, 1132–1151.

Levine, R. A., & Campbell, D. T. (1972). *Ethnocentrism: Theories of Conflict, Ethnic Attitudes and Group Behavior*. New York: Wiley.

Moscovici, S., & Zavalloni, M. (1969). The group as a polarizer of attitudes. *Journal of Personality and Social Psychology*, 12, 125–135.

Myers, D. G. (1973). Summary and bibliography of experiments on group-induced response shift. *Catalog of Selected Documents in Psychology*, 3, 123.

Myers, D. G. (1978). Polarizing effects of social comparison. *Journal of Experimental Social Psychology*, 14, 554–563.

Myers, D. G., & Arenson, S. J. (1972). Enhancement of dominant risk tendencies in group discussion. *Psychological Reports*, 30, 615–623.

Myers, D. G., & Bishop, G. D. (1970). Discussion effects on racial attitudes. *Science*, 169, 778–789.

Myers, D. G., & Lamm, H. (1976). The group polarization phenomenon. *Psychological Bulletin*, 83, 602–627.

Osgood, C. E., & Tannenbaum, P. H. (1955). The principles of congruity in the prediction of attitude changes. *Psychological Review*, 62, 42–55.

Perlman, D., & Oskamp, S. (1971). The effects of picture content and exposure frequency on evaluations of negroes and whites. *Journal of Experimental Social Psychology*, 7, 503–512.

Petersen, K., & Dutton, J. E. (1975). Certainty, extremity, intensity: Neglected variables in research on attitude-behavior consistency. *Social Forces*, 54, 393–414.

Petty, R. E., & Krosnick, J. A. (Eds.) (in press). *Attitude Strength: Antecedents and Consequences*, Hillsdale, NJ: Erlbaum.

Roberts, J. V. (1984). Public opinion and capital punishment: The effects of attitudes upon memory. *Canadian Journal of Criminology*, 26, 283–291.

Sarat, A., & Vidmar, N. (1976). Public opinion, the death penalty, and the eighth amendment: Testing the Marshall hypothesis. *Wisconsin Law Review*, 171, 171–206.

Sherif, M., Harvey, O. J., White, B. J., Hood, W. R., & Sherif, C. W. (1961). *Intergroup Cooperation and Competition: The Robbers Cave Experience*. Norman, OK: University Book Exchange.

Stoner, J. A. (1961). A comparison of individual and group decision involving risk (Unpublished master's thesis, Massachusetts Institute of Technology). Cited in D. G. Marquis (1960), Individual responsibility and group decisions involving risk. *Industrial Management Review*, 3, 8–23.

Tesser, A. (1978). Self-generated attitude change. In L. Berkowitz (Ed.), *Advances in Experimental Social Psychology* (Vol. 11, pp. 289–338). New York: Academic Press.

Tesser, A., & Leone, C. (1977). Cognitive schemas and thought as determinants of attitude change. *Journal of Experimental Social Psychology*, 13, 340–356.

Vinokur, A., & Burnstein, E. (1974). The effects of partially shared persuasive arguments on group induced shifts: A group problem solving approach. *Journal of Personality and Social Psychology*, 29, 305–315.

Received June 13, 1994
Revision received December 9, 1994
Accepted December 19, 1994 ■

PART 4B

Productivity

Many groups in work settings are assigned productivity tasks, such as building houses, that involve creating tangible products that can be evaluated against external standards. These tasks require both cognitive activity (e.g., deciding how to allocate material and human resources) and coordinated physical activity on the part of group members. Many analyses of group productivity employ input-process-output models. A good example is Hackman's (1987) model of group effectiveness, which specifies how features of the organizational context (e.g., a training system that enhances members' expertise) and the group's design (e.g., the right mix of members) affect interactions among group members, which in turn affect the group's effectiveness.

Although Hackman suggests that group interactions can improve as well as inhibit group performance, more attention has focused on "process loss" than on "process gain." In an influential analysis, Steiner (1972) suggested two reasons for process loss, which he defined as the difference between a group's potential productivity and its actual productivity. *Coordination loss* occurs because group members do not combine their individual responses in the optimal way (e.g., carpenters building a house do not perform their subtasks in the right order). *Motivation loss* occurs because group members do not exert maximal effort on the task (e.g., some carpenters slack off because they think no one will notice their laziness). Much of the work on motivation loss has dealt with "social loafing," which occurs when people exert *less* effort while working together than while working alone. Although social loafing occurs on a range of cognitive and physical tasks, it can be reduced or eliminated in several ways. These include increasing (a) the identifiability and uniqueness of individual contributions, (b) the ease of evaluating these contributions, (c) the task involvement and accountability of members, and (d) task attractiveness (Parks & Sanna, 1999).

Some recent work has focused on motivation gain, which occurs when people exert *more* effort while working together than while working alone. For example, more capable group members sometimes work extra hard when they view the group's task as important and believe that other members are unmotivated. This phenomenon is called "social compensation" (Williams & Karau, 1991). In addition, less capable group members sometimes work extra hard when their performance is especially important (i.e., on "conjunctive tasks," where the group's performance depends on the performance of its weakest member). This phenomenon is called the "Kohler effect" (Hertel, Kerr, & Messe, 2000).

Research on group productivity has not been limited to identifying factors that produce motivation loss and gain. Another important line of research focuses on the determinants and consequences of group goal setting. Some of this work examines the process by which group members develop shared goals, whereas other work examines the influence of these goals on group performance and member satisfaction. For example, group goals (like individual goals) have more impact on performance when they are specific and challenging. Researchers generally assume that group goals do not influence performance and satisfaction directly, but instead

have an indirect impact on them through their influence on group members' behavior during task completion.

Group productivity is a popular research topic in part because teams play such an important role in many business organizations. Teams deserve special attention because they differ in potentially important ways from the laboratory groups that social psychologists usually study. For example, teams: generally work on more meaningful and complex tasks; exist for longer periods of time and thus experience more developmental changes and member turnover; have clearer norms, roles, and status systems, and provide more important rewards to their members. Another difference is that teams, compared to typical laboratory groups, are more likely to contain members who differ widely in their task-relevant knowledge and skills. Because of this diversity, team members must learn about one another's special competencies before they can coordinate their actions effectively (i.e., minimize the likelihood of coordination loss and maximize the likelihood of coordination gain). A shared understanding of "who knows what" in teams is sometimes called *transactive memory*. Building on Wegner's (1987) pioneering analysis of this phenomenon, group researchers have investigated such issues as how training team members together affects the development of transactive memory and thereby influences team performance (e.g., Liang, Moreland, & Argote, 1995).

Transactive memory can be viewed as one component of "shared mental models," which include members' knowledge about the group's task and equipment, individual members' abilities and responsibilities, and the setting in which the group operates (Mohammed & Dumville, 2001). Shared mental models have received substantial attention recently because they are assumed to influence group performance. Although there is some evidence that they can do so (Mathieu, Heffner, Goodwin, Salas, & Cannon-Bowers, 2000), many questions remain about how shared mental models should be defined and measured, what factors affect their development, and when they are most likely to influence group performance (Cannon-Bowers & Salas, 2001).

Researchers have also sought to answer many other questions about to team productivity (Levine & Moreland, 1998). These include how to select and train team members, how to manage team continuity and change, how to enhance communication within teams, how to identify team problems, and how to assess team performance. Special attention has been given to the role of stress in teams (Kerr & Tindale, 2004). Evidence indicates, for example, that stress often improves the quantity of what a team produces (while degrading its quality), focuses the attention of team members on central features of its task, and causes members to use simplified, heuristic forms of information processing. One common source of stress in teams is time pressure. A relevant line of research involves *social entrainment*, in which teams fail to adjust their behavior when time pressures change (Kelly & McGrath, 1985). Another line of research involves the *need for closure*, or the tendency for groups (and individuals) to prefer clear and unambiguous solutions (Kruglanski & Webster, 1996). This need, which increases under stressful work conditions, can affect teams in several ways,

for example by increasing the rejection of opinion deviates who threaten team consensus (Kruglanki & Webster, 1991).

Several techniques have been developed to improve group productivity (Levine & Moreland, 1998). Team development encompasses several activities, including problem identification, sensitivity training, and role analysis. Quality circles, popularized by Japanese businesses, involve regular meetings at which group members identify production problems and discuss ways to solve them. Finally, autonomous work groups (or self-managing work teams) give members substantial control over how their tasks are managed and executed. Although none of these techniques works in every case, each has strong advocates and appears to be useful in some situations.

After they create a joint product, group members often reflect on its quality and the process used to create it. These reflections, in turn, influence their subsequent thoughts and behaviors. For example, the identification of members with their group depends heavily on its performance, increasing with success and decreasing with failure. Members also make different attributions depending on whether their group succeeds or fails (Leary & Forsyth, 1987). A self-serving, or egocentric, bias leads members to attribute group success to their own contributions and failure to other causes. A group-serving, or sociocentric, bias leads members to attribute group success to everyone's contributions and failure to other causes. Such attributions can have important consequences for how members allocate rewards and punishments following task completion.

REFERENCES

Cannon-Bowers, J. A., & Salas, E. (2001). Reflections on shared cognition. *Journal of Organizational Behavior*, *22*, 195–202.

Hackman, J. R. (1987). The design of work teams. In J. Lorsch (Ed.), *Handbook of organizational behavior* (pp. 315–342). Englewood Cliffs, NJ: Prentice Hall.

Hertel, G., Kerr, N. L., & Messe, L. A. (2000). Motivation gains in performance groups: Paradigmatic and theoretical developments on the Kohler effect. *Journal of Personality and Social Psychology*, *79*, 580–601.

Kelly, J. R., & McGrath, J. E. (1985). Effects of time limits and task types on task performance and interaction of four-person groups. *Journal of Personality and Social Psychology*, *49*, 395–407.

Kerr, N. L., & Tindale, R. S. (2004). Group performance and decision making. *Annual Review of Psychology*, *55*, 623–655.

Kruglanski, A. W., & Webster, D. M. (1991). Group members' reactions to opinion deviates and conformists at varying degrees of proximity to decision deadline and of environmental noise. *Journal of Personality and Social Psychology*, *61*, 212–225.

Kruglanski, A. W., & Webster, D. M. (1996). Motivated closing of the mind: "Seizing" and "freezing." *Psychological Review*, *103*, 263–283.

Leary, M. R., & Forsyth, D. R. (1987). Attributions of responsibility for collective endeavors. In C. Hendrick (Ed.), *Review of personality and social psychology* (Vol. 8, pp. 167–188). Newbury Park, CA: Sage.

Levine, J. M., & Moreland, R. L. (1998). Small groups. In D. T. Gilbert, S. T. Fiske, & G. Lindzey (Eds.), *The handbook of social psychology* (4th ed., pp. 415–469). Boston, MA: McGraw-Hill.

Liang, D. W., Moreland, R. L., & Argote, L. (1995). Group versus individual training and group performance: The mediating role of transactive memory. *Personality and Social Psychology Bulletin*, *21*, 384–393.

Mathieu, J. E., Heffner, T. S., Goodwin, G. F., Salas, E., & Cannon-Bowers, J. A. (2000). The influence of shared mental models on team process and performance. *Journal of Applied Psychology*, *85*, 273–283.

Mohammed, S., & Dumville, B. C. (2001). Team mental models in a team knowledge framework: Expanding theory and measurement across disciplinary boundaries. *Journal of Organizational Behavior*, *22*, 89–106.

Parks, C. D., & Sanna, L. J. (1999). *Group performance and interaction*. Boulder, CO: Westview Press.

Steiner, I. D. (1972). *Group process and productivity*. New York: Academic Press.

Wegner, D. M. (1987). Transactive memory: A contemporary analysis of the group mind. In B. Mullen & G. R. Goethals (Eds.), *Theories of group behavior* (pp. 185–208). New York: Springer-Verlag.

Williams, K. D., & Karau, S. J. (1991). Social loafing and social compensation: The effects of expectations of coworker performance. *Journal of Personality and Social Psychology*, *61*, 570–581.

Readings

The first paper in this section, by Latané, Williams, and Harkins (1979), describes research on an interesting form of "process loss" caused by the tendency of group members to exert less effort while working together than while working alone. This research was stimulated by early work showing that group members working on a rope-pulling task (where success depends on the sum of members' efforts and there was no division of labor) expended less energy per person as the size of the group increased. This finding is intriguing because it flies in the face of the popular belief that being in a group increases people's motivation to work hard. Latané and his colleagues were particularly intrigued by the finding because of its relevance to *social impact theory*, which predicts that when group members are the targets of external pressure, that pressure will be divided among the members. The larger the size of the group, the less pressure each member will feel, which in turn will produce less individual effort (social loafing). This reduced effort is similar to that observed in studies of bystander intervention during emergencies, where people are less likely to render aid if others are present than if they are not.

To explore social loafing in work groups, Latané and his colleagues conducted two laboratory experiments. In the first experiment, groups were seated in a soundproofed room and asked to make as much noise as possible by shouting or clapping during a series of trials. Each participant shouted or clapped alone, in pairs, in groups of four, and in groups of six. The main dependent variable was how much noise the participants made. Not surprisingly, the more people there were in a group, the more total noise they produced. But as group size increased, the average amount of noise produced by *each person* decreased. Why? One possibility, suggested by social impact theory, is that working with others reduced group members' motivation and effort (motivation loss). But another possibility also exists. Maybe working with others reduced group members' ability to coordinate their responses (coordination loss).

In their second experiment, Latané and his colleagues tested the relative impact of motivation loss and coordination loss on shouting by people working alone, in pairs, and in groups of six. The two-person and six-person groups were run in two different ways. In one case, participants actually shouted with others, as in the first experiment. In the second case, participants *thought* they were shouting with others, but in fact shouted alone. In these "pseudo groups," there was no possibility of coordination loss. When participants actually shouted together, their total output increased with group size, but their average output per person decreased, just as in the first experiment. This decrease presumably was due again to some combination of motivation and coordination loss. When participants thought they were shouting with others, but were not (pseudo groups), they also produced less noise per person than when they knew they were shouting alone, indicating the important role of motivation loss by itself. Comparisons of performance reductions in actual groups versus pseudo groups indicated that

about half the reduction in actual groups was due to coordination loss and about half was due to motivation loss.

In the second paper, Weingart (1992) investigated the impact of group goals on group performance. She tested an input–process–output model in which group goals and task complexity influence group planning and member effort, which in turn affect group performance. Weingart's predictions regarding member effort were straightforward—a more difficult group goal produces greater member effort, which in turn facilitates group performance (Hypotheses 1 and 2). In contrast, her predictions about group planning were complex. She identified three components of planning (amount, quality, and timing) and argued that they are influenced by group goals and task complexity. For example, Weingart predicted that the quality of planning would be lower when goal difficulty and task complexity were high rather than low (Hypothesis 4). And she argued that the impact of planning on group performance would vary as a function of task complexity. For example, she predicted that the amount of planning would have a more positive impact on group performance as task complexity increased (Hypothesis 7).

To test these and other predictions, Weingart conducted an experiment in which four-person groups were asked to build small structures using simple materials (e.g., Tinkertoys, macaroni, glue). She manipulated the difficulty of each group's goal (easy vs. difficult) and the complexity of its task (simple vs. complex). Videotapes of the work sessions provided information about member effort and the three components of planning. For example, amount of planning was defined as how often participants spoke about the quality and use of supplies, individual performance plans, and group performance plans. Group performance was the number of structures that a group completed. The results of the experiment were complex, but provided some support for Weingart's predictions. She found, for example, that group goal difficulty influenced group performance through member effort and that task complexity influenced performance through the amount of planning and member effort.

The third paper in this section, by Moreland (1999), focused on the role of transactive memory in group performance. Moreland argued that transactive memory, defined as a shared awareness of who knows what, has several potential benefits for groups, including improved planning, better coordination, and more efficient problem solving. Indirect evidence for the impact of transactive memory has been found in studies showing that groups perform better when their members have worked together before, probably because they are more familiar with one another's strengths and weaknesses. To explore transactive memory in work groups in more direct ways, Moreland and his colleagues conducted several experiments in which members of newly-formed groups were trained either together or apart on a complex task.

In the first experiment, three-person groups were asked to assemble a radio using a circuit board and dozens of electronic components. In the training phase of the experiment, members of some groups were trained individually on the task, whereas members of other groups were trained together. In the

test phase, which occurred a week later, members of each group jointly completed a memory test about the task and then assembled a radio together. The results indicated that groups whose members were trained together remembered more about assembling the radio and made fewer assembly errors than did groups whose members were trained individually. Videotapes of the groups working on the task during the test phase were used to derive three indicators of transactive memory—memory differentiation, task coordination, and task credibility (trust). Analyses of these indicators showed that transactive memory was stronger in groups whose members were trained together rather than apart. Moreover, causal analyses revealed that the performance benefits of group training were mediated by transactive memory. In other words, training methods no longer mattered when differences among groups in transactive memory were taken into account.

In the second experiment, Moreland and his colleagues added two new conditions to those used in the first experiment. One of these involved individual training followed by a team-building exercise. This condition was designed to encourage group development without producing transactive memory. The other involved group training followed by the reassignment of members to new groups. This condition was designed to disable the transactive memory produced by group training, leaving only generic learning about how to perform the task with others. During the test phase, performance was better in the simple group training condition than in any of the other conditions, indicating that the effects of group training were not due to group development or the learning of generic strategies. As before, causal analyses showed that performance differences across conditions were mediated by transactive memory.

The third experiment was designed to measure directly how much team members knew about one another's task-relevant knowledge, which was only inferred from members' behavior in the previous experiments. This experiment was identical to the first one, except that participants reported their beliefs about one another's radio-building skills at the beginning of the test phase and then built the radio by themselves. The results showed that group training indeed created transactive memory—people who were trained together had more complex, accurate, and consensual beliefs about the radio-building skills of their fellow group members than did people who were trained individually. Taken as a whole, these experiments provide convincing evidence for the role of transactive memory in group performance.

Discussion Questions

1. Although researchers have devoted more attention to process loss than to process gain, there are cases in which a group's performance exceeds what is expected on the basis of its members' skills. When might process gain occur?
2. We know that a group's goals can influence its performance, but what factors lead some groups to adopt more challenging goals?
3. Consider the impact of stress on group performance. When is stress helpful, and when is it harmful? Do different forms of stress (e.g., time pressure, danger) have different effects on performance? Do group leaders ever try to manage the stress their followers experience, and, if so, then how do they do this?
4. Certain kinds of shared knowledge seem to facilitate group performance. But is more always better? Are there times when group performance is better if some members are kept in the dark about some things?
5. Groups that exist for any length of time experience personnel turnover involving the exit of old members and the entry of new ones. What are the costs and benefits of turnover for groups working on different kinds of tasks (e.g., routine versus novel tasks, simple versus complex tasks)?

Suggested Readings

Hinsz, V. B. (1995). Group and individual decision making for task performance goals: Processes in the establishment of goals in groups. *Journal of Applied Social Psychology*, *25*, 353–370.

Hollenbeck, J. R., Ilgen, D. R., Sego, D. J., Hedlund, J., Major, D. A., & Phillips, J. (1995). Multilevel theory of team decision making: Decision performance in teams incorporating distributed expertise. *Journal of Applied Psychology*, *80*, 292–316.

Karau, S. J., & Kelly, J. R. (1992). The effects of time scarcity and time abundance on group performance quality and interaction process. *Journal of Experimental Social Psychology, 28,* 542–571.

Kerr, N. L. (1983). Motivation losses in small groups: A social dilemma analysis. *Journal of Personality and Social Psychology, 45,* 819–828.

Littlepage, G. E., Robison, W., & Reddington, K. (1997). Effects of task experience and group experience on group performance, member ability, and recognition of expertise. *Organizational Behavior and Human Decision Processes, 69,* 133–147.

Many Hands Make Light the Work: The Causes and Consequences of Social Loafing

Bibb Latané, Kipling Williams, and Stephen Harkins

Two experiments found that when asked to perform the physically exerting tasks of clapping and shouting, people exhibit a sizable decrease in individual effort when performing in groups as compared to when they perform alone. This decrease, which we call social loafing, is in addition to losses due to faulty co-ordination of group efforts. Social loafing is discussed in terms of its experimental generality and theoretical importance. The widespread occurrence, the negative consequences for society, and some conditions that can minimize social loafing are also explored.

There is an old saying that "many hands make light the work." This saying is interesting for two reasons. First, it captures one of the promises of social life—that with social organization people can fulfill their individual goals more easily through collective action. When many hands are available, people often do not have to work as hard as when only a few are present. The saying is interesting in a second, less hopeful way—it seems that when many hands are available, people actually work less hard than they ought to.

Over 50 years ago a German psychologist named Ringelmann did a study that he never managed to get published. In rare proof that unpublished work does not necessarily perish, the results of that study, reported only in summary form in German by Moede (1927), have been cited by Dashiell (1935), Davis (1969), Köhler (1927), and Zajonc (1966) and extensively analyzed by Steiner (1966, 1972) and Ingham, Levinger, Graves, and Peckham (1974). Apparently Ringelmann simply asked German workers to pull as hard as they could on

This research was supported by National Science Foundation Grant GS40194.

The authors would like to thank Lewis Hinkle for technical assistance and Edward Diener, John Harvey, Norbert Kerr, Robert Kidd, George Levinger, Thomas Ostrom, Richard Petty, and Ladd Wheeler for their valuable comments.

S. Harkins is now an assistant professor of psychology at Northeastern University.

Requests for reprints should be sent to Bibb Latané, Behavioral Sciences Laboratory, Ohio State University, 404B West 17th Avenue, Columbus, Ohio 43210.

a rope, alone or with one, two, or seven other people, and then he used a strain gauge to measure how hard they pulled in kilograms of pressure.

Rope pulling is, in Steiner's (1972) useful classification of tasks, maximizing, unitary, and additive. In a maximizing task, success depends on how much or how rapidly something is accomplished and presumably on how much effort is expended, as opposed to an optimizing task, in which precision, accuracy, or correctness are paramount. A unitary task cannot be divided into separate subtasks—all members work together doing the same thing and no division of labor is possible. In an additive task, group success depends on the *sum* of the individual efforts, rather than on the performance of any subset of members. From these characteristics, we should expect three people pulling together on a rope with perfect efficiency to be able to exert three times as much force as one person can, and eight people to exert eight times as much force.

Ringelmann's results, however, were strikingly different. When pulling one at a time, individuals averaged a very respectable 63 kg of pressure. Groups of three people were able to exert a force of 160 kg, only two and a half times the average individual performance, and groups of eight pulled at 248 kg, less than four times the solo rate. Thus the collective group performance, while increasing somewhat with group size, was substantially less than the sum of the individual efforts, with dyads pulling at 93% of the sum of their individual efforts, trios at 85%, and groups of eight at only 49%. In a way somewhat different from how the old saw would have it, many hands apparently made light the work.

The Ringelmann effect is interesting because it seems to violate both common stereotype and social psychological theory. Common stereotype tells us that the sense of team participation leads to increased effort, that group morale and cohesiveness spur individual enthusiasm, that by pulling together groups can achieve any goal, that in unity there is strength. Social psychological theory holds that, at least for simple, well-learned tasks involving dominant responses, the presence of other people, whether as co-workers or spectators, should facilitate performance. It is thus important to find out whether Ringelmann's effect is replicable and whether it can be obtained with other tasks.

The Ringelmann effect is also interesting because it provides a different arena for testing a new theory of social impact (Latané, 1973). Social impact theory holds that when a person stands as a target of social forces coming from other persons, the amount of social pressure on the target person should increase as a multiplicative function of the strength, immediacy, and number of these other persons. However, if a person is a member of a group that is the target of social forces from outside the group, the impact of these forces on any given member should diminish in inverse proportion to the strength, immediacy, and number of group members. Impact is divided up among the group members, in much the same way that responsibility for helping seems to be divided among witnesses to an emergency (Latané & Darley, 1970). Latané further suggests that just as psychophysical reactions to external stimuli can be described in terms of a power law (Stevens, 1957), so also should reactions to social stimuli, but with an exponent having an absolute value less than 1, so that the nth person should have less effect than the $(n - 1)$th. Ringelmann's asking his workers to pull on a rope can be considered social pressure. The more people who are the target of this pressure, the less pressure should be felt by any one person. Since people are likely to work hard in proportion to the pressure they feel to do so, we should expect increased group size to result in reduced efforts on the part of individual group members. These reduced efforts can be called "social loafing"—a decrease in individual effort due to the social presence of other persons. With respect to the Ringelmann phenomenon, social impact theory suggests that at least some of the effect should be due to reduced efforts on the part of group participants, and that this reduced effort should follow the form of an inverse power function having an exponent with an absolute value less than one.

The Ringelmann effect is interesting for a third reason: If it represents a general phenomenon and is not restricted to pulling on a rope, it poses the important practical question of when and why collective efforts are less efficient than individual ones. Since many components of our standard of life are produced through one form or another of collective action, research identifying the causes and conditions of inefficient group output and suggesting strategies to overcome these inefficiencies is clearly desirable.

For these three and other reasons, we decided to initiate a program of research into the collective performance of individuals in groups.

Experiment 1

Clap Your Hands and Shout Out Loud

One of the disadvantages of Ringelmann's rope pulling task is that the equipment and procedures are relatively cumbersome and inefficient. Therefore, we decided to keep our ears open for other tasks that would allow us to replicate the Ringelmann finding conceptually and would provide the basis for extended empirical and theoretical analysis. We chose cheering and clapping, two activities that people commonly do together in social settings and that are maximizing, unitary, and additive. As with rope pulling, output can be measured in simple physical units that make up a ratio scale.

Method

On eight separate occasions, groups of six undergraduate males were recruited from introductory psychology classes at Ohio State University; they were seated in a semicircle, 1 m apart, in a large soundproofed laboratory and told, "We are interested in judgments of how much noise people make in social settings, namely cheering and applause, and how loud they seem to those who hear them. Thus, we want each of you to do two things: (1) Make noises, and (2) judge noises." They were told that on each trial "the experimenter will tell you the trial number, who is to perform and whether you are to cheer (Rah!) or clap. When you are to begin, the experimenter will count backwards from three and raise his hand. Continue until he lowers it. We would like you to clap or cheer for 5 seconds as loud as you can." On each trial, both the performers and the observers were also asked to make magnitude estimates of how much noise had been produced

(Stevens, 1966). Since these data are not relevant to our concerns, we will not mention them further.

After some practice at both producing and judging noise, there were 36 trials of yelling and 36 trials of clapping. Within each modality, each person performed twice alone, four times in pairs, four times in groups of four, and six times in groups of six. These frequencies were chosen as a compromise between equating the number of occasions on which we measured people making noise alone or in groups (which would have required more noise-making in fours and sixes) and equating the number of individual performances contributing to our measurements in the various group sizes (which would have required more noisemaking by individuals and pairs). We also arranged the sequence of performances to space and counterbalance the order of conditions over each block of 36 trials, while making sure that no one had to perform more than twice in a row.

Performances were measured with a General Radio sound-level meter, Model 1565A, using the C scale and the slow time constant, which was placed exactly 4 m away from each performer. The C scale was used so that sounds varying only in frequency or pitch would be recorded as equally loud. Sound-level meters are read in decibel (dB) units, which are intended to approximate the human reaction to sound. For our purposes, however, the appropriate measure is the effort used in generating noise, not how loud it sounds. Therefore, our results are presented in terms of dynes/cm^2, the physical unit of work involved in producing sound pressure.

Because people shouted and clapped in full view and earshot of each other, each person's performance could affect and be affected by the others. For this reason, the group, rather than the individual, was the unit of analysis, and each score was based on the average output per person. Results were analyzed in a $4 \times 2 \times 2$ analysis of variance, with Group Size (1, 2, 4, 6), Response Mode (clapping vs. shouting), and Replications (1, 2) as factors.

Results

Participants seemed to adapt to the task with good humor if not great enthusiasm. Nobody refused to clap or shout, even though a number seemed somewhat embarrassed or shy about making these noises in public. Despite this, they did manage to produce a good deal of noise. Individuals averaged 84 dB (C) clapping and 87 dB cheering, while groups of six clapped at 91 dB and shouted at 95 dB (an increment of 6 dB represents a doubling of sound pressure).

As might be expected, the more people clapping or cheering together, the more intense the noise and the more the sound pressure produced. However, it did not grow in proportion to the number of people: The average sound pressure generated *per person* decreased with increasing group size, $F (3, 21) = 41.5, p < .001$. People averaged about 3.7 dynes/cm² alone, 2.6 in pairs, 1.8 in foursomes, and about 1.5 in groups of six (Figure 16.1). Put another way, two-person groups performed at only 71% of the sum of their individual capacity, four-person groups at 51%, and six-person groups at 40%. As in pulling ropes, it appears that when it comes to clapping and shouting out loud, many hands do, in fact, make light the work.

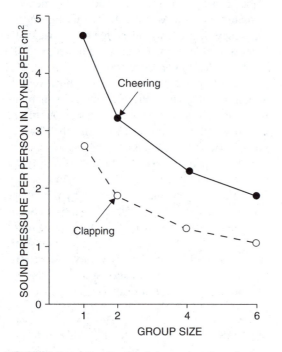

FIGURE 16.1 ■ Intensity of noise as a function of group size and response mode, Experiment 1.

People also produced about 60% more sound power when they shouted than when they clapped, $F (1, 7) = 8.79, p < .01$, presumably reflecting physical capacity rather than any psychological process. There was no effect due to blocks of trials, indicating that the subjects needed little or no practice and that their performance was not deleteriously affected by fatigue. In addition, there were no interactions among the variables.

Discussion

The results provide a strong replication of Ringelmann's original findings, using a completely different task and in a different historical epoch and culture. At least when people are making noise as part of a task imposed by someone else, voices raised together do not seem to be raised as much as voices raised alone, and the sound of 12 hands clapping is not even three times as intense as the sound of 2.

Zajonc's (1965) elegant theory of social facilitation suggests that people are aroused by the mere presence of others and are thus likely to work harder (though not necessarily to achieve more) when together. Although social facilitation theory might seem to predict enhanced group performance on a simple task like clapping or shouting, in the present case it would not predict any effect due to group size, since the number of people present was always eight, six participants and two experimenters. Evaluation apprehension theory (Cottrell, 1972) would also not predict any effect as long as it is assumed that co-actors and audience members are equally effective in arousing performance anxiety. Therefore, these theories are not inconsistent with our position that an unrelated social process is involved. The results of Experiment 1 also can be taken as support for Latané's (1973) theory of social impact: The impact that the experimenters have on an individual seems to decrease as the number of coperformers increases, leading to an apparent drop in individual performance, a phenomenon we call social loafing.

However, there is an alternative explanation to these results. It may be, not that people exert less effort in groups, but that the group product suffers as a result of group inefficiency. In his invaluable theoretical analysis of group productivity, Steiner (1972) suggests that the discrepancy between a group's potential productivity (in this case n times the average individual output) and its actual productivity may be attributed to faulty social process. In the case of Ringelmann's rope pull, Steiner identifies one source of process loss as inadequate social coordination. As group size increases, the number of "coordination links," and thus the possibility of faulty coordination (pulling in different directions at different times), also increases. Steiner shows that for Ringelmann's original data the decrement in obtained productivity is exactly proportional to the number of coordination links.

Ingham et al. (1974) designed an ingenious experiment to determine whether the process losses found in rope pulling were mainly due to problems of coordinating individual efforts and the physics of the task, or whether they resulted from reductions in personal exertion (what we have called social loafing). First, they conducted a careful replication of Ringelmann's original rope-pulling study and found similar results—dyads pulled at 91% of the sum of their individual capacities, trios at 82%, and groups of six at only 78%.

In a second experiment, Ingham et al. cleverly arranged things so that only the individual's perception of group size was varied. Individuals were blindfolded and led to believe that others were pulling with them, but in fact, they always pulled alone. Under these conditions, of course, there is no possibility of loss due to faulty synchronization. Still there was a substantial drop in output with increases in perceived group size: Individuals pulled at 90% of their alone rate when they believed one other person was also pulling, and at only 85% with two to six others believed pulling. It appears that virtually all of the performance decrement in rope pulling observed by Ingham et al. can be accounted for in terms of reduced effort or social loafing.

With respect to clapping and especially shouting, however, there are several possible sources of coordination loss that might have operated in addition to social loafing: (a) Sound cancellation will occur to the extent that sound pressure waves interfere with each other, (b) directional coordination losses will occur to the extent that voices are projected toward different locations, and (c) temporal coordination losses will occur to the extent that moment-to-moment individual variations in intensity are not in synchrony. Our second experiment was designed to assess the relative effects of coordination loss and social loafing in explaining the failure of group cheering to be as intense as the sum of individual noise outputs.

Experiment 2

Coordination Loss or Reduced Effort?

For Experiment 2 we arranged things so that people could not hear each other shout; participants were asked to wear headphones, and during each trial a constant 90-dB recording of six people shouting was played over the earphones, ostensibly to reduce auditory feedback and to signal each trial. As a consequence, individuals could be led to believe they were shouting in groups while actually shouting alone. Ingham et al. (1974) accomplished this through the use of "pseudo-subjects," confederates who pretended to be pulling with the participants but who in fact did not pull any weight at all. That is an expensive procedure—each of the 36 participants tested by Ingham et al. required the services of 5 pseudosubjects as well as the experimenter. We were able to devise a procedure whereby, on any given trial, one person could be led to believe that he was performing in a group, while the rest thought he was performing alone. Thus, we were able to test six real participants at one time.

Additionally, although we find the interpretation offered by Ingham et al. plausible and convincing, the results of their second experiment are susceptible to an alternative explanation. When participants were not pulling the rope, they stood and watched the pseudosubjects pull. This would lead people accurately to believe that while they were pulling the rope, idle participants would be watching (Levinger, Note 1). Thus, as the number of performers decreased, the size of the audience increased. According to Cottrell's evaluation apprehension hypothesis (1972), the presence of an evaluative audience should enhance performance for a simple, well-learned task such as rope pulling, and, although there is little supportive evidence, it seems reasonable that the larger the audience, the greater the enhancement (Martens & Landers, 1969; Seta, Paulus, & Schkade, 1976). Thus, it is not clear whether there was a reduced effort put forth by group members because they believed other people were pulling with them, or an increase in the effort exerted by individuals because they believed other people were watching them. In Experiment 2, therefore, we arranged to hold the size of the audience constant, even while varying the number of people working together.

Method

Six groups of six male undergraduate volunteers heard the following instructions:

> In our experiment today we are interested in the effects of sensory feedback on the production of sound in social groups. We will ask you to produce sounds in groups of one, two, or six, and we will record the sound output on the sound-level meter that you can see up here in front. Although this is not a competition and you will not learn your scores until the end of the experiment, we would like you to make your sounds as loud as possible. Since we are interested in sensory feedback, we will ask you to wear blindfolds and earphones and, as you will see, will arrange it so that you will not be able to hear yourself as you shout.

> We realize it may seem strange to you to shout as loud as you can, especially since other people are around. Remember that the room is sound-proofed and that people outside the room will not be able to hear you. In addition, because you will be wearing blindfolds and headsets, the other participants will not be able to hear you or to see you. Please, therefore, feel free to let loose and really shout. As I said, we are interested in how loud you can shout, and there is no reason not to do your best. Here's your chance to really give it a try. Do you have any questions?

Once participants had donned their headsets and blindfolds, they went through a series of 13 trials, in which each person shouted four times in a group of six, once in a group of two, and once by himself. Before each trial they heard the identification letters of those people who were to shout.

Interspersed with these trials were 12 trials, two for each participant, in which the individual's headset was switched to a separate track on the stereophonic instruction tape. On these trials, everybody else was told that only the focal person should shout, but that individual was led to believe either that one other person would shout with him or that all six would shout.

Thus, each person shouted by himself, in actual groups of two and six, and in pseudogroups of two and six, with trials arranged so that each person would have approximately equal rest periods between the trials on which he performed. Each trial was preceded by the specification of who was to perform. The yells were coordinated by a tape-recorded voice counting backwards from three, followed by a constant 90-dB 5-sec recording of the sound of six people shouting. This background noise made it impossible for performers to determine whether or how loudly other people were shouting, or, for that matter, to hear themselves shout. Each trial was terminated by the sound of a bell. This sequence of 25 trials was repeated three times, for a total of 75 trials, in the course of which each subject shouted 24 times.

As in Experiment 1, the data were transformed into dynes/cm^2 and subjected to analyses of variance, with the group as the unit of analysis and each score based on the average output per person. Two separate 3×3 analyses of variance with group size (1, 2, 6) and trial block (1–3) were run, one on the output of trials in which groups actually shouted together, and one on the pseudogroup trials in which only one person actually shouted.

Results

Overall, participants shouted with considerably more intensity in Experiment 2 than in Experiment 1, averaging 9.22 dynes/cm^2 when shouting alone, as compared to 4.73 dynes/cm^2, $t(12) = 4.05$, $p < .01$. There are several plausible reasons for this difference. The new rationale involving the effects of reduced sensory feedback may have interested or challenged individuals to perform well. The constant 90-dB background noise may have led people to shout with more intensity, just as someone listening to music through headphones will often speak inappropriately loudly (the Lombard reflex). The performers may have felt less embarrassed because the room was soundproof and the others were unable to see or hear them. Finally, through eliminating the possibility of hearing each other, individuals could no longer be influenced by the output of the others, thereby lifting the pressure of social conformity.

As in Experiment 1, as the number of actual performers increased, the total sound output also increased, but at a slower rate than would be expected from the sum of the individual outputs. Actual groups of two shouted at only 66% of capacity, and groups of six at 36%, $F(2, 10) = 226$, $p < .001$. The comparable figures for Experiment 1 are 71% and 40%. These similarities between experiments suggest that our procedural changes, even though they made people unable to hear or see each other, did not eliminate their feeling of being in a group or reduce the amount of incoordination or social loafing.

The line connecting the solid circles in Figure 16.2 shows the decreased output per person when actually performing in groups. The dashed line along the top represents potential productivity—the output to be expected if there were no losses due to faulty coordination or to social loafing. The striped area at the bottom represents the obtained output per person in actual groups. Output is obviously lower than potential productivity, and this decrease can be considered as representing the sum of the losses due to incoordination and to reduced individual effort.

In addition to shouting in actual groups, individuals also performed in pseudogroups in which they believed that others shouted with them but in which they actually shouted alone, thus preventing coordination loss from affecting output. As shown in Figure 16.2, people shouted with less intensity in pseudogroups than when alone, $F(2, 10) = 37.0, p < .0001$. Thus, group size made a significant difference even in pseudogroups in which coordination loss is not a factor and only social loafing can operate.

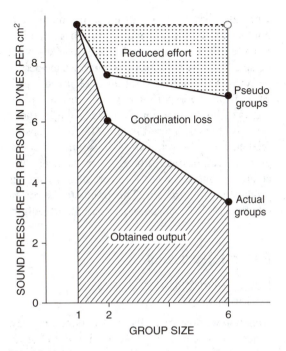

FIGURE 16.2 ■ Intensity of sound produced per person when cheering in actual or perceived groups of 1, 2, and 6, as a result of reduced effort and faulty co-ordination of group efforts, Experiment 2.

When performers believed one other person was yelling, they shouted 82% as intensely as when alone, and when they believed five others to be yelling, they shouted 74% as intensely. The stippled area defined at the top of Figure 16.2 by the data from the pseudogroups represents the amount of loss due to social loafing. By subtraction, we can infer that the white area of Figure 16.2 represents the amount of loss due to faulty coordination. Since the latter comprises about the same area as the former, we can conclude that, for shouting, half the performance loss decrement is due to incoordination and half is due to social loafing.

Discussion

Despite the methodological differences between Experiments 1 and 2, both experiments showed that there is a reduction in sound pressure produced per person when people make noise in groups compared to when alone. People in Experiment 1 applauded and cheered in full view of each other, with all the excitement, embarrassment, and conformity that goes along with such a situation. In Experiment 2, no one could see or hear any other person. Only the experimenters could see the people perform. And finally, the rationale changed drastically, from the experimenters' interest in "judgments of how much noise people make in social settings" to their interest in "the effects of sensory feedback on the production of sound in social groups." Yet, despite differences in the task characteristics and supposed purpose, the two studies produced similar results. This points to the robust nature of both the phenomenon and the paradigm.

General Discussion

Noise Production as Group Performance

Although we do not usually think about it that way, making noise can be hard work, in both the physical and the psychological sense. In the present case, the participants were asked to produce sound pressure waves, either by rapidly vibrating their laryngeal membranes or by vigorously striking their hands together. Although superficially similar in consequence, this task should not be confused with more normal outbreaks of shouting and clapping that occur as spontaneous outbursts of exuberant expressiveness. Our participants shouted and clapped because we asked them to, not because they wanted to.

This effortful and fatiguing task resulted in sound pressure waves, which, although invisible, can be easily and accurately measured in physical units that are proportional to the amount of work performed. The making of noise is a useful task for the study of group processes from the standpoint both of production and of measurement—people are practiced and skilled at making noise and can do so without the help of expensive or cumbersome apparatus, and acoustics and audio engineering are sufficiently advanced to permit sophisticated data collection. We seem to have found a paradigm wherein people get involved enough to try hard and become somewhat enthusiastic, yet the task is still effortful enough so that they loaf when given the opportunity.

The Causes of Social Loafing

The present research shows that groups can inhibit the productivity of individuals so that people reduce their exertions when it comes to shouting and clapping with others. Why does this occur? We suggest three lines of explanation, the first having to do with attribution and equity, the second with submaximal goal setting, and the third with the lessening of the contingency between individual inputs and outcomes.

1. Attribution and equity. It may be that participants engaged in a faulty attribution process, leading to an attempt to maintain an equitable division of labor. There are at least three aspects of the physics and psychophysics of producing sound that could have led people to believe that the other persons in their group were not working as hard or effectively as themselves. First, individuals judged their own outputs to be louder than those of the others, simply because they were closer to the sound source. Second, even if everyone worked to capacity, sound cancellation would cause group outputs to seem much less than the sum of their individual performances. Finally, the perception of the amount of sound produced in a group should be much less than the actual amount—growing only as the .67 power of the actual amount of sound, according to Stevens's psychophysical power law (1975).

These factors may have led individuals to believe that the other participants were less motivated or less skillful than themselves—in short, were shirkers or incompetents. Thus, differences in the perception of sound production that were essentially the result of physical and psychophysical processes may have been mistakenly attributed to a lack of either skill or motivation on the part of the others, leading individuals to produce less sound in groups because there is no reason to work hard in aid of shirkers or those who are less competent.

This process cannot explain the results of Experiment 2, since the capacity to judge the loudness of one's own output, much less that of others, was severely impaired by the 90-dB background masking noise used to signal the trials. However, rather than "discovering" social loafing while participating in the experiment, the participants may have arrived with the preexisting notion that people often do not pull their own weight in groups. Thus, despite being unable to hear or see one another, lack of trust and the propensity to attribute laziness or ineptitude to others could have led people to work less hard themselves.

2. Submaximal goal setting. It may be that despite our instructions, participants redefined the task and adopted a goal, not of making as much noise as possible, but merely of making enough noise or of matching some more or less well-defined standard. Individuals would clearly expect it to be easier to achieve this goal when others are helping, and might work less hard as a consequence. This, of course, would change the nature of noise production from what Steiner (1972) would term a *maximizing* task to an *optimizing* task. A maximizing task makes success a function of how much or how rapidly something is accomplished. For an optimizing task, however, success is a function of how closely the individual or group approximates a predetermined "best" or correct outcome. If participants in our experiments perceived sound production as an optimizing rather than a maximizing task, they might feel the optimal level of sound output could be reached more easily in groups than alone, thereby allowing them to exert less effort.

The participants in Experiment 2 could hear neither themselves nor others and would not be able to determine whether their output was obnoxious or to develop a group standard for an optimal level. Furthermore, in both experiments, the experimenters reiterated their request to yell "as loud as you can, every time," over and over again. Before the first trial they would ask the group how loud they were supposed to yell. In unison, the group would reply, "As loud as we can!" We think it unlikely that participants perceived the task to be anything other than maximizing.

3. Lessened contingency between input and outcome. It may be that participants felt that the contingency between their input and the outcome was lessened when performing in groups. Individuals could "hide in the crowd" (Davis, 1969) and avoid the negative consequences of slacking off, or they may have felt "lost in the crowd" and unable to obtain their fair share of the positive consequences for working hard. Since individual scores are unidentifiable when groups perform together, people can receive neither precise credit nor appropriate blame for their performance. Only when performing alone can individual outputs be exactly evaluated and rewarded.

Let us assume that group members expect approval or other reward proportional to the total output of a group of n performers, but that since individual efforts are indistinguishable, the reward is psychologically divided equally among the participants, each getting $1/n$ units of reward. Under these assumptions, the average group, if it performed up to capacity and suffered no process loss, could expect to divide up n times the reward of the average individual, resulting in each member's getting $n \times 1/n$, or n/n, units of reward, the same amount as an individual.

Although the total amount of reward may be the same, the contingency on individual output is not. Any given individual under these assumptions will get back only one nth of his own contribution to the group; the rest will be shared by the others. Even though he may also receive unearned one nth of each other person's contribution, he will be tempted, to the extent that his own performance is costly or effortful, to become a "free rider" (Olson, 1965). Thus, under these assumptions, if his own performance cannot be individually monitored, an individual's incentive to perform should be proportional to $1/n$.

Seligman (1975) has shown that animals and people become lethargic and depressed when confronted with tasks in which they have little or no control over the outcomes. Likewise, in our experiments, people may have felt a loss of control over their fair share of the rewards when they performed in groups, leading them also to become, if not lethargic and depressed, at least less enthusiastic about making lots of noise.

Since people were asked to shout both alone and in groups, they may have felt it smart to save their strength in groups and to shout as lustily as possible when scores were individually identifiable, marshalling their energy for the occasions when they could earn rewards. This line of reasoning suggests that if inputs were made identifiable and rewards contingent on them, even when in groups, it would be impossible for performers to get a free ride and they would have an incentive to work equally hard in groups of different sizes.

Social Loafing and Social Impact Theory

Each of these three lines of explanation may be described in terms of Latané's (1973) theory of social impact. If a person is the target of social forces, increasing the number of other persons also in the target group should diminish the pressures on each individual because the impact is divided among the group members. In a group performance situation in which pressures to work come from outside the group and individual outputs are not identifiable, this division of impact should lead each individual to work less hard. Thus, whether the subject is dividing up the amount of work he thinks should be performed or whether he is dividing up the amount of reward he expects to earn with his work, he should work less hard in groups.

The theory of social impact further stipulates the form that the decrease in output should follow. Just as perceptual judgments of physical stimuli follow power functions (Stevens, 1957), so also should judgments of social stimuli, and the exponent of the psychosocial power function should have an exponent of less than one, resulting in a marginally decreasing impact of additional people. Thus, social impact theory suggests that the amount of effort expended on group tasks should decrease as an inverse power function of the number of people in the group. This implication cannot be tested in Experiment 1 or with the actual groups of Experiment 2, inasmuch as coordination loss is confounded with social loafing. However, a power function with an exponent of $-.14$ accounted for 93% of the variance for the pseudogroups of Experiment 2. It appears that social impact theory provides a good account of both the existence and the magnitude of social loafing.

The Transsituational and Transcultural Generality of Social Loafing

The present research demonstrates that performance losses in groups occur with tasks other than rope pulling and with people other than prewar German workers. There are, in addition, other instances of experimental research that demonstrate similar cases of social loafing. For example, Marriott (1949) and Campbell (1952) have shown that factory workers produce less per person in larger groups than in smaller ones. Latané and Darley (1970) have found that the likelihood that a bystander will intervene in a situation in which someone requires assistance is substantially reduced by the addition of other bystanders who share in the responsibility for help. Wicker (1969) has found that the proportion of members taking part in church activities is lower in large than in small churches, presumably because the responsibility for taking part is more diffuse. Similarly, Petty, Harkins, Williams, and Latané (1977) found that people perceived themselves as exerting less cognitive effort on evaluating poems and editorials when they were among groups of other unidentifiable evaluators than when they alone were responsible for the task.

These experimental findings have demonstrated that a clear potential exists in human nature for social loafing. We suspect that the effects of social loafing have far-reaching and profound consequences both in our culture and in other cultures. For example, on collective farms (kolkhoz) in Russia, the peasants "move all over huge areas, working one field and one task one day, another field the next, having no sense of responsibility and no direct dependence on the results of their labor" (Smith, 1976, p. 281). Each peasant family is also allowed a private plot of up to an acre in size that may be worked after the responsibility to the collective is discharged. The produce of these plots, for which the peasants are individually responsible, may be used as they see fit. Although these plots occupy less than 1% of the nation's agricultural lands (about 26 million acres), they produce 27% of the total value of Soviet farm output (about $32.5 billion worth) (Yemelyanov, 1975, cited in

Smith, 1976, p. 266). It is not, however, that the private sector is so highly efficient; rather, it is that the efficiency of the public sector is so low (Wädekin, 1973, p. 67).

However, before we become overly pessimistic about the potential of collective effort, we should consider the Israeli kibbutz, an example that suggests that the effects of social loafing can be circumvented. Despite the fact that kibbutzim are often located in remote and undeveloped areas on the periphery of Israel to protect the borders and develop these regions, these communes have been very successful. For example, in dairying, 1963 yields per cow on the kibbutz were 27% higher than for the rest of Israel's herds, and in 1960 yields were 75% higher than in England. In 1959, kibbutz chickens were producing 22% of the eggs with only 16% of the chickens (Leon, 1969). The kibbutz and the kolkhoz represent the range of possibilities for collective effort, and comparisons of these two types of collective enterprise may suggest conditions under which per person output would be greater in groups than individually.

Social Loafing as a Social Disease

Although some people still think science should be value free, we must confess that we think social loafing can be regarded as a kind of social disease. It is a "disease" in that it has negative consequences for individuals, social institutions, and societies. Social loafing results in a reduction in human efficiency, which leads to lowered profits and lowered benefits for all. It is "social" in that it results from the presence or actions of other people.

The "cure," however, is not to do away with groups, because despite their inefficiency, groups make possible the achievement of many goals that individuals alone could not possibly accomplish. Collective action is a vital aspect of our lives: From time immemorial it has made possible the construction of monuments, but today it is necessary to the provision of even our food and shelter. We think the cure will come from finding ways of channeling social forces so that the group can serve as a means of intensifying individual responsibility rather than diffusing it.

REFERENCE NOTE

1. Levinger, G. Personal communication, June 1976.

REFERENCES

Campbell, M. Group incentive payment schemes: The effects of lack of understanding and group size. *Occupational Psychology*, 1952, *26*, 15–21.

Cottrell, N. Social facilitation. In C. McClintock (Ed.), *Experimental social psychology*. New York: Holt, Rinehart & Winston, 1972.

Dashiell, J. F. Experimental studies of the influence of social situations on the behavior of individual human adults. In C. Murchison (Ed.), *A handbook of social psychology*. Worcester, Mass.: Clark University Press, 1935.

Davis, J. H. *Group performance*. Reading, Mass.: Addison-Wesley, 1969.

Ingham, A. G., Levinger, G., Graves, J., & Peckham, V. The Ringelmann effect: Studies of group size and group performance. *Journal of Experimental Social Psychology*, 1974, *10*, 371–384.

Köhler, O. Ueber den Gruppenwirkungsgrad der menschlichen Körperarbeit und die Bedingung optimaler Kollektivkroftreaktion. *Industrielle Psychotechnik*, 1927, *4*, 209–226.

Latané, B. *A theory of social impact*. St. Louis, Mo.: Psychonomic Society, 1973.

Latané, B., & Darley, J. M. *The unresponsive by-stander: Why doesn't he help?* New York: Appleton-Century-Crofts, 1970.

Leon, D. *The kibbutz: A new way of life*. London: Pergamon Press, 1969.

Marriott, R. Size of working group and output. *Occupational Psychology*, 1949, *23*, 47–57.

Martens, R., & Landers, D. M. Coaction effects on a muscular endurance task. *Research Quarterly*, 1969, *40*, 733–737.

Moede, W. Die Richtlinien der Leistungs-Psychologie. *Industrielle Psychotechnik*, 1927, *4*, 193–207.

Olson, M. *The logic of collective action: Public goods and the theory of groups*. Cambridge, Mass.: Harvard University Press, 1965.

Petty, R., Harkins, S., Williams, K., & Latané, B. The effects of group size on cognitive effort and evaluation. *Personality and Social Psychology Bulletin*, 1977, *3*, 579–582.

Seligman, M. *Helplessness*. San Francisco: Freeman, 1975.

Seta, J. J., Paulus, P. B., & Schkade, J. K. Effects of group size and proximity under cooperative and competitive conditions. *Journal of Personality and Social Psychology*, 1976, *34*, 47–53.

Smith, H. *The Russians*. New York: Ballantine Books, 1976.

Steiner, I. D. Models for inferring relationships between group size and potential group productivity. *Behavioral Science*, 1966, *11*, 273–283.

Steiner, I. D. *Group process and productivity*. New York: Academic Press, 1972.

Stevens, S. S. On the psychological law. *Psychological Review*, 1957, *64*, 153–181.

Stevens, S. S. A metric for the social consensus. *Science*, 1966, *151*, 530–541.

Stevens, S. S. *Psychophysics: Introduction to its perceptual, neural and social prospects.* New York: Wiley, 1975.

Wädekin, K. *The private sector in Soviet agriculture.* Los Angeles: University of California Press, 1973.

Wicker, A. N. Size of church membership and members support of church behavior settings. *Journal of Personality and Social Psychology*, 1969, *13*, 278–288.

Zajonc, R. B. Social facilitation. *Science*, 1965, *149*, 269–274.

Zajonc, R. B. *Social psychology: An experimental approach.* Belmont, Calif.: Brooks/Cole, 1966.

Received June 23, 1978 ■

Impact of Group Goals, Task Component Complexity, Effort, and Planning on Group Performance

Laurie R. Weingart

This study tested a model asserting that goal difficulty and task component complexity influence group performance by affecting the effort exerted by group members, the amount and quality of their planning, and the timing of their planning (preplanning versus in-process planning). Hypotheses derived from this model were tested in a 2 × 2 experimental design. Fifty-six groups of 4 students each worked for 15 min building Tinkertoy structures. Results showed that group-goal difficulty influenced group performance through effort; task component complexity influenced performance through the amount of planning performed by group members and the level of effort invested in their work; and the quality of the group's planning process also influenced group performance.

Several studies have shown that group goals can improve group performance (e.g., Becker, 1978; Klein & Mulvey, 1989; Latham & Yukl, 1975; Pritchard, Jones, Roth, Stuebing, & Ekeberg, 1988; Weingart & Weldon, 1991; Weldon, Jehn, & Pradhan, 1991). However, very little is known about the behaviors that mediate this effect. In this article, a model of group goals

This research was based on my doctoral dissertation at the J. L. Kellogg Graduate School of Management, Northwestern University. I wish to thank the members of my dissertation committee: Elizabeth Weldon, Jeanne Brett, Larry L. Cummings, and Michael Roloff for their guidance, and three anonymous reviewers for their helpful comments on earlier versions of this article.

Correspondence concerning this article should be sent to Laurie R. Weingart, Graduate School of Industrial Administration, Carnegie Mellon University, Pittsburgh, Pennsylvania 15213.

and group performance is presented. This model suggests four mediators (effort and the amount, quality, and timing of planning) and considers the impact of task component complexity as a moderator of the group-goal effect. The goals of this article are threefold: (a) to develop a theory of group goals and task complexity, (b) to describe a study that tested the theory, and (c) to suggest future research in this area.

The model presented in this article is consistent with Hackman and Morris's (1975) input–process–output model of group performance effectiveness. Hackman and Morris suggested that three summary variables mediate the relationship between input variables (group norms, task design, and group composition) and the effectiveness of group performance: the application of performance strategies, effort, and group members' knowledge and skill. This article examines the effects of two input variables—group goals (a group norm) and task component complexity—on the quantity of performance through the mediating processes of the amount, quality, and timing of planning (task performance strategies) and group member effort. Hackman and Morris (1975) also suggested that critical task characteristics influence which summary variables are important determinants of performance effectiveness for the task at hand. In this article, the role of task component complexity is discussed as a "critical task contingency" (Hackman & Morris, 1975, p. 88) that moderates the impact of planning on task performance.

A Model of Group Goals, Task Complexity, and Group Performance

A model of the influence of group goals and task complexity on group performance on an unfamiliar task is shown in Figure 17.1. This model identifies four behaviors proposed to mediate the group-goal effect: (a) the effort invested in task performance by group members, (b) the time at which planning takes place, (c) the amount of planning performed, and (d) the quality of the planning process. Although other mediators of the group-goal–performance relationship may exist (Weldon & Weingart, in press), this model is focused on effort and planning because they are believed to be powerful determinants of the goal–performance relationship (Earley, Northcraft, Lee, & Lituchy, 1990; Earley, Wojnaroski, & Prest, 1987; Locke, Shaw, Saari, & Latham, 1981).

This model also shows the moderating and direct effects of task component complexity. Component complexity is one of three aspects of task complexity described by Wood (1986). Component complexity is the number of unique acts required to perform the task (Wood, 1986). An act is unique when the specific knowledge and skills required to perform other acts do not generalize to that act (Naylor & Dickinson, 1969; Wood, 1986). This model shows that the processes that account for the group-goal effect vary with task component complexity. Each mediator and the effects of goal difficulty and task complexity are described in the following paragraphs.

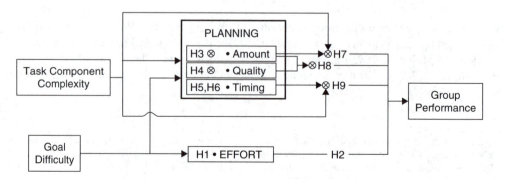

FIGURE 17.1 ■ A model of group goal and task component complexity effects on group performance. ⊗ – Interactive effect.

Effort

Effort has two components: intensity and duration. When a production task is involved, intensity is measured by the rate of work (i.e., number of task-relevant acts performed per unit of time; Bryan & Locke, 1967; Garland, 1982; Locke & Latham, 1990), and duration is measured by the total time spent working. Therefore, an increase in either is an increase in effort.

It has been suggested that group-goal difficulty affects both the intensity and duration of group members' efforts when they are motivated to meet a goal (Weldon & Weingart, in press), and the results of several individual and group goal-setting studies support this hypothesis (Earley et al., 1987; Earley, Northcraft et al., 1990; Locke et al., 1981; Weingart & Weldon, 1991; Weldon et al., 1991). In those studies, self-reports of effort increased with increased goal level, and performance improved, suggesting that effort mediated the goal–performance relationship. However, because these studies did not measure effort objectively, it is impossible to determine whether the increase in performance was actually due to effort, as reported. In this study, effort was examined by an external rater to verify earlier subjective reports.

> *Hypothesis 1.* As group-goal difficulty increases, effort will increase.
> *Hypothesis 2.* As effort increases, group performance will increase.

Planning

According to McGrath (1984), planning is an activity "that requires the group to lay out a course of action by which it can attain an already chosen objective" (p. 127). This definition is similar to the process of developing task performance strategies described by Hackman and Morris (1975). In their view, planning or strategy development is a process that occurs before and independent of actual task performance. However, planning can also occur as group members work on a task. Therefore, in this model, I make a distinction between preplanning and in-process planning. In addition, McGrath (1984) and Hackman and Morris

(1975) did not distinguish between the development of individual and group plans, even though group performance involves both types of plans. Planning for group performance focuses on coordinating group members, including the delegation of subtasks, integration of individual outputs, and timing of coordination (Guetzkow, 1968). Planning for individual performance involves developing performance routines for each group member, including the identification of task-relevant acts, how to perform acts, and information cues necessary to perform the task. Individual planning has been shown to mediate the individual goal–performance relationship (Earley et al., 1987; Earley, Northcraft et al., 1990).

The model presented here suggests that goal difficulty and task component complexity have direct and interactive effects on planning in groups. In the next sections, I examine how these factors influence the amount of planning, the timing of planning (in-process versus preplanning), and the quality of the planning process in groups.

Amount of planning. When group members do not have a pre-existing plan for task performance because the task is unfamiliar, and they do not have an independent block of time to develop a plan, they must allocate some time during the performance session to planning. In this situation, the amount of planning performed should increase with task component complexity because there are more unique acts to plan for (individual-level plans), requiring greater differentiation and coordination of subtasks among group members (group-level plan). However, this might not occur when the group is working toward a difficult goal because pressures to produce quick results can drive out planning (March, 1959, as reported in Shure, Rogers, Larsen, & Tassone, 1962). When working toward a difficult goal, group members are expected to prefer performing task-related acts over planning, because performing results in tangible products, which immediately affect performance. Consistent with this reasoning, Shure et al. (1962) found that groups performing under high task demands and without separate planning sessions did little planning compared with groups working with separate planning sessions. Similarly, Hackman, Brousseau, and Weiss (1976) found that groups working toward cash prizes did not spontaneously engage in planning unless they were instructed to do so. In addition, Baumler (1971) showed that interdependent individuals working on a business game with individual goals engaged in less group planning than did those without goals. Reductions in planning with increasing goal difficulty are even more likely for unfamiliar tasks, because both planning and performing require the active use of cognitive resources, whereas well-learned tasks do not require planning and can be performed without much thought (Kanfer & Ackerman, 1989; Lane, 1982).

This suggests that specific goal difficulty moderates the relationship between task component complexity and the amount of planning performed. When goal difficulty is low, group members are likely to respond to increased task complexity by engaging in more planning. However, when a difficult goal is assigned, performance activities are likely to take precedence over planning, and planning may be low regardless of the level of task complexity.

Hypothesis 3. When goal difficulty is low, the amount of planning will be low and will increase with task component complexity. When goal difficulty is high, the amount of planning will remain low regardless of task component complexity.

Quality of the planning process. Smith, Locke, and Barry (1990) suggested five factors that characterize high-quality group planning, including effective communication and interaction between organizational members, a future orientation, and a systematic analysis of the organization's strengths, weaknesses, opportunities, and threats. They suggest that a high-quality planning process is comprehensive and considers the roles of, and incorporates input from, group members.

Goal difficulty and task component complexity were expected to interact to affect the quality of the planning process. This hypothesis was based on research showing that individuals often develop poor strategies for tasks of moderate to high complexity when difficult goals are assigned (Earley, Connelly, & Ekegren, 1989; Earley & Lee, 1987;

Earley & Perry, 1987; Huber, 1985). These effects are particularly strong when individuals are unfamiliar with the complex task (Earley, Lee, & Hanson, 1990). Locke and Latham (1990) explained these findings by suggesting that challenging goals "create a level of arousal that interferes with the cognitive processes involved in the selection and development of a task-specific plan" (p. 312). These same findings were expected to hold for groups so that the combination of a difficult goal and complex task would produce low-quality planning.

Hypothesis 4. The quality of the planning process will be low when both task component complexity and goal difficulty are high, compared with when tasks are simple or goals are easy.

Timing of planning. Timing of planning is the sequence of planning and performing that the group uses to perform the task. This study focused on two types of planning: preplanning and in-process planning. Preplanning takes place before group members begin working on the task, such that plan modification during implementation is not expected (Faludi, 1973). It "is a process of deciding in advance what is to be done, how it is to be done, and who is going to do it" (Steiner, 1971, p. 4). In-process planning occurs during task performance (Faludi, 1973) and proceeds by determining the first few actions to be taken and then implementing those actions. The remainder of the plan for future actions is developed and adapted as information is generated from performing the task (Freidmann, 1966). In-process planning allows group members to make immediate progress on the task because they do not need to develop a complete plan before performing.

Group-goal difficulty and task component complexity were hypothesized to have independent, direct effects on timing of planning. First, when goal difficulty increased, but the time allotted to perform the task remained constant, group members were expected to become more concerned about making immediate progress toward the goal. Because preplanning interferes with immediate progress toward the goal, group members working toward difficult goals were expected to engage in in-process planning rather than preplanning.

Second, task complexity was expected to have a positive effect on the amount of in-process planning. A large amount of information needs to be considered when planning for the performance of a complex task. To avoid this difficulty, group members may plan only portions of the task at a time. In addition, performing an unfamiliar, complex task can result in high uncertainty concerning what should be done (Galbraith, 1977). An unfamiliar task of high component complexity will be characterized by high uncertainty because the gap between the information required and the information available will be large. In-process planning reduces this uncertainty because information gained while working on the task can be integrated into the plan.

> *Hypothesis 5.* As goal difficulty increases, the proportion of total planning time spent in in-process planning will increase.
> *Hypothesis 6.* As task component complexity increases, the proportion of total planning time spent in in-process planning will increase.

Planning, task complexity, and group performance. The relationships between the amount, quality, and timing of planning and group performance should depend on task complexity. First, the amount of planning engaged in by group members plays a less important role in determining performance for a simple task than for a complex task because fewer acts need to be planned and coordinated. Second, the extent to which planning actually improves performance depends on the quality of the planning process. Smith et al. (1990) found that when the planning process was of high quality, the amount of time spent planning and group performance were positively related. However, when the planning process was of low quality, this relation was negative. Thus, the quality of the planning process should moderate the relationship between the amount of planning and group performance.

Finally, the impact of timing of planning on group performance was expected to be moderated by the component complexity of the task. Because in-process planning reduces up-front knowledge requirements and decreases the high level of uncertainty associated with a task of high component complexity, in-process planning should lead to better performance than preplanning when a task is complex (Lindblom, 1959). When task component complexity is low, in-process planning and preplanning should be equally effective because the previously stated benefits of in-process planning are not realized on a simple task.

> *Hypothesis 7.* The amount of planning will be more positively related to group performance as task component complexity increases.
> *Hypothesis 8.* The amount of planning will be positively related to group performance when the quality of the planning process is high. When the quality of the planning process is low, the amount of planning will be negatively related to group performance.
> *Hypothesis 9.* At high levels of task component complexity, in-process planning will enhance group performance. At low levels of task component complexity, in-process planning will have no effect.

Assumptions underlying the model. The validity of this model requires the following assumptions. First, the task environment must remain stable so that task demands do not change. Second, group members must have the skills and abilities necessary to plan and perform the task. Third, group members must accept the group goal as something they intend to achieve. Finally, feedback about progress toward the goal during task performance must be available. Without feedback, the group will be unable to evaluate its progress toward the goal, the effectiveness of its plan, or the adequacy of its effort.

Method

Subjects

Two-hundred and twenty-four undergraduates (56 groups of 4 people each) from two universities in the midwestern United States participated in this study. Subjects were paid $5.00 or received class credit for their participation, depending on the university. Four subjects volunteered for each experimental session, and each group of 4 was randomly assigned to one of four conditions in a 2 (component complexity) × 2 (goal level) design.

Task

Each group of 4 subjects was asked to build an assigned number of structures using Tinkertoys, pipe cleaners, aluminum foil, string, styrofoam balls, wooden craft sticks, cardboard triangles, macaroni, popcorn kernels, scissors, and glue. They were given a detailed color illustration of the structure to be built and were allowed 15 min to plan and perform the task. A video camera recorded the work session.

Experimental Conditions

The four experimental conditions presented either an easy or difficult group goal and a high or low level of task component complexity. Component complexity was operationalized as the number of unique acts required to build a structure, while holding constant the total number of acts across the two structures. The total number of acts and the number of unique acts were determined in a pretest by observing a group performing the task and identifying the acts that were performed by individual group members. The simple structure required the performance of 26 acts, 3 of which were unique (i.e., connect Tinkertoys, glue sticks together, and stick into styrofoam). The complex structure also required 26 acts; however, 11 of those acts were unique (see the Appendix for the list of required acts).

Goal difficulty was manipulated by varying the number of structures to be build during a 15-min work session. Pretest results were used to determine the level of an easy goal that could be attained by over 80% of the groups and a difficult goal that could be attained by under 20% of the groups. Groups in the difficult-goal condition were asked to build nine structures in 15 min. Groups in the easy-goal condition were asked to build three structures in 15 min.

Procedure

Subjects were scheduled for one 35-min experimental session. They were told they would work together to build structures from the available materials. The group was shown an illustration of the structure. The concept of component complexity, the number of unique acts required to build each structure, and the complexity of the structure was explained. Supplies required to build the structures were then shown to the group. Next, subjects were told they had 15 min to build nine structures (a difficult goal) or three structures (an easy goal).

Subjects then completed a preexperimental questionnaire designed to assess their understanding of the two manipulations and their acceptance of the group goal. Next, group members were brought into a room containing a video camera, a large table, all necessary supplies, and an illustration of the structure to be built, and began working on the task. Subjects were informed when 2 min remained in the work session. At the end of the work session, the experimenter counted the completed structures. Then, subjects individually filled out a postexperimental questionnaire.

Self-Report Measures

Manipulation checks. The effectiveness of the component complexity manipulation was assessed in a preexperimental questionnaire by asking subjects to report the number of unique actions required to build each structure. Subjects also completed a three-item scale that assessed their understanding of the component complexity of the structure (α = .83). Subjects were asked how complex the model would be to assemble and if they believed each structure required very few or very many unique actions. The complexity items were measured on either 5- or 7-point scales; therefore, responses to each item were converted to z scores and combined into a single scale. Subjects also reported the level of the assigned goal and responded to a two-item scale that was designed to assess their understanding of the difficulty of the goal (α = .67). Subjects were asked how difficult the goal was and whether they believed the group could attain the goal.

Group-goal commitment. Subjects completed a five-item scale, in the preexperimental questionnaire, designed to measure commitment to working toward attainment of the group's goal (α = .79) and adapted from Hollenbeck, Williams, and Klein (1989). Subjects responded on 7-point Likert-type scales ranging from *strongly agree* to *strongly disagree*.

Task uncertainty. Subjects responded to three items, within the postexperimental questionnaire, designed to assess the level of uncertainty experienced regarding how to perform the task ($\alpha = .59$).

Mediating Variables

Effort. Effort was measured by counting the number of task-relevant physical actions performed by each group member during the first 15 s of every minute that the group worked on the task. The task-relevant actions counted as one unit of effort were similar to the task-relevant acts required to build each model; however, differences stemming from varied performance strategies existed.[1] Each action that required the exertion of effort and resulted in progress toward completing a structure was counted as a unit of effort.

For each 15-s period, a coder watched the videotape and counted the number of task-relevant actions performed by each group member. The measures of effort were averaged across group members. These averages were summed across time periods to determine the total effort exerted. One coder coded all the groups, and a second coder coded one-third of the groups. The effort scores across the coders were highly correlated ($r = .94, p < .001$).

Amount of planning. To test the hypothesized model, the planning variables were partitioned to parallel the characteristics of the task. The present task involved three components: group performance, individual performance, and use of supplies. Because differences across task components could not be identified with a composite measure of planning, each component was examined separately.

Written transcripts of all conversation among group members while working on the task were produced from work-session videotapes. Three

measures were created by counting the number of statements concerning (a) the quality and use of supplies, (b) individual performance plans identifying and clarifying acts to be performed; and (c) group performance plans discussing who was going to perform an act and how individual outputs would be integrated. Any statement that was not coded as planning was coded as miscellaneous.

Two undergraduate research assistants, unaware of the hypotheses, individually coded the content of the transcripts of the work sessions. First, coders were instructed to assign codes to each speaking turn (the unit of observation). Second, a single unit could receive two or more codes if warranted. Third, a single unit could be given the same code twice, but this could occur only if the subject topic of the unit changed (e.g., planning for gluing sticks versus attaching balls). Fourth, questions asked by group members were not counted as planning, but answers to the questions were. Questions about the plan were excluded because they did not directly determine a component of the plan, but rather resulted in answers that did.

Each assistant identified units and coded for content one-half of the transcripts. Both assistants independently coded nine transcripts, which were used to assess coding reliability. Reliability for unit identification (Folger, Hewes, & Poole, 1984) was high, with little disagreement about the number of units (Guetzkow's $U = .0099$; Guetzkow, 1950). Interpretive reliability (Folger et al., 1984), representing the consistency with which codes were assigned to units and corrected for chance agreement (Cohen, 1960), was .80 for supplies, .68 for acts, and .76 for coordination.

Planning quality. Two additional assistants independently viewed the videotapes and rated the quality of each group's planning. They completed a nine-item questionnaire for each group, modeled after one used by Smith et al. (1990) and designed to identify the quality of the planning process related to the identification of supplies, the development of individual performance plans, and the development of group performance plans. Five-point scales were used for each item; sample

---

[1] These differences removed the possibility of a confound between the measurement of effort and performance. The discovery of more (or less) efficient ways of performing the task resulted in varying relationships between effort and performance.

items ranged from *subdivision of the task was not discussed* (1) to *subdivision of the task was discussed* (5) and *resources were not considered* (1) to *resources were specifically considered* (5).

The interrater Pearson correlations used to estimate agreement were all significant and ranged from .39 to .77 ($M = .59$, $SD = .13$). The ratings for each item were averaged across coders.

A principal-components analysis was performed to assess the internal validity of the scales used to measure planning quality. A three-component solution was sought, and an oblique rotation was used because components were expected to be correlated. Three components were obtained, explaining 61% of the total variance. These components were made up of items slightly different from those hypothesized and were labelled *Planning quality—Individual roles* (Component 1, three items, $\alpha = .79$), *Planning quality—Supplies* (Component 2, two items, $\alpha = .55$), and *Planning quality—Group Coordination* (Component 3, four items, $\alpha = .74$). The correlation between Components 1 and 2 was .019; the correlation of these components with Component 3 was .38 and $-.01$, respectively.

Timing of planning. The amount of preplanning engaged in by group members was determined by counting the number of planning statements that occurred before any group member performed any task-relevant act. In-process planning was operationalized as any subsequent planning statements. The first task-relevant act occurred when the first two pieces of the model were put together to form one piece. A measure of the proportion of time spent in in-process planning as opposed to preplanning was created by dividing the number of in-process planning statements by the total number of planning statements.

Group Performance

Group performance was measured by counting the number of structures completed by the group in the allotted 15 min. Examination of the variance of group performance within each treatment group showed that the assumption of homogeneity of variance across goal conditions was not met (for the easy goal, $s^2 = 0.96$; for the difficult goal, $s^2 = 4.58$; Cochran's $C = .825$, $p < .001$). A log transformation was applied to the performance data to eliminate the differences in variance across the goal conditions (for the easy goal, $s^2 = .001$, and for the difficult goal, $s^2 = .004$).

Results

Manipulation Checks

Group members' ability to accurately report and evaluate goal difficulty and task component complexity was assessed to ensure that the manipulations before the work session were salient.

Goal difficulty. Ninety-eight percent ($n = 218$) of the subjects reported their assigned group goal accurately. Subjects in the difficult-goal condition reported a more difficult goal ($M = 4.24$, $SD = 0.94$) than did subjects in the easy-goal condition ($M = 2.94$, $SD = .93$), $F(1, 199) = 101.5$, $p < .001$. Task complexity also affected goal difficulty reports. Group members rated the goal as more difficult in the high-complexity condition ($M = 3.73$, $SD = 1.04$, $n = 99$) than in the low-complexity condition ($M = 3.42$, $SD = 1.21$, $n = 104$), $F(1, 199) = 6.99$, $p < .01$.

Task complexity. Ninety-seven percent ($n = 214$) of the subjects gave accurate reports of the number of unique acts required to build each structure. Subjects in the high-complexity condition rated the structure as more complex ($M = .72$, $SD = .50$) than did subjects in the low-complexity condition ($M = -.69$, $SD = .54$), $F(1, 200) = 373.44$, $p < .001$.[2] No other effects were significant.

Group Members' Commitment to the Group Goal

Subjects were moderately committed to working toward goal attainment ($M = 4.51$, $SD = 0.85$). No differences in goal commitment were found across experimental conditions.

---

[2] This scale is reported in standardized form.

Task Uncertainty

Subjects reported higher uncertainty regarding how to perform the task in the high-complexity condition ($M = 5.33$, $SD = 0.97$) than in the low-complexity condition ($M = 4.97$, $SD = 1.11$), $F(1, 220) = 6.62$, $p < .01$.

Test of the Model

Means, standard deviations, and correlations among variables are presented in Table 17.1. Cell means and standard deviations are listed in Table 17.2.

To test the model presented in Figure 17.1, nine hierarchical regression analyses were performed (see Table 17.3). The first equation examined the antecedents of effort (Hypothesis 1) in a three-step hierarchical regression. In the second, third, and fourth equations, hierarchical regressions were performed to test the impact of the interaction between goal difficulty and task component complexity on each of the amount-of-planning variables (Hypothesis 3). In the fifth, sixth, and seventh equations, hierarchical regressions were performed to test the impact of the interaction between goal difficulty and task component complexity on each of the quality-of-planning variables (Hypothesis 4). The eighth equation examined the antecedents of timing of planning (goal difficulty

[Hypothesis 5] and task complexity [Hypothesis 6]). The ninth regression equation examined the antecedents of group performance (effort [Hypothesis 2], Amount of Planning × Task Complexity [Hypothesis 7], Amount of Planning × Quality of Planning [Hypothesis 8], and Task Complexity × Timing of Planning [Hypothesis 9]). Goal difficulty was included in the ninth equation to account for other mediators (e.g., cooperation) not examined in this study (Weldon & Weingart, in press).

Results from Equation 1 support Hypothesis 1. Goal difficulty had a positive effect on effort. Results from Equation 9 showed that Hypothesis 2 was also supported; effort had a positive effect on group performance. An independent test of the role of effort as a mediator of the goal difficulty–performance relationship was conducted using a variation of a procedure suggested by Baron and Kenny (1986). First, effort was regressed on goal difficulty ($r = .75$, $p < .001$). Second, the residual of group performance (after partialing out other variables in the model) was regressed on goal difficulty ($r = .62$, $p < .001$). Finally, the residual of group performance was regressed on goal difficulty and effort ($\beta = .36$, $p < .05$; $\beta = .34$, $p < .05$; respectively). Because goal difficulty preceded effort temporally in this study, and the relationship between goal difficulty and performance

TABLE 17.1. Means, Standard Deviations, and Correlations Among Variables

Variable	M	SD	1	2	3	4	5	6	7	8	9	10	11
1. Performance	4.57	2.06	–										
2. Log (performance)	1.16	0.06	–	–									
3. Task component complexity	–	–	–	−.07	–								
4. Goal difficulty	–	–	–	.60**	.00	–							
5. Effort	17.56	6.09	–	.66**	−.29*	.75**	–						
Amount of planning													
6. Supplies	12.61	8.91	–	−.04	.38**	−.10	−.20	–					
7. Individual	20.29	8.95	–	.05	−.03	−.10	.05	.32**	–				
8. Group	9.16	5.59	–	.17	.14	.18	.20	.49**	.33**	–			
Quality of planning													
9. Supplies	2.12	0.67	–	.04	.47**	.11	−.07	.41**	.15	.28*	–		
10. Individual role	2.44	0.62	–	.20	−.10	.06	.14	−.09	.11	.31**	−.11	–	
11. Group coordination	1.74	0.40	–	.30*	−.34**	.31**	.41**	−.12	.24*	.35**	−.15	.44**	–
12. In-process planning	0.83	0.09	–	.11	−.09	.34**	.29*	.12	.37**	.17	−.01	−.15	.16

Note: $N = 56$ groups.
*$p \leq .05$, **$p \leq .01$.

TABLE 17.2. Cell Means and Standard Deviations of Dependent Variables

	Task component complexity			
	Low		High	
Variable	*M*	*SD*	*M*	*SD*
Easy-goal condition				
Performance	3.50	1.29	3.21	0.58
Log (performance)	1.13	0.04	1.12	0.02
Effort	15.00	4.67	11.12	1.65
In-process planning	0.81	0.09	0.79	0.12
Amount of planning				
Supplies	11.29	9.17	15.71	10.31
Individual	21.14	7.94	21.14	11.57
Group	8.50	4.52	7.86	6.37
Quality of planning				
Supplies	1.79	0.55	2.30	0.75
Roles	2.56	0.44	2.25	0.50
Coordination	1.79	0.35	1.44	0.25
Difficult-goal condition				
Performance	5.93	2.23	5.64	2.13
Log (performance)	1.20	0.06	1.19	0.06
Effort	23.62	4.00	20.51	3.96
In-process planning	0.88	0.07	0.86	0.08
Amount of planning				
Supplies	7.14	3.98	16.29	8.42
Individual	20.00	7.80	18.86	8.78
Group	8.21	5.77	12.07	5.06
Quality of planning				
Supplies	1.82	0.52	2.57	0.57
Roles	2.44	0.71	2.51	0.77
Coordination	1.96	0.40	1.77	0.42

Note: N = 56 groups.

decreased, $t(53) = 8.34$, $p < .01$ (Williams's modification of the Hotelling test [Kenny, 1987]) but remained significant when effort was included in the equation, effort partially mediated the goal–performance relationship. Equation 1 also showed that increased task component complexity resulted in less effort.

Equations 2, 3, and 4 showed that Hypothesis 3 was not supported. Task component complexity did not interact with goal difficulty to influence amount of planning for supplies, individual performance plans, or the group's performance plan. However, task component complexity did have an unexpected direct positive effect on the amount of planning about supplies.

Results of Equations 5, 6, and 7 did not support Hypothesis 4. Goal difficulty did not interact with task component complexity to affect the quality of planning about supplies, individual performance, or group performance. However, direct effects were found. Goal difficulty had a positive impact on the quality of planning about group coordination. Increased task component complexity led to ratings of higher quality planning for the use of supplies and lower quality planning for group coordination.

Equation 8 supported Hypothesis 5. Goal difficulty increased in-process planning. Equation 8 also showed that timing of planning did not vary with component complexity. Thus, Hypothesis 6 was not supported.

Equation 9 (Step 2) showed that the amount of planning about supplies interacted with task complexity to influence group performance. Decomposition of the model (using a method suggested by Stolzenberg, 1980) showed that the amount of planning about supplies had a positive effect on performance for the simple structure ($\beta = .53$). For the complex structure, the amount of planning about supplies had a negative effect on performance ($\beta = -.26$). This finding was opposite that predicted in Hypothesis 7.

Step 2 of Equation 9 also showed that the amount of planning about individual performance interacted with the quality of planning about individual roles to influence group performance. The relationship between the amount of planning for individual performance and actual group performance became stronger as the quality of planning for individual roles improved. This result supported Hypothesis 8 because the amount of planning was negatively related to performance when planning was of the lowest quality.[3] However, Hypothesis 9 was not supported, because task component

---

[3] Step 2 of Equation 9 also shows that amount of planning for individual performance, the quality of planning for roles, and the timing of planning had significant negative effects on performance. However, these direct effects were not interpreted because they did not reach significance until interactions involving those variables were added to the equation (see Cohen, 1978, for a discussion of the interpretation of partialed products).

Table 17.3. Regression Analysis of Group Goal Model

Dependent variable/ independent variable	β^a	ΔR^2	F^b	R^2	F
Impact of goal difficulty and task complexity on mediators					
Equation 1: Effort					
Step 1					
Goal difficulty (GD)	.75**				
Task component complexity (TCC)	−.29***			.64	47.16**
Step 2					
TCC × GD	.05	.00	0.15	.64	30.98**
Equation 2: Amount of planning—supplies (AP–S)					
Step 1					
GD	−.10				
TCC	.38**			.16	4.97**
Step 2					
TCC × GD	.23	.02	1.12	.18	3.69*
Equation 3: Amount of planning—individual (AP–I)					
Step 1					
GD	−.10				
TCC	−.03			.01	0.28
Step 2					
TCC × GD	−.05	.00	0.05	.01	0.20
Equation 4: Amount of planning—group (AP–G)					
Step 1					
GD	.18				
TCC	.14			.05	1.47
Step 2					
TCC × GD	.35	.04	2.36	.09	1.79
Equation 5: Quality of planning—supplies (QP–S)					
Step 1					
GD	.11				
TCC	.47**			.24	8.27**
Step 2					
TCC × GD	.15	.01	0.47	.25	5.64**
Equation 6: Quality of planning—roles (QP–R)					
Step 1					
GD	.06				
TCC	−.10			.01	0.34
Step 2					
TCC × GD	.27	.02	1.30	.03	0.66

Dependent variable/ independent variable	β^a	ΔR^2	F^b	R^2	F
Equation 7: Quality of planning—coordination (QP–C)					
Step 1					
GD	.31*				
TCC	−.34**			.21	7.19**
Step 2					
TCC × GD	.19	.01	0.38	.22	5.30**
Equation 8: In-process planning					
Step 1					
GD	.34*				
TCC	−.09			.12	3.78*
Step 2					
TCC × GD	.00	.00	0.99	.12	2.47
Impact of group goal, task complexity, and mediators on group performance					
Equation 9: Log (performance)					
Step 1					
Effort	.51**				
Timing	−.15				
AP–S	.11				
AP–I	.09				
AP–G	−.08				
QP–S	−.01				
QP–R	.10				
QP–C	.02				
TCC	.06				
GD	.29			.50	4.53**
Step 2[c]					
Effort	.35*				
Timing	−.34				
AP–S	.26				
AP–I	−1.47*				
AP–G	.61				
QP–S	−.16				
QP–R	−.89*				
QP–C	.24				
TCC	.02				
GD	.52**				
TCC[d] × AP–S	−.90*				
TCC × AP–I	.06				
TCC × AP–G	−.20				
TCC × Timing	0.58				
AP–S × QP–S	.46				
AP–I × QP–R	2.02**				
AP–G × QP–C	−.69	.15	4.24*	.65	4.23**

[a] Standardized beta weights are reported. [b] This F statistic refers to the change in R^2 attributable to each step. [c] The variables entered in Step 1 of this equation are relisted in Step 2 to display the change in betas estimated for main effects that occurred after the interactions were added to the equation.
* $p \le .05$. ** $p \le .01$.

complexity did not interact with timing of planning as estimated in Equation 9. Finally, Equation 9 showed that goal difficulty had a direct positive effect on group performance. Overall, 65% of the variance in group performance was explained.

Discussion

The results of this study are diagrammed in Figure 17.2. These results provided partial support for the model and are discussed in relation to the more general input–process–output model proposed by Hackman and Morris (1975).

Effort

Effort was found to be an important mediating process in the input–performance relationship (Hackman & Morris, 1975) for groups working on this task. The data revealed four important findings regarding effort. First, group-goal difficulty influenced group performance through the effort exerted by group members (Hypotheses 1 and 2 were supported). Based on an independent measure of effort, these results show the importance

of effort in performance groups, which supports previous findings based on self-reports. Second, group members working on the complex task exerted less effort than did those working on the simple task. This result might have occurred because, although the structures were designed to require an equal number of acts and differed only in the number of unique acts, group members building the simple structure performed more actions than did group members building the complex structure. It may be that the design of the simple structure required the performance of more codable actions than did the complex structure.

Third, effort was the only significant mediator of the positive relationship between a group goal and group performance on this task. Goal difficulty also had a direct positive effect on performance not mediated by effort or planning. This finding suggests that other mediators should be explored. For example, Weldon and Weingart (in press) suggested that cooperation, morale-building communication, and concern for task dimensions not related to the goal also mediate the group-goal–performance relationship.

Fourth, effort was the only process variable having a significant zero-order correlation with group

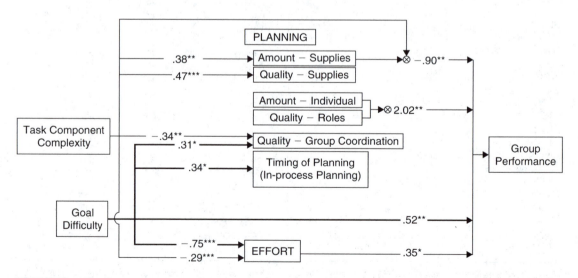

FIGURE 17.2 ■ Significant regression coefficients. Bold lines represent goal difficulty effects. *$p \le .05$, ** $p \le .01$, ***$p \le .001$.

performance, suggesting that performance for both structures was determined more by effort than by planning. This may have occurred because the two tasks (i.e., structures) were not different enough from one another in complexity to warrant large differences in planning behavior. However, the results from the regression analysis show that planning did influence performance after the effects of other variables were removed from performance. This suggests that planning had an effect on performance independent of goal difficulty and effort but that the amount of variance in performance explained by planning was small.

Amount of Planning

The second process variable examined in this study, the amount of planning performed by group members, did not behave as expected. Less planning was expected to occur when a group was working toward a difficult goal on a complex task because of planning's potential interference with task performance (Hypothesis 3). However, group members working on the complex task did not plan less under difficult goal conditions. These results contradict those of Shure et al. (1962). This contradiction may be due to differences in the cost of planning in the two experiments (Weldon et al., 1991). As Weldon et al. pointed out, group members could plan only through written notes in Shure et al.'s study, and writing these notes interfered with task performance, making planning quite costly. In the current task, planning may not have been as disruptive, because group members could plan verbally while performing some acts physically. As a result, increasing goal difficulty did not reduce planning.

However, task complexity did influence planning about supplies. Group members engaged in more planning about supplies when working on the complex task than they did when working on the simple task. This is not surprising because the complex task involved more unique acts, which required a greater variety of supplies. Increased planning about supplies did not influence performance in the manner predicted by the theory. It was hypothesized

(Hypothesis 7) that increased planning would contribute more to the performance of a complex than a simple task. Instead, the opposite occurred. Discussing the high variety of supplies required to build the complex structure appears to have led to confusion and reduced performance, whereas discussing the few types of supplies required for the simple structure may have served to clarify the task. These results point to the need for further research exploring the critical contingency (Hackman & Morris, 1975) of task complexity in determining whether planning is an important determinant of group performance.

Quality of Planning

Task complexity and goal difficulty influenced the quality of planning but did not interact as hypothesized (Hypothesis 4). A difficult goal combined with a complex task did not interfere with high-quality planning. Given that the goal was quite difficult, it is possible that the high-complexity task was not complex enough to produce this result. Or, it may be that the quality of the plan developed is more important than the quality of the planning process. Future research should distinguish between the quality of the planning process and the quality of the plan produced and should test their relative effects.

Instead of the hypothesized interaction, the results show the direct effects of input variables on group interaction processes suggested in Hackman and Morris's (1975) model of group performance effectiveness. Three direct effects were found. First, group members working toward a difficult goal engaged in higher quality planning for coordination than did those working toward an easy goal. Therefore, increased goal difficulty motivated group members to focus on developing an effective plan for the reintegration of subtasks. Second, task component complexity reduced the quality of planning for coordination. One explanation for this finding is that group members' focus on supplies interfered with their concern for group coordination because of the time constraints. The negative (but nonsignificant) correlation between quality of planning about supplies and quality of planning about coordination ($r = -.15$) lends some support to this explanation. Third, groups working on the complex task engaged in higher quality planning for supplies than did groups working on the simple task. Just as increased task complexity motivated more planning about supplies, it also motivated higher quality planning about supplies.

Although the quality of planning for coordination and the quality of planning for the use of supplies were influenced by goal difficulty and task complexity, neither aspect of planning quality was related to group performance (counter to Hypothesis 8). It may be that high-quality planning for coordination was not necessary for this task because coordination was possible through direct observation of co-workers' progress on their individual subtasks. However, when group members cannot freely observe their co-workers' performance, explicit, comprehensive planning for coordination should be necessary for interdependent work. Future research should test the relationship between quality of planning and performance under these different conditions.

However, the quality of planning for individual roles did interact with the amount of planning for individual activities to influence group performance (Hypothesis 8). As the quality of planning for individual roles increased, the relationship between the amount of planning and performance became stronger, yet planning about individual performance was not related to the level of the group goal or to the complexity of the task. It is possible that individual goals, in combination with group goals, are necessary to motivate individual performance planning because individual goals serve to focus group members on individual performance (Matsui, Kakuyama, & Onglatco, 1987; Mitchell & Silver, 1990).

Timing of Planning

Timing of planning was influenced by the difficulty of the group's goal, supporting Hypothesis 5. Groups working toward a difficult goal engaged in less preplanning than did those working toward an easy goal. Thus, it appears that the difficult goal

increased group members' concern about making immediate progress on the task. To cope with this concern, group members altered when they planned rather than decrease how much they planned. However, group members did not increase their in-process planning in response to higher task complexity (counter to Hypothesis 6), even though they reported more uncertainty about the high- than the low-complexity task. Although group members in the low-complexity condition experienced more certainty about the task, it is possible that they still experienced enough uncertainty to avoid preplanning. Or, it may be that group members' concern about immediate progress on the task was so strong that it overwhelmed any thoughts of pre-planning that the low-complexity groups may have entertained.

Because group members engaged in very little preplanning, supporting previous research showing that groups do not spontaneously engage in formal planning (Hackman et al., 1976), and because there was little variance in preplanning across groups, the relationship between timing of planning and group performance could not be ascertained. Additional research using groups that engage in preplanning is necessary to address the relationship between timing of planning and group performance.

Conclusions

This article contributes to the group goal-setting and group performance literature in several ways. First, this study demonstrates the importance of planning for individual roles. Previous group goal-setting studies have not mentioned this aspect of planning; instead, they have focused on planning for group performance (e.g., Smith et al., 1990) or have not made distinctions between planning for individual versus group performance (e.g., Weldon et al., 1991). By distinguishing these two types of planning, it was discovered that planning for group coordination was not important to actual group performance in this study. This result may change for tasks with higher coordination requirements (e.g., Mitchell & Silver, 1990), in that the nature of the task determines whether effort or planning is important to group performance (Hackman &

Morris, 1975). Thus, this result should hold for tasks with lower coordination demands, such as those used in this study.

Second, this article addresses the role of in-process planning in the performance process. Previous group performance research has primarily focused on planning as a process that occurs before task performance (e.g., Hackman & Morris, 1975; McGrath, 1984) rather than examining how plans are developed and modified during task performance. However, this study shows that in-process planning can be central in performance groups and might constitute a larger percentage of planning than does preplanning. Future research should focus on conditions that motivate preplanning as opposed to in-process planning and on conditions that influence the effectiveness of each one. For example, providing independent blocks of planning time (Shure et al., 1962), or limiting the time pressure to produce products, might motivate groups to preplan, and the amount of time pressure and planning's interference with the performance process might determine the appropriateness of preplanning versus in-process planning.

Third, rather than examine planning for performance of the task as a whole, as has been done in past research, planning for individual performance, group performance, and the use of supplies was studied. This is important because results showed that the amount and quality of planning differed across distinct aspects of the task. It is possible that group members engage in more and higher quality planning for task characteristics that are salient. Research is needed to further address planning for specific aspects of performance. To do this, theory that guides the identification and examination of task characteristics important to planning must be developed.

Fourth, this study shows that the mediating roles of different aspects of planning cannot be assumed. Whereas Hackman and Morris (1975) suggested that behavioral norms can be altered to influence task performance strategies and that alterations in task design influence effort, this study shows that both goal difficulty (a behavioral norm) and task complexity (an aspect of task design) influenced the amount and quality of planning for various aspects of the task. However, only the amount of planning about supplies was related to performance. This finding shows that a group goal and the task itself do not necessarily cue group members to behave in ways that actually contribute to group performance. Instead, it seems that a goal cues planning for salient task characteristics, even though salient task characteristics are not always the most important ones for effective task performance. A theory explaining which task characteristics are most salient when working toward a group goal versus those that are important to group performance should be developed.

Fifth, this study employed objective measures of group process. This differs from most group goal-setting studies, which have simply made inferences about the processes that mediate the group-goal effect (e.g., Becker, 1978) or have collected self-reports of group process (e.g., Smith et al., 1990). Independent measures are useful because they provide direct observation of process, avoiding potentially biased self-reports and incorrect inferences. To truly understand the group goal-setting effect, independent, more objective measures are essential.

In generalizing the results of this study, some issues should be noted. First, additional factors that are not mediators of the group-goal effect may influence group performance. Although this model was not designed to explain all the variance in task performance, future research should focus on other important determinants of group performance, in addition to group goals. Other factors include different types of task complexity (i.e., coordinative and dynamic complexity), structural and cultural characteristics of the organization, and the technology available to the work group.

In addition, this study focused on the introduction of a goal to an ad hoc group working on an unfamiliar task under high time pressure. Additional research is needed to determine whether these findings generalize to existing groups working on familiar and unfamiliar tasks with less time pressure. Moreover, this study examined performance during only one work session. As the task becomes more familiar over time, the role of effort and planning in the goal–performance relationship may change. Additional research should address this issue.

REFERENCES

Baron, R. M., & Kenny, D. A. (1986). The moderator–mediator variable distinction in social psychological research: Conceptual, strategic, and statistical considerations. *Journal of Personality and Social Psychology, 51,* 1173–1182.

Baumler, J. V. (1971). Defined criteria of performance in organizational control. *Administrative Science Quarterly, 16,* 340–348.

Becker, L. J. (1978). Joint effect of feedback and goal setting on performance: A field study of residential energy conservation. *Journal of Applied Psychology, 63,* 428–433.

Bryan, J. F., & Locke, E. A. (1967). Goal setting as a means of increasing motivation. *Journal of Applied Psychology, 51,* 274–277.

Cohen, J. (1960). A coefficient of agreement for nominal scales. *Educational and Psychological Measurement, 20,* 37–46.

Cohen, J. (1978). Partialed products *are* interactions; partialed powers *are* curve components. *Psychological Bulletin, 85,* 858–866.

Earley, P. C., Connelly, T., & Ekegren, G. (1989). Goals, strategy development, and task performance: Some limits on the efficacy of goal setting. *Journal of Applied Psychology, 74,* 24–33.

Earley, P. C., & Lee, C. (1987). *Expertise training in goal setting: Importance of expertise in strategy development.* Unpublished manuscript.

Earley, P. C., Lee, C., & Hanson, L. A. (1990). Joint moderating effects of job experience and task component complexity: Relations among goal setting, task strategies, and performance. *Journal of Organizational Behavior, 11,* 3–15.

Earley, P. C., Northcraft, G. B., Lee, C., & Lituchy, T. R. (1990). Impact of process and outcome feedback on the relation of goal setting to task performance. *Academy of Management Journal, 33,* 87–105.

Earley, P. C., & Perry, B. C. (1987). Work plan availability and performance: An assessment of task strategy priming on subsequent task completion. *Organizational Behavior and Human Decision Processes, 39,* 279–302.

Earley, P. C., Wojnaroski, P., & Prest, W. (1987). Task planning and energy expended: Exploration of how goals influence performance. *Journal of Applied Psychology, 72,* 107–114.

Faludi, A. (1973). *Planning theory.* New York: Pergamon Press.

Folger, J. P., Hewes, D. E., & Poole, M. S. (1984). Coding social interaction. In B. Dervin & M. Voigt (Eds.), *Progress in communication studies* (pp. 115–161). Norwood, NJ: Ablex.

Freidmann, J. (1966). The institutional context. In B. M. Gross (Ed.), *Action under planning* (pp. 31–67). New York: McGraw-Hill.

Galbraith, J. R. (1977). *Organization design.* Reading, MA: Addison-Wesley.

Garland, H. (1982). Goal levels and task performance: A compelling replication of some compelling results. *Journal of Applied Psychology, 67,* 245–248.

Guetzkow, H. (1950). Unitizing and categorizing problems in coding qualitative data. *Journal of Clinical Psychology, 6,* 47–58.

Guetzkow, H. (1968). Differentiation of roles in task-oriented groups. In D. Cartwright & A. Zander (Eds.), *Group dynamics: Research and theory* (pp. 512–526). New York: Harper & Row.

Hackman, J. R., Brousseau, K. R., & Weiss, J. A. (1976). The interaction of task design and group performance strategies in determining group effectiveness. *Organizational Behavior and Human Performance, 16,* 350–365.

Hackman, J. R., & Morris, C. G. (1975). Group tasks, group interaction process, and group performance effectiveness: A review and proposed integration. In L. Berkowitz (Ed.), *Advances in experimental social psychology* (Vol. 8, pp. 45–99). New York: Academic Press.

Hollenbeck, J. R., Williams, C. R., & Klein, H. J. (1989). An empirical examination of the antecedents of commitment to difficult goals. *Journal of Applied Psychology, 74,* 18–23.

Huber, V. L. (1985). Effects of task difficulty, goal setting, and strategy on performance of a heuristic task. *Journal of Applied Psychology, 70,* 492–504.

Kanfer, R., & Ackerman, P. L. (1989). Motivation and cognitive abilities: An integrative/aptitude–treatment interaction approach to skill acquisition. *Journal of Applied Psychology, 74,* 657–690.

Kenny, D. A. (1987). *Statistics for the social and behavioral sciences.* Boston: Little, Brown.

Klein, H. J., & Mulvey, P. W. (1989, August). *Performance goals in group settings: An investigation of group and goal processes.* Paper presented at the 48th Annual Meeting of the Academy of Management, Washington, DC.

Lane, D. M. (1982). Limited capacity, attention allocation, and productivity. In W. Howell & E. Fleishman (Eds.), *Information processing and decision making* (pp. 121–156). Hillsdale, NJ: Erlbaum.

Latham, G. P., & Yukl, G. A. (1975). Assigned versus participative goal setting with educated and uneducated woods workers. *Journal of Applied Psychology, 60,* 299–302.

Lindblom, C. E. (1959). The science of "muddling through." *Public Administration Review, 19,* 79–88.

Locke, E. A., & Latham, G. P. (1990). *A theory of goal setting and task performance.* Englewood Cliffs, NJ: Prentice-Hall.

Locke, E. A., Shaw, K. N., Saari, L. M., & Latham, G. P. (1981). Goal setting and task performance: 1969–1980. *Psychological Bulletin, 90,* 125–152.

Matsui, T., Kakuyama, T., & Onglatco, M. L. (1987). Effects of goals and feedback on performance in groups. *Journal of Applied Psychology, 72,* 407–415.

McGrath, J. E. (1984). *Groups: Interaction and performance.* Englewood Cliffs, NJ: Prentice-Hall.

Mitchell, T. R., & Silver, W. S. (1990). Individual and group goals when workers are interdependent: Effects on task strategies and performance. *Journal of Applied Psychology, 75,* 185–193.

Naylor, J. C., & Dickinson, T. L. (1969). Task structure, work structure, and team performance. *Journal of Applied Psychology, 53,* 167–177.

Pritchard, R. D., Jones, S. D., Roth, P. L., Stuebing, K. K., & Ekeberg, S. E. (1988). Effects of group feedback, goal setting, and incentives on organizational productivity. *Journal of Applied Psychology, 73*, 139–145.

Shure, G. H., Rogers, M. S., Larsen, I. M., & Tassone, J. (1962). Group planning and task effectiveness. *Sociometry, 25*, 263–282.

Smith, K. G., Locke, E. A., & Barry, D. (1990). Goal setting, planning, and organizational performance: An experimental simulation. *Organizational Behavior and Human Decision Processes, 46*, 118–134.

Steiner, G. A. (1971). *Comprehensive managerial planning*. Oxford, OH: Planning Executives Institute.

Stolzenberg, R. M. (1980). The measurement and decomposition of causal effects in nonlinear and nonadditive models. In K. F. Schuessler (Ed.), *Sociological methodology* (pp. 459–488). San Francisco: Jossey-Bass.

Weingart, L. R., & Weldon, E. (1991). Processes that mediate the relationship between a group goal and group member performance. *Human Performance, 4*, 33–54.

Weldon, E., Jehn, K., & Pradhan, P. (1991). Processes that mediate the relationship between a group goal and improved group performance. *Journal of Personality and Social Psychology, 61*, 555–569.

Weldon, E., & Weingart, L. R. (in press). Group goals and group performance. *British Journal of Social Psychology*.

Wood, R. E. (1986). Task complexity: Definition of a construct. *Organizational Behavior and Human Decision Processes, 37*, 60–82.

Appendix

Required Acts for Each Structure

Unique act	No. of repetitions
Simple structure	
1. Connect Tinkertoys	10
2. Glue sticks	6
3. Stick styrofoam	10
Complex structure	
1. Connect Tinkertoys	9
2. Glue sticks	2
3. Stick styrofoam	2
4. Glue macaroni or popcorn	3
5. Wrap pipe cleaner	1
6. Wrap aluminum foil	1
7. Cut thread	1
8. Thread needle	1
9. String styrofoam balls	3
10. Tie thread at ends	2
11. Put paper into Tinkertoy	1

Received August 31, 1990
Revision received February 21, 1992
Accepted February 26, 1992 ■

Transactive Memory: Learning Who Knows What in Work Groups and Organizations

Richard L. Moreland*

In many organizations, work that was once done by individuals is now done by groups. These groups include top management teams, cross-functional teams, self-managed work teams, and special task forces. The trend toward group work in organizations has generated a parallel trend toward group research among many social scientists, especially organizational psychologists (see Levine & Moreland, 1990; Sanna & Parks, 1997). Much of that research focuses on work group performance. Organizations often use groups to improve worker productivity and the available evidence suggests that this goal is often achieved (see Carr, 1992; Hoerr, 1989; Katzenbach & Smith, 1993; Montebello & Buzzota, 1993; Wellins, Byham, & Dixon, 1994). However, work groups sometimes fail (see Dubnicki & Limburg, 1991; Dumaine, 1994; Hackman, 1998; Vogt & Hunt, 1988) and even when they seem to succeed, further improvements in worker productivity may still be possible. A careful theoretical analysis of work group performance, investigating causal factors that could be managed by an organization, is thus potentially valuable (Dunphy & Bryant, 1996).

Improving the Performance of Work Groups by Managing Their Composition

Several theoretical models of work group performance have been offered (e.g., Cohen, 1994; Gladstein, 1984; Hackman, 1987). These models differ from one another in various ways, but most of them identify group composition as an important factor. Composition refers to the number and types of workers who belong to the group (Moreland & Levine, 1992a). Many individual characteristics, including not only the workers' abilities but also their demographic characteristics, opinions, and personality traits, might be relevant to a group's tasks. The group's performance of such tasks could thus be improved by altering its composition for those characteristics. Changes to both the central tendency and the variability of group members might be helpful. For example, the group's central tendency could be improved by (a) hiring workers with desirable characteristics or firing workers with undesirable characteristics, (b) training workers in ways that strengthen desirable characteristics or weaken undesirable characteristics, or (c) linking the group to outsiders with desirable characteristics (see Ancona & Caldwell, 1988). Changes in group

*University of Pittsburgh.

variability could also be made, using similar tactics, but such changes can influence performance in more complex ways (Moreland, Levine, & Wingert, 1996). Although diversity can improve a group's performance, such gains are often offset by losses arising from conflict among group members.

Altering a work group's composition is an appealing strategy, but it may not always be practical. Fortunately, another strategy is usually possible (see Hackman & Morris, 1975), namely making better use of whatever characteristics a group's members already possess. This requires that someone know not only which worker characteristics are relevant to the group's tasks, but also how those characteristics are distributed among group members. Traditionally, a manager was always assumed to have and use such knowledge. But in many organizations, work groups are now becoming self-managed (Lawler, Mohrman, & Ledford, 1992; Manz & Sims, 1993; *Training and Development*, 1994). In these groups, which may not have a leader, who is responsible for identifying task-relevant characteristics and evaluating their distribution among group members (see Kozlowski, Gully, Salas, & Cannon-Bowers, 1996; Saavedra & Kwun, 1993)? The latter task can be especially difficult in an era when the activities of many work groups are rapidly changing (Herr, 1993; Parker, Wall, & Jackson, 1997; Waller, 1997), temporary employees come and go more often (Barsness, 1996; Feldman, 1995; Mantel, 1994), and regular group members are likely to be diverse (Jackson & Alvarez, 1993).

Perhaps the performance of some work groups, especially self-managed teams, could be improved by helping members learn more about one another so that they could make better use of the group's human resources. Among those resources, the task knowledge of group members, often referred to as the group's "intellectual capital" or "knowledge assets" (Marquardt, 1996; Stewart, 1995a), seems especially important. An analysis of how group members could share task knowledge with one another can be found in Wegner's work on transactive memory (see Wegner, 1987, 1995; Wegner, Giuliano, & Hertel, 1985).

Transactive Memory and Work Group Performance

Wegner was the first to analyze transactive memory, especially as it occurs in couples. He noted that people often supplement their own memories, which are limited and can be unreliable, with various external aids. These include objects (e.g., address or appointment books) and other people (e.g., friends or coworkers). Wegner was especially interested in the use of people as memory aids. He speculated that a transactive memory system may develop in many groups to ensure that important information is remembered. This system combines the knowledge possessed by individual group members with a shared awareness of who knows what. So when group members need information, but cannot remember it themselves or doubt that their memories are accurate, they can turn to each other for help. A transactive memory system can thus provide a group's members with more and better information than any of them could remember alone.

The potential benefits of transactive memory for a work group's performance are clear. When group members know more about each other, they can plan their work more sensibly, assigning tasks to the people who will perform them best. Coordination ought to improve as well because workers can anticipate rather than simply react to each other's behavior (see Murnighan & Conlon, 1991; Wittenbaum, Vaughan, & Stasser, 1998). As a result, they can work together more efficiently, even if task assignments are unclear. Finally, problems should be solved more quickly and easily when workers know more about one another because they can then match problems with the people most likely to solve them (see Moreland & Levine, 1992b). Once those people are identified, they can be asked for help or the problems can simply be given to them to solve.

If these claims seem unconvincing, then just imagine a work group (e.g., subjects in most laboratory experiments on group performance) whose members are ignorant about who knows what. In such a group, sensible planning would not be possible. Tasks might be assigned to people at random, or maybe on the basis of such irrelevant cues as appearance or demeanor. The group might fail to plan its work at all, allowing people to work at whatever tasks they liked best (see Weingart, 1992). It would be surprising if either of these options led to an optimal use of the group's resources. Coordination would probably suffer as well, as confused members struggled to make sense of each other's behavior, and problems might become more troublesome, as unqualified members tried to solve them.

Do work groups really perform better when their members know who is good at what? Unfortunately, research on transactive memory is scarce. Most of that research involves couples rather than groups (see Hollingshead, 1998; Wegner, Erber, & Raymond, 1991), and tasks that are not much like those faced by most workers. There is, however, some indirect evidence that transactive memory can improve a group's performance. It comes from research on group decision making that investigates whether the quality of a group's decisions is related to how well its members can recognize expertise (see Libby, Trotman, & Zimmer, 1987; Stasser, Stewart, & Wittenbaum, 1995; Yetton & Bottger, 1982). Expertise recognition is clearly an important part of transactive memory because it not only guides group members to those individuals who have useful information, but also allows members to evaluate whatever information they obtain by considering its sources. And decision making clearly plays an important role in many of the tasks that work groups perform (Guzzo & Salas, 1995).

In general, groups make wiser decisions when their members are better at recognizing expertise. Some of the most interesting work in this area is done by Henry (see Henry, 1993, 1995a, 1995b; Henry, Strickland, Yorges, & Ladd, 1996), and by Littlepage and his colleagues (Littlepage, Schmidt, Whisler, & Frost, 1995; Littlepage & Silbiger, 1992; Littlepage, Robison, & Reddington, 1997). In Henry's research, subjects are usually asked to answer trivia questions (e.g., When was the safety pin invented?), first alone and then in small groups. Afterwards, they evaluate one another's expertise.

The ability of group members to recognize expertise is assessed by comparing those evaluations with measures of actual expertise. Henry has been especially interested in discovering ways to improve the recognition of expertise by groups. I will consider that issue later on, but for now, two general findings from Henry's research seem noteworthy. First, a group's members can form (without discussion) shared beliefs about their relative expertise, and those beliefs are often accurate. Second, groups make better decisions when their members' beliefs about relative expertise are more accurate.

Littlepage and his colleagues usually ask subjects in their research to solve problems posed by hypothetical scenarios (e.g., Desert Survival) involving the survival of a group in a dangerous environment after a traumatic event. Subjects solve these problems alone at first, then in groups. Afterwards they evaluate one another's expertise. The ability of group members to recognize expertise is again assessed by comparing these evaluations with measures of real expertise. Like Henry, Littlepage and his colleagues find that group members form shared beliefs about their relative expertise. Those beliefs are not always accurate, however, perhaps because the decision-making task in these studies is relatively complex. Nevertheless, Littlepage and his colleagues do find, like Henry, that groups make better decisions when their members' beliefs about relative expertise are more accurate.

These and other findings suggest that transactive memory systems, which reflect the ability of group members to recognize expertise, may indeed be valuable for work groups. But how do such systems develop, and can they be managed? In most work groups, the development of transactive memory systems is probably a slow and gradual process. As workers spend time together, performing the same or similar tasks, they become familiar with one another. Each person's strengths and weaknesses are noted and then taken into account as group members learn to work together productively. Although no one has yet studied this process directly, many studies have shown that groups perform better if their members are more familiar with one another (see

Argote, 1993; Barsness, 1996; Goodman & Shah, 1992; Gruenfeld, Mannix, Williams, & Neale, 1996; Jehn & Shah, 1997; Kanki & Foushee, 1989; Larson, Foster-Fishman, & Keys, 1994; Murnighan & Conlon, 1991; Watson, Kumar, & Michaelsen, 1993; Watson, Michaelsen, & Sharp, 1991). Kanki and Foushee (1989), for example, found that the performance benefits of keeping an aircrew's members together across simulated flights were strong enough to overcome such dangers as boredom and fatigue. Goodman and his colleagues (see Goodman & Shah, 1992) found in several studies that coal mining crews whose members worked together more often were more productive and had fewer accidents. Finally, Murnighan and Conlon (1991) found that the best string quartets in Britain, as measured by such criteria as album sales, concert bookings, and newspaper or magazine reviews, were those whose members had played together longest.

There are, of course, several reasons why familiarity among its members might help a group to perform better. Familiarity often strengthens group cohesion, for example, which can improve group performance (Mullen & Copper, 1994). None of the studies I just cited actually showed that familiarity was helpful because it helped group members to recognize one another's expertise. Moreover, familiarity is sometimes harmful rather than helpful for group performance (see Katz, 1982; Kim, 1997; Leedom & Simon, 1995) and it does not always improve the recognition of expertise among group members (see Libby, Trotman, & Zimmer, 1987; Littlepage, Schmidt, Whisler, & Frost, 1995). Findings such as these may be anomalies, but they can also provide valuable evidence about boundary conditions for the effects of familiarity on expertise recognition (and transactive memory systems).

Let us suppose, for a moment, that transactive memory systems do develop in work groups as their members become more familiar with each other and that the performance of such groups improves as a result. What are the implications of all this for managers? One clear implication is that work groups should be kept intact as much as possible. Efforts should be made to minimize turnover in existing groups, for example, because the arrival

of new members and the departure of old members can disrupt transactive memory systems by changing the distribution of task-relevant knowledge within a group. It is impossible to eliminate turnover, so efforts should also be made to improve group socialization processes in ways that help newcomers and oldtimers become familiar with one another, thereby restoring the transactive memory systems in their groups. Suggestions for such changes are offered by Levine and Moreland, in chapter 12 of this volume (Thompson, Levine, & Messick, 1999). Finally, when new work groups are formed, their members should be trained together rather than apart (Moreland, Argote, & Krishnan, 1998) so that transactive memory systems develop more quickly. If the members of a new group are trained separately or in special groups created solely for training purposes, they will know less about one another and thus have more trouble working together productively.

Transactive Memory Through Group Training

My own research over the past few years has focused on transactive memory systems in newly formed work groups. Linda Argote, from Carnegie Mellon University, has been my collaborator in all this research, and several graduate students have helped with it as well (see Liang, Moreland, & Argote, 1995; Moreland, Argote, & Krishnan, 1996, 1998). We were intrigued by the fact that many organizations ask employees to work in groups, yet few organizations provide training for such work. Moreover, the group training that is provided often seems misguided because it is based on two dubious assumptions, namely that employees can be taught a generic set of social skills that will allow them to adapt to any work group, and that adapting to a work group is unrelated to learning how that group's tasks are performed. If these assumptions are indeed wrong, then group work requires a different kind of training—employees should learn to perform tasks in the same groups where they will be working. We have explored this issue in several laboratory experiments on small groups whose members were trained to perform a complex task. In these experiments, various versions of group and individual training were provided and their effects on group performance were compared. Our two general predictions were that work groups would perform better if their members were trained together rather than apart and that the performance benefits of such training would depend on the development of transactive memory systems.

Experiment One

The subjects in our first experiment (Liang, Moreland, & Argote, 1995) were 90 students from undergraduate business courses at Carnegie Mellon University. These students were randomly assigned to small work groups, each containing three persons of the same sex. Each group was asked to assemble the AM portion of an AM-FM radio, using materials from a radio kit. That kit included a circuit board and dozens of electronic components. The subjects were asked to insert each component into its proper place on the circuit board and then to wire all of the components together.

Two types of training were provided. Half of the groups were randomly assigned to an individual training condition and the other half were assigned to a group training condition. In the individual training condition, group members were trained separately, whereas in the group training condition, they were trained together. The content of training was exactly the same in both conditions.

The experiment was carried out in two hour-long sessions held a week apart. The first session focused on training and the second session focused on testing. In the individual training condition, each subject participated in a personal training session, but later worked with other subjects in a group for the testing session. In the group training condition, the members of each group participated in both sessions together.

At the start of the experiment, subjects were told that the purpose of our research was to examine how training affects work group performance. Everyone knew that they would return later to perform the task as a group. Subjects in the individual training condition did not know who the members of that group would be, whereas subjects in the group training conditions expected to remain in the same group.

Each training session began with the experimenter demonstrating how to assemble the radio. Subjects were allowed to ask questions during this demonstration, which lasted for about 15 minutes. They were then given up to 30 minutes to practice assembling a radio themselves. In the group training condition, subjects worked together on one radio. After subjects completed their practice radios, the experimenter evaluated those radios, identifying any assembly errors and explaining how to correct them.

The testing session began with a memory test. Each group was given 7 minutes to recall how to assemble the radio. Group members collaborated on this task, recording what they remembered on a single sheet of paper. We then asked each group to actually assemble a radio. Thirty minutes were allotted for this task; subjects were told to work as quickly as possible, but also to minimize assembly errors. While assembling their radios, groups were not allowed to review their recall sheets or consult with the experimenter. Cash prizes were offered as incentives for good task performance. Finally, every subject completed a brief questionnaire that provided background information and assessed beliefs about the group and its task.

Three measures of group performance were collected and analyzed, namely (a) how well each group recalled the procedure for assembling a radio, (b) how quickly each group assembled its radio, and (c) how many assembly errors each group made. We found no differences between training conditions in how quickly the groups assembled their radios, but there were significant differences in both procedural recall and assembly errors. As expected, groups whose members were trained together recalled more about how to assemble a radio, and made fewer assembly errors, than did groups whose members were trained apart.

Videotapes of the groups working on their radios allowed us to explore several factors that could have produced these performance effects. We were most interested in three factors associated with the operation of transactive memory systems. The first of these factors was *memory differentiation*, or the tendency for group members to specialize in remembering different aspects of the assembly process. For example, one person might remember where radio components should be inserted in the circuit board, while another person remembers how those components should be wired together. The second factor was *task coordination*, or the ability of group members to work together efficiently on the radio. There should be less confusion, fewer misunderstandings, and greater cooperation in groups with stronger transactive memory systems. The final factor was *task credibility*, or the level of trust among group members in one another's radio knowledge. In groups with stronger transactive memory systems, members should make fewer public claims of expertise, be more open to one another's suggestions, and criticize one another's work less often.

Three other factors that seemed relevant to group performance and might have varied across training conditions were also coded from the videotapes. The first factor was *task motivation*, or how eager group members were to win the prizes we offered by assembling their radio quickly and accurately. The second factor was *group cohesion*, or the level of attraction among group members. The final factor was *social identity*, or the tendency for subjects to think about themselves as group members rather than individuals.

Two judges (one blind to both our hypotheses and the training conditions), were given a list of behaviors exemplifying these six factors. With those behaviors in mind, the judges watched each videotape and made an overall rating of the group on each factor. The only exception was social identity, which was evaluated by counting how often personal versus collective pronouns (e.g., "I" vs. "We") were used by group members while they assembled their radio. The ratio of collective pronouns to all pronouns was computed and used as a measure of social identity (see Cialdini et al., 1976; Veroff, Sutherland, Chadiha, & Ortega, 1993). The coding reliability for all six factors was assessed by computing intraclass correlations. Those correlations indicated good reliability in the judges' evaluations. Scores on the three transactive memory factors were strongly correlated, so they were made into a composite index by averaging them

together for each group. We did not assume that the other three factors were related, nor did they prove to be correlated with each other, so they were examined separately in our analyses.

Did training affect how group members behaved while they assembled their radios? As we expected, scores on all three of the transactive memory factors, and on the transactive memory index, were significantly higher in the group training condition. Among the other three factors, only social identity differed significantly across training conditions. Higher social identity scores were found for groups whose members were trained together rather than apart.

These findings suggested that the effects of group training on performance may indeed have been mediated by transactive memory. To explore that issue, we performed a series of multiple regression analyses (see Baron & Kenny, 1986) in which training methods were represented by a dummy variable, transactive memory was measured using the composite index, and group performance was measured by assembly errors. We began by regressing first assembly errors and then transactive memory index scores on training methods. Training methods had significant effects in both analyses, as the results described earlier suggest. Assembly errors were then regressed on training methods and transactive memory index scores simultaneously. The effects of transactive memory on assembly errors remained significant, but the effects of training methods became nonsignificant, indicating that the effects of training methods on group performance were mediated by transactive memory. In other words, training methods no longer mattered when variability among groups in transactive memory was taken into account. Analogous regression analyses involving the social identity factor were also performed, but their results provided no evidence of mediation.

This experiment provided direct evidence that a group's performance can be improved by training its members together rather than apart. As we expected, groups remembered more about how to assemble the radios, and produced radios with fewer flaws, when their members were trained together. We also expected and found stronger transactive memory systems in groups whose members were trained together. The members of those groups were more likely to specialize at remembering different aspects of their task, coordinate their work activities better, and show greater trust in one another's expertise. Finally, transactive memory systems were responsible for the positive effects of group training on group performance, just as we expected.

Experiment Two

Our second experiment was designed with three goals in mind. First, it was important to replicate the results of our initial experiment, so we recreated the same individual and group training conditions and reexamined their effects on group performance.

A second goal was to evaluate alternative explanations for our results. Newly formed groups often experience special problems, such as anxiety about acceptance, interpersonal conflicts, and uncertainty about group norms (LaCoursiere, 1980; Tuckman, 1965), that can limit their performance. Training the members of a work group together provides more time for them to resolve these problems. This suggests that enhanced development might contribute to the performance advantages of group training. Another alternative explanation for our results involves strategic learning. Working in groups creates a variety of coordination problems (see Wittenbaum, Vaughan, & Stasser, 1998). Some of those problems can be solved through simple strategies that are relevant to almost any group (see, for example, Johnson & Johnson, 1998). These generic strategies, which include building commitment to the group and organizing its activities, require little knowledge about any specific group. Training the members of a work group together provides them with more opportunities to employ such strategies. This suggests that strategic learning might contribute as well to the performance advantages of group training.

To evaluate these alternative explanations, two new training conditions were developed for the second experiment. One of these was identical to the individual training condition except that a brief team-building exercise was conducted after the training session. This exercise (see McGrath, 1993) was meant to foster group development. Group members were asked to create a quiz that the university could use to evaluate students who wanted to serve as mentors for freshmen during their fall orientation. Another new condition was identical to the group training condition except that each group was scrambled between its training and testing sessions—subjects who were trained together were separated by reassigning everyone to new groups. This change was not announced until the end of the training session.

The team-building condition was meant to encourage group development without providing the kinds of information group members needed to develop transactive memory systems. The reassignment condition was meant to disable whatever transactive memory systems group members had already developed by making such systems irrelevant, leaving strategic learning as the only major benefit of group training. If group development and/or strategic learning are indeed responsible for the performance advantages of group training, then the performance of groups in these two new conditions should be good. But if the performance advantages of group training depend on transactive memory systems, then the performance of those groups should be poor. Groups lacked transactive memory systems in the team-building condition, and in the reassignment condition, those systems were no longer relevant.

The third goal for this experiment was to explore the impact of turnover on transactive memory systems. One benefit of such systems is that each member of a work group can rely on the others for information about various aspects of the task. But what if someone leaves the group, taking with him or her valuable knowledge that nobody else possesses? This problem could have arisen in the reassignment condition, where groups experienced sudden and dramatic turnover after their training sessions. By analyzing how those groups reacted to that challenge, we hoped to learn something about the effects of turnover on group training and performance.

The subjects for this experiment were 186 students enrolled in introductory psychology courses at the University of Pittsburgh. Many of the procedures were the same as those in our first experiment. Once again, subjects were randomly assigned to small, same-sex work groups. The task and materials were the same and each group again participated in both training and testing sessions. However, the training sessions in this experiment were modified slightly for groups in the individual training conditions. Rather than participating in separate sessions, the members of these groups were trained in the same room at the same time, but could not observe or interact with one another while they practiced assembling their radios. This made the experiences of subjects in the individual and group training conditions more comparable. Another minor procedural modification involved the testing sessions. At the beginning of each session, before working on their recall sheets, all subjects were asked to complete a brief questionnaire. Aside from these two changes, the training and testing sessions (including time limits) were carried out just as they were before.

Our initial analyses focused on evaluating the two new training conditions. On their questionnaires, the subjects made ratings indicating their agreement or disagreement with the answers to various questions about their groups. Some of those questions involved feelings about group development (e.g., "Does this work group seem more like one group or three separate individuals?"), whereas others involved thoughts about transactive memory systems (e.g., "How much do you think the other members of this work group know about your skills at assembling the radio?"). The ratings in each of these categories were strongly correlated, so they were averaged together (first within subjects and then within groups) to create indices of group development and transactive memory for each group. Scores on the group development index were significantly higher in the group training and the team-building conditions than in the individual training or the reassignment conditions. And scores on the transactive memory index were significantly higher in the group training condition than in the individual training, team-building, or reassignment conditions.

These two new conditions thus seemed to affect groups in the ways that we hoped. The team-building condition encouraged group development without producing transactive memory systems, whereas the reassignment condition disabled transactive memory systems by making them irrelevant.

Our next set of analyses focused on group performance. Once again, no differences were found in how quickly groups in different training conditions assembled their radios. There were, however, significant differences in procedural recall and assembly errors. As we expected, group training led to better performance on both of these measures than did any of the other training methods, which did not differ from one another.

Videotapes of the groups were again rated by two judges, using the same procedures as before. Intraclass correlations again indicated that these ratings were made reliably. Because scores on the three transactive memory factors were again correlated strongly, they were again averaged together to create a composite index for each group. As we expected, scores on that index were significantly higher in the group training condition than in the other three conditions, which did not differ from one another. As for the other three factors, only social identity differed significantly across training conditions. Scores on that factor were higher in the group training and team-building conditions than in the individual training or reassignment conditions.

Were the effects of training methods on group performance mediated by transactive memory? Multiple regression analyses were again used to explore that issue. Once again, group performance was measured by assembly errors and the composite index served to measure transactive memory. But in these analyses, training methods were represented by three dummy variables, using a coding scheme (Cohen & Cohen, 1983) that contrasted the group training condition with the other three training conditions. As before, we began by using training methods to predict assembly errors, and then transactive memory index scores, in separate analyses. Training methods had significant effects in both analyses. We then used training methods and transactive memory index scores to predict assembly errors simultaneously. The effects of transactive memory were significant, but the effects of training methods became nonsignificant. Analogous regression analyses involving the social identity factor were also performed, but produced no evidence of mediation by that factor. So, once again, differences in group performance across training conditions were mediated by the operation of transactive memory systems, just as we expected.

The first goal for this experiment, to replicate the results of our first experiment, was thus achieved. Once again, groups whose members were trained (and remained) together outperformed groups whose members were trained in other ways, and this performance advantage depended on the operation of transactive memory systems. Another goal for this experiment was to evaluate the contributions of group development and generic learning to the performance advantages of group training. Those contributions appeared to be minimal. Groups in both the new training conditions (where transactive memory systems were either missing or disabled) performed much worse than those in the group training condition and no better than those in the individual training condition. The weak performance of groups in the reassignment condition can be taken as evidence that generic training programs, which assume that experimental learning about work groups will transfer from one group to another, are unlikely to succeed. Finally, this experiment gave us a glimpse of how turnover can affect the operation of transactive memory systems. Groups in the reassignment condition experienced sudden and dramatic turnover, disabling their transactive memory systems and thereby harming their performance. But the damage was less severe than it might have been. Although these groups performed worse than groups in the group training condition, they performed about as well as groups in the individual and team-building conditions.

Experiment Three

Our first two experiments suggested that group training really can help workers to learn who knows what about a task. But no direct measures of such

knowledge were collected in either experiment. Instead, we measured several behaviors related to the operation of transactive memory systems and then *inferred* that such systems were stronger in groups where such behaviors were more common. The primary goal for our third experiment was thus to measure more directly what the members of a work group actually know about one another. We expected to find, as our earlier results suggested, that group members would know more about one another if they were trained together rather than apart. We also expected such knowledge to be *shared* more often if group members were trained together. Shared knowledge is a key feature of transactive memory systems (see Wegner, 1987, 1995). A secondary goal for this experiment was to see what role social loafing (see Karau & Williams, 1993) might play in group training and performance. Training a work group's members together could encourage some of them to take advantage of the others by learning only those aspects of a task that seem most interesting. Because such workers never expect to perform the whole task on their own, they may hope that other members of the group will compensate for their ignorance by performing whatever aspects of the task they failed to learn.

The subjects for this experiment were 78 students enrolled in introductory psychology courses at the University of Pittsburgh. Many of the procedures were identical to those in our first two experiments. The subjects were again assigned randomly to small, same-sex work groups. The task and materials were the same and every group participated in both training and testing sessions. During the first session, each group received either individual or group training, and training sessions were conducted in the same manner as our second experiment. But a week later, when the testing sessions were held, important procedural changes were made. We began these sessions by asking every subject to complete a brief questionnaire. Up to 10 minutes were allotted for this task. Then, as usual, the subjects were asked first to complete a recall sheet and then to assemble a radio as quickly and accurately as possible. The standard time limits were imposed on both tasks. But in this experiment, the subjects were asked to perform those tasks *individually*. In fact, they were not allowed to observe or talk with one another while working at either task. This was an unpleasant surprise for the subjects, who were told during their training sessions that they would later be working on the radios in groups.

The questionnaire measured in various ways what each group's members knew about one another's radio expertise. The first question simply asked subjects to describe, in their own words, each person's strengths and weaknesses at building radios. Responses to this question were later rated by two judges (one blind to training conditions) for their overall level of detail. Intraclass correlations indicated that these ratings were made reliably. In the next part of the questionnaire, subjects were asked to rate how skillful each member of their group was at different aspects of building a radio. These ratings included how much each person could remember about the procedure for assembling radios, how quickly that person could assemble a radio, and how many errors such a radio would contain. The third part of the questionnaire was similar except that subjects were asked to rank each member of their group (from best to worst) for those same skills. The questionnaire ended with two unusual questions regarding the distribution of expertise among group members. One question asked subjects to guess what percentage of the knowledge needed to build a radio well was possessed by everyone in their group (shared knowledge), rather than by just some members (unshared knowledge). The other question asked subjects to rate how similar the errors would be in radios built by different members of their group.

Responses from the questionnaires were used to produce three indices for each group. These measured (a) the *complexity* of group members' beliefs about one another's radio expertise, (b) the *accuracy* of those beliefs, and (c) the level of *agreement* about the distribution of expertise. The complexity index was produced using the first question and the last two questions on the questionnaire. Subjects' responses on each question were first averaged within groups, then standardized (because the questions used different response formats), and finally (because they were strongly correlated) averaged together to produce a complexity index. As we expected, complexity was significantly greater in groups whose members were trained together rather than apart. When group members were trained together, they wrote more detailed analyses of one another's strengths and weaknesses at building radios, guessed that less of the information needed to build radios was known by everyone in their group, and expected more dissimilar errors to occur if the members of their group built radios alone.

The accuracy index was produced using the various rating and ranking questions on the questionnaire. The rating questions involved such radio-building skills as procedural recall, speed of assembly, and assembly errors. Subjects' answers to those questions revealed their *beliefs* about how strong those skills were in each group member. Because each of the subjects later completed a recall sheet and built a radio alone, objective information was available about how strong those skills really were. This made it possible to measure the accuracy of subjects' beliefs about one another. For a given skill, we first correlated a subject's ratings of the group's members with their actual performance. This yielded three correlations for each subject, reflecting that person's accuracy at perceiving the skills of every group member. Next, the subject's correlations were transformed (using Fisher's r-to-Z procedure) and averaged together. The resulting figures were then averaged within groups to produce a single score for each group. Subjects' responses to the ranking questions on the questionnaire were processed in much the same way. The result of these computations was a set of six accuracy scores for each group, derived from its members' ratings or rankings of three radio-building skills. Those scores were strongly correlated, so they were averaged together to yield an accuracy index for each group. As we expected, significantly greater accuracy was found in groups whose members were trained together rather than apart.

The agreement index was produced in a similar way. Once again, we used the rating and ranking questions, but this time each subject's responses were correlated with those of the other group members rather than with any actual performance information. This produced three correlations for each subject, reflecting that person's agreement with other members about the distribution of skills within the group. These scores were processed in the same way as before, creating a set of six agreement scores for each group. Those scores were also strongly correlated, so once again we averaged them together to produce an agreement index for each group. Significantly greater agreement was found in groups whose members were trained together rather than apart, as we expected.

These results show that training a work group's members together rather than apart can indeed help to produce a transactive memory system. When group members were trained together, they had more complex beliefs about the distribution of radio-building skills within their group. In particular, they were more likely to see one another as unique individuals, each with special skills that other group members might not possess. Beliefs about the distribution of radio-building skills were also more accurate, and more likely to be shared, in groups whose members were trained together. The advantages of creating a work group whose members share complex, yet accurate beliefs about who is good at what are easy to imagine. Such a group should perform very well.

An assumption underlying our earlier experiments was that indirect and direct measures of transactive memory systems would be strongly correlated. That is, behaviors involving memory differentiation, task coordination, and task credibility should occur more often in groups whose members have complex, accurate, and shared beliefs about one another's expertise. Was that assumption correct? All the subjects in our third experiment worked alone during their testing sessions, so no videotapes of group performance were made. However, we did make videotapes of the training sessions in that experiment. Videotapes of groups whose members were trained together were thus evaluated by two judges, one blind to the research hypotheses. These judges rated the same three behavioral factors as in our earlier experiments, using the same procedures. Once again, intraclass correlations indicated that these evaluations were

made reliably. Because scores on the three factors were strongly correlated, each group's scores were averaged to create a composite index. That index was then correlated with the questionnaire indices of complexity, accuracy, and agreement for each group. All these correlations were positive and significant, suggesting that indirect, behavioral measures of transactive memory systems (like those used in our earlier experiments) can detect their operation in work groups.

Finally, this experiment also provided some information about how social loafing might affect group training and performance. As noted earlier, the usual performance measures (procedural recall, speed of assembly, assembly errors) were collected from every subject during the testing sessions. Although performance on these measures was a bit worse in groups whose members were trained together rather than apart, none of those differences was significant, whether individuals or groups were used as the units of analysis. We should not dismiss the problem of social loafing, but these results suggest that it is not severe. Apparently, group members learn their task about as thoroughly whether they are trained together or apart.

Alternate Routes to Transactive Memory

Our first three experiments showed that a transactive memory system can substantially improve a work group's performance, and that training the group's members together is a reliable way to produce such a system. Given those findings, we considered several directions for future research. The impact of turnover among workers on transactive memory systems, for example, seemed worth exploring in more detail. As time passes, turnover is inevitable for most work groups, and as we noted earlier, turnover can be harmful when a group's performance depends on its transactive memory system. As members come and go, that system must be modified to reflect changes in the distribution of expertise within the group. When turnover is frequent and/or unexpected, such modifications may be difficult to make, raising doubts among group members about who really knows what. A group that relied on such knowledge to perform its tasks might thus have more trouble coping with turnover than a group whose members never knew much about one another's expertise. Of course, when turnover is infrequent and/or expected, a group with a transactive memory system may be able to use that system to its advantage. For example, if someone is expected to leave the group, then a transactive memory system should help the group to identify what task knowledge is about to be lost and respond in ways that will limit the harmful effects of that loss. One tactic might be to arrange for the person who is leaving to transfer his or her task knowledge to other group members. Another tactic might be to seek a new member whose task knowledge resembles that of the person who is leaving. In either case, a transactive memory system would be helpful to the group, both for identifying what kinds of knowledge are relevant and for generating consensus about which tactic to use.

Thoughts about turnover, however, put us in a pragmatic frame of mind and led us to consider other ways in which transactive memory systems might develop in work groups. Training a group's members together and then keeping them together seems appealing in principle, but may be difficult or impossible in practice. What are the alternatives? Why not, for example, try to provide the members of a newly formed group the same kinds of information about one another that they would have acquired through group training? One approach is to simply inform everyone in the group about what role each member should play when the group's task is performed. Stasser, Stewart, and Wittenbaum (1995) used this approach in an experiment on information sharing. Groups of college students were given clues about a hypothetical murder and then asked to use that information to discover who (among several suspects) committed the crime. Within each group, some clues were distributed to everyone, whereas other clues were distributed in ways that provided each member with expertise on a different suspect. The latter clues were critical for solving the crime. Every group was informed that its members might receive different sets of clues. Information about exactly who knew what, however, varied from one group to another. In some

groups, but not others, each member was privately informed about his or her own area of expertise. And in some groups, but not others, everyone's area of expertise was publicly announced. Simply informing everyone about their own expertise had little impact on group performance, but announcing everyone's expertise helped group members to talk about more of the critical clues and thereby solve the crime. In other words, providing the kind of information found in transactive memory systems improved group performance.

While planning our fourth experiment, we chose a subtler approach, namely to provide groups with information that could be used to identify the distribution of expertise among their members. But that information was not organized or summarized in any simple way, forcing each group to draw its own conclusions about who knew what. This experiment is still in progress, but should be completed soon, with help from Sean Fitzgerald and Larissa Myaskovsky. Some preliminary findings are worth reporting here, however, if only to clarify the issues that concern us.

At present, 120 subjects (about two thirds of our target sample) have taken part in the experiment. All of the subjects are students enrolled in introductory psychology classes at the University of Pittsburgh. Many of the procedures are identical to those in our earlier experiments. Subjects are again randomly assigned to small, same-sex work groups. The task and materials are the same and every group participates in both training and testing sessions. During its first session, each group receives either individual or group training, and training sessions are conducted in the same manner as our second experiment. But a week later, during the testing sessions, some procedural changes are made. Half of the groups that received individual training, and all of the groups that received group training, are treated just as before. But the other half of the individual training groups are given feedback about the skills of their members. This feedback takes the form of a chart that shows how well group members built radios during the training session. Five skills (resistors, capacitors, transistors, other components, wiring) form the chart's rows and three rankings (first place, second place, third place) form its columns. Every cell in the chart contains the name of a group member, along with (in parentheses) a score revealing how well that person performed that aspect of radio building. These scores are calculated by subtracting the number of errors that person made from the number of points that could have been earned. Higher scores thus indicate better performance.

Groups in the feedback condition have 5 minutes to review their charts. We were not sure whether or how the information on those charts would be used, but as it turns out, most groups seem very interested in that information, reviewing and discussing the chart's contents as long as they can. And we have the impression (confirmed in the debriefing sessions) that many groups summarize their charts by simply identifying who is best at each aspect of the task.

From this point on, the procedure is similar to that in our second experiment. Each group is asked first to complete a recall sheet and then to assemble a radio as quickly and accurately as possible. The standard time limits are imposed on both tasks. Afterwards, all subjects are given 5 minutes to complete a brief questionnaire. That questionnaire is similar to the one in our second experiment, but also contains two new questions. One question asks subjects to rate how much the experimenter wanted their group to succeed. This question was included because we feared that groups in the feedback condition might perform well because the experimenter, who provided them with a potentially useful chart, seemed to be helping them succeed. The other question asks subjects how difficult it was to communicate with one another about the task. We included this question because one of our colleagues, Sara Kiesler at Carnegie Mellon University, suggested that an important advantage of training group members together may be the development of *jargon*—special ways of talking about the task that help workers to perform it more quickly and easily (see Lyon, 1974).

As in our earlier experiments, each group is videotaped while it works on its radio. The three behaviors related to transactive memory are being rated again, by judges blind to the research hypotheses and/or training conditions, along with three behaviors related to how subjects talk about the task. Those behaviors are (a) the overall level of task, rather than socioemotional, communication in the group; (b) apparent miscommunication among group members about the task; and (c) the use of task jargon. We are interested in whether any performance advantages remain significant even when these three behaviors are taken into account.

This experiment is not yet complete, but one important finding is emerging: Groups in the feedback condition build radios nearly as well as groups whose members were trained together, and groups in both of those conditions build radios much better than do groups whose members were trained apart. This finding suggests that there is indeed more than one way for transactive memory systems to develop in work groups. It also suggests some interesting questions about what kinds of feedback groups need for such systems to arise. Does everyone need to receive the kind of feedback contained in our charts, or would it be sufficient to provide that feedback to just one group member? Does it matter who that person is? Could the feedback in our charts be simplified? It may be sufficient to simply identify the person who is best at each aspect of the task, or even just the person whose task performance is best overall.

This last option reminded us of Henry's research on the recognition of expertise. As I noted earlier, much of that research involves a standard paradigm. Subjects are asked to answer a series of trivia questions, first alone and then in small groups. Afterwards, they evaluate one another's expertise. Comparisons between these evaluations and measures of actual expertise are then made to see how well groups can recognize expertise among their members. Using this paradigm, Henry has studied several interventions, some rather subtle, that might help groups to better recognize expertise. For example, Henry (1995b) studied two interventions involving changes in subjects' behavior during group discussions. In the first intervention, subjects were asked to develop several possible answers for each trivia question, then evaluate the likely accuracy of each answer, and finally share those evaluations with other members during group discussions. Henry believed that evaluating the relative merits of their own answers might help subjects to evaluate the relative merits of answers proposed by others. In a second intervention, subjects were asked to evaluate the answers proposed by other group members for each trivia question, and then choose (as part of the group discussion) which person seemed to have the best answer. Finally, subjects in a control condition received no instructions about how to behave, either alone or in their groups. Were the interventions helpful? The results were mixed. The second intervention produced high levels of expertise recognition, but did not surpass the control condition in that regard. The first intervention was less helpful, but still produced levels of expertise recognition that were higher than would be expected by chance.

Other interventions that Henry has studied, such as providing subjects with continuous feedback about the correct answers to the trivia questions (Henry, Strickland, Yorges, & Ladd, 1996; see also Blickensderfer, Cannon-Bowers, & Salas, 1997), or asking subjects to share, during their group discussions, any information they possess that seems relevant to those questions (Henry, 1995a), also appear to be helpful. These findings imply that there are several ways to help work groups develop transactive memory systems and thereby improve their performance. If providing a group's members direct access to information about who knows what is impossible, or seems likely to produce harmful side-effects (e.g., destabilizing group structure or causing conflict among group members), then more subtle and indirect means of fostering transactive memory systems are apparently available.

Transactive Memory Systems in Organizations

Before closing the chapter, it seems worthwhile to speculate about transactive memory systems in organizations. Do such systems develop within organizations, and if so, is it possible to manage them? Many organizations are investing considerable time, energy, and money in efforts to answer these questions (see Stewart, 1995a, 1995b, 1997). Some speculation, supported by any relevant theory

or research that can be found, may thus be warranted.

If transactive memory systems can develop in organizations, then they may well differ from the transactive memory systems of work groups. Organizations are obviously larger than work groups, for example, so their transactive memory systems should contain more (and more varied) sources of task knowledge. As a result, workers are likely to have more trouble identifying who knows what in organizations than in work groups. Organizations are less cohesive than work groups as well and tend to evoke weaker commitment from their members (Moreland & Levine, in press). People who work for the same organization, but belong to different work groups, may thus be less willing to share their task knowledge (Constant, Sproull, & Kiesler, 1996). Finally, transactive memory systems in organizations have an educational quality that is rarely found in the transactive memory systems of work groups. Once knowledge about a task has been transferred from one worker to another in an organization, the latter person is usually expected to use that knowledge independently, without returning to its source. But in a work group, someone may repeatedly ask for the same task knowledge from the same source. Transactive memory systems are thus used by work group members to make their tasks easier, rather than to learn more about those tasks.

How do transactive memory systems operate in organizations? There are several ways in which a worker, seeking knowledge about a task, might proceed. These options can be divided into two broad categories, reflecting two different approaches to the problem (see Marquardt, 1996; Robinson & Weldon, 1993). The general goal of the *interpersonal approach* is to locate a specific person (or persons) in the organization and then obtain whatever information is needed from him or her. The general goal of the *technological approach* is to obtain whatever information is needed through the use of computers. These two approaches overlap to some extent, of course. For instance, a worker who takes an interpersonal approach may sometimes rely on computers to reach his or her goal, whereas a worker who takes a technological approach may sometimes rely on people. But even if the distinction between these two approaches is rough, it may still be helpful, given how little is known about transactive memory systems in organizations.

Interpersonal Approaches

When someone is searching for task knowledge in an organization, how might the interpersonal approach be implemented? That person could start with the members of his or her own work group, asking not what they know themselves, but rather whether they know of anyone outside the group who might be helpful. Ancona and her colleagues (see Ancona, 1990; Ancona & Caldwell, 1988, 1992) have shown that successful work groups try to manage the flow of information and other resources across their boundaries by developing special activities and roles. In a study of new product development teams, for example, Ancona and Caldwell (1988) found that scout, ambassador, sentry, and guard activities occurred more often in successful teams, and that workers in those teams were more likely to play immigrant, captive, and emigrant roles. Many of these activities and roles, especially scouting and immigration, could generate information about an organization that would help work group members to enter its transactive memory system. Organizations should thus consider how to foster such activities and roles because of the benefits they can yield for work groups.

There are, of course, many other ways in which a work group's members could obtain information about their organization's transactive memory system (see Marquardt, 1996). Most organizations, for example, keep workers informed about recent events by publishing (perhaps electronically) periodic newsletters that everyone receives. Those newsletters often contain information about the accomplishments of various work groups or workers, thereby revealing who knows what in the organization. Presenting such information in the form of stories, which people appear to process more readily (see Martin, 1982), could draw more attention to that information and help workers to remember it better. Special events, such as parties, picnics, or colloquia, and certain activities, such as training exercises, can also help

workers in an organization to learn more about each other, thereby strengthening the organization's transactive memory system. Sutton and Hargadon (1996), for example, studied a product design firm in which brainstorming sessions were often held. Although the major purpose of those sessions was to produce ideas, the researchers found that brain-storming produced other benefits as well, including the development and maintenance of organizational memories. Some of those memories focused on who knew what in the organization. Finally, the transactive memory systems of some organizations are easier for workers to use because of structural features (e.g., linking arrangements, matrix organization) or practices (e.g., job rotation, cross-functional teams) that bring people from different segments of those organizations into contact with one another more often.

Finally, some people may have broader knowledge than others about what is going on in their organizations. Such knowledge often includes information about who knows what. In his chapter for this volume, for example, Burt focuses on workers who occupy structural holes in the social networks of their organizations. These workers have many weak ties (see Granovetter, 1973) with people or groups who might not otherwise come into contact with one another. As a result, they can provide valuable guidance for anyone seeking task knowledge within their organizational domains. Some organizations have formalized such activities by creating special roles, such as an ombudsman (Marquardt, 1996), whose duty is to help knowledge seekers reach someone who can provide the necessary information. In other organizations, special units (see Stewart's, 1995a, description of the PPO division at Hewlett-Packard) have been created for the same purpose. In all these organizations, workers know just where to go for information about who knows what.

My analysis of the interpersonal approach has focused so far on the identification of people in an organization who may possess the task knowledge that a worker needs. But once those people have been identified, will that worker ask them for help? Maybe he or she is too shy, would feel embarrassed to admit ignorance about the task, or is worried about becoming indebted to others for their help. And if such help is requested, are the people who can provide it willing to do so? In many organizations, those who seek task knowledge and those who can provide it are strangers who have little in common besides their employer. Task knowledge can also become a source of power (Eisenberg & Phillips, 1991; Krackhardt, 1990), something to keep rather than give away. Some workers may also keep task knowledge to themselves because they worry about how others might use it. Finally, unless they are actually rewarded by the organization for sharing their task knowledge with others, workers who do so must behave altruistically. Given all these potential problems, is knowledge about tasks ever shared? There is some evidence that it is (see Constant, Sproull, & Kiesler, 1996), especially when those who are asked to share what they know are strongly committed to the organization (Organ, 1988). There can also be several intangible rewards for workers who share their task knowledge. These rewards include personal growth (when questions from others lead to new insights), stronger self-esteem, greater prestige in the organization, and the expectation that favors will someday be repaid.

Technological Approaches

Computers have changed almost every aspect of organizations, including how workers seek and find information about their tasks. The technological approach to organizational systems of transactive memory can be implemented in several ways. First, ordinary e-mail is often used by workers seeking task knowledge (see Constant, Sproull, & Kiesler, 1996). Someone can send out a request for information to everyone in the organization, or just to people on relevant distribution lists. Once the request has gone out, all that remains is to await replies. Variations on this approach (see Stewart, 1995b) include using a private forum created for the organization by a commercial Internet provider, such as Compu-Serve, or posting and reading messages of many kinds (e.g., news, gossip, war stories, or descriptions of best practices) using software designed for information sharing, such as Lotus Notes. Once replies to a message are received,

they must be sorted for helpfulness, credibility of source, and so on. The person who requested help may then recontact some of the people who replied to his or her message, seeking clarification or elaboration of the information that was provided. In this way, a technological approach may slowly become more interpersonal. But note that such a transformation is not inevitable; people who seek and provide task information in this way need never meet and may never exchange further messages with one another. In some cases, they may even remain anonymous.

Another technological approach, one that seems a bit more sophisticated, is the use of electronic Yellow Pages. Several organizations (see Stewart, 1995a) have worked hard at developing these information resources, again using Lotus Notes or similar software. Many kinds of information, ranging from personal resumes to instructions or guidelines, and from frequently asked questions to news items, can be found in an organization's Yellow Pages. An important advantage, however, is that all of this information has been organized using keywords, so that when a specific kind of task knowledge is required, someone can enter the relevant keywords into his or her computer and either find that knowledge directly or identify other people within the organization who may possess it (note that only the latter process actually involves transactive memory). Of course, this approach works best when the information in the organization's Yellow Pages is both comprehensive and accurate, an optimal set of keywords was used to organize that information, and the worker who needs information uses the proper keywords to search for it. One can become confused by it all, so some organizations now supplement their Yellow Pages by offering personalized assistance to users (see Stewart's, 1995a, description of the Knowledge Coordinators at NatWest Markets).

Finally, several organizations (especially large consulting firms) have recently developed complex software designed to help workers learn everything that anyone in their organization knows about various tasks (see Stewart, 1997). An organizational intranet is incorporated into many of these programs so that users can jump quickly from one web page to another on their computers, following associational links among people or work groups, tasks, procedures, equipment, and so on. Again, not all web page chains involve transactive memory—some workers find the information that they need on the intranet itself, whereas others use the intranet to discover where such information can be found. Only the latter workers have learned who knows what in their organization.

What Works Best?

At this point, it is impossible to tell whether interpersonal or technological approaches are more effective for workers who are seeking task knowledge through the transactive memory systems of their organizations. Evidence regarding the effectiveness of either approach is scarce and seldom very convincing. For example, organizations favoring the technological approach often praise it highly, but that praise may reflect their concerns about the costs associated with that approach rather than its actual value. It is not necessary, of course, to "choose" one approach over the other, except that organizations with limited resources may want to know how those resources could be used most wisely. In that spirit, a brief summary of the major strengths and weaknesses of each approach seems worthwhile.

A major strength of the interpersonal approach is that knowledge about a task can be shared in ways that are tailored to a worker's specific needs. In other words, the transfer of knowledge is customized, so that the person who requested information learns exactly what he or she wanted to know. Misunderstandings can also be detected and corrected relatively quickly. A major disadvantage of this approach is that task knowledge may not be shared at all. The person who needs information may not know who to ask for it, and even when an information source can be identified, problems may still arise if the person who needs the information is afraid to request it, or the person who has the information declines to provide it. The thoughts and feelings of workers about their jobs, themselves, and one another are notoriously difficult to manage, yet they can play a vital role in the

interpersonal approach to transactive memory systems. As for the technological approach, a major strength is how much knowledge about tasks it can provide. In principle, there is no limit to the amount of information that can be stored in an organization's intranet. That information is standardized, rather than customized, and readily available to anyone who has computer access, regardless of the relationship (if any) between that person and whoever stored the information. A major disadvantage of this approach is that it can be very costly (see Stewart, 1995b), both to store all the information initially and then to update that information as time passes.

There is a clear need for more and better evidence regarding these (and perhaps other) approaches to transactive memory systems in organizations. Gathering such evidence may be difficult, but the rewards are likely to be high, well worth the effort required.

REFERENCES

Ancona, D. G. (1990). Outward bound: Strategies for team survival in an organization. *Academy of Management Journal, 33,* 334–365.

Ancona, D. G., & Caldwell, D. F. (1988). Beyond task and maintenance: Defining external functions in groups. *Group and Organizational Studies, 13,* 468–494.

Ancona, D. G., & Caldwell, D. F. (1992). Bridging the boundary: External activity and performance in organizational teams. *Administrative Science Quarterly, 37,* 634–665.

Argote, L. (1993). Group and organizational learning curves: Individual, system, and environmental components. *British Journal of Social Psychology, 32,* 31–51.

Baron, R. M., & Kenny, D. A. (1986). The moderator-mediator variable distinction in social psychological research: Conceptual, strategic, and statistical considerations. *Journal of Personality and Social Psychology, 51,* 1173–1182.

Barsness, Z. I. (1996). *The impact of contingent workers on work group effectiveness: A process model of the relationship between group composition and group effectiveness.* Unpublished doctoral dissertation, Northwestern University, Evanston, IL.

Blickensderfer, E., Cannon-Bowers, J. A., & Salas, E. (1997). Theoretical bases for team self-correction: Fostering shared mental models. In M. Beyerlein (Ed.), *Advances in interdisciplinary studies of work teams* (pp. 249–279). Greenwich, CT: JAI.

Carr, C. (1992). *Teampower: Lessons from America's top companies in putting teampower to work.* Englewood Cliffs, NJ: Prentice-Hall.

Cialdini, R. B., Borden, R. J., Thorne, A., Walker, M. R., Freeman, S., & Sloan, L. R. (1976). Basking in reflected glory: Three (football) field studies. *Journal of Personality and Social Psychology, 34*, 366–375.

Cohen, J., & Cohen, P. (1983). *Applied multiple regression/correlation analyses for the behavioral sciences*. Hillsdale, NJ: Lawrence Erlbaum Associates.

Cohen, S. G. (1994). Designing effective self-managing work teams. In M. Beyerlein (Ed.), *Advances in interdisciplinary studies of work teams* (Vol. 1, pp. 67–102). Greenwich, CT: JAI.

Constant, D., Sproull, L., & Kiesler, S. (1996). The kindness of strangers: The usefulness of electronic weak ties for technical advice. *Organization Science, 7*, 119–135.

Dubnicki, C., & Limburg, W. J. (1991, September/October). How do healthcare teams measure up? *Healthcare Forum, 34*, 10–11.

Dumaine, B. (1994, September 5). The trouble with teams. *Fortune, 130*, 86–92.

Dunphy, D., & Bryant, B. (1996). Teams: Panaceas or prescriptions for improved performance? *Human Relations, 49*, 677–699.

Eisenberg, E. M., & Phillips, S. R. (1991). Miscommunications in organizations. In N. Coupland, H. Giles, & J. M. Wiemann (Eds.), *Miscommunications and problematic talk* (pp. 244–258). Newbury Park, CA: Sage.

Feldman, D. C. (1995). Managing part-time and temporary employment relationships: Individual needs and organizational demands. In M. Landon (Ed.), *Employees, careers, and job creation: Developing growth-oriented human resource strategies and programs* (pp. 121–141). San Francisco: Jossey-Bass.

Gladstein, D. (1984). Groups in context: A model of task group effectiveness. *Administrative Science Quarterly, 29*, 499–517.

Goodman, P. S., & Shah, S. (1992). Familiarity and work group outcomes. In S. Worchel, W. Wood, & J. A. Simpson (Eds.), *Group process and productivity* (pp. 276–298). Newbury Park, CA: Sage.

Granovetter, M. S. (1973). The strength of weak ties. *American Journal of Sociology, 78*, 1360–1380.

Gruenfeld, D. H., Mannix, E. A., Williams, K. Y., & Neale, M. A. (1996). Group composition and decision making: How member familiarity and information distribution affect process and performance. *Organizational Behavior and Human Decision Processes, 67*, 1–15.

Guzzo, R. A., & Salas, E. (1995). *Team effectiveness and decision making in organizations*. San Francisco, CA: Jossey-Bass.

Hackman, J. R. (1987). The design of work teams. In J. W. Lorsch (Ed.), *Handbook of organizational behavior* (pp. 315–342). Englewood Cliffs, NJ: Prentice-Hall.

Hackman, J. R. (1998). Why teams don't work. In R. S. Tindale, L. Heath, J. Edwards, E. Posavac, F. B. Bryant, Y. Suarez-Balcazar, E. Henderson-King, & J. Myers (Eds.), *Theory and research on small groups* (pp. 245–267). New York: Plenum.

Hackman, J. R., & Morris, C. G. (1975). Group tasks, group interaction process, and group performance effectiveness: A review and proposed integration. In L. Berkowitz (Ed.), *Advances in experimental social psychology* (Vol. 8, pp. 45–99). New York: Academic Press.

Henry, R. A. (1993). Group judgment accuracy: Reliability and validity of post-discussion confidence judgments. *Organizational Behavior and Human Decision Processes, 56*, 11–27.

Henry, R. A. (1995a). Improving group judgment accuracy: Information sharing and determining the best member. *Organizational Behavior and Human Decision Processes, 62*, 190–197.

Henry, R. A. (1995b). Using relative confidence judgments to evaluate group effectiveness. *Basic and Applied Social Psychology, 16*, 333–350.

Henry, R. A., Strickland, O. J., Yorges, S. L., & Ladd, D. (1996). Helping groups determine their most accurate member: The role of outcome feedback. *Journal of Applied Social Psychology, 26*, 1153–1170.

Herr, E. L. (1993). Contests and influences on the need for personal flexibility for the 21st century. *Canadian Journal of Counseling, 27*, 219–235.

Hoerr, J. (1989, July 10). The payoff from teamwork. *Newsweek*, 56–62.

Hollingshead, A. B. (1998). Retrieval processes in transactive memory systems. *Journal of Personality and Social Psychology, 74*, 659–671.

Jackson, S. E., & Alvarez, E. B. (1993). Working through diversity as a strategic imperative. In S. E. Jackson (Ed.), *Diversity in the workplace: Human resource initiatives* (pp. 13–29). New York: Guilford.

Jehn, K. A., & Shah, P. P. (1997). Interpersonal relationships and task performance: An examination of mediating processes in friendship and acquaintance groups. *Journal of Personality and Social Psychology, 72*, 775–790.

Johnson, W., & Johnson, R. T. (1998). Cooperative learning and social interdependence theory. In R. S. Tindale, L. Heath, J. Edwards, E. Posavac, F. B. Bryant, Y. Suarez-Balcazar, E. Henderson-King, & J. Myers (Eds.), *Theory and research on small groups* (pp. 9–35). New York: Plenum.

Kanki, B. G., & Foushee, H. C. (1989). Communication as group process mediator of aircrew performance. *Aviation, Space, and Environmental Medicine, 4*, 402–410.

Karau, S. J., & Williams, K. D. (1993). Social loafing: A meta-analytic review and theoretical integration. *Journal of Personality and Social Psychology, 65*, 681–706.

Katz, R. (1982). The effects of group longevity on project communication and performance. *Administrative Science Quarterly, 27*, 81–104.

Katzenbach, J. R., & Smith, D. K. (1993). *The wisdom of teams: Creating the high-performance organization*. Cambridge, MA: Harvard Business School Press.

Kim, P. H. (1997). When what you know can hurt you: A study of experiential effects on group discussion and performance. *Organizational Behavior and Human Decision Processes, 69*, 165–177.

Kozlowski, S. W. J., Gully, S. M., Salas, E., & Cannon-Bowers, J. A. (1996). Team leadership and development: Theory, principles, and guidelines for training leaders and teams. In M. Beyerlein (Ed.), *Advances in interdisciplinary studies of work teams* (Vol. 3, pp. 253–291). Greenwich, CT: JAI.

Krackhardt, D. (1990). Assessing the political landscape: Structure, cognition, and power in organizations. *Administrative Science Quarterly, 35*, 342–369.

LaCoursiere, R. (1980). *The life cycle of groups: Group developmental stage theory.* New York: Human Sciences.

Larson, J. R., Jr., Foster-Fishman, P. G., & Keys, C. B. (1994). Discussion of shared and unshared information in decision-making groups. *Journal of Personality and Social Psychology, 67*, 446–461.

Lawler, E. E., Mohrman, S. A., & Ledford, G. E. (1992). *Employee involvement and total quality management.* San Francisco: Jossey-Bass.

Leedom, D. K., & Simon, R. (1995). Improving team coordination: A case for behavior-based training. *Military Psychology, 7*, 109–122.

Levine, J. M., & Moreland, R. L. (1990). Progress in small group research. *Annual Review of Psychology, 41*, 585–634.

Liang, D. W., Moreland, R. L., & Argote, L. (1995). Group versus individual training and group performance: The mediating role of transactive memory. *Personality and Social Psychology Bulletin, 21*, 384–393.

Libby, R., Trotman, K. T., & Zimmer, I. (1987). Member variation, recognition of expertise, and group performance. *Journal of Applied Psychology, 72*, 81–87.

Littlepage, G. E., Robison, W., & Reddington, K. (1997). Effects of task experience and group experience on group performance, member ability, and recognition of expertise. *Organizational Behavior and Human Decision Processes, 69*, 133–147.

Littlepage, G. E., Schmidt, G. W., Whisler, E. W., & Frost, A. G. (1995). An input-process-output analysis of influence and performance in problem-solving groups. *Journal of Personality and Social Psychology, 69*, 877–889.

Littlepage, G. E., & Silbiger, H. (1992). Recognition of expertise in decision-making groups: Effects of group size and participation patterns. *Small Group Research, 23*, 344–355.

Lyon, E. (1974). Work and play: Resource constraints in a small theater. *Urban Life and Culture, 3*, 71–97.

Mantel, B. (1994, September 5). Workplace issues for temporary workers. In E. Weiss (Executive Producer), *All things considered.* Washington, DC: National Public Radio.

Manz, C. C., & Sims, H. P. (1993). *Business without bosses: How self-managing teams are building high-performance companies.* New York: Wiley.

Marquardt, M. J. (1996). *Building the learning organization: A systems approach to quantum improvement and global success.* New York: McGraw-Hill.

Martin, J. (1982). Stories and scripts in organizational settings. In A. Hastorf & I. Isen (Eds.), *Cognitive social psychology* (pp. 255–305). New York: Elsevier.

McGrath, J. E. (1993). The JEMCO Workshop: Description of a longitudinal study. *Small Group Research, 24*, 285–306.

Montebello, A. R., & Buzzotta, V. R. (1993, March). Work teams that work. *Training and Development*, 59–64.

Moreland, R. L., Argote, L., & Krishnan, R. (1996). Socially shared cognition at work: Transactive memory and group performance. In J. L. Nye & A. M. Brower (Eds.), *What's social about social cognition? Research on socially shared cognition in small groups* (pp. 57–84). Thousand Oaks, CA: Sage.

Moreland, R. L., Argote, L., & Krishnan, R. (1998). Training people to work in groups. In R. S. Tindale, L. Heath, J. Edwards, E. Posavac, F. B. Bryant, Y. Suarez-Balcazar, E. Henderson-King, & J. Myers (Eds.), *Theory and research on small groups* (pp. 36–60). New York: Plenum.

Moreland, R. L., & Levine, J. M. (1992a). The composition of small groups. In E. J. Lawler, B. Markovsky, C. Ridgeway, & H. A. Walker (Eds.), *Advances in group processes* (Vol. 9, pp. 237–280). Greenwich, CT: JAI.

Moreland, R. L., & Levine, J. M. (1992b). Problem identification by groups. In S. Worchel, W. Wood, & J. A. Simpson (Eds.), *Group process and productivity* (pp. 17–47). Newbury Park, CA: Sage.

Moreland, R. L., & Levine, J. M. (in press). Socialization in organizations and work groups. In M. Turner (Ed.), *Groups at work: Advances in theory and research.* Mahwah, NJ: Lawrence Erlbaum Associates.

Moreland, R. L., Levine, J. M., & Wingert, M. L. (1996). Creating the ideal group: Group composition effects at work. In E. H. Witte & J. H. Davis (Eds.), *Understanding group behavior: Small group processes and interpersonal relations* (pp. 11–35). Mahwah, NJ: Lawrence Erlbaum Associates.

Mullen, B., & Copper, C. (1994). The relation between group cohesiveness and performance: An integration. *Psychological Bulletin, 115*, 210–227.

Murnighan, J. K., & Conlon, D. E. (1991). The dynamics of intense work groups: A study of British string quartets. *Administrative Science Quarterly, 36*, 165–186.

Organ, D. W. (1988). *Organizational citizenship behavior: The good soldier syndrome.* Lexington, MA: Lexington.

Parker, S. K., Wall, T. D., & Jackson, P. R. (1997). "That's not my job": Developing flexible employee work orientations. *Academy of Management Journal, 40*, 899–929.

Robinson, S., & Weldon, E. (1993). Feedback seeking in groups: A theoretical perspective. *British Journal of Social Psychology, 32*, 71–86.

Saavedra, R., & Kwun, S. K. (1993). Peer evaluation in self-managing work groups. *Journal of Applied Psychology, 78*, 450–462.

Sanna, L. J., & Parks, C. D. (1997). Group research trends in social and organizational psychology: Whatever happened to intragroup research? *Psychological Science, 8*, 261–267.

Stasser, G., Stewart, D., & Wittenbaum, G. M. (1995). Expert roles and information exchange during discussion: The importance of knowing who knows what. *Journal of Experimental Social Psychology, 31*, 244–265.

Stewart, T. A. (1995a, Nov. 27). Getting real about brainpower. *Fortune, 132*, 201–203.

Stewart, T. A. (1995b, Oct. 30). Mapping corporate brainpower. *Fortune, 132*, 209–212.

Stewart, T. A. (1997, Sep. 29). Does anyone around here know … ? *Fortune*, *136*, 279–280.

Sutton, R. J., & Hargadon, A. (1996). Brainstorming groups in context: Effectiveness in a produce design firm. *Administrative Science Quarterly*, *41*, 685–718.

Thompson, L. L., Levine, J. M., & Messick, D. M. (Eds.). (1999). *Shared cognition in organizations*. Mahwah, NJ: Lawrence Erlbaum Associates.

Trends that will influence workplace learning and performance in the next five years. (1994, May). *Training and Development*, *48*, 29–32.

Tuckman, B. W. (1965). Developmental sequence in small groups. *Psychological Bulletin*, *63*, 384–399.

Veroff, J., Sutherland, L., Chadiha, L., & Ortega, R. M. (1993). Newlyweds tell their stories: A narrative method for assessing marital experiences. *Journal of Social and Personal Relationships*, *10*, 437–457.

Vogt, J. F., & Hunt, B. D. (1988, May). What *really* goes wrong with participative work groups? *Training and Development Journal*, 96–100.

Waller, M. J. (1997). Keeping the pins in the air: How work groups juggle multiple tasks. In M. Beyerlein (Ed.), *Interdisciplinary studies of work teams* (Vol. 4, pp. 217–247). Greenwich, CT: JAI.

Watson, W. E., Kumar, K., & Michaelsen, L. K. (1993). Cultural diversity's impact on interaction process and performance: Comparing homogeneous and diverse task groups. *Academy of Management Journal*, *36*, 590–602.

Watson, W. E., Michaelsen, L. K., & Sharp, W. (1991). Member competence, group interaction, and group decision making: A longitudinal study. *Journal of Applied Psychology*, *76*, 803–809.

Wegner, D. M. (1987). Transactive memory: A contemporary analysis of the group mind. In B. Mullen & G. R. Goethals (Eds.), *Theories of group behavior* (pp. 185–208). New York: Springer-Verlag.

Wegner, D. M. (1995). A computer network model of human transactive memory. *Social Cognition*, *13*, 319–339.

Wegner, D. M., Erber, R., & Raymond, P. (1991). Transactive memory in close relationships. *Journal of Personality and Social Psychology*, *61*, 923–929.

Wegner, D. M., Giuliano, T., & Hertel, P. T. (1985). Cognitive interdependence in close relationships. In W. J. Ickes (Ed.), *Compatible and incompatible relationships* (pp. 253–276). New York: Springer-Verlag.

Weingart, L. R. (1992). Impact of group goals, task component complexity, effort, and planning on group performance. *Journal of Applied Psychology*, *77*, 682–693.

Wellins, R. S., Byham, W. C., & Dixon, G. R. (1994). *Inside teams: How 20 world-class organizations are winning through teamwork*. San Francisco: Jossey-Bass.

Wittenbaum, G. M., Vaughan, S. I., & Stasser, G. (1998). Coordination in task-performing groups. In R. S. Tindale, L. Heath, J. Edwards, E. Posavac, F. B. Bryant, Y. Suarez-Balcazar, E. Henderson-King, & J. Myers (Eds.), *Theory and research on small groups* (pp. 177–204). New York: Plenum.

Yetton, P. W., & Bottger, P. C. (1982). Individual versus group problem solving: An empirical test of a best-member strategy. *Organizational Behavior and Human Performance*, *29*, 307–321.

PART 4C

Leadership

There is much theory and research on leadership. Some of this work focuses on the emergence and acceptance of leaders, but most of it focuses on their effectiveness. Leadership is clearly an important factor in group performance; some people view it as the *most* important factor. As a result, much time and effort and money have gone into research designed to resolve such issues as why some leaders are more effective than others and whether anything can be done to improve a leader's effectiveness. No final resolutions of those issues have been achieved, but a lot has been learned.

Work on leadership effectiveness can be organized in several ways (see Chemers, 2000; Yukl, 1989), but one method involves categorizing such work according to the underlying assumptions that are made about the likely source of effectiveness. When this is done, three broad approaches are apparent. One approach emphasizes the leader—effectiveness is assumed to reflect a characteristic that is stronger in good leaders than in poor ones. Another approach emphasizes the relationships between leaders and followers— effectiveness is assumed to reflect the ability of some leaders to establish satisfying relationships with their best followers. Finally, the third approach emphasizes followers—effectiveness is assumed to be more subjective than objective, reflecting beliefs among followers about how well they are led.

Leaders

The average person believes that effective leaders are simply those who have the "right stuff." But what *is* that stuff? Researchers have studied many *personal qualities* of leaders (see Stodgill, 1974), from their physical attributes (e.g., height, strength, sex), to their abilities, to their personality characteristics. And some personal qualities do seem to be associated with effective leadership. Broadly speaking, these qualities involve the ability, sociability, and motivation of leaders. Effective leaders thus tend to be more capable, more socially skilled, and more concerned about their groups than are poor leaders. It is worth noting, however, that relatively few of the many personal qualities studied by researchers turned out to relate significantly to leadership effectiveness. Even when good and poor leaders differed significantly in some quality, the actual difference between them was not very large— good and poor leaders were more similar than different. As a result, measuring some quality in a set of people and then using that information to predict how effectively they would lead was seldom successful. Finally, studies of transitions from one group to another showed that people who led one group effectively were sometimes ineffective at leading other groups (and vice versa), despite the fact that their personal qualities were (presumably) unchanged.

Findings such as these persuaded many researchers that the personal qualities of leaders were not so important after all, and so some researchers moved on to study the *behavior* of leaders. What do leaders actually *do* that might cause groups to succeed or fail? Many specific leader behaviors were identified, but most of them can be classified as task or social/emotional in nature. Task behaviors include organizing and monitoring the activities of followers, setting deadlines for them, and evaluating their performance. Social/emotional activities include asking followers for input, showing sensitivity to their needs, and resolving conflicts among them. But which type of behavior is most helpful—task or social/emotional? The evidence was mixed. In some studies, task behavior was more helpful than social/emotional behavior, but in other studies, the reverse was true.

Maybe the optimal pattern of behavior for leaders varies across situations, and so an effective leader is someone who adapts his or her behavior to whatever situation arises in a group. This notion led to the development of several *contingency theories* of leadership effectiveness (e.g., Fiedler, 1967; House, 1991; Vroom & Yetton, 1973). Fiedler's theory generated the most research, much of which supported his claims that (a) most leaders prefer task *or* social/emotional behaviors and have difficulty acting in both ways; (b) situations vary in the control that they offer to leaders (i.e., how easy it is to be an effective leader); and (c) task-oriented leaders are more effective in extreme situations (high or low control), whereas relationship-oriented leaders are more effective in moderate situations (medium control).

Leader–Follower Relationships

In Fiedler's theory, an important factor in situational control is the quality of relations between the leader and other group members. Maybe such relations matter even more than his theory suggests— effective leadership may depend primarily on the ability of a leader to develop satisfying relationships with some followers. But what makes a relationship satisfying or unsatisfying? According to *social exchange theory* (see Brehm, 1992), relationship satisfaction is influenced by the rewards and costs that the partners exchange with one another: each partner seeks a relationship that maximizes the ratio of rewards to costs that he or she receives. The behavior of leaders and followers can produce many kinds of rewards and costs for the people involved. From the leader's viewpoint, for example, obedience by followers is rewarding, whereas defiance is costly. And from the viewpoint of followers, a leader's praise is rewarding, whereas criticism is costly. To be effective, a leader should thus try to generate more rewards and fewer costs for followers, especially those whose knowledge and skills are most valuable. Their relationships with him or her will then seem more satisfying, and they will work harder to help the group succeed.

This approach to leadership effectiveness can be seen in research by Hollander and others (see Hollander, 1985) on such topics as elected versus appointed leaders and "idiosyncracy credits" (group members are more tolerant of costly behavior from people whose past behavior was more rewarding), and in research investigating leader–member exchange (LMX) theory (Liden, Sparrowe & Wayne, 1997). One major finding from the latter research, which focuses on work groups, is that followers are often divided into two separate cliques, the "ingroup" and the "outgroup." Each clique has a distinct exchange relationship with the leader. Members of the ingroup have a much warmer and more collegial relationship with the leader than do members of the outgroup— ingroup members are more likely to be treated as

trusted friends whose opinions are important and whose outcomes matter. This finding raises several interesting issues, such as how a leader chooses who should belong to the ingroup versus the outgroup and how someone in the outgroup can move to the ingroup.

Followers

A closer consideration of the relationships between leaders and followers led some researchers to focus on the followers themselves. A leader's effectiveness, after all, is not always easy to judge. Such judgments can be very subjective, and followers may be the people whose opinions about leaders matter most. How, then, do followers evaluate their leaders' effectiveness? Maybe leadership is simply an *attribution* made by followers for group outcomes that they want to explain (Calder, 1977). These leadership attributions are guided by *prototypes* and *scripts* in the minds of followers. When an important outcome occurs in a group, and someone's appearance and recent behavior match the leader prototypes and scripts of other group members, then the outcome may be attributed to that person's leadership. And the more positive the outcome is, the more effective his or her leadership will seem.

Much work on leadership prototypes, scripts, and attributions has been done (e.g., Brown & Lord, 2001; Wofford & Goodwin, 1994). Recently, a few theorists have even suggested that leadership effectiveness is *entirely* subjective (see Gemmill & Oakley, 1992; Meindl, 1995). That is, leaders may do nothing that really helps or harms groups. Followers believe in leadership, however, because they like to think that someone has control over their group, rather than admitting that group success or failure depends on uncontrollable factors. A belief in leaders may thus be one form of the illusion of control (see Presson & Benassi, 1996), but at the group rather than the individual level.

REFERENCES

Brehm, S. (1992). *Intimate relationships*. New York: McGraw-Hill.

Brown, D. J., & Lord, R. G. (2001). Leadership and cognition: Moving beyond first-order constructs. In M. London (Ed.), *How people evaluate others in organizations* (pp. 181–202). Mahwah, NJ: Lawrence Erlbaum Associates, Inc.

Calder, B. J. (1977). An attribution theory of leadership. In B. M. Staw & G. R. Salancik (Eds.), *New directions in organizational behavior* (pp. 179–204). Chicago: St. Clair Press.

Chemers, M. M. (2000). Leadership research and theory: A functional integration. *Group Dynamics, 4*, 27–43.

Fiedler, F. E. (1967). *A theory of leadership effectiveness*. New York: McGraw-Hill.

Gemmill, G., & Oakley, J. (1992). Leadership: An alienating social myth? *Human Relations, 45*, 113–129.

Hollander, E. P. (1985). Leadership and power. In G. Lindzey & E. Aronson (Eds.), *The handbook of social psychology* (3rd ed., Vol. 2, pp. 485–537). New York: Random House.

House, R. J. (1971). A path-goal theory of leader effectiveness. *Administrative Science Quarterly, 16*, 321–338.

Liden, R.C., Sparrowe, R.T., & Wayne, S.J. (1997). Leader–member exchange theory: The past and potential for the future. *Research in Personnel and Human Resources Management, 15*, 47–119.

Meindl, J. R. (1995). The romance of leadership as a follower-centric theory: A social constructionist approach. *Leadership Quarterly, 6*, 329–341.

Presson, P., & Benassi, V. (1996). Illusion of control: A meta-analytic review. *Journal of Social Behavior and Personality, 3*, 493–510.

Stodgill, R. (1974). *Handbook of leadership*. New York: Free Press.

Vroom, V. H., & Yetton, P. W. (1973). *Leadership and decision making*. Pittsburgh: University of Pittsburgh Press.

Wofford, J. D., & Goodwin, V. L. (1994). A cognitive interpretation of transactional and transformational leadership theories. *Leadership Quarterly, 5*, 161–186.

Yukl, G. (1989). Managerial leadership: A review of theory and research. *Journal of Management, 15*, 251–289.

Readings

The first paper in this set, by Zaccaro, Foti, and Kenny (1991), describes a laboratory experiment on the emergence of leaders in groups. The issue was whether a person who becomes the leader of one group would also emerge as the leader of other groups, indicating that he or she has some personal quality associated with leadership. If that were the case, then the researchers also wanted to identify that personal quality. They thought that it might be *self-monitoring*, a personality trait that involves someone's ability to sense what others want from him or her in a social situation and then give it to them. A person who could do that might well seem like a potential leader to other group members and might actually lead the group well.

To explore these issues, the researchers divided a sample of college students into a dozen "sets," each containing nine persons. Each set of students then participated in a separate laboratory session lasting for two days. The first day began with a written test measuring each student's level of self-monitoring. Next, the students were assigned to three groups, with three students per group. Each group was then given one of four tasks, which differed in the kinds of leadership behavior required for optimal group performance. After completing their task, group members were given questionnaires that asked them to evaluate the leadership potential of each person in the group and to describe how often each person had exhibited specific leader behaviors. After a break, the researchers disbanded the original groups and reassigned the students to new groups. This was done in such a way that none of the groups contained students who had worked together before. Each group was then given a task to perform. This was done in such a way that none of the students worked on the same task as before. Group members then completed the questionnaire again, ending the first day of the experiment. On the second day, new groups worked on other tasks under these same general procedural constraints. By the end of the experiment, each student had thus worked on all four tasks, in four completely different groups.

Three kinds of data analyses were performed. First, a *social relations analysis* was performed on the leadership potential evaluations produced by each group. The goal of that analysis was to determine how much the variability in those evaluations depended on who made them (sources), whom they described (targets), and different combinations of sources and targets. The results showed that a significant amount of variability in the evaluations was related to whom they described, indicating that there was at least some consensus within the groups about the leadership potential of their members. A follow-up analysis examined how stable the evaluations of each student's leadership potential were across the groups to which he or she belonged. The results showed considerable stability, indicating that certain students tended to emerge as the leader of every group that they joined.

In a second set of data analyses, evaluations of leadership potential were correlated with descriptions of specific leader behaviors for each type of task. The goal of these analyses was to determine whether students whose behavior matched the requirements for whatever task a group was performing were more likely than others to be viewed as leaders. Although these correlations were generally weak, they tended to be stronger when there was a match rather than a mismatch between leader behavior and task requirements. This suggests that the emergence of a leader depends in part on his or her ability to provide whatever a group needs to perform its task successfully.

A final set of data analyses involved correlations between students' self-monitoring scores and the evaluations of leadership potential that they received from others. These correlations were generally small, but all of them were positive and some of them were significant, especially those involving the overall self-monitoring scores and subsidiary scores for acting ability. Apparently, self-monitoring was a stronger trait among students who emerged as group leaders than among students who were only followers.

The second paper in this set, by Fiedler (1965), describes his *contingency theory* of leadership effectiveness and offers a narrative review of research that seems to validate that theory. According to Fiedler, the most important characteristic of a leader is his or her *leadership style*. Some leaders are task-oriented—their primary goal is to help the group get a lot of work done, even if they are disliked as a result. A task-oriented leader tends to be critical, directive, and autocratic. Other leaders are relationship-oriented—their primary goal is to make group members happy, even if less work gets done as a result. A relationship-oriented leader tends to be considerate, permissive, and democratic. A person's leadership style could be assessed in many ways, but Fiedler has often relied on a measure called the Least Preferred Coworker (LPC) Scale. On that scale, people are asked to think about a coworker (past or present) who limited their productivity at a job. They then evaluate that person on a variety of rating scales, each of which reflects a dimension that has positive and negative endpoints (e.g., warm vs. cold, pleasant vs. unpleasant). A higher score on the measure indicates more positive ratings of the coworker on these dimensions. Fiedler argued (and evidence indicates) that LPC scores reflect people's leadership styles. People with higher LPC scores tend to be relationship-oriented leaders. They are able to like a coworker with positive personal qualities, even if that person limits their productivity, because getting work done is not their primary goal. In contrast, people with lower LPC scores tend to be task-oriented leaders. Because their primary goal *is* to get work done, they cannot like a coworker who limits their productivity. Put another way, task-oriented leaders evaluate coworkers in terms of their impact on personal productivity, whereas relationship-oriented leaders consider other factors as well.

Are task-oriented or relationship-oriented leaders more effective? Fiedler believed that the answer depends on such situational factors as leader–member relations, task structure, and position power. Leader–member relations reflect how well the leader is liked and respected by his or her followers. Task structure reflects how well the group knows what it is supposed to be doing. It includes goal clarity (are task requirements clearly stated or otherwise known to the group?), goal path multiplicity (how many ways are there to perform the task?), solution specificity (how many performance outcomes are acceptable?), and decision verifiability (can the group tell whether it

has performed the task well?). Finally, position power reflects the leader's formal authority over followers (e.g., the ability to hire or fire, promote or demote). These three factors together comprise the *favorability* of a situation for effective leadership; leader–member relations have the most impact on situational favorability, and position power has the least. Situational favorability can be measured in several ways, but in much of his research, Fiedler relied on questionnaires that asked group members to describe leader–member relations, task structure, and position power.

How, exactly, are leadership style and situational favorability related? Fiedler argued that when situational favorability is extreme, either very high or very low, a task-oriented leader should be most effective. In contrast, a relationship-oriented leader should be most effective in a situation of moderate favorability. Fiedler tested these predictions in two ways, as described in the paper. First, he reviewed the results from prior studies of groups in which (a) leaders completed the LPC scale; (b) measures of group performance (a proxy for leadership effectiveness) were available; and (c) one could infer, from other information about the groups, something about leader–member relations. Fiedler found that correlations between leaders' LPC scores and measures of group performance tended to be less positive (task-oriented leaders were more effective) when leader–member relations were good or poor, rather than moderate.

Next, with cooperation from the Belgian Navy, Fiedler performed a field experiment to test his contingency model. Many temporary crews were created, each led by a single sailor. All of the leaders completed the LPC scale, so their leadership styles were known, and the crews were created in ways that varied their leader–member relations, task structure, and position power. Fiedler did not manipulate leader–member relations, but rather measured them by means of a questionnaire completed by group leaders. Task structure was manipulated by asking some of the crews to perform tasks that were both familiar and rather clear (planning the optimal sea routes for ships visiting several ports), or unfamiliar and rather unclear (writing recruiting materials to persuade men to join the Navy). Position power was manipulated by appointing as crew leaders men whose rank was high (petty officers) or low (new recruits). Finally, the favorability of the situation for the crews was also manipulated by assigning to them sailors whose language preferences (French or Dutch) were the same or different. The crews were rank-ordered for situational favorability, and then their task performance (a proxy for leadership effectiveness) was correlated with the LPC scores of their leaders. As Fiedler predicted, these correlations tended to be negative (task-oriented leaders were more effective) among crews in highly favorable or unfavorable situations, but positive (relationship-oriented leaders were more effective) among crews in moderately favorable situations.

The third paper in this set, by Hains, Hogg, and Duck (1997), describes a laboratory experiment on leadership effectiveness and acceptance. Two theoretical approaches to these phenomena were contrasted. The first approach (see Brown & Lord, 2001) suggests that there are broad stereotypes about what an effective leader is like—how such a person ought to look and act. For example, many people expect a successful business manager to be male, tall, clean-shaven, and well-dressed, and to be insightful, make decisions quickly, and accept blame when mistakes are made. Group members who match such stereotypes more closely may thus be more likely to become leaders, and their leadership may be more likely to seem effective.

The second approach is *self-categorization theory*, which was described earlier in connection with the paper on group cohesion by Prentice, Miller, and Lightdale (1994). According to the theory, group phenomena occur when people categorize themselves as members of the same group and behave accordingly. This process creates a prototype, or shared image of the kind of person who embodies whatever qualities make the group distinctive. Prototypes could play a role in leadership similar to the one played by leader stereotypes, except that stereotypes apply to sets of groups and may be slow to change, whereas prototypes apply to specific groups and can change quickly, if people compare their own group to different outgroups. Self-categorization theory suggests that within a group, the person who matches the group prototype most closely is most likely to become group leader. On a sports team that sees itself as especially aggressive, for example, the most aggressive player is likely to become the team's leader. Once a leader has emerged in this way, he or she may well be effective, or at least appear to be effective, because (a) other members feel attracted to someone who represents their group so well and thus allow that person to exert a lot of influence, and (b) the role of prototype matching in leadership is often subtle, so the leader's influence over other members may be misattributed to his or her personal qualities, such as charisma, rather than to prototypicality.

To contrast these two approaches to leadership, Hains and her colleagues manipulated three variables, namely (a) the salience of group membership, which was assumed to affect the importance of group prototypes; (b) the perceived stereotypicality of a group's leader; and (c) the perceived prototypicality of that leader. College students were asked to consider whether the police should have more power in the community. Group salience was manipulated by leading some of the students (but not others) to believe that they would soon participate in a classroom debate between small groups about this issue. To manipulate perceived leader stereotypicality and prototypicality, the researchers first collected a variety of information about the students, including their personal opinions about police powers, and then randomly assigned them to small groups. One student from each group was then (supposedly) chosen at random by the researchers to become its leader, and group members were provided with (false) information about that person. Leader stereotypicality was manipulated by informing students that the leaders of their groups had described themselves earlier as similar or dissimilar to the kind of person who generally makes an effective leader (e.g., someone who plans carefully). Leader prototypicality was manipulated by informing students that the leaders of their groups had opinions about the police that were representative or not representative of the opinions held by other members. The students then completed several measures of leader acceptance and expected leader effectiveness.

Similar results were found on both sets of measures. There were strong effects of leader stereotypicality, which were independent from those of the other variables. Leaders who seemed more stereotypical were better accepted by followers and were expected to be more effective. Leader prototypicality had weaker, but still significant effects. Leaders who seemed more prototypical were also better accepted and expected to be more effective, but these effects depended on how salient group membership was to the students. Prototypical leaders were better accepted and expected to be more effective only when group salience was high (making group prototypes more important). When group salience was low, the prototypicality of leaders no longer mattered.

The results of this experiment suggest that both approaches to leadership are valid. The support for self-categorization theory is particularly interesting, however, because it raises many issues regarding leadership that have not been considered. Hains and her colleagues noted, for example, that the social environment of groups may be more important than is generally thought. Because a group's prototype includes whatever characteristics make that group distinctive from other groups, any changes in the kinds of groups to which the group is compared will necessarily alter its prototype as well. For example, if other sports teams in a league become more aggressive, then the team that was once most aggressive may focus on other qualities of its members, such as their unusual strength. As a result, strength may become more important to the team's prototype, which could lead to a change in leadership—the player who led the team because he or she was so aggressive might be replaced by whichever player is strongest. Canny leaders may even take advantage of this process by attempting to hold the real and/or perceived social environments of their groups constant, so that the prototypes in their groups do not change, allowing them to remain leaders.

The final paper in this set, by Meindl, Ehrlich, and Dukerich (1985), describes six studies, some correlational and others experimental, on the "romance" of leadership. What is so romantic about leadership? Meindl and his colleagues make the surprising claim that leaders have little or no real impact on the performance of groups, especially large groups, such as business organizations or government agencies. Whether such groups succeed or fail depends on factors that cannot be controlled by any single person. For example, the performance of a business organization depends largely on such factors as the number and strength of its competitors, the health of the economy, restrictions imposed by government regulations, and so on. There is some evidence, in fact, that turnover in the CEOs of such organizations seldom makes much difference—companies that are succeeding generally continue to do well after leadership changes, and companies that are failing generally continue to do poorly. Why, then, do people believe so strongly in leadership? Meindl and his colleagues argue that leadership is a romantic notion that people embrace because it helps them to cope with some of the anxiety associated with group membership. People who work for a large organization would hate to

think that its fate depends on factors that no one can control. It is more comforting to think that someone, such as the leader of the organization, can help it to succeed. Even if the organization fails, workers may prefer to think that its failure was due to poor leadership rather than to uncontrollable factors.

To test their claim, Meindl and his colleagues first performed a set of archival studies, all correlational in nature, in which the popularity of leadership as a topic in (a) articles from the *Wall Street Journal*, (b) dissertations by students in business schools, and (c) articles from general business publications, was measured. These measures were then correlated with broad indicators of organizational performance. Several significant correlations were found, indicating that when organizations performed unusually well or poorly, more attention was devoted to leadership. Apparently, people often see leadership effectiveness as a critical factor in organizational performance.

Next, the researchers performed a set of laboratory experiments, all using a similar paradigm. College students were given materials that described an organization whose recent performance was unusually good or poor. Brief information about the leader of that organization was also provided. The students were then asked to explain why the organization succeeded or failed by attributing its performance to various factors, such as leadership effectiveness, worker productivity, the state of the economy, and so on. The results indicated that leadership attributions were generally more popular than attributions of other kinds and that they were especially popular when an organization's performance was extreme (good or poor). Once again, people seemed to see leadership effectiveness as a key factor in organizational performance.

So, people believe in leaders, even though leaders may not have much real impact on the performance of groups. Are leaders good for anything at all, other than providing comfort to anxious followers? Some analysts have argued that leaders have a symbolic value that may be important. Aside from serving as symbols themselves of the groups that they lead, leaders can use symbolism to make group goals clearer and more appealing to members. This could strengthen the commitment of members to their group and thereby improve its performance.

Discussion Questions

1. Have you ever belonged to a group whose formal leader was not actually the person that led the group? What kinds of problems did that create? How could such problems be solved?
2. Do you belong to any groups whose leaders seem especially effective or ineffective? If so, then what are those leaders actually doing to affect the performance of these groups? Do you think anyone else in those groups could do similar things?
3. Some groups (e.g., psychotherapy groups) have more than one formal leader. What are some of the possible advantages and disadvantages of this practice?
4. According to social exchange theory, the health of a relationship depends not only on how satisfied participants are with the rewards and costs they are receiving, but also with any alternative relationships that are available to them, and the investments (e.g., time, energy, money, lost opportunities) that they have made in their relationship. How might alternative relationships and investments influence the health of the relationships between a leader and his or her followers, and how might that change the leader's effectiveness?
5. Setting aside how effective a leader *actually* is, what can a leader do to *seem* more effective to followers? Are followers likely to be deceived? Why or why not?

Suggested Readings

Chemers, M. W., Watson, C. B., & May, S. T. (2000). Dispositional affect and leadership effectiveness: A comparison of self-esteem, optimism, and efficacy. *Personality and Social Psychology Bulletin, 26,* 267–277.

Fiedler, F. E. (1978). The contingency model and the dynamics of the leadership process. In L. Berkowitz (Ed.), *Advances in experimental social psychology* (Vol. 11, pp. 60–112). New York: Academic Press.

Jacobsen, C., & House, R. J. (2001). Dynamics of charismatic leadership: A process theory, simulation model, and tests. *Leadership Quarterly, 12,* 75–112.

Kerr, S., & Jermier, J. M. (1978). Substitutes for leadership: Their meaning and measurement. *Organizational Behavior and Human Performance, 22,* 375–403.

Pfeffer, J. (1981). Management as symbolic action: The creation and maintenance of organizational paradigms. In L. L. Cummings & B. M. Staw (Eds.), *Research in organizational behavior* (Vol. 3, pp. 1–52). Greenwich, CT: JAI Press.

Self-Monitoring and Trait-Based Variance in Leadership: An Investigation of Leader Flexibility Across Multiple Group Situations

Stephen J. Zaccaro, Roseanne J. Foti, and David A. Kenny*

Response flexibility as a basis for leadership was examined. Ss were 108 students who completed the self-monitoring scale and four group tasks, interacting with different people on each task. Tasks required as leader styles either initiating structure, consideration, persuasion, or production emphasis. After each task, group members rated each other on perceived leadership and on four scales corresponding to the aforementioned leader styles. Results indicated that 59% of the variance in leadership emergence was trait based; for two of the four tasks, leader rankings were significantly correlated with task-relevant behaviors; and self-monitoring was significantly correlated both with average leader rankings and with task-relevant behaviors on two of the tasks. These findings suggest that trait-based variance in leadership may be due to social perceptiveness and response flexibility.

Trait explanations of leader emergence are generally regarded with little esteem by leadership theorists. Much of this disdain can be attributed to the results of two research traditions in the leadership literature. The first emphasized the search for specific personal qualities that differentiate leaders from followers. Reviews of this research by Stogdill (1948) and Mann (1959)

Stephen J. Zaccaro and Roseanne J. Foti share equal responsibility for the work described in this article. Their work was supported in part by the College of Arts and Sciences Small Grant program at Virginia Polytechnic Institute and State University. The work of David A. Kenny was supported in part by National Science Foundation Grant BNS-8807462.

We thank Neil Hauenstein, Ted Gessner, Robert Holt, Michael Mumford, and June Tangney for their comments and suggestions on earlier drafts of this article. We also thank Marta Carter, Melissa Kitner-Triolo, Jennifer Fletcher, Michelle Rohrbach, Mimi Buchanan, Peter Dori, Michelle Fulton, and Andy Garlington for their assistance as data collectors.

Correspondence concerning this article should be addressed to either Roseanne J. Foti, Department of Psychology, Virginia Polytechnic Institute and State University, Blacksburg, Virginia 24061, or Stephen J. Zaccaro, Department of Psychology, George Mason University, Fairfax, Virginia 22030.

* University of Connecticut.

argued instead for the importance of the group situation over particular traits in leader emergence. The second research tradition used "rotation designs" to vary aspects of the group and examine the association between leadership in one situation and leader emergence in other situations. After completing one such study, Barnlund (1962) concluded that leadership depended not on individual traits but rather on situational variables.

This last view illustrates what has been the dominant perspective in the literature, that leaders were individuals chosen by group members because they responded best to situational demands (e.g., Barnlund, 1962). Although we do not explicitly reject this view, we suggest that trait explanations of emergent leadership also have considerable viability. Indeed, two recent studies indicated significant evidence for both specific leadership traits (Lord, De Vader, & Alliger, 1986) and cross-situational consistency (Kenny & Zaccaro, 1983).

The present study investigates the relationship between perceived leader status across different group situations and individual sensitivity to social demands. Our proposal is that leaders are more adept than followers at perceiving group requirements and selecting appropriate responses to these demands. We investigate self-monitoring (Snyder, 1974, 1979) as a construct that reflects such leader characteristics.

Evidence for Trait-Based Approaches to Leadership

Leader Qualities

The earliest tradition in leadership research is perhaps the search for personal qualities that distinguish leaders from nonleaders (e.g., Terman, 1904). Characteristics studied most frequently included intelligence, dominance, adjustment, and masculinity. Reviews of this literature, however, emphasized the failure to find consistent support for any particular trait (Mann, 1959; Stogdill, 1948). For example, after reviewing 124 studies, Stogdill (1948) concluded, "the evidence suggests that leadership is a relation that exists between persons in a social situation, and that persons who are leaders in one

situation may not be leaders in another situation" (p. 64). Mann (1959) focused on seven personality factors—intelligence, adjustment, extraversion, dominance, masculinity, conservatism, and sensitivity—and, after reviewing 1,400 associations, found that no trait had a median correlation higher than .25 with leadership criteria.

Lord et al. (1986) argued that the Mann and Stogdill reviews obfuscated the differences between leadership perceptions and leader effectiveness. Although traits may or may not affect performance, they do have a demonstrated influence on perceptions of leadership (Lord, Foti, & De Vader, 1984). They also pointed out that the findings of Mann and Stogdill were interpreted too negatively. Indeed, despite each review's forceful conclusion to the contrary, both did report consistent associations between personal qualities, particularly intelligence, and indexes of leadership. Moreover, Lord et al. (1986) argued that Mann's findings of low associations between traits and leadership could be attributed to sampling error, unreliability, and range restriction. Whereas Mann found that leadership had a median correlation of .25 with intelligence and .15 with masculinity, Lord et al. reported the frequency weighted correlations corrected for unreliability to be .52 and .34, respectively. Significant correlations were found between leadership and intelligence, dominance, and masculinity–femininity. Thus, they concluded that "personality traits are associated with leadership perceptions to a higher degree and more consistently than the popular literature indicates" (p. 407).

Cross-Situational Consistency

The reported failure of early studies to find leadership traits led to investigations of cross-situational stability in leader emergence. These studies typically rotated individuals through several different group situations (e.g., Barnlund, 1962; Bell & French, 1950; Borgatta, Bales, & Couch, 1954; Carter & Nixon, 1949). In these studies, leader choices in one session were correlated with those in other sessions. Whereas most of this research provided evidence for cross-situational consistency, Barnlund (1962), using the most elaborate rotation design (i.e., varying both group membership and task), concluded that his results "tend to support the view that leadership is dependent upon situational variables" (p. 52).

Kenny and Zaccaro (1983) reanalyzed Barnlund's data using a quantitative model of social relations (Kenny, 1988; Kenny & La Voie, 1984). This model decomposes an individual's interpersonal rating into three components plus a constant: (a) the extent to which a person sees others as leaders (rater effect); (b) the extent to which a person is seen as a leader by others (ratee effect); and (c) the relationship between rater and ratee (interaction or relationship effect). Using Barnlund's reported correlations, Kenny and Zaccaro (1983) estimated the association between ratee effects across group situations and found that 49% to 82% of leadership variance could be attributed to some stable characteristic(s) of the emergent leader.

This finding disputes the conclusion made by Barnlund that leadership was not stable. Nonetheless, the assumption of cross-situational stability in leader emergence has not been investigated fully in published rotation designs. In these studies, factors such as participant characteristics (in the rotation set), contextual cues, and time-related variables were kept constant (Kenny & Zaccaro, 1983). Given this deficiency, there is a clear need for studies that assess whether trait-based variance in leader emergence can be found across a range of rotation conditions. Accordingly, the present investigation assesses the stability assumption of leader trait theories in 12 separate rotation sets.

Leader Dispositions and Response Flexibility

Social Perceptiveness and Behavioral Flexibility

The model proposed by Kenny and Zaccaro (1983) for the rotation design assesses only the degree to which the same individuals are perceived as leaders across varying situations, not the specific qualities possessed by these individuals. We suggest that if the stability assumption of trait theories is true, then proposed characterological profiles of leaders should reflect the ability to respond effectively in diverse situations. That is, emergent leaders may have the capability to recognize what group members expect of them in each group situation (i.e., social perceptiveness) and respond accordingly (i.e., behavioral flexibility; Kenny & Zaccaro, 1983). These characteristics would explain cross-situational consistency in leader emergence and situational specificity in leader behaviors.

Although sensitivity to social situations has not been entirely ignored in the leadership literature, the few reports are not conclusive. In his review, Stogdill (1948) concluded that "alertness to the surrounding environment and understanding of situations are intimately associated with leadership ability, *yet very little is understood regarding the nature of these processes*" (p. 49; italics added). Stogdill also noted several studies suggesting that "ready adaptability to changing situations is a factor which may be associated with leadership capacity" (p. 49). Mann (1959) also concluded that methodological and conceptual problems with studies on interpersonal sensitivity indicated a need for further research. The present study addresses this need by incorporating self-monitoring into a rotation-design investigation of leader emergence.

Self-Monitoring

Snyder (1974, 1979) identified an individual difference characteristic called self-monitoring, which indicates an ability to monitor and control one's expressive behaviors. More specifically, self-monitoring includes three characteristics: a concern for social appropriateness, a sensitivity to social cues, and an ability to control one's behavior in response to those cues (Briggs, Cheek, & Buss, 1980; Snyder, 1974, 1979). Research has shown that high self-monitors (a) are better able to present themselves in socially desirable ways (Lippa, 1978); (b) are able to adapt to new situations more effectively than low self-monitors (Snyder, 1979); and (c) are more likely than low self-monitors to speak first in interactions and to initiate more conversation sequences (Ickes & Barnes, 1977), all behaviors typical of leaders.

To date there have been a limited number of studies that associated self-monitoring with leadership emergence (Ellis, 1988; Ellis, Adamson, Deszca, & Cawsay, 1988; Foti & Cohen, 1986; Garland & Beard, 1979). These studies provided tentative evidence for a relationship between self-monitoring and leader emergence, but they did not vary actual group situations. Only Foti and Cohen (1986) manipulated leader style requirements (i.e., task-oriented versus considerate). Thus, it cannot be ascertained whether high self-monitors would continue to emerge as leaders across different group situations.

The present study extends these investigations by incorporating a rotation design experiment. After completing the self-monitoring scale, subjects in 12 separate rotation sets worked on four different group tasks. Each task required, as a primary behavioral style, either initiating structure, consideration, persuasion, or production emphasis. Group composition was varied for each task. After each session, subjects indicated their perceptions of leadership in the group and the behavioral styles displayed by each group member.

On the basis of previous research (Foti & Cohen, 1986; Kenny & Zaccaro, 1983), we offer three hypotheses. The first is that there will be a significant proportion of trait-based variance in leader emergence scores across the 12 rotation sets. The second is that leader rankings and ratings, averaged across tasks, will be correlated with perceived levels of the leadership behaviors specifically required by each group task; leader status, however, will be uncorrelated with behaviors not specified by task characteristics. Furthermore, because self-monitoring is linked to such flexibility, our third hypothesis is that self-monitoring scores will be positively associated with leader emergence across tasks, within rotations.

Method

Subjects

The subjects were 108 undergraduates from a large southeastern university. Students received course credit and monetary compensation (i.e., $5) for their participation in the study. Nine subjects participated in each rotation, for a total of 12 rotations. All-male groups were used in 6 of the rotations; all-female groups were used in the remaining 6 sets.

Tasks

Subjects in a rotation set were rotated through four group situations, each involving a different task. Three-person groups completed each task. Furthermore, group composition was varied such that a person worked in a group with each other person only once. The tasks were chosen to reflect four different leadership requirements: initiating structure, consideration, persuasion, and production emphasis. In pilot research, subjects completed one of the tasks and were asked to rank four leadership styles in order of importance (1 = *most important*, 4 = *least important*) for successful completion of the task. To facilitate these judgments, subjects were provided with a definition of each style and several behavioral examples.

The data from the pilot studies indicated that on the four tasks, an average of 70.4% of the subjects ranked as most important the style targeted as primarily required for task success. No alternate or nontargeted style on any task was ranked as most important by more than 28% of the subjects. (Initiating structure was ranked first by 28% of the subjects on the discussion task; consideration, i.e., the required style, was ranked first by 67%.) An analysis was completed comparing the frequency of subjects who ranked the targeted leadership style as most important with those who similarly ranked any of the alternate styles. The results indicated that on each of the four tasks, a significant majority perceived the proposed required leadership style as most important for task completion (chi-squares ranged from 10.88 to 45.63, all *ps* < .01). Taken together, these data suggest that the tasks used in this study reflected four different primary leadership styles.

The first task was a modified version of a manufacturing game (Foti & Cohen, 1986; cf. Pepinsky, Hemphill, & Shevitz, 1958). The purpose of the game was to purchase raw materials (Lego blocks), manufacture toy products (i.e., jeeps, robots, or boats), and sell the completed products back to a buyer for a profit. There were three performance sessions, each 15 min in duration. Participants started with $10,000 in play money and a price list for the first session. Costs of the raw materials and prices of the finished products changed for each subsequent session. Each group was given 5 min before the first session, and 2 min before Sessions 2 and 3, to discuss the task and their plan of action. Pilot work indicated that the predominant leader style required on this task was initiating structure.

The second task involved brainstorming options to the following question: "Should children with AIDS [acquired immune deficiency syndrome] be allowed to attend school?" Group members were asked to prepare a set of recommendations that considered the needs of children, parents, peers, school personnel, and the community. All group members were to be encouraged to contribute opinions and options. The predominant behavioral style for this task was consideration.

The third task required group members to simulate a township school board (e.g., Marshall & Foti, 1989). The board was meeting to determine the best possible uses for surplus funds. After receiving the same background information about the schools in the community, each group member was given a separate proposal to present before the board. Presenters had 10 min to prepare arguments and 5 min to persuade the group toward a particular course of action. After all three presentations were made, the group discussed the proposals and prepared a written recommendation. Persuasion was the predominant leader behavior style for this task.

The final task was "moon tent" assembly (Kolb, Rubin, & McIntyre, 1984; Zaccaro, 1984). This task required subjects to fold paper in a certain number of steps until an object resembling a tent was completed. Members placed completed products in separate containers near each work station. Groups were told that they were competing against the other groups to make the most moon tents. Members of the winning group would receive additional extra credit for their courses. (At the end of the experiment, all groups received the extra

points.) The performance period lasted for 20 min. However, at the midpoint, the group took a break and experimenters counted up the number of moon tents made. Each group was then told that they were second in production among the three groups. This was done to facilitate in the group an emphasis on increasing production speed. Pilot work indicated production emphasis to be the relevant leader style for this task.

Procedure

Twelve sets of nine subjects completed the tasks over a 2-day period. On Day 1, experimenters explained what subjects would be doing and administered a consent form and the self-monitoring questionnaire. After completing the self-monitoring questionnaire, subjects were assigned to a three-person group. All three groups then completed one of the four tasks. After each task was completed, group members were asked to rate each of their two peers and themselves on perceptions of leadership and on displayed initiating structure, consideration, production emphasis, and persuasion behaviors. They also ranked each group member (including themselves) in order of leader preference if the group were asked to meet a second time to work on the same kind of task. The second task session concluded the first day of the experiment. Each subject was assigned to a different group so that he or she did not work with the same group members twice.

On the next day, subjects returned to complete the final two task sessions. Again, group membership was established in each session so that no person ever worked with another individual more than once. The order of assigned tasks was counterbalanced across days and across sessions within each day. After the last task session, subjects were debriefed as to the purpose of the study.

Measures

Self-monitoring was measured using a 25-item true–false questionnaire described in Snyder (1974). A factor analysis of this scale has indicated three factors: extraversion, other directiveness, and acting (Briggs et al., 1980). In this study, leader scores were correlated with the full scale and with each of the subscales. Cronbach's alpha for the entire scale was .67.

Leader emergence was measured in two ways. First, leadership perceptions were measured using the five-item General Leadership Impression scale (GLI; Lord et al., 1984). A sample item asked, "How much did this individual contribute to the effectiveness of the group?" Group members rated each other member and themselves on these items (although self-ratings were excluded from all analyses). Responses were made on 5-point Likert rating scales with anchors ranging from *extreme amount* to *nothing*. Previous research has shown this scale to have high internal consistency (Cronbach's alpha = .88).

For a second measure of leader emergence, group members were asked to complete the following: "If you were asked to meet a second time with this same group to work on the same kind of task, please rank in order, your preference for a group leader. Indicate your choice by putting the number assigned to each group member in the space provided. Please include yourself in the ranking." Subjects then gave a rank of 1 to their top choice for the leadership position, 2 to their second choice, and 3 to their last choice.

Displayed initiating structure, consideration, persuasion, and production emphasis behaviors were measured using four 10-item subscales from the Leader Behavior Description Questionnaire (LBDQ; Stogdill, 1963). Subjects rated themselves and their peers by indicating on 5-point scales (ranging from *always* to *never*) the frequency of specific leader behaviors. The internal consistencies of these subscales have been well documented (Schriesheim & Kerr, 1974; Stogdill, 1963).

Data Analysis

The analyses used to determine the proportion of trait-based variance in leader emergence were based on the social relations model (Kenny, 1988; Kenny & La Voie, 1984). This model decomposes ratings into rater, ratee, relationship, and group effects. Of direct interest for this study is the proportion of stable ratee variance, or the degree to which there was agreement among perceptions, across group situations, of a ratee's leadership. The measure for this trait-based variance is λ^2. (See Kenny & Zaccaro, 1983, for additional details.) In the present study, λ^2 was estimated using the ROTO computer program (Kenny, 1989). This program computes variances for each rotation and then averages them across rotations. The resulting mean is then tested to determine if it is significantly different from zero (with degrees of freedom equal to the number of rotations minus one).

To test Hypothesis 2, within-task correlations were computed between leader emergence scores (i.e., rankings and ratings) averaged across group situations and ratings on the four LBDQ dimensions. Hypothesis 3 was assessed through correlations between self-monitoring scores and leader ratings and rankings averaged across group situations. In the aforementioned analyses, perceptions of one person's leadership were assessed relative to others in the rotation set; thus, possible variability due to the effect of rotation set was removed from both rankings and ratings such that within rotations leader emergence scores averaged to zero. This means, however, that although such variability was no longer present in these scores, it was still present in self-monitoring scores and in the peer LBDQ ratings. Therefore, variance due to the rotation set was also partialed out of both sets of measures.

In the analyses, all leadership scores were calculated as the average of peer ratings or rankings. Because of bias due to self-enhancement, self-ratings and self-rankings were excluded from these derived measures. Also, including these self-perceptions would contaminate the correlation between self-monitoring and leader emergence, because the rater becomes both the source and target for the personality and influence ratings.

Although the directions of our correlations were predicted, we used the more conservative two-tailed probability values to evaluate all observed correlations. The degrees of freedom for these analyses were 95 (i.e., number of subjects minus number of rotations minus one).

Results

Before examining the stability of leader emergence across different situations, it is necessary to determine the amount of variance, averaged across rotations, in perceived leadership within group situations that is attributable to the rater, the ratee, and their relationship. (Relational variance also includes random error; see Kenny & La Voie, 1984.) The analyses completed on leadership scores indicate that 40% of the variance in ratings, $t(11) = 3.13, p < .01$, and 38% of the variance in rankings, $t(11) = 7.32, p < .01$, represented ratee effects. Proportions of variance due to relationship effects were .53, $t(11) = 5.81, p < .01$, and .62, $t(11) = 8.89, p < .01$, in ratings and rankings, respectively. The proportion of rater-based variance in ratings (.07) was not significant. (No rater-based variance can exist in leader rankings.) These results indicate that a significant proportion of leadership variance was due to aspects of the ratee, or the person perceived as a leader.

The important question for this study is whether this effect is stable. That is, do perceptions of the ratee as a leader in one situation match perceptions of the ratee in other group situations, where both task and membership have been varied? In support of Hypothesis 1, analyses completed on individual ratings indicated a significant amount of stable or trait-based variance in leader emergence, $\lambda^2 = .59, t(11) = 2.43, p < .05$. A similar effect was reported for leadership rankings, $\lambda^2 = .43, t(11) = 2.76, p < .05$. These data indicate a significant tendency for a person to be seen as a leader across different group situations.

The matrix of within-task correlations computed between leader emergence scores averaged across tasks and task-specific LBDQ ratings is shown in Table 19.1. Support for Hypothesis 2 would be indicated by a pattern of larger correlations on the diagonal than off the diagonal. The diagonal elements indicate a match between task type and leadership style. To facilitate interpretation, rankings were reverse scored such that 3 represented the top rank and 1 the lowest.

Results from the leader rankings indicate the expected pattern. On two of the four tasks, group

TABLE 19.1. Within-Task Correlations of Overall Leader Rankings and Ratings With Task-Specific Leader Behavior Description Questionnaire (LBDQ) Responses

	Task			
LBDQ subscale	SBS	MG	AIDS	MT
Rankings				
Persuasion	.20*	.07	.18	.09
Initiating structure	.15	.18	.15	.11
Consideration	.06	.09	.35**	.04
Production emphasis	.13	−.03	.14	.16
Ratings				
Persuasion	.18	.15	.16	−.04
Initiating structure	.13	.19	.25*	.08
Consideration	.15	.01	.31**	.07
Production emphasis	.02	.04	.14	.11

Note: $N = 108$. SBS = school board simulation; MG = manufacturing game; AIDS = acquired immune deficiency syndrome discussion task; MT = moon tent production. Rankings ranged from 3 (highest) to 1 (lowest).
*$p < .05$ (two-tailed test). ** $p < .01$ (two-tailed test).

members who received the top leadership rank averaged across tasks were rated significantly higher than nonleaders on the behavioral style that was most appropriate for each task. For example, pilot studies indicated that persuasion was the most appropriate style for the school board simulation task. The results with rankings indicate that leaders received higher peer ratings for persuasion on this task than nonleaders and that this relationship was not significant for the other three leadership styles. Indeed, for each of the tasks, the largest correlation was between average leader rank and the relevant task-required LBDQ dimension (i.e., the diagonal correlation). However, the diagonal correlation did not reach statistical significance on the manufacturing game ($r = .18, p < .10$) and the moon tent assembly task ($r = .16, p < .12$). No off-diagonal correlation was statistically significant. We note, though, that some of these correlations approached the magnitude of the diagonal correlations.

The same pattern of larger correlations on the diagonal than off the diagonal emerged for leader ratings. However, the only significant diagonal correlation was for the AIDS discussion task. Moreover, the off-diagonal correlation between leader ratings and initiating structure was significant on

TABLE 19.2. Correlations Between Self-Monitoring and Leader Emergence

	Leadership perceptions	
Scale	Rankings[a]	Ratings
Self-monitoring	.22*	.15
Extraversion	.18	.15
Acting	.21*	.14
Other directiveness	.08	.00

[a] Rankings ranged from 3 (highest) to 1 (lowest).
*$p < .05$ (two-tailed).

TABLE 19.3. Within-Task Correlations Between Self-Monitoring and Task-Specific Leader Behavior Description Questionnaire (LBDQ) Peer Ratings

	Task			
LBDQ subscale	SBS	MG	AIDS	MT
Persuasion	.15	.08	.12	.12
Initiating structure	.05	.25*	.14	.07
Consideration	.10	.10	.24*	−.07
Production emphasis	.08	.10	.14	.12

Note: $N = 108$. SBS = school board simulation; MG = manufacturing game; AIDS = acquired immune deficiency syndrome discussion task; MT = moon tent production.
*$p < .05$ (two-tailed).

this same task. Thus, the correlations with leader ratings indicate weaker support for Hypothesis 2.

Regarding Hypothesis 3, support for the notion of leader flexibility can be found in the correlations between self-monitoring and leader emergence scores. These correlations are shown in Table 19.2. Leader rankings were correlated significantly with scores on the self-monitoring scale. The correlation with the acting subscale was also significant. Scores on the extraversion and other-directiveness subscales were not related to leader emergence. Associations between self-monitoring and ratings on the GLI scale did not reach statistical significance. Thus, these data provide partial support for Hypothesis 3.

Prior studies suggested that the relationship between self-monitoring and leader emergence may vary by gender (e.g., Garland & Beard, 1979). Accordingly, moderated regression analyses were completed to test this possibility. The results indicated that gender had no moderating influences on the relationships between leader rankings or ratings and self-monitoring, extraversion, acting, and other directiveness, respectively.

A critical question for the present study is whether self-monitoring reflects a greater sensitivity to changing task requirements. In order to address this question, two analyses were conducted. First, we computed a measure of variance among each person's leader dimension scores across tasks. If high self-monitors were changing their behavioral styles to fit the appropriate task demands, then self-monitoring should be positively correlated with this measure. The correlation between

self-monitoring scores and the LBDQ variance was .18 ($p < .10$). Thus, high self-monitors showed somewhat more flexibility in peer behavioral ratings than low self-monitors.

Self-monitoring scores were then correlated with mean LBDQ ratings for each task to determine whether this flexibility by high self-monitors was tied to task behavioral requirements. These correlations are shown in Table 19.3. Here again, the diagonal elements indicate a match between task type and the appropriate leadership style. For two of the four tasks, the manufacturing game and the AIDS discussion task, high self-monitors received higher peer ratings for the corresponding leadership style (initiating structure and consideration, respectively) than low self-monitors. Taken together, these results provide partial support for the prediction that high self-monitors adapt their behavior to changing situations.

Discussion

The results of the present study clearly support Hypothesis 1 that emergent leadership is stable across group situations and can be attributed to individual characteristics. Our data confirm Kenny and Zaccaro's (1983) finding of significant trait-based variance in leadership. The present study goes beyond earlier research, however, by demonstrating stable leader emergence across multiple rotation sets.

Kenny and Zaccaro (1983) suggested as a characteristic of leaders the capability to recognize different group requirements (social perceptiveness) and respond accordingly (behavioral flexibility). Our results tentatively support this argument, in that individuals ranked as leaders were more likely than nonleaders to display relevant or required behaviors for two of the four group tasks. Furthermore, one variable reflecting such a characteristic, self-monitoring, was associated with leadership rankings. Our findings move beyond traditional interactionist and trait views of leadership by suggesting that leaders behave in accordance with a group's functional requirements, but that some group members may be better than others at perceiving these requirements and responding accordingly. Thus, we account for response specificity to situational demands and cross-situation generality in leader status.

The data from leader ratings were less supportive of our hypotheses than those from the rankings. However, we observed a tendency in several groups for members to give each other very similar if not identical ratings, a strategy not possible with the rankings. Such a tendency would attenuate the possible correlations with leader ratings.

Also, our conclusions should be tempered by the observations that the overall correlations were not large and that some of the within-task correlations did not appear to differ greatly from one another. Our point, however, is not that leaders adopt one behavioral style to the exclusion of all others. Multiple styles are likely to be required and demonstrated on different group tasks. Our data suggest, though, a general tendency for leaders to be perceived as demonstrating the style primarily required on any one task more so than followers.

Finally, we note the limitations imposed by the experimental controls required for this study. For example, potentially emergent leaders faced four different tasks, each with unfamiliar group members. The tasks afforded little domain-specific knowledge and limited use of related cognitive capacities. Furthermore, the newness of the group inhibited fully accurate perceptions of social requirements. These factors can act to constrain the range of possible behavioral responses and the magnitude of the resultant correlations. Thus, our findings need to be evaluated with these points in mind.

We suggest that additional attention be directed toward other behavioral differences between leaders and nonleaders as group situations change. The relatively low correlations shown in Tables 19.1 and 19.3 suggest that the behavioral dimensions assessed in this study reflected only a small part of these differences. We urge, therefore, that other activity patterns linked more closely to the requirements posed by situational change be examined. For example, as situations change, we expect that leaders more than nonleaders would engage in such responses as information searching, acquisition, utilization, and communication (cf. Mumford, Fleishman, Zaccaro, Levin, & Hein, 1990). These behaviors are not directly assessed by the traditional behavioral indexes used here. Also such responses may more accurately reflect differences between high and low self-monitors. Thus, further research should focus on a wider range of behavioral dimensions.

Our data are in accordance with a transactional approach to leadership (Hollander & Julian, 1968). According to this approach, the leader provides a resource for the group by facilitating leadership functions, among which is directing the task. Although, as we have found here, the leader's contributions may vary with task demands, the leader is likely to be perceived by other group members as providing the resources needed for attainment of common goals. This approach necessitates viewing the leadership process as an interaction of individual and situational determinants. Specifically, what is important are the leader characteristics perceived as relevant by other group members.

Our focus on leadership perceptions emphasizes laypeople's conceptualizations of leadership, that is, their implicit leadership theories. Previous work has demonstrated that leadership ratings of both fictitious and real supervisors may be more a function of raters' implicit theories than leaders' actual behavior (Eden & Leviatan, 1975; Rush, Thomas, & Lord, 1977; Weiss & Adler, 1981). Attempting to develop a cognitive definition of implicit leadership theory, Lord, Foti, and Phillips (1982) argued that implicit theories were simply a type of category system. Their theory emphasized the role of leadership categories and prototypes in explaining leadership perceptions and distortions in memory about leader behavior. Extensive work in this area has shown that people share a core set of characteristics (i.e., prototypes) perceived as being related to leadership (Foti, Fraser, & Lord, 1982; Lord et al., 1984). These characteristics include intelligence, determination, and decisiveness. Thus, this line of research shows personality characteristics as being important perceptual constructs that should predict leadership perceptions and therefore leadership emergence.

Our findings suggest self-monitoring as one of these personality characteristics. A growing literature has linked self-monitoring and leader emergence (Ellis, 1988; Ellis et al., 1988; Foti & Cohen, 1986; Foti & Rueb, 1990). However, we note that although our leader stability coefficient (i.e., cross-situation ratee variance) was relatively high (.59), the observed correlations with self-monitoring were relatively low (Table 19.2). We suggest that the proposed leader capabilities of social perceptiveness and behavioral flexibility reflect a complex network or constellation of traits and characteristics of which only one was examined here. Further research should perhaps focus on additional personality variables linked to the aforementioned proposed capabilities. Also, more traditional leader variables such as intelligence, dominance, and achievement motivation should be included (cf. Foti & Rueb, 1990; Lord et al., 1984; Sorrentino, 1973; Sorrentino & Field, 1986). Thus, the emphasis ought to be on a multivariate approach to individual characteristics facilitating leader emergence. Such an approach can be more successful in identifying dispositional patterns that produce the amount of stable variance observed here in cross-situational leader emergence.

We clearly acknowledge that the study of leadership emergence is perceptual in nature. Although we believe the study of perceptions is important in its own right, care must be exercised in generalizing our findings on the relationship between self-monitoring and leader emergence to other areas of leadership. Our results do not directly imply that traits would predict the performance of a leader's work group, attainment of group goals, or any other measures of leader effectiveness. We urge, however, that future research be directed toward objective measures of leadership behaviors (Bales & Strodtbeck, 1951; Lord, 1977) displayed by high and low self-monitors.

In conclusion, while supporting the fact that leaders match their style to fit the situation is not original (cf. House & Mitchell, 1974; Vroom & Yetton, 1973), demonstrating this as an individual difference tied to leader emergence is new. Our contention is that self-monitoring is one fruitful approach to studying the leadership process, because it incorporates both a trait and a situation view of leadership. Other approaches adopting a similar perspective should advance understanding of leader qualities and leader emergence.

REFERENCES

Bales, R. F., & Strodtbeck, F. L. (1951). Phases in group problem-solving. *Journal of Abnormal and Social Psychology, 46*, 485–495.

Barnlund, D. C. (1962). Consistency of emergent leadership in groups with changing tasks and members. *Speech Monographs, 29*, 45–52.

Bell, G. B., & French, R. L. (1950). Consistency of individual leadership position in small groups of varying membership. *Journal of Abnormal and Social Psychology, 45*, 764–767.

Borgatta, E. F., Bales, R. L., & Couch, A. S. (1954). Some findings relevant to the great man theory of leadership. *American Sociological Review, 19*, 755–759.

Briggs, S. R., Cheek, J. M., & Buss, A. H. (1980). An analysis of the self-monitoring scale. *Journal of Personality and Social Psychology, 38*, 679–686.

Carter, L. F., & Nixon, M. (1949). An investigation of the relationship between four criteria of leadership ability for three different tasks. *Journal of Psychology, 27*, 245–261.

Eden, D., & Leviatan, U. (1975). Implicit leadership theory as a determinant of the factor structure underlying supervisory behavior scales. *Journal of Applied Psychology, 60*, 736–741.

Ellis, R. J. (1988). Self-monitoring and leadership emergence in groups. *Personality and Social Psychology Bulletin, 14*, 681–693.

Ellis, R. J., Adamson, R. S., Deszca, G., & Cawsay, T. F. (1988). Self-monitoring and leader emergence. *Small Group Behavior, 19*, 312–324.

Foti, R. J., & Cohen, B. A. (1986, August). Self-monitoring and leadership emergence. In J. Kennedy (Chair), *Attempting to solve the leadership puzzle*. Symposium conducted at the 94th Annual Convention of the American Psychological Association, Washington, DC.

Foti, R. S., Fraser, S. L., & Lord, R. G. (1982). Effects of leadership labels and prototypes on perceptions of political leaders. *Journal of Applied Psychology, 67*, 326–333.

Foti, R. J., & Rueb, J. (1990, April). *Self-monitoring, traits, and leader emergence*. Paper presented at the annual meeting of the Society for Industrial and Organizational Psychology, Miami, FL.

Garland, H., & Beard, J. F. (1979). Relationship between self-monitoring and leader emergence across two task situations. *Journal of Applied Psychology, 64*, 72–76.

Hollander, E. P., & Julian, J. W. (1968). Leadership. In E. Borgatta & W. W. Lambert (Eds.), *Handbook of personality theory and research* (pp. 33–69). Chicago: Rand McNally.

House, R. J., & Mitchell, T. R. (1974). Path goal theory of leadership. *Contemporary Business, 3*, 81–98.

Ickes, W. J., & Barnes, R. D. (1977). The role of sex and self-monitoring in unstructured dyadic interactions. *Journal of Personality and Social Psychology, 35*, 315–330.

Kenny, D. A. (1988). Interpersonal perception: A social relations analysis. *Journal of Social and Personal Relationships, 5*, 247–261.

Kenny, D. A. (1989). ROTO: *A FORTRAN program for the analysis of group rotation data*. Storrs: University of Connecticut.

Kenny, D. A., & La Voie, L. (1984). The social relations model. In L. Berkowitz (Ed.), *Advances in experimental social psychology* (Vol. 18, pp. 141–182). San Diego, CA: Academic Press.

Kenny, D. A., & Zaccaro, S. J. (1983). An estimate of variance due to traits in leadership. *Journal of Applied Psychology, 68*, 678–685.

Kolb, D. A., Rubin, I. M., & McIntyre, J. M. (1984). *Organizational psychology: An experiential approach to organizational behavior* (4th ed.). Englewood Cliffs, NJ: Prentice-Hall.

Lippa, R. (1978). The effects of expressive control on expressive consistency and on the relation between expressive behavior and personality. *Journal of Personality, 46*, 438–461.

Lord, R. G. (1977). Functional leadership behavior: Measurement and relation to social power and leadership perceptions. *Administrative Science Quarterly, 22*, 114–133.

Lord, R. G., De Vader, C. L., & Alliger, G. M. (1986). A meta-analysis of the relation between personality traits and leadership: An application of validity generalization procedures. *Journal of Applied Psychology, 71*, 402–410.

Lord, R. G., Foti, R. J., & De Vader, C. L. (1984). A test of leadership categorization theory: Internal structure, information processing, and leadership perceptions. *Organizational Behavior and Human Performance, 34*, 343–378.

Lord, R. G., Foti, R. J., & Phillips, J. S. (1982). A theory of leadership categorization. In J. G. Hunt, U. Sekaran, C. Schriesheim (Eds.), *Leadership: Beyond establishment views* (pp. 104–121). Carbondale: Southern Illinois University.

Mann, R. D. (1959). A review of the relationships between personality and performance in small groups. *Psychological Bulletin, 56*, 241–270.

Marshall, P., & Foti, R. (1989, March). *The relationship of self-monitoring and task experience to leader emergence*. Paper presented at the 35th Annual Meeting of the Southeastern Psychological Association, Washington, DC.

Mumford, M. D., Fleishman, E. A., Zaccaro, S. J., Levin, K. Y., & Hein, M. B. (1990). *Taxonomic efforts in the description of leader behavior: A synthesis and functional interpretation*. Manuscript submitted for publication.

Pepinsky, P. N., Hemphill, J. K., & Shevitz, R. N. (1958). Attempts to lead, group productivity, and morale under conditions of acceptance and rejection. *Journal of Abnormal and Social Psychology, 57*, 47–54.

Rush, M. C., Thomas, J. C., & Lord, R. G. (1977). Implicit leadership theory: A potential threat to the internal validity of leader behavior questionnaires. *Organizational Behavior and Human Performance, 20*, 93–110.

Schriesheim, C. A., & Kerr, S. (1974). Psychometric properties of the Ohio State leadership scales. *Psychological Bulletin, 81*, 756–765.

Snyder, M. (1974). The self-monitoring of expressive behavior. *Journal of Personality and Social Psychology, 30*, 526–537.

Snyder, M. (1979). Self-monitoring processes. In L. Berkowitz (Ed.), *Advances in experimental social psychology* (Vol. 12, pp. 86–128). San Diego, CA: Academic Press.

Sorrentino, R. M. (1973). An extension of a theory of motivation to the study of emergent leadership. *Journal of Personality and Social Psychology, 26*, 356–368.

Sorrentino, R. M., & Field, N. (1986). Emergent leadership over time: The functional value of positive motivation. *Journal of Personality and Social Psychology, 50*, 1091–1099.

Stogdill, R. M. (1948). Personal factors associated with leadership: A survey of the literature. *Journal of Psychology, 25*, 35–71.

Stogdill, R. M. (1963). *Manual for the Leader Behavior Description Questionnaire—Form XII: An experimental revision*. Columbus: Bureau of Business Research, Ohio State University.

Terman, L. (1904). A preliminary study of the psychology and pedagogy of leadership. *Pedagogical Seminary, 11*, 413–451.

Vroom, V. H., & Yetton, P. W. (1973). *Leadership and decision making*. Pittsburgh, PA: University of Pittsburgh Press.

Weiss, H. M., & Adler, S. (1981). Cognitive complexity and the structure of implicit leadership theories. *Journal of Applied Psychology, 66*, 69–78.

Zaccaro, S. J. (1984). Social loafing: The role of task attractiveness. *Personality and Social Psychology Bulletin, 10*, 99–106.

Received November 13, 1989
Revision received October 9, 1990
Accepted October 26, 1990 ■

The Contingency Model: A Theory of Leadership Effectiveness

Fred E. Fiedler

Leadership, as a problem in social psychology, has dealt primarily with two questions, namely, how one becomes a leader, and how one can become a *good* leader, that is, how one develops effective group performance. Since a number of excellent reviews (e.g., Stogdill, 1948; Gibb, 1954; Mann, 1959; Bass, 1960) have already dealt with the first question we shall not be concerned with it in the present paper.

The second question, whether a given leader will be more or less effective than others in similar situations, has been a more difficult problem of research and has received correspondingly less attention in the psychological literature. The theoretical status of the problem is well reflected by Browne and Cohn's (1958) statement that "leadership literature is a mass of content without coagulating substances to bring it together or to produce coordination. . . ." McGrath (1962), in making a similar point, ascribed this situation to the tendency of investigators to select different variables and to work with idiosyncratic measures and definitions of leadership. He also pointed out, however, that most researchers in this area have gravitated toward two presumably crucial clusters of leadership attitudes and behaviors. These are the critical, directive, autocratic, task-oriented versus the democratic, permissive, considerate, person-oriented type of leadership. While this categorization is admittedly oversimplified, the major controversy in this area has been between the more orthodox viewpoint—reflected in traditional supervisory training and military doctrine that the leader should be decisive and forceful, that he should do the planning and thinking for the group, and that he should coordinate, direct, and evaluate his men's actions—and the other viewpoint—reflected in the newer human-relations-oriented training and in the philosophy behind nondirective and brain-storming techniques—which stresses the need for democratic, permissive, group-oriented leadership techniques. Both schools of thought have strong adherents and there is evidence supporting both points of view (Gibb, 1954; Hare, 1962).

This article was written especially for this book (Proshansky & Seidenberg, 1965) while the author was a Ford Faculty Research Fellow at the University of Louvain, Belgium (1963–1964). The present paper is based mainly on research conducted under the Office of Naval Research Contracts 170-106, N6-ori-07135 (Fred E. Fiedler, Principal Investigator) and RN177-472, Nonr 1834 (36) (Fred E. Fiedler, C. E. Osgood, L. M. Stolurow, and H. C. Triandis, Principal Investigators). The writer is especially indebted to his colleagues, A. R. Bass, L. J. Cronbach, M. Fishbein, J. E. McGrath, W. A. T. Meuwese, C. E. Osgood, H. C. Triandis, and L. R. Tucker, who offered invaluable suggestions and criticisms at various stages of the work.

While one can always rationalize that contradictory findings by other investigators are due to poor research design, or different tests and criteria, such problems present difficulties if they appear in one's own research. We have, during the past thirteen years, conducted a large number of studies on leadership and group performance, using the same operational definitions and essentially similar leader attitude measures. The inconsistencies which we obtained in our own research program demanded an integrative theoretical formulation which would adequately account for the seemingly confusing results.

The studies which we conducted used as the major predictor of group performance an interpersonal perception or attitude score which is derived from the leader's description of his most and of his least preferred co-workers. He is asked to think of all others with whom he has ever worked, and then to describe first the person with whom he worked best (his most preferred co-worker) and then the person with whom he could work least well (his least preferred co-worker, or LPC). These descriptions are obtained, wherever possible, before the leader is assigned to his team. However, even where we deal with already existing groups, these descriptions tend to be of individuals whom the subject has known in the past rather than of persons with whom he works at the time of testing.

The descriptions are typically made on 20 eight-point bipolar adjective scales, similar to Osgood's Semantic Differential (Osgood et al., 1957), e.g.,

called the Assumed Similarity between Opposites, or ASo, indicates the degree to which the individual perceives the two opposites on his co-worker continuum as similar or different. The second score is simply based on the individual's description of his least preferred co-worker, LPC, and indicates the degree to which the subject evaluates his LPC in a relatively favorable or unfavorable manner. The two measures are highly correlated (.80 to .95) and will here be treated as interchangeable.

We have had considerable difficulty in interpreting these scores since they appear to be uncorrelated with the usual personality and attitude measures. They are, however, related to the Ohio State University studies' "Initiation of structure" and "Consideration" dimensions (Stogdill and Coons, 1957). Extensive content analyses (Julian and McGrath, 1963; Morris, 1964) and a series of studies by Hawkins (1962) as well as still unpublished research by Bass, Fiedler and Krueger have given consistent results. These indicate that the person with high LPC or ASo, who perceives his least preferred co-worker in a relatively favorable, accepting manner, tends to be more accepting, permissive, considerate, and person-oriented in his relations with group members. The person who perceives his most and least preferred co-workers as quite different, and who sees his least preferred co-worker in a very unfavorable, rejecting manner tends to be directive, controlling, task-oriented, and managing in his interactions.

Pleasant	8	:	7	:	6	:	5	:	4	:	3	:	2	:	1	Unpleasant
Friendly	8	:	7	:	6	:	5	:	4	:	3	:	2	:	1	Unfriendly

These items are scaled on an evaluative dimension, giving a score of 8 to the most favorable pole (i.e., Friendly, Pleasant) and a score of 1 to the least favorable pole. Two main scores have been derived from these descriptions. The first one, which was used in our earlier studies, is based on the profile similarity measure D (Cronbach and Gleser, 1953) between the descriptions of the most and of the least preferred co-worker. This score,

ASo and LPC scores correlated highly with group performance in a wide variety of studies, although, as mentioned above, not consistently in the same direction. For example, the sociometrically chosen leader's ASo score correlated −.69 and −.58 with the percentage of games won by high school basketball teams and −.51 with the accuracy of surveying of civil engineer teams (Fiedler, 1954), and the melter foreman's ASo score correlated $-.52$ with tonnage output of open-hearth shops (Cleven and Fiedler, 1956). These negative correlations indicate that *low* ASo or LPC scores were associated with good group performance, i.e., that these groups performed better under managing, directive leaders than under more permissive, accepting leaders. However, while the ASo score of the sociometrically accepted company managers also correlated negatively $(-.70)$ with the net income of consumer cooperatives, the board chairman's ASo score under the same circumstances correlated $+.62$ (Godfrey, Fiedler, and Hall, 1959). Thus, groups with different tasks seemed to require different leader attitudes. In a more recent study of group creativity in Holland, the leader's LPC score correlated with performance $+.75$ in religiously homogeneous groups with formally appointed leaders, but $-.72$ in religiously heterogeneous groups; and while the correlation was $+.75$ in homogeneous groups with appointed leaders it was $-.64$ in homogeneous groups having emergent (sociometrically nominated) leaders (Fiedler, Meuwese, and Oonk, 1961).

The results of these investigations clearly showed that the direction and magnitude of the correlations were contingent upon the nature of the group-task situation which confronted the leader. The problem resolved itself then into (a) developing a meaningful system for categorizing group-task situations; (b) inducing the underlying theoretical model which would integrate the seemingly inconsistent results obtained in our studies; and (c) testing the validity of the model by adequate research.

Development of the Model

Key Definitions

We shall here be concerned with "interacting" rather than "co-acting" task groups. By an interacting task group we mean a face-to-face team situation (such as a basketball team) in which the members work *interdependently* on a common goal. In groups of this type, the individual's contributions cannot readily be separated from total group performance. In a co-acting group, however, such as a bowling or a rifle team, the group performance is generally determined by summing the members' individual performance scores.

We shall define the leader as the group member who is officially appointed or elected to direct and coordinate group action. In groups in which no one has been so designated, we have identified the informal leader by means of sociometric preference questions such as asking group members to name the person who was most influential in the group, or whom they would most prefer to have as a leader in a similar task.

The leader's effectiveness is here defined in terms of the group's performance on the assigned primary task. Thus, although a company manager may have, as one of his tasks, the job of maintaining good relations with his customers, his main job, and the one on which he is in the final analysis evaluated, consists of the long-range profitability of the company. Good relations with customers, or high morale and low labor turnover may well contribute to success, but they would not be the basic criteria by this definition.

The Categorization of Group-Task Situations

Leadership is essentially a problem of wielding influence and power. When we say that different types of groups require different types of leadership we imply that they require a different relationship by which the leader wields power and influence. Since it is easier to wield power in some groups than in others, an attempt to categorize groups might well begin by asking what conditions in the group-task situation will facilitate or inhibit the leader's exercise of power. On the basis of our previous work we postulated three important aspects in the total situation which influence the leader's role.

1. Leader-member relations. The leader who is personally attractive to his group members, and who is respected by his group, enjoys considerable power (French, 1956). In fact, if he has the confidence and loyalty of his men he has less need of official rank. This dimension can generally be measured by means of sociometric indices or by group atmosphere scales (Fiedler, 1962) which indicate the degree to which the leader experiences the group as pleasant and well disposed toward him.

2. Task structure. The task generally implies an order "from above" which incorporates the authority of the superior organization. The group member who refuses to comply must be prepared to face disciplinary action by the higher authority. For example, a squad member who fails to perform a lawful command of his sergeant may have to answer to his regimental commander. However, compliance with a task order can be enforced only if the task is relatively well structured, i.e., if it is capable of being programmed. One cannot effectively force a group to perform well on an unstructured task such as developing a new product or writing a good play.

Thus, the leader who has a structured task can depend on the backing of his superior organization, but if he has an unstructured task the leader must rely on his own resources to inspire and motivate his men. The unstructured task thus provides the leader with much less effective power than does the highly structured task.

We operationalized this dimension by utilizing four of the aspects which Shaw (1962) recently proposed for the classification of group tasks. These are (a) decision *verifiability*, the degree to which the correctness of the solution can be demonstrated objectively; (b) *goal clarity*, the degree to which the task requirements are clearly stated or known to the group; (c) *goal path multiplicity*, the degree to which there are many or few procedures available for performing the task (reverse scoring); and (d) *solution specificity*, the degree to which there is one rather than an infinite number of correct solutions (e.g., solving an equation vs. writing a story). Ratings based on these four dimensions have yielded interrater reliabilities of .80 to .90.

3. Position power. The third dimension is defined by the power inherent in the position of leadership irrespective of the occupant's personal relations with his members. This includes the rewards and punishments which are officially or traditionally at the leader's disposal, his authority as defined by the group's rules and bylaws, and the organizational support given to him in dealing with his men. This dimension can be operationally defined by means

of a check list (Fiedler, 1964) containing items such as "Leader can effect promotion or demotion," "Leader enjoys special rank and status in real life which sets him apart from, and above, his group members." The median interrater agreement of four independent judges rating 35 group situations was .95.

A Three-Dimensional Group Classification

Group-task situations can now be rated on the basis of the three dimensions of leader-member relations, task structure, and position power. This locates each group in a three-dimensional space. A rough categorization can be accomplished by halving each of the dimensions so that we obtain an eight-celled cube (Fig. 20.1). We can now determine whether the correlations between leader attitudes and group performance within each of these eight cells, or octants, are relatively similar in magnitude and direction. If they are, we can infer that the group classification has been successfully accomplished since it shows that groups falling within the same octant require similar leader attitudes.

A previous paper has summarized 53 group-task situations which are based on our previous studies (Fiedler, 1964). These 53 group-task situations have been ordered into the eight octants. As can be seen from Table 20.1, groups falling within the same octant show correlations between the

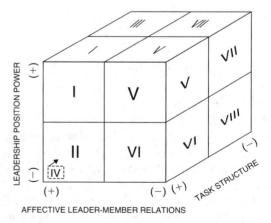

FIGURE 20.1 ■ A model for the classification of group-task situations.

leader's ASo or LPC score and the group performance criterion which are relatively similar in magnitude and direction. We can thus infer that the group classification has been accomplished with at least reasonable success.

Consideration of Figure 20.1 suggests a further classification of the cells in terms of the effective power which the group-task situation places at the leader's disposal, or more precisely, the favorableness of the situation for the leader's exercise of his power and influence.

Such an ordering can be accomplished without difficulty at the extreme poles of the continuum. A liked and trusted leader with high rank and a structured task is in a more favorable position than is a disliked and powerless leader with an ambiguous task. The intermediate steps pose certain theoretical and methodological problems. To collapse a three-dimensional system into an undimensional one implies in Coombs' terms a partial order or a lexicographic system for which there is no unique solution. Such an ordering must, therefore, be done either intuitively or in accordance with some reasonable assumptions. In the present instance we have postulated that the most important dimension in the system is the leader-member relationship since the highly liked and respected leader is less in need of position power or the power of the higher authority incorporated in the task structure. The second most important dimension is the task

structure, since a leader with a highly structured task does not require a powerful leader position. (For example, privates or noncommissioned officers in the army are at times called upon to lead or instruct officers in certain highly structured tasks—such as demonstrating a new weapon or teaching medical officers close order drill—though not in unstructured tasks—such as planning new policies on strategy.) This leads us to order the group-task situations first on leader-member relations, then on task structure, and finally on position power. While admittedly not a unique solution, the resulting ordering constitutes a reasonable continuum which indicates the degree of the leader's effective power in the group.[1]

A Contingency Model for Predicting Leadership Performance

As was already apparent from Table 20.1, the relationship between leader attitudes and group performance is contingent upon the accurate classification of the group-task situation. A more meaningful model of this contingency relationship emerges when we now plot the correlation between LPC or ASo and group performance on the one hand, against the octants ordered on the effective power or favorableness-for-the-leader dimension on the other. This is shown in Figure 20.2. Note

TABLE 20.1. Median Correlation between Leader LPC and Group Performance in Various Octants

	Leader-member relations	Task structure	Position power	Median correlation	Number of relations included in median
Octant I	Good	Structured	Strong	−.52	8
Octant II	Good	Structured	Weak	−.58	3
Octant III	Good	Unstructured	Strong	−.41	4
Octant IV	Good	Unstructured	Weak	.47	10
Octant V	Mod. Poor	Structured	Strong	.42	6
Octant VI	Mod. Poor	Structured	Weak		0
Octant VII	Mod. Poor	Unstructured	Strong	.05	10
Octant VIII	Mod. Poor	Unstructured	Weak	−.43	12

---

[1] Another cell should be added which contains real-life groups which reject their leader. Exercise of power would be very difficult in this situation and such a cell should be placed at the extreme negative end of the continuum. Such cases are treated in the section on validation.

that each point in the plot is a *correlation* predicting leadership performance or group effectiveness. The plot therefore represents 53 *sets of groups* totaling over 800 separate groups.

As Figure 20.2 shows, managing, controlling, directive (low LPC) leaders perform most effectively either under very favorable or under very unfavorable situations. Hence we obtain negative correlations between LPC and group performance scores. Considerate, permissive, accepting leaders obtain optimal group performance under situations intermediate in favorableness. These are situations in which (a) the task is structured, but the leader is disliked and must, therefore, be diplomatic; (b) the liked leader has an ambiguous, unstructured task and must, therefore, draw upon the creativity and cooperation of his members. Here we obtain positive correlations between LPC and group performance scores. Where the task is highly structured

and the leader is well liked, nondirective behavior or permissive attitudes (such as asking how the group ought to proceed with a missile count-down) is neither appropriate nor beneficial. Where the situation is quite unfavorable, e.g., where the disliked chairman of a volunteer group faces an ambiguous task, the leader might as well be autocratic and directive since a positive, nondirective attitude under these conditions might result in complete inactivity on the part of the group. This model, thus, tends to shed some light on the apparent inconsistencies in our own data as well as in data obtained by other investigators.

Empirical Tests: Extension of the Model

The basic hypothesis of the model suggests that the directive, controlling, task-oriented (low LPC)

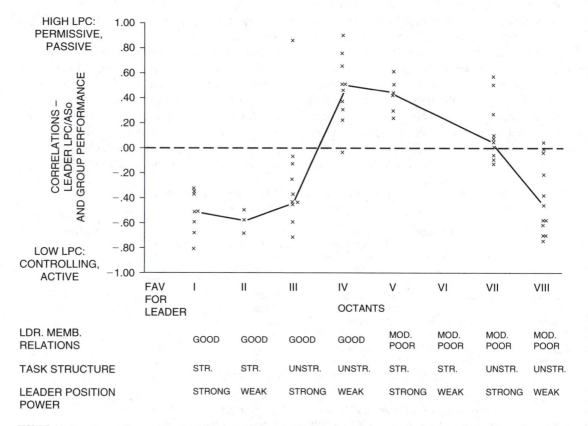

FIGURE 20.2 ■ Correlations of leader LPC and group performance plotted against octants, that is, favorableness of group-task situation for leader.

leader will be most successful in group-task situations which are either very favorable or else very unfavorable for the leader. The permissive, considerate, human-relations-oriented (high LPC) leader will perform best under conditions which are intermediate in favorableness. This hypothesis was tested by reanalyzing data from previous studies as well as by a major experiment specifically designed to test the model. Both are briefly described below.

Reanalyses of Previous Studies

As we indicated before, there is reason to believe that the relationship between the leader and his members is the most important of the three dimensions for classifying group-task situations. The problem of exercising leadership will be a relatively easy one in group-task situations in which the leader is not only liked by his crew and gets along well with his group, but in which the task is structured and the leader has a relatively powerful position. The situation will be somewhat more difficult if the leader under the latter circumstances has an only moderately good relationship with his group members, and it will be quite difficult if the leader-member relations are very poor, i.e., if the group members reject or actively dislike the leader. Ordinarily this does not occur in laboratory studies. It does happen, however, that real-life groups strongly reject leaders—sometimes to the point of sabotaging the task. Since such a situation would present a very difficult problem in leadership, we would expect better performance from the task-oriented, controlling leader, and hence a negative correlation between the leader's ASo of LPC score and his group's performance. This result appeared in one study of bomber crews for which we already

had the appropriate data, and it was tested by new analyses in two other studies.

Bomber crew study. A study of B-29 bomber crews was conducted (Fiedler, 1955) in which the criterion of performance consisted of radar bomb scores. This is the average circular error or accuracy of hitting the target by means of radar procedures. The crews were classified on the basis of the relationship between the aircraft commander and his crew members. The crews were ordered on whether or not (a) the aircraft commander was the most chosen member of the crew, and (b) the aircraft commander sociometrically endorsed his key men on his radar bombing team (the radar observer and navigator).

The results of this analysis are presented in Table 20.2. It can be seen that the correlations between ASo and crew performance are highly negative in crews having very good and very poor leader-group relations, but they tend to be positive in the intermediate range.

Antiaircraft artillery crews. A second set of data came from a study of antiaircraft artillery crews (Hutchins and Fiedler, 1960). The criterion of crew performance consisted of scores indicating the "location and acquisition" of unidentified aircraft. These crews were subdivided on the basis of leader-crew relations by separately correlating the leader's LPC score with group performance (a) for the ten crews which most highly chose their crew commander, (b) the ten which were in the intermediate range, and (c) the ten crews which gave the least favorable sociometric choices to their leader. Correlation coefficients (Rho) of $-.34$, $+.49$,

TABLE 20.2. Correlations between Aircraft Commander's (AC's) ASo Score and Radar Bomb Scores under Different Patterns of Sociometric Choices in B-29 Bomber Crews

	Rho	N
AC is most preferred crew member and chooses keymen (K)	$-.81$	10
AC is most preferred crew member and is neutral to K	$-.14$	6
AC is most preferred crew member and does not choose K	$.43$	6
AC is not most preferred crew member but chooses K	$-.03$	18
AC is not most preferred crew member and is neutral to K	$-.80$	5
AC is not most preferred crew member and does not choose K	$-.67$	7

and −.42 were obtained respectively for the three sets of artillery crews. Here again there is a clear indication that controlling and directive leaders perform most effectively under very favorable or unfavorable leader-group relations (negative correlations between LPC and group performance), whereas more permissive and accepting leaders obtain optimal group performance when leader-group relations are intermediate in favorableness (positive correlations between LPC and group performance).

Consumer cooperative companies. Finally we reanalyzed data from a study of 31 consumer cooperatives (Godfrey, Fiedler, and Hall, 1959) in which the criterion of performance consisted of the percentage of company net income over a three-year period. The companies were subdivided into those

in which the general manager was sociometrically chosen (a) by his board of directors as well as by his staff of assistant managers, (b) by his board but not his staff, or (c) by his staff but not his board, and (d) the companies in which the general manager was rejected, or not chosen, by both board of directors and staff. The findings shown in Table 20.3 are clearly consistent with those reported above for the two studies of military personnel.

The results of these three investigations are summarized in Figure 20.3. It can be seen that the task-oriented, managing, low LPC leaders performed best under very favorable and under very unfavorable situations, while the permissive, considerate leaders performed best under conditions intermediate in favorableness. These data, therefore, clearly support the hypothesis derived from the model.

TABLE 20.3. Correlations between General Manager's ASo Score and Company Net Income

	Rho	N
Gen. Mgr. is chosen by board and staff (ASo Perf.)	−.67	10
Gen. Mgr. is chosen by board, but rejected by staff	.20	6
Gen. Mgr. is rejected by board, but chosen by staff	.26	6
Gen. Mgr. is rejected by board and staff	−.75	7

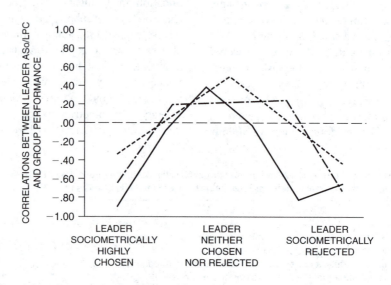

FIGURE 20.3 ■ Correlations between leader LPC or ASo scores and group performance under three conditions of leader acceptance by the group in studies of bomber crews, antiaircraft artillery crews, and consumer cooperatives.

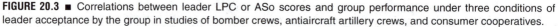

Experimental Test of the Contingency Model

In cooperation with the Belgian naval forces we recently conducted a major study which served in part as a specific test of the model. Only aspects immediately relevant to the test are here described. The investigation was conducted in Belgium where the French- and Dutch-speaking (or Flemish) sectors of the country have been involved in a long-standing and frequently acrimonious dispute. This conflict centers about the use of language, but it also involves a host of other cultural factors which differentiate the 60 percent Flemish- and 40 percent French-speaking population groups in Wallonie and Brussels. This "linguistic problem," which is rooted in the beginning of Belgium's natural history, has in recent years been the cause of continuous public controversy, frequent protest meetings, and occasional riots.

The linguistic problem is of particular interest here since a group consisting of members whose mother tongue, culture, and attitudes differ will clearly present a more difficult problem in leadership than a group whose members share the same language and culture. We were thus able to test the major hypothesis of the model as well as to extend the research by investigating the type of leadership which linguistically and culturally heterogeneous groups require.

Design. The experiment was conducted at the naval training center at Ste. Croix-Bruges.[2] It utilized 48 career petty officers and 240 recruits who had been selected from a pool of 546 men on the basis of a pretest in which we obtained LPC, intelligence, attitude, and language comprehension scores.

The experiment was specifically designed to incorporate the three major group classification dimensions shown in Figure 20.1, namely, leader-member relations, position power, and task structure. It also added the additional dimension of group homogeneity vs. heterogeneity. Specifically, 48 groups had leaders with high position power (petty officers) while 48 had leaders with low position power (recruits); 48 groups began with the unstructured task, while the other 48 groups began with the two structured tasks; 48 groups were homogeneous, consisting of three French- or three Dutch-speaking men, while the other 48 groups were heterogeneous, consisting of a French-speaking leader and two Flemish members, or a Dutch-speaking, Flemish leader and two French-speaking members. The quality of the leader-member relations was measured as in our previous studies by means of a group atmosphere scale which the leader completed after each task session.

Group performance criteria. Two essentially identical structured tasks were administered. Each lasted 25 minutes and required the groups to find the shortest route for a ship which, given certain fuel capacity and required ports of call, had to make a round trip calling at respectively ten or twelve ports. The tasks were objectively scored on the basis of sea miles required for the trip. Appropriate corrections and penalities were assigned for errors.

The unstructured task required the groups to compose a letter to young men of 16 and 17 years, urging them to choose the Belgian navy as a career. The letter was to be approximately 200 words in length and had to be completed in 35 minutes. Each of the letters, depending upon the language in which it was written, was then rated by Dutch- or

---

[2] This investigation was conducted in collaboration with Dr. J. M. Nuttin (Jr.) and his students while the author was a Ford Faculty Research Fellow at the University of Louvain, 1963–1964. The experiment, undertaken with permission of Commodore L. Petitjean, then Chief of Staff of the Belgian naval forces, was carried out at the Centre de Formation Navale, Ste. Croix-Bruges. The writer wishes to express his special gratitude and appreciation to the commandant of the center, Captain

V. Van Laethem, who not only made the personnel and the facilities of the center available to us, but whose active participation in the planning and the execution of the project made this study possible. We are also most grateful to Dr. U. Bouvier, Director of the Center for Social Studies, Ministry of Defense, and to Capt. W. Cafferata, USN, of the U.S. Military Assistance and Advisory Group, and to Cmdr. J. Robison, U.S. Naval Attaché in Brussels, who provided liaison and guidance.

by French-speaking judges on style, the use of language, as well as interest value, originality, and persuasiveness. Estimated reliability was .92 and .86 for Dutch- and French-speaking judges, respectively.

It should be noted in this connection that the task of writing a letter is not as unstructured as might have been desirable for this experiment. The form of any letter of this type is fairly standardized, and its content was, of course, suggested by the instructions. The navy officers with whom we consulted throughout the study considered it unwise, however, to give a highly unstructured task, such as writing a fable or proposing a new policy, since tasks of this nature were likely to threaten the men and to cause resentment and poor cooperation. High and low task structure is, therefore, less well differentiated in this study than it has been in previous investigations.

Results. The contingency model specifies that the controlling, managing, low LPC leaders will be most effective either in very favorable or else in relatively unfavorable group-task situations, while the permissive, considerate, high LPC leaders will be more effective in situations intermediate in difficulty.

The basic test of the hypothesis requires, therefore, that we order the group-task situations represented in this experiment in terms of the difficulty which they are likely to present for the leader. Since there are 16 cells in the design, the size of the sample within each cell (namely, 6 groups) is, of course, extremely small. However, where the conditions are reasonably replicated by other cells, the relationship can be estimated from the median rank-order correlations.

The hypothesis can be tested more readily with correlations of leader LPC and group performance in homogeneous groups on the more reliably scorable second structured task. These conditions approximate most closely those represented in Figure 20.3, on bomber and antiaircraft crews and consumer cooperatives. We have here made the fairly obvious assumption that the powerful leader or the leader who feels liked and accepted faces an easier group-task situation than low-ranking leaders and those who see the groups as unpleasant and

tense. Each situation is represented by two cells of six groups each. Arranging the group-task situations in order of favorableness for the leader then gives us the following results:

> High group atmosphere and high position
> power . . . −.77, −.77
> High group atmosphere and low position
> power . . . +.60, +.50
> Low group atmosphere and high position
> power . . . +.16, +.01
> Low group atmosphere and low position
> power . . . −.16, −.43

These are, of course, the trends in size and magnitude of correlations which the model predicts. Low LPC leaders are again most effective in favorable and unfavorable group-task situations; the more permissive, considerate, high LPC leaders were more effective in the intermediate situations.

Extending the model to include heterogeneous groups requires that we make a number of additional assumptions for weighting each of the group-task dimensions so that all 48 cells (i.e., 16 cells × 3 tasks) can be reasonably ordered on the same scale. We have here assigned equal weights of 3 to the favorable poles of the major dimension, i.e., to homogeneity, high group atmosphere, and high position power. A weight of 1 was assigned to the first structured task, and a weight of 2 to the second structured task on the assumption that the structured task makes the group-task situation somewhat more favorable than the unstructured task, and that the practice and learning effect inherent in performing a second, practically identical, task will make the group-task situation still more favorable for the leader. Finally, a weight of 1 was given to the "second presentation," that is, the group task which occurred toward the end of the session, on the assumption that the leader by that time had gotten to know his group members and had learned to work with them more effectively, thus again increasing the favorableness of his group-task situation to a certain extent.

The resulting weighting system leads to a scale from 12 to 0 points, with 12 as the most favorable pole. If we now plot the median correlation coefficients of the 48 group-task situations against the scale indicating the favorableness of the situation for the leader, we obtain the curve presented in Figure 20.4.

As can be seen, we again obtain a curvilinear relationship which resembles the one shown in Figure 20.2. Heterogeneous groups with low position power and/or poor leader-member relations fall below point .00 on the scale, and thus tend to perform better with controlling, directive, low LPC leaders. Only under otherwise very favorable conditions do heterogeneous groups perform better

with permissive, considerate, high LPC leaders, that is, in group-task situations characterized by high group atmosphere as well as high position power, four of the six correlations (66%) are positive, while only five of eighteen (28%) are positive in the less favorable group-task situations.

It is interesting to note that the curve is rather flat and characterized by relatively low negative correlations as we go toward the very unfavorable end of the scale. This result supports Meuwese's (1964) recent study which showed that correlations between leader LPC as well as between leader

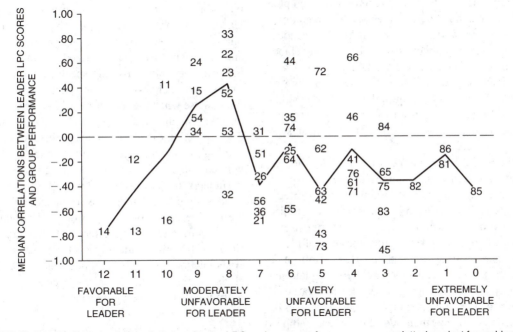

FIGURE 20.4 ■ Median correlations between leader LPC and group performance scores plotted against favorableness-for-leader scale in the Belgian Navy study. The code is explained in the table.

Code in Fig. 20.4

Composition	1st Digit				2nd Digit		
	Pos. pow.	High group atmos.	Low group atmos.		Task	1st pres.	2nd pres.
Homo.	High	1	5		Str. I	1	2
Homo.	Low	2	6		Str. II	3	4
Het.	High	3	7		Unstr.	5	6
Het.	Low	4	8				

intelligence and group performance tend to become attenuated under conditions of relative stress. These findings suggest that the leader's ability to influence and control the group decreases beyond a certain point of stress and difficulty in the group-task situation.

Discussion

The contingency model seeks to reconcile results which up to now had to be considered inconsistent and difficult to understand. We have here attempted to develop a theoretical framework which can provide guidance for further research. While the model will undoubtedly undergo modifications and elaboration as new data become available, it provides an additional step toward a better understanding of leadership processes required in different situations. We have here tried to specify exactly the type of leadership which different group-task situations require.

The model has a number of important implications for selection and training as well as for the placement of leaders and organizational strategy. Our research suggests, first of all, that we can utilize a very broad spectrum of individuals for positions of leadership. The problem becomes one of placement and training rather than of selection since both the permissive, democratic, human-relations-oriented and the managing, autocratic, task-oriented leaders can be effectively utilized. Leaders can be trained to recognize their own style of leadership as well as the conditions which are most compatible with their style.

The model also points to a variety of administrative and supervisory strategies which the organization can adopt to fit the group-task situation to the needs of the leader. Tasks can, after all, be structured to a greater or lesser extent by giving very specific and detailed, or vague and general, instructions; the position power of the group leader can be increased or decreased and even the congeniality of a group and its acceptance of the leader can be affected by appropriate administrative action, e.g., increasing or decreasing the group's homogeneity.

The model also throws new light on phenomena which were rather difficult to fit into our usual ideas about measurement in social psychology. Why, for example, should groups differ so markedly in their performance on nearly parallel tasks? The model—and our data—show that the situation becomes easier for the leader as the group moves from the novel to the already known group-task situations. The leaders who excel under relatively novel and therefore more difficult conditions are not necessarily those who excel under those which are more routine, or better known, and therefore more favorable. Likewise, we find that different types of task structure require different types of leader behavior. Thus, in a research project's early phases the project director tends to be democratic and permissive: everyone is urged to contribute to the plan and to criticize all aspects of the design. This situation changes radically in the more structured phase when the research design is frozen and the experiment is underway. Here the research director tends to become managing, controlling, and highly autocratic and woe betide the assistant who attempts to be creative in giving instructions to subjects, or in his timing of tests. A similar situation is often found in business organization where the routine operation tends to be well structured and calls for a managing, directive leadership. The situation becomes suddenly unstructured when a crisis occurs. Under these conditions the number of discussions, meetings, and conferences increases sharply so as to give everyone an opportunity to express his views.

At best, this model is of course only a partial theory of leadership. The leader's intellectual and task-relevant abilities, and the members' skills and motivation, all play a role in affecting the group's performance. It is to be hoped that these other important aspects of group interaction can be incorporated into the model in the not too distant future.

REFERENCES

BASS, B. M. *Leadership, psychology and organizational behavior.* New York: Harper & Row, 1960.

BROWNE, C. G., and COHN, T. S. (Eds.). *The study of leadership.* Danville, Ill.: Interstate Printers and Publishers, 1958.

CLEVEN, W. A., and FIEDLER, F. E. Interpersonal perceptions of open hearth foremen and steel production. *J. appl. Psychol.*, 1956, *40*, 312–314.

CRONBACH, L. J., and GLESER, GOLDENE, C. Assessing similarity between profiles. *Psychol. Bull.*, 1953, *50*, 456–473.

FIEDLER, F. E. Assumed similarity measures as predictors of team effectiveness. *J. abnorm. Soc. Psychol.*, 1954, *49*, 381–388.

FIEDLER, F. E. The influence of leader-keymen relations on combat crew effectiveness. *J. abnorm. Soc. Psychol.*, 1955, *51*, 227–235.

FIEDLER, F. E. Leader attitudes, group climate, and group creativity. *J. abnorm. Soc. Psychol.*, 1962, *65*, 308–318.

FIEDLER, F. E. A contingency model of leadership effectiveness. In L. Berkowitz (Ed.), *Advances in experimental social psychology*, New York: Academic Press, 1964.

FIEDLER, F. E., and MEUWESE, W. A. T. The leader's contribution to performance in cohesive and uncohesive groups. *J. abnorm. Soc. Psychol.*, 1963, *67*, 83–87.

FIEDLER, F. E., MEUWESE, W. A. T., and OONK, SOPHIE. Performance of laboratory tasks requiring group creativity. *Acta Psychologica*, 1961, *18*, 100–119.

FRENCH, J. R. P., JR. A formal theory of social power. *Psychol. Rev.*, 1956, *63*, 181–194.

GIBB, C. A. Leadership. In G. Lindzey (Ed.), *Handbook of social psychology*, Vol. 2. Reading, Mass.: Addison-Wesley, 1954.

GODFREY, ELEANOR P., FIEDLER, F. E., and HALL, D. M. *Boards, management, and company success.* Danville, Ill.: Interstate Printers and Publishers, 1959.

HARE, A. P. *Handbook of small group research.* New York: The Free Press of Glencoe, 1962.

HAWKINS, C. A study of factors mediating a relationship between leader rating behavior and group productivity. Unpublished Ph.D. dissertation, Univer. Of Minnesota, 1962.

HUTCHINS, E. B., and FIEDLER, F. E. Task-oriented and quasi-therapeutic role functions of the leader in small military groups. *Sociometry*, 1960, *23*, 293–406.

JULIAN, J. W., and McGRATH, J. E. *The influence of leader and member behavior on the adjustment and task effectiveness of negotiation groups.* Urbana, Ill.: Group Effectiveness Research Laboratory, Univer. Of Illinois, 1963.

McGRATH, J. E. *A summary of small group research studies.* Arlington, Va.: Human Sciences Research Inc., 1962 (Litho.).

MANN, R. D. A review of the relationship between personality and performance in small groups. *Psychol. Bull.*, 1959, *56*, 241–270.

MEUWESE, W. A. T. The effect of the leader's ability and interpersonal attitudes on group creativity under varying conditions of stress. Unpublished doctoral dissertation, Univer. Of Amsterdam, 1964.

MORRIS, C. G., II. The effects of leader attitudes on the behavior of problem solving groups and their leaders. Unpublished MA thesis, Univer. of Illinois, 1964.

OSGOOD, C. E., SUCI, G. A., and TANNENBAUM, P. H. *The measurement of meaning.* Urbana, Ill.: Univer. Of Illinois Press, 1957.

PROSHANSKY, H., and SEIDENBERG, B. (Eds.). *Basic studies in social psychology.* New York: Holt, Rinehart & Winston, 1965.

SHAW, M. E. Annual Technical Report, 1962. Gainesville, Fla.: Univer. Of Florida, 1962 (Mimeo.).

STOGDILL, R. M. Personal factors associated with leadership: a survey of the literature. *J. Psychol.*, 1948, *25*, 35–71.

STOGDILL, R. M., and COONS, A. E. Leader behavior: its description and measurement. Columbus, Ohio: Ohio State University, *Res. Monogr. No. 88*, 1957.

Self-Categorization and Leadership: Effects of Group Prototypicality and Leader Stereotypicality

Sarah C. Hains, Michael A. Hogg, and Julie M. Duck

A self-categorization model of leadership is introduced (leaders have the prototypical characteristics of a psychologically salient in-group) and contrasted with leadership categorization theory (leaders have the appropriate stereotypical properties of a leader schema) in a $2 \times 2 \times 2$ experiment. Under conditions of high or low group salience, and in anticipation of a group activity, subjects evaluated the leadership effectiveness of a randomly nominated leader who was group prototypical or nonprototypical and whose behavior was stereotypical or nonstereotypical of a leader schema. As predicted from the authors' self-categorization analysis, group prototypicality was a significant basis for leadership for subjects who identified with the group but not for those who did not. There was a general effect, consistent with leader categorization theory, whereby stereotypical leaders were perceived to be more effective than nonstereotypical leaders. However, as predicted, this effect was weaker under high group identification.

Leadership has long been a popular focus of research for the social sciences (e.g., Eagly, Karau, & Makhijani, 1995; Graumann & Moscovici, 1986; Hunt, Baliga, Dachler, & Schriesheim, 1988), particularly for social and organizational psychology (e.g., Bass, 1990; House & Baetz, 1990; Stogdill, 1974; Yukl, 1981). In recent years, however, it has waned in popularity as a focus for social psychological research and is instead more commonly studied in other disciplines

Note: Thanks go to Sarah Nicoll and Katy White for helping run sessions. Some of the data reported in this article were presented by the first author at the April 1995 Inaugural Conference of the Society of Australasian Social Psychologists, Hobart, TAS, Australia. Address correspondence to Michael A. Hogg, School of Psychology, University of Queensland, Brisbane, QLD 4072, Australia, e-mail mike@psy.uq.edu.au.

(see Levine & Moreland, 1990). This may reflect a recent tendency for social psychologists to pay more attention to individual cognition (e.g., Fiske, 1993b; Fiske & Taylor, 1991) and intergroup behavior (e.g., Brewer & Miller, 1996) than to intragroup processes and group structure (see Moreland, Hogg, & Hains, 1994). The present article describes how self-categorization theory (Turner, 1985; Turner, Hogg, Oakes, Reicher, & Wetherell, 1987), a social-cognitive intergroup theory, can be used to cast light on leadership as a characteristic of intragroup structure.

The history of leadership research in social psychology has largely been a struggle between personality and situational perspectives. Although personality perspectives have produced a handful of personality correlates of leadership (e.g., Mullen, Salas, & Driskell, 1989), these are generally weak, and many scholars now agree that personality is a relatively poor predictor of leadership (Stogdill, 1974; Yukl, 1981). Situational perspectives (e.g., Bales, 1950; Sherif, 1966) have fared somewhat better; almost anyone can be an effective leader if the circumstances are right. In the 1960s, drawing on research that described the actual behavior of leaders (e.g., Bales, 1950; Lippitt & White, 1943; Stogdill, 1974), Fiedler (1965, 1971, 1981) introduced his contingency theory—an interactionist model that considers the effectiveness of a particular leadership style to be contingent on the favorability of the situation that the leader faces. Commentators tend to agree that Fiedler's model is generally well supported (e.g., Strube & Garcia, 1981) despite some continuing controversy (e.g., Peters, Hartke, & Pohlmann, 1985).

In many respects, social psychology quietly closed the book on leadership at this point, and social psychologists turned their attention to other topics. One notable exception has been leader categorization theory (Lord, 1977, 1985; Lord & Alliger, 1985; Lord, Foti, & DeVader, 1984; Nye & Forsyth, 1991; Palich & Hom, 1992; Phillips & Lord, 1981). This theory is firmly grounded in contemporary social cognition. It states that people have preconceptions about how effective leaders should behave in general and in more specific leadership situations. These preconceptions are cognitive schemas of types of leaders (i.e., categories of leaders that are represented as person-schemas) that operate in the same way as other schemas (see Fiske & Taylor, 1991). People are categorized as leaders on the basis of the perceived match between their behavior or character and the prototypic attributes (i.e., schema) of a preexisting leader category (e.g., Rush & Russell, 1988). Once someone is categorized, the relevant leadership schema generates further assumptions about that person's behavior. The perceived effectiveness of an incumbent leader depends on the extent to which the person's leadership attributes are congruent with the perceiver's salient leadership schema. Leadership schemas vary in situational inclusiveness; subordinate schemas are applicable only to specific situations, whereas superordinate schemas are applicable to a wide range of situations. Although leadership schemas are cognitive representations that may be widely shared, they are not closely tied to defining properties of specific social groups. For example, Rush and Russell (1988) found that leadership perceptions among people enrolled in graduate business courses were more strongly influenced by leadership schemas than by actual characteristics of specific leaders or of the groups they led.

This perspective treats leader categories as nominal categories—that is, as abstract cognitive clusterings of instances that share attributes but do not have any psychological existence as a real social group. Indeed, the notion of a social group of leaders really makes little sense; who would lead and who would follow? Leadership is viewed as a product of individual information processing, not as a structural property of real groups or as an intrinsic or emergent property of psychological group membership (see Hogg, 1996a).

One facet of leadership that seems to have been underemphasized by many perspectives, including leader categorization theory, is that leadership may be a structural feature of in-groups that is generated by group belongingness. Leadership processes and perceptions may rest on a structural differentiation of groups into leader(s) and followers that is at least partly generated by psychological processes associated with the experience of group membership. If so, then having the prototypical or normative characteristics of a salient in-group (i.e., being a prototypical in-group member) may be at least as important for leadership as having the prototypical characteristics of a particular type of leader (i.e., being congruent with the schema of a nominal leader category).

This suggests that group identification may play an important role in leadership dynamics. Self-categorization theory (Turner, 1985; Turner et al., 1987), a development of social identity theory (e.g., Hogg & Abrams, 1988; Tajfel & Turner, 1979; Turner, 1982), attributes group behavior to a depersonalization of perception, affect, and behavior that is produced by categorizing the self and others in terms of in-group/out-group distinctions. Self-categorization transforms the self-concept from a structure based on individuality to one based on group prototypicality (e.g., group normativeness). To avoid confusion, we will henceforth replace the term *prototypicality* used by leader categorization theorists with *stereotypicality* and reserve the term *prototypicality* to refer to our self-categorization theory usage.

Although the self-categorization/social identity perspective is usually associated with research on intergroup behavior, broad social categories, and stereotyping, it also offers a general perspective for analyzing group-mediated social psychological phenomena (e.g., Hogg, 1996a; Hogg & Abrams, 1988; Hogg, Terry, & White, 1995). Several such analyses can be found, focusing on, for example, social influence (Turner, 1991), small-group processes (Hogg, 1992, 1996b), attitudes (Terry & Hogg, 1996), and the social self-concept (Abrams, 1994). A self-categorization analysis of intragroup differentiation and structure has not yet, however, been fully developed (Brewer, 1991, 1993; Hogg, 1996a; Hogg, Terry, & White, 1995). Thus, a self-categorization analysis of leadership, which is one of the most fundamental structural features of groups, not only is useful for understanding leadership as a group process, but also is a test of the theory's utility in intragroup contexts.

A self-categorization analysis of leadership has recently been presented by Hogg (1996a). Leaders are individuals who have disproportionate influence, often because of their prestige and power, over the attitudes, behaviors, and destiny of in-group members. A group leader should thus be the individual who occupies the contextually most prototypical group position—as this is the position that embodies the behaviors to which most group members conform. In-group prototypes are closely tied to the social comparative context (i.e., the people, attributes, and categories that are the contextually salient basis of social information processing) because, for self-categorization theory, they embody the optimal balance between maximization of intragroup similarities and intergroup differences (i.e., prototypes are governed by the principle of metacontrast). If the comparative context remains relatively stable, then so does the prototype, and so the same person will remain in the leadership (i.e., most influential) position. This is a relatively passive process; the leader does not lead in an active sense but merely embodies the aspirations, attitudes, and behaviors of the group.

However, leadership is more than merely being a prototypical group member; it also involves the active exercise of individual power. People occupying prototypical positions may acquire such power in at least two ways: (a) They are socially attractive (Hogg, 1992, 1993; Hogg, Cooper-Shaw, & Holzworth, 1993; Hogg & Hains, 1996; Hogg & Hardie, 1991), so people in the group are more likely to comply with their suggestions, requests, and orders; (b) they are perceived to have charismatic/leadership personalities, due to attribution processes that cause members to attribute a leader's influence to the person rather than to the position that he or she occupies (cf. the fundamental attribution error; Ross, 1977). Indeed, because prototypical members are often figural against the background of less prototypical members, the fundamental attribution error may be especially strong for them (e.g., Taylor & Fiske, 1978). Once leaders are perceived to be charismatic and to have power, the dispositional attribution of power may be reinforced. People with relatively less power in a given context (i.e., followers) are motivated to redress their perceived lack of control. One way in which they can do this is by focusing attention on those who do have power (i.e., leaders) to discover highly diagnostic individuating information (i.e., dispositional information) about those with power (e.g., Fiske, 1993a; Fiske & Dépret, 1996).

The longer a person remains in a leadership position, the stronger these factors will become; social attraction will be stronger and more consensual, and personal attribution will be more entrenched and pervasive in its consequences. Having acquired power in these ways, the person occupying the prototypical position will be able to adopt the more active aspects of leadership, including the power to be innovative and constructively deviant and to maintain his or her leadership position by influencing the social comparative context and thus his or her prototypicality. Additionally, groups with consensual prototypes are more likely to have entrenched leaders, due to the consensuality of perceptions of and feelings for the leader by the group. In groups without consensual prototypes, there will be greater dissensus of perceptions of and feelings for the leader. As a result, the leader may have less power and may occupy a less stable position. Leadership schemas (cf. leadership categorization theory) will also have a role to play; once someone has been categorized as a leader on the basis of the processes just described, leadership schemas may generate additional assumptions about that person's personality and behavior.

This theory of leadership (Hogg, 1996a) is as yet untested. However, it integrates within one conceptual framework several themes that already exist in the leadership literature. These include the idea that leaders should adhere to group norms (e.g., Hollander, 1958) and be representative members of the group (e.g., Eagly et al., 1995; Eagly, Makhijani, & Klonsky, 1992) but that they should also be innovative and thus deviant (e.g., Bray, Johnson, & Chilstrom, 1982; Hollander, 1958; see Levine, 1989); the idea that leaders are liked more if they are similar to their followers (e.g., Eagly et al., 1995; Eagly et al., 1992; Pavitt & Sackaroff, 1990) and that people who acquire status through leadership become more attractive (e.g., Humphrey, 1985; Messé, Kerr, & Sattler, 1992; Sande, Ellard, & Ross, 1986); and the idea that group members may systematically credit effective leadership

characteristics to someone who merely occupies the leadership role (e.g., Meindl, 1990, 1995; Pfeffer, 1977). Although the theory has a number of interrelated components, at its core lies the notion, derived from self-categorization theory, that group prototypicality has an important role in leadership. Specifically, more prototypical group members are more likely to become leaders, and more likely to be perceived as effective leaders, than are less prototypical group members.

The present study focuses on the role of group prototypicality in perceived leadership effectiveness. The specific aim of the study is to show that perceived leadership effectiveness is more strongly related to the group prototypicality of the leader under conditions in which group membership is made salient than under conditions in which individuality is salient. Schemas for leadership behavior will also influence perceived leadership effectiveness but will be unrelated or inversely related to the salience of group membership. The independent variables of salience of in-group membership, in-group prototypicality of the leader, and leader stereotypicality (schema congruence) of the leader were orthogonally manipulated in an experimental paradigm that was loosely based on earlier group polarization studies by Hogg, Turner, and Davidson (1990) and McGarty, Turner, Hogg, David, and Wetherell (1992). Under conditions of high or low group salience, subjects anticipated joining a discussion group and were given information about the group's leader that described him or her as a prototypical or nonprototypical group member (group prototypicality) and as possessing or not possessing qualities congruent with a general leadership schema (leader stereotypicality). In addition to checks on the manipulations, the principal dependent measures focused on anticipatory perceptions and evaluations of the leader's behavior and effectiveness.

From our self-categorization analysis of leadership, at least two hypotheses can be derived. The main prediction is for a Salience × Prototypicality interaction on perceived leadership effectiveness (Hypothesis 1). Under conditions of high group salience, the group prototypicality of the leader becomes an important basis for evaluating leadership effectiveness, such that prototypical leaders are perceived as more effective than non-prototypical leaders. Under conditions of low group salience, the group prototypicality of the leader assumes much less importance, such that there are no differences in the perceived effectiveness of prototypical and nonprototypical leaders. In other words, high salience will increase the perceived effectiveness of prototypical leaders and diminish the perceived effectiveness of nonprototypical leaders.

A second and less critical prediction is for a Salience × Leader Stereotypicality interaction on perceived leader effectiveness (Hypothesis 2). Under conditions of low group salience, the leader stereotypicality of the leader's behavior will be attended to such that more stereotypical leaders will be perceived as more effective than less stereotypical leaders. In the high-salience condition, however, stereotypicality will be less important, and so there will be less difference between stereotypical and nonstereotypical leaders. In other words, low salience will increase the perceived effectiveness of stereotypical leaders and diminish the perceived effectiveness of nonstereotypical leaders. This interaction will occur against the background of a strong main effect for leader stereotypicality, in which perceptions of leadership effectiveness are influenced by general beliefs about the characteristics of good leaders (i.e., superordinate leadership schemas).

Method

Subjects and Design

Subjects were 58 male and 126 female introductory psychology students who participated in partial fulfillment of course requirements. They were randomly assigned to conditions formed by the 2 × 2 × 2 between-subjects manipulation of three independent variables: (a) group salience, (b) group prototypicality of the leader, and (c) leader stereotypicality (schema congruence). In anticipation of a class discussion (low salience) or a group discussion and intergroup competition

(high salience), subjects were given carefully constructed feedback, based on their responses to a first questionnaire, about a target person who was purportedly chosen randomly as their leader (manipulation of group prototypicality and leader stereotypicality of the leader). They then completed a second questionnaire measuring the effectiveness of the manipulations (including group identification) and evaluations of the leader. Each experimental session contained approximately 20 subjects and was run by a female experimenter. Because of differences in verbal instructions, high- and low-salience subjects were run in separate sessions, but every session contained both levels of the other two independent variables.

Procedure

Subjects sat at tables and were instructed not to communicate with one another unless asked to do so. The experiment was introduced as a study of group decision making and discussion in high-salience conditions and as a study of individual decision making and discussion in low-salience conditions. High-salience subjects expected the class to be divided into two groups, according to their initial positions on the issue of "increased police powers." Each group would then discuss that issue to reach a consensual position, and this would be followed by an intergroup competition during which each group presented a defense of its own position to the experimenter. Low-salience subjects expected a class discussion in which each person competed with every other person to defend his or her own personal position on the issue.

First, subjects were familiarized with the issue of increased police powers by reviewing some general information about the issue. They then completed the first questionnaire, which obtained (a) demographic information, (b) information that allowed us to categorize subjects in the high-salience conditions, (c) information to lend credence to subsequent feedback provided to subjects about the group prototypicality and leader stereotypicality of the leader, and (d) information checking that the leader stereotype was applicable to the experimental situation. Subjects indicated how much they supported an increase in police powers (on a scale from 1 = *totally against* to 30 = *totally support*) and high-salience subjects also identified which side of the issue they were on (for or against) to reinforce a sense of commitment to one or the other group as regards the issue. The issue of increased police powers was chosen after pilot data ($N = 48$) revealed an approximately normal distribution (about the scale midpoint of 15.5) of opinions in the relevant student population. We thus assumed that there would be an approximately 50-50 split of high-salience subjects into groups for and against increased police powers. This was confirmed: 44 were for, and 51 were against. We chose to use a 30-point scale, with no midpoint, to allow fine gradations of opinion and to constrain high-salience subjects to choose a side on the issue.

The first questionnaire also obtained information about schemas for leadership behavior. Subjects read a leader profile that listed five behaviors identified by Cronshaw and Lord's (1987) extensive review as representing the most superordinate category of leader—that is, typical leader behaviors for a broad range of situations: (a) delays actions on decisions, (b) carefully plans what to do, (c) emphasizes group goals, (d) coordinates group's activities, and (e) lets other group members know what is expected of them. These behaviors were sufficiently general properties of leadership, in our opinion, to be equally relevant to the task and situational requirements in both the high- and the low-salience conditions. Subjects answered three questions (on 9-point scales) about this profile. The first question asked subjects to indicate how well this profile described their own leadership style (self-stereotypicality). This was primarily to lend credence to our ability to provide feedback about the stereotypicality of the leader but was also a useful check on subject differences between conditions. The other two questions checked that subjects did indeed view this profile as being stereotypical of an effective leader. Subjects indicated how much they would prefer a leader who had this profile (stereotypical leader preference) and how much they would prefer a leader who

had the opposite profile (nonstereotypical leader preference).

Questionnaires were collected and taken away, ostensibly to be examined. High-salience subjects were told that they would be formed into groups on the basis of whether they were for or against increased police powers. While this took place, and in preparation for their discussions, subjects completed a couple of interim tasks. High-salience subjects were given 2 min to think about and write down arguments in support of their group's position on the issue. They were then told to spend a few moments thinking about the type of people in their group and how they might be similar to one another but different from people in the other group. Low-salience subjects thought about and wrote down arguments in support of their personal position on the issue and then thought about the type of people they were and how they differed from other people. Although these were primarily designed as filler tasks, they also served to reinforce the manipulation of salience by helping high-salience subjects to focus on their group membership and by helping low-salience subjects to focus on their uniqueness and individuality (see Hogg & Hains, 1996; Hogg & Hardie, 1991).

Having ostensibly examined the first questionnaire and prepared additional materials, the experimenter next told high-salience subjects that they were fairly evenly split into two groups: for and against. Low-salience subjects were told that there was a range of attitudes in the class but that most people were somewhere near the middle. In this way, the perceived diversity of group positions was approximately the same for both high- and low-salience participants. A second and final questionnaire was then administered—ostensibly to distribute additional information and to obtain anticipatory thoughts and feelings before the class discussion (low-salience condition) or group discussion and intergroup competition (high-salience condition). This was a two-part questionnaire, with 30 items (most involving 9-point rating scales).

Part A of the questionnaire measured the perceived group prototype by asking subjects to indicate "the position on the topic of increased police powers which you believe best represents the position of members of your group" (on a scale from 1 = *totally against* to 30 = *totally support*). The remaining questions measured the effectiveness of the manipulation of group salience. There were three direct checks on the manipulation, which asked subjects to what extent they (a) felt like a group member rather than a distinct individual, (b) saw the competitive discussion as inter- or intragroup (group discussion), and (c) perceived two distinct groups or a number of distinct individuals to be present (on a scale ranging from 1 = *much more individual* to 9 = *much more group*). Salience was also checked more indirectly through its impact on group identification, which was measured by 11 questions taken from recent social identity/self-categorization research (e.g., Hogg et al., 1993; Hogg & Hains, 1996; Hogg & Hardie, 1991). Subjects indicated (on a scale ranging from 1 = *not very much* to 9 = *very much*) (a) how committed they felt to their group (commitment), (b) how happy they were with their choice of group (in low salience, their personal position on the issue), (c) how similar they felt they were to their group (similar), (d) how much they liked their group (like), (e) how well they fitted in their group (fit), (f) how cohesive they expected their group to be (cohesive), (g) how important their group was to them (importance), (h) how much they identified with their group (identify), (i) how glad they were to be with their group (glad), (j) how much they saw themselves belonging with their group (belong), and (k) how well they matched the representative position of their group (self-prototypicality).

After completing Part A of the questionnaire, high-salience subjects were told that a leader for each group had been randomly selected to collate group arguments and to present the group's position to the experimenter during the intergroup competition. Low-salience subjects were told that a leader had been randomly selected from the class to collate individual arguments and to present the variety of rationales representing the class's position to the experimenter. Although identification of the leader was ostensibly deferred until the discussion began, Part B of the questionnaire also presented some information about this person, so

that people could form an impression of him or her and answer questions about their impressions. The information was ostensibly gleaned from responses to the first questionnaire. The leader was identified by a code number, which was not the subject's own code number.

There were four different configurations of leader feedback, formed by the orthogonal manipulation of group prototypicality and leader stereotypicality. Prototypical and nonprototypical leaders were located differently on the 30-point attitude scale, depending on the salience condition and on whether the subject was against (1 to 15 on the scale) or for (16 to 30 on the scale) increased police powers. For high-salience subjects against increased powers, the prototypical leader occupied a position of 8, and the nonprototypical leader occupied a position of 15, whereas for low-salience subjects against increased powers, it was the other way around. For high-salience subjects for increased powers, the prototypical leader occupied a position of 23, and the nonprototypical leader occupied a position of 16, whereas for low-salience subjects for increased powers, it was the other way around. These positions were chosen on the basis of pilot data ($N = 48$) showing that 8 and 23 were the most prototypical positions for high-salience subjects against and for increased powers, respectively, and that 15.5 was the most prototypical position for low-salience subjects.

Leader stereotypicality was manipulated independently of leader prototypicality. The stereotypical leader was described as someone who, on the first questionnaire, circled 8 and the nonstereotypical leader as someone who circled 2 on the 9-point scale (ranging from 1 = *not very similar* to 9 = *very similar*) measuring how similar to the stereotypical leadership profile subjects considered their own behavior to be. Although the leader stereotypicality information was supposedly based on a leader's match to a multidimensional profile, the information was provided for subjects in this unidimensional form to make this manipulation comparable in strength and complexity to the group prototypicality manipulation.

After studying the leader feedback information, subjects answered questions (on 9-point scales) about their perceptions of the leader. Leader prototypicality was directly measured by a single question: "How well does the leader match the group position?" (leader prototypicality). This was followed by three questions concerning subjects' approval or endorsement of the leader: "How representative is the leader of the group?" (representative), "How appropriate is the leader's position for leadership?" (leader appropriateness), and "How relevant to leadership is his/her position?" (relevance). There was also one question concerning how similar subjects felt they were to the leader (similar to leader). Finally, there were 10 specific questions measuring perceived leadership effectiveness. Subjects were asked to what extent the leader (a) had qualities for good leadership (qualities), (b) matched their image of a good leader (fit image), (c) behaved as a leader should (behave), and (d) would be an effective leader (effective). They were also asked questions about (e) liking for the leader (like leader), (f) overall goodness of the leader (good leader), (g) support for the leader (support leader), (h) endorsement of the leader (endorse), (i) willingness to defer to the leader (defer), and (j) expectations of being influenced by the leader (influence).

Once subjects completed the second questionnaire, they were informed that the study was over and that the discussion would not be occurring at that time. Full debriefing revealed that all subjects were naive regarding the experimental hypotheses.

Results

The key dependent measures were perceived leadership evaluations, but before discussing these, we need to check on background conditions and the effectiveness of the three experimental manipulations.

Checks on Background Conditions and Manipulations

An initial analysis performed on all dependent measures revealed no differences between subjects who were for or against increased police powers. This variable was, therefore, excluded from subsequent

analyses. A three-way (Group Salience × Group Prototypicality × Leader Stereotypicality) ANOVA on subjects' attitudes toward increased police powers revealed no significant differences between conditions. The average position across the experiment was a reassuring 15.40 ($SD = 7.27$), almost identical to the scale midpoint of 15.50.

No predictions were made for gender, and there were no statistically significant differences between cells in the proportion of subjects who were male (26% through 38%). Because data analyses with gender covaried out (i.e., ANCOVA) did not change the results reported below, we decided to exclude gender as a variable.

Leader stereotypicality. The perceived leader stereotypicality of the behavior profile presented at the start of the study was checked by two measures: how much subjects would prefer a leader who fit the profile (stereotypical leader preference) and how much subjects would prefer a leader who fit the opposite profile (nonstereotypical leader preference). For the manipulation to be effective, we would expect subjects in all conditions to show a large and significant preference for the stereotypical leader profile over the nonstereotypical leader profile. A four-way (Salience × Prototypicality × Stereotypicality × Stereotypical-Nonstereotypical Leader Preference) ANOVA with repeated measures on the last factor revealed a strong main effect for the repeated measure; subjects felt they would prefer someone who had the described leadership style more than someone who did not ($Ms = 6.89$ and 2.42), $F(1, 176) = 536.79$, $p < .001$. This confirms that the leadership profile was indeed viewed as stereotypical of a good leader. The absence of a two-way interaction with salience confirms that although high-salience subjects already had slightly different expectations from low-salience subjects about the forthcoming group task, the leader stereotype was viewed as equally stereotypical and appropriate by both sets of subjects.

There was only one other significant effect: a three-way interaction for salience, stereotypicality, and the repeated measure, $F(1, 176) = 8.44$, $p < .01$. The effect was tiny (accounting for 5% of variance) relative to the main effect for the repeated measure (75% of variance) and can probably be attributed to random differences among cells, because leader stereotypicality had not yet been manipulated. On stereotypical leader preference, the salience by stereotypicality interaction was significant, $F(1, 176) = 6.55$, $p < .05$, but it was small (eta-square = .04), and Newman-Keuls revealed that no two means differed significantly. The means for the low-salience-stereotypical, high-salience-nonstereotypical, high-salience-stereotypical, and low-salience-nonstereotypical cells were 7.24, 7.08, 6.76, and 6.45, respectively. The Salience × Stereotypicality interaction on nonstereotypical leader preference was a mirror image (the two measures were negatively correlated, $r (184) = -.46$, $p < .001$). The comparable cell means were 2.11, 2.16, 2.85, and 2.57, respectively. This interaction was significant, $F(1, 176) = 5.81$, $p < .05$, but the effect size was again small (eta-square = .03) and no two means differed significantly.

Because the measure of stereotypical leader preference was correlated with the measure of how well the behavioral profile described the subject's own leadership style (self-stereotypicality), $r(184) = .36$, $p < .001$, it is not surprising that the same Salience × Stereotypicality interaction emerged on self-stereotypicality, $F(1, 176) = 5.95$, $p < .05$. This effect was also small (eta-square = .03), and no two means differed significantly. The extent to which subjects felt the behavioral profile described their own leadership style decreased from the low-salience-stereotypical to the high-salience-nonstereotypical to the high-salience-stereotypical to the low-salience-nonstereotypical cells ($Ms = 6.16$, 5.84, 5.41, and 5.34, respectively). There were no other significant effects on self-stereotypicality. Precautionary data analyses with self-stereotypicality as a covariate did not significantly change the results reported below, confirming that the results cannot be attributed to differences in how leader stereotypical subjects viewed themselves to be.

Group prototypicality. Subjects were asked to estimate the position on the 30-point attitude scale that represented the group prototype. We calculated the absolute difference between the estimated prototype and the scale midpoint of 15.5 and conducted a three-way ANOVA on these difference scores. There was only one significant effect, a main effect for group salience, $F(1, 176) = 123.41$, $p < .001$, eta-square = .41. Low-salience subjects estimated the group prototype to be 2.65 scale points from the midpoint (i.e., at approximately 13 or 18 on the 30-point scale), whereas high-salience subjects estimated it at 6.78 scale points from the scale midpoint (i.e., approximately 9 or 22 on the 30-point scale). This confirms that subjects would see prototypical leaders (presented as occupying positions of 15 or 16 for low-salience subjects and 8 or 23 for high-salience subjects) as indeed closer to the relevant group prototype than non-prototypical leaders.

Group prototypicality was also checked by the question asking how well the leader matched the group position (leader prototypicality). A three-way ANOVA revealed only one significant effect, a main effect for prototypicality. The leader was seen as more prototypical of the group in the high- than low-prototypical condition ($Ms = 7.09$ and 4.69, respectively), $F(1, 176) = 90.56$, $p < .001$, eta-square = .34. These findings confirm that the manipulation of the group prototypicality of the leader was successful.

Group salience. There were three items designed to check directly the effectiveness of the salience manipulation. These items asked whether subjects (a) felt like a group member rather than a distinct individual, (b) saw the competitive discussion as inter- or intragroup (group discussion), and (c) perceived two distinct groups or several distinct individuals as present. Factor analysis (with orthogonal varimax rotation) of these items produced a single factor (eigenvalue 1.75, factor loadings of .64, .80, and .84, respectively) that accounted for 58.4% of the variance. We computed a composite measure of salience as the weighted average of the constituent variables (items were weighted by their factor loadings). The reliability of this scale was weak ($\alpha = .63$) but acceptable. A three-way (Salience × Prototypicality × Stereotypicality) ANOVA on this composite scale revealed only one significant effect, a main effect for salience, $F(1, 176) = 18.62$, $p < .001$, eta-square $= .10$, which confirmed the effectiveness of the salience manipulation. High-salience subjects felt group membership was more salient than did low-salience subjects ($Ms =$ 3.74 and 3.05, respectively).

The effectiveness of the salience manipulation was also checked more indirectly by the following 11 items measuring group identification: commitment, happy, similar, like, fit, cohesive, importance, identify, glad, belong, and self-prototypicality. Factor analysis (with orthogonal varimax rotation) of these items produced one major factor (eigenvalue of 4.87, 44.2% variance accounted for) that stood out clearly from the rest of the field (eigenvalues of 1.14, 1.03, 0.77, etc.). For this reason, we decided to specify a single-factor solution, which produced factor loadings ranging from .80 to .35 around a mean of .65. We computed a scale from the weighted average of the 11 items (weighted by factor loadings). The reliability of this scale was high ($\alpha = .87$), and deletion of items did not improve reliability. A three-way ANOVA on this composite scale revealed only one significant effect, a main effect for salience, $F(1, 176) =$ 29.08, $p < .001$, eta-square $= .14$. High-salience subjects identified more strongly than low-salience subjects with their group ($Ms = 3.45$ and 2.92, respectively). These checks on salience confirm that the manipulation had the intended effects of making the group more salient and, consistent with self-categorization/social identity theory, of causing subjects to identify with it more strongly.

Overall, our checks of background conditions and manipulations were successful. Background conditions were as intended, and all three experimental manipulations worked as planned. However, there was one unintended effect. Against the background of a predicted strong and significant preference for the stereotypical leader profile over the nonstereotypical leader profile (eta-square $= .75$), there was a weaker but significant unpredicted variation in the magnitude of this difference between conditions formed by the interaction of salience and stereotypicality (eta-square $= .05$). We computed a new variable representing the difference between the measures of stereotypical leader preference and nonstereotypical leader preference (the latter

was subtracted from the former) and reran the three-way ANOVAs reported below but with this difference score as a covariate (i.e., ANCOVA). The results reported below were not significantly changed.

Leader Evaluations

Leader effectiveness. The following 10 items directly measured the perceived effectiveness of the leader: qualities, fit image, behave, effective, like leader, good leader, support leader, endorse, defer, and influence. Factor analysis (with orthogonal varimax rotation) of these items produced a single factor with eigenvalue greater than 1.00 (eigenvalue 5.41), which accounted for 45.1% of variance. Factor loadings ranged from .86 to .45 around a mean of .70. We computed a scale from the weighted average of the 10 items (weighted by factor loadings). The reliability of this scale was high ($\alpha = .88$) and was not improved by deletion of items. A three-way ANOVA on this composite scale revealed two significant main effects. There was a strong effect for leader stereotypicality, $F(1, 176) = 49.49$, $p < .001$, eta-square $= .22$. Subjects expected a stereotypical leader to be more effective ($M = 4.23$) than a nonstereotypical leader ($M = 3.53$). And there was a weaker effect for prototypicality, $F(1, 176) = 4.19$, $p < .05$, eta-square $= .02$. Subjects expected a prototypical leader to be more effective ($M = 3.98$) than a nonprototypical leader ($M = 3.77$).

Of most interest to us was the significant interaction of salience and prototypicality, $F(1, 176) = 18.63$, $p < .001$, eta-square $= .10$. This interaction is illustrated in Figure 21.1. Low-salience subjects did not expect prototypical leaders to be more effective than nonprototypical leaders ($Ms = 3.80$ and 4.03, respectively), whereas high-salience subjects did ($Ms = 4.14$ and 3.53, respectively). Salience significantly increased perceived leadership effectiveness for prototypical leaders, and significantly reduced it for nonprototypical leaders. All pairs of means except 3.80 and 4.03 differed significantly by Newman-Keuls, $p < .05$. This finding confirms Hypothesis 1.

There were no other significant effects on the composite measure, and, with one exception,

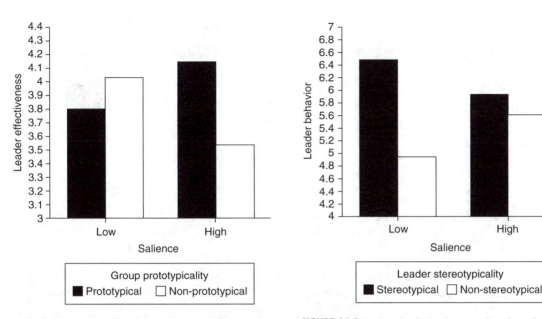

FIGURE 21.1 ▪ Leader effectiveness as a function of group salience and group prototypicality.

FIGURE 21.2 ▪ Leader behavior as a function of group salience and leader stereotypicality.

significant effects on constituent measures replicated those on the composite measure. The exception is worth reporting because it supports Hypothesis 2. There was a significant interaction of salience and stereotypicality on the measure of whether the leader might behave as a leader should, $F(1, 176) = 7.65$, $p < .01$, eta-square = .04. This interaction is illustrated in Figure 21.2. High-salience subjects did not expect a stereotypical leader to behave more like a leader than a nonstereotypical leader ($Ms = 5.91$ and 5.59, respectively), whereas low-salience subjects did ($Ms = 6.47$ and 4.93, respectively). Reduced salience significantly improved perceptions of the stereotypical leader and significantly worsened them for the nonstereotypical leader. All means except 5.91 and 5.59 differed significantly by Newman-Keuls, $p < .05$. Although this effect supports Hypothesis 2, the absence of a significant Salience × Stereotypicality effect on the composite measure or on other constituent measures indicates a failure to obtain overall support for Hypothesis 2.

Leader appropriateness, relevance, and representativeness. Three-way ANOVAs were conducted on the general measures of (a) how relevant to leadership the leader's position was (relevance), (b) how

appropriate his or her position was for leadership (leader appropriateness), and (c) how representative the leader was of the group (representative). These items measured the extent to which subjects felt they could accept, approve of, or endorse the leader and thus are closely related to leader effectiveness.

On relevance, there was a main effect for prototypicality, $F(1, 176) = 9.12$, $p < .05$, eta-square = .05, which was qualified by an interaction with salience, $F(1, 176) = 15.53$, $p < .001$, eta-square = .08. The interaction is plotted in Figure 21.3. Although subjects in the low-salience condition did not feel that a prototypical leader was more relevant as a leader than a nonprototypical leader ($Ms = 5.73$ and 6.02, respectively), high-salience subjects did ($Ms = 6.94$ and 5.04, respectively). Salience had the effect of significantly increasing the perceived leadership relevance of a prototypical leader and of significantly reducing the perceived relevance of a nonprototypical leader. All pairs of means except 5.73 and 6.02 differed significantly by Newman-Keuls, $p < .05$. A remarkably similar effect emerged on appropriateness. There were main effects for salience and for prototypicality, $F(1, 176) = 11.35$, $p < .01$, eta-square = .06, and

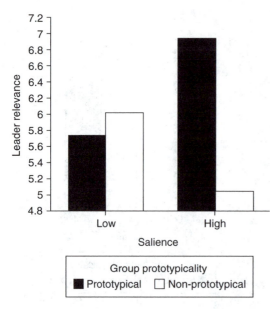

FIGURE 21.3 ■ Leader relevance as a function of group salience and group prototypicality.

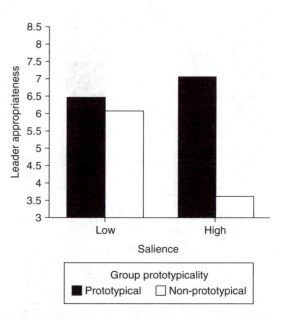

FIGURE 21.4 ■ Leader appropriateness as a function of group salience and group prototypicality.

$F(1, 176) = 52.30$, $p < .001$, eta-square = .23, respectively, which were qualified by their interaction, $F(1, 176) = 31.46$, $p < .001$, eta-square = .15. The interaction is plotted in Figure 21.4. Although subjects in the low-salience conditions did not feel that a prototypical leader was more appropriate as a leader than a nonprototypical leader ($Ms = 6.47$ and 6.07, respectively), high-salience subjects did ($Ms = 7.04$ and 3.62, respectively, $p < .05$); only the latter difference was significant by Newman-Keuls, $p < .05$. Salience had the effect of significantly (by Newman-Keuls) reducing the perceived appropriateness of a leader who was nonprototypical but not significantly altering perceptions of a prototypical leader. There were no other significant effects on relevance and appropriateness.

These findings, which confirm Hypothesis 1, are remarkably similar to those reported above for the measure of leader effectiveness. In addition, however, they suggest the intriguing possibility (see Figure 21.4) that group members are more likely to downgrade and reject leaders who are nonprototypical than to upgrade and accept leaders who are prototypical.

A slightly different pattern of results to those reported for relevance and appropriateness emerged on the measure of representativeness. There was a significant main effect for prototypicality, $F(1, 176) = 9.77$, $p < .01$, eta-square = .05: The leader was seen to be more representative of group members in the high- than low-prototypical condition ($Ms = 5.78$ and 5.14, respectively). There was also a significant main effect for leader stereotypicality, $F(1, 176) = 22.69$, $p < .001$, eta-square = .11, which was accounted for by the interaction with salience, $F(1, 176) = 24.35$, $p < .001$, eta-square = .12. The interaction is plotted in Figure 21.5. Subjects in the high-salience condition whose leader was nonstereotypical evaluated the leader as significantly (by Newman-Keuls) less representative of the group ($M = 4.29$) than did subjects in the other three conditions ($Ms = 6.24$ for high salience stereotypical, 5.75 for low salience nonstereotypical, and 5.69 for low salience stereotypical). One way to interpret this is in terms of in-group bias; the leader schema used in this study was positively evaluated, and so to favor a salient in-group, someone who does not have these favorable qualities (i.e., is nonstereotypical) must be seen

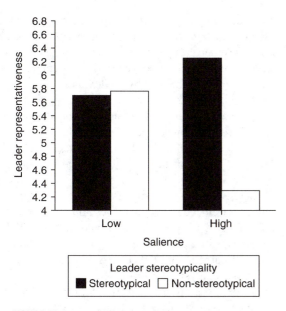

FIGURE 21.5 ■ Leader representativeness as a function of group salience and leader stereotypicality.

as less representative than someone who does. There were no other significant effects on this measure.

Taken together, these leader evaluation results show the following. First, group prototypicality of the leader was a strong and significant basis for leader evaluation in terms of leadership effectiveness and approval in salient groups, whereas it was unimportant in nonsalient groups (Hypothesis 1). Second, people evaluated stereotypical leaders as more effective and appropriate than nonstereotypical leaders (Hypothesis 2). Third, although the stereotypicality effect was largely unaffected by group salience, it did disappear under high salience on one isolated measure (leadership behavior) of leader effectiveness (Hypothesis 2). And fourth, high-salience-nonstereotypical leaders were viewed as less representative of the group than stereotypical or low-salience-nonstereotypical leaders.

Self-Leader Similarity

A three-way ANOVA on the single item measuring how similar subjects felt they were to the leader (similar to leader) revealed two main effects. High-salience subjects felt less similar than low-salience subjects to the leader ($Ms = 4.89$ and 5.42, respectively), $F(1, 176) = 4.86$, $p < .05$, eta-square $= .03$, and subjects felt more similar to a stereotypical than to a nonstereotypical leader ($Ms = 5.66$ and 4.65, respectively), $F(1, 176) = 19.62$, $p < .001$, eta-square $= .10$. The former finding may reflect intragroup differentiation into leaders and followers in a salient group, whereas the latter finding probably reflects the fact that subjects preferred the stereotypical behavioral profile to the nonstereotypical one.

Discussion

In this article, we argued, from self-categorization theory, that although leaders are often chosen or evaluated on the basis of whether they possess attributes congruent with some general leadership schema, this may assume less importance when group membership is a salient basis of self-definition. Then, the extent to which the person is a prototypical member of the group will assume greater importance.

Our main hypothesis (Hypothesis 1) was well supported across relevant measures. Under conditions of high salience, perceptions of leadership effectiveness and leadership acceptance were influenced by the perceived prototypicality of the leader; prototypical leaders were expected to be more effective and acceptable than nonprototypical leaders. Under conditions of low salience, however, leadership effectiveness was uninfluenced by the perceived prototypicality of the leader; prototypical and nonprototypical leaders were expected to be equally effective and acceptable.

In general, group salience significantly improved the expected effectiveness of prototypical leaders and significantly worsened the expected effectiveness of nonprototypical leaders. Interestingly, on one measure (how appropriate the leader's position was), the effect was asymmetrical, with salience worsening perceptions of the nonprototypical leader but leaving perceptions of the prototypical leader unchanged. This apparent rejection of a nonprototypical leader hints at the possibility that a "black sheep" effect (e.g., Marques, 1990; Marques & Paez, 1994), based on depersonalized social attraction (Hogg, 1992, 1993), may influence the dynamics of leadership. In further support of this idea, salience also significantly weakened the perceived representativeness of a nonstereotypical leader—that is, someone who did not possess the desirable characteristics of the leader schema and, therefore, would not contribute favorably to the group's reputation.

The second hypothesis (Hypothesis 2) was less strongly supported; the expected main effect for leader stereotypicality was found, but the predicted interaction between salience and stereotypicality emerged only on one measure. Overall, people expected that leaders who possessed stereotypical attributes would be more effective than nonstereotypical leaders. However, on the single measure of leader behavior, this effect disappeared under conditions of high group salience—that is, increased salience significantly reduced the expected effectiveness of stereotypical leaders and significantly increased the expected effectiveness of nonstereotypical leaders.

These effects were obtained against the background of effective manipulation of the independent variables of group salience, group prototypicality, and leader stereotypicality. Manipulation checks revealed significant main effects only for the relevant independent variables—with the one exception of a Salience × Stereotypicality interaction on the stereotypicality check. However, the interaction was small (eta-square = .05) relative to the stereotypicality main effect (eta-square = .75), and reanalysis of the data with the stereotype check as a covariate (2 × 2 × 2 ANCOVA) did not significantly change the results. Although not designed as a check on the salience manipulation, the measure of leader representativeness revealed additional support for the manipulation in the form of in-group bias; subjects in the high-salience condition considered the leader who did not possess the stereotypical (and desirable) leader attributes to be less representative of the group than the leader who did possess these attributes.

The strong main effect for stereotypicality on perceived leader effectiveness is consistent with leader categorization theory; people used schemas about leadership to determine who would be an effective leader. However, group salience also had a strong effect on leader perceptions, which was consistent with our social identity/self-categorization analysis. When group membership was salient, perceptions of leader effectiveness and acceptance were strongly influenced by contextually relevant in-group defining features (i.e., group prototypes). Being an effective or accepted leader in a salient group is thus not only, or merely, a matter of having stereotypical leadership characteristics, but also a matter of being a prototypical in-group member.

There was also some suggestion that stereotypical leader attributes may have less importance in a salient group. This finding is inconsistent with leader categorization theory but quite consistent with self-categorization theory. Although not crucial to our analysis, we expect that this last effect would be more pronounced in contexts in which the group was stronger (i.e., meaningful, enduring, cohesive, central to social identity) than in this study. Under those conditions, group salience should more firmly redirect attention from leader stereotypicality to group prototypicality. This would be consistent with data reported by Hogg, Hardie, and Reynolds (1995), who found that identity salience in a quasi-minimal group study caused subjects to shift their cognitive focus for interindividual evaluation from interpersonal to group prototypical dimensions.

One last finding was that high-salience subjects perceived themselves to be significantly less similar to the leader than did low-salience subjects. A mechanical reading of social identity/self-categorization theory might predict the opposite: Self-categorization accentuates perceived self-prototype similarity, and who is more prototypical than the leader? In contrast, we suggest that leadership is more than just being prototypical (note that the leaders in this experiment not only varied in prototypicality but were also explicitly identified as leaders). Leadership involves a fundamental structural differentiation between leader and follower roles within a group, a differentiation that becomes more pronounced as the group becomes more salient. Thus, people who strongly identify with a group are more likely to recognize and affirm this structural differentiation and accentuate perceived intragroup differences between self and leader (see Hogg, 1996a, 1996b). This idea has yet to be explored from a social identity/self-categorization perspective.

In the present study, we tried to equate the amount of information provided about the group prototypicality and leader stereotypicality of the leader by providing relatively little information on both. To investigate further the extent to which these factors are inversely related in salient groups, future studies might benefit from the use of stronger group contexts. In particular, it would be valuable to employ a richer multidimensional prototype that is more consistent with the "fuzzy set" notion of a prototype that is assumed by self-categorization theory. The present study also operationalized leadership in a very minimal way; the leaders did not actually perform a task on which they exhibited leadership, and there was no interaction within the group or between leaders and followers. Leadership effectiveness and acceptance were measured only in anticipation of interaction, and there was, of course, no objective measure of how effective or how well accepted the leaders were. Many of these limitations of the present study would be overcome by a quasi-naturalistic laboratory paradigm (e.g., Hogg et al., 1993) or a field-oriented approach involving naturally occurring groups (e.g., Fielding & Hogg, 1997; Pavitt & Sackaroff, 1990). However, the artificiality of the groups in the present experiment intentionally optimizes control and facilitates comparison with other leader categorization and social identity/self-categorization studies.

The model of leadership introduced in this article is a dynamic one that suggests that although group prototypicality is essential to leadership, there may be other processes at work. For instance, the model describes how attributional processes may transform prototype-based leaders into true charismatic leaders—thus recognizing the human tendency to perceive leaders as people who have a broad and enduring capacity to lead. This model, which thus addresses both the emergence and the decline of leaders, as well as perceptions of leader effectiveness and acceptability, remains to be investigated in subsequent studies. However, the present study does provide evidence for the role of group prototypicality in leadership.

There are a number of other directions for future research (Hogg, 1996b). According to self-categorization theory, the group prototype maximizes the metacontrast between intergroup differentiation and intragroup homogenization and should, therefore, be displaced from a relevant comparison out-group (e.g., Hogg et al., 1990; McGarty et al., 1992). Thus, if the intergroup frame of reference for an experimental group were manipulated, the prototypical position would change, and so would the leadership position. This would be a function of group salience, and there would be a latency effect in leadership acceptance reflecting the dispositional attribution of leadership capability. Of course, outside the laboratory, leaders are not merely passive casualties of changing social contexts. Established leaders would be expected to actively manipulate the salient social context themselves by making relevant those out-groups that make themselves appear more prototypical and/or their leadership rivals less prototypical.

Another direction for future research would be to focus on the effect of group cohesiveness on leadership. On the basis of our model, we would predict that increased cohesiveness would be associated with marked prototype-based leadership endorsement and evaluation, greater and more consensual social attraction for the leader, and a stronger tendency to attribute leadership dispositionally. Together, these processes would grant the leader substantial charisma and power. Stereotypes of appropriate leadership behavior would assume diminished importance relative to group prototypicality. If the prototype failed to embody characteristics that encouraged appropriate leadership behaviors, the circumstances would be precisely those that might engender groupthink, or perhaps bizarre leadership cults.

REFERENCES

Abrams, D. (1994). Social self-regulation. *Personality and Social Psychology Bulletin, 20*, 473–483.

Bales, R. F. (1950). *Interaction process analysis: A method for the study of small groups*. Reading, MA: Addison-Wesley.

Bass, B. M. (1990). *Bass and Stogdill's handbook of leadership: Theory, research and managerial applications.* New York: Free Press.

Bray, R. M., Johnson, D., & Chilstrom, J. T., Jr. (1982). Social influence by group members with minority opinions: A comparison of Hollander and Moscovici. *Journal of Personality and Social Psychology, 43,* 78–88.

Brewer, M. B. (1991). The social self: On being the same and different at the same time. *Personality and Social Psychology Bulletin, 17,* 475–482.

Brewer, M. B. (1993). The role of distinctiveness in social identity and group behaviour. In M. A. Hogg & D. Abrams (Eds.), *Group motivation: Social psychological perspectives* (pp. 1–16). Hemel Hempstead, UK: Harvester Wheatsheaf.

Brewer, M. B., & Miller, N. (1996). *Intergroup relations.* Buckingham, UK: Open University Press.

Cronshaw, S. F., & Lord, R. G. (1987). Effects of categorization, attribution, and encoding processes on leadership perceptions. *Journal of Applied Psychology, 72,* 97–106.

Eagly, A. H., Karau, S. J., & Makhijani, M. G. (1995). Gender and the effectiveness of leaders: A meta-analysis. *Psychological Bulletin, 117,* 125–145.

Eagly, A. H., Makhijani, M. G., & Klonsky, B. G. (1992). Gender and the evaluation of leaders: A meta-analysis. *Psychological Bulletin, 111,* 3–22.

Fiedler, F. E. (1965). A contingency model of leadership effectiveness. In L. Berkowitz (Ed.), *Advances in experimental social psychology* (Vol. 1, pp. 149–190). San Diego, CA: Academic Press.

Fiedler, F. E. (1971). *Leadership.* Morristown, NJ: General Learning.

Fiedler, F. E. (1981). Leadership effectiveness. *American Behavioral Scientist, 24,* 619–632.

Fielding, K. S., & Hogg, M. A. (1997). Social identity, self-categorization and leadership: A field study of small interactive groups. *Group Dynamics: Theory, Research, and Practice, 1,* 39–51.

Fiske, S. T. (1993a). Controlling other people: The impact of power on stereotyping. *American Psychologist, 48,* 621–628.

Fiske, S. T. (1993b). Social cognition and social perception. *Annual Review of Psychology, 44,* 155–194.

Fiske, S. T., & Dépret, E. (1996). Control, interdependence and power: Understanding social cognition in its social context. *European Review of Social Psychology, 7,* 31–61.

Fiske, S. T., & Taylor, S. E. (1991). *Social cognition* (2nd ed.). New York: McGraw-Hill.

Graumann, C. F., & Moscovici, S. (Eds.) (1986). *Changing conceptions of leadership.* New York: Springer-Verlag.

Hogg, M. A. (1992). *The social psychology of group cohesiveness: From attraction to social identity.* Hemel Hempstead, UK: Harvester Wheatsheaf, and New York: New York University Press.

Hogg, M. A. (1993). Group cohesiveness: A critical review and some new directions. *European Review of Social Psychology, 4,* 85–111.

Hogg, M. A. (1996a). Intragroup processes, group structure and social identity. In W. P. Robinson (Ed.), *Social groups and identities: Developing the legacy of Henri Tajfel* (pp. 65–93). Oxford, UK: Butterworth-Heinemann.

Hogg, M. A. (1996b). Social identity, self-categorization, and the small group. In E. H. Witte & J. Davis (Eds.), *Understanding group behavior: Vol. 2. Small group processes and interpersonal relations* (pp. 227–253). Mahwah, NJ: Lawrence Erlbaum.

Hogg, M. A. (1997). *Leadership processes in groups: Self-categorization and the role of depersonalization.* Unpublished research proposal to the Australian Research Council, University of Queensland, Brisbane.

Hogg, M. A., & Abrams, D. (1988). *Social identifications: A social psychology of intergroup relations and group processes.* London and New York: Routledge.

Hogg, M. A., Cooper-Shaw, L., & Holzworth, D. W. (1993). Studies of group prototypicality and depersonalized attraction in small interactive groups. *Personality and Social Psychology Bulletin, 17,* 175–180.

Hogg, M. A., & Hains, S. C. (1996). Intergroup relations and group solidarity: Effects of group identification and social beliefs on depersonalized attraction. *Journal of Personality and Social Psychology, 70,* 295–309.

Hogg, M. A., & Hardie, E. A. (1991). Social attraction, personal attraction, and self-categorization: A field study. *Personality and Social Psychology Bulletin, 17,* 175–180.

Hogg, M. A., Hardie, E. A., & Reynolds, K. J. (1995). Prototypical similarity, self-categorization, and depersonalized attraction: A perspective on group cohesiveness. *European Journal of Social Psychology, 25,* 159–177.

Hogg, M. A., Terry, D. J., & White, K. M. (1995). A tale of two theories: A critical comparison of identity theory with social identity theory. *Social Psychology Quarterly, 58,* 255–269.

Hogg, M. A., Turner, J. C., & Davidson, B. (1990). Polarized norms and social frames of reference: A test of the self-categorization theory of group polarization. *Basic and Applied Social Psychology, 11,* 77–100.

Hollander, E. P. (1958). Conformity, status, and idiosyncrasy credit. *Psychological Review, 65,* 117–127.

House, R. J., & Baetz, M. L. (1990). Leadership: Some empirical generalizations and new research directions. In L. L. Cummings & B. M. Staw (Eds.), *Leadership, participation, and group behavior* (pp. 1–84). Greenwich, CT: JAI.

Humphrey, R. (1985). How work roles influence perception: Structural-cognitive processes and organizational behavior. *American Sociological Review, 50,* 242–252.

Hunt, J. G., Baliga, B. R., Dachler, H. P., & Schriesheim, C. A. (Eds.) (1988). *Emerging leadership vistas.* Lexington, MA: D. C. Heath.

Levine, J. M. (1989). Reaction to opinion deviance in small groups. In P. B. Paulus (Ed.), *Psychology of group influence* (2nd ed., pp. 187–231). Hillsdale, NJ: Lawrence Erlbaum.

Levine, J. M., & Moreland, R. L. (1990). Progress in small group research. *Annual Review of Psychology, 41,* 585–634.

Lippitt, R., & White, R. (1943). The "social climate" of children's groups. In R. G. Barker, J. Kounin, & H. Wright (Eds.), *Child behavior and development* (pp. 485–508). New York: McGraw-Hill.

Lord, R. G. (1977). Functional leadership behavior: Measurement and relations to social power and leadership perceptions. *Administrative Science Quarterly, 22,* 114–133.

Lord, R. G. (1985). An information processing approach to social perception, leadership and behavioral measurement in organizations. *Research in Organizational Behavior, 7,* 87–28.

Lord, R. G., & Alliger, G. M. (1985). A comparison of four information processing models of leadership and social perceptions. *Human Relations, 38,* 47–65.

Lord, R. G., Foti, R. J., & DeVader, C. L. (1984). A test of leadership categorization theory: Internal structure, information processing, and leadership perceptions. *Organizational Behavior and Human Performance, 34,* 343–378.

Marques, J. M. (1990). The black-sheep effect: Out-group homogeneity in social comparison settings. In D. Abrams & M. A. Hogg (Eds.), *Social identity theory: Constructive and critical advances* (pp. 131–151). Hemel Hempstead, UK: Harvester Wheatsheaf, and New York: Springer-Verlag.

Marques, J. M., & Paez, D. (1994). The "black sheep effect": Social categorization, rejection of ingroup deviates and perception of group variability. *European Review of Social Psychology, 5,* 37–68.

McGarty, C., Turner, J. C., Hogg, M. A., David, B., & Wetherell, M. S. (1992). Group polarization as conformity to the prototypical group member. *British Journal of Social Psychology, 31,* 1–20.

Meindl, J. R. (1990). On leadership: An alternative view of the conventional wisdom. In B. M. Staw & L. L. Cummings (Eds.), *Research in organizational behavior* (Vol. 12, pp. 159–203). Greenwich, CT: JAI.

Meindl, J. R. (1995). The romance of leadership as follower-centric theory: A social constructionist perspective. *Leadership Quarterly, 6,* 329–341.

Messé, L. A., Kerr, N. L., & Sattler, D. N. (1992). "But some animals are more equal than others": The supervisor as a privileged status in group contexts. In S. Worchel, W. Wood, & J. A. Simpson (Eds.), *Group process and productivity* (pp. 203–223). Newbury Park, CA: Sage.

Moreland, R. L., Hogg, M. A., & Hains, S. C. (1994). Back to the future: Social psychological research on groups. *Journal of Experimental Social Psychology, 30,* 527–555.

Mullen, B., Salas, E., & Driskell, J. E. (1989). Salience, motivation, and artifact as contributions to the relation between participation rate and leadership. *Journal of Experimental Social Psychology, 25,* 545–559.

Nye, J. L., & Forsyth, D. R. (1991). The effects of prototype-based biases on leadership appraisals: A test of leader-ship categorization theory. *Small Group Research, 22,* 360–379.

Palich, L. E., & Hom, P. W. (1992). The impact of leader power and behavior on leadership perceptions: A lisrel test of an expanded categorization theory of leadership model. *Group and Organization Management, 17,* 279–296.

Pavitt, C., & Sackaroff, P. (1990). Implicit theories of leadership and judgments of leadership among group members. *Small Group Research, 21,* 374–392.

Peters, L. H., Hartke, D. D., & Pohlmann, J. T. (1985). Fiedler's contingency theory of leadership: An application

of the meta-analytic procedure of Schmidt and Hunter. *Psychological Bulletin, 97,* 274–285.

Pfeffer, J. (1977). The ambiguity of leadership. *Academy of Management Review, 2,* 104–112.

Phillips, J. S., & Lord, R. G. (1981). Causal attributions and perceptions of leadership. *Organizational Behavior and Human Performance, 28,* 143–163.

Ross, L. (1977). The intuitive psychologist and his shortcomings. In L. Berkowitz (Ed.), *Advances in experimental social psychology* (Vol. 10, pp. 174–220). San Diego, CA: Academic Press.

Rush, M. C., & Russell, J. E. A. (1988). Leader prototypes and prototype-contingent consensus in leader behavior descriptions. *Journal of Experimental Social Psychology, 24,* 88–104.

Sande, G. N., Ellard, J. H., & Ross, M. (1986). Effect of arbitrary assigned status labels on self-perceptions and social perceptions: The mere position effect. *Journal of Personality and Social Psychology, 50,* 684–689.

Sherif, M. (1966). *In common predicament: Social psychology of intergroup conflict and cooperation.* Boston, MA: Houghton-Mifflin.

Stogdill, R. (1974). *Handbook of leadership.* New York: Free Press.

Strube, M. J., & Garcia, J. E. (1981). A meta-analytic investigation of Fiedler's contingency model of leadership effectiveness. *Psychological Bulletin, 90,* 307–321.

Tajfel, H., & Turner, J. C. (1979). An integrative theory of intergroup conflict. In W. G. Austin & S. Worchel (Eds.), *The social psychology of intergroup relations* (pp. 33–47). Monterey, CA: Brooks/Cole.

Taylor, S. E., & Fiske, S. T. (1978). Salience, attention, and attribution: Top of the head phenomena. In L. Berkowitz (Ed.), *Advances in experimental social psychology* (Vol. 11, pp. 249–288). San Diego, CA: Academic Press.

Terry, D. J., & Hogg, M. A. (1996). Group norms and the attitude-behavior relationship: A role for group identification. *Personality and Social Psychology Bulletin, 22,* 776–793.

Turner, J. C. (1982). Towards a cognitive redefinition of the social group. In H. Tajfel (Ed.), *Social identity and intergroup relations* (pp. 15–40). Cambridge, UK: Cambridge University Press.

Turner, J. C. (1985). Social categorization and the self-concept: A social cognitive theory of group behavior. In E. J. Lawler (Ed.), *Advances in group processes: Theory and research* (Vol. 2, pp. 77–122). Greenwich, CT: JAI.

Turner, J. C. (1991). *Social influence.* Milton Keynes, UK: Open University Press.

Turner, J. C., Hogg, M. A., Oakes, P. J., Reicher, S. D., & Wetherell, M. S. (1987). *Rediscovering the social group: A self-categorization theory.* Oxford, UK, and New York: Blackwell.

Yukl, G. (1981). *Leadership in organizations.* Englewood Cliffs, NJ: Prentice Hall.

Received December 12, 1995
Revision accepted November 13, 1996 ■

The Romance of Leadership

James R. Meindl, Sanford B. Ehrlich, and Janet M. Dukerich

This research is an attempt to explore and understand the prominence of the concept of leadership in our collective consciousness. In three archival studies, we examined the attention and interest in leadership as reflected in a variety of publications, in conjunction with national, industry, and firm variations in performance. In a series of experimental studies, we examined the effects of performance outcome levels on the strength of leadership attributions. The results of these studies supported an attributional perspective in which leadership is construed as an explanatory concept used to understand organizations as causal systems; results were interpreted in terms of a romanticized conception of leadership.*

The sheer volume of theory and research devoted to the study of leadership over the decades is testimony to its prominence in our collective efforts to understand and improve organizations. However, it has become apparent that, after years of trying, we have been unable to generate an understanding of leadership that is both intellectually compelling and emotionally satisfying. The concept of leadership remains largely elusive and enigmatic. Critics have made us aware of a range of scientific deficiencies that have plagued relevant theories and research, citing poor methodology, conceptual problems, definitional ambiguities, inappropriate focus, lack of coherence, and so on (e.g., Bennis, 1959; Stogdill, 1974; Miner, 1975; Greene, 1976; Karmel, 1978; McCall and Lombardo, 1978). Others have told us that leadership is best construed as a mere

substitute for and, thus, is functionally equivalent to other, more mundane organizational arrangements and processes (e.g., Kerr and Jermier, 1978). Still others confront us with disturbing evidence that our assumptions about the direct instrumental potency of leadership on organizational outcomes have vastly outstripped reality (e.g., Lieberson and O'Connor, 1972; Salancik and Pfeffer, 1977). Finally, there are persuasive arguments that cause one to suspect that the greater relevance of leadership as a concept for organizational science is that it is a phenomenologically important aspect of how observers and participants understand, interpret, and otherwise give meaning to organizational activities and outcomes (Calder, 1977; Pfeffer, 1977; Pfeffer and Salancik, 1978). Despite these assaults on traditional views, it appears that the concept of

* We are grateful to three anonymous *ASQ* reviewers for their helpful comments.

leadership is a permanently entrenched part of the socially constructed reality that we bring to bear in our analysis of organizations. And there is every sign that the obsessions with and celebrations of it will persist. The purpose of this analysis is to shed some light on this collective commitment to leadership.

In our view, the social construction of organizational realities has elevated the concept of leadership to a lofty status and level of significance. Such realities emphasize leadership, and the concept has thereby gained a brilliance that exceeds the limits of normal scientific inquiry. The imagery and mythology typically associated with the concept is evidence of the mystery and near mysticism with which it has been imbued. A sample listing of some articles on leadership that were found in recent volumes of the *Index of Business Publications* reflects this imagery: "Leadership and Magical Thinking"; "Black Art of Leadership"; "I Think Continually of Those Who Are Great"; "Protean Managerial Leadership"; and "Casting Out Organizational Demons: An Exorcise in Leadership."

It appears that as observers of and as participants in organizations, we may have developed highly romanticized, heroic views of leadership—what leaders do, what they are able to accomplish, and the general effects they have on our lives. One of the principal elements in this romanticized conception is the view that leadership is a central organizational process and the premier force in the scheme of organizational events and activities. It amounts to what might be considered a faith in the potential if not in the actual efficacy of those individuals who occupy the elite positions of formal organizational authority. The romanticization of leadership is hinted at in the observations made by a number of social and organizational analysts who have noted the esteem, prestige, charisma, and heroism attached to various conceptions and forms of leadership (e.g., Weber, 1946; Klapp, 1964; House, 1977; Burns, 1978; Goode, 1978; McCall and Lombardo, 1978; Staw and Ross, 1980; March, 1981). We suspect that the romanticized conception of leaders and leadership is generalized and prevalent. The argument being advanced here is that the concept of leadership is a perception that plays a part in the way people attempt to make sense out of organizationally relevant phenomena. Moreover, in this sense-making process, leader-ship has assumed a romanticized, larger-than-life role.

An important part of the sense-making process involves an attempt to generate causal attributions for organizational events and occurrences (Thompson and Tuden, 1959; Weick, 1979). The possibility of taking an attributional perspective on leadership was first raised by Calder (1977) and by Pfeffer (1977). Since then, there has been a growing body of research and theory devoted to attributional analyses of leadership (see McElroy, 1982; Lord and Smith, 1983, for recent reviews). However, that literature, with but few exceptions (e.g., Phillips and Lord, 1981), has not dealt in a direct way with the basic issue raised by Calder and by Pfeffer, which we are addressing here: namely, leadership is perhaps best construed as an explanatory category that can be used to explain and account for organizational activities and outcomes. Staw (1975) reached a similar conclusion, but in a more general context, by arguing that the self-reported opinions and beliefs of organizational actors and observers regarding causality may in fact constitute attributional inferences rather than actual causal determinants of events and occurrences. Unfortunately, most researchers have responded by focusing narrowly on the methodological ramifications of this view (e.g., DeNisi and Pritchard, 1978; Downey, Chacko, and McElroy, 1979; Binning and Lord, 1980; McElroy and Downey, 1982), for the most part ignoring the wider, underlying implication that many organizational behavior concepts can be used by individuals to form coherent explanations of events and occurrences. This is precisely the premise from which the present analysis proceeds.

The significance placed on leadership is a response to the ill-structured problem of comprehending the causal structure of complex, organized systems. Imagine for a moment the problem faced by an observer who must comprehend a large and complex system: there are many causal forces to consider and they occur together in highly intricate and overlapping networks, complete with multiple inputs and outcomes, numerous feedback loops, and all existing in some dynamic state of flux. Total comprehension of the system will easily be beyond the power of the observer. In such a task, the particular understanding that is gained will depend at least as much on the characteristics of the observer as it does on the system itself. Our informal, implicitly held models and perhaps our more formal theories, as well, are limited responses to the task of comprehending the causal complexities that characterize all organizations. Of course, the potential ways in which an understanding can be achieved are many, and it would be difficult to choose among them on a purely rational, logical basis. However, what is attended to and what causal factors emerge as the "figure" against the background of all other possibilities, even if arbitrary with respect to the system, is not random but is a process guided by the psychology and sociology of the observer. In effect, the results represent a systematic bias about how a system is understood, how relevant events and outcomes are defined and explained, and to what factors they are attributed. The term "bias" is used here in the way Schlenker (1982: 205) defined it: "A bias in the interpretation and explanation of events is a subjective tendency to prefer one interpretation over another; such an interpretation may or may not be an error according to some 'objective' criterion for assessing the event." Such preferences occur, in part, because of the ambiguity of relevant information and the perceived importance of events. The romanticized conception of leadership results from a biased preference to understand important but causally indeterminant and ambiguous organizational events and occurrences in terms of leadership. Accordingly, in the absence of direct, unambiguous information that would allow one rationally to infer the locus of causality, the romanticized conception of leadership permits us to be more comfortable in associating leaders—by ascribing to them control and responsibility—with events and outcomes to which they can be plausibly linked.[1]

The Present Research

The research reported here examined the hypothesis that the relative prominence of the use of leadership in understanding complex, organized systems varies to a significant degree with the performance levels of such systems. Generally speaking, the need to understand and make sense should correspond to the occurrence of salient events (Anderson, 1983). It is possible that observers are generally prone to overestimate the impact of leadership in their explanations of events; however, it seems likely that variations in events would be important for uncovering any bias toward understanding events in terms of leadership. One implication of a heroic, larger-than-life view of leadership is that its effects on an organization are not trivial. That is, associations between leadership and events will be consistent with the romanticized conception and will therefore be most appealing when those events are in some way defined as extraordinary (i.e., large cause, large effect). We reasoned that the romanticized conception will have greatest sway in extreme cases—either very good or very poor performance—causing observers to understand these events in terms of leadership. A stronger emphasis on leadership should occur under conditions in which high-magnitude outcomes obtain, and weaker preferences should be found when low-magnitude outcomes obtain. We know from past research that leaders are often held responsible and are "scapegoated" for poor organizational performance (e.g., Gamson and Scotch, 1964). Other evidence suggests that information about performance is sometimes used to infer the good and bad quality of leadership that must have existed (e.g., Staw, 1975). Thus, we expected that a bias toward leadership could be systematically related to performance levels in a positive or negative way. These ideas were tested in a series of archival and experimental studies.

---

[1] This collective, idealized representation of leadership bears a certain similarity to what has been examined under the general rubric of "implicit leadership theories" (e.g., Rush, Thomas, and Lord, 1977; Staw and Ross, 1980); however, we presumed the conception to be much more generic, powerful, and less well articulated.

Archival Studies

In the archival studies, we attempted to find evidence of the bias represented in the romanticized conception of leadership by explaining how, if at all, an interest in leadership is associated with the performance of firms, industries, and the national economy. In order to do so, we examined published sources and dissertations for the appearance of leadership as a topic of interest and attention. The working assumption was that an analysis of the correspondence between attention to leadership and performances could provide an indirect and very broad indication of the extent to which outcomes are collectively understood in terms of and attributed to leadership. In Study 1, we examined the relative emphasis on corporate leaders and leadership in the popular press. In Studies 2 and 3, we focused on the correspondence between variations in national economic performance and the general emphasis placed on leadership by young scholars and by the business community in general. All three studies were designed to test the hypothesis that the amount of interest in and attention devoted to leadership in the publications studied would vary directly or inversely with general performance.

Study 1: The Popular Press

Method

For this study, we examined titles of articles published in the *Wall Street Journal*, from 1972 through 1982, on a sample of 34 business firms drawn from the Fortune 500 list of large U.S. corporations. We measured the amount of attention and publicity this well-known publisher of business news devoted to the topic of corporate leadership and determined whether or not that attention bore any relationship to performance levels—defined here in general terms of the sales or profit growth of the firms and industries involved. The *Wall Street Journal* was chosen because it has an impeccable reputation as a highly credible source of business news, it has an extraordinary readership, and it is perhaps one of the most powerful, leading publications in the world (Neilson and Neilson, 1973). For performance

data for the same period, we relied on the *Value Line Investment Survey*.

Our selection of firms was guided by several considerations. First, we attempted to sample a range of different industries, with several sample firms in each industry. We also tried to choose firms that showed a range of different performance curves over the time period. Finally, we wanted to select firms that we felt would have received ample press coverage during those years. We had originally sampled 35 firms; however, we realized later that we had unwittingly selected one firm that was a wholly owned subsidiary, and it was therefore dropped. The final sample of firms is listed in Table 22.1.

Emphasis on leadership. To get an estimate of the extent to which corporate leadership was emphasized for a given firm in a given year, we used the annual index of the *Wall Street Journal*, which contains a listing by title, under each large corporation, of every article on the corporation appearing in the *WSJ* in that year. Our procedure was to read the titles under the headings for each firm in the sample and for every year. An article was classified as leadership oriented (LA) if its title included a keyword or phrase that appeared in a "dictionary," developed specifically for this research, containing

TABLE 22.1. Sample of firms

Abbott Labs	Ford Motor Company
Allied Chemical	General Electric
American Airlines	General Mills
American Cyanamid	General Motors
American Home Products	Hewlett-Packard
American Motors	IBM
Armco	Lilly
Bethlehem Steel	Lockheed
Boeing	McDonnell-Douglas
Bristol Myers	McGraw-Edison
Burroughs	NCR
Chrysler	Pan Am
Continental Airlines	RCA
Data General	Republic Steel
Delta Airlines	Texas Instruments
DuPont	U.S. Steel
Eastern Airlines	Westinghouse

a short, selected list of items. The items included references to names of corporate officers, references to senior executive positions, and phrases such as "top management," "senior executive," "top brass," and other descriptors commonly used to refer to corporate leadership. In some cases, whether or not an item was a keyword depended on its use in the context of the title. For example, the word "management" was included if it referred to the administrators of the firm, but it was excluded when the referent was a process, as in "the management of innovation." If the title did not include a listed item, then the article was assigned to an "other" (OA) category. Two coders had the task of scanning the titles and coding articles. Each coder was assigned responsibility for tabulating the frequencies in each category on a firm-by-firm, yearly basis, for half the sample. The two coders underwent several preliminary exercises in which they were asked to search and classify the articles from a number of pages of the *Index*, using the dictionary to guide their decisions. These exercises led to some modifications in the dictionary. In subsequent trial runs, each coder independently searched and classified the articles from two pages selected at random from the *Index*. The extent of their agreement was scored, revealing an error rate of less than 3 percent. The coders' tabulations summarizing the number of articles classified as LA relative to the number of articles classified as OA was taken as a rough indication of the degree to which leadership was being emphasized. This emphasis was captured in a "Leadership Quotient" (LQ), equivalent to the ratio, (LA/OA) × 100.

Of course, there are some obvious, inherent limitations in using titles to classify articles. If nothing else, measurement error would be increased through any misclassifications. However, there are several considerations that justified its use and provided us with at least some reassurance about its

suitability for this research. First, this method allowed us to scan and code a very large number of references in a reasonable period of time, thus enabling us to expand the number of data points far beyond that possible through an analysis of the actual contents of articles. Second, titles are usually intended to highlight the main themes of an article, which suggests that there is a reasonable correspondence between title and content. Third, even if the correspondence between titles and content is a loose one, references to leaders in the title head of an article symbolically emphasize the concept of leadership, increasing its prominence relative to other concepts and thereby producing an implicit association between top management and whatever information then appears in the article or elsewhere about the firm. Fourth, our method is conceptually consistent with the systems used by a number of well-known and popular library data bases. For example, the *Social Sciences Citation Index* (*SSCI*) and the *Educational Resources Information Center* (*ERIC*) data bases both make use of title-keyword systems to classify publications into a variety of content areas.[2] Although these considerations cannot give us perfect confidence, when taken together they allowed us to feel reasonably comfortable with our title scan and classification procedure.

Results and Discussion

A total of 33,248 articles about the firms in our sample appeared in the *WSJ* over the period examined. Of those, 2,832 had titles that were coded as emphasizing things other than leadership (OA). The average number of articles for any given firm, in any given year, was 88.90. Of those, an average of 7.57 were coded as LA, ranging from a minimum of zero to a maximum of 59. The average number of OA articles was 81.33, ranging from a minimum of 6 to a maximum of 995. The average yearly LQ was 14.48 percent, ranging from a minimum of

---

[2] Unlike the *SSCI* data base, which relies exclusively on a title-keyword system, the *ERIC* data base uses both a title-keyword system and a controlled vocabulary system. Under the controlled vocabulary system, assignment to a particular content area ("access code") is made by a coder who reads publications for their content themes. We conducted separate searches

of the *ERIC* data base using the keyword descriptor method and the controlled vocabulary method to retrieve the number of entries on a yearly basis, for every year the data base was available (1966–1983), under the access code "leadership." The number of entries retrieved under each system were highly correlated, $r(16\ df) = .94, p < .001$.

0 percent to a maximum of 70 percent. The comparable figure for mean annual sales growth was 13.33 percent, ranging from a low of -45.57 percent to a high of 131.03 percent.

Year-wise analysis. To find evidence that a general emphasis on leadership is associated with performance, we examined the yearly LQs for the entire sample of firms in conjunction with their yearly performances. The results indicated that LQ scores were positively related to performance, measured here in terms of yearly annual sales growth, $r(9 \text{ df}) = .53, p < .05$. This suggests that years in which companies are on average doing well are also the years in which leadership on average tends to be more highly emphasized.

Analysis by industry. To examine the relative emphasis on leadership with respect to different industry performances, we classified the 34 firms in our sample into ten major industrial groupings on the basis of the first two digits of their SIC designations. The mean annual increase in sales performance across these industries was 10.37 percent, with a standard deviation of 2.70 percent, ranging from a high of 15.80 percent, to a low of 6.92 percent. The number of firms in our sample in the same industrial group was quite small: usually three or four, but in one case two, and in another case six. Even so, a one-way ANOVA revealed that the mean LQ varied substantially across the industry groups, $F(9,34) = 2.28, p < .05$. Moreover, the variance in LQ appears to be systematically related to industry performance: a planned comparison revealed that firms associated with the five highest performance industries had, on average, significantly higher LQs than those firms associated with the lowest performance industries, $F(1,33) = 8.99, p < .01$. That finding was corroborated by a significant correlation between average firm LQ and industry performance, $r(8 \text{ df}) = .64, p < .05$.

Company-by-company analysis. To examine how the emphasis on leadership may vary in relationship to a firm's own performances over time and how that relationship may vary across firms, we conducted separate analyses for each firm, correlating

LQ with annual performance. Since we have data available for only 11 years, the potential degrees of freedom available for these analyses are quite small (df $= 9$). However, we felt that the 34 replications could provide us with a reasonably good estimate of the pervasiveness of the expected effect. Given the inherent difficulties of specifying a priori what definition of performance will be used to make inferences about and associations to the leaders of any given firm, and since performance of a single firm is often judged in terms of how well it is doing relative to others in its own industry, we expanded the general performance outcomes for this analysis to include growth in profits and sales relative to the comparable industry-wide figures. The results of these analyses indicated that for 25 of the 34 firms (74 percent), LQ was significantly ($p < .09$ or greater) associated with at least some of our definitions of performance. If 50 percent is used as an extremely conservative expected value, then a simple one-degree-of-freedom chi-square test suggests this is a nonrandom pattern; $\chi^2(1 \text{ df}) = 6.89, p < .019$. Also, of the 25 firms showing an association between LQ and performance, 16 (64 percent) were positive, and the remaining 9 (36 percent) were negative.

Within-year analysis. Our final analysis focused on the covariation of LQ and performance across companies in each of the 11 years. The data summarized in Table 22.2 show that, in every year examined, LQ was correlated ($p < .08$ or greater) with performance outcomes. In eight of those years, the significant correlations were negative, indicating that in each of those years, the poorer the performance, the more leadership was emphasized. In the remaining three years, the significant correlations were positive, such that the better the performances, the greater the emphasis on leadership.

The four sets of analyses gave us an opportunity to gain somewhat different perspectives on the data and provided us with different focal points for examining the tendency to associate leadership with performance. In each of the analyses, the weight of evidence supported our expectations that the emphasis on a firm's top management will vary significantly with performance levels. The industry

TABLE 22.2. Within-year Analysis: Direction of Significant Correlations between Leadership Quotient and Company Performance Measures

Year										
1972	1973	1974	1975	1976	1977	1978	1979	1980	1981	1982
neg*	neg	neg	neg	neg	neg*	pos	pos	pos	neg	neg

*$p < .08$; all others are $p < .05$ or greater.

and the year-wise analyses revealed that an emphasis on leadership increases with increasingly positive performance. The within-company and within-year analyses introduced additional evidence that, on some occasions and for some firms, leadership is more likely to be emphasized when performances are poor. These two major patterns of results, when taken together, provided us with initial support for the proposition that the perceived causal priority of and attributions to leadership in understanding organizational events and occurrences are likely to occur when performances are either very good or very bad.

Study 2: Dissertation Topics

With the evidence obtained from Study 1, we turned our attention to exploring the societal aspect of our theory, which suggests that the level of collective interest and significance invested in the concept of leadership is responsive to fluctuations in the general economic performance of the entire nation. In order to test that notion, we chose, in this study, to track the level of interest in leadership through the dissertation topics young scholars chose. We assumed that the commitment and devotion represented by a dissertation topic would provide us with a glimpse of the collective investment in the concept of leadership.

Method

We counted the number of doctoral dissertations devoted to the topic of leadership and related it to the general economic conditions over the years 1929–1983. Our primary source of information was *Dissertation Abstracts International (DAI)*, an internationally recognized reference tool that summarizes and indexes virtually all the current dissertations accepted in the U.S. and Canada (*DAI User's Guide*, 1983). We used the subject index, which lists and groups dissertations into over 200 specialized subject headings, one of which is "leadership." The number of dissertations appearing every year under that heading ("LD") formed the basis of our analysis. However, because *DAI* did not give comparable data that would allow us to estimate easily the total number of dissertations in all the social sciences, we obtained an estimate from another source, *American Doctoral Dissertations*. We used their annual figures to find the total number of social science dissertations accepted each year ("TD"). In order to estimate general economic conditions, we relied on figures published by the Economic Statistics Bureau of Washington, DC, in their *Handbook of Basic Economic Statistics*, to compute year-to-year percentage changes in the GNP (delta GNP). This measure was chosen because it is a very broad and familiar indicator of swings in the nation's economy.

Results and Discussion

From 1929 to 1983 there was a dramatic increase in the number of dissertations awarded. In 1929, there were under 2,000; in 1979, there were over 35,000. This historical trend showed up in our preliminary analysis as a very strong correlation between years and TD, $r = .91, p < .001$, and LD, $r = .81$, $p < .001$. Thus, in light of this strong historical trend, we controlled for years, through partial correlations, to examine the relationship between economic conditions and interest in leadership. We also formed a ratio, LD/TD, which yielded a leadership quotient ($LQ_{dissertations}$) conceptually similar to that used in Study 1. It also seemed reasonable to expect a lag of several years between economic conditions and completed dissertations, although

TABLE 22.3. Lagged Partial Correlations between LQ$_{dissertations}$ and Changes in the General Economy (Delta GNP)

	Lag					
0	+1	+2	+3	+4	+5	+6
−15	−22	−28*	−27*	−39**	−17	−02

*$p < .05$; **$p < .01$.

we could not specify exactly what that lag would be. On the basis of these considerations, our analyses focused on the lagged (0 to +6 years) partial correlations between delta GNP and LQ$_{dissertations}$, controlling for linear, historical trends. Table 22.3 shows that the relationship between delta GNP and LQ$_{dissertations}$ was negative, indicating that downturns in the growth of the economy were subsequently followed by a greater interest in leadership, relative to all other topics and after controlling for historical trends. This relationship becomes reliable after a two-year lag, reaching its highest level in the plus-fourth year, and then drops off. These results, then, suggest that there is an association between good or bad economic times and the interest in leadership, at least among scholars choosing dissertation topics.

Study 3: General Business Periodicals

This study was conceptually similar to Study 2. This time, however, our strategy was to focus more specifically on the business community. Accordingly, we deliberately chose an available data base that was much wider in scope than that used in Study 2 and captured to a greater degree the interests of the general business community in the topic of leadership. Given the results of Study 2, we expected that the negative relationship between the state of the general economy and interest in leadership would be replicated here. This strategy allowed us to observe whether or not the general business community's collective interest in leadership is also responsive to fluctuations in the national economy. If so, then we could have added confidence in the generalizability of our guiding hypothesis. In addition, the study afforded us an opportunity to determine if interest is such that it tends to emphasize leadership to a greater degree during good or during bad economic times.

Method

We examined the annual volumes from 1958 to 1983 of the *Business Periodical Index* (*BPI*), published by the H. W. Wilson Company, which consists of subject entries for a wide range of business-oriented publications. In 1981 alone, the contents of over 250 different periodicals were indexed and grouped into hundreds of subject headings, one of which is "leadership." Although scholarly journals such as *ASQ* and *AMJ* are indexed, the majority of the publications indexed are nonacademic and practitioner-oriented. For example, this index includes popular periodicals, such as *Barrons, Business Week, Forbes*, and *Fortune*, as well as more specialized, often industry-specific publications, such as *Chemical Week, Electronics World*, and *Pipeline and Gas Journal*. Because of these characteristics, this database was chosen over others, such as *ERIC*, or *SSCI*. In addition, the index was published from 1958 to the present—the longest running period we could find.

As in Study 2, obtaining a yearly estimate of the interest in leadership entailed a simple count of the number of titles listed under the subject heading, "leadership" (LA$_{BPI}$). However, no published data were available on the total number of articles indexed (TA$_{BPI}$), and this had to be estimated. Fortunately, because the format, page size, and type size have remained the same across volumes and years, we were able to obtain the average number of entries per page by drawing a sample of 50 pages (two pages for every year) and then counting the number of entries on each ($M = 65.24$; $SD = 7.15$). We then multiplied the number of pages in each volume by the average number of entries per page to arrive at a yearly estimate of TA$_{BPI}$.

Results and Discussion

There has been a strong growth in the number of business periodicals published over the years, and this historical trend was reflected in our data by

TABLE 22.4. Lagged Partial Correlations between LQ$_{BPI}$ and Changes in the General Economy (Delta GNP)

			Lag			
0	+1	+2	+3	+4	+5	+6
.67***	.48**	.52**	.02	−.33	−.35	−.02

*p < .05; **p < .01; ***p < .001.

the zero-order correlations between years and TA$_{BPI}$, $r = .88$, $p < .001$, and LA$_{BPI}$, $r = .83$, $p < .001$. In an analysis parallel to that in the previous study, we examined the relationship between LQ$_{BPI}$ (LA/TA) and delta GNP, controlling for that linear historical trend. The partial correlations were lagged in the same manner as in Study 2 (0 to +6 years), although little delay was anticipated, given that the intent of the majority of the periodicals is to stay current. The results, summarized in Table 22.4, show that, as in Study 2, there appeared to be some association between economic performance and interest in leadership, after controlling for historical trends. However, unlike in the previous study, the relationship is predominantly positive, suggesting that the interest in leadership in the general business community, at least in terms of publications, seems to be at its greatest levels when there are upswings in the nation's economic growth. Apparently, the relationship is more immediate in time than that found with the dissertation data, which is not surprising, given the differences in the nature and goals of those publications. However, why LQ$_{dissertations}$ in Study 2 varied inversely and why in this study LQ$_{BPI}$ varied directly with delta GNP is intriguing. Perhaps those patterns represent some underlying differences between academic and practitioner-oriented views. Whatever the case, the relationships are not likely to represent random associations and are both generally consistent with our expectations, if not in direction, at least in terms of degree.

Experimental Studies

The preceding archival studies provided reasonably clear evidence of a general relationship between performance outcomes and degree of emphasis on leadership. The following series of experiments was designed to test more precisely the notion that the use of leadership as an explanatory concept—in the form of casual attributions—varies with performance. In particular, given the theoretical arguments and the pattern of positive and negative relationships uncovered in the archival studies, we sought to determine if, under controlled experimental conditions, leadership attributions would indeed be more likely to occur—and thereby create a stronger association—when performance is either very good or very bad. In the three experiments reported here, business school students were presented with minimal information and were asked to account for instances of performance that varied in terms of the magnitude of outcomes. In each case, they were asked to consider a leader as a possible reason for the outcome event. For comparison purposes, individuals' attributions to alternative determinants of performance other than to the leader were also obtained. Study 4 provided a partial test of the hypothesis by examining attributional patterns when observers were presented with information that varied the magnitude of *positive* performance outcomes. Study 5 provided a more complete test of the hypothesis by replicating and extending Study 4 and included conditions that varied the magnitude of *negative* as well as positive performance outcomes. Studies 4 and 5 laid the groundwork for Study 6, which attempted to replicate the pattern of results under more refined conditions and began to explore the role of expectations on leadership attributions. Although Studies 4 and 5 were preliminary, because they were instrumental to the development of Study 6, we will briefly describe them here.

Study 4

Method

Fifty-nine undergraduates enrolled in an introductory organizational behavior course at a large northeastern university participated in this study. Their mean age was 21.90 years, and on the average they reported having the equivalent of 2.56 years of work experience.

Subjects were randomly assigned to read one of three different versions of an extremely brief organizational performance-related vignette. Each version contained the same summary description of an organizational unit and its members, including the leader. The vignettes differed only in terms of the information they provided on performance outcomes, which were defined in terms of sales increase. Low, moderate, and high magnitude effects were conveyed to subjects by providing them with information that the unit had experienced either a slight (2 percent), moderate (10 percent), or large (25 percent) increase in sales performance. The vignettes read as follows:

> John Smith is the Director of Sales for a major northeastern appliance firm. John assumed this position five years ago following his attainment of an MBA degree. Prior to his MBA, John had completed a bachelor's degree in Marketing. In this position he has gained the respect of both his subordinates and superiors. On his last evaluation John was rated as a capable worker and his subordinates have indicated that they enjoy working for him. John currently is in charge of five subordinates. All of the subordinates working in John's department have a good working knowledge of marketing principles as demonstrated by their prior and current work experience. At the end of the fourth quarter, new customer accounts had shown a slight/moderate/large increase (2%/10%/25%) during the year, over last year's performance.

Immediately after reading the vignettes, subjects were asked to rate (on a 7-point scale) the extent to which they considered the leader to be an important causal determinant of the performance outcome.[3] And, in order to insure that subjects were aware of and at least considered other, perhaps competing explanations for the outcome, parallel questions asked them to express the extent to which alternative, plausible factors may have contributed to the outcome, including other actors (subordinates), environmental factors (general economy),

and anything else they felt should be considered (other). Responses to these last questions were considered together as "alternative" attributions and were therefore aggregated, for conceptual and analytic purposes.

Results and Discussion

Attributions ("leader" vs. "alternatives") were examined conjointly with outcome effects (low, moderate, and high magnitudes) in a 3×2 ANOVA. The data in Table 22.5 reveal that the general level of attribution making did not differ across the three magnitude conditions (overall low $M = 5.08$; overall moderate $M = 4.93$; overall large $M = 5.03$), $F(1,56) = .21$; ns. The analysis also revealed that in general, attributions to leader (overall $M = 5.27$) were preferred to attributions to alternatives (overall $M = 4.75$), $F(1,56) = 11.59$, $p < .001$. Most importantly, however, and as expected, the main effects were qualified by an interaction between type of attribution and magnitude of outcome, $F(2,56)$, $p < .06$, indicating that larger magnitude outcomes caused *greater* use of the leader as an explanation and *less* use of alternative explanations. A planned comparison between the leader and alternative attributions in the large magnitude condition ($M = 5.50$ and $M = 4.55$, respectively) was significant, $F(1,56) = 13.43$, $p < .001$. These two types of attributions were not reliably different in the other low and moderate magnitude conditions.

Thus, the pattern of results provided initial support for the hypothesis that the preference to use leaders in understanding organizational outcomes

TABLE 22.5. Mean Attributions in Each Magnitude Condition: Study 4

	Magnitude of Increase		
Attributions*	Low (N = 19)	Moderate (N = 20)	High (N = 20)
Leader	5.10	5.20	5.50
Alternatives	5.00	4.67	4.55

* 7-point scales; higher scores indicate stronger attributions.

---

[3] We considered using open-ended response measures; however, recent evidence suggests that structured, scale measures

similar to those used here are generally preferable to other methods for assessing attributions (Elig and Frieze, 1979).

increases with increasingly large magnitudes of positive effects. Although, by itself, the increase in attributions to the leader was not great, the trend upward is compelling when compared with the "baseline" provided by the use of alternative explanations. Such comparisons reveal that the increase in leadership attributions occurred despite the fact that attributions to alternatives decreased.

Study 5

The support found in Study 4, although suggestive, is limited by the fact that only positive performance conditions were examined. In its general form, the hypothesis is indifferent to the direction of performance changes—the effect should occur in the negative as well as in the positive cases. Accordingly, the goal in Study 5 was to further verify the hypothesis by examining attributional responses for negative performance cases, as well, especially in light of the negative associations uncovered in our archival studies.

Method

One hundred and sixteen undergraduates enrolled in introductory organizational behavior and human resource courses participated in this study. Their mean age was 22.32 years, and on average they reported having the equivalent of 2.24 years of work experience.

The vignettes used in Study 4 were modified to accommodate the inclusion of negative as well as positive outcomes of varying degrees. That resulted in six different versions: large negative (25 percent decrease), moderate negative (10 percent decrease), small negative (2 percent decrease), small positive (2 percent increase), moderate positive (10 percent increase), and large positive (25 percent increase) effects. Thus, the descriptions subjects received ranged from very poor sales performance at the high-magnitude, negative end, to very good sales performance at the high-magnitude, positive end. On the basis of feedback obtained from initial pretesting, the brief description of the leader was made consistent with the general positive or negative direction of performance change, in order to insure that he remained an equally plausible explanation for all outcome effects. Thus, in three cases of increased performance, a somewhat positive impression was conveyed; in the decreased performance cases, a somewhat negative impression was conveyed. Of course, the description of the leader within each type (increase versus decrease in performance) was held constant.

Immediately after reading the vignettes, subjects were asked to rate the performance of the unit on a 7-point scale, from "extremely poor" to "extremely good." As in Study 4, subjects were then asked to attribute performance outcomes to the leader and to alternative causes.

Results and Discussion

The performance and attribution data are summarized in Table 22.6. Our prediction was that the greatest level of leader attributions would occur at

TABLE 22.6. Mean Perceived Performance and Attributions in Each Performance Outcome Condition: Study 5

	Performance Condition					
Dependent variable	Large decrease (N = 19)	Moderate decrease (N = 19)	Slight decrease (N = 20)	Slight increase (N = 18)	Moderate increase (N = 20)	Large increase (N = 20)
Attributions*						
Leader	5.00	4.26	4.55	4.94	5.05	5.10
Alternatives	3.82	3.96	4.07	4.09	3.91	3.80
Perceived performance[†]	2.47	3.11	3.55	5.17	5.55	6.35

* 7-point scales; higher scores indicate stronger attributions.
[†] 7-point scales; higher scores indicate better perceived performance.

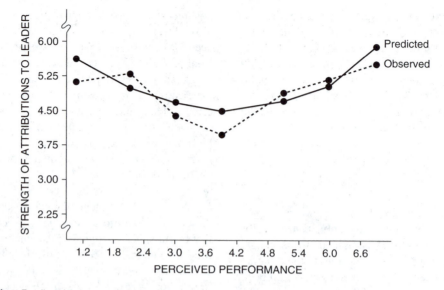

FIGURE 22.1 ■ Predicted values and mean attributions to leader at each level of perceived performance: Study 5.

both extremes of the performance continuum—i.e., where positive and negative magnitudes are greatest—implying a curvilinear relationship between performance level and leader attributions. The means across the six conditions suggest such a pattern did indeed occur.[4] However, the most sensitive and useful test compares subjects' own perceptions of performance outcomes with the strength of their attributions to the leader. Accordingly, an orthogonal polynomial regression analysis was conducted, using subjects' own perceptions of performance to predict the extent to which leadership was used as an explanatory concept. The hypothesis, in this case, is a quadratic (2° polynomial) model. Linear, quadratic, and cubic models were examined, and, as predicted, the only coefficient to reach significance was associated with the quadratic component, $\beta = 3.09(1.02)$; $t = 3.02$, $p < .001$. In addition, goodness-of-fit tests for the polynomial model at each degree were conducted.

These tests estimated the *lack* of fit of models at each degree, relative to the residual MS from fitting polynomials of higher degrees. Thus, a high F ratio is an indication of a poor fit. These tests revealed that the linear model produced a significantly poor fit, $F(2,112) = 4.87$, $p = .009$, while the quadratic model provided the best fit, $F(1,112) = .62$, $p = .43$. A scatter plot of the data confirmed the U-shaped distribution of scores. Figure 22.1 shows the mean attributions for subjects at each perceived performance level. Similar analyses conducted on the alternative attributions indicated that such curvilinear trends did not occur, lending added support to the hypotheses.

As an even better test of the hypothesis, the perceived performances were used to predict subjects' preferences for using the leader as a causal explanation *relative* to their tendency to make alternative attributions. Accordingly, a parallel regression analysis was conducted using the difference

---

[4]A 1 × 6 ANOVA on the performance ratings revealed a significant main effect, $F(5, 110) = 77.22$, $p < .001$, attesting to the efficacy of the manipulation. The attribution measures were examined in a 2 × 6 ANOVA (one within factor: two types of attributions; one between factor: six performance levels). This analysis revealed a significant main effect for type of attribution, such that leader attributions (overall $M = 4.82$)

were generally stronger than attributions to alternative causes (overall $M = 3.94$), $F(1, 110) = 55.38$, $p < .001$. The main effect for performance level was not significant, $F(5, 110) = .99$, $p = .42$; ns, indicating that the level of attributions to all sources did not vary across conditions. The interaction between attribution and performance was marginal, $F(5, 110) = 2.01$, $p < .08$.

between the leader and alternative attributions as the dependent variable. Again, the quadratic component was significant, $\beta = 4.60(1.22)$; $t = 3.76$, $p < .001$. Also as expected, the subsequent fit test revealed a poor linear fit, $F(2, 112) = 7.34$, $p < .001$, but a good fitting quadratic model, $F(1, 112) = .57$, $p = .45$. These results, then, paralleled those of the previous regression analyses.

When taken together, the results provided good support for the hypothesis that larger outcomes—whether they are positive or negative—are most likely to lead observers to make the inference that a leader was an important cause. Nevertheless, several issues remained, and those became the focus of Study 6.

Study 6

This final study had two general objectives. One was to replicate the pattern of results found in the previous experiments under somewhat more refined conditions. The vignettes used in those experiments raised some issues that could be relevant to the observed effects. One issue concerned the salience and general prominence of the leader in the vignettes. Upon reflection, we had not paid much attention to the positioning and length of the leader's description in the vignettes. It was possible that we had unwittingly and artificially inflated the extent to which the leader was subsequently considered as an important causal determinant of performance. That is a concern, because other research indicates that attributions in general are highly sensitive to the contextual properties of causal information, such as saliency and primacy (e.g., Jones et al., 1968; Taylor and Fiske, 1978; McArthur, 1981). In fact, it is precisely for those reasons that the "main effects" for type of attribution (leader versus alternatives) observed in Studies 4 and 5 must be treated with caution. A less likely, but nevertheless present possibility is that extreme outcomes may somehow have been attributed to the leader in response to such artificial, externally induced prominence, rather than being the results of internal processes (e.g., Phillips and Lord, 1981). A related issue was the description of the

leader: in Study 5, in order to insure that the leader remained an equally plausible, potential causal determinant across the entire span of positive and negative performance conditions, he was portrayed somewhat positively in the three positive, increased performance conditions and somewhat negatively in the three negative, decreased performance conditions. Although this is not necessarily a problem, Study 6 allowed us to make use of an alternative strategy in which all descriptive information on the leader was deleted from the various vignettes, and we were able to clear up any ambiguities that might have been associated with the previous strategy.

A second general purpose was to examine the role of performance expectations in making leader attributions. Other literature (e.g., Jones and Davis, 1965; Jones et al., 1971; Pyszczynski and Greenberg, 1981; Hastie, 1984; Weiner, 1985) suggests that spontaneous attribution making is exacerbated by, among other things, the degree to which events depart from observers' general and normative expectations. Surprising, extraordinary events increase the need to search for plausible causal determinants. In the present context, expectations may be strongly related to the magnitude of the performance outcome and to the subsequent tendency to make attributions to the leader and perhaps to alternative causes, as well. One reasonable hypothesis is that the more extreme performances deviated from observers' less extreme expectations of what performance changes are typical for an organization. If that is true, then perhaps it is the size of deviation from expectations—not simply the magnitude of performance—that is responsible for the observed pattern of leadership attributions. Although that reasoning is not inconsistent with the general perspective taken in this analysis, it does suggest that some attempt should be made to take into account observers' expectations, along with performance outcomes, in order to examine their effects on attributions.

Method

Seventy-two undergraduate business majors in sections of an evening introductory organizational behavior course participated in this experiment.

Their mean age was 25.0 years, and on average they reported having nearly five (4.87) years of full-time work experience.

The vignettes used in the previous studies were modified, in order to decrease the prominence of the leader relative to other potential causal determinants, by weaving into the text the mention of the leader, along with a number of other causal determinants. The final vignettes read as follows:

> The Gemini Corporation is a large volume manufacturer of household appliances. They have been in business for a number of years and have several plants located throughout the country. The appliance industry is characterized by an environment whose market and economic factors have been changing over the past few years. Sales is one of the functional departments within this corporation and is headed by a Director, John Smith, who assumed this position at the beginning of the last fiscal year. At about the same time, a new group of sales representatives were hired and reported directly to Mr. Smith. At the end of the fiscal year, gross sales had shown a slight/moderate/large increase/decrease (2%/10%/25%) over last year's performance.

As a further precaution, subjects were asked on the rating form itself to consider all of the potential causes before they made their attributional ratings of the impact of any single causal determinant.

Before making these ratings, however, subjects were first asked to rate the performance of the unit, as in the previous studies. And, in order to assess the extent to which the level of performance deviated from their own implicit and general expectations, after rating the unit's performance they were also asked to rate (on a 7-point scale) how surprising they found the increase or decrease in performance.

Results and Discussion

Initial analyses. A series of analyses of variance was conducted on the six performance conditions, examining attributions, expectations, and perceived performance. These data are summarized in Figure 22.2. A one-way ANOVA of the perceived performance attested to the efficacy of the manipulation, $F(5, 66) = 9.65, p < .001$. A similar analysis of the expectation measure revealed a significant effect of performance condition on expectations, $F(5, 66) = 3.14, p = .013$. Attributions were examined in a two-way analysis of variance with one between factor (performance) and one within factor (leader versus alternative attributions). This analysis revealed a significant main effect for performance outcome, $F(5, 66) = 2.55, p = .036$, and for type of attribution, $F(1, 66) = 7.49, p = .008$. Moreover, both main effects were qualified by a significant interaction, $F(5, 66) = 2.42, p = .045$.

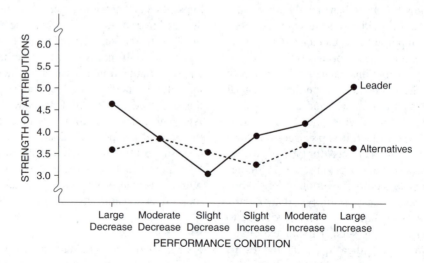

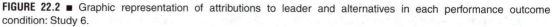

FIGURE 22.2 ■ Graphic representation of attributions to leader and alternatives in each performance outcome condition: Study 6.

Expectations and performance. First, in order to establish the relationship between performance and expectations, a polynomial regression analysis was conducted in which rated performance was used to predict the reported deviations from expectations. This analysis revealed that the coefficient on the quadratic component was significant, $\beta = 2.989(1.26)$; $t(69) = 2.38$, $p < .025$. Moreover, the goodness-of-fit tests indicated that the linear model provided a significant poor fit, $F(2.89)$, $p = .062$, while the U-shaped model ($2°$ polynomial) provided the best fit, $F(1.68) = .19$, $p = .67$. Thus, extremely good and extremely poor performance were judged to be more surprising and therefore represented larger deviations from subjects' general expectations.

Leader attributions. The next task was to incorporate expectations into the model specified by the original hypothesis. However, the polynomial regression technique used in the previous experiment to test the predicted curvilinear relationship between perceived performance and leader attributions did not lend itself to the inclusion of more than a single predictor variable and, therefore, could not be used to control and test for the additional effect of expectations. Consequently, a more traditional multiple-regression procedure was employed as a reasonable approximation of the model. First, the relationship between leader attributions and perceived performance was estimated by including the performance variable and its squared term as predictors of leader attributions. If the hypothesized "quadratic" relationship were true, then a significant, but negative coefficient should be obtained on the performance variable, *in combination* with a significant but positive coefficient on the squared term. With only these two predictor terms, the overall equation was significant, $R^2 = .347$; $F(2.69) = 18.30$, $p < .001$. More importantly, however, and as expected, the coefficient associated with the performance term was significant and negative, $\beta = -2.41(.438)$, $p < .001$; and the coefficient associated with the squared term was significant and positive, $\beta = .322(.545)$, $p < .001$. In effect, then, these results replicated those of the previous study and, in light of the changes made in the

vignettes, provided us with more confidence in the validity and generalizability of the effect.

The overall equation remained significant when the expectation ratings were added into the above model as a predictor, $R^2 = .344$; $F(3, 68) = 13.41$, $p < .001$. However, the coefficient associated with the expectation rating was not significant, $\beta = .1829(.110)$, $p = .103$. The negative coefficient on the performance term remained significant, $\beta = -2.24(.444)$, $p < .001$, as did the positive coefficient on the squared term, $\beta = .297(.559)$, $p < .001$. Thus one must conclude that although extreme performances deviated from expectations and were generally viewed as more surprising than lower magnitude performances, in this case, such deviations probably did not, by themselves, have a large independent effect on the strength of leader attributions. Moreover, when controlling for expectations, the observed relationship between the magnitude of outcomes and the tendency to understand performance in terms of leadership persisted.

A plausible argument is that when faced with explaining a large magnitude outcome, individuals make more attributions to all relevant sources. According to that line of reasoning, the level of leadership attributions may simply be an artifact of a more general trend. Consequently, we performed one final set of analyses that attempted to control for individuals' general tendency to make attributions to all sources. In order to do that, the same set of variables was used to predict a ratio in which the strength of leadership attributions was divided by the strength of attributions to all other sources. This ratio roughly parallels the LQ measure used in the previous archival studies. According to the hypothesis, extreme performances should be associated with higher ratios. The prediction model was also significant for this dependent variable, $R^2 = .283$, $p < .001$. And, as with the previous dependent variable, the coefficient associated with the expectation term was not significant $\beta = .238(.458)$, $p = .604$. However, as predicted, the coefficient on the performance term was significant and negative, $\beta = -.811(.184)$, $p < .001$; and the coefficient associated with the squared term was significant and positive, $\beta = .109(.232)$, $p < .001$. This last analysis, then, indicated that extreme performances did indeed lead to a proportional increase in the preference to use the leader as a causal explanation and provided a strong confirmation of our expectations.

General Discussion

The romanticized conception of leadership suggests that leaders do or should have the ability to control and influence the fates of the organizations in their charge. This assumption of control and the responsibility it engenders is a double-edged sword: not only does it imply giving credit for positive outcomes, but it also entails laying blame for negative ones (Salancik and Meindl, 1984). Our experimental studies revealed that pattern. However, the results of our archival studies suggest that one or the other tendency, for whatever reasons, may predominate in any given case. The negative and positive associations in Studies 2 and 3, respectively, between an interest in leadership and the state of the national economy are particularly intriguing. The positive association uncovered in Study 3 suggests that the popular press that serves the general business community contributes to the credit-giving aspect of the romanticized view. Of course, the popular press is in part a reflection of the community it serves, and firms, by their own activities, can prompt an interest in and association to leadership factors. Thus, the finding that leadership is accentuated during times of economic prosperity is, in retrospect, not so difficult to understand. By the same token, the scholarly community may have less reason to favor giving credit over laying blame. In fact, the negative association between an interest in the topic of leadership and economic prosperity may reflect the problem-oriented response of young scholars to hard times.

Others (e.g., Pfeffer, 1977; Pfeffer and Salancik, 1978) have suggested that the tendency to ascribe high levels of control and influence to leaders arises from private needs to find causes among human actors. Accordingly, the exacerbation of those needs would tend to foster the development of a romantic conception in which leadership was indeed believed to be highly significant. In fact, a subsequent analysis of our experimental studies revealed that attributions to different personal causal agents (in this case, leader and subordinates) tended to be positively correlated ($r = .20$, .22, and .37 in Studies 4, 5, and 6, respectively), as this general line of reasoning would suggest. A romanticized view of leadership is probably also an outgrowth of a general faith in human organizations as potentially effective and efficient value-producing systems that fulfill the various interests of their participants and perhaps, also, society at large. The potency and promise of human organizations and all the values they represent come to be symbolized in the formal hierarchy of authority and the officials who occupy the elite positions of power and status (Milgram, 1974). Given this, a faith in the significance of leadership may be one manifestation of internalized values about the validity of organizations and therefore, by implication, the roles occupied by people who are charged with the responsibility to maintain and control them.

Because observers are prone to overestimate the amount of control that leaders exert, particularly when the event or outcome in question is especially significant, a subscription to a romanticized view could be dysfunctional to the goals of an "objective" or rational assessment of important but causally indeterminant events. At the same time, however, it seems possible that an excessive belief in the potency of leadership could also be functional for those who will occupy positions of formal authority and status. If we assume that on some occasions leadership can, in reality, make a difference—but that we cannot be sure when—then it may be important for organizations to have leaders who operate, at some level, on the assumption that they do make a difference and that they are in control. Without the benefits of a working assumption that conveys a sense of efficacy and control, the initiation of and persistence in potentially relevant activity would be considerably more difficult. The end result may be somewhat depressed functioning and a sense of helplessness in situations in which control is in fact possible.

The present research may begin to provide us with some new insights about the reason for changing leadership or decisions to extend an incumbent's tenure in response to perceived variations in an organization's fortunes. For example, there is a small, but somewhat paradoxical literature that attempts to understand the causes and consequences of managerial succession. Several theoretical perspectives have been offered (e.g., Grusky, 1963; Gamson and Scotch, 1964; Gordon and Rosen, 1981), all of them based on more or less implicit assumptions about the attributions of relevant and powerful others to leadership factors in response to poor organizational performance. In fact, the theories and the empirical studies make a convincing case that poor performance increases the probability and rate of successions (Grusky, 1963; Helmich and Brown, 1972; Lieberson and O'Connor, 1972; Helmich, 1974, 1977; Osborn et al., 1981). There is less theoretical agreement about the effect of succession on subsequent organizational performance. Conventional wisdom implies that the effect on performance of changing leaders should be positive, since such events are ostensibly guided by the positive intentions and expectations of those in a position to induce them. Some (e.g., Grusky, 1963) argue that successions are disruptive to so many important processes that subsequent performances will decline. Still others (e.g., Gamson and Scotch, 1964) emphasize the symbolic aspects of successions and consider them exercises in "ritualistic scapegoating" that involve processes that are only incidentally or tangentially relevant for subsequent performance. The available empirical evidence tends to run contrary to the conventional wisdom, suggesting that although poor performances may often precipitate successions, such events have little or negative effects on subsequent performance (e.g., Allen, Panian, and Lotz, 1979; Brown, 1982). The paradox is that, despite the absence of clearly instrumental effects, successions are nevertheless a popular response to poor performance. At least a part of that paradox can be understood as reflecting an inclination to construe events and outcomes in terms of leadership. Pfeffer (1977) argued that the limited impact that many leadership successions have on performance outcomes is due in large part to the lack of variability in the pool of individuals from which both the incumbent and successor have

been drawn. One interesting and testable hypothesis precipitated by the present analysis is that interested parties are very likely to overperceive the degree of relevant variation in that pool, seeing more heterogeneity than really exists between the old and the new leader and among the potential successors. Given the romanticization of leadership, it is less difficult to understand the optimistic faith in the effectiveness of successions—the shifting of commitment from the old to the new leader and the maintenance of positive expectations for outcomes, even in the face of contrary evidence.

Needless to say, organizations have always been influenced by their environments, yet it is only recently—within the last ten years—that organizational dependencies have been fully appreciated in our theoretical perspectives (e.g., Aldrich, 1979; Hall, 1982; Pfeffer and Salancik, 1978). In Study 1, the average company sales growth performance over the 11-year period and the corresponding figures for relevant industries were strongly correlated, $R(9 \text{ df}) = .80, p > .01$. That is not surprising, given the number of industries sampled and the size of the firms in our sample that were chosen to represent these industries. However, it does provide a rough indication that a given firm's fate, in terms of performance, is closely tied to external factors affecting whole industries, as opposed to being under the direct, unique control of its top management. As expected, however, we were able to find evidence that there is nevertheless a tendency to link leadership not only with variations in company performance, but also with the performance of entire industries, which are undoubtedly affected by factors well beyond the control of any single firm or management. Other researchers have also found systematic evidence indicating that traditional views have overestimated the amount of variance in performance outcomes that is logically and empirically attributable to leadership (e.g., Lieberson and O'Connor, 1972; Salancik and Pfeffer, 1977). Such evidence shifts attention and the locus of control away from top-level leaders and the positions they occupy to other causal entities and forces not directly tied to the qualities and activities of leadership. The implication is that perhaps leadership is not as important as we normally think—at least not in the traditional sense (Pfeffer, 1978, 1981). That implication is provocative, because it contradicts the romanticized conception of leadership, and some resistance to it is predictable. To the extent that observers are psychologically invested in a romanticized view of leadership, then, we might expect selective perceptions, confirmatory biases, and other processes (Ross, 1977) to be present that cause the observer to avoid or resist information and evidence that diminishes the significance of leadership to organizational functioning. Consider the reaction of Burke (1979: 121) to Pfeffer (1978):

> Pfeffer indeed went out on a limb by proclaiming that leaders do not matter that much. Many variables other than the leader per se account for organizational outcomes. Moreover, "leadership is the outcome of an attribution process in which observers—in order to achieve a feeling of control over their environment—tend to attribute outcomes to persons rather than to context, and the identification of individuals with leadership positions facilitates this attribution process" (p. 31). An interesting belief, interpretation, hypothesis, or whatever, but methinks Pfeffer broke the limb and fell off. In other words, in an apparent attempt to be provocative, Pfeffer seems to have leaned too heavily toward iconoclasm.

It is possible to take the position that leadership may in fact contribute to a large portion of the variance that is controllable and thus warrants intense attention. However, the results of our analysis suggest that the faith in leadership is likely to exceed the reality of control and will be used to account for variance that is in fact uncontrollable. This is a convenient state of affairs for managements motivated to do just that. Salancik and Meindl (1984) presented evidence documenting the attempt by top managements to create an illusion of control through the manipulation of causal reasoning around performance issues. Such motivations appear to be strongest among managements whose firms have displayed the sorts of erratic performance histories that would imply little real control. Our analysis suggests that what otherwise might be considered patently obvious attempts to create the illusions of control where

none exists is likely to be complemented by a high degree of receptivity among observers.

When considering the "symbolic role" of management (Pfeffer and Salancik, 1978; Pfeffer, 1981), the greater significance of leadership lies not in the direct impact on substantive matters but in the ability to exert control over the meanings and interpretations important constituencies give to whatever events and occurrences are considered relevant for the organization's functioning (Pondy, 1978; Daft and Weick, 1984). The manipulation of language and other organizationally relevant symbols allows leaders to manage the political and social processes that maintain organized activity in the face of potentially disruptive forces (Pondy et al., 1982). One plausible hypothesis is that the development of a romanticized conception of leadership causes participants more readily to imbue the symbolic gestures of leaders with meaning and significance. Accordingly, the psychological readiness to comprehend things in terms of leadership, whatever dysfunctions it represents, may play an important role in determining the ultimate effectiveness of symbolism as a political tool, benefiting most those leaders who are adept at its manipulation.

Conclusion

There has been in recent years some question concerning the viability of leadership, both as a concept and as an area of inquiry. Indeed, there is ample reason to modify our traditional assumptions about the instrumental potency of leadership factors in the larger scheme of things. Given the present analysis, however, it appears that the obsession with the concept will not easily be curtailed. While there are some obvious limitations to the studies reported here, together they provide reasonably coherent and compelling evidence for the premise that a romanticized conception of leadership is an important part of the social reality that is brought to bear in our informal analysis of organizations—and perhaps in our more formal theories as well. Ironically, though, a heroic vision of what leaders and leadership are all about virtually guarantees that a satisfying understanding will remain beyond the grasp of our best scientific efforts, particularly since the thrust of scientific inquiry is to do away with mysteries. The major effect is to objectify, quantify, and in some cases trivialize the unique import of leadership. In that sense, the product of such efforts is contrary and antithetical to the romanticized conception. And, if our analysis is correct, the continuing infatuation with leadership, for whatever truths it yields about the qualities and behavior of our leaders, can also be used to learn something about the motivations of followers. It may be that the romance and the mystery surrounding leadership concepts are critical for sustaining follower-ship and that they contribute significantly to the responsiveness of individuals to the needs and goals of the collective organization.

REFERENCES

Aldrich, Howard E. 1979 Organizations and Environments. Englewood Cliffs, NJ: Prentice-Hall.

Allen, Michael P., Sharon K. Panian, and Roy E. Lotz 1979 "Managerial succession and organizational performance: A recalcitrant problem revisited." Administrative Science Quarterly, 24: 167–180.

Anderson, Craig A. 1983 "The causal structure of situations: The generation of plausible causal attributions as a function of type of event situation." Journal of Experimental Social Psychology, 19: 185–203.

Bennis, Warren 1959 "Leadership theory and administrative behavior: The problem of authority." Administrative Science Quarterly, 4: 259–301.

Binning, John F., and Robert G. Lord 1980 "Boundary conditions for performance cue effects on group process rating: Familiarity versus type of feedback." Organizational Behavior and Human Performance, 26: 115–130.

Brown, M. Craig 1982 "Administrative succession and organizational performance: The succession effect." Administrative Science Quarterly, 27: 1–16.

Burke, W. Warner 1979 Review of Morgan W. McCall and Michael M. Lombardo (eds.), Leadership: Where Else Can We Go? Journal of Applied Behavioral Science, 15: 121–122.

Burns, John M. 1978 Leadership. New York: Harper & Row.

Calder, Bobby J. 1977 "An attribution theory of leadership." In Barry M. Staw and Gerald R. Salancik (eds.), New Direction in Organizational Behavior: 179–204. Chicago: St. Clair.

Daft, Richard L., and Karl E. Weick 1984 "Toward a model of organizations as interpretation systems." Academy of Management Review, 9: 284–295.

DeNisi, Angelo S., and Robert D. Pritchard 1978 "Implicit theories of performance as artifacts in survey research: A replication and extension." Organizational Behavior and Human Performance, 21: 358–366.

Downey, Kirk, H. Thomas I. Chacko, and James C. McElroy 1979 "Attribution of the 'causes' of performance: A constructive, quasi-longitudinal replication of the Staw (1975) study." Organizational Behavior and Human Performance, 24: 287–299.

Elig, Timothy W., and Irene Hanson Frieze 1979 "Measuring causal attributions for success and failure." Journal of Personality and Social Psychology, 37: 621–634.

Gamson, William A., and Norman A. Scotch 1964 "Scapegoating in baseball." American Journal of Sociology, 70: 69–72.

Goode, William J. 1978 The Celebration of Heroes. Berkeley, CA: University of California Press.

Gordon, Gil E., and Ned Rosen 1981 "Critical factors in leadership succession." Organizational Behavior and Human Performance, 27: 227–254.

Greene, Charles N. 1976 "Disenchantment with leadership research: Some causes, recommendations, and alternative directions." In J. G. Hunt and L. L. Larson (eds.), Leadership: The Cutting Edge: 57–67. Carbondale, IL: Southern Illinois University Press.

Grusky, Oscar 1963 "Managerial succession and organizational effectiveness." American Journal of Sociology, 69: 21–31.

Hall, Richard H. 1982 Organizations: Structures and Process, 3rd ed. Englewood Cliffs, NJ: Prentice-Hall.

Hastie, Reid 1984 "Causes and effects of causal attributions." Journal of Personality and Social Psychology, 46: 44–56.

Helmich, Donald L. 1974 "Organizational growth and succession patterns." Academy of Management Journal, 17: 771–775. 1977 "Executive succession in the corporate organization: A current integration." Academy of Management Review 2: 252–266.

Helmich, Donald L., and Brown W. B. 1972 "Successor type and organizational change in the corporate enterprise." Administrative Science Quarterly, 17: 371–381.

House, Robert J. 1977 "A 1976 theory of charismatic leadership." In J. G. Hunt and L. L. Larson (eds.), Leadership: The Cutting Edge: 189–207. Carbondale, IL: Southern Illinois University Press.

Jones, Edward E., and Keith E. Davis 1965 "From acts to dispositions: The attribution process in person perception." In L. Berkowitz (ed.), Advances in Experimental Social Psychology, 2: 219–266. New York: Academic Press.

Jones, Edward E., Leslie Rock, Kelly O. Shaver, George Goethals, and Ward L. M. 1968 "Pattern of performance and ability attribution: An unexpected primacy effect." Journal of Personality and Social Psychology, 10: 317–340.

Jones, Edward E., Steven Worchel, George R. Goethals, and Judy Grumet 1971 "Prior expectancy and behavior extremity as determinants of attitude attribution." Journal of Experimental Social Psychology, 7: 59–80.

Karmel, Barbara 1978 "Leadership: A challenge to traditional research methods and assumptions." Academy of Management Review, 3: 475–482.

Kerr, Steven, and John M. Jermier 1978 "Substitutes for leadership: Their meaning and measurement." Organizational Behavior and Human Performance, 22: 375–403.

Klapp, Orrin E. 1964 Symbolic Leaders. Chicago: Aldine.

Lieberson, Stanley, and James F. O'Connor 1972 "Leadership and organizational performance: A study of large corporations." American Sociological Review, 37: 117–130.

Lord, Robert G., and Jonathan E. Smith 1983 "Theoretical information processing and situational factors affecting attribution theory models of organizational behavior." Academy of Management Review, 8: 50–60.

March, James G. 1981 "How we talk and how we act: Administrative theory and administrative life." Unpublished manuscript, Stanford University.

McArthur, Leslie Z. 1981 "What grabs you? The role of attention in impression formation and causal attribution." In E. T. Higgins, C. P. Herman, and M. P. Zanna (eds.), Social Cognition: The Ontario Symposium, 1: 201–246. Hillsdale, NJ: Erlbaum.

McCall, Morgan W., Jr., and Michael M. Lombardo (eds.) 1978 Leadership: Where Else Can We Go? Durham, NC: Duke University Press.

McElroy, James C. 1982 "A typology of attribution leadership research." Academy of Management Review, 7: 413–417.

McElroy, James C., and Kirk Downey H. 1982 "Observation in organizational research: Panacea to the performance-attribution effect?" Academy of Management Journal, 25: 822–835.

Milgram, Stanley 1974 Obedience to Authority. New York: Harper & Row.

Miner, John B. 1975 "The uncertain future of the leadership concept: An overview." In J. G. Hunt and L. L. Larson (eds.), Leadership Frontiers: 197–208. Kent, OH: Kent State University Press.

Neilson, Winthrop, and Frances Neilson 1973 What's News—Dow Jones. Radnor, PA: Chilton.

Osborn, Richard N., Lawrence R. Jauch, Thomas N. Martin, and William F. Glueck 1981 "The event of CEO succession, performance and environmental conditions." Academy of Management Journal, 24: 183–191.

Pfeffer, Jeffrey 1977 "The ambiguity of leadership." Academy of Management Review, 2: 104–112. 1978 "The ambiguity of leadership." In Morgan W. McCall and Michael M. Lombardo (eds.), Leadership: Where Else Can We Go?: 13–34. Durham, NC: Duke University Press. 1981 "Management as symbolic action: The creation and maintenance of organizational paradigms." In L. L. Cummings and B. M. Staw (eds), Research in Organizational Behavior, 3: 1–52. Greenwich, CT: JAI Press.

Pfeffer, Jeffrey, and Gerald R. Salancik 1978 The External Control of Organizations: A Resource Dependence Perspective. New York: Harper & Row.

Phillips, James S., and Robert G. Lord 1981 "Causal attributions and perceptions of leadership." Organizational Behavior and Human Performance, 28: 143–163.

Pondy, Louis R. 1978 "Leadership is a language game." In M. W. McCall, Jr., and M. M. Lombardo (eds.), Leadership: Where Else Can We Go?: 87–99. Durham, NC: Duke University Press.

Pondy, Louis R., Peter Frost, Gareth Morgan, and Thomas Dandridge (eds.) 1982 Organizational Symbolism. Greenwich, CT: JAI Press.

Pyszczynski, T. A., and Gerald Greenberg 1981 "Role of disconfirmed expectancies in the instigation of attributional processing." Journal of Personality and Social Psychology, 40: 31–38.

Ross, Lee 1977 "The intuitive psychologist and his shortcomings: Distortions in the attribution process." In Leonard Berkowitz (ed.), Advances in Experimental Social Psychology, 10: 174–220. New York: Academic Press.

Rush, Michael C., Jay C. Thomas, and Robert L. Lord 1977 "Implicit leadership theory: A potential threat to the internal validity of leader behavior questionnaires." Organizational Behavior and Human Performance, 20: 92–110.

Salancik, Gerald R., and James R. Meindl 1984 "Corporate attributions as strategic illusions of management control." Administrative Science Quarterly, 29: 238–254.

Salancik, Gerald R., and Jeffrey Pfeffer 1977 "Constraints on administrative discretion: The limited influence of mayors on city budgets." Urban Affairs Quarterly, 12: 475–498.

Schlenker, Barry R. 1982 "An identity-analytic approach to the explanation of social conduct." In Leonard Berkowitz (ed.), Advances in Experimental Social Psychology. 15: 194–248. New York: Academic Press.

Staw, Barry M. 1975 "Attribution of the 'causes' of performance: A general alternative interpretation of cross-sectional research on organizations." Organizational Behavior and Human Performance, 13: 414–432.

Staw, Barry M., and Jerry Ross 1980 "Commitment in an experimenting society: A study of the attribution of leadership from administrative scenarios." Journal of Applied Psychology, 65: 249–260.

Stogdill, Ralph M. 1974 Handbook of Leadership. New York: Free Press.

Taylor, Shelly E., and Susan G. Fiske 1978 "Salience, attention, and attribution: Top of the head phenomena." In L. Berkowitz (ed.), Advances in Experimental Social Psychology, 11: 250–288. New York: Academic Press.

Thompson, James D., and Tuden A. 1959 "Strategies, structures, and processes of organizational decision." In J. D. Thompson, P. B. Hammond, R. W. Hawkes, B. H. Lunker, and A. Tuden (eds), Comparative Studies in Administration: 195–216. Pittsburgh: Pittsburgh University Press.

Weber, Max 1946 "The sociology of charismatic authority." In H. H. Gerth and C. W. Mills (eds), From Max Weber: Essays in Sociology: 245–252. New York: Oxford University Press.

Weick, Karl E. 1979 The Social Psychology of Organizing, rev. ed. Reading, MA: Addison-Wesley.

Weiner, Bernard E. 1985 "Spontaneous causal thinking." Psychological Bulletin, 97: 74–84.

PART 5

Group Ecology

The ecology of groups is often neglected by researchers. Every group occupies a setting of some kind, however, and no group can be fully understood unless its setting is analyzed. Analyses of settings reveal many environmental factors, which can be categorized as physical, social, or temporal in nature. Most research on such factors has treated them as causes for various effects in groups. But groups sometimes attempt to control the settings that they occupy, which means that environmental factors could also be treated as effects.

Physical Environments

To understand a group, it is often helpful to know where it operates. Is the group usually found indoors or outdoors? When the group is indoors, what kinds of rooms does it occupy? How are they decorated? What portions of the group's space belong to particular group members, rather than to everyone?

Most research on the physical environments of groups treats them as causes rather than effects. For example, several researchers have studied crowding (Paulus & Nagar, 1989), in residential areas, college dorms, and prisons, as well as in laboratories. When group members feel more crowded, they often exhibit greater stress, worse performance (especially on complex tasks), and more conflict. These effects may be mediated by the loss of control, cognitive overload, or behavioral constraints that come with crowding. A related area of research focuses on groups that work in extreme environments, such as outer space, underground/underwater, and combat zones (Harrison & Connors, 1984). Groups that work in these environments often have stronger leaders, greater cohesion, and more conformity pressure. These effects may reflect attempts by groups to control conflicts among their members, which allows everyone to concentrate on the threatening environment around them. Office environments have also been studied (Sundstrom, 1986), in the belief that such factors as temperature, lighting, floor space, and noise could affect the job satisfaction of group members, which in turn might affect the productivity of their groups. There is indeed evidence for these effects, though they are often small in size. Finally, there is a growing interest in how computer technology influences work groups (McGrath & Hollingshead, 1993). Several kinds of technology have been studied, but the strongest evidence involves email, which affects work groups by reducing their overall communication, equalizing participation levels, and emphasizing informational (rather than normative) influence. There is little evidence, however, that email affects group productivity.

There is much less research on attempts by groups to control their environments, though such control is possible in many cases. For example, groups can seek more pleasant environments and avoid less pleasant ones, as when a family moves from a small house to a larger one. And some groups can change their environments in ways that make them more pleasant, as when a fraternity buys better sound equipment for its party room. Finally, any group can interpret its environment in ways that might make it seem more or less pleasant. A group of office workers, for example, might focus on the

fact that their carpeting is old and ragged, ignoring their new desks and chairs.

Several researchers have studied *territoriality* (Brown, Lawrence, & Robinson, 2005; Taylor, 1988), another way in which groups can control their environments. Many groups, including youth gangs and gated neighborhoods, establish territories and then defend them against outsiders. Groups are more likely to be territorial when their composition is homogenous and stable, they are cohesive, and they have a strong sense of social identity. A group can also apportion its territory among members. This is often done on the basis of status (consider who gets the best rooms in a sorority house). Territoriality is alleged to serve many purposes for groups. A group that can establish a territory and defend it against outsiders could (a) protect valuable resources; (b) improve living/working conditions; (c) gain privacy; (d) control social interactions; (e) become more cohesive; and (f) express its social identity. But there is little evidence that territoriality actually produces these benefits for groups or their members.

Temporal Environments

Much of the research in this area focuses on group development, a topic of special interest to clinical and counseling psychologists, who often use groups in their practices (Lacoursiere, 1980). This work has generated many models of group development. In most of these models, a sequence of developmental stages is proposed, through which all groups must pass. Although this work is often interesting, it is open to criticism. For example, many researchers study just a few groups (often only one), in which they were themselves members (often leaders). And the models proposed by these researchers are often unclear about important issues, such as the number of developmental stages, the behavioral themes associated with those stages, the rate at which development occurs, and so on. Finally, *why* do groups develop? Many models assume that group development is a recapitulation of individual development during childhood. Other factors that might shape group development, such as the arrival of new members or the departure of old ones, or changes in the physical or social environment of the group, are rarely acknowledged. A recent trend in research on group development, namely a focus on task rather than therapy groups, is promising, in part because it has avoided some of these problems.

The goal of research on group development is to learn whether and how groups change over time, but it is important to note that every group operates at some developmental level and that its level of development might affect other aspects of group life (Worchel, Coutant-Sassic, & Grossman, 1991). For example, reactions to deviance could be harsher in a newly-formed group, because its members are struggling to develop and obey norms about how they should behave, but milder in a group that has been around for awhile, because its members are interested in distinguishing themselves from one another. All of this suggests that group researchers should be cautious about interpreting their findings without first considering the developmental levels of the groups they have observed.

Other research on temporal environments examines the formation or dissolution of groups. In a review and analysis of work on group formation,

Moreland (1987) argued that it should not be viewed as an event, but rather as a *process*, one involving social integration. Social integration can take several forms (environmental, behavioral, affective, cognitive), and so the challenge is to discover how different forms of social integration work together to create a particular group. Research on group dissolution is rare, unfortunately. It may be a process of social disintegration. If so, then Moreland's analysis of group formation (reversed) might also explain group dissolution. But dissolution may be more complex than that, involving special processes that must be studied in their own right.

Finally, a few researchers have studied the impact of time limits on groups. Karau and Kelly (2004) have integrated that work in an attentional focus model. According to their model, time pressure leads group members to focus on a restricted range of task cues and to focus on task completion as their primary goal. The range of task cues is restricted not when those cues first occur, but later on, when group members negotiate what is important and what is not. And the focus on task completion often produces a worse outcome than a group might otherwise achieve.

Although the passage of time affects groups in many ways, groups are not helpless time travelers. There is some evidence that they often attempt to control time. McGrath and Rotchford (1983) argue that groups face three general temporal problems, namely uncertainty, conflicts of interest among members, and scarcity. These problems can be solved through scheduling, synchronization, and allocation (respectively). A few studies suggest that work groups are more productive when they devote more effort to solving temporal problems.

Social Environments

Nearly all of the research in this area involves intergroup relations. Several reviews of this work are available (e.g., Hogg, 2003), including *Intergroup Relations* by Hogg and Abrams (2001) in the same series as this one. Literally hundreds of studies on intergroup relations have been done, and though they have produced much valuable information, two general problems are worth noting. First, many researchers seem to assume that groups relate to one another in a social vacuum. Most studies involve just two groups, each separate from the other. However, many groups are actually bound together in some way, because they share members, have "weak ties" (relationships that bind individuals from the two groups to one another), or are embedded in the same social network. And other groups or individuals intervene at times in intergroup relations, if they believe that their own outcomes might be affected. Thus, relations between groups can be quite complex, involving multiple actors related to one another in a variety of ways.

Second, many researchers seem to assume that intergroup relations are always competitive, yet there is considerable evidence of cooperation between groups. Such cooperation may be indirect, as when one group imitates another or uses another group for the purpose of social comparison. Cooperation can also be direct, as when groups exchange valuable resources, form alliances to attain common goals, or merge to form new groups. These and other positive forms of intergroup relations should be studied more often by researchers.

Setting aside these problems, what does research on intergroup relations reveal? The picture is grim—groups often fight with one another, in civil and not so civil ways. One source of conflict is competition for scarce resources. But such competition may be unnecessary for conflict to occur. Research on social categorization shows that simply making group memberships salient to people is often enough to create biases that favor the ingroup over outgroups—people tend to help members of their own group and (less often) to harm members of other groups (Wilder, 1986). Why? Social identity theory, which was described earlier, offers one explanation. According to that theory, everyone wants their own group to compare favorably with other groups, so that they can develop or maintain a positive social identity. One way to accomplish that goal is to help one's own group and harm other groups. And once biases arise, they frequently become self-fueling. Although few researchers have studied revenge, it is another source of conflict between groups. When one group harms another, that harm is likely to be remembered, motivating the group that was harmed to "pay back" what was done to it, sometimes with "interest."

How can intergroup conflict be reduced or eliminated? Maybe it cannot, given how easily such conflict is produced and how likely it is to persist or even escalate. There is considerable interest in this problem among theorists and researchers, however, leading to several proposals. Ironically, one possible solution is to use social categorization, the original cause for so many conflicts between groups. If the members of groups that are in conflict can be led to *recategorize* themselves as members of the same larger group, then their biases may weaken, especially if a new larger outgroup can also be identified (although that is likely to create intergroup conflict at another level ...). There is evidence that such recategorization can indeed be helpful (Gaertner, Dovidio, Nier, Banker, Ward, Houlette, & Loux, 2000).

Other, smaller areas of research on the social environments of groups can be found as well. For example, some researchers study groups embedded in large organizations, focusing on such issues as how these groups balance their own interests against those of their organization, on whose success they also depend. Cultural differences between groups are also studied by some researchers. For example, do families play a different role in the lives of Japanese than in the lives of Americans? Another area of research involves groups that overlap because they share members. A single person can belong to several different groups. This produces interdependence among those groups, because the person's experiences in one group affect his or her behavior in the other groups. Consider families, for example. Although child development seems to occur primarily in the family, it can also be affected by other groups to which children (e.g., school friends) and their parents (e.g., coworkers) belong (Bronfenbrenner, 1986). Finally, groups can be influenced by a variety of outsiders, such as prospective and ex-members, friends and relatives, customers or clients, and enemies. The mere presence of such persons can affect a group, as when group members close ranks to confront an enemy. More direct forms of influence are also possible, as when people are recruited into groups by their friends.

Nearly all of the work discussed so far treats the social environment of groups as a cause, rather than an effect. Can groups ever control their social environments, and if so, then how is that done? A few scholars have considered this issue (e.g., Wageman, 1999), but much remains to be learned.

REFERENCES

Bronfenbrenner, U. (1986). Ecology of the family as a context for human development: Research perspectives. *Developmental Psychology, 22*, 723–742.

Brown, G., Lawrence, R. B., & Robinson, S. L. (2005). Territoriality in organizations. *Academy of Management Review, 30*, 577–594.

Gaertner, S. L., Dovidio, J. F., Nier, J. A., Banker, B. S., Ward, C. M., Houlette, M., & Loux, S. (2000). The Common Ingroup Identity Model for reducing intergroup bias: Progress and challenges. In D. Capozza, & R. Brown (Eds.), *Social identity processes: Trends in theory and research* (pp. 133–148). London, UK: Sage.

Harrison, A. A., & Connors, M. M. (1984). Groups in exotic environments. In L. Berkowitz (Ed.), *Advances in experimental social psychology* (Vol. 8, pp. 49–87). Orlando, FL: Academic Press.

Karau, S. J., & Kelly, J. R. (2004). Time pressure and team performance: An attentional focus integration. In B. Mannix, M. Neale, & S. Blount (Eds.), *Research on managing groups and teams: Time in groups* (pp. 185–212). Oxford, UK: Elsevier.

Lacoursiere, R. B. (1980). The *life cycle of groups: Group developmental stage theory*. New York: Human Sciences Press.

McGrath, J. E., & Hollingshead, A. B. (1993). *Groups interacting with technology: Ideas, evidence, issues, and an agenda*. Thousand Oaks, CA: Sage.

McGrath, J. E., & Rotchford, N. (1983). Time and behavior in organizations. In L. L. Cummings, & B. M. Staw (Eds.), *Research in organizational behavior* (Vol. 5, pp. 57–101). Greenwich, CT: JAI Press.

Moreland, R. L. (1987). The formation of small groups. In C. Hendrick (Ed.), *Review of personality and social psychology* (Vol. 8, pp. 80–109). Newbury Park, CA: Sage.

Paulus, P., & Nagar, D. (1989). Environmental influences on groups. In P. Paulus (Ed.), *Psychology of group influence* (pp. 111–142). Hillsdale, NJ: Lawrence Erlbaum Associates, Inc.

Sundstrom, E. (1986). *Workplaces: The psychology of the physical environment in offices and factories*. Cambridge: Cambridge University Press.

Taylor, R. B. (1988). *Human territorial functioning: An empirical, evolutionary perspective on individual and small group territorial cognitions, behaviors, and consequences*. Cambridge: Cambridge University Press.

Wageman, E. (Ed.) (1999). *Research on managing groups and teams: Groups in context*. Oxford, UK: Elsevier.

Wilder, D. A. (1986). Social categorization: Implications for creation and reduction of intergroup bias. In L. Berkowitz (Ed.), *Advances in experimental social psychology* (Vol. 19, pp. 291–355). Orlando, FL: Academic Press.

Worchel, S., Coutant-Sassic, D., & Grossman, M. (1991). A developmental approach to groups: A model and illustrative research. In S. Worchel, W. Wood, & J. A. Simpson (Eds.), *Group process and productivity* (pp. 181–202). Thousand Oaks, CA: Sage.

Readings

The first paper in this set, by McKenna and Bargh (1998), describes several studies of Internet newsgroup participation among people with concealable stigmas. These are people with personal qualities that are socially undesirable, such as sexual deviance or political extremism, but not obvious to others. People with concealable stigmas are often lonely. They do not know for sure how many others are like themselves, but they realize that such people are disliked, because they overhear many negative comments about them by those who are "normal." This creates a problem for people with these stigmas—they want to meet and befriend others like themselves, but are afraid to try, because that might require them to reveal their undesirable personal qualities and thus risk disapproval. Internet newsgroups offer a solution to this problem. On the Internet, people with concealable stigmas can search anonymously for newsgroups whose members share their personal qualities. If they find some, which is likely given the thousands of newsgroups that exist, they can simply read the messages posted by others for awhile. Later on, when they feel more comfortable, they can participate more actively by discussing their thoughts and feelings with other newsgroup

members, who are likely to understand them. This line of reasoning led McKenna and Bargh to the general prediction that people with concealable stigmas would identify strongly with relevant newsgroups on the Internet and maybe experience some personal benefits as a result.

In their first study, McKenna and Bargh counted how often people posted messages to newsgroups and evaluated how they reacted to any feedback that those messages evoked. People with concealable stigmas posted more messages to their newsgroups than did people with more conspicuous stigmas (e.g., obesity) or people without stigmas. People with concealable stigmas were also more sensitive than others to the kinds of feedback they received— the more positive that feedback was, the more likely they were to post additional messages. In their second study, McKenna and Bargh surveyed people whose concealable stigmas involved sexual deviance. The researchers located Internet newsgroups dedicated to such persons and asked members who had posted messages to those newsgroups (posters), as well as members who had not posted any messages (lurkers), to complete a questionnaire. A causal analysis of the data revealed several findings. First, posters identified more strongly with their newsgroups than did lurkers. Second, posters had more self-acceptance than lurkers, felt less socially isolated and estranged from society, and were more likely to have "come out." Finally, nearly all these effects of posting were mediated by newsgroup identification. That is, people with a concealable stigma did not derive many benefits from posting messages to relevant newsgroups unless posting led them to identify more strongly with those groups.

McKenna and Bargh's third study was similar, but this time they surveyed people whose concealable stigmas involved political extremism rather than sexual deviance. Once again, posters identified more strongly with their newsgroups than did lurkers. And posters again had more self-acceptance than lurkers, felt less socially isolated and estranged from society, and were more likely to have come out. Finally, newsgroup identification mediated all the benefits of posting messages. The results of these studies thus confirmed that people with concealable stigmas do seek out and participate in relevant Internet newsgroups and that such participation can produce some benefits for them, so long as it strengthens their group identification.

The second paper in this set, by Arrow (1997), describes a field experiment on the development of groups. Do groups, like individuals, change systematically as they age? Many psychologists believe that they do, and there are literally dozens of theories about that phenomenon. Arrow divides these theories into four categories. *Robust equilibrium theories* claim that when groups form, they experience some initial fluctuations in structure and dynamics, but then settle down and experience little change afterwards. *Life cycle theories* claim that all groups pass through a similar series of sequential stages in their structure and dynamics. *Punctuated equilibrium theories* claim that the structure and dynamics of groups are generally stable, changing only in response to critical events (e.g., failure at an important task, conflict with another group, loss of key members). Crises such as these cause groups to change their structure and dynamics, which then remain stable until new crises occur. Finally, *adaptive response theories* claim that the structure and dynamics of groups change all the time as groups try to adjust to changes (large or small) in their environments.

Arrow studied 20 small groups of students in an undergraduate course on behavior in organizations. Each group initially contained three or four students and the course lasted for 13 weeks. Groups met weekly for two hours to work on special assignments. Toward the end of each meeting, members also completed questionnaires that measured different aspects of group structure and dynamics. As the course progressed, changes occurred in the composition of the groups and in their communication methods. For example, a few groups gained or lost members early in the course (during the drop/add period), and the researchers later moved some of the students from one group to another for awhile and then moved them back. And for the first half of the course, the members of some groups communicated only by email, while the members of other groups communicated entirely face-to-face. About halfway through the course, the researchers reversed these communication conditions briefly and then changed them back.

Arrow wondered how well different theories about group development could describe any changes that she observed in the structure and dynamics of these groups (as described by the students on the questionnaires). The research setting was not well suited, she thought, for testing life cycle theories, so she did not try to do so. To test robust equilibrium theories, Arrow simply evaluated the stability of the groups' initial structure and dynamics. She tested punctuated equilibrium theories by examining how groups reacted to the "crisis" created by changing communication methods halfway through the course, and she tested adaptive response theories by examining how groups reacted to poor grades on the special assignments they worked on during the weekly meetings. A complex pattern of results emerged. Groups whose members communicated by email were described best by robust equilibrium theories, whereas groups whose members communicated face-to-face were described best by punctuated equilibrium theories. There was little evidence of adaptive responses to poor grades among the groups, perhaps because their members did not view their special assignments as very important.

The third paper in this set, by Moreland and Levine (2001), describes theory and research on work group socialization. Group socialization is similar to group development in that temporal changes occur in both cases. But whereas group development involves changes in the group as a whole, group socialization involves changes in relationships that the group has with each of its members. Moreland and Levine described group socialization as the "passage" of an individual through the group, from the time when that person is merely thinking about joining the group, through the time that he or she actually spends in the group, to the time when membership is just a memory.

The paper is divided into three sections. The first section offers a narrative review of both theory and research on the socialization tactics used by organizations and by new workers, and on commitment, a major outcome of the socialization

process. The tactics that organizations use during socialization include orientation sessions, training programs, mentoring, and information dissemination. The evidence suggests that these tactics do not work very well—commitment to organizations among new workers is often weak. This suggests that organizations should attempt to recruit new workers whose commitment is already strong, rather than recruiting a broader selection of workers and then trying to strengthen their commitment through socialization. The tactics used by new workers during socialization include surveillance or feedback seeking, developing mentoring relationships with old timers, and collaborating with one another. These tactics are sometimes impractical, however, and when they are used, the evidence suggests that they are often ineffective. Finally, research on commitment suggests that it is quite complex. For example, it can take different forms, focus on different targets, and rise or fall over time.

In the second section of their paper, Moreland and Levine argue that work groups are the key to understanding organizational socialization and thus deserve more attention. Why? One reason is that the process of organizational socialization occurs primarily in the context of work groups. Another reason is that work group socialization, which occurs at the same time as organizational socialization, is likely to matter more to most new workers. Moreland and Levine offer a general model of group socialization that they believe can be applied to work groups. According to that model, group socialization involves three psychological processes: *evaluation*, *commitment*, and *role transitions*. First, the group and the individual evaluate the rewards and costs of their relationship with one another. These evaluations produce feelings of commitment, which can rise and fall over time as circumstances change. If commitment rises or falls far enough, then a decision criterion is crossed. Decision criteria mark the boundaries between different roles that the person can play in the group (prospective member, new member, full member, marginal member, ex-member). After a role transition occurs, evaluations begin again, producing further changes in commitment and additional role transitions. In this way, it is possible for a person to experience five phases of group membership (investigation, socialization, maintenance, resocialization, remembrance), separated by four role transitions (entry, acceptance, divergence, exit).

The last section of the paper provides a narrative review of theoretical and empirical papers on group socialization by Moreland, Levine, and their colleagues. In their theoretical papers, they either analyze particular components of the socialization model (e.g., commitment, role transitions) in more detail or use that model to reveal new things about other aspects of groups (e.g., minority influence, group culture, intergroup relations). In their empirical papers, they describe research inspired by the model. For example, Moreland, Levine, and their colleagues have studied how earlier group memberships affect later behavior when people consider joining other groups; why people who are thinking about joining a group are often overly optimistic about what will happen to them in that group; and how prospective and new members are treated by groups that are understaffed or overstaffed.

The final paper in this set, by Ancona and Caldwell (1988), focuses on *boundary-spanning activities* in work teams. These activities involve efforts by team members to control the flow of resources (e.g., people, information, funds) across the boundary that separates their team from its social environment. According to Ancona and Caldwell, theory and research on groups have emphasized too much what goes on inside groups and have not emphasized enough what goes on around them. This is problematic, because insofar as groups rely on external resources, boundary-spanning activities may be critical to their success.

Ancona and Caldwell performed a "comparative case analysis" of several product development teams in various technological industries. Dozens of team leaders from several organizations were interviewed, and people from two of those teams were asked to record all of their interactions with outsiders for one week. All of these data were then used to identify three kinds of boundary-spanning activities, each associated with a distinct set of roles. First, some teams used *scouts* and *ambassadors* to import and/or export information, resources, or support. Scouts sought feedback about their team from outsiders, gathered other information that might be relevant to the team, and developed "mental models" relating causes and effects in the team's environment. Ambassadors created channels of communication with outsiders, coordinated and negotiated a team's efforts to work with others in the organization, and managed the impressions that people within the organization formed about the team. Second, some teams used *sentries* and *guards* to control the flow of resources across organizational boundaries. Sentries focused on resources flowing into the team, while guards focused on resources flowing out. For example, sentries arranged for resources to enter a team and to be distributed among its members, modified resources so that they would be more useful to the team (e.g., "translating" information so that team members could understand it more easily), and buffered the team from resources that might be harmful (e.g., disturbing information). In contrast, guards decided whether outside requests for resources from the team were legitimate, arranged for legitimate requests to be met, and protected the team by keeping certain resources (e.g., secrets) away from outsiders. Finally, some teams used *immigrants*, *captives*, and *emigrants* to control resources by changing the composition of their own and/or other teams. Immigrants and captives were outsiders brought into the team because they possessed valuable resources (e.g., skills, knowledge, contacts). Immigrants entered the team voluntarily; captives were forced to become team members. Emigrants were members of the team who were sent out to participate in other teams within the organization.

Ancona and Caldwell also discussed several possible causes and effects of these boundary-spanning activities. At the individual level, for example, some people are more likely than others to become scouts because of their personality characteristics (e.g., sociability) or similarities to outsiders. And scouting activities provide career opportunities for such persons, because they learn more about the organization and develop broader social networks within it. At the team level, the team's task and its internal processes could both affect its boundary-spanning activities. For example, such activities are more likely to occur in teams whose tasks seem more important and less likely to occur in teams with greater cohesion (which can produce an inward focus). The most important effect of boundary-spanning activities on teams is better performance, especially among teams that are more dependent on external resources. Finally, at the organizational level, boundary-spanning activities are more likely to occur when workers belong to multiple teams and when the organization requires coordination/cooperation among teams. As for their effects, boundary-spanning activities can help to distribute resources across an organization and can produce more standardization among teams.

Discussion Questions

1. Most social psychological research on small groups involves artificial groups whose members have no past or expected future together. How might that affect the members of those groups?
2. Suppose that the development of a particular group could be predicted in advance. How could a leader or manager make use of such knowledge?
3. Do you belong to any groups whose members communicate primarily by computer? How do you think these groups differ from those whose members communicate face-to-face?

4. Some theorists believe that groups can become "place-dependent" if they occupy the same space for a long period of time. What does that mean, do you think, and why does it happen? Is place dependence a strength or a weakness of groups?
5. Imagine two people who are friends, despite the fact that they belong to groups that are in conflict with one another. What stresses would these people experience, and how might they try to resolve them? Which relationships are ultimately stronger—friendships or group memberships? Why?

Suggested Readings

Elsbach, K. D. (2004). Interpreting workplace identities: The role of office décor. *Journal of Organizational Behavior, 25*, 99–128.

Flaherty, M. (2003). Time work: Customizing temporal experience. *Social Psychology Quarterly, 66*, 17–33.

Gersick, C. J. G. (1988). Time and transition in work teams: Toward a new model of group development. *Academy of Management Journal, 31*, 9–41.

Hartstone, M., & Augoustinos, M. (1995). The minimal group paradigm: Categorization into two versus three groups. *European Journal of Social Psychology, 25*, 179–193.

Wright, S. C., Aron, A., McLaughlin-Volpe, T., & Ropp, S. A. (1997). The extended contact effect: Knowledge of cross-group friendships and prejudice. *Journal of Personality and Social Psychology, 73*, 73–90.

Coming Out in the Age of the Internet: Identity "Demarginalization" Through Virtual Group Participation

Katelyn Y. A. McKenna and John A. Bargh

Internet newsgroups allow individuals to interact with others in a relatively anonymous fashion and thereby provide individuals with concealable stigmatized identities a place to belong not otherwise available. Thus, membership in these groups should become an important part of identity. Study 1 found that members of newsgroups dealing with marginalized–concealable identities modified their newsgroup behavior on the basis of reactions of other members, unlike members of marginalized–conspicuous or mainstream newsgroups. This increase in identity importance from newsgroup participation was shown in both Study 2 (marginalized sexual identities) and Study 3 (marginalized ideological identities) to lead to greater self-acceptance, as well as coming out about the secret identity to family and friends. Results supported the view that Internet groups obey general principles of social group functioning and have real-life consequences for the individual.

I just thought, "Oh God. What if they pick up that I'm gay?" It was that fear and shame. . . . I watched the whole Gay Pride march in Washington in 1993, and I wept when I saw that.

I mean I cried so hard, thinking "I wish I could be there," because I never felt like I belonged anywhere.—Ellen DeGeneres, *Time* magazine interview.

Katelyn Y. A. McKenna, Department of Telecommunications, Ohio University; John A. Bargh, Department of Psychology, New York University.

This research was supported by the Alexander von Humboldt Foundation and was conducted while we were visitors at the University of Konstanz, Germany. Portions of this research were presented at the annual meeting of the Society for Experimental Social Psychology, Toronto, October 1997. National Science Foundation Grant SBR-9409448 also supported the research.

We are indebted to Patrick Shrout for his generous advice and assistance with the causal modeling analyses; thanks also go to Roy Baumeister, Kay Deaux, Noah Glassman, Peter Gollwitzer, and Henry Jean-Paul Hammelbeck for feedback on an earlier version of this article. Peter Gollwitzer kindly provided us with computer and technical support facilities at Konstanz. Finally, we are grateful to the hundreds of Internet newsgroup members whose cooperation was essential in this research.

Correspondence concerning this article should be addressed to Katelyn Y. A. McKenna, who is now at the Department of Psychology, New York University, 6 Washington Place, 7th Floor, New York, New York 10003. Electronic mail may be sent to mckenna@psych.nyu.edu.

A variety of motivations might explain why one identifies with a social group (e.g., Brewer, 1991; Deaux, 1996; Hogg & Abrams, 1993). Among the most prominently discussed motives are to gain self-esteem, to reduce uncertainty about oneself, and to fulfill the basic need to belong. For those with mainstream and culturally valued identities, opportunities for group identification are readily available. Yet for those who possess culturally stigmatized identities, especially identities that are concealable from others (Frable, 1993; Jones et al., 1984), this is not the case. Such stigmatized individuals are likely to quite strongly possess all of these central motivations to belong to a group of similar others, but are unable to do so because of the concealable and potentially embarrassing nature of their identity.

For those with concealable and culturally devalued identities (e.g., people with epilepsy, former prison inmates, those with nonmainstream sexual interests or political views), it is not possible to look around and see others who are similar to oneself in this important way (Frable, 1993). Moreover, because of the potentially embarrassing nature of the self aspect, it is not easy to make the first move and disclose this aspect to others to find those who are similar. There are real risks to one's important close relationships at home and at work in such self-disclosure (Derlega, Metts, Petronio, & Margulis, 1993, pp. 73–88; Pennebaker, 1990, chap. 9). Therefore, the individual feels isolated and different and is barred from the benefits of sharing with similar others.

The Emergence of Virtual Groups

Recently, however, a new variety of group has emerged that provides those with stigmatized identities an opportunity to share in the benefits of group membership. These *virtual groups* have developed on the Internet in the form of newsgroups. Today, over 30,000 different newsgroups exist, covering general as well as quite specific interests, among them topics that an individual would likely find embarrassing to reveal to others in real life.

The numbers of people participating in virtual groups is substantial and growing rapidly. Most North American households now own at least one computer, and over 40 million people are *on-line*, that is, connected to the Internet, able to send and receive electronic mail (E-mail), and able to read and post messages in newsgroups (Dowe, 1997). Worldwide, the number of people on-line is doubling every year, and estimates are that 10% of the world's population will be on-line by the turn of the century ("Making a Business," 1997).

In a recent book, Turkle (1995) argued that the emergence of the Internet has enabled the exploration of aspects of one's identity that formerly had to remain hidden because of societal disapproval. In virtual groups, where people can be anonymous and do not deal in face-to-face interactions, individuals can admit to having marginalized, or nonmainstream, proclivities that they hide from the rest of the world. For the first time, they can reap the benefits of joining a group of similar others: feeling less isolated and different, disclosing a long secret part of oneself, sharing one's own experiences and learning from those of others, and gaining emotional and motivational support (Archer, 1987; Derlega et al., 1993; E. E. Jones et al., 1984).

The Nature of Marginalized Identities

Brewer (1991) argued that an individual has the need to feel connected to others, to have a sense of group belonging, and to feel like a special, valued member of a group. Therefore, feeling different from the membership of a valued group (such as mainstream society) is problematic for the individual, in that certain aspects of identity may need to be hidden in order to achieve group acceptance and approval. Such conflicts between the public persona and the private self, argued Horney (1946), are the major cause of unhappiness and neuroses.

In an insightful analysis of marginalized identities, Frable (1993) distinguished between those that are *concealable* and those that are *conspicuous* to others. Whether an individual is able to keep the stigmatized identity from others has several important psychological ramifications. First of all, unlike persons with conspicuous stigmas (e.g., obesity), those with hidden conditions are not able to see similar others in their environment, so there is no visible sign of others who share the stigmatized feature. Second, those with a concealable stigma are more likely to hear the negative comments and opinions of others concerning the stigma than are those with conspicuous marginal statuses. People are more likely to express negative opinions about a social group to a person they do not know is a member of that group. Hearing such opinions is likely to reinforce the negative effect of the marginalized identity on the individual's self-esteem.

Consequently, people with visible stigmas are able to see that there are similar others and so do not feel so unique or alone, but people with concealable stigmas cannot and so tend to feel more different from other people. Frable (1993) confirmed this prediction in two studies. In one, participants with qualities that were culturally stigmatized but concealable (e.g., people with epilepsy, incest survivors) showed a considerably reduced tendency toward false consensus compared both to participants with a culturally valued or conspicuous condition (e.g., obesity, a visible scar) and a non-marginalized identity control condition. Those with concealable marginal identities were the least likely to feel that others shared their preferences for mundane items such as ham salad sandwiches. In the second study, participants with concealable cultural stigmas endorsed as self-descriptive more items related to uniqueness (e.g., *rare, outsider*) than did other participants.

Motivational Bases for Identifying With a Virtual Group

In Tajfel's (1982) original model of social identity, the central motivational impetus for identifying with a social group was the gain in self-esteem the identification brought (Deaux, 1996; Hogg & Abrams, 1990). A person continued to be a group member so long as the group added positive features to the person's social identity. Hogg and Abrams (1990, 1993) argued that self-esteem is not the only motivation possible for group identification: uncertainty reduction, power, self-efficacy, and

greater self-knowledge are others. Other researchers have since pointed to still another motivational basis, a basic need to belong (Baumeister & Leary, 1995; Brewer, 1991).

All of these motivations for group identification are likely to be operative—and strongly so—for the person with a marginalized and concealable identity. First, the primary need to belong to the society at large is frustrated to the extent the individual feels different from others. Second, in the absence of a visible set of others with whom to compare him- or herself, the individual is likely to be uncertain about this important aspect of identity and will be motivated to reduce this uncertainty (see Archer, 1987; Hogg & Abrams, 1993). Third, the general motive to hold a positive self-image (e.g., Sedikides, 1993) is thwarted by including this negative group identity. Thus, attempts to connect with others who share that identity and do not view it negatively will figure prominently in efforts to reduce the stigma and thereby increase self-esteem (Jones et al., 1984, p. 133).

Identity Importance and Self-Esteem

But suppose a stigmatized individual finds an Internet newsgroup where others with the same stigmatized identity post messages that share relevant personal experiences and convey identity-enhancing attitudes and beliefs. Identifying with this virtual group alone may still not be enough to produce positive changes in self-esteem and greater acceptance of this aspect of self.

Deaux and her colleagues have argued for the role of involvement in the group or the subjective importance of the identity as a mediator of the benefits of identification on self-esteem (e.g., Bat-Chava, 1994; Deaux, 1996; Ethier & Deaux, 1994). According to Tajfel's (1982) theory, incorporating the group identity into one's social identity is sufficient to increase self-esteem. However, Deaux (1996, p. 793) has demonstrated that unless individual differences in the importance of the identity are taken into account, the effect of identification alone is negligible.

For instance, in Ethier and Deaux's (1994) study of first-year university students who held the Hispanic identity, the strength of ethnic identification was positively related to participation in Hispanic cultural groups and activities, as well as to individual self-esteem. Ethier (1995) further showed that variations in the importance of the mother identity were related to differences in the amount of time that new mothers spent taking care of their babies. Further, Bat-Chava (1994) found no overall relationship between identification as a deaf person and self-esteem; only when the identity was important to the individual (as determined by the amount of involvement in the deaf community) was there an increase in self-esteem.

Why Disidentification is not an Option

If the stigmatized identity is concealable, why doesn't the individual just remove this aspect of identity? After all, according to Tajfel (1982), if a group identity contributes negatively to self-esteem, an individual then no longer identifies with that group. However, in their treatment of social stigma, E. E. Jones et al. (1984) described several reasons why concealable negative identities cannot be so easily discarded. Principally, the person feels guilt at keeping a secret from his or her spouse, family, and close friends; and infers from his or her concealment behavior that this aspect of self must be shameful (see Derlega et al., 1993, p. 95). This creates a vicious cycle that increases the vigilance against revealing this identity. Yet the great and continuous effort exerted to keep these secret aspects from public view causes the individual to continuously focus on those very aspects, keeping them in mind as a salient part of self-definition. Having to remain vigilant against revealing negative self-features does not permit the person to forget about or de-emphasize this aspect of identity—quite the contrary. Research by Wegner and his colleagues (e.g., Wegner, 1994; Wegner & Erber, 1992) on ironic effects of mental control attempts has documented such consequences. To guard against revealing a secret aspect of self, one must keep the secret continually in mind

(as what not to say, talk about, or reveal). The side effect of this vigilance is to make the taboo topic more accessible in memory than if the suppression attempts had never been made.

A Process Model of "Demarginalization"

Given that "leaving the field" is not an option and that the stigmatized identity is likely to continue as a very salient component of the self, the individual remains highly motivated to identify with a group of similar others. Thus, we hypothesized that people with concealable stigmatized identities would be more likely to become involved in Internet newsgroups and would consider membership in such virtual groups to be more important to their lives than would people with marginalized–conspicuous and mainstream identities, as indicated by their behavioral reactions to evaluative feedback from other group members. This prediction was tested in Study 1.

Studies 2 and 3 tested a process model of identity demarginalization (see Figure 23.1). The dependent variables in both studies were the degree of self-acceptance of the marginalized identity and the revelation of this formerly secret part of the self to close others. Recent response time evidence reported by Smith and Henry (1996) bolstered the axiom of social identity theory that social group memberships are incorporated into the psychological self to the extent that the individual feels like a member of the group (i.e., it has become an in-group for that person). Thus, to the extent that newsgroup participation leads to stronger group identification, the individual should come to accept this identity as part of, instead of distinct from, his or her self-concept. Study 2 focused on marginalized sexual interests and identities. Study 3 replicated Study 2 but surveyed members of newsgroups concerned with marginal political views and ideologies.

On the basis of the work by Deaux and her colleagues, we hypothesized that among the people who identify with a marginalized social group via the Internet, those who participated actively in that group would benefit more in terms of

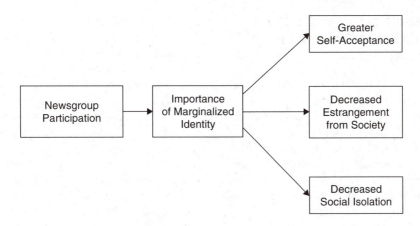

FIGURE 23.1 ■ A process model of identity demarginalization.

self-acceptance and self-esteem than those who do not. Whereas group participation and identity importance are more or less reciprocally linked in Deaux's model, we posit a directional Participation → Importance relation. In contrast to the groups studied by Deaux and her colleagues, such as Hispanics and new mothers, in which one is a de facto member of the group according to objective criteria, the only way that people with concealable marginalized identities can belong to the group is by participating in it. In other words, one must join the group prior to any gains in the importance of the group to one's social identity. This is the only way that the other group members can know about one's membership in the group. Wicklund and Gollwitzer (1982) have discussed and shown how group memberships do not become psychologically real until the person makes them a social reality, that is, by having others notice and acknowledge one's membership in the group.

Moreover, this greater self-acceptance or demarginalization of the identity was expected to cause the individual to be more likely to come out about the identity to those people in real life whose opinions matter most to him or her, such as family and friends, as individuals are motivated to make their important identities a social reality, instead of just a private affair (Gollwitzer, 1986). Finally, membership in the marginalized newsgroup should reduce the individual's feelings of being different from others (see Frable, 1993) and so should also reduce

the person's estrangement from society and feelings of social isolation.

To distinguish between those who become actively involved in a virtual group and those who do not, we took advantage of the fact that newsgroups are composed of two types of members, those who post, providing the reading material for others, and those who "lurk," simply reading the material posted by others.[1] Some of the lurkers will eventually "delurk" and become posters themselves, whereas others will remain in the shadows (see Jones, 1995).[2]

---

[1] In view of the seemingly pejorative undertone of the label *lurker*, we should point out that it is not our term but instead the standard term among newsgroup members for those who read but do not post. The term is rarely used in a disparaging manner, especially in marginalized newsgroups. Posters in such newsgroups are usually highly aware of the potentially negative consequences of "going public" (see Kelly & McKillop, 1996) and so can understand the choice to remain a lurker. Moreover, lurkers themselves typically title their own first post a "delurk."

[2] We know of no previous study comparing newsgroup lurkers and posters, and so little is known as to why some individuals are more likely to remain nonparticipant lurkers. We can, however, offer some possibilities. First, it may be that lurkers are less likely to have anonymous Internet accounts (where a pseudonym is used instead of the person's real name). Second, in our discussions with newsgroup members, it seemed that lurkers were just more shy in general and more worried about the evaluative reactions of other members should they post compared with those who do post.

Study 1: Degree of Involvement in Marginalized Versus Mainstream Virtual Groups

The present study assessed whether there are differences in the ways that participants in mainstream versus marginalized–conspicuous and marginalized–concealable newsgroups respond to feedback from others. Because those who post in newsgroups concerned with marginalized–concealable stigmas have few, if any, venues to express this part of themselves, the opinions of others within their newsgroup should be of greater importance to them than to posters in either mainstream or marginalized–conspicuous newsgroups. Therefore, we predicted that the positivity of the responses to posters in the concealable-stigma groups would have a greater effect on their subsequent posting behavior. It also follows from the hypothesis of greater group importance that there should be a higher overall frequency of posting per person in marginalized–concealable versus mainstream or marginalized–conspicuous newsgroups.

Method

Sampling of newsgroups. Twelve newsgroups were selected for study: four mainstream, four marginalized–conspicuous, and four marginalized–concealable newsgroups. With one exception (*soc.support.fat-acceptance*), all belonged to the alt. newsgroup hierarchy.[3] At the time of the study, there were approximately 650 alt. newsgroups. This number was reduced by eliminating "binary" newsgroups (in which mainly pictures are posted) and personals newsgroups (which are similar to the personal advertisement sections of magazines and newspapers). The newsgroup sample population was further restricted to those in which there were

at least 100 posts per week to ensure there would be sufficient data for analysis.[4] This left a final population of 53 newsgroups.

Four of these newsgroups concerned visible stigmas that are generally recognized as undesirable and "marked" conditions (see Frable, 1993; Jones et al., 1984): obesity (*soc.support.fat-acceptance*), stuttering (*alt.support.stuttering*), cerebral palsy (*alt.support.cerebral-palsy*), and baldness (*alt.baldspot*). This set of newsgroups thus represented marginalized but conspicuous identities.

Next, to determine which of the remaining newsgroups represented marginalized–concealable identities and which represented mainstream (nonstigmatized) interests, we first divided the list of 53 newsgroups on the basis of whether the average person would be unwilling to post in the newsgroup using his or her real name because of potential discovery and embarrassment. We included the names of the 15 potential marginal newsgroups and 10 potential mainstream newsgroups on a list that we then posted to 5 highly trafficked mainstream newsgroups (e.g., *alt.cooking. recipes*). In this post, we asked potential respondents to mark those groups on the list in which they would be unwilling to post using their real name and to send this list back to us via E-mail. We received 55 responses. There was substantial agreement as to which newsgroups were culturally stigmatized and which were mainstream. From the newsgroups marked by over 90% of respondents, four were randomly selected to be our sample of marginalized newsgroups: *alt.drugs, alt.homosexual, alt.sex.bondage,* and *alt.sex.spanking*. (Consistent with these findings, Pennebaker [1990, chap. 9] detailed the social censure faced by homosexuals and people with deviant sexual interests and the resultant stress they endure keeping it secret.) Four mainstream groups were randomly selected from

---

[3] These are among the most popular newsgroups for the average user, as they require no special expertise or knowledge (the comp. newsgroups, for example, are frequented mainly by those with an in-depth interest and knowledge of computer science).

[4] This number includes only the posts specifically directed to that particular newsgroup (with content relevant to the interest of the newsgroup) and does not include advertisements that are simultaneously cross-posted to a large number of newsgroups (known as *spam*).

those marked by less than 5% of the respondents: *alt.culture.us.1970s, alt.parents-teens, alt. politics. economics*, and *alt.tv.melrose-place*.

Coding of posts. A content analysis was conducted on all original posts in these 12 newsgroups, as well as on the follow-up responses to each original post, made during a 3-week period. Together, an original post and those made in response to it are known as a "thread."[5] So that only posts relevant to the topic of the group were analyzed, threads cross-posted to more than three groups were not coded, nor were any personals or advertisements. We chose a time period of 3 weeks because there is often a delay of as much as 4 days before a given post reaches all the available newsgroup servers, and responses to those posts may occur over as much as a 10-day period.

Responses to each original post were coded by four judges (blind to the research hypotheses) as either positive, mixed (containing both positive and negative elements), or negative in evaluative tone. A total of 485 threads were coded, each consisting of one original post and an average of three responses (for a total of 1,888 posts). Postings in the marginalized–concealable newsgroups (236 threads) outnumbered those in the mainstream (97 threads) and marginalized–conspicuous (152 threads) newsgroups. To establish intercoder reliability, 30 threads (10 marginal–concealable, 10 marginal–conspicuous, 10 mainstream) were randomly selected and coded by all four coders. Intercoder agreement was quite high at 97%.

The dependent variable was the frequency with which the original poster continued to post over the 3-week period, following the feedback regarding his or her original post.

Results

For each thread, the positivity of posted responses was the number of positive minus the number of mixed and negative responses combined. Mixed

and negative responses were grouped together because of the statistical rarity of exclusively negative responses (less than 0.4 per thread). Thus, the positivity index reflected the extent to which there were more (or less) exclusively positive posts than posts containing at least some criticism.

Posting frequency. A simultaneous regression analysis was then conducted, with total posts per poster being the dependent variable and newsgroup marginality (coded as mainstream = −1, marginal–conspicuous = 0, and marginal–concealable = 1) and positivity of feedback being the predictor variables. Consistent with the hypothesized greater importance of marginalized–concealable newsgroups to their members, a significantly greater number of posts per person was found in the marginal–concealable ($M = 5.5$) than in either the marginal–conspicuous ($M = 2.8$) or the mainstream ($M = 1.9$) newsgroups: $\beta = .18$, $t(481) = 4.03$, $p < .0001$. (Note that because these means reflect the number of posts per author, they are already adjusted for the total numbers of posts and authors in the various newsgroups.) Planned comparisons confirmed that the marginalized–concealable newsgroup members were reliably more frequent posters on average compared to posters in the other two newsgroups combined, $F(1, 482) = 32.33$, $p < .0001$. There was no reliable difference in posting frequency between the marginalized–conspicuous and mainstream newsgroups, $F(1, 482) = 1.42$, *ns*.

Responsiveness to feedback. The main effect for feedback positivity was not reliable: $\beta = .07$, $t(481) = 1.58$, $p = .12$. Thus, overall the positivity of group feedback did not modify the poster's subsequent behavior. However, there was a reliable Newsgroup Marginality × Feedback interaction: $\beta = .23$, $t(481) = 4.82$, $p < .00001$. As predicted, the group feedback influenced the member's subsequent posting behavior only in the marginalized–concealable newsgroups (see Figure 23.2). The correlation between positivity of feedback and subsequent posting frequency was $r = .38$ ($p < .001$, two-tailed) for the marginalized–concealable newsgroups but was negligible and nonsignificant

---

[5] Responses to an original post are easily identifiable by their subject headers, which begin with "Re:" and are followed by the subject header of the original post.

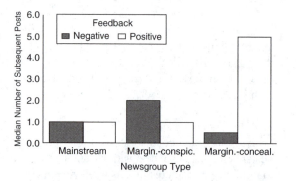

FIGURE 23.2 ■ Effects of feedback from newsgroup members on participants' subsequent posting behavior (Study 1). Margin.-conspic. = marginalized–conspicuous; margin.-conceal. = marginalized–concealable.

for the marginalized–conspicuous ($r = -.07$, $p > .25$) and mainstream ($r = .17$, $p = .11$) newsgroups.

Newsgroup demographics. Because people self-selected themselves into the three types of newsgroups, it is important to rule out alternative explanations for the observed effects in terms of demographic differences between newsgroup members. It could be, for example, that those who participate in the marginalized–concealable newsgroups are primarily teenage males, whereas those who participate in the mainstream groups are mainly middle-age females. If so, our obtained differences in posting frequency and responsiveness to group feedback might be due to factors other than the relevance of the newsgroups to marginalized identities.

Accordingly, we tracked each newsgroup for several additional days and coded all posts revealing the gender and age of the poster. Age was obtained mainly through delurk posts, in which a person typically includes a brief self-description, but we noted age whenever a poster mentioned it. Gender was deduced principally from the poster's first name, excluding any ambiguous names. A given poster contributed only once to this set of data, not each time he or she posted.

The three types of newsgroups showed similar demographic features. Age was the most infrequently mentioned feature (57 times across all newsgroups), but the available ages for posters across the three newsgroup types were comparable, with

TABLE 23.1. Comparison of Mean Survey Responses by Marginalized Sexual (Study 2) and Ideological (Study 3) Newsgroup Members

	Type of marginalized identity		
Dependent measure	Sexual	Ideological	*t*
Age (years)	37	34	<1
Percentage male	61	83	3.42***
Time reading news-group (in months)	18.2	14.5	1.81†
Time posting (in months; posters only, *df* = 159)	14.4	14.1	<1
Importance (1–7) to self of			
Newsgroup	4.8	4.0	3.05***
Members' opinion of self	3.8	2.9	3.09***
Interacting with group	4.6	3.9	2.45***
Time per day in group (1–4)	2.1	2.0	<1
Self-acceptance due to newsgroup (1–7)	4.5	3.5	3.43****
Percentage who came out	37	63	3.64****
Social isolation index (1–5)	2.4	2.2	1.64†
Estrangement index (1–4)	1.6	1.7	1.16

Note: For all comparisons except time posting, *df* = 225.
†*p* < .10 (marginally significant). *** *p* < .01. **** *p* < .001.

a mean of 37 years for the mainstream groups, 39 years for the marginalized–concealable groups, and 34 years for the marginalized–conspicuous groups. However, because of the difficulty in obtaining age information from posts, we asked about age (and gender) in the two survey studies that follow (Studies 2 and 3). As can be seen in Table 23.1, those results confirmed that the mean age of concealable–marginalized newsgroup members was in the mid-30s.

Gender was more readily available information, derivable from the posts of 315 individual posters. The mainstream group posters were 67% male, the marginalized–conspicuous groups were 63% male, and the marginalized–concealable groups were 64% male. Again, the types of groups consisted of comparable proportions of men and women. Finally, it was also possible to check the domains from which the posts and threads that had served as the data for Study 1 originated. (Domains are indicated by the final extension on an electronic address, such as ".edu" for academic locations in the United States and ".com" or ".net" for commercially provided addresses.) The great majority of posts—over 80%—in all newsgroups were from commercial accounts (.com and .net), which represent a much broader demographic range of participants than do academic (.edu) accounts. Thus it was not the case that posters in one or the other type of newsgroup came predominantly from academic locations (which are characterized by several demographic differences in comparison with posters from commercial domains, such as level of education and computer literacy). In sum, it seems unlikely that demographic differences were responsible for the results of Study 1.

Discussion

We hypothesized that because their concealable stigmatized identity does not make the benefits of group membership easily available elsewhere, as compared with people with mainstream or marginalized–conspicuous identities, those with marginalized–concealable identities would identify more strongly with relevant Internet newsgroups and would consider such groups to be more important to their identity. As Internet newsgroups are the virtual or "cyber-equivalent" of nonelectronic groups, such as ethnic campus or deaf-adult organizations, we indexed the importance of newsgroup identity, as did Ethier and Deaux (1994) and Bat-Chava (1994), by the degree of the individual's involvement or participation in the group. Because one participates in virtual groups by posting messages and responses, we predicted that members of marginalized–concealable newsgroups would post more per person overall than would members of mainstream or marginalized–conspicuous newsgroups. Similarly, we also hypothesized that the (positive or negative) feedback given to members of marginalized–concealable newsgroups by other members of the group would matter more to them than it would to members of the other types of newsgroups, and thus the feedback would show a greater impact on the marginalized–concealable newsgroup members' subsequent posting behavior. The results of our

study of posting behavior in 12 Internet newsgroups, comprising an analysis of nearly 1,900 posts, confirmed both predictions.

The results of Study 1 established that virtual groups do matter to individuals with marginalized–concealable identities, more so than they matter to those with visible stigmas or mainstream identities. Studies 2 and 3 were conducted to assess the consequences of participating in marginalized virtual groups for an individual's self-esteem and acceptance of that aspect of his or her identity. Study 2 was conducted with individuals who post and read posts in newsgroups dealing with concealable–marginalized sexual orientations, whereas Study 3 replicated Study 2 with individuals who post and read posts in newsgroups concerning concealable–marginalized ideological orientations.

Study 2: Demarginalization of Sexual Identities

In this study, we examined whether individual differences in virtual group involvement were related to differential gains in self-esteem and self-acceptance and reduced social isolation. Whereas we assumed (and here tested) that all newsgroup members share the stigmatized identity, our major hypothesis was that posters, because of their greater group involvement, would find the group more important to their identity and, consequently, feel greater self-acceptance and less estrangement from society than lurkers. We further predicted that this reconciliation of the private, marginalized identity with the public self would cause people to be more likely to come out about this identity to their real-life family and friends.

Method

Respondents. From the set of marginalized newsgroups determined by the initial survey in Study 1, the three most popular newsgroups dealing with marginalized sexual identities (in terms of numbers of posts) were selected to be the focus of Study 2: *alt.homosexual, alt.sex.bondage,* and *alt. sex.spanking.* The survey sample consisted of posters and lurkers.

Measures. To ensure that members of these news-groups felt marginalized in this aspect of their identity, we first asked all respondents to rate how embarrassed they would be if this aspect of their identity were to be revealed to those around them (i.e., if they were "outed"). This rating was made on a 3-point scale, from *not at all embarrassed* (1) to *extremely embarrassed* (3). Participants were also asked to rate, on a 7-point scale (1 = *not at all*, 7 = *very much*), the extent to which they felt society as a whole attaches a stigma to the aspect of identity covered by the newsgroup.

The remainder of the survey contained 17 items designed to assess the relationship among (a) involvement in the group (i.e., participation: poster vs. lurker), (b) the importance of the newsgroup to identity, (c) feelings of social isolation, and (d) self-acceptance of (and coming out about) the marginalized identity. We strove to keep the questionnaire brief to encourage a high response rate (i.e., reducing the time burden on our volunteer respondents).

Four questions addressed the importance of newsgroup membership to the respondent's social identity. On response scales ranging from *not at all important* (1) to *very important* (7), respondents rated how important the newsgroup was to them, the importance they placed on interaction with other members of the newsgroup, and the importance they placed on the way other members of the newsgroup perceive them. The final item related to importance was the amount of time per day the respondent spent reading, posting, or both in the newsgroup, which was rated on a 4-point scale ranging from *0 to 15 min* (1) to *more than an hour* (4). Responses to each of these four items were first standardized and then averaged to compose the importance index (see *Structural equation modeling procedure* for the rationale behind using this index variable).

In order to measure the level of social isolation, or feelings of being different from others, three items were included. The first came from Dean's (1961) Social Isolation Scale: "Sometimes I feel all alone in the world." The remaining two were taken from the General Alienation Scale of Jessor and Jessor (1977): "I sometimes feel uncertain about who I really am" and "Most people don't

seem to accept me when I am just being myself." Responses to each item were made on a 5-point scale ranging from *strongly disagree* (1) to *strongly agree* (5). To create the social isolation index, scores on each scale were first separately standardized and then averaged.

The final dependent variable was the individual's feelings of estrangement from society. This was conceptualized as a variable distinct from social isolation because several previous studies have found little or no correlation between isolation–alienation and estrangement (see Robinson, Shaver, & Wrightsman, 1991). We used three of the four items from the Cultural Estrangement Scale of Kohn and Schooler (1983), which assesses the extent to which an individual rejects or feels removed from the dominant social values. (There were many missing responses on the item concerning shared religious background.) The respondent answered either *rarely* or *frequently* to the following three items: "According to your general impression, how often do your ideas and opinions about important matters differ from those of your relatives?" "How often do your ideas and opinions differ from those of your friends?" and "How often do your ideas and opinions differ from those of most people in your country?" Each scale was standardized prior to the average being taken to constitute the estrangement index.

The self-acceptance index was based on two additional questions that concerned the degree to which belonging to the newsgroup had enabled the respondent to accept the marginalized identity as part of him- or herself. On a 7-point scale, the respondent rated the extent to which he or she had come to accept this aspect of identity as a direct result of the newsgroup. Coming out was measured by whether or not a respondent had told friends and family about this marginalized aspect of his or her identity, again as a direct result of the news-group (*yes* or *no*). We had originally intended to create a single self-acceptance index by averaging these two scores (after standardization); however, the coefficient alpha obtained was insufficient to justify this index (see *Results and Discussion*), and the two measures were treated as distinct outcome variables in the structural equation model.

The questionnaire also included five questions regarding the respondent's age, gender, country of origin, length of time reading the newsgroup (in months), and length of time posting in the newsgroup (in months).

Procedure. To include both posters and lurkers in the survey, we used two different methods of obtaining responses. Posters can be identified and reached through their E-mail addresses, which appear in the articles they post. Over a 3-week period (which was 6 months after the completion of Study 1), questionnaires were E-mailed to everyone who posted in the selected newsgroups (N = 160). As in Study 1, we excluded from the sample those whose posts were cross-posted to three or more newsgroups and posters of advertisements.

Because there is no way of knowing who is reading but not posting to a newsgroup, lurkers cannot be identified and contacted directly. Thus, in order to reach them, a copy of the questionnaire was posted in each of the three newsgroups, requesting lurkers to complete and return the survey. The questionnaire was reposted every 3 days over the 3-week period.

Results and Discussion

Sample characteristics. Of the 160 questionnaires sent to posters, 103 were completed and returned, for a 64% response rate. A total of 49 lurkers responded to the posted questionnaire, for a total sample size of 152. The sample was composed of 92 men and 58 women. The age of respondents ranged from 18 to 68, with the average age being 37 years (see Table 23.1). Posters had generally been reading posts in the newsgroup longer (M = 19.5 months) than their lurker counterparts (M = 15.6 months).

Feelings of marginalization. The mean rating of how embarrassed the respondent would be if others found out about his or her particular interest was 1.9 on the 3-point scale (N = 124), with a 95% confidence interval of 1.80 to 2.04. Thus, the respondents generally reported moderate embarrassment concerning their interest in the newsgroup. They

also endorsed the belief that society stigmatizes their sexual preference, with a mean of 5.3 on the 7-point scale (95% confidence interval of 5.1 to 5.5). It is important to note that posters and lurkers produced nearly identical means on both questions; both ts < 1. These results serve as a manipulation check on our classification of these newsgroups as representing marginalized aspects of identity.

Creation of indexes. The four items related to the importance of the newsgroup to the respondent's identity were significantly intercorrelated (average r = .54, all ps < .001). The more important the newsgroup was to the respondent, the greater was the importance of interacting with the other members; likewise the more the respondent cared about the way he or she was perceived by other members of the newsgroup, the more other members' opinions of the respondent mattered to him or her and the more time the respondent spent per day in the newsgroup. The importance index had an associated reliability coefficient (Cronbach's alpha) of .81.

The three items constituting the social isolation index also intercorrelated at an acceptable level (average r = .34, all ps < .001), as did the three items making up the cultural estrangement index (average r = .28, all ps < .001). The coefficient alphas for the social isolation index (.60) and estrangement index (.54) were modest but above the level considered sufficient for basic research by Nunnally (1967, p. 226). It should be noted as well that these are standard measures of isolation and estrangement, that have been used in many prior studies of these concepts.

The items involving self-acceptance of the marginalized identity and the extent to which the individual had come out to his or her close friends and family as a direct result of the newsgroup did not intercorrelate sufficiently to be combined into a single index: r = .15, p < .04, coefficient α = .24. Therefore, they were treated as separate outcome variables in the structural equation model.

Structural equation modeling procedure. To test the hypothesized mediational model of identity demarginalization, we conducted a structural equation modeling analysis of the relations between participation in the newsgroups (lurker vs. poster), importance of group identity, self-acceptance, coming out, estrangement, and social isolation. Correlations among the four outcome variables can be found in the left half of Table 23.2, and these low values confirm that the variables are tapping separate aspects of experience.

The model tested is shown in Figure 23.3. Several aspects of the modeling procedure should be noted. First, a saturated model was estimated such that all possible paths were included (paths not shown were nonsignificant at $p > .25$) and the disturbances in the outcomes were free to covary.

TABLE 23.2. Correlations Among Outcomes Variables in Studies 2 and 3

Variable	1	2	3	4
1. Self-acceptance	–	.33*	−.06	.04
2. Coming out	.15	–	−.30*	.13
3. Estrangement	−.16*	−.04	–	.28*
4. Social isolation	.11	.05	.22*	–

Note: Values below the diagonal correspond to Study 2 ($N = 152$); values above the diagonal correspond to Study 3 ($N = 77$). * $p < .05$.

In other words, our estimation procedure permitted any direct effects of participation (i.e., those not mediated by identity importance) to emerge. Second, identity importance is included as an index variable instead of as a latent variable represented by the four separate importance-related items because those four items were related to the outcome variables in unique ways as well as through the variance the items share. For example, three of the four importance-related items had a small negative correlation with social isolation, but the time per day variable showed a small positive correlation. This violates an assumption that latent variables' separate indicators point to the outcome variables in a similar fashion; consequently, the latent variable version of the model fit the data poorly. In any event, the results of the latent variable analysis were highly similar to those shown in Figure 23.3.

Participation and identity importance. The outcome of the structural equations analysis strongly supported the hypothesized model. First, as predicted, the importance of the newsgroup to the respondent's identity was substantially greater for

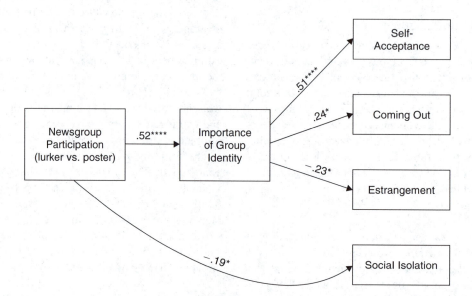

FIGURE 23.3 ■ Demarginalization of sexual identities (Study 2): Structural equation model of the relations between group participation, importance of group identity, self-acceptance, disclosing the identity to close others, social estrangement, and social isolation. Absolute values of all omitted paths <.13. * $p < .05$. **** $p < .001$.

those who participated actively in the group (i.e., posters) than for those who only read the posts (i.e., lurkers). Posters found the newsgroup itself and interaction with other members of the newsgroup to be more important to their lives (see Table 23.3) than lurkers did. Posters spent more time per day in the newsgroup, and the way the posters were viewed by other members mattered more to them. However, lurkers were mainly left out of this first and crucial part of the demarginalization process.

To ensure that the effect of active participation in the marginalized group on identity importance was not attributable merely to the tendency of posters to have been group members (reading the newsgroup posts) longer than have lurkers, we performed the following subsidiary analyses. First, how long lurkers had been reading the newsgroup posts had no relation to the importance index ($r = -.06$, $p > .25$), nor did the length of time posters had been reading the newsgroup matter to its importance for their identity ($r = .06$, $p > .25$). However, for posters, the length of time posting in the newsgroup did predict newsgroup importance ($r = .31$, $p < .001$). Thus, for posters it was the subset of time they had participated, and not the total time they had been reading the newsgroup posts, that mattered for identity importance. The conclusion that can be drawn from the data supports the proposed model: Not only is the group identity more important for those who participate than for those who lurk, but also the longer one has participated, the greater the importance of the group identity.

This result is also important in that it supports the causal direction in our model from participation to identity importance, instead of the other way around. It is highly unlikely that higher levels of identity importance could produce longer newsgroup participation. The latter is mainly a function of how long the individual has been connected to the Internet; some came online earlier than others (e.g., in 1993 rather than 1995). From our discussions in these newsgroups during data collection, it is clear the respondents did not know about the existence of their particular newsgroup (or even Internet newsgroups in general) prior to gaining access to the Internet. Thus, it must be the case

that increasing the amount of time participating in the newsgroup increases the importance of that identity for the individual.

Consequences of identity importance. The next step of the model calls for identity importance to mediate between group membership and its benefits. Figure 23.3 shows that the more important was the marginalized identity, the greater was the self-acceptance of the identity, the more likely was the individual to share this new social identity with family and friends, and the less estranged from society the person felt. These effects are in harmony with Deaux's (1993, 1996) postulated mediational role of identity importance for the positive effects of group membership on the self-concept and for the behavioral consequences of group identity.

The lack of reliable direct paths between participation and self-acceptance, coming out, and estrangement further demonstrated that it is because of the increase in identity importance that one reaches this greater state of openness with close others. A crucial alternative explanation for the effect of participation on demarginalization, one in terms of some preexisting individual difference between posters and lurkers, is thereby ruled out. It is possible that people who are posters, compared with lurkers, are simply more willing to come out of the shadows, and so they would be more likely to come out to family and friends as well. Yet being a poster in and of itself did not have a separate, direct effect on self-acceptance and coming out to others, only an effect mediated by identity importance. Moreover, the items measuring self-acceptance and coming out were explicitly phrased in terms of being consequences of newsgroup membership, not of prior conditions on which posters and lurkers could have differed.

There was one direct effect of participation in the group, however, that was not mediated by identity importance. Posters, more than lurkers, had decreased feelings of social isolation. Thus, at least with these forms of marginalized identities, there are benefits of group involvement that accrue regardless of how important the identity becomes to oneself. As Schachter's (1959) affiliation research showed, just making contact with others reduces feelings of isolation—identification with the group is not needed. Why this would be more true of participants than of lurkers, who also can see in the newsgroup that they are not alone, might be because participation causes others (in the newsgroup) to notice one's manifestation of the new identity—a key factor in making it feel like a real part of the self (Gollwitzer, 1986).

Study 3: Demarginalization of Ideological Identities

According to etiquette books, sex and politics are at the top of the list of topics that one should avoid in polite conversation. Therefore, to replicate the results of Study 2 (which focused on marginalized sexual identities), in Study 3 we turned to newsgroups concerned with marginal, nonmainstream political and ideological beliefs. The proposed model of identity demarginalization was intended to apply to any concealable marginal aspect of identity, not only those related to sexual preference. Holding "subversive" political beliefs that are generally unpopular in one's society has long been a major secret source of identity for people across generations and political systems.

Method

The identical questionnaire used in Study 2 was again distributed to posters and lurkers, but in a different set of newsgroups and E-mail "listservs." (Listservs are a form of private newsgroup conducted via personal E-mail, such that only members can read and respond to messages.) In Study 3, we focused on newsgroups with an ideologically marginalized character. Among the newsgroups selected for study were those catering to a belief in governmental cover-ups, a belief in extraterrestrial visitors, and a belief in governmental cover-ups of extraterrestrial visits. Also included were groups on the topics of White supremacy, citizen militias, and the cultural group skinheads. The specific newsgroups were *alt.conspiracy, alt.skinheads, alt.conspiracy.area51, alt.*

politics.nationalism.white, misc.activism.militia, and the RISKERS listserv.[6]

The survey sample consisted of posters and lurkers. Over a 3-week period, questionnaires were E-mailed to all those who posted in the selected groups. As before, cross-posts and advertisements were excluded. Additionally, only those posters and lurkers who appeared to adhere to the stated ideology of the particular newsgroup were sampled. Questionnaires were sent to 170 posters in the six newsgroups. Finally, in order to reach lurkers, a copy of the questionnaire was posted in each of the newsgroups every 3 days during the period of study.

Results

Sample characteristics. Of the questionnaires sent to posters, there were 10 responses from *alt. conspiracy*, 7 from *alt.conspiracy.area51*, 9 from *misc.activism.militia*, 15 from *alt.politics.nationalism.white*, 9 from *alt.skinheads*, and 9 from the RISKERS listserve, for a total of 59 returned surveys (see next paragraph). A total of 18 lurkers responded to the posted survey, for a total sample size of 77. The sample was composed of 13 women and 64 men. The age of respondents ranged from 15 to 62, with the average age being 34 years (see Table 23.1). The overwhelming majority of respondents lived in the United States. Posters had generally been reading longer than lurkers ($Ms = 16.1$ vs. 9.4 months).

Feelings of marginalization. The mean rating of how embarrassed the respondent would be if others found out about his or her particular interest was 1.4 on the 3-point scale ($N = 52$), with a 95% confidence interval of 1.2 to 1.7. Thus, the respondents generally reported some, but lower, amounts of embarrassment concerning their newsgroup interest than had respondents in Study 2. However, the Study 3 respondents felt that society attaches considerable stigma to their ideological beliefs, with a mean of 5.0 on the 1–7 scale (95% confidence

---

[6] RISKERS is an acronym for Real Interest Secrets Kept Entire Reality Sovereign.

interval of 4.5 to 5.4). Once again, these results were the same for posters and lurkers (both $ps > .24$).

Comparison of Study 2 and Study 3 samples. The overall response rate for posters was 35%, considerably lower than in Study 2. The lower response rate is worthy of comment as it points to one important difference between the newsgroups of Study 2 and Study 3. Following posted notification about the survey, several posters in the ideological newsgroups posted exhortations not to participate because they suspected we were agents of the FBI, CIA, or another government agency seeking information to use against the group.

Although this behavior was certainly consistent with the suspiciousness and skepticism members of these groups have for government, it made data collection more difficult. After influential members of the newsgroups submitted these posts, very few surveys were returned. In response, we wrote by E-mail to posters who had questioned our intent and posted messages in the various newsgroups to reassure potential respondents that we were not affiliated with any government agency. Only then did group members begin to complete and return the surveys.

The groups differed in other interesting ways, as shown in Table 23.1. Whereas most ideological group respondents were male, the sexual group sample was more evenly balanced between the genders. Also, on average, the relevant newsgroup was more important to individuals with marginalized sexual identities than to those with marginalized ideological identities. Perhaps this is due to the extensive media coverage of militia groups and White supremacy groups in North America and Europe, making those with marginalized political identities more conspicuous in society and newsgroups less needed to provide the group identity (see Frable, 1993).

The other notable comparison is that the ideological groups were not reliably more estranged from society, as one might expect. However, this may be because the marginalized sexual and ideological groups are both fairly highly estranged; the means reflect that 70% of the time for ideological group members and 60% of the time for the sexual identity group members the response *frequently* was selected for questions dealing with how often the person feels cut off from family, friends, and country.

Creation of indexes. All indexes were computed in the same way as they were in Study 2 to provide an exact replication. Within the indexes, the component items intercorrelated at an acceptable level: average $r = .39$ among the four importance index items (coefficient $\alpha = .71$), average $r = .37$ for the three social isolation index items (coefficient $\alpha = .62$), and average $r = .29$ among the three estrangement index items (coefficient $\alpha = .57$). The right half of Table 23.2 reports the correlations between the four outcome variables, which again indicate that they represent separate aspects of experience. Using these indexes, we estimated a structural model identical to the one we estimated in Study 2.

Participation and identity importance. Despite the substantially different type of marginalized identity studied, the results replicated the major findings of Study 2 (see Figure 23.4). The critical paths for the hypothesized model of demarginalization were again strongly significant: Among the newsgroup members (posters and lurkers), those who actively participated in the electronic newsgroup came to consider the group identity more important than did those who did not actively participate. Compared with lurkers, the average poster considered the newsgroup more important to his or her life, was more affected by the other members' opinions of him or her, and spent more time per day in the newsgroup (see Table 23.3); multivariate $F(1, 180) = 10.19$, $p = .0017$. As in the research by Deaux (e.g., 1996), active involvement in a group resulted in a stronger bond forged between the group identity and the individual's sense of self.

As in Study 2, differences in the length of time a person has been involved with the newsgroup did not account for the observed effect of participation on identity importance. Overall, length of time reading the newsgroup did not correlate with the importance index, $r = .05$, $p > .25$. Neither

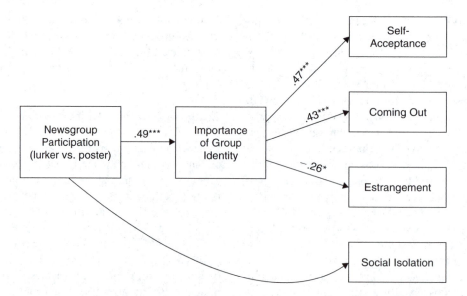

FIGURE 23.4 ■ Demarginalization of ideological identities (Study 3): Structural equation model of the relations between group participation, importance of group identity, self-acceptance, disclosure of the identity to close others, social estrangement, and social isolation. Absolute values of all omitted paths < .15. * $p < .05$. *** $p < .01$.

TABLE 23.3. Means of Dependent Variables of Studies 2 and 3 by Participation Status (Lurker vs. Poster)

Dependent measure	Lurker	Poster	$F(1, 225)^a$
Importance index (standardized)	−0.7	0.3	48.38****
Newsgroup to self (1–7)	3.9	4.8	
Interaction with members (1–7)	2.8	5.0	
Members' opinion of self (1–7)	2.7	3.8	
Time per day in group[b]	1.6	2.3	
Self-acceptance due to newsgroup (1–7)	3.8	4.3	5.59**
Percentage who came out	36	49	3.17††
Estrangement index (1–2)	1.7	1.6	1.21
Social isolation index (1–5)	2.4	2.2	3.29††

[a] None of these main effects of participation varied as a function of type of newsgroup studied (i.e., Study 2 vs. Study 3); all interaction $ps > .21$. [b] Scale values for time per day spent in newsgroup were as follows: 1 = 0–15 min, 2 = 16–30 min, 3 = 31–60 min, 4 = more than one hour per day.
†† $p = .07$ (marginally significant). ** $p = .02$. **** $p < .001$.

did this relation hold for lurkers alone, ($r = .11$, $p > .25$) or for posters alone, ($r = 2.07$, $p > .25$). However, as in Study 2, the number of months a person had been posting did predict identity importance, ($r = .22$, $p = .07$). The longer a person had

been posting, the more important the group identity became to him or her. This result demonstrates the positive effect of active participation on the transformation of identity. Moreover, this result is inconsistent with an alternative interpretation of our findings in terms of preexisting differences between posters and lurkers.

The consequences of identity importance. As in Study 2, the four outcome variables—self-acceptance, coming out, estrangement, and social isolation—showed only low intercorrelations (see the right half of Table 23.2) and so constituted distinct potential consequences of newsgroup participation and identity importance. Figure 23.4 shows that identity importance was again strongly predictive of self-acceptance, of coming out to friends and family, and of feelings of estrangement, whereas the direct effects of participation were not reliable. Thus, the effect of group participation on self-acceptance of the marginalized identity was again mediated by the strength of the group identification.

In contrast to the results of Study 2, there was no direct effect of participation on social isolation nor one mediated by identity importance. We conjecture that the lack of effect of identity importance on social isolation in Study 3 is due to the fact that isolation from society (or at least the government) is the very theme of the set of ideological newsgroups we studied. Any increase in importance of these particular identities could therefore have increased feelings of social isolation as much as decreased them.

General Discussion

The results of the three studies paint a consistent picture of the effect of Internet newsgroups on the transformation of an individual's social identity. Study 1 showed that newsgroups concerned with concealable marginalized identities were more important to the lives of their members, as indicated by the amount of active participation (average number of posts) by each member and by the impact that positive and negative feed-back from other members had on each member's behavior. Studies 2 and 3 went further, examining the transformational ability of Internet group participation on these concealable marginalized identities. Consistent with the model of Deaux and her colleagues, group involvement (posting vs. lurking) led to increased importance of the group identity, which in turn increased self-acceptance of that identity.

It is hard to understate the power of the identity transformation effect obtained in Studies 2 and 3. As a direct result of Internet newsgroup membership and participation, over 37% of participants in Study 2 and 63% of those in Study 3 revealed to others what had been an embarrassing secret about themselves. This is particularly remarkable in the context of Study 2, because sexual preferences are often formed early in life. Given that the mean age in that sample was 37 years, involvement in those Internet newsgroups caused these people to reveal something to close family members and friends that many of them had kept hidden well into their adult lives.

Out interpretation of this phenomenon is in terms of identity demarginalization, a process by which participation in a group of similar others creates changes in one's identity—specifically, the acquisition of a positive group identity where there was formerly only isolation and feelings of being different. That our participants moved so dramatically to inform others in their life about this new identity is consistent with the premises of self-completion theory (Wicklund & Gollwitzer, 1982). According to that model, important identities need to be realized and expressed in daily life. The individual is motivated to have others notice this identity in order to make it a social reality (Brunstein & Gollwitzer, 1996; Gollwitzer, 1986). The participants in our studies were motivated to come back to real life with their Internet life to verify their identity and make it "real."

Our data thus support the more active theories of the self, in which the individual is motivated to construct and hold his or her identities, in contrast to more purely informational theories of the self. For those with marginalized identities, degree of participation in the newsgroup, through its effect on identity importance, reliably predicted which group members would disclose this formerly hidden aspect of self to important others in their lives.

The Reality of the Virtual

Whether virtual or electronic groups operate by the same principles as real-life or "face-to-face" groups has been a debating point for some years among researchers of computer-mediated communication (CMC), which concerns E-mail interactions (Kiesler, Siegel, & McGuire, 1984; Lea & Spears, 1995; Spears, Lea, & Lee, 1990; Walther, Anderson, & Park, 1994). Some authors, for example, have argued that the relative lack of social cues in E-mail interactions leads to a greater incidence of antisocial behaviors than would occur in face-to-face interactions, presumably because of deindividuation (Kiesler et al., 1984). However, others have found that despite (or perhaps even because of) the greater anonymity of CMC, group members form and adhere to norms just as they do in face-to-face groups (Spears et al., 1990).

Our findings are consistent with the position that the principles that apply to face-to-face group processes also apply to electronic modes of group participation. Just as with nonelectronic group identities (e.g., Deaux, 1996), virtual groups are important to the daily lives of their members, and virtual group identities become an important part of the self. As with real-life groups, the positive versus negative feedback of group members shapes one's subsequent behavior to the extent that belonging to that group matters to the individual (Study 1). In addition, just as individuals with conspicuous marginalized identities feel less different and more self-accepting than do those with concealable marginalized identities because of the visible presence of similar others in the environment (Frable, 1993), the existence of marginalized-content newsgroups increases self-acceptance by making visible what was previously hidden (Studies 2 and 3).

Not only do virtual groups operate the same way real-life groups do, but as our findings also show, what happens in one group or sphere affects behavior in the other. In their spontaneous comments, many respondents in Studies 2 and 3 mentioned that it was the lack of an equivalent group to belong to in real life that caused them to seek out their newsgroup and to identify strongly with it. Similarly, the changes in identity caused by virtual group membership (and especially participation) had ramifications for the individual's real-life relationships, making him or her more likely to share this previously hidden identity. This bidirectional flow of influence between the two spheres belies the claim by many (e.g., Beninger, 1987; Stoll, 1995) that the Internet can give only the illusion of community—that social activity via the computer serves only to increase isolation and to cause the deterioration of the individual's real-life relationships.

While our findings make the case for the reality of the virtual, it must nonetheless be acknowledged that there are key differences between virtual and real-life group processes. Kiesler et al. (1984) were among the first to note the deindividuating effects of the relative anonymity of E-mail communication. Just as delivering bad or unwelcome news is easier to do by telephone or letter than in person, it is easier to disagree or to make negative or aggressive comments over E-mail than face-to-face (see also Diener, 1980). However, the

greater anonymity of Internet group participation can also have benefits. As Turkle (1995) compellingly argued, it also allows for the exploration of identity aspects that were previously closed to the individual, which can lead to a more multifaceted and richer self-concept. As explained in her analysis, the Internet allows individuals—removed from the public consequences of their statements, opinions, and behavior—to try out different personae and to experience how others react to such personae in real life (e.g., "gender-bending," in which individuals portray themselves as members of the opposite sex). In our studies, individuals used the shelter of anonymity to express those important aspects of themselves that might well be sanctioned if expressed for attribution—that is, publicly and nonanonymously (see, e.g., Kelly & McKillop, 1996).

The Benefits of Participation

Through participation in an Internet group that shares a marginalized aspect of one's identity, that part of the self is transformed, becoming more acceptable. As participants in the marginalized newsgroup find the newsgroup to be increasingly more important to their identity, they begin to feel that this aspect of themselves is more socially acceptable than they had thought. This reduces the inner conflict between the marginalized self aspect and cultural standards and allows the individual to be more open about that aspect with important others, such as family and friends.

In her revision of psychoanalytic theory, Horney (1946) argued that just such conflicts between the self and public standards were the major cause of neurosis, anxiety, and unhappiness. Years later, E. E. Jones et al. (1984, p. 135) noted similarly that possession of a stigmatized identity made the individual less able to cope with the stresses of daily life because self-esteem was reduced. Pennebaker (1989) also argued for a negative effect of identity concealment on coping, but for different reasons: Not only does the act of concealment require continuous effort, thus becoming a long-term stressor, but concealment also prevents the individual from bringing the aspect into the open, where it can be dealt with.

From these theoretical statements, one would expect that over time, concealing an important aspect of the self from others would have negative health consequences. Pennebaker (1989, 1990) found that bringing concealed identities into the open, even anonymously (as in his experimental situation), significantly reduced reported health symptoms in a long-term follow-up. Also, a study by Larson and Chastain (1990) showed that individuals who scored the highest on a personality scale measuring tendencies of self-concealment also reported a greater number of bodily symptoms (e.g., headaches, colds), were more anxious, and were more likely to be depressed than those scoring low on the scale.

Self-disclosure can also provide social validation of one's beliefs and feelings, at least among similar others, as in the Internet groups we studied (Archer, 1987). It can also bring feelings of acceptance from those confided in, information useful in dealing with problems associated with the identity, and motivational support in the form of encouragement (Derlega et al., 1993, p. 101). On Internet newsgroups, only posters would be expected to share in these benefits, as lurkers do not engage in any such self-disclosure, underscoring again the benefits of group participation.

This is not to say that revealing secrets about oneself always leads to positive outcomes and is without risks. Often the person confided to reacts badly at learning this new information, and the relationship is changed or even ended (Kelly & McKillop, 1996). Rejection by others following disclosure can lead to increased feelings of isolation and lowered self-worth. Recognition of this possible outcome is clearly why our participants in Studies 2 and 3 kept their marginalized identities to themselves for so long. The potential negative reactions of others must be weighed against the positive gains from self-disclosure in any decision to come out (see Pennebaker, 1990, chap. 8).

Is the Virtual Entirely Virtuous?

In the *Time* magazine article (Handy, 1997) in which Ellen DeGeneres came out as a lesbian and announced that her popular television character would follow suit, the television evangelist Jerry Falwell denounced both actions. That same month, the Oklahoma City bombing trial of an avowed citizen's militia member began, and 38 cult members committed suicide on the basis of their beliefs about the existence of extraterrestrials. The newsgroups we studied included those related to the marginalized sexual identities, beliefs in the existence of extraterrestrials, and antigovernment activism prominent in all of these well-publicized events. Is the demonstrated effect of such newsgroups to increase an individual's acceptance of these nonmainstream identities, to provide social support and validation of such beliefs, and to encourage real-life behavior consistent with these identities an unequivocally good thing?

The answer, of course, depends on one's valuation of the marginalized identity in question. Almost by definition, mainstream society will not value marginalized identities and will place a negative value on any mechanism that encourages their open expression. At the same time, our findings show that individuals with these identities place a high value on their relevant newsgroups and reap personal benefits of self-esteem and self-acceptance.

Thus, whatever position one takes regarding the values of the various marginalized identities, the psychological effects of virtual group participation for the individual are nonetheless real. In all likelihood they will be an increasingly common feature of life in the age of the Internet.

REFERENCES

Archer, R. L. (1987). Commentary: Self-disclosure, a very useful behavior. In V. L. Derlega & J. H. Berg (Eds.), *Self-disclosure: Theory, research, and therapy* (pp. 329–342). New York: Plenum.

Bat-Chava, Y. (1994). Group identification and the self-esteem of deaf adults. *Personality and Social Psychology Bulletin, 20,* 494–502.

Baumeister, R. F., & Leary, M. R. (1995). The need to belong: Desire for interpersonal attachments as a fundamental human motivation. *Psychological Bulletin, 117,* 497–529.

Beninger, J. R. (1987). Personalization of mass media and the growth of pseudo-community. *Communication Research, 14,* 352–371.

Brewer, M. B. (1991). The social self: On being the same and different at the same time. *Personality and Social Psychology Bulletin, 17,* 475–482.

Brunstein, J. C., & Gollwitzer, P. M. (1996). Effects of failure on subsequent performance: The importance of self-defining goals. *Journal of Personality and Social Psychology, 70,* 395–407.

Dean, D. (1961). Alienation: Its meaning and measurement. *American Sociological Review, 26,* 753–758.

Deaux, K. (1993). Reconstructing social identity. *Personality and Social Psychology Bulletin, 19,* 4–12.

Deaux, K. (1996). Social identification. In E. T. Higgins & A. W. Kruglanski (Eds.), *Social psychology: Handbook of basic principles* (pp. 777–798). New York: Guilford Press.

Derlega, V. J., Metts, S., Petronio, S., & Margulis, S. T. (1993). *Self-disclosure.* London: Sage.

Diener, E. (1980). De-individuation: The absence of self-awareness and self-regulation in group members. In P. Paulus (Ed.), *The psychology of group influence* (pp. 1160–1171). Hillsdale, NJ: Erlbaum.

Dowe, T. (1997, January). The Netizen. *Wired, 5,* 53–56, 184–185.

Ethier, K. A. (1995). *Becoming a mother: Identity acquisition during the transition to parenthood.* Unpublished doctoral dissertation, City University of New York.

Ethier, K. A., & Deaux, K. (1994). Negotiating social identity when contexts change: Maintaining identification and responding to threat. *Journal of Personality and Social Psychology, 67,* 243–251.

Frable, D. E. S. (1993). Being and feeling unique: Statistical deviance and psychological marginality. *Journal of Personality, 61,* 85–110.

Gollwitzer, P. M. (1986). Striving for specific identities: The social reality of self-symbolizing. In R. Baumeister (Ed.), *Public self and private self* (pp. 143–159). New York: Springer.

Handy, B. (1997, April 14). He called me Ellen Degenerate? *Time, 149,* 56–57.

Hogg, M. A., & Abrams, D. (1990). Social motivation, self-esteem, and social identity. In D. Abrams & M. A. Hogg (Eds.), *Social identity theory: Constructive and critical advances* (pp. 28–47). New York: Springer.

Hogg, M. A., & Abrams, D. (1993). Towards a single-process uncertainty-reduction model of social motivation in groups. In M. A. Hogg & D. Abrams (Eds.), *Group motivation: Social psychological perspectives* (pp. 173–190). London: Harvester Wheatsheaf.

Horney, K. (1946). *Our inner conflicts: A constructive theory of neurosis.* London: Routledge & Kegan Paul.

Jessor, R., & Jessor, S. L. (1977). *Problem behavior and psychosocial development.* New York: Academic Press.

Jones, E. E., Farina, A., Hastorf, A. H., Markus, H., Miller, D. T., & Scott, R. A. (1984). *Social stigma: The psychology of marked relationships.* New York: Freeman.

Jones, S. G. (Ed.). (1995). *CyberSociety: Computer-mediated communication and community.* Thousand Oaks, CA: Sage.

Kelly, A. E., & McKillop, K. J. (1996). Consequences of revealing personal secrets. *Psychological Bulletin, 120,* 450–465.

Kiesler, S., Siegel, J., & McGuire, T. (1984). Social psychological aspects of computer-mediated communication. *American Psychologist, 39,* 1123–1134.

Kohn, M. L., & Schooler, C. (1983). *Work and personality: An inquiry into the impact of social stratification.* Norwood, NJ: Ablex.

Larson, D. G., & Chastain, R. L. (1990). Self-concealment: Conceptualization, measurement, and health implications. *Journal of Social and Clinical Psychology, 9,* 439–455.

Lea, M., & Spears, R. (1995). Love at first byte? Building personal relationships over computer networks. In J. T. Wood & S. Duck (Eds.), *Under-studied relationships: Off the beaten track* (pp. 197–240). London: Sage.

Making a business of the bit buffet. (1997, March 8). *The Economist, 342,* 81.

Nunnally, J. C. (1967). *Psychometric theory.* New York: McGraw-Hill.

Pennebaker, J. W. (1989). Confession, inhibition, and disease. In L. Berkowitz (Ed.), *Advances in experimental social psychology* (Vol. 22, pp. 211–244). New York: Academic Press.

Pennebaker, J. W. (1990). *Opening up: The healing power of confiding in others.* New York: Morrow.

Robinson, J. P., Shaver, P. R., & Wrightsman, L. (Eds.). (1991). *Measures of personality and social psychological attitudes* (Vol. 1). New York: Academic Press.

Schachter, S. (1959). *The psychology of affiliation: Experimental studies of the sources of gregariousness.* Stanford, CA: Stanford University Press.

Sedikides, C. (1993). Assessment, enhancement, and verification determinants of the self-evaluation process. *Journal of Personality and Social Psychology, 65,* 317–338.

Smith, E. R., & Henry, S. (1996). An in-group becomes part of the self: Response time evidence. *Personality and Social Psychology Bulletin, 22,* 635–642.

Spears, R., Lea, M., & Lee, S. (1990). De-individuation and group polarization in computer-mediated communication. *British Journal of Social Psychology, 29,* 121–134.

Stoll, C. (1995). *Silicon snake oil.* New York: Doubleday.

Tajfel, H. (1982). Instrumentality, identity, and social comparisons. In H. Tajfel (Ed.), *Social identity and intergroup relations* (pp. 483–507). Cambridge, England: Cambridge University Press.

Turkle, S. (1995). *Life on the screen: Identity in the age of the Internet.* New York: Simon & Schuster.

Walther, J. B., Anderson, J. F., & Park, D. W. (1994). Interpersonal effects in computer-mediated interaction: A meta-analysis of social and anti-social communication. *Communication Research, 21,* 460–487.

Wegner, D. M. (1994). Ironic processes of mental control. *Psychological Review, 101,* 34–52.

Wegner, D. M., & Erber, R. (1992). The hyperaccessibility of suppressed thoughts. *Journal of Personality and Social Psychology, 63,* 903–912.

Wicklund, R. A., & Gollwitzer, P. M. (1982). *Symbolic self-completion.* Hillsdale, NJ: Erlbaum.

Received November 17, 1997
Revision received March 3, 1998
Accepted March 12, 1998 ■

Stability, Bistability, and Instability in Small Group Influence Patterns

Holly Arrow

Three models of change and continuity in group structure are tested using existing longitudinal data on 20 small groups. Groups met face to face or via a computer-mediated communication system for 13 weeks. Computer-mediated groups fit the robust equilibrium pattern best, with initial fluctuations in the influence hierarchy followed by a more stable structure that persisted despite changes in operating conditions. Face-to-face groups fit a bistable punctuated equilibrium pattern best, retaining their initial influence structure until an environmental cue triggered a shift. Contrary to the predictions of this model for radical change, adjustments were modest. Poor performance on tasks failed to trigger changes predicted by the adaptive response model, probably because outcomes were not very important to group members.

When a number of persons have come together to form a group, their behavior never holds to its first pattern.

> Homans, 1950, p. 109

Lasting patterns can appear as early as the first few seconds of a group's life.

> Gersick, 1988, p. 33

Holly Arrow, Department of Psychology, University of Illinois at Urbana–Champaign.

This article is based on my master's thesis, submitted to the University of Illinois, Urbana–Champaign, in 1994. I thank Joseph E. McGrath and Stanley Wasserman, who supervised the thesis. The research on which it is based was supported in part by National Science Foundation grants BNS 91-06501, IRI 91-07040, and SBR 93-10184 and by a National Science Foundation Graduate Research Fellowship.

I also thank Deborah H. Gruenfeld, Andrea B. Hollingshead, Joseph E. McGrath, and Kathleen O'Connor, who planned and conducted the JEMCO Workshop study; Paul Franz, Kevin Gehrt, Martha Orland, Mike Samonds, Kristy Steimel, Brian Thomson, and others who assisted in the collection and processing of data: Joan Alster for statistical consulting; and Jennifer Berdahl for her advice.

A set of six papers analyzing different data from the same longitudinal study have been published as a special issue of *Small Group Research* (Vol. 24, August 1993). None of the analyses reported here have been previously published elsewhere.

Correspondence concerning this article should be addressed to Holly Arrow, who is now at Department of Psychology, 1227 University of Oregon, Eugene, Oregon 97403. Electronic mail may be sent via the Internet to harrow@darkwing.uoregon.edu

Traditional models of group development—the patterning of change and continuity in group structure and behavior over time—propose that groups follow a fixed sequence of stages (Bales, 1970; Bennis & Shepard, 1956; Tuckman, 1965; Tuckman & Jensen, 1977; see Mennecke, Hoffer, & Wynne, 1992, for a review). These models typically presume a stable group composition and context and ignore external causes of change. Changes in group composition or other interventions are treated as externalities that disrupt the ideal path of development (Hill & Gruner, 1973). Yet most naturally occurring groups with an extended history experience temporary or permanent changes of membership and cope (or fail to cope) with other changes in tasks, technology, and operating conditions over time. Proponents of non-sequential group development models emphasize the importance of contingencies in the environment that influence a group's developmental path (e.g., Gersick, 1991; McGrath, 1991; Poole & Roth, 1989a, 1989b). According to these theorists, differences in group composition or task type should result in different patterns of change and continuity in group structure (patterns of interpersonal relations) and task behavior over time. Changes in these contingencies during the group's history should evoke responses by the group. To better understand the impact of both initial conditions and changes in conditions, they call for more research exploring the possibility of multiple developmental paths (Cissna, 1984; McCollom, 1995; McGrath & O'Connor, 1996; Poole & Roth, 1989b).

The Dynamics of Group Structure: A Multiple-Path Approach

This study takes up that challenge, using existing data from 20 groups of similar size and composition that met weekly for 13 weeks (see McGrath, 1993). Half the groups met face to face, and half used a computer conferencing system. Several of the groups had unplanned changes in group composition in the first few weeks, and with one exception, all had one or more absences. In addition, operating conditions were changed for all

groups in two planned interventions. This article addresses three questions: (a) For task groups with a fixed duration operating in a changing environment, do patterns of change and continuity in group structure correspond to a particular model of group development? (b) Does communication medium affect which developmental pattern is followed? and (c) Does early disruption of group composition affect group development?

A better understanding of the contingencies underlying group development is important because different models identify different periods during which groups will be receptive to, resistant to, or disrupted by interventions. Supervisors who oversee and support work groups, for example, could benefit from knowing when groups need to be buffered from change and when they will welcome assistance in adapting to a changing environment. Imposed changes in group composition should have different effects on relational patterns and task performance depending on the timing of change (Arrow & McGrath, 1995).

Established findings in social psychology, such as people's tendency to view in-group members as more heterogeneous than out-group members (Linville & Jones, 1980), and people's tendency to cooperate with in-group members and compete with out-group members (Tajfel & Turner, 1986), have been shown to depend on the stage of group development for the in-group in question (see Worchel, 1994, for a discussion of such group development effects).

Because the literature provides literally dozens of theories of group development (Hill & Gruner, 1973, claim to have identified over 100), theory-driven investigation requires some initial consolidation. The next section extracts four basic models from the plethora of existing theories, and derives concrete, testable predictions for changes and continuity in group structure.

Four Models of Change and Continuity in Group Structure

The four models draw on typologies of both group development and organizational development

TABLE 24.1. Characteristics of Change Among the Four Models of Group Development

Model	Source of change	Nature of change	Source of continuity
Robust equilibrium	Internal forces	Initial fluctuations	Internal forces
Life cycle	Internal forces	Gradual, ongoing	External disruption
Punctuated equilibrium	External cues	Radical, abrupt	Internal forces
Adaptive response	External cues	Immediate or delayed response	External forces

(Allmendinger & Hackman, in press; McCollom, 1995; Mennecke et al., 1992; Miller & Friesen, 1980; Wanous, Reichers, & Malik, 1984). They are also informed by complexity theory (Cowan, Pines, & Meltzer, 1994) and dynamical systems theory, which identify basic patterns of change and evolution in both living and nonliving systems (Goerner, 1994).

The four models differ in their relative emphasis on internal and external causes of change. They also differ in whether and under what circumstances they predict abrupt change, gradual change, or relative stability in group structure. Sources and characteristics of change and continuity in the four models are summarized in Table 24.1. Although the empirical study that follows examines change and continuity in only one aspect of group structure—the patterning of interpersonal influence—the models presented here are intended to apply to group structure more generally. Broadly defined, *group structure* refers to the pattern of relations among group members (Levine & Moreland, 1990). Theories of group development have addressed aspects such as leader–follower relations (e.g., Bion, 1961; Mann, Gibbard, & Hartman, 1967); status and role systems (e.g., McGrath, 1991); distribution of influence and power (e.g., Poole & Roth, 1989b; Worchel, 1994); cohesiveness (e.g., Poole & Roth, 1989b; Tuckman, 1965); and conflict (e.g., Mann et al., 1967; Tuckman, 1965).

Model 1: Robust Equilibrium

The robust equilibrium model posits a brief period of fluctuation followed by a steady state. After an initial period of instability in relational structures, a stable influence hierarchy and role system will emerge and persist. Shocks that might disrupt the group's structure will be dampened by the group, hence variations will be small. *Equilibrium* is the normal state of the group; *robust* refers to the persistence of a stable structure despite changes in the environment.

The robust equilibrium model emphasizes internal causes of development in the initial period and structural stability and continuity thereafter. From a dynamical systems perspective, the group moves toward a single attractor (Abraham, Abraham, & Shaw, 1990) and stays in the region of closely similar structures, with minor fluctuations. Equilibrium in this case is not rigidity but the stability achieved by an active, self-regulating system.

Theoretical and empirical roots

Equilibrium and homeostatic models have a long history in social and organizational psychology—from field theory (Lewin, 1951), to the equilibrium problem (Bales, 1953), to open systems theory (Katz & Kahn, 1978), which draws in turn on general systems theory (Berrien, 1976; von Bertalanffy, 1968). More recent work extends this line of theorizing (e.g., Carley, 1991). Although equilibrium models acknowledge change (usually treated as gradual) as an aspect of group functioning, the emphasis is on achieving and actively maintaining a stable state. In organizational theory, institutional models (e.g., Zucker, 1977, 1987) stress the power of institutional processes to buffer established organizations against change and ensure continuity. Robust equilibrium also fits the population ecology approach to organizational change (Hannan & Freeman, 1977, 1984), which proposes that stable systems are the most "fit." This theory proposes that changes in a population of organizations occur as new organizations are formed and unsuccessful ones (especially unstable ones) dissolve, and not through changes within established groups.

Some equilibrium models have been tested empirically. In a four-meeting study of five-person groups, Bales (1955) found that a simple, tentative group structure emerged (if at all) toward the end of the first meeting. This structure was challenged in the second meeting, resulting in either a confirmation of the first structure or an exchange of status positions between the top two or three members. Not all groups studied reached an equilibrium state, but the presumption in this study was that all groups were striving to achieve "an equilibrated role structure" (Bales, 1955). More recent theorizing on robust equilibrium in large groups (e.g., Carley, 1991) propose contingencies such as complexity and initial cultural homogeneity that determine the length of time before "perfect social stability" is reached.

Psychological processes underlying the model

One explanation for the robust equilibrium pattern in initially unstructured groups can be found in the changing expectations of groups members about one another (McGrath, Berdahl, & Arrow, 1996). According to expectation states theory (Berger, Conner, & Fisek, 1974) and social role theory (Eagly & Karau, 1991), when strangers first come together in a group, members use easily observed status characteristics such as gender, race, or age as a basis for establishing the initial leadership and influence hierarchy. As members gain information on the actual abilities of one another through interaction, the structure may be adjusted to match the relevant skills of different members. In line with the robust equilibrium model, the outcome of this adjustment process would then be adopted as the normative structure for interpersonal relations in the group. Of course, when members' behavior is shaped by the expectations of others, this can reinforce preconceptions (Ridgeway, 1991).

Adjustments based on imposed stereotypes may worsen the fit between relational patterns such as role and status systems and actual member skills and abilities.

A "constructural" explanation for robust equilibrium (Carley, 1991) proposes that stability emerges as members with initially distinct knowledge bases share information of all kinds with one another. Equilibrium in knowledge and behavior is established as shared knowledge overtakes unique information as a proportion of information contained in the group. This process presumes, of course, that membership remains quite stable.

Predictions

The robust equilibrium model defines equilibrium as a point of arrival that will be achieved within the first few meetings. According to this model, groups will show much stronger week-to-week continuity in structure once members have found their place in the status structure. Substantial changes in the environment may cause transient changes in the group structure, but the group will quickly revert to its normal pattern. Poor fit between an established structure and environmental demands will lead to failure, not adaptive change.

Model 2: Life Cycle

Life cycle models posit that groups pass through stages characterized by different structural patterns. In the first stage, an initial structure forms. In the second, this structure is contested and adjusted. In the third stage, the group settles on a normative structure. In the fourth stage, the group focuses on task performance, and over time, the structure becomes increasingly inflexible. Different groups may take more or less time to work through these stages. In the last stage, the structure changes again as the group dissolves the bonds that hold it together.

According to this model, change is the normal condition for groups, and this change follows an internal logic, with the resolution of each stage initiating the next. Life cycle changes do not rely on environmental cues, and the model emphasizes gradual as opposed to sudden or radical change. Environmental changes should have little effect on group development, although strong external shocks might retard progress.

Theoretical and empirical roots

The life cycle model is abstracted from group theories that fall into the categories of linear-progressive and life cycle models (Mennecke et al., 1992). Probably the best known is Tuckman's (1965) four-stage model, later expanded to five stages (Tuckman & Jensen, 1977): forming, storming, norming, performing, and adjourning. Other theories in this vein posit three stages (e.g., Hill & Gruner, 1973), six stages (Bennis & Shepard, 1956; Worchel, 1994), or four (e.g., LaCoursiere, 1980). Organizational life cycle literature (see Whetten, 1987, for a review) also is unresolved on the number of stages. More broadly, the model is congruent with the idea of gradual, progressive change that pervades theories of child development, organizational theories of growth and decline, cumulative scientific development, and biological evolution (see Gersick, 1991, for a summary). Variants on the life cycle model include what Mennecke and colleagues (1992) term *recurring cycle models*. Some of these focus on the history of the group as a whole (e.g., Worchel, 1994); others focus on recurrent project cycles (e.g., Bales & Strodtbeck, 1951; Bion, 1961; see McGrath & O'Connor, 1996, for a review). For short-term groups with a single project, of course, the distinction is moot.

Psychological processes underlying the model

The life cycle model presumes that different psychological problems or issues are prominent at different periods in the group's life (Bennis & Shepard, 1956; Burnand, 1990) and that these issues have implications for the structure of interpersonal relations in a group, including influence patterns. Change is internally generated and follows a fixed developmental sequence. The emergence of structure in the first stage, for example, addresses members' discomfort in an ambiguous situation. Once uncertainty is reduced, a power struggle ensues to test the appropriateness of the initial structure (Stage 2). Once a stable structure is confirmed

(Stage 3), performance becomes the main issue (Stage 4). In the final stage, attention shifts to the emotional issue of leave-taking, and the structure developed to facilitate performance dissolves.

Predictions

Groups that fit the life cycle model should undergo changes in structure, including fluctuation in influence patterns, in the first few meetings. After the conflict period is resolved, influence patterns should become increasingly stable until just before the group disbands. In the last few sessions, the group structure should dissolve. The emergence and transformation of group structure should be unrelated to changes in task, technology, or other operating conditions. A big change might temporarily interrupt group evolution, however, "freezing" existing patterns while group development is disrupted.

Model 3: Punctuated Equilibrium

In the punctuated equilibrium model, group structure is characterized by strong inertial forces that generate a stable equilibrium "punctuated" by periods of sudden, rapid change. According to this model, whatever structure emerges in a group's first interaction will persist whether or not it is optimal, or even satisfactory, for performance. Moderate changes in the environment will have no effect on group structure. However, when a shock to the system jolts the group out of its usual fixed pattern, an abrupt and radical restructuring will occur. The new structure that emerges will then persist unchanged until the next crisis. Alternately, a group may abruptly unravel and dissolve (extinction). This model combines continuity and abrupt change. Internal processes promote continuity, whereas external causes trigger change.

Theoretical and empirical roots

This model draws on punctuated equilibrium theories in biological evolution (Eldredge & Gould, 1972; Gould, 1989) and group development (Gersick, 1988, 1989) that emphasize revolutionary rather than incremental change. Gersick found that both laboratory (1989) and naturally occurring (1988) project groups held to the pattern of interaction established in their first meeting until the project's temporal midpoint. In an extension of the theory, other triggers for change are proposed: a strong external intervention, a change in group composition, or any dramatically novel state of affairs (Gersick & Hackman, 1990). A variation of this model proposes that serious disequilibrium can be generated either by external fluctuations or from internal events such as serious interpersonal conflicts among group members (Smith & Gemmill, 1991).

Punctuated equilibrium models in organizational theory (Miller & Friesen, 1980; Tushman & Romanelli, 1985) specify gradual change during the equilibrium period that consolidates and exaggerates whatever tendencies (e.g., toward innovation or formalization) are established at the outset. A small number of *gestalts*, which are coherent organizational patterns of interlocking environmental demands, group structure, and task strategy (Miller & Friesen, 1980), are proposed to act as attractors that organizational forms converge toward over time. Groups in which members have unequal influence, for example, will become more unequal over time, whereas groups that tend initially toward subgroup cliques will become more divided over time. These organizational development models emphasize declining performance and threats to organizational survival as forces that rouse the organization to counteract inertial forces and adopt a different organizational design. Research in this tradition (e.g., Haveman, 1992) stresses the positive benefits of group or organizational restructuring in response to environmental changes.

Psychological processes underlying the model

The rapid onset of a persistent equilibrium state is explained by the application of a schema or framework for behavior (Gersick, 1988) that is shared among members. This framework may include implicit agreements about what roles should be played and how role assignment should be decided. Instead of developing norms over several sessions, members simply enact a shared script or routine

(Gersick & Hackman, 1990) based on past experience. This script is then reinforced as part of the normative structure of the group (Bettenhausen & Murnighan, 1985). Such shared frameworks or imported routines provide a prepackaged structure that enables the group to turn its attention immediately to task performance, rather than taking the time and energy to develop a customized structure tailored to the task, the environment, and the needs and abilities of individual members. Incremental changes during these periods are designed to increase the fit between structural variables, technology, control systems such as norms, and strategy (Tushman & Romanelli, 1985).

The rapid change periods can be explained by a dual process model. Some strong cue triggers a switch from automatic processing to intentional processing (Bargh, 1994; Shiffrin & Schneider, 1977), and group members abruptly notice problems in the fit between environmental demands and group functioning (including inappropriate structures) that have previously been ignored. This galvanizes members to make rapid and fundamental changes to improve the fit. The restructured group then resumes habitual task performance.

This analysis of underlying process also suggests a contingency that will determine whether or not a group follows the punctuated equilibrium pattern. When members lack an appropriate script or disagree on the basis for assigning members to positions, instant equilibrium is unlikely.

Predictions

Starting from the very first meeting, group structure should persist virtually unchanged from week to week, unless a marked change in the environment triggers a restructuring. After a brief unsettled transition, a new stable structure will emerge and persist. Groups will not return to their prior structure after the disruption. Hence patterns before and after a restructuring will show little similarity.

A strong external shock, a change in leadership (Miller & Friesen, 1980), persistent poor performance (Tushman & Romanelli, 1985), or a salient temporal milestone can trigger the instability and rapid change that allows a group to adjust its structure. For groups with a fixed life span and defined tasks, the midpoint can provide the trigger for restructuring (Gersick, 1988, 1989).

Model 4: Adaptive Response

The adaptive response model posits that groups actively create and adjust their structure in response to internal and external contingencies. According to this model, groups create or adopt structures to fit their task, their technology, and environmental demands. If operating conditions change, the group will adjust its structure in response. Whether the group exhibits structural stability, gradual change, or abrupt change depends on whether the demands of the environment remain stable, change slowly, or change abruptly.

If the task demands tight coordination among members, for example, groups will need a more formal, explicit communication and influence structure. Different decision rules, which imply different influence patterns, may be adopted for different types of decisions. Differential emphasis on task and social activity during periods of intense work or the socialization of new members may trigger members to take on different roles, which may change their relative influence in the group. Groups will also alter their structure in response to threat or failure.

The speed of adaptive response (immediate or delayed) will depend on how adept the group is at recognizing a change in circumstances and making needed adjustments. Detailed crisis contingency plans, for example, may be established. Gersick and Hackman (1990) proposed that groups that face frequent major changes may develop a meta-level habit that provides routines for switching to different frameworks. In organizations in which emergency situations are common, for example, specific routines may be developed and practiced. A hospital has one set of check-in procedures for the run-of-the-mill sick or injured, for example, and another for patients who arrive in critical condition. Military personnel have different norms for wartime versus peacetime operations.

Theoretical and empirical roots

The adaptive response model draws on the task performance school typified by Steiner (1972); sociotechnical theory (Trist & Bamforth, 1951; see also Hulin & Roznowski, 1985); the contingency theory of decision development (Poole & Roth, 1989b); and organizational adaptation models (Lawrence & Lorsch, 1967; Pfeffer & Salancik, 1978).

Steiner (1972) noted that different task structures imply different weights for the contributions of different members; different influence structures should thus be optimal for different task types. In organizational settings, task and technology are closely intertwined: Technology shapes the tasks to be performed (Hulin & Roznowski, 1985). However, the two can be varied independently in the laboratory. Kiesler and Sproull (1992) found that status differences were smaller in groups using computer-mediated communication (CMC) than in face-to-face (FTF) groups performing the same task (other studies, e.g., Berdahl & Craig, 1996, have found opposite effects; see McGrath & Hollingshead, 1994, for a review). Differences in structure based on communication technology would be expected on the basis of sociotechnical theory, which stresses the mutual adjustment and structuring of technical and social systems.

Contingency theory, which focuses on decision development, emphasizes that developmental paths are contingent and that groups actively seek to fit environmental demands (Poole & Roth, 1989b). Hybrid models such as time, interaction, and performance (TIP) theory (McGrath, 1991) include both stages or phases (as in the life cycle model) and task and context contingencies for the appearance and ordering of stages. In dynamical-systems terms, the adaptive response model stresses the flexible switching of groups among a large array of possible structures (Kelso, 1995).

Psychological processes underlying the model

Adaptive response can be explained using an information-processing perspective. Group members scan the environment for information relevant to task performance and group survival. Once the situation is defined as fitting a particular category, group members jointly enact an appropriate script. If the conditions persist unchanged, the group continues to reenact the script. If conditions change, group members will switch to a new script. Changes in structure will occur when different scripts specify different types of structure (e.g., concentration of power vs. equally weighted contributions).

Predictions

Because this model views environmental demands and operating conditions, not internal development, as primary, groups should change only in response to a perceived change in conditions or when performance is perceived to be poor. If operating conditions are stable and performance satisfactory, the group should not restructure.

The JEMCO Workshop Study: 20 Groups Under Stable and Changing Conditions

Existing data from an ongoing research program on time, task, and technology in work groups (McGrath, 1993) were used to test the robust equilibrium, punctuated equilibrium, and adaptive response models for 20 small groups that met for 13 consecutive weeks. (The life cycle model, unfortunately, could not be tested given the limitations of the data.) The groups were similar in size (3 or 4 persons) and composition (all but 1 included both sexes) and performed identical tasks in a fixed sequence. Given the experimentally imposed similarity in purpose, tasks, and meeting schedule among groups, adherence to a single developmental model seemed likely. Multiple developmental paths were also considered plausible, however, because of differences in communication technology, levels of membership change, and quality of task performance.

Method

Procedure

Participants were 81 students (37 men, 44 women) in an advanced course on the social psychology of organizations, who met weekly for 13 weeks in 3- or 4-person teams as the laboratory portion of the class. Members were assigned to teams on a quasi-random basis, given the constraints of student

schedules. All groups except one included both sexes. The research component of the course was clearly described in the course catalog and on the first day of class.

The 13 weekly team meetings lasted 2 hr each. Members were asked to consider themselves employees in the fictional "JEMCO" (J.E. McGrath Company) consulting organization, and each week their teams completed a consulting task for a fictional client. Task materials included a brief case description and detailed instructions about what type of solution or advice to generate. They were also told how the products would be scored.

In Week 3, for example, group members read about a fictional company with a high incidence of alcohol abuse among employees. Groups were then asked to select among several policies designed to deal with the problem and to detail the reasons for their choices in a group rationale that explained why their choice would fit the company's criteria better than the alternatives. The rationale was scored for persuasiveness by multiple raters. In week 10, groups were asked to apply the decision rules outlined in Vroom and Yetton's (1973) normative theory of leadership to four different scenarios and determine which management styles would be considered feasible. Choices were scored for consistency with the theory. (For detailed descriptions of the tasks for each week, see McGrath, 1993.)

After completing the group task each week, all members completed a standard questionnaire, which included questions about the relative influence of different members and the perceived quality of performance.

Experimental conditions and manipulations

Communications technology. The 13 weeks of the study included both planned manipulations in communications medium and in membership, and unplanned week-to-week changes such as absences. An overview is given in Table 24.2. Half of the groups were assigned to meet face to face in small rooms in which their interactions were videotaped; the other half communicated via a computer conferencing system that allowed each member to

TABLE 24.2. The JEMCO Workshop Study: Planned and Unplanned Changes and Manipulations

Week	Manipulations and membership change
1	Assignment to groups
2	5 groups get new members due to student drop/add; 3 absences
3	1 group gets a new member due to drop/add; 2 groups lose members
4	1 group loses a member; 1 absence
5	3 absences
6	6 absences (week before spring break); 1 drop
7	Communication medium switched; 3 absences
8	Role manipulation—week excluded from analyses
9	Role manipulation—week excluded from analyses; groups return to regular medium
10	2 absences
11	Member switch—each group traded a regular member for a temporary guest, round robin fashion; 6 absences
12	Member switch continues; 5 absences
13	Members return to regular groups; 2 groups (besides the chronic problem cases) fail to meet because of member absences

Note: JEMCO = J. E. McGrath Company (name of fictional consulting company). Two of the original 22 groups were excluded because of chronic attendance problems.

send messages to all other members. In weeks 7 and 8, groups switched locations and used the other communication technology; in Week 9 they returned to their original setting and communication technology. This change in communication technology is relevant to those models that predict a change in group structure when there is a major change in operating conditions. Week 7 was also the temporal midpoint of the 13-week study.

Roles, status, and leadership. Groups were left to develop their own status systems and were not assigned specific roles, with one exception. In Weeks 8 and 9, groups performed role-playing negotiation tasks in which members were assigned to predetermined roles. One member had final decision making power. In these weeks, relations between members were structured by the experimenters and did not reflect the naturally occurring

structure of the group. Hence these weeks were excluded from the analyses.

Membership change and continuity. In Weeks 11 and 12, one member from each group was switched to another group that was using the same communication technology as his or her regular group. Guest members returned to their usual groups in Week 13. In the first 2 weeks, 8 of the groups changed composition as students added or dropped the course or were absent for the second meeting. Over the 13 weeks, most of the groups had one or two absences. Two of the 22 groups in the original study had chronic attendance problems, with only 1 member showing up some weeks. These groups (1 FTF, 1 CMC) were excluded from analyses, leaving 10 groups for each communication condition.

Measures

Performance, perceived performance, and cohesiveness. Each of the weekly tasks called for a different group product. Because products were scored differently from week to week, all product scores were converted to z scores. Each week, members rated the quality of task performance, their satisfaction with the group product, and their confidence in their group's performance on a 7-point scale. Internal consistency of this three-item scale of perceived performance quality was .95 (Cronbach's α for standardized variables).

Influence structure. Each week, each member ranked all group members, including self, from 1 (*most influential*) to n (*least influential*) in group decision making. Judgments for each target member were averaged to yield a mean rank for each member, each week. Although not used in the analyses reported in this study, measurements of other aspects of structure were also available in the data set. The relative amount of influence for each member correlated positively with relative participation (.71), relative value of member contributions (.78), and relative interpersonal popularity (.55). All correlations were significant at the $p < .0001$ level. Thus influence structure can be considered a representative aspect of a cluster of attributes distinguishing relative member importance in the group.

Member judgments about one another's influence were arranged in a member-by-member matrix for each group. Intermember agreement about relative influence was calculated by comparing each pair of rows, summing the number of agreements, and dividing by the maximum agreements possible for a group of that size. This measure of interrater agreement yielded 52% agreement in judgments (exact matches in rankings of same target) for face-to-face groups and 47% agreement for computer-mediated groups. By chance, 17% agreement would be expected. Inspection of the matrices indicated that a common source of disagreement was members rating themselves as more influential than they were rated by others.

Continuity and change in influence structures. Kendall's Tau (Kendall, 1963) was used to measure similarity in the relative influence scores of members across weeks as indicated by their mean rank for each week. The coefficient is sensitive to inversions in order (Member A switches places with Member B as most influential) but indifferent to actual values (ranks, in this case). This is important because mean rank is sensitive to group size, which might change between weeks if a member was absent. For each group, the index was calculated for each pair of meetings that had at least two members in common. Values can range from -1 (*complete inversion*) to $+1$ (*ordering preserved across weeks*).

This measure ignores information on whether members changed their assessment of one another's relative influence from week to week, unless multiple members changed their judgments in the same direction. To capture this detailed information on the patterning of judgments by each member about each other member, an additional measure of change was calculated. Judgments were arranged in a sociomatrix with rows for judges and columns for targets of judgments. The quadratic assignment procedure (QAP) correlation (Hubert & Schultz, 1976) was then used to calculate the similarity in sociomatrices between weeks. The algorithm available in *UCINET IV* (Borgatti, Everett, & Freeman,

1992) computes Pearson correlation coefficients using corresponding cells of two sociomatrices. For each group, QAP correlations were calculated for each week-to-week comparison for which the sociomatrices had at least three cells in common. This measure also can take values from -1 to $+1$.

To capture changes in both the overall influence hierarchy and in member-to-member judgments about relative influence, Kendall's Tau and QAP correlation scores (which correlated .66) were averaged to yield a "structural similarity" index of continuity in influence structures across weeks.

Results

The analyses reported next examined whether the groups fit the patterns predicted by one or more of the models. Although multiple developmental paths were considered possible, all groups in the data set were of similar size and composition and performed identical tasks in the same order. Robust equilibrium, the midpoint version of punctuated equilibrium, and the performance contingency for adaptive response were tested. Because Weeks 8 and 9 had to be excluded from analyses, the data set was judged inadequate for a fair test of the life cycle model. Ambiguity about the timing of transitions between stages also made concrete predictions for the life cycle model impossible without a host of relatively arbitrary assumptions about where transitions should fall. Communication medium and early membership change were investigated as possible factors influencing the developmental patterns of the groups.

Robust equilibrium supported for computer-mediated groups

For the robust equilibrium model, Week 1 structure was predicted to have low similarity to structure in Weeks 3 to 13. So scores on the structural similarity index should be low when comparing influence patterns in Week 1 with patterns for Weeks 3 to 13. Structure during Weeks 3 to 13 was expected to be stable, so structural similarity scores were predicted to be high for all week-to-week comparisons among Weeks 3 to 13. Week 2 was considered ambiguous, as the model does not specify how quickly equilibrium will be attained. The dependent variable for analyses was the mean similarity scores for week-to-week comparisons that were, according to the model, supposed to show either low or high continuity in influence patterns. The low and high categories were treated as two levels of a within-groups "model" factor. Communication medium (FTF or CMC) was included as a between-groups factor.

A 2 (communication medium) × 2 (theoretically low or high structural similarity) analysis of variance indicated a Medium × Model interaction for structural similarity, $F(1, 18) = 7.55, p < .02$. Computer-mediated groups fit the predicted pattern, with structure in Weeks 3 to 13 showing substantially higher continuity than that between Week 1 and subsequent weeks. This pattern of initial fluctuation followed by relative stability fits the robust equilibrium model. In face-to-face groups, in contrast, structure in weeks 3 to 13 showed lower week-to-week continuity, violating the predicted pattern. Table 24.3 shows the means and standard deviations.

Feeble support for punctuated equilibrium with a midpoint transition

The "midpoint transition" version of the punctuated equilibrium model was tested following the same procedure, but with different week-to-week

comparisons coded as low or high. Structure in Weeks 1–6 (before the transition) and in Weeks 7–13 (after the transition) was expected to show high interweek similarity. Comparisons of structure in weeks before and after the midpoint, however, were expected to show relatively low structural similarity.

Results indicated a main effect across groups for model factor (low or high) for the punctuated equilibrium model, $F(1, 18) = 4.65, p < .05$. There was no significant effect for communication medium, although effect size for the model was somewhat larger for the face-to-face groups than for the computer-mediated groups (see Table 24.3 for means). Although the midpoint appears to have inspired some adjustments to structure beyond the normal week-to-week variability, the groups do not show a marked midpoint transition. Readers should keep in mind that the midpoint corresponded to the imposed change in communication media. Thus the results also indicate that the manipulation of communication technology had relatively mild effects on the stability of influence structures.

Adaptive response to poor performance not supported

Unlike the robust and punctuated equilibrium models, which allow relatively straightforward predictions, change and continuity for the adaptive

TABLE 24.3. Similarity in Influence Structure for Week-by-Week Comparisons That the Models Predicted Would Show High or Low Continuity

Model	Face-to-face (n = 10)		Computer-mediated (n = 10)	
	M	SD	M	SD
Robust equilibrium				
Week 1 compared with Weeks 3–13 (low)	.23	.20	.09	.31
Weeks 3–13 compared (high)	.17	.20	.28	.22
Punctuated equilibrium				
Weeks 1–6 compared with Weeks 7–13 (low)	.14	.22	.20	.28
Weeks 1–6 compared; 7–13 compared (high)	.25	.18	.26	.21

Note: Structural similarity scores could take values ranging from −1 to +1. Maximum values were restricted by low interrater reliability (.52 face-to-face, .47 computer-mediated communication) in member judgments about relative influence. When high scores are substantially higher than low scores, the patterns of change and continuity in influence scores fit the predictions of the model.

response model depend on task, technology, and environmental contingencies and on group perceptions. Unacceptably poor performance is one spur to adaptive change. However, performance deficits per se do not necessarily drive change; perceived deficits do. If groups responded to good performance by sticking with their current structure and strategy, and responded to poor performance with adjustments in structure, we would expect perceived performance at Time t to be positively correlated with structural stability at Time $t + 1$.

To test this possibility, correlation coefficients were calculated between perceived performance in Weeks 1 through 5 with structural stability (compared with the prior week) in Weeks 2 through 6, respectively (later weeks were excluded because technology and membership manipulations confused the picture). Two of the five correlations were positive, three were negative, and none were significant. Increasing the lag to 2 weeks, four correlations were calculated, between perceived performance in Weeks 1 to 4 and structural stability for Weeks 3 through 6, respectively. All four correlations were positive, but not significantly so at the .05 level adjusted for multiple comparisons. Relations between structural stability and *cumulative* perceived performance (calculated by averaging judgments in all prior weeks) also failed to show significant effects, although all correlations were positive. Failure to adjust based on perceived performance problems turned out to be

wise: Standardized product scores and perceived quality of performance were negatively correlated ($-.33, p > .1, n = 20$) for Weeks 1 through 6.

Early member change as a contingency affecting development

To investigate the possible impact of early stability or instability in membership on the subsequent development of groups, the analyses for robust equilibrium and punctuated equilibrium were rerun with member stability as an additional factor. The general linear model procedure in SAS (SAS Institute, 1989) was used to accommodate the unequal cell sizes. Results indicate a Model × Medium × Member Stability interaction for structural stability, $F(1, 16) = 9.45, p < .01$. Early member change had no effect on the tendency of groups to adhere to punctuated equilibrium predictions, but it did affect the tendency of computer-mediated groups to follow robust equilibrium patterns. The seven CMC groups with consistent member composition fit the model well; the three CMC groups with early membership change did not fit model predictions (see Table 24.4). Mean continuity for the latter were high because of a single high-continuity group.

Discussion

The questions that motivated the study of the 20 task groups were (a) Do patterns of change and

TABLE 24.4. Similarity in Influence Structure for Week-to-Week Comparisons Specified by the Robust Equilibrium Model, for Computer-Mediated Groups With and Without Early Membership Change

	Computer-mediated groups ($n = 10$)			
	Early member Change ($n = 3$)		Early member stability ($n = 7$)	
Robust equilibrium	M	SD	M	SD
Week 1 with Weeks 3–13 (low)	.44	.33	−.06	.12
Weeks 3–13 (high)	.37	.34	.25	.17

Note: Structural similarity scores could take values ranging from −1 to +1. Maximum values were restricted by low interrater reliability (.52 face-to-face, .47 computer-mediated communication) in member judgments about relative influence. When high scores are substantially higher than low scores, the patterns of change and continuity in influence scores fit the predictions of the robust equilibrium model.

continuity in group structure correspond to a particular model of group development? (b) Does communication medium affect which developmental pattern is followed? and (c) Does early disruption of group composition affect group development? The data set used allowed a test of the robust equilibrium model, the midpoint version of the punctuated equilibrium model, and the poor performance contingency for the adaptive response model. A limitation of the study is its focus on changes in a single aspect of structure—influence patterns. However, high correlations between influence, participation, value of member contributions, and popularity indicate that other aspects of structure were closely related to influence patterns.

Groups overall showed a slight change in the stability of influence patterns corresponding to the punctuated equilibrium model, with a somewhat larger change for FTF groups: The magnitude of change, however, hardly qualifies as a "restructuring." Communication medium did matter: Changes in influence patterns in CMC groups fit the robust equilibrium model quite well, but only if early membership composition was consistent.

The groups examined in this study were small, fixed-term teams whose members met once a week over the course of a semester. Unlike the single-project groups studied by Gersick (1988, 1989), these groups showed only slight evidence of a punctuated equilibrium midpoint pattern. Interpretation of the apparent tendency to adjust group structure is also muddied by the correspondence of the midpoint with an outside intervention that changed the groups' communication technology. Thus we don't know whether the groups were showing a modest adaptive response to a change in technology or a feeble response to a temporal cue. The groups also differed from those studied by Gersick in another way. Instead of working on a single large project, they received a new task each week that had to be completed by the end of the meeting. Thus they did not need to rely on temporal cues to pace themselves over the course of a semester.

One explanation for the computer-mediated groups' adherence to the robust equilibrium pattern, showing early instability in influence structure instead of "instant" equilibrium, is that members had no consensus script for how to run a task group communicating on computers. Lacking the rich interpersonal cues of the face-to-face medium, they may have found it more difficult to evaluate contributions from different members in making decisions, as diffuse status cues such as race, gender, and physical attractiveness were either unavailable or much weaker. Upper level students assigned to face-to-face groups, however, were likely to have past experience working in similar classroom project groups and thus could adopt an acceptable structure quickly. Faced with the switch to computer mediation in Week 7, however, they may have found that their established influence patterns did not work as well. A separate study of these groups (O'Connor, Gruenfeld, & McGrath, 1993) found that conflict increased when groups were switched to an unfamiliar medium, supporting this interpretation.

Groups did not adjust their influence structure in response to perceived performance problems. Performance on the tasks had no impact on students' course grades, however, so the incentive to make corrective changes was weak. The range of possible contingencies affecting influence structures is much broader than performance. Indeed, one of the assumptions underlying the adaptive response model—that groups adapt their structure to fit the demands of task, technology, and other environmental features—was supported by the different paths taken by groups using different communication media.

This study articulated four general models of group development, specified predictions for versions of three of the models, and compared the fit of observed structural change patterns with the predicted patterns. The life cycle model could not be tested adequately with this data.

Longitudinal studies can help researchers to better understand the multiple paths that groups take in elaborating and transforming the pattern of interpersonal relations. Many more comparisons across multiple groups studied over time will be necessary to identify which features of groups and their environments predispose them toward one pattern or another. Variables not addressed in the current study, for example, include the purpose for which the groups were formed and the relative importance of the members, the technology, and the group tasks in shaping group structure (see Arrow & McGrath, 1995, for a typology of groups based on these distinctions).

All studies of group development over time, whether they focus on many groups or few, stable or rapidly changing conditions, could benefit from deriving concrete, testable predictions from a few core models and testing those predictions systematically. More attention to the underlying processes purported to drive change and maintain continuity may yield a better basis for theorizing about the types of conditions that predispose groups to follow one model or another.

It is, of course, expensive in time and resources to gather longitudinal data on multiple groups under controlled conditions. However, as the JEMCO Workshop paradigm illustrates (McGrath, 1993), it is possible to accomplish this within a classroom context. Content coding of published case studies supplemented by retrospective questionnaires (an approach followed by Miller & Friesen, 1980) and archival analysis supplemented by sample surveys and interviews (Allmendinger & Hackman, in press) are some promising multimethod strategies for studying naturally occurring groups and sorting out the contingencies determining different basic patterns of development. More traditional experimental approaches using groups that meet for only a brief period have also succeeded in demonstrating group development effects (Worchel, 1994). The generality of group development patterns for groups of markedly different duration remains, however, an open question, one amenable to empirical research.

REFERENCES

Abraham, F. D., Abraham, R. H., & Shaw, C. S. (1990). *A visual introduction to dynamical systems theory for psychology*. Santa Cruz, CA: Aerial Press.

Allmendinger, J., & Hackman, J. R. (in press). Organizations in changing environments: The case of East German symphony orchestras. *Administrative Science Quarterly*.

Arrow, H., & McGrath, J. E. (1995). Membership dynamics in groups at work: A theoretical framework. In B. M. Staw & L. L. Cummings (Eds.), *Research in Organizational Behavior*, *17*, 373–411. Greenwich, CT: JAI Press.

Bales, R. F. (1953). The equilibrium problem in small groups. In T. Parsons, R. F. Bales, & E. A. Shils (Eds.), *Working papers in the theory of action* (pp. 111–161). Glencoe, IL: Free Press.

Bales, R. F. (1955). Adaptive and integrative changes as sources of strain in social systems. In A. P. Hare, E. F. Borgatta, & R. F. Bales (Eds.), *Small groups: Studies in social interaction* (pp. 127–131). New York: Knopf.

Bales, R. F. (1970). *Personality and interpersonal behavior*. New York: Holt, Rinehart & Winston.

Bales, R. F., & Strodtbeck, F. L. (1951). Phases in group problem solving. *Journal of Abnormal and Social Psychology*, *46*, 485–495.

Bargh, J. A. (1994). The four horsemen of automaticity: Awareness, intention, efficiency and control in social cognition. In R. S. Wyer, Jr., & T. K. Srull (Eds.), *Handbook of social cognition* (2nd ed.; Vol. 1, pp. 1–40). Hillsdale, NJ: Erlbaum.

Bennis, W. G., & Shepard, H. A. (1956). A theory of group development. *Human Relations*, *9*, 415–437.

Berdahl, J. L., & Craig, K. M. (1996). Equality of participation and influence in groups: The effects of communication medium and sex composition. *Computer Supported Cooperative Work (CSCW)*, *4*, 179–202.

Berger, J., Conner, T., & Fisek, M. H. (Eds.) (1974). *Expectations states theory: A theoretical research program*. Cambridge, MA: Winthrop.

Berrien, F. K. (1976). A general systems approach to organizations. In M. D. Dunnette (Ed.), *Handbook of industrial and organizational psychology* (pp. 41–62). Chicago: Rand McNally College Publishing.

Bettenhausen, K. L., & Murnighan, J. K. (1985). The emergence of norms in competitive decision-making groups. *Administrative Science Quarterly*, *30*, 350–372.

Bion, W. R. (1961). *Experiences in groups and other papers*. New York: Basic Books.

Borgatti, S. B., Everett, M. G., & Freeman, L. C. (1992). *UCINET IV Version 1.0*. Columbia, SC: Analytic Technologies.

Burnand, G. (1990). Group development phases as working through six fundamental human problems. *Small Group Research*, *21*, 255–273.

Carley, K. (1991). A theory of group stability. *American Sociological Review*, *56*, 331–354.

Cissna, K. N. (1984). Phases in group development: The negative evidence. *Small Group Behavior*, *15*, 3–32.

Cowan, G. A., Pines, D., & Meltzer, D. (Eds.). (1994). *Complexity: Metaphors, models, and reality*. Santa Fe Institute Studies in the Sciences of Complexity, Proceedings Volume 19. Reading, MA: Addison-Wesley.

Eagly, A. H., & Karau, S. J. (1991). Gender and the emergence of leaders: A meta-analysis. *Journal of Personality and Social Psychology*, *60*, 685–710.

Eldredge, N., & Gould, S. J. (1972). Punctuated equilibria: An alternative to phyletic gradualism. In T. J. M. Schopf (Ed.), *Models in paleobiology* (pp. 82–115). San Francisco: Freeman, Cooper, & Co.

Gersick, C. J. G. (1988). Time and transition in work teams: Toward a new model of group development. *Academy of Management Journal, 31,* 9–41.

Gersick, C. J. G. (1989). Marking time: Predictable transitions in task groups. *Academy of Management Journal, 32,* 274–309.

Gersick, C. J. G. (1991). Revolutionary change theories: A multilevel exploration of the punctuated equilibrium paradigm. *Academy of Management Review, 16,* 10–36.

Gersick, C. J. G., & Hackman, J. R. (1990). Habitual routines in task-performing groups. *Organizational Behavior and Human Decision Processes, 47,* 65–97.

Goerner, S. (1994). *Chaos and the evolving ecological universe.* Langhorne, PA: Gordon & Breach.

Gould, S. J. (1989). Punctuated equilibrium in fact and theory. *Journal of Social Biological Structure, 12,* 117–136.

Hannan, M. T., & Freeman, J. (1977). The population ecology of organizations. *American Journal of Sociology, 82,* 929–964.

Hannan, M. T., & Freeman, J. (1984). Structural inertia and organizational change. *American Sociological Review, 49,* 149–164.

Haveman, H. A. (1992). Between a rock and a hard place: Organizational change and performance under conditions of fundamental environmental transformation. *Administrative Science Quarterly, 37,* 48–75.

Hill, W. F., & Gruner, L. (1973). A study of development in open and closed groups. *Small Group Behavior, 4,* 355–381.

Homans, G. C. (1950). *The human group.* New York: Harcourt, Brace & World.

Hubert, L., & Schultz, J. (1976). Quadratic assignment as a general data analysis strategy. *British Journal of Mathematical and Statistical Psychology, 29,* 190–241.

Hulin, C. L., & Roznowski, M. (1985). Organizational technologies: Effects on organizations' characteristics and individuals' responses. In B. M. Staw & L. L. Cummings (Eds.), *Research in Organizational Behavior, 7,* 39–85. Greenwich, CT: JAI Press.

Katz, D., & Kahn, R. L. (1978). *The social psychology of organizations* (2nd ed.). New York: Wiley.

Kelso, J. A. S. (1995). *Dynamic patterns: The self-organization of brain and behavior.* Cambridge, MA: MIT Press.

Kendall, M. G. (1963). *Rank correlation methods* (3rd ed.). London: Griffin.

Kiesler, S., & Sproull, S. (1992). Group decision making and communication technology. *Organizational Behavior and Human Decision Processes, 52,* 96–123.

LaCoursiere, R. B. (1980). *The life cycle of groups: Group developmental stage theory.* New York: Human Sciences Press.

Lawrence, P. R., & Lorsch, J. W. (1967). *Organization and environment.* Boston: Harvard University Press.

Levine, J. M., & Moreland, R. L. (1990). Progress in small group research. *Annual Review of Psychology, 41,* 585–634.

Lewin, K. (1951). *Field theory in social science.* Westport, CT: Greenwood Press.

Linville, P. W., & Jones, E. E. (1980). Polarized appraisals of out-group members. *Journal of Personality and Social Psychology, 38,* 689–703.

Mann, R. D., Gibbard, G. S., & Hartman, J. J. (1967). *Interpersonal styles and group development.* New York: Wiley.

McCollom, M. (1995). Reevaluating group development: A critique of familiar models. In J. Gillette & M. McCollom (Eds.), *Groups in context: A new perspective on group dynamics* (pp. 133–154). Lanham, MD: University Press of America.

McGrath, J. E. (1991). Time, interaction, and performance (TIP): A theory of groups. *Small Group Research, 22,* 147–174.

McGrath, J. E. (1993). The JEMCO workshop: Description of a longitudinal study. *Small Group Research, 24,* 285–306.

McGrath, J. E., Berdahl, J. L., & Arrow, H. (1996). Traits, expectations, culture and clout: The dynamics of diversity in work groups. In S. E. Jackson & M. N. Ruderman (Eds.), *Diversity in work teams: Research paradigms for a changing workplace* (pp. 17–45). Washington, DC: American Psychological Association.

McGrath, J. E., & Hollingshead, A. B. (1994). *Groups interacting with technology.* Newbury Park, CA: Sage.

McGrath, J. E., & O'Connor, K. M. (1996). Temporal issues in work groups. In M. West (Ed.), *Handbook of work group psychology* (pp. 25–52). London: Wiley.

Mennecke, B. E., Hoffer, J. A., & Wynne, B. E. (1992). The implications of group development and history for group support system theory and practice. *Small Group Research, 23,* 524–572.

Miller, D., & Friesen, P. H. (1980). Momentum and revolution in organizational adaptation. *Academy of Management Journal, 23,* 591–614.

O'Connor, K. M., Gruenfeld, D. H. & McGrath, J. E. (1993). The experience and effects of conflict in continuing work groups. *Small Group Research, 24,* 362–382.

Pfeffer, J., & Salancik, G. R. (1978). *The external control of organizations: A resource dependence perspective.* New York: Harper & Row.

Poole, M. S., & Roth, J. (1989a). Decision development in small groups: IV. A typology of decision paths. *Human Communication Research, 15,* 323–356.

Poole, M. S., & Roth, J. (1989b). Decision development in small groups: V. Test of a contingency model. *Human Communication Research, 15,* 549–589.

Ridgeway, C. (1991). The social construction of status value: Gender and other nominal characteristics. *Social Forces, 70,* 367–386.

SAS Institute, Inc. (1989). *SAS/STAT® User's Guide* (Version 6, 4th ed., Vol. 2). Cary, NC: Author.

Shiffrin, R. M., & Schneider, W. (1977). Controlled and automatic human information processing: II. Perceptual learning, automatic attending, and a general theory. *Psychological Review, 84,* 127–190.

Smith, C., & Gemmill, G. (1991). Change in the small group: A dissipative structure perspective. *Human Relations, 44,* 697–716.

Steiner, I. D. (1972). *Group process and productivity.* New York: Academic Press.

Tajfel, H., & Turner, J. C. (1986). The social identity theory of intergroup behavior. In S. Worchel & W. G. Austin (Eds.),

Psychology of intergroup relations (2nd ed., pp. 7–24). Chicago: Nelson-Hall.

Trist, E. L., & Bamforth, K. W. (1951). Some social and psychological consequences of the longwall methods of coal-getting. *Human Relations*, *4*, 3–38.

Tuckman, B. W. (1965). Developmental sequence in small groups. *Psychological Bulletin*, *63*, 384–399.

Tuckman, B. W., & Jensen, M. A. C. (1977). Stages of small-group development revisited. *Group & Organization Studies*, *2*, 419–427.

Tushman, M. L., & Romanelli, E. (1985). Organizational evolution: A metamorphosis model of convergence and reorientation. In B. M. Staw & L. L. Cummings (Eds.), *Research in Organizational Behavior*, *7*, 171–222. Greenwich, CT: JAI Press.

von Bertalanffy, L. (1968). *General systems theory* (Rev. ed.). New York: George Braziller.

Vroom, V. H., & Yetton, P. W. (1973). *Leadership and decision making*. Pittsburgh, PA: University of Pittsburgh Press.

Wanous, J. P., Reichers, A. E., & Malik, S. D. (1984). Organizational socialization and group development: Toward an integrative perspective. *Academy of Management Review*, *9*, 670–683.

Whetten, D. A. (1987). Organizational growth and decline processes. *Annual Review of Sociology*, *13*, 335–358.

Worchel, S. (1994). You can go home again: Returning group research to the group context with an eye on developmental issues. *Small Group Research*, *25*, 205–223.

Zucker, L. G. (1977). The role of institutionalization in cultural persistence. *American Sociological Review*, *42*, 726–743.

Zucker, L. G. (1987). Institutional theories of organization. *Annual Review of Sociology*, *13*, 443–464.

Received January 30, 1996
Revision received July 26, 1996
Accepted July 26, 1996 ■

Socialization in Organizations and Work Groups

Richard L. Moreland and John M. Levine*

Socialization is a process of mutual adjustment that produces changes over time in the relationship between a person and a group. Because socialization occurs in groups of many kinds, it has been analyzed by scholars from many disciplines and professions (Bell & Price, 1975; Putallaz & Wasserman; 1990; Scott & Scott, 1989). Much of the best work, though, has been done by organizational psychologists. The purpose of this chapter is to offer a fresh perspective on that work by emphasizing the role of work groups in the socialization process. We begin with a brief review of recent theory and research on organizational socialization, focusing on the tactics used by organizations and their employees, and on commitment, the emotional bond that links organizations and employees to one another. Next, we make two surprising claims about organizational socialization, namely that it occurs largely in work groups, and that it is less important than work group socialization. These claims reflect clear evidence that much of what organizations and employees know about each other is learned in the context of work groups, and that work groups have a stronger influence than organizations on the behavior of most employees. Finally, we describe a model of group socialization (Moreland & Levine, 1982) that is relevant to work groups and could thus enhance many analyses of organizational socialization.

Theoretical and empirical work on that model is reviewed, and some issues regarding the model's application to work groups is discussed.

Organizational Socialization: A Brief Review

Several good reviews of theory and research on organizational socialization are available (e.g., Anderson & Thomas, 1996; Ashford & Taylor, 1990; Bauer, Morrison, & Callister, 1998; Fisher, 1986; Saks & Ashforth, 1997; Wanous & Colella, 1989), so we focus here on three topics that seem especially important. First, what tactics do organizations use during the socialization process, and how successful are they at achieving their socialization goals? Second, what tactics do new employees use during the socialization process, and how successfully are their socialization goals achieved? Finally, what is commitment, how does it arise, and how does it affect employees' behavior?

Organizational Tactics

Many socialization tactics can be used by organizations. One way to study such tactics is to consider the underlying strategies that they reflect. This can be accomplished by first examining the

* University of Pittsburgh.

relationships among socialization tactics and then considering their strategic implications. Several studies of this sort can be found (e.g., Allen & Meyer, 1990; Ashforth & Saks, 1996; Baker, 1995; Baker & Feldman, 1990; Black & Ashford, 1995; Jones, 1986; Mignerey, Rubin, & Gorden, 1995; Zahrly & Tosi, 1989). In this work, descriptions by new employees of the socialization tactics used in their organizations were analyzed using a set of dimensions proposed by Van Maanen and Schein (1979; see also Van Maanen, 1978). Those dimensions are collective versus individual, formal versus informal, sequential versus random, fixed versus variable, serial versus disjunctive, and investiture versus divestiture. Collective tactics provide newcomers with shared experiences during socialization, whereas individual tactics allow socialization experiences to vary from one newcomer to another. Formal tactics involve structured training that occurs outside the workplace, whereas informal tactics involve unstructured training that occurs while newcomers are on the job. Sequential and fixed tactics, as opposed to random and variable tactics, clarify for newcomers what steps socialization requires and how long the process takes. Serial tactics use old-timers to train newcomers for familiar jobs, whereas disjunctive tactics force newcomers to learn about the familiar jobs on their own. Finally, investiture tactics affirm newcomers by suggesting that they are already valuable to the organization, whereas divestiture tactics challenge newcomers by suggesting that their value depends on completing the socialization process successfully.

These dimensions are interdependent, and their relationships can be informative. Jones (1986), for example, identified two clusters of socialization tactics that may reflect distinct organizational strategies. When *institutional tactics* (collective, formal, sequential, fixed, serial, and investiture) are used by an organization, newcomers are more likely to adopt a custodial role orientation, viewing socialization as a process requiring personal rather than organizational change (see Nicholson, 1984). But when an organization uses *individual tactics* (individual, informal, variable, random, disjunctive, and divestiture), newcomers are more likely to adopt an innovative role orientation, viewing socialization as a process that requires some organizational change as well. The available evidence confirms these role orientation effects and suggests that institutional tactics can also improve the organizational commitment and job attitudes of newcomers. However, these and other effects are often weak, depend on just a few tactics within each cluster, and fade over time. And there is little evidence that other important outcomes, such as job performance, absenteeism, or turnover, are affected by the use of institutional versus individual tactics.

A more direct way to study the tactics that organizations use during socialization is to focus on specific tactics and examine their effects. Much of this work involves four tactics: orientation sessions, training programs, mentoring, and information dissemination. In many organizations, special orientation sessions are held to welcome newcomers, educate them about the organization, and perhaps strengthen their organizational commitment. These are often formal, ritualistic events (Trice & Beyer, 1984), but they can be informal as well, and they need not be pleasant. Initiations are orientations of a sort, for example, and they can be traumatic (see Rohlen, 1973). Orientation sessions seem to be a common socialization tactic, yet employees do not view such sessions as helpful, nor is there much evidence for their benefits (see Louis, Posner, & Powell, 1983; Nelson & Quick, 1991; Posner & Powell, 1985; Saks, 1994; Wanous, 1993). And although there are good reasons to believe that initiating newcomers could be useful, perhaps by strengthening organizational commitment through the resolution of cognitive dissonance, the evidence is again weak. For example, Feldman (1977) asked hospital employees to recall events during socialization that they regarded as initiations into their jobs or their work groups. Employees who experienced initiations were no more likely than others to feel competent at their jobs or accepted by their work groups. There is even some evidence that stressful initiations can weaken commitment to a group (Lodewijkz & Syroit, 1997).

Training programs are designed primarily to help employees acquire or improve job skills, a goal that is often achieved (Grant, 1995; Guzzo,

Jette, & Katzell, 1985). But as Feldman (1989) and others have noted, training can play a role in socialization as well, whether it is meant to or not. Training has some symbolic value—the resources spent on training send messages to newcomers about their potential value to an organization and can thus affect their organizational commitment. And newcomers can learn much about their organization from the ways in which it trains them. Is the training well organized? Who are the trainers? How challenging is the training? What does the organization expect from employees, and what happens if its expectations are not met? Finally, when a training program succeeds, newcomers' job skills improve, so they feel less anxious, more self-confident, and so on. These changes could also affect the socialization process and its outcomes. How important are training programs for socialization? Most organizations offer their employees no training at all, and employees who are trained seldom view that experience as helpful (Louis et al., 1983; Nelson & Quick, 1991). However, some studies suggest that training can be a useful socialization tactic (Saks, 1995, 1996; Tannenbaum, Mathieu, Salas, & Cannon-Bowers, 1991). Saks (1996), for example, asked new accountants from several companies how much training they received and how helpful it was to them. Both of these variables had beneficial effects on such socialization outcomes as organizational commitment, job satisfaction, and turnover intentions. Training also helped newcomers to feel less anxious, which may explain why it improved some of their other outcomes. Few of these effects were strong, but they do show that training programs can be useful socialization tools.

Mentoring occurs when older employees (mentors) develop special helping relationships with younger employees (protégés). Mentors can help their protégés in many ways (Kram, 1988). For example, they can provide training, reveal hidden aspects of an organization, interpret ambiguous work experiences, act as advocates or guardians, and offer sympathy. Such help makes new employees more likely to succeed (see, for example, Whitely & Coetsier, 1993), in part by improving their socialization. Although mentoring is a natural phenomenon, there are ways in which it might be managed by organizations. When these management attempts succeed, mentoring becomes a socialization tactic. For example, an organization can encourage mentoring by educating employees about benefits, by providing models of successful mentor/protégé relationships, by rewarding mentors for their helpfulness, and so on (Kram, 1985). A more direct approach is to match protégés with mentors and then try to regulate their relationships with one another. Guidelines for mentoring programs can be found in several sources (e.g., Lawrie, 1987; Phillips-Jones, 1983; Zey, 1985), along with descriptions of some actual programs (e.g., Geiger-Dumond & Boyle, 1995). These programs raise complex issues, such as who should participate, how protégés and mentors are best matched, what mentoring activities to prescribe, and how to respond if mentoring relationships fail. If such issues are not resolved, a mentoring program will be ineffective and may even do more harm than good. Mentoring programs *can* succeed (Noe, 1988), of course, but a revealing study by Chao, Walz, and Gardner (1992) suggested that informal mentoring relationships may be more helpful to newcomers than formal relationships that are created through mentoring programs (see also Kizilos, 1990). In fact, doubts about the value of such programs have led Kram (1985) and others to argue that most organizations should just encourage mentoring, rather than trying to regulate it.

Finally, the dissemination of information to new employees is another socialization tactic that can be used by organizations. Through newsletters, bulletin boards, mailings (paper or electronic), manuals, and special reports, organizations can distribute information of several kinds, including news, announcements of organizational policies and goals, descriptions of employee benefits or services, suggestions for improving job performance, and so on. Few researchers have studied the effects of such information on newcomers (see Jablin, 1987), but the available evidence is not encouraging. Jablin (1984), for example, found that new employees in nursing homes wanted more information about their jobs than they actually received. And even when organizations provide information to newcomers, it may not be very help-ful. Burke and Bolf (1986) asked employees from several organizations to recall how valuable infor-mation obtained from different sources was for learning their jobs. The information that employees received from their organizations (e.g., reports, manuals, public relations materials) was evaluated less positively than information from other sources, such as supervisors and coworkers. Similar results were later reported by Ostroff and Kozlowski (1992) and Kramer (1993a).

Several socialization tactics are thus available to organizations, but just how successful are most organizations at achieving their socialization goals? Research on the socialization strategies and tac-tics used by organizations indicates that their impact on new employees is weak. Other evidence also suggests that organizations are not socializ-ing their employees effectively. For example, Reichheld (1996) argued that years of downsizing have produced a loyalty crisis in many American corporations—employees no longer feel very com-mitted to the organizations for which they work. Robinson and Rousseau (1994), in fact, showed that soon after most employees are hired, they come to believe that the implicit contracts governing their employment were violated. They lose trust in their organizations as a result and may decide to break such contracts themselves. Finally, many organizations struggle to cope with high levels of turnover among new employees (see Chao, 1988; Wanous, 1992), who may well misbehave before they leave by indulging in absenteeism, substance abuse, sabotage, or theft (Crino, 1994; DuPont, 1989; Jones & Boye, 1994). An organization can always modify its socialization tactics, of course, in an effort to achieve better outcomes. Wanous (1993) and Kram (1985), for example, have offered sug-gestions for improvements in orientation sessions and mentoring, respectively. But given the appar-ent difficulty of socializing new employees effec-tively, it may be wiser for most organizations to emphasize recruiting instead (Chatman, 1991; Schneider, Goldstein, & Smith, 1995; see also Mulford, Klonglan, Beal, & Bohlen, 1968; Mulford, Klonglan, & Warren, 1972), searching for workers who already have whatever qualities

are desired. Recent work on how to identify work-ers whose experiences or personalities incline them to become more committed to organiza-tions reflects this alternative (see, for example, James & Cropanzano, 1994; Lee, Ashford, Walsh, & Mowday, 1992; Mael & Ashforth, 1995).

Tactics of New Employees

Because new employees tend to be younger, less experienced, and lower in status than other work-ers, one might assume that they have little influence on the socialization process, but that would be a mistake (see Bell & Staw, 1989; Jablin, 1984). In fact, newcomers can influence socialization in both unintentional and intentional ways (see Levine, Moreland, & Choi, in press). Unintentional influ-ence occurs when organizations change their socialization tactics to accommodate newcomers of different types, or when different types of new-comers respond to the same socialization tactics in distinct ways. Effects of both kinds could involve many personal characteristics (e.g., sex, prior job experience, status), but most researchers have focused on newcomers' personalities. Self-efficacy, for instance, can apparently influence socialization by shaping the role orientations of newcomers (Brief & Aldag, 1981; Jones, 1986; Saks, 1994; 1995). Jones found that the use of institutional tac-tics by organizations was more likely to produce custodial role orientations among newcomers with lower levels of self-efficacy. Similarly, Saks (1994) found that training had stronger effects on new-comers' coping abilities, job performance, and turnover intentions when their levels of self-efficacy were lower. Other personality characteristics, such as a tolerance for ambiguity (Ashford & Cummings, 1985; Reichers, 1987) or self-monitoring (Snyder, 1995), might influence the socialization process as well. For example, newcomers with higher self-monitoring levels may know more about what organizations want from them and may be more willing or able to provide it (cf. Zaccaro, Foti, & Kenny, 1991).

New employees can also influence the socializa-tion process intentionally through their own tactics. Several complex analyses of these socialization tactics can be found (Ashford & Taylor, 1990; Comer, 1991; Feldman & Brett, 1983; Miller & Jablin, 1991), but for our purposes, a simple summary may be sufficient—newcomers can engage in surveillance or feedback seeking, encourage mentoring by oldtimers, or collaborate with one another.

A careful surveillance of people and events in an organization can be very helpful to new employees (see Gundry & Rousseau, 1994). Newcomers who watch what happens to other workers, for example, can often benefit from observational learning, acquiring new behaviors and accepting those most likely to be rewarded. Anyone can serve as a model for newcomers, but they tend to observe and imitate people who appear competent or successful (Weiss, 1977). Surveillance also allows for social comparison, especially with other newcomers who seem particularly successful (upward comparisons) or unsuccessful (downward comparisons). Either type of comparison can be encouraging or discouraging, depending on the target person. Upward comparisons are encouraging, and downward comparisons are discouraging, if newcomers identify with that person and thus believe that they could experience similar outcomes. But upward and downward comparisons have the opposite effects if newcomers do not identify with the target person. Finally, surveillance helps newcomers to develop and test mental models of the workplace (see Cannon-Bowers, Tannenbaum, Salas, & Volpe, 1995; Louis, 1980). As those models improve, they generate more accurate predictions about life at work, building newcomers' confidence and helping them adjust to their jobs.

Surveillance is relatively easy and tends to be covert, so that newcomers can hide their lack of knowledge about the organization from others. A more dangerous tactic, but one that often provides more information, is feedback seeking. Newcomers can and do ask a variety of questions during socialization. Miller and Jablin (1991) asserted that newcomers seek answers to three types of questions, namely referent (*What does it take to succeed?*), appraisal (*Am I successful?*), and relational (*Am I accepted?*). Unfortunately, there may be costs associated with asking these and other questions (Ashford & Cummings, 1983). For example,

Morrison and Bies (1991) suggested that the mere act of asking appraisal questions can affect how newcomers are viewed by others. Under some conditions, they may seem ignorant and insecure, whereas under other conditions, they may seem conscientious and eager to improve. And of course, the answers to appraisal questions are important as well. If newcomers receive negative feedback, for example, their reputations can be damaged, along with their self-esteem. Information, in other words, usually comes at a price. Miller and Jablin described some ways in which newcomers can make feedback seeking less costly. These include asking questions indirectly, starting and/or joining casual conversations about work (which might produce answers to questions not yet asked), and talking with outsiders who are familiar with the organization (e.g., customers, suppliers, union officials).

As noted earlier, mentoring can also help new employees to succeed, but some workers (especially women and minorities) may have trouble finding older colleagues who are willing and able to become their mentors. That is one reason why many organizations have tried to develop formal mentoring programs. Is there anything that newcomers could do to attract mentors on their own? If so, then mentoring could become a socialization tactic for them. Unfortunately, the development of mentoring relationships is rarely studied, so very little is known about this tactic. Kram (1983) interviewed mentors and protégés in a public utility firm and found that their relationships often began when young workers fantasized about working closely with older colleagues whom they admired and respected. If opportunities for such collaboration later arose, a mentoring relationship often developed, especially when the senior person seemed interested in his or her partner and was asked for advice or aid by that person. Additional insights into the development of mentoring relationships may come from work on leader–member exchange theory (see Dienesch & Liden, 1986; Scandura & Schriesheim, 1994). Leaders can relate to followers in different ways—"outgroup" relationships are much less collegial than "ingroup" relationships, which resemble mentoring relationships. Several studies have shown that leaders tend to develop ingroup relationships with followers who seem competent, similar to themselves, and likable (Deluga & Perry, 1994; Dockery & Steiner, 1990; Liden, Wayne, & Stilwell, 1993; Wayne & Ferris, 1990; see also Tepper, 1995). In a study of employees in several organizations, for example, Deluga and Perry found that better quality relationships arose between supervisors and their subordinates when the latter workers performed their jobs well and used various ingratiation tactics, such as flattering supervisors and agreeing with their opinions. These findings suggest that new employees may indeed use mentoring as a socialization tactic, if older colleagues who would make good mentors are available and newcomers can impress them favorably.

Finally, when several new employees enter an organization at about the same time, they can collaborate with one another to make the socialization process easier. Newcomers may, for example, offer one another information, advice, encouragement, aid, and protection. In these and other ways, they can become "mentors" for one another, especially when regular mentors are unavailable (Kram & Isabella, 1985; Ostroff & Kozlowski, 1993). Collaboration is not inevitable—newcomers who believe they are competing for acceptance by oldtimers may treat one another harshly. But more often, newcomers seem willing to help each other, perhaps because the fact that they are all "new" is so salient (see Moreland, 1985). When newcomers are similar to one another, spend much time together, and are treated alike by oldtimers, they could form a group of their own, embedded in the organization (Feldman, 1989). Such a group can be valuable, because its members are especially likely to help one another (Dornbusch, 1955). But a group of newcomers might also develop its own special culture, which may be incongruent with that of the organization and thus interfere with the socialization process. In fact, if a group of newcomers becomes cohesive and its members are sufficiently disenchanted with the organization, they may even work together to demand that it change (see Dunham & Barrett, 1996).

New employees, like the organizations for which they work, thus have access to several socialization tactics, but how successful are most newcomers at achieving their socialization goals? The evidence we mentioned earlier, indicating that turnover and misbehavior among employees are serious problems in many organizations, implies that newcomers often fail to adjust to work. The socialization tactics used by newcomers may contribute to this problem—research suggests that those tactics are seldom effective. Ostroff and Kozlowski (1992), for example, found that although surveillance (observing others and experimentation) was a popular tactic among newcomers, its use was unrelated to their organizational commitment, job satisfaction, work adjustment, or turnover intentions. Moreover, newcomers who used that tactic experienced greater stress than those who did not. Many researchers have also studied how feedback seeking affects newcomers' socialization outcomes. Although some studies suggest that this tactic is beneficial (Morrison, 1993a, 1993b), its effects are rather weak, and other studies show no benefits at all (Ashford & Black, 1996; Brett, Feldman, & Weingart, 1990; Mignery et al., 1995). Kramer (1993a) actually found that the adjustment of transferred employees improved only when they received feedback that was unsolicited! Mentoring is obviously useful, but only for those few newcomers lucky enough to become protégés. There is little evidence as yet that mentoring can be tactical—even competent and likable newcomers may have difficulty establishing mentoring relationships. Finally, collaboration among newcomers can be problematic as well. Newcomers may have limited contact with one another, for example, or believe that it is better to compete rather than cooperate. Even when collaboration is possible, it may be unwise for newcomers to rely on each other for advice or information, because they usually know far less than other employees about the organization. In fact, when researchers ask newcomers to evaluate their socialization experiences, collaboration is not described as very helpful (Louis et al., 1983; Nelson & Quick, 1991; see also Settoon & Adkins, 1997).

Commitment

Commitment plays a vital role in socialization because it links organizations to employees emotionally and thus provides the conduit through which influence flows in either direction. Perhaps for that reason, commitment has become a very popular topic, producing far more theoretical and empirical work than we can consider here. Guest (1992), Mathieu and Zajac (1990), Morrow (1993), and Randall (1990) offer summaries of that work. Commitment is generally regarded as a characteristic of employees rather than organizations; researchers study how employees feel about their organizations, not how organizations feel about their employees. Much of the interest in commitment also appears to be pragmatic; researchers study commitment because of its potential value to organizations. When employees feel more committed to an organization, they are more likely to act in ways that could help that organization achieve its goals. Evidence suggests that employee commitment is indeed an asset for organizations because it is related to several desirable outcomes, such as higher levels of motivation, satisfaction, and prosocial behavior; better job performance; and less tardiness, absenteeism, and turnover. Two caveats regarding this evidence should be noted, however. First, commitment has much weaker effects on some outcomes (e.g., job performance) than on others (e.g., satisfaction), and its effects often seem inconsistent, varying from one setting to another (see Randall, Fedor, & Longenecker, 1990). Second, commitment is more complex than it once appeared. It is now clear that there are different components (dimensions) of organizational commitment, that someone could be committed to many groups in and around an organization, and that commitment to an organization can change in important ways over time. Each of these discoveries deserves some discussion.

Early analyses of commitment (see Mowday, Steers, & Porter, 1979) implied that it was a unidimensional construct, but most theorists now see it as multidimensional. O'Reilly and Chatman (1986), for example, argued that compliance, identification, and internalization are three bases for the attachment of employees to organizations. Compliance involves a desire for the extrinsic rewards of employment, identification involves a desire to affiliate with the organization and other employees,

and internalization involves congruence between personal and organizational values. There is some evidence that these are indeed distinct aspects of commitment (see Harris, Hirschfeld, Feild, & Mossholder, 1993), although identification and internalization can be difficult to distinguish. These three aspects of commitment do seem to have different antecedents and consequences as well. Caldwell, Chatman, and O'Reilly (1990), for example, found that identification and internalization reflect rigorous recruitment and selection procedures and value systems in organizations, whereas compliance reflects strong career and reward systems. And the effects of identification and internalization on such employee outcomes as job satisfaction, prosocial behavior, and turnover are more positive than the effects of compliance on those same outcomes (Becker, 1992; Becker, Randall, & Riegel, 1995; Harris et al., 1993). Another analysis, by Meyer and Allen (1991), distinguished among affective, continuance, and normative commitment. Affective commitment involves emotional attachment to, identification with, and involvement in an organization. Continuance commitment involves the perceived costs of leaving an organization. Normative commitment involves feelings of obligation to stay in an organization. There is evidence that these three aspects of commitment are also distinct (Dunham, Grube, & Castaneda, 1994; Hackett, Bycio, & Hausdorf, 1994; Meyer, Allen, & Gellatly, 1990) and that they have separate antecedents and consequences as well (Meyer, Bobocel, & Allen, 1991; Meyer, Paunonen, Gellatly, Goffin, & Jackson, 1989; Randall et al., 1990). For example, affective commitment reflects positive work experiences, continuance commitment reflects investments (e.g., pension contributions) or employment alternatives, and normative commitment reflects personal values (e.g., loyalty). Job performance relates positively to affective commitment and negatively to continuance commitment, whereas prosocial behavior relates positively to both affective and normative commitment, but not to continuance commitment.

Although Meyer and Allen's (1991) analysis of commitment has generated more research than

O'Reilly and Chatman's (1986) analysis, it would be difficult to choose which approach is "best" at this point. Each approach has its critics (see Jaros, Jermier, Koehler, & Sincich, 1993; Vandenberg, Self, & Seo, 1994), and there are several other analyses of commitment that also seem worthy of consideration. For example, some analysts view commitment as a set of positive employee behaviors that reflect efforts to cope with the decision to work for one organization rather than another (see Salancik, 1977). This approach, based loosely on cognitive dissonance theory, suggests that commitment should be stronger when decisions about jobs are made publicly and voluntarily and seem irrevocable. These factors do appear to influence commitment in these ways (Kline & Peters, 1991). In contrast, Rusbult and her colleagues analyzed commitment from the perspective of social exchange theory. According to their approach, commitment to an organization is stronger when work satisfaction is high (employment generates more rewards than costs), employment alternatives are unattractive, and large investments have been made. Investments are resources that an employee could not recover if he or she left the organization; they may be intrinsic to work (e.g., time and energy spent on the job) or extrinsic (e.g., friendships with other employees). Evidence for this analysis of commitment can also be found (Farrell & Rusbult, 1981; Rusbult & Farrell, 1983; Rusbult, Farrell, Rogers, & Mainous, 1988). Finally, Ashforth and Mael (1989; see also Dutton, Dukerich, & Harquail, 1994) suggested that organizational identification may be more important than commitment for predicting many employee outcomes. Their analysis, drawn from social identity and self-categorization theory, emphasizes cognitive rather than emotional processes, especially the tendency for some employees to incorporate distinctive characteristics of organizations into their self-concepts. Research exploring the causes and effects of organizational identification has produced intriguing results (see Mael & Ashforth, 1995; Mael & Tetrick, 1992).

The discovery that commitment to an organization can take different forms, each with its own effects on employees' outcomes, is clearly important. Another discovery that may be just as important had its origins in a paper by Reichers (1985), who argued that multiple commitments can affect the outcomes of many employees. Employees may feel committed not only to the organization where they work, but also to other entities in and around that organization, such as work groups, supervisors, top management, clients, unions, friends or family members, and so on. A particular outcome, such as turnover, can thus depend not only on organizational commitment, but also on these other commitments. This suggests a need to develop *commitment profiles* for employees, so that better predictions can be made about their outcomes. Becker and his colleagues created such profiles and used them successfully in a series of studies (Becker, 1992; Becker & Billings, 1993; Becker, Billings, Eveleth, & Gilbert, 1996; Becker et al., 1995). Becker (1992), for example, found that commitments to work groups, supervisors, and top management were related to a variety of employee outcomes, including job satisfaction, prosocial behavior, and interest in quitting, even after organizational commitment was taken into account. The existence of multiple commitments also suggests a need to explore the ways in which they are related to one another. Reichers (1986) noted that such commitments can create both psychological and social conflicts for employees and that work outcomes may well depend on how those conflicts are resolved. The complex relationships among commitments to organizations and other entities have been studied recently by some researchers (e.g., Hunt & Morgan, 1994; Yoon, Baker, & Ko, 1994). We will discuss that work later, as it applies to the feelings of employees about organizations versus work groups.

Finally, it is essential to realize that commitment changes in important ways over time. This discovery may seem prosaic at first, because an employee's commitment is probably always rising or falling in response to events at work. But consider how complex changes in commitment might become in the context of the other discoveries just discussed. Over time, different aspects of commitment could change independently, some rising and others falling (Allen & Meyer, 1993).

In fact, changes could even occur in the whole structure of commitment, making it difficult to compare an employee's feelings about an organization at different points in his or her career (see Meyer et al., 1990; Vandenberg & Self, 1993). Similarly, commitments to different entities could change independently (Gregersen, 1993), and the number or kinds of entities to which someone feels committed could change too, altering the relative impact of that person's organizational commitment on various work outcomes. The implications of these and other changes for socialization are just beginning to be explored, but they seem important.

Socialization in Work Groups

As this brief review suggests, much has been learned about organizational socialization, especially in recent years. This progress reflects a general willingness among researchers to acknowledge the problems apparent in earlier work and then modify their methodologies in ways that help to solve those problems. For example, a common feature of earlier work on organizational socialization was a narrow *temporal perspective* that led most researchers to focus on the entry experiences of new employees. These experiences are important, of course, but they are only part of a larger socialization process and thus should be analyzed in broader and more complex ways. Fortunately, this problem has become less serious as more longitudinal studies of organizational socialization are performed. Several examples of such studies can now be found (e.g., Bauer & Green, 1994; Nelson, Quick, & Eakin, 1988; Nelson & Sutton, 1990; Settoon & Adkins, 1997; Vandenberg & Self, 1993), and their results provide insights into the socialization process. Another problematic feature of earlier work on organizational socialization was a narrow *social perspective* that led most researchers to study how organizations influence new employees, rather than how new employees try to influence their organizations. But this problem has also become less serious, as more researchers study newcomers' efforts to control the socialization process (e.g., Ashford & Black, 1996;

Fagenson, 1988; Wanous, 1989), and more theorists analyze ways in which that process can change work groups and organizations (see Feldman, 1994; Levine & Moreland, 1985; Levine et al., in press; Sutton & Louis, 1987).

Despite these and other improvements, organizational socialization research still suffers from several problems. An especially serious problem, in our opinion, is that the *contexts* in which such socialization occurs are ignored by many researchers. In particular, there is too little work on the important role that small work groups (formal or informal) can play in the socialization process (Anderson & Thomas, 1996). Although some theorists (e.g., Feldman, 1981, 1989; Van Maanen & Schein, 1979) have discussed that role, their remarks have not led to much research. We would like to make two claims about organizational socialization, claims that may seem surprising at first, but that are supported by considerable evidence. First, we believe that the socialization process occurs primarily in work groups, which can control what and how organizations and employees learn about one another. Second, we believe that work group socialization has a stronger impact than organizational socialization on the behavior of most employees.

Work Groups as Contexts for Organizational Socialization

Where does organizational socialization occur? Research on the socialization process is often decontextualized—contexts are either ignored or are assumed to have trivial effects. Organizations and their employees seem to influence one another directly in such research, as if each worker were involved in a close, personal relationship with his or her organization. But in most organizations, this is simply impossible. Instead, the relationships between an organization and its employees are usually more distant and impersonal. Such relationships can thus be shaped by various contextual factors. Small work groups, formal and informal, seem especially important in this regard. In fact, much evidence suggests that the process of organizational socialization occurs primarily within such groups.

A series of studies by Ancona and her colleagues (Ancona, 1990; Ancona & Caldwell, 1988, 1992) provide some evidence relevant to this claim. These studies investigate how work groups try to manage the flow of information and resources across their boundaries with other groups and individuals from the same organization. Boundary management can be accomplished in various ways, but many groups develop special activities and roles for this purpose. In a study of new product development teams, for example, Ancona and Caldwell (1988) found that *scout, ambassador, sentry*, and *guard activities* occurred more often in more successful teams and that workers from those teams were more likely to play *immigrant, captive*, and *emigrant* roles. Scouts gathered information for a group about the organization in which it operated, whereas ambassadors provided (favorable) information about the group to that organization. Sentries and guards controlled both the amount and type of information that entered or left a group, respectively. Finally, both immigrants and captives were employees from other parts of the organization who were brought into the group to reduce levels of uncertainty or dependence, whereas emigrants were employees sent out of the group to work elsewhere in the organization for similar reasons. These and other efforts by work groups to manage their boundaries (see also Sundstrom, deMeuse, & Futrell, 1990) have important implications for organizational socialization. To some extent, every group can control what the organization learns about an employee and what he or she learns about the organization by regulating the person's contacts with workers outside the group and restricting what information the person and the organization receive about each other (Feldman, 1981).

Another set of relevant findings comes from research on social information processing theory (see Salancik & Pfeffer, 1978; Zalesny & Ford, 1990). According to that theory, an employee's opinion about a job is often influenced by the opinions of his or her coworkers. Such influence can be direct, as when one group member persuades another to share his or her opinion about a job, or more indirect, as when someone in the group calls attention to specific job characteristics, offers explanations for events at work, reminds everyone about past events or generates expectations for future events, and so forth. It would not be surprising if employees' opinions about organizations were affected in similar ways. Organizations can be difficult to understand, making employees (especially newcomers) susceptible to social influence as they search for meaning in their work experiences (Louis, 1980). Even when work groups cannot control the flow of information across their boundaries, they can still alter the interpretation of that information and thereby influence the socialization process (Feldman, 1981). Messages from an organization to its employees, efforts to create new organizational programs or practices, and even evaluations of an organization by outsiders can thus vary considerably in their meaning or importance for employees in different work groups. Consider, for example, research by Fulk and her colleagues (Fulk, 1993; Schmitz & Fulk, 1991) on reactions to new communication technologies. After surveying scientists and engineers from several organizations, Fulk (1993) found that work group memberships were powerful predictors of attitudes and behavior toward electronic mail. Similar results involving other aspects of organizational life can be found in studies by Baba (1995) and Rentsch (1990).

Finally, there is good evidence that most of the tactics used by organizations and their employees during the socialization process depend on work groups. In some organizations, socialization is neglected, forcing employees to acquire whatever information they may need from other sources, such as coworkers or outsiders (Chao, 1988). And many organizations, using the socialization tactics described earlier, provide employees with information that is not very useful, because it is irrelevant, vague, or erroneous (Comer, 1991; Darrah, 1994; Dirsmith & Covaleski, 1985). Employees in such organizations must again depend on other sources, such as coworkers, for the information that they need. Organizational socialization tactics *can* provide employees with useful information, of course, but that information is usually delivered by supervisors and coworkers during work group interactions. Many new employees, for example, undergo work group initiations designed to test their commitment to those groups (see Vaught & Smith, 1980). And training in most organizations is rather informal, occurring while new employees are working at their jobs (Moreland, Argote, & Krishnan, 1998). Mentoring usually involves efforts by supervisors to help new employees who work for them (Kram, 1988), and information dissemination is often "aided" by social networks among employees (Noon & Delbridge, 1993). The socialization tactics used by new employees, including surveillance, feedback seeking, mentoring, and collaboration, also tend to occur in work groups, because they often involve supervisors or coworkers. Several researchers have surveyed new employees about their socialization experiences to discover which experiences were most helpful (Burke & Bolf, 1986; Comer, 1991; Louis et al., 1983; Nelson & Quick, 1991; Ostroff & Kozlowski, 1992, 1993). A very common finding in such research is that interactions with supervisors and coworkers are more helpful than experiences involving the organization as a whole. Many other studies (e.g., Chatman, 1991; Dansky, 1996; George & Bettenhausen, 1990; Kram & Isabella, 1985; Kramer, 1993a, 1993b; Morrison, 1993b) also show that coworkers are an integral part of the socialization process. Taken altogether, this work suggests that organizational socialization takes place largely in work groups.

Work Group Socialization is the Key

An organization can be viewed as a collection of allied work groups whose activities and outcomes are interdependent. This perspective reveals an important aspect of organizational socialization, namely that it can involve the passage of an employee through several groups, from the organization itself to the various work groups (formal and informal) that it contains. In a *holographic* organization (Albert & Whetten, 1985), work groups resemble one another because they embody the organization's central features, so socialization is relatively simple. An employee can relate to different groups (and they can relate to that person)

in similar ways. But in an *ideographic* organization, work groups tend to be more distinctive, making socialization more complex. Some theorists believe every work group is unique (see Levine & Moreland, 1991, 1999), but a more common claim is that the work groups in most organizations can be sorted into clusters or *subcultures*, each with a different approach to organizational life. Several analyses of organizational subcultures can be found (see Johns & Nicholson, 1982; Louis, 1983; Van Maanen & Barley, 1985), focusing on why they develop and how they affect organizations and employees. And several studies of organizational subcultures (e.g., Baba, 1995; Fulk, 1993; Gregory, 1983; Rentsch, 1980; Sackman, 1992) offer clear evidence for their existence and importance. Baba, for example, studied how employees in a large manufacturing corporation reacted to proposed changes in procedures for developing new products. Those reactions varied from one work group to another, and much of that variability reflected the "ecological zones" in which groups operated. Adaptations to local operating conditions apparently led groups from each zone to interpret the new procedures differently and to react to them accordingly.

All of this suggests that organizational socialization and work group socialization can be distinct processes for many employees. While organizations and employees are adjusting to one another, analogous adjustments are also occurring in work groups. This raises an interesting question: Which process is more important? Work group socialization seems more important to us for two related reasons. First, employees are generally more committed to their work groups than they are to their organizations. Second, work groups often have more influence on employees than do organizations. So, if the goal of studying socialization in organizations is to predict and/or control how employees think, feel, and act, then work groups and their members clearly deserve more attention.

Are employees really more committed to their work groups than to their organizations? There are several good reasons to suspect that work group commitment is stronger. Much of an employee's time, especially in this era of teamwork (see Lawler, Mohrman, & Ledford, 1992), is spent in work groups whose members become familiar and attractive as a result (Moreland & Beach, 1992). And in many organizations, employee compensation systems now take work group performance into account, making outcome dependence among group members a salient issue. Work groups are also more likely than organizations to satisfy the psychological needs of employees. These include the need to belong (Baumeister & Leary, 1995; see also Riordan & Griffeth, 1995), the need to be distinctive (Brewer, 1993), and the need to exert control (Lawler, 1992). Lawler, for example, noted that people typically have more control over group than organizational events, so they often feel more attached to groups than to organizations. Finally, organizational socialization can be stressful (Katz, 1985; Louis, 1980; Nelson, 1987), and coworkers, especially work group members, are an important source of encouragement, advice, and aid for employees who seek social support (Nelson et al., 1988; see also Nelson, Quick, & Joplin, 1991). We focused here on employees' commitment to work groups versus organizations, but work groups are probably more committed than organizations to employees as well, for many of the same reasons.

Few researchers have measured how committed employees are to both work groups *and* organizations, but the available evidence suggests that work group commitment is stronger. Zaccaro and Dobbins (1989), for example, found that group commitment was stronger than organizational commitment among college students in a military training program. Becker (1992) studied the employees of a military supply company, measuring their commitments (both levels and types) to the organization, its top management, and their supervisors and work groups. Commitment to work groups was stronger than commitment to supervisors, top management, or the organization. In a similar study of hospital workers, Gregersen (1993) found that their commitment to customers and coworkers was stronger than their commitment to supervisors, top management, or the organization. Finally, Barker and Tompkins (1994) found that employees in a small manufacturing organization were more

committed to their work groups (self-managed teams) than to the organization as a whole.

More research of this sort is clearly needed, especially concerning whether different *types* of commitment link employees to work groups and organizations. A related issue is how work group and organizational commitment are related to one another. Commitment to a work group could strengthen or weaken an employee's commitment to the organization in which that group is embedded. Or work group and organizational commitment could be unrelated, with distinct causes and effects. The available evidence, although complex and often difficult to interpret, suggests that work group and organizational commitment are indeed independent in many settings (see Becker & Billings, 1993; Hunt & Morgan, 1994; Mathieu, 1991; Meyer & Allen, 1988; Randall & Cote, 1991; Wright, 1990; Yoon et al., 1994; Zaccaro & Dobbins, 1989; see also Mathieu & Zajac, 1990; Reichers, 1986). Apparently, commitment to work groups has little impact on the organizational commitment of most employees and vice versa.

Are employees really more influenced by their work groups than by their organizations? The fact that work group commitment is often stronger than organizational commitment is one reason to suspect that they are. Another reason is that coworkers, because they have more contact with an employee than anyone else in the organization, are more capable of monitoring that person's behavior and taking corrective action when necessary. Finally, some theorists (Ashforth & Mael, 1989; Feldman, 1981; Fisher, 1986; Katz, 1985; see also Feldman, 1976; Ostroff & Kozlowski, 1992) argue that adjusting to work groups is an early, critical step in organizational socialization. There is much to learn about every work group (see Cannon-Bowers et al., 1995; Chao, O'Leary-Kelly, Wolf, Klein, & Gardner, 1994; Levine & Moreland, 1991, 1999), and employees who neglect this task are often rejected by coworkers. Regardless of how well they relate to the organization as a whole, such employees are thus less likely to succeed at their jobs. Once again, we focused here on how employees are influenced by work groups versus organizations, but it seems likely that employees also have more influence on work groups than they do on organizations.

Many studies indicate that work groups indeed have more influence on employees than do organizations. These studies can be sorted into two categories. The first category contains studies showing that employees from different work groups in the same organization often think, feel, and act in distinct ways. Some of the studies cited earlier on social information processing and organizational subcultures belong in this category, along with studies of the differences among work groups in such employee behaviors as job performance (George & Bettenhausen, 1990; Joyce & Slocum, 1984); prosocial behavior (Becker et al., 1995; George, 1990; George & Bettenhausen, 1990; see also Brief & Motowidlo, 1986); tardiness (Becker et al., 1995); and absenteeism (George, 1990; Markham & McKee, 1995; see also Johns & Nicholson, 1982; Nicholson & Johns, 1985). The second category contains studies showing that work group norms are good predictors of employee behaviors (e.g., Baratta & McManus, 1992; Blau, 1995; Kidwell, Mossholder, & Bennett, 1997; Lusch, Boyt, & Schuler, 1996; Martocchio, 1994; Mathieu & Kohler, 1990). In a study of public transit authority drivers, for example, Mathieu and Kohler found that the average levels of work group absenteeism were related to individual absenteeism levels, even after demographic characteristics, prior absenteeism records, job involvement and satisfaction, and organizational commitment were taken into account. More dramatic evidence for the power of work groups could be found in situations where organizations and groups make conflicting demands on employees (see Bearman, 1991; Roethlisberger & Dickson, 1939). When employees choose to act in ways that please their coworkers, but displease the organization, the importance of work group socialization becomes quite clear. Of course, work groups are not omnipotent, and some employees may be less sensitive than others to their influence. These include marginal group members, who are not strongly committed to their groups, and employees with experience in several groups, who often have a more "cosmopolitan" perspective on their work.

A Model of Group Socialization

We have made two claims about organizational socialization, namely that it occurs largely in work groups and that it is less important than work group socialization for employees. If these claims are correct, then much of the work on organizational socialization is misguided because it has ignored the critical role of work groups in the socialization process. Perhaps that is why so much research on organizational socialization has produced results that seem weak or inconsistent. A better understanding of the socialization process may thus require a familiarity with theory and research on small groups (Feldman, 1989). A general model of group socialization would be especially helpful; fortunately, one is already available.

We have developed a model (Moreland & Levine, 1982) that both describes and explains the process of group socialization. In that model, the relationship between a group and an individual is assumed to change in systematic ways over time, and both parties are viewed as potential influence agents. The model applies best to small, autonomous, and voluntary groups whose members interact regularly, are behaviorally interdependent, have feelings for each other, and share a common perspective on the world. Groups of many kinds, including work groups, sports teams, self-help groups, or cults, can thus be analyzed using the model.

Basic Processes

Our model is built around three psychological processes—*evaluation, commitment*, and *role transition*. Evaluation involves attempts by the group and the individual to assess and maximize one another's rewardingness. Evaluation produces feelings of commitment, which rise and fall over time. When commitment reaches a critical level (decision criterion), a role transition occurs. The relationship between the group and the individual is transformed, and both parties begin to evaluate one another again, often in different ways than before. Thus, a cycle of socialization activity is created, one that propels the individual through the group.

For the group, evaluation involves assessing individual contributions to the achievement of group goals. This includes identifying the goals to which a person can contribute and the behavioral dimensions on which such contributions will be measured, developing normative expectations for each of those dimensions, and finally comparing the person's expected and actual behavior. If someone fails to meet a group's expectations, attempts may be made to modify his or her behavior. A similar evaluation process is carried out by the individual, who focuses on group contributions to the satisfaction of personal needs. Through their mutual evaluations, both the group and the individual develop a general sense of the rewardingness of their relationship.

Evaluations are not limited to the present. The group and the individual may also recall how rewarding their relationship was in the past and speculate about how rewarding it will be in the future. Evaluations can extend to alternative relationships (actual or potential) as well—other individuals are evaluated by the group, and other groups are evaluated by the individual. All of these evaluations can influence commitment through three comparisons. For either the group or the individual, commitment is stronger to the extent that (a) their past relationship was more rewarding than other relationships in which they were or could have been involved; (b) their present relationship is more rewarding than other relationships in which they are or could be involved; and (c) their future relationship is expected to be more rewarding than other relationships in which they will or can be involved. A more detailed analysis of how these three comparisons combine to produce an overall feeling of commitment can be found in Moreland and Levine (1982). Our approach to commitment is simpler than those of many organizational psychologists (whose work we reviewed earlier) because we have not distinguished among different types of commitment. But simplicity is often a virtue, and our approach is flexible enough to capture (as rewards or costs of group membership) most of the sources of commitment identified by organizational psychologists. A more detailed analysis of these matters can also be found in Moreland and Levine (1982).

Commitment has important consequences for both the group and the individual. When a group is strongly committed to an individual, it is likely to accept that person's needs, work hard to satisfy them, feel warmly toward the person, and try to gain (or retain) the person as a member. And when an individual is strongly committed to a group, he or she is likely to accept that group's goals, work hard to achieve them, feel warmly toward the group, and try to gain or maintain membership. Problems can arise if commitment levels diverge. Such divergence occurs when the group's commitment to the individual grows stronger than his or her commitment to the group, or vice versa. Because of these problems, each party may monitor the other's commitment (see Eisenberger, Fasolo, & Davis-LaMastro, 1990; Shore & Wayne, 1993) and respond to any divergence by changing its own commitment or trying to change the commitment of its partner.

Changes in commitment are also important, because they can transform the relationship between a group and an individual. These transformations are governed by *decision criteria*, or specific levels of commitment that mark the boundaries between different membership roles the person could play in the group. The group will try to initiate a role transition when its commitment to an individual reaches its decision criterion. And the individual will make a similar effort when his or her commitment to a group reaches a personal decision criterion. Role transitions often involve ceremonies or other activities (see Trice & Beyer, 1984) that signify these changes in the relationship between the group and the individual.

After a role transition, the group and the individual relabel their relationship and may well change their expectations for one another's behavior. Evaluations continue, producing more changes in commitment and maybe other role transitions. In this way, the individual can go through five distinct phases of group membership (investigation, socialization, maintenance, resocialization, remembrance), separated by four transitions (entry, acceptance, divergence, exit). Figure 25.1 provides a typical example of how the relationship between a group and an individual might change over time.

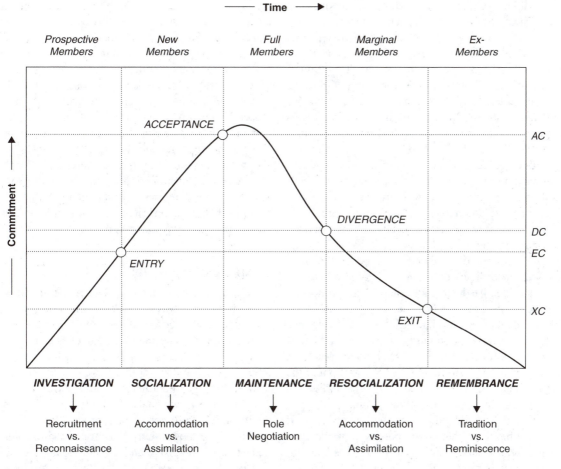

FIGURE 25.1 ■ The socialization process for a typical group member.

Passage Through a Group

Group membership begins with a period of investigation. During investigation, the group engages in recruitment, searching for individuals who can contribute to the achievement of group goals. The individual, as a prospective member, engages in reconnaissance, searching for groups that can contribute to the satisfaction of personal needs. If the commitment levels of both parties rise to their respective entry criteria (EC), entry occurs and the person becomes a new group member.

Entry marks the end of investigation and the beginning of socialization. The group and the individual try during socialization to change one another in ways that might make their relationship more rewarding (Moreland & Levine, 1989). The group wants the individual to contribute more to the achievement of its goals, whereas the individual wants the group to contribute more to the satisfaction of his or her needs. To the extent that these efforts succeed, the individual experiences assimilation and the group experiences accommodation. If the commitment levels of both parties rise to their respective acceptance criteria (AC), acceptance occurs and the person becomes a full member of the group.

Acceptance marks the end of socialization and the beginning of maintenance. The group and the individual negotiate during maintenance about functional roles (e.g., leader) for the individual that might maximize both the achievement of group goals and the satisfaction of personal needs. If role negotiation succeeds, the commitment levels of both parties rise and maintenance continues, perhaps indefinitely. But if role negotiation fails, commitment levels fall. If they reach the respective divergence criteria (DC) of both parties, divergence occurs and the individual becomes a marginal member of the group.

Divergence marks the end of maintenance and the beginning of resocialization. During resocialization, the group and the individual try again to change one another so that the group's goals are more likely to be achieved and the individual's needs are more likely to be satisfied. If enough assimilation and accommodation occur, the commitment levels of both parties may rise again to their respective divergence criteria. This produces a special role transition (*convergence*) that allows the individual to regain full membership. Convergence is rare, however. Commitment levels usually continue to fall (as in Figure 25.1) until they reach the respective exit criteria (XC) of the group and the individual. Exit then occurs and the individual becomes an ex-member of the group.

Group membership ends with a period of remembrance, when both parties look back at their relationship. The group recalls the individual's contributions to the achievement of its goals, whereas the individual recalls the group's contributions to the satisfaction of his or her needs. Some of these memories may be incorporated into group traditions and/or individual reminiscences. If they still have an influence on one another's outcomes, then both parties may also evaluate their current relationship. Over time, feelings of commitment between the group and the individual eventually stabilize, often at a low level.

Figure 25.1 is an idealized representation of how the relationship between group and an individual might change over time and thus masks several complexities (see Moreland & Levine, 1982). For example, group and individual commitment levels may undergo sudden shifts, rather than changing gradually. Group and individual decision criteria are sometimes unstable, and changes in decision

criteria could affect how long individuals spend in various membership phases. If two adjacent criteria are similar, for example, the membership phase they demarcate will be short, and it will not occur at all if the criteria are identical. Some decision criteria can also vary in their relative positions, which would change the order in which related role transitions occur. There are situations, for instance, in which exit might occur during the investigation or socialization phase of membership. And finally, the figure suggests that the group and the individual have the same set of decision criteria and are equally committed to one another throughout their relationship. When decision criteria or commitment levels diverge, conflict is likely to occur.

Exploring the Model

We have explored our model of group socialization in several ways. Much of this work, which includes both theoretical and empirical papers, is reviewed in Levine and Moreland (1994). In some of our theoretical papers, we expanded the model by analyzing its basic processes in more detail. In an early paper on role transitions (Moreland & Levine, 1984), we analyzed the strains associated with anticipating, scheduling, producing, and then adjusting to these events. Role transitions are simplest when the group and the individual have the same decision criteria and are usually committed to one another. But what if decision criteria and/or commitment levels differ? Role transitions then become more complicated and might produce strain. Imagine, for example, that neither the group nor the individual is ready for a role transition. They may still anticipate that transition by developing expectations about whether it will occur at all, how and when it might occur, and so on. Group and individual expectations can differ considerably when the commitment level of one party is much closer to its decision criterion. Strain may arise as a result, and it should increase with the difference in the distances separating the commitment levels of the group and the individual from their decision criteria. Now imagine that either the group *or* the individual, but not both, is ready for a role transition. Strain may arise around issues of scheduling, as one party tries to hasten the role transition while the other tries to delay it. Strain should now increase with the *sum* of the distances separating the commitment levels of the group and the individual from their decision criteria. Finally, imagine that the group and the individual are both ready for a role transition. Producing a role transition requires decisions about where that event will occur, who will participate in it, how they should act, and so on. And after a role transition ends, the group and the individual must both adjust to their new relationship. Producing and adjusting to a role transition can be difficult if the commitment level of one party is much closer to its decision criterion, so strain may again arise. As before, that strain should increase with the difference in the distances separating the commitment levels of the group and the individual from their decision criteria.

A later paper (Moreland, Levine, & Cini, 1993) focused on commitment. Although social exchange theory guided our original analysis of commitment, other theories may be relevant too and could reveal different aspects of that process. Self-categorization theory (see Hogg & McGarty, 1990; Turner, 1985), for example, has been applied to a related phenomenon, namely group cohesion. Hogg (1987) argued that cohesion depends on how well a group's members match its *prototype*—a shared mental image of someone with the characteristics that make the group unique. Cohesion is stronger insofar as group members seem (to one another) to match that prototype more closely. Perhaps an analogy to commitment can be made. A group's commitment to an individual may depend on how prototypical the person seems to other group members. And an individual's commitment to a group may depend on the person's self-perceived prototypicality, or on how prototypical the other group members seem to him or her. This analysis suggests that commitment can change because of shifts in a group's prototype. Such shifts might involve changes in who belongs to the ingroup or relevant outgroups, or changes in which outgroups are most salient. Shifts of either sort would alter the perceived prototypicality of everyone in the group and thereby change the group's commitment to each individual and each individual's commitment

to the group. Identity theory (Stryker, 1987; Stryker & Serpe, 1982) may also be relevant to commitment. According to that theory, social roles (e.g., group memberships) are often incorporated into the self as *identities*. Commitment to an identity depends on the number, intensity, and value of whatever personal relationships would be lost if the relevant role were no longer played. As the overall damage associated with the loss of those relationships increases, commitment grows stronger. A group's commitment to an individual may thus reflect its members' beliefs about how their relationships (with one another and outsiders) would be affected if that person moved further into or out of the group. And similarly, an individual's commitment to a group may reflect that person's beliefs about how such movement would affect his or her own relationships. This analysis suggests that changes in commitment are sometimes caused by shifts in the social networks that surround and permeate most groups. These shifts, which might occur if the composition of a network changed or if its participants developed new relationships with one another, would alter the interpersonal consequences of membership for everyone in the group. Each individual's commitment to the group, and the group's commitment to each individual, would be influenced as a result.

Besides expanding our model of group socialization by analyzing such processes as role transitions and commitment in more detail, we have also extended the model to other small group phenomena. In an early paper, for example, we explored how group socialization can affect minority influence, or innovation (Levine & Moreland, 1985). Innovation was defined as any significant change an individual produces in the structure, dynamics, or performance of a group. Each of the basic processes in our model offers some general insights into this phenomenon. An analysis of commitment, for example, clarifies when innovation attempts will be made and whether they will succeed. Attempts to change a group are more likely to occur when someone's commitment to the group is weak, although very weak commitment can cause a person to give up on a group entirely. And if someone makes an innovation attempt, it is more likely to succeed when the group's commitment to the person is strong. Success is especially likely when the group is more committed to the person than he or she is to the group. Our model offers some specific insights into innovation as well, revealing a variety of ways in which it might occur during each phase of group membership. Attempts to change a group by prospective members during investigation, and by ex-members during remembrance, are particularly interesting because people who do not belong to a group are often ignored as potential innovators. Innovation during investigation can be unintentional, as when prospective members ask questions about a group that lead members to consider making changes in it (see Feldman, 1994; Sutton & Louis, 1987), or intentional, as when prospective members demand changes from a group *anticipatory accommodation*) before they will join it. Conceding to these demands can have serious consequences for a group, beyond attracting new members. For example, the group may have trouble retaining those members if the changes they were promised are not made. And if those changes are made, other group members may feel alienated because their own recruitment was less rewarding or angry because they dislike how the group has changed. Innovation during remembrance can also be unintentional, as when someone's departure from a group changes its dynamics or performance (see Staw, 1980), or when fond memories of an ex-member lead a group to evaluate current members more harshly or to raise its decision criteria. Intentional innovation can also occur, as when successful ex-members improve a group's performance by offering advice or aid. Recently, we have offered a detailed analysis of how newcomers can produce innovation in the groups they have entered (Levine et al., in press).

In another paper (Moreland & Levine, 1988), we examined the relationship between group socialization and group development. These phenomena are identical in dyads, where there is just one relationship changing over time. In larger groups, socialization and development are related, but distinct. Group socialization involves temporal changes in the relationships between a group and each of its members, whereas group development involves temporal changes in the group as a whole. Each phenomenon can affect the other in various ways. Consider the possible effects of group socialization on group development. Socializing new members and resocializing marginal members could interfere with a group's development by absorbing valuable resources. And if new or marginal members produce accommodation in a group, its development could be affected by whatever changes are made. Although they do not belong to a group, prospective or ex-members could affect its development as well. For example, prospective members can facilitate development by demanding improvements in a group before they join, whereas ex-members can delay development by demanding that a group remain as it was when they belonged. The possible effects of group development on group socialization should also be considered. If development indeed occurs in a series of stages, as many theorists have argued (see Tuckman, 1965; Tuckman & Jensen, 1977), some socialization activities simply may not occur during certain stages of development. During the forming stage, for example, investigation activities may be common, but socialization, maintenance, and resocialization activities are unlikely because they depend on norms that have not yet developed. Remembrance activities are also unlikely when someone leaves a group during its forming stage. When a socialization activity occurs during more than one developmental stage, it may also vary from one stage to another. For example, compared to a group in the performing stage, a group in the adjourning stage often feels less secure, and may thus demand less assimilation from new or marginal members, lower acceptance and divergence criteria for them, and permit them to produce more accommodation.

The role of group socialization in maintaining work group cultures was examined in yet another paper (Levine & Moreland, 1991). A group's culture, we argued, includes socially shared knowledge and related customs. In work groups, shared knowledge provides the answers to questions that employees often ask about their group (*Are we successful?*), its members (*Who is best at what?*), and the work they perform (*Which tasks really matter?*). Customs, which include routines (everyday procedures), accounts (stories about important issues), jargon (unusual words or gestures), rituals (ceremonies marking important events), and symbols (objects with special meanings), embody this shared knowledge, often in very subtle ways. All of this suggests that someone entering a work group may have much to learn, and that acceptance is likely to be delayed until the person understands, appreciates, and participates in the group's culture. The transfer of cultural information from oldtimers to newcomers is an important socialization activity, and our model is helpful in identifying variables that can affect that process. These variables include the personal characteristics of newcomers and oldtimers and the socialization tactics that they employ. For example, some newcomers may already be familiar with a work group because of prior contact with the group or its members. And when further information is required, newcomers who are more motivated (stronger commitment to the group) or capable (better social skills) are more likely to seek and obtain it. Experience, motivation, and ability are important characteristics among oldtimers as well. Oldtimers are more likely to provide helpful information about the group, for example, when they have dealt with similar newcomers in the past, when they want current newcomers to gain acceptance, and when they understand the group's culture well (perhaps because they helped to shape it). Whatever their personal characteristics, newcomers and oldtimers can also improve the transfer of cultural information through various socialization tactics. Newcomers' tactics include evoking help from oldtimers by behaving in role-congruent ways (e.g., anxious and dependent), developing close relationships with oldtimers who might be helpful, and collaborating with one another. Oldtimers' tactics include training newcomers, "encapsulating" newcomers by making them spend most of their time (on and off the job) with group members, and testing what newcomers have learned about the group's culture, then rewarding or punishing them accordingly. We have also analyzed how organizations can improve the socialization practices of work

groups that are embedded within them (Levine & Moreland, 1999).

Finally, in a recent paper (Levine, Moreland, & Ryan, 1998), we explored the influence of group socialization on intergroup relations. Conflict is common between groups, especially when there is competition for scarce resources. Because members are a scarce resource for many groups, some conflicts are related to efforts by groups to gain and retain members. One situation where such conflicts often arise is when two groups are recruiting the same prospective member. Each group can focus on its own relationship with that individual and try to raise the person's commitment or lower the person's entry criterion. But each group can also focus on the individual's relationship with its competitor and attempt to lower the person's commitment to that group or raise the person's entry criterion for that group. The latter tactics are difficult and can be risky. A prospective member may be suspicious of one group's efforts to disparage another, so subtlety is often required. A group may pretend, for example, to be unaware that the individual is being recruited by a competitor, so that its criticism of that group seems less self-serving. Or a group may arrange for outsiders (with no apparent links to either group) to make pointed comparisons between the groups that favor itself. Whatever tactics are used, the group's competitor may well learn about them (perhaps from the prospective member) and then retaliate. As a result, both groups might lose the prospective member, and they could be harmed in other ways as well. Another situation where conflicts arise is when a group recruits someone who is already in another group, but cannot belong to both groups. In this case, the group must somehow weaken the prospective member's relationship with its competitor, maybe by lowering the person's commitment to that group or raising the person's exit criterion for that group. But achieving those goals may be even more dangerous than before. Resistance to the group's recruiting efforts can come from both the individual (who may view the group as an "outgroup," or worry that changing groups will seem like a betrayal) and from the group to which he or she already belongs. That group may again retaliate, perhaps by trying to turn the tables and recruit someone from its competitor. Finally, conflicts can also arise in situations where groups share a member. Competition here involves efforts to control the individual's time, energy, and other assets, rather than to persuade the person to stay in one group and leave the other. A group may become anxious if someone's commitments seem to be changing in ways that favor another group. Responses to such changes can vary widely, depending on the group's own commitment to that person. A group will probably work harder to improve its relationship with someone to whom it is strongly committed. Compromises might even be made with the other group if the alternative is losing that member. But if these efforts fail, then anxiety can turn to anger, directed at both the individual and the group that he or she prefers.

Our exploration of the model is not limited to theoretical work—we have also collected and analyzed data on the socialization process in many kinds of small groups. Most of this empirical work focused on the first two phases of group membership, namely investigation and socialization, and rather than testing the model directly, we have often used it instead as a tool for generating interesting hypotheses about socialization activities. In one project (Pavelchak, Moreland, & Levine, 1986), we studied the influence of earlier group memberships on later reconnaissance activities. During summer orientation sessions, all of the students entering our university were asked to complete a questionnaire assessing their experiences in high school groups and expectations about college groups. Later on, a representative sample of students was interviewed by telephone about their behavior at an activities fair, which the university offered at the start of the fall term to help new students learn more about campus groups. Three reconnaissance activities were explored using these data. Reconnaissance begins with efforts by the individual to identify potentially desirable groups. We found that such efforts often depended on earlier experiences in other groups—students whose high school group experiences were more positive (enjoyable and important) could name more college groups that they might

join, and were more likely to have already chosen a group that they would join. These effects were mediated, however, by the belief that memberships in college groups were valuable for achieving the students' goals. After some prospective groups have been identified, the individual must evaluate how rewarding it might be to belong to those groups. Once again, earlier experiences (especially in similar groups) proved to be important. Students who had already chosen a college group to join were optimistic overall, expecting the rewards of membership to far outweigh its costs, but weaker optimism was found among students who belonged to similar groups in high school (see Premack & Wanous, 1985), and the levels of optimism among these students reflected the positivity of their experiences in those groups. Finally, when commitment to a group reaches the individual's entry criterion, he or she will attempt join that group. There is evidence (see Fazio & Zanna, 1981) that attitudes formed on the basis of direct experience affect behavior more strongly than do attitudes formed in other ways. Among the students who wanted to join a specific college group, we thus expected greater effort to actually join that group by students who belonged to a similar group in high school. That is indeed what we found. When students were interviewed about the activities fair, those who had direct experience with their chosen group (through membership in a high school analog) were more likely than others to state that they went to the fair to visit that group, visited the group at the fair, and left their names with the group to encourage further contact.

One of the most remarkable findings from the project just described was how optimistic prospective members were about the groups they wanted to join. Many students could not (or would not) name a single cost of group membership, and when such costs were named, they were regarded as less probable and powerful than the rewards of group membership. Such optimism can be dangerous, because it often leads to disappointment and leaves many newcomers poorly prepared for the problems of group life (see Wanous, Poland, Premack, & Davis, 1992). It would be helpful to learn *why* prospective members are so optimistic, so in a later project (Brinthaupt, Moreland, & Levine, 1991), we studied three potential sources of optimism in college students' evaluations of campus groups they were about to join. These were (a) recruiting efforts by those groups; (b) feelings of cognitive dissonance about joining groups that might be unsatisfying; and (c) an illusion that the future will generally be better for the self than for others (Taylor & Brown, 1988; Weinstein, 1980). Students planning to join a campus group were given a questionnaire that measured their expectations about that group and experiences with it. For example, they were asked to name the possible rewards and costs of group membership, for both themselves and for the average student, and then to evaluate every reward and cost for probability and strength. We also asked students about their group's recruiting activities (e.g., Was the group described by its members primarily in positive terms?), and any reasons they might have for feeling dissonant about joining the group (e.g., Did you devote much time and energy to the group as a prospective member?). As in our earlier project, students were very optimistic about their chosen groups, naming more rewards than costs of membership and evaluating the rewards as more probable and powerful than the costs. There was little evidence that this optimism was due to recruiting efforts or cognitive dissonance. With some exceptions, students reported weak recruiting efforts by their chosen groups and few reasons for feeling dissonant about becoming group members. Neither of these factors was strongly related to students' optimism levels either. However, illusions about the self did seem to be an important source of optimism. Students expected group membership to be much better for themselves than for the average student, even when the same rewards and costs were evaluated.

Aside from studying the socialization activities of individuals, we have also studied such activities by groups. For example, one project (Cini, Moreland, & Levine, 1993) investigated how staffing levels can affect the behavior of groups toward prospective and new members. This project reflected an interest in research showing that members of understaffed groups work harder at a wider variety of tasks, and thus feel more important and involved, than do members of groups that are optimally staffed or overstaffed (see Schoggen, 1989). We were interested in whether staffing differences produce differential treatment of prospective and new group members. When understaffing occurs, a group may try to cope by altering its socialization practices in ways that make it easier for people to enter the group and then become full members. To explore this possibility, we interviewed the leaders of nearly 100 student groups at our university. We asked them several questions related to staffing levels, such as how large their groups actually were, how big or small those groups could become before problems occurred, what those problems were and how they might be solved, and so on. We also asked leaders questions about the typical socialization practices in their groups, especially the ways in which their prospective and new members were treated. Regarding staffing levels, we found that most leaders believed their groups were understaffed and that leaders were more concerned about understaffing than overstaffing. The most common problems associated with understaffing were poor group performance, fatigue and burnout, a loss of resources (from stakeholders), and member homogeneity. Such problems were typically solved by simply recruiting more members or by reorganizing the group. The most common problems associated with overstaffing were apathy and boredom, alienation, disorganization, strained resources, and clique formation. These problems were most often solved by building commitment among group members, recruiting fewer or better members, punishing deviates more harshly, or subdividing the group. Regarding socialization tactics, we found that prospective and new members were indeed treated more favorably by groups with lower staffing levels. Those groups wanted more new members, sought fewer special qualities in prospective members, had lower entry criteria, and tended to allow entry at any time. Groups with lower staffing levels also demanded less from new members. In these groups, newcomers' behavior was evaluated less carefully, they were treated more leniently when problems arose, and acceptance criteria were lower.

Conclusions

We began this chapter with a brief review of recent work on organizational socialization. That review focused on the tactics used by organizations and their new employees during socialization and on the commitment of new employees to their organizations. Much has been learned about the socialization process in organizations, but the results are somewhat discouraging. Many socialization tactics used by organizations and employees seem to be ineffective, and although some employees do become committed to their organizations, the impact of that commitment on their incomes is modest. Moreover, many organizations suffer high levels of turnover (especially among new employees) and employee misbehavior of various sorts. The socialization process in these organizations is apparently failing and must somehow be improved.

We think that it is time to analyze organizational socialization in a different way. In our opinion, much of the work in this area ignores the critical role of small work groups in the socialization process. There is now good evidence that organizational socialization occurs primarily within such groups and that work group socialization is more important for many employees than is organizational socialization. This suggests a need for new research, guided by a general model of group socialization, that investigates the socialization process in work groups. We have developed such a model and used it (in a series of papers) to explore not only socialization, but other group phenomena as well.

As a tool for analyzing organizational socialization, our model has four major strengths. First, and most importantly, it focuses on small groups. If our claims about work group socialization are correct, and it really is the key to understanding how new employees and organizations adjust to one another, then our model provides a useful theoretical approach. Second, our model has two features that should help to expand the temporal and social perspectives of psychologists who study organizational socialization. It acknowledges that the relationship between a group and an individual often extends over a long period of time, from investigation (when both parties speculate about their future relationship) through remembrance (when both parties remember their past relationship). And it acknowledges that the group and the individual are both sources and targets of influence throughout their relationship with one another—the individual can affect the group, just as it can affect him or her. Third, our model has proven useful in exploring several phenomena that are relevant to organizational socialization and that have already been analyzed by others in that context. These phenomena include innovation by new group members (see Levine & Moreland, 1985; Levine et al., in press; Nicholson, 1984), and unrealistic optimism in prospective group members (see Brinthaupt et al., 1991; Pavelchak et al., 1986; Wanous, 1992). Finally, an emphasis on work group socialization may reveal new ways in which the socialization process could be improved for new employees and their organizations. Nelson, Quick, and Eakin (1988), for example, suggested that team building and social support interventions in work groups could help make socialization less stressful for new employees.

Of course, our model may also have weaknesses that could limit its value for analyzing organizational socialization. For example, the model was not developed specifically for that purpose, and insofar as work groups have special characteristics, it may become necessary to stretch the model accordingly. One potential problem in this regard is that work groups are seldom wholly autonomous or voluntary—groups cannot always choose who to admit or eject, and workers are not always free to enter or leave a group. This suggests some interesting ways in which organizational socialization might shape work group socialization. By hiring and firing different kinds of employees, for example, an organization may force its work groups to allow the entry of people who evoke only weak commitment or the exit of people who evoke strong commitment. Jackson, Stone, and Alvarez (1993) analyzed the former phenomenon and its impact on group socialization in the context of recent efforts by many organizations to improve the diversity of their workforce. When minority workers enter a work group, its level of relational dissimilarity rises, and this may alter the ways in which newcomers and oldtimers relate to one another. Jackson and her colleagues argued, for example, that as relational dissimilarity rises, socialization becomes less open and direct, inhibiting both assimilation and accommodation and thereby delaying acceptance. Recent efforts by many organizations to downsize their workforce may have an impact on work group socialization as well. Research in both of these areas could be very fruitful. Another possible weakness in our model is its approach to commitment, which is simpler than those found in most recent work on organizational socialization. It may be necessary to consider how different dimensions of commitment, and multiple commitments to entities in and out of work groups, influence the socialization process. Finally, because empirical work on our model has lagged behind theoretical work, several of the model's assumptions (e.g., the effects of group and individual decision criteria in producing role transitions) have not yet been tested.

In our opinion, these weaknesses are clearly outweighed by the model's strengths, and so we urge those who study the process and outcomes of organizational socialization to consider how socialization in smaller groups might be relevant. Organizational psychology is already the source of much of the best work on other small group processes (see Levine & Moreland, 1990; 1998; Sanna & Parks, 1997). It is now time to include socialization as one of those processes.

ACKNOWLEDGMENTS

We would like to thank Linda Argote, Thomas Becker, Daniel Feldman, Marlene Turner, and John Wanous for their comments on an earlier version of the chapter. Copies of this or other papers we have written on group socialization can be obtained from either author at the Psychology Department, University of Pittsburgh, Pittsburgh, Pennsylvania, 15260.

REFERENCES

Albert, S., & Whetten, D. A. (1985). Organizational identity. In L. L. Cummings & B. M. Staw (Eds.), *Research in organizational behavior* (Vol. 7, pp. 263–295). Greenwich, CT: JAI.

Allen, N. J., & Meyer, J. P. (1990). Organizational socialization tactics: A longitudinal analysis of links to a newcomer's commitment and role orientation. *Academy of Management Journal*, *33*, 847–858.

Allen, N. J., & Meyer, J. P. (1993). Organizational commitment: Evidence of career stage effects? *Journal of Business Research*, *26*, 49–61.

Ancona, D. G. (1990). Outward bound: Strategies for team survival in an organization. *Academy of Management Journal*, *33*, 334–365.

Ancona, D. G., & Caldwell, D. F. (1988). Beyond task and maintenance: Defining external functions in groups. *Group and Organization Studies*, *13*, 468–494.

Ancona, D. G., & Caldwell, D. F. (1992). Bridging the boundary: External activity and performance in organizational teams. *Administrative Science Quarterly*, *37*, 634–665.

Anderson, A., & Thomas, H. D. C. (1996). Work group socialization. In M. A. West (Ed.), *Handbook of work group psychology* (pp. 423–450). Chichester, England: Wiley.

Ashford, S. J., & Black, J. S. (1996). Proactivity during organizational entry: The role of desire for control. *Journal of Applied Psychology*, *81*, 199–214.

Ashford, S. J., & Cummings, L. L. (1985). Feedback as an individual resource: Personal strategies of creating information. *Organizational Behavior and Human Performance*, *32*, 370–398.

Ashford, S. J., & Taylor, M. S. (1990). Adaptation to work transitions: An integrative approach. In G. R. Ferris & K. M. Rowland (Eds.), *Research in personnel and human resources management* (Vol. 8, pp. 1–39). Greenwich, CT: JAI.

Ashforth, B. E., & Mael, F. (1989). Social identity theory and the organization. *Academy of Management Review*, *14*, 20–39.

Ashforth, B. E., & Saks, A. M. (1996). Socialization tactics: Longitudinal effects on newcomer adjustment. *Academy of Management Journal*, *39*, 149–178.

Baba, M. L. (1995). The cultural ecology of the corporation: Explaining diversity in work group responses to organizational transformation. *Journal of Applied Behavioral Science*, *31*, 202–233.

Baker, H. E., & Feldman, D. C. (1990). Strategies of organizational socialization and their impact on newcomer adjustment. *Journal of Managerial Issues*, *2*, 198–212.

Baker, W. K. (1995). Allen and Meyer's 1990 longitudinal study: A reanalysis and reinterpretation using structural equation modeling. *Human Relations*, *48*, 169–186.

Baratta, J. E., & McManus, M. A. (1992). The effect of contextual factors on individuals' job performance. *Journal of Applied Social Psychology*, *22*, 1702–1710.

Barker, J. R., & Tompkins, P. K. (1994). Identification in the self-managing organization: Characteristics of target and tenure. *Human Communication Research*, *21*, 223–240.

Bauer, T. N., & Green, S. G. (1994). Effects of newcomer involvement in work-related activities: A longitudinal study of socialization. *Journal of Applied Psychology*, *79*, 211–223.

Bauer, T. N., Morrison, E. W., & Callister, R. R. (1998). Organizational socialization: A review and directions for future research. In G. R. Ferris (Ed.), *Research in personnel and human resources management* (Vol. 16, pp. 149–214). Stamford, CT: JAI.

Baumeister, R. F., & Leary, M. R. (1995). The need to belong: Desire for interpersonal attachments as a fundamental human motivation. *Psychological Bulletin, 117*, 497–529.

Bearman, P. S. (1991). Desertion as localism: Army unit solidarity and group norms in the U.S. Civil War. *Social Forces, 70*, 321–342.

Becker, T. E. (1992). Foci and bases of commitment: Are they distinctions worth making? *Academy of Management Journal, 35*, 232–244.

Becker, T. E., & Billings, R. S. (1993). Profiles of commitment: An empirical test. *Journal of Organizational Behavior, 14*, 177–190.

Becker, T. E., Billings, R. S., Eveleth, D. M., & Gilbert, N. L. (1996). Foci and bases of employee commitment: Implications for job performance. *Academy of Management Journal, 39*, 464–482.

Becker, T. E., Randall, D. M., & Riegel, C. D. (1995). The multidimensional view of commitment and the theory of reasoned action: A comparative evaluation. *Journal of Management, 21*, 617–638.

Bell, C. G., & Price, C. M. (1975). *The first term: A study of legislative socialization.* Beverly Hills, CA: Sage.

Bell, N. E., & Staw, B. M. (1989). People as sculptors versus sculpture: The role of personality and personal control in organizations. In M. B. Arthur, D. T. Hall, & B. S. Lawrence (Eds.), *The handbook of career theory* (pp. 232–251). Cambridge, England: Cambridge University Press.

Black, J. S., & Ashford, S. J. (1995). Fitting in or making jobs fit: Factors affecting mode of adjustment for new hires. *Human Relations, 48*, 421–437.

Blau, G. (1995). Influence of group lateness on individual lateness: A cross-level examination. *Academy of Management Journal, 38*, 1483–1496.

Brett, J., Feldman, D. C., & Weingart, L. R. (1990). Feedback-seeking behavior of new hires and job changers. *Journal of Management, 16*, 737–749.

Brewer, M. (1993). The role of distinctiveness in social identity and group behavior. In M. A. Hogg & D. Abrams (Eds.), *Group motivation: Social psychological perspectives* (pp. 1–16). New York: Harvester Wheatsheaf.

Brief, A. P., & Aldag, R. J. (1981). The "self" in work organizations: A conceptual review. *Academy of Management Review, 6*, 75–88.

Brief, A. P., & Motowidlo, S. J. (1986). Prosocial organizational behaviors. *Academy of Management Review, 11*, 710–725.

Brinthaupt, T. M., Moreland, R. L., & Levine, J. M. (1991). Sources of optimism among prospective group members. *Personality and Social Psychology Bulletin, 17*, 36–43.

Burke, R. J., & Bolf, C. (1986). Learning within organizations: Sources and content. *Psychological Reports, 59*, 1187–1198.

Caldwell, D. F., Chatman, J., & O'Reilly, C. A. (1990). Building organizational commitment: A multiform study. *Journal of Occupational Psychology, 63*, 245–261.

Cannon-Bowers, J. A., Tannenbaum, S. I., Salas, E., & Volpe, C. E. (1995). Defining competencies and establishing team training requirements. In R. Guzzo & E. Salas (Eds.), *Team effectiveness and decision making in organizations* (pp. 333–380). San Francisco: Jossey-Bass.

Chao, G. T. (1988). The socialization process: Building newcomer commitment. In M. London & E. Mone (Eds.), *Career growth and human resource strategies* (pp. 31–47). Westport, CT: Quorum Press.

Chao, G. T., O'Leary-Kelly, A. M., Wolf, S., Klein, H. J., & Gardner, P. D. (1994). Organizational socialization: Its content and consequences. *Journal of Applied Psychology, 79*, 730–743.

Chao, G. T., Walz, P. M., & Gardner, P. D. (1992). Formal and informal mentorships: A comparison on mentoring functions and contrast with nonmentored counterparts. *Personnel Psychology, 45*, 619–636.

Chatman, J. A. (1991). Matching people and organizations: Selection and socialization in public accounting firms. *Administrative Science Quarterly, 36*, 459–484.

Cini, M., Moreland, R. L., & Levine, J. M. (1993). Group staffing levels and responses to prospective and new group members. *Journal of Personality and Social Psychology, 65*, 723–734.

Comer, D. R. (1991). Organizational newcomers' acquisition of information from peers. *Management Communication Quarterly, 5*, 64–89.

Crino, M. D. (1994). Employee sabotage: A random or preventable phenomenon? *Journal of Managerial Issues, 6*, 311–330.

Dansky, K. H. (1996). The effect of group mentoring on career outcomes. *Group and Organization Management, 21*, 5–21.

Darrah, C. (1994). Skill requirements at work: Rhetoric versus reality. *Work and Occupations, 21*, 64–84.

Deluga, R. J., & Perry, J. T. (1994). The role of subordinate performance and ingratiation in leader–member exchanges. *Group and Organization Management, 19*, 67–86.

Dienesch, R. M., & Liden, R. C. (1986). Leader–member exchange model of leadership: A critique and further development. *Academy of Management Review, 11*, 618–634.

Dirsmith, A. J., & Covaleski, M. A. (1985). Informal communications, nonformal communications, and mentoring in public accounting firms. *Accounting, Organizations, and Society, 10*, 149–169.

Dockery, T. M., & Steiner, D. D. (1990). The role of the initial interaction in leader–member. *Group and Organization Studies, 15*, 395–413.

Dornbusch, S. M. (1955). The military academy as an assimilating institution. *Social Forces, 33*, 316–321.

Dunham, R. B., Grube, J. A., & Castaneda, M. B. (1994). Organizational commitment: The utility of an integrative definition. *Journal of Applied Psychology, 79*, 370–380.

Dunham, R. S., & Barrett, A. (1996, January 29). The house freshmen. *Business Week*, pp. 24–31.

DuPont, R. L. (1989). Never trust anyone under 40: What employers should know about drugs in the workplace. *Policy Review, 48*, 52–57.

Dutton, J. E., Dukerich, J. M., & Harquail, C. V. (1994). Organizational images and member identification. *Administrative Science Quarterly*, *39*, 239–263.

Eisenberger, R., Fasolo, P., & Davis-LaMastro, V. (1990). Perceived organizational support and employee diligence, commitment, and innovation. *Journal of Applied Psychology*, *75*, 51–59.

Fagenson, E. A. (1988). The power of a mentor: Protégés and nonprotégés' perceptions of their own power in organizations. *Group and Organization Studies*, *13*, 182–194.

Farrell, D., & Rusbult, C. E. (1981). Exchange variables as predictors of job satisfaction, job commitment, and turnover: The impact of rewards, costs, alternatives, and investments. *Organizational Behavior and Human Performance*, *28*, 78–95.

Fazio, R. H., & Zanna, M. P. (1981). Direct experience and attitude–behavior consistency. In L. Berkowitz (Ed.), *Advances in experimental social psychology* (Vol. 14, pp. 161–202). New York: Academic Press.

Feldman, D. C. (1976). A contingency theory of socialization. *Administrative Science Quarterly*, *21*, 433–452.

Feldman, D. C. (1977). The role of initiation activities in socialization. *Human Relations*, *11*, 977–990.

Feldman, D. C. (1981). The multiple socialization of organization members. *Academy of Management Review*, *6*, 309–318.

Feldman, D. C. (1989). Careers in organizations: Recent trends and future directions. *Journal of Management*, *15*, 135–156.

Feldman, D. C. (1994). Who's socializing whom? The impact of socializing newcomers on insiders, work groups, and organizations. *Human Resource Management Review*, *4*, 213–233.

Feldman, D. C., & Brett, J. M. (1983). Coping with new jobs: A comparative study of new job hires and job changers. *Academy of Management Journal*, *26*, 258–272.

Fisher, C. D. (1986). Organizational socialization: An integrative review. In G. R. Ferris & K. M. Rowland (Eds.), *Research in personnel and human resources management* (Vol. 4, pp. 101–145). Greenwich, CT: JAI.

Fulk, J. (1993). Social construction of communication technology. *Academy of Management Journal*, *36*, 921–950.

Geiger-Dumond, A. H., & Boyle, S. K. (1995, March). Mentoring: A practitioner's guide. *Training and Development*, 51–54.

George, J. M. (1990). Personality, affect, and behavior in groups. *Journal of Applied Psychology*, *75*, 107–116.

George, J. M., & Bettenhausen, K. (1990). Understanding prosocial behavior, sales performance, and turnover: A group-level analysis in a service context. *Journal of Applied Psychology*, *75*, 698–709.

Grant, L. (1995, May 22). A school for success. *U.S. News and World Report*, pp. 53–55.

Gregersen, H. B. (1993). Multiple commitments at work and extra-role behavior during three stages of organizational tenure. *Journal of Business Research*, *26*, 31–47.

Gregory, K. L. (1983). Native-view paradigms: Multiple cultures and culture conflicts in organizations. *Administrative Science Quarterly*, *28*, 359–376.

Guest, D. E. (1992). Employee commitment and control. In J. F. Hartley & G. M. Stephenson (Eds.), *Employment relations: The psychology of influence and control at work* (pp. 111–135). Oxford, England: Basil Blackwell.

Gundry, L. K., & Rousseau, D. M. (1994). Critical incidents in communicating culture to newcomers: The meaning is the message. *Human Relations*, *47*, 1063–1088.

Guzzo, R. A., Jette, R. D., & Katzell, R. A. (1985). The effects of psychologically based intervention programs on worker productivity: A meta-analysis. *Personnel Psychology*, *38*, 275–291.

Hackett, R. D., Bycio, P., & Hausdorf, P. A. (1994). Further assessments of Meyer and Allen's (1991) three-components model of organizational commitment. *Journal of Applied Psychology*, *79*, 15–23.

Harris, S. G., Hirschfeld, R. R., Field, H. S., & Mossholder, K. W. (1993). Psychological attachment: Relationships with job characteristics, attitudes, and preferences for newcomer development. *Group and Organization Management*, *18*, 459–481.

Hogg, M. A. (1987). Social identity and group cohesiveness. In J. C. Turner, M. A. Hogg, P. J. Oakes, S. D. Reicher, & M. S. Wetherell (Eds.), *Rediscovering the social group: A self-categorization theory* (pp. 89–110). Oxford, England: Basil Blackwell.

Hogg, M. A., & McGarty, C. (1990). Self-categorization and social identity. In D. Abrams & M. A. Hogg (Eds.), *Social identity theory: Constructive and critical advances* (pp. 10–27). New York: Springer-Verlag.

Hunt, S. D., & Morgan, R. M. (1994). Organizational commitment: One of many commitments or key mediating construct? *Academy of Management Journal*, *37*, 1568–1587.

Jablin, F. M. (1984). Assimilating new members into organizations. In R. N. Bostrom (Ed.), *Communication yearbook* (Vol. 8, pp. 594–626). Newbury Park, CA: Sage.

Jablin, F. M. (1987). Organizational entry, assimilation, and exit. In G. M. Goldhaber & G. A. Barnett (Eds.), *Handbook of organizational communication* (pp. 679–740). Norwood, NJ: Ablex.

Jackson, S. E., Stone, V. K., & Alvarez, E. B. (1993). Socialization amidst diversity: Impact of demographics on work team oldtimers and newcomers. In L. L. Cummings & B. M. Staw (Eds.), *Research in organizational behavior* (Vol. 15, pp. 45–109). Greenwich, CT: JAI.

James, K., & Cropanzano, R. (1984). Dispositional group loyalty and individual action for the benefit of an ingroup: Experimental and correlational evidence. *Organizational Behavior and Human Decision Processes*, *60*, 179–205.

Jaros, S. J., Jermier, J. M., Koehler, J. W., & Sincich, T. (1993). Effects of continuance, affective, and moral commitment on the withdrawal process: An evaluation of eight structural equation models. *Academy of Management Journal*, *36*, 951–995.

Johns, G., & Nicholson, N. (1982). The meaning of absence: New strategies for theory and research. In B. M. Staw & L. L. Cummings (Eds.), *Research in organizational behavior* (Vol. 4, pp. 127–172). Greenwich, CT: JAI.

Jones, G. R. (1986). Socialization tactics, self-efficacy, and newcomers' adjustment to organizations. *Academy of Management Journal, 29,* 262–279.

Jones, J. W., & Boye, M. W. (1994). Job stress, predisposition to steal, and employee theft. *American Journal of Health Promotion, 8,* 331–333.

Joyce, W. F., & Slocum, J. W. (1984). Collective climate: Agreement as a basis for defining aggregate climates in organizations. *Academy of Management Journal, 27,* 721–742.

Katz, R. (1985). Organizational stress and early socialization experiences. In T. Beehr & R. Bhagat (Eds.), *Human stress and cognition in organizations: An integrative perspective* (pp. 117–139). New York: Wiley.

Kidwell, R. E., Mossholder, K., & Bennett, N. (1997). Cohesiveness and organizational citizenship behavior: A multilevel analysis using work groups and individuals. *Journal of Management, 23,* 775–793.

Kizilos, P. (1990, April). Take my mentor, please! *Training,* 49–55.

Kline, C. J., & Peters, L. H. (1991). Behavioral commitment and tenure of new employees: A replication and extension. *Academy of Management Journal, 34,* 194–204.

Kram, K. W. (1983). Phases of the mentor relationship. *Academy of Management Journal, 26,* 608–625.

Kram, K. E. (1985). Improving the mentoring process. *Training and Development Journal, 39,* 40–43.

Kram, K. E. (1988). *Mentoring at work: Developmental relationships in organizational life.* Lanham, MD: University Press of America.

Kram, K. E., & Isabella, L. A. (1985). Mentoring alternatives: The role of peer relationships in career development. *Academy of Management Journal, 28,* 110–132.

Kramer, M. W. (1993a). Communication after job transfers: Social exchange processes in learning new roles. *Human Communication Research, 20,* 147–174.

Kramer, M. W. (1993b). Communication and uncertainty reduction during job transfers: Learning and joining processes. *Communication Monographs, 60,* 178–198.

Lawler, E. E., Mohrman, S. A., & Ledford, G. E. (1992). *Employee involvement and total quality management.* San Francisco: Jossey-Bass.

Lawler, E. J. (1992). Affective attachments to nested groups: A choice process theory. *American Sociological Review, 57,* 327–339.

Lawrie, J. (1987). How to establish a mentoring program. *Training and Development Journal, 41,* 25–27.

Lee, T. W., Ashford, S. J., Walsh, J. P., & Mowday, R. T. (1992). Commitment propensity, organizational commitment, and voluntary turnover: A longitudinal study of organizational entry processes. *Journal of Management, 18,* 15–32.

Levine, J. M., & Moreland, R. L. (1985). Innovation and socialization in small groups. In S. Moscovici, G. Mugny, & E. Van Avermaet (Eds.), *Perspectives on minority influence* (pp. 143–169). Cambridge, England: Cambridge University Press.

Levine, J. M., & Moreland, R. L. (1990). Progress in small group research. *Annual Review of Psychology, 41,* 585–634.

Levine, J. M., & Moreland, R. L. (1991). Culture and socialization in work groups. In L. B. Resnick, J. M. Levine, & S. D. Teasley (Eds.), *Perspectives on socially shared cognition* (pp. 257–279). Washington, DC: APA.

Levine, J. M., & Moreland, R. L. (1994). Group socialization: Theory and research. In W. Stroebe & M. Hewstone (Eds.), *European review of social psychology* (Vol. 5, pp. 305–336). Chichester, England: Wiley.

Levine, J. M., & Moreland, R. L. (1998). Small groups. In D. Gilbert, S. Fiske, & G. Lindzey (Eds.), *The handbook of social psychology* (4th ed., Vol. 2, pp. 415–469). Boston: McGraw-Hill.

Levine, J. M., & Moreland, R. L. (1999). Knowledge transmission in work groups: Helping newcomers to succeed. In L. Thompson, J. Levine, & D. Messick (Eds.), *Shared cognition in organizations: The management of knowledge* (pp. 267–296). Mahwah, NJ: Lawrence Erlbaum Associates.

Levine, J. M., Moreland, R. L., & Choi, H-S. (in press). Group socialization and newcomer innovation. In M. Hogg & S. Tindale (Eds.), *Blackwell handbook in social psychology (Vol. 3): Group processes.* Oxford: Blackwell.

Levine, J. M., Moreland, R. L., & Ryan, C. S. (1998). Group socialization and intergroup relations. In C. Sedikides, J. Schopler, & C. A. Insko (Eds.), *Intergroup cognition and intergroup behavior* (pp. 283–308). Mahwah, NJ: Lawrence Erlbaum Associates.

Liden, R. C., Wayne, S. J., & Stilwell, D. (1993). A longitudinal study on the early development of leader–member exchanges. *Journal of Applied Psychology, 78,* 662–674.

Lodewijkz, H., & Syroit, J. (1997). Severity of initiation revisited: Does severity of initiation increase attractiveness in real groups? *European Journal of Social Psychology, 27,* 275–300.

Louis, M. R. (1980). Surprise and sense-making: What newcomers experience in entering unfamiliar organizational settings. *Administrative Science Quarterly, 25,* 226–251.

Louis, M. R. (1983). Organizations as culture-bearing milieux. In L. R. Pondy, P. J. Frost, G. Morgan, & T. C. Dandridge (Eds.), *Organizational symbolism* (pp. 39–54). Greenwich, CT: JAI.

Louis, M. R., Posner, B. Z., & Powell, G. N. (1983). The availability and helpfulness of socialization practices. *Personnel Psychology, 36,* 857–866.

Lusch, R. F., Boyt, T., & Schuler, D. (1996). Employees as customers: The role of social controls and employee socialization in developing patronage. *Journal of Business Research, 35,* 179–187.

Mael, F. A., & Ashforth, B. E. (1995). Loyal from day one: Biodata, organizational identification, and turnover among newcomers. *Personnel Psychology, 48,* 309–333.

Mael, F. A., & Tetrick, L. E. (1992). Identifying organizational identification. *Educational and Psychological Measurement, 52,* 813–824.

Markham, S. E., & McKee, G. H. (1995). Group absence behavior and standards: A multilevel analysis. *Academy of Management Journal, 38*, 1174–1190.

Martocchio, J. J. (1994). The effects of absence culture on individual absence. *Human Relations, 47*, 243–262.

Mathieu, J. E. (1991). A cross-level nonrecursive model of the antecedents of organizational commitment and satisfaction. *Journal of Applied Psychology, 76*, 607–618.

Mathieu, J. E., & Kohler, S. S. (1990). A cross-level examination of group absence influences on individual absence. *Journal of Applied Psychology, 75*, 217–220.

Mathieu, J. E., & Zajac, D. M. (1990). A review and meta-analysis of the antecedents, correlates, and consequences of organizational commitment. *Psychological Bulletin, 108*, 171–194.

Meyer, J. P., & Allen, N. J. (1988). Links between work experiences and organizational commitment during the first year of employment: A longitudinal analysis. *Journal of Occupational Psychology, 61*, 195–209.

Meyer, J. P., & Allen, N. J. (1991). A three-component conceptualization of organizational commitment. *Human Resources Management Review, 1*, 61–89.

Meyer, J. P., Allen, N. J., & Gellatly, I. R. (1990). Affective and continuance commitment to the organization: Evaluation of measures and analysis of concurrent and time-lagged relations. *Journal of Applied Psychology, 75*, 710–720.

Meyer, J. P., Bobocel, D. R., & Allen, N. J. (1991). Development of organizational commitment during the first year of employment: A longitudinal study of pre- and post-entry influences. *Journal of Management, 17*, 717–733.

Meyer, J. P., Paunonen, S. V., Gellatly, I. R., Goffin, R. D., & Jackson, D. N. (1989). Organizational commitment and job performance: It's the nature of the commitment that counts. *Journal of Applied Psychology, 74*, 152–156.

Mignerey, J. T., Rubin, R. B., & Gorden, W. I. (1995). Organizational entry: An investigation of newcomer communication behavior and uncertainty. *Communication Research, 22*, 54–85.

Miller, V. C., & Jablin, F. M. (1991). Information seeking during organizational entry: Influences, tactics, and a model of the process. *Academy of Management Review, 16*, 92–120.

Moreland, R. L. (1985). Social categorization and the assimilation of "new" group members. *Journal of Personality and Social Psychology, 48*, 1173–1190.

Moreland, R. L., Argote, L., & Krishnan, R. (1998). Training people to work in groups. In R. S. Tindale, L. Heath, J. Edwards, E. J. Posavac, F. B. Bryant, Y. Suarez-Balcazar, E. Henderson-King, & J. Meyers (Eds.), *Theory and research on small groups* (pp. 37–60). New York: Plenum.

Moreland, R. L., & Beach, S. R. (1992). Exposure effects in the classroom: The development of affinity among students. *Journal of Experimental Social Psychology, 28*, 255–276.

Moreland, R. L., & Levine, J. M. (1982). Group socialization: Temporal changes in individual–group relations. In L. Berkowitz (Ed.), *Advances in experimental social psychology* (Vol. 15, pp. 137–192). New York: Academic Press.

Moreland, R. L., & Levine, J. M. (1984). Role transitions in small groups. In V. L. Allen & E. Van de Vliert (Eds.), *Role transitions: Explorations and explanations* (pp. 181–195). New York: Plenum.

Moreland, R. L., & Levine, J. M. (1988). Group dynamics over time: Development and socialization in small groups. In J. McGrath (Ed.), *The social psychology of time: New perspectives* (pp. 151–181). Newbury Park, CA: Sage.

Moreland, R. L., & Levine, J. M. (1989). Newcomers and old-timers in small groups. In P. Paulus (Ed.), *Psychology of group influence* (pp. 143–186). Hillsdale, NJ: Lawrence Erlbaum Associates.

Moreland, R. L., Levine, J. M., & Cini, M. (1993). Group socialization: The role of commitment. In M. A. Hogg & D. Abrams (Eds.), *Group motivation: Social psychological perspectives* (pp. 105–129). New York: Harvester Wheatsheaf.

Morrison, E. W. (1993a). Longitudinal study of the effects of information seeking on newcomer socialization. *Journal of Applied Psychology, 78*, 173–183.

Morrison, E. W. (1993b). Newcomer information seeking: Exploring types, modes, sources, and outcomes. *Academy of Management Journal, 36*, 557–589.

Morrison, E. W., & Bies, R. J. (1991). Impression management in the feedback seeking process: A literature review and research agenda. *Academy of Management Review, 16*, 522–541.

Morrow, P. C. (1993). *The theory and measurement of work commitment*. Greenwich, CT: JAI.

Mowday, R. T. L., Steers, R. M., & Porter, L. W. (1979). The measurement of organizational commitment. *Journal of Vocational Behavior, 14*, 224–227.

Mulford, C. L., Klonglan, G. E., Beal, G. N., & Bohlen, J. M. (1968). Selectivity, socialization, and role performance. *Sociology and Social Research, 53*, 68–77.

Mulford, C. L., Klonglan, G. E., & Warren, R. D. (1972). Socialization, communication, and role performance. *Sociological Quarterly, 13*, 74–80.

Nelson, D. L. (1987). Organizational socialization: A stress perspective. *Journal of Organizational Behavior, 8*, 311–324.

Nelson, D. L., & Quick, J. C. (1991). Social support and newcomer adjustment in organizations: Attachment theory at work? *Journal of Organizational Behavior, 12*, 543–554.

Nelson, D. L., Quick, J. C., & Eakin, M. E. (1988). A longitudinal study of newcomer role adjustment in U.S. organizations. *Work & Stress, 2*, 239–253.

Nelson, D. L., Quick, J. C., & Joplin, J. R. (1991). Psychological contracting and newcomer socialization: An attachment theory foundation. *Journal of Social Behavior and Personality, 6*, 55–72.

Nelson, D. L., & Sutton, C. (1990). Chronic work stress and coping: A longitudinal study and suggested new directions. *Academy of Management Journal, 33*, 859–869.

Nicholson, N. (1984). A theory of work role transitions. *Administrative Science Quarterly, 29*, 172–191.

Nicholson, N., & Johns, G. (1985). The absence culture and the psychological contract—who's in control of absence? *Academy of Management Review, 10,* 397–407.

Noe, R. A. (1988). An investigation of the determinants of successful assigned mentoring relationships. *Personnel Psychology, 41,* 457–479.

Noon, M., & Delbridge, R. (1993). News from behind my hand: Gossip in organizations. *Organization Studies, 14,* 23–36.

O'Reilly, C. A., & Chatman, J. (1986). Organizational commitment and psychological attachment: The effects of compliance, identification, and internalization on prosocial behavior. *Journal of Applied Psychology, 71,* 492–499.

Ostroff, C., & Kozlowski, S. W. J. (1992). Organizational socialization as a learning process: The role of information acquisition. *Personnel Psychology, 45,* 849–874.

Ostroff, C., & Kozlowski, S. W. J. (1993). The role of mentoring in the information-gathering processes of newcomers during early organizational socialization. *Journal of Vocational Behavior, 42,* 170–183.

Pavelchak, M., Moreland, R. L., & Levine, J. M. (1986). Effects of prior group memberships on subsequent reconnaissance activities. *Journal of Personality and Social Psychology, 50,* 56–66.

Phillips-Jones, L. (1983). Establishing a formalized mentoring program. *Training and Development Journal, 37,* 38–42.

Posner, B. Z., & Powell, G. N. (1985). Female and male socialization experiences: An initial investigation. *Journal of Occupational Psychology, 58,* 81–85.

Premack, S. L., & Wanous, J. P. (1985). A meta-analysis of realistic job preview experiments. *Journal of Applied Psychology, 70,* 706–718.

Putallaz, M., & Wasserman, A. (1990). Children's entry behavior. In S. R. Asher & J. D. Coie (Eds.), *Peer rejection in childhood* (pp. 60–89). New York: Cambridge University Press.

Randall, D. M. (1990). The consequences of organizational commitment: A methodological investigation. *Journal of Organizational Behavior, 11,* 361–378.

Randall, D. M., & Cote, J. (1991). Interrelationships of work commitment constructs. *Work & Occupations, 18,* 194–211.

Randall, D. M., Fedor, D. B., & Longenecker, C. O. (1990). The behavioral expression of organizational commitment. *Journal of Vocational Behavior, 36,* 210–224.

Reichers, A. E. (1985). A review and reconceptualization of organizational commitment. *Academy of Management Review, 10,* 465–476.

Reichers, A. E. (1986). Conflict and organizational commitments. *Journal of Applied Psychology, 71,* 508–514.

Reichers, A. E. (1987). An interactionist perspective on newcomer socialization rates. *Academy of Management Review, 12,* 278–287.

Reichheld, F. (1996). *The loyalty effect.* Cambridge, MA: Harvard Business School Press.

Rentsch, J. R. (1990). Climate and culture: Interaction and qualitative differences in organizational meanings. *Journal of Applied Psychology, 75,* 668–681.

Rickman, S. A. (1992). Culture and subcultures: An analysis of organizational knowledge. *Administrative Science Quarterly, 37,* 140–161.

Riordan, C. M., & Griffeth, R. W. (1995). The opportunity for friendship in the workplace: An underexplored construct. *Journal of Business and Psychology, 10,* 141–154.

Robinson, S. L., & Rousseau, D. M. (1994). Violating the psychological contract: Not the exception but the norm. *Journal of Organizational Behavior, 15,* 245–259.

Roethlisberger, F. J., & Dickson, W. J. (1939). *Management and the worker.* Cambridge, MA: Harvard University Press.

Rohlen, T. P. (1973). "Spiritual education" in a Japanese bank. *American Anthropologist, 75,* 1542–1562.

Rusbult, C. E., & Farrell, D. (1983). A longitudinal test of the investment model: The impact on job satisfaction, job commitment, and turnover of variations in rewards, costs, alternatives, and investments. *Journal of Applied Psychology, 68,* 429–438.

Rusbult, C. E., Farrell, D., Rogers, G., & Mainous, A. G. (1988). Impact of exchange variables on exit, voice, loyalty, and neglect: An integrative model of responses to declining job satisfaction. *Academy of Management Journal, 31,* 599–627.

Saks, A. M. (1994). Moderating effects of self-efficacy for the relationship between training method and anxiety and stress reactions of newcomers. *Journal of Organizational Behavior, 15,* 639–654.

Saks, A. M. (1995). Longitudinal investigation of the moderating and mediating effects of self-efficacy on the relationship between training and newcomer adjustment. *Journal of Applied Psychology, 80,* 211–225.

Saks, A. M. (1996). The relationship between the amount and helpfulness of entry training and work outcomes. *Human Relations, 49,* 429–451.

Saks, A. M., & Ashforth, B. E. (1997). Organizational socialization: Making sense of the past and present as a prologue for the future. *Journal of Organizational Behavior, 51,* 234–279.

Salancik, G. R. (1977). Commitment and the control of organizational behavior and belief. In B. M. Staw & G. R. Salancik (Eds.), *New directions in organizational behavior* (pp. 1–74). Chicago: St. Clair Press.

Salancik, G. R., & Pfeffer, J. (1978). A social information processing approach to job attitudes and task design. *Administrative Science Quarterly, 23,* 224–253.

Sanna, L. J., & Parks, C. D. (1997). Group research trends in social and organizational psychology: What ever happened to intragroup research? *Psychological Science, 8,* 261–267.

Scandura, T. A., & Schriesheim, C. A. (1994). Leader–member exchange and supervisor career mentoring as complementary constructs in leadership research. *Academy of Management Journal, 37,* 1588–1602.

Schoggen, P. (1989). *Behavior settings: A revision and extension of Roger G. Barker's ecological psychology.* Stanford, CA: Stanford University Press.

Scott, W. A., & Scott, R. (1989). *Adaptation of immigrants: Individual differences and determinants.* Oxford, England: Pergamon.

Schmitz, J., & Fulk, J. (1991). Organizational colleagues, media richness, and electronic mail: A test of the social influence model of technology use. *Communication Research, 18,* 487–523.

Schneider, B., Goldstein, H. W., & Smith, D. B. (1995). The ASA framework: An update. *Personnel Psychology, 48,* 747–774.

Settoon, R. P., & Adkins, C. L. (1997). Newcomer socialization: The role of supervisors, coworkers, friends, and family members. *Journal of Business and Psychology, 11,* 507–526.

Shore, L. M., & Wayne, S. J. (1993). Commitment and employee behavior: Comparison of affective commitment and continuance commitment with perceived organizational support. *Journal of Applied Psychology, 78,* 774–780.

Snyder, M. (1995). Self-monitoring: Public appearances versus private realities. In G. G. Brannigan & M. R. Merrens (Eds.), *The social psychologists: Research adventures* (pp. 35–50). New York: McGraw-Hill.

Staw, B. (1980). The consequences of turnover. *Journal of Occupational Behavior, 1,* 253–273.

Stryker, S. (1987). Identity theory: Developments and extensions. In K. Yardley & T. Honess (Eds.), *Self and identity: Psychosocial perspectives* (pp. 89–103). New York: Wiley.

Stryker, S., & Serpe, R. T. (1982). Commitment, identity, salience, and role behavior: Theory and research example. In W. Ickes & E. S. Knowles (Eds.), *Personality, roles, and social behavior* (pp. 199–218). New York: Springer-Verlag.

Sundstrom, E., deMeuse, K. P., & Futrell, D. (1990). Work teams: Applications and effectiveness. *American Psychologist, 45,* 120–133.

Sutton, R. I., & Louis, M. R. (1987). How selecting and socializing newcomers influences insiders. *Human Resource Management, 26,* 347–361.

Tannenbaum, S. I., Mathieu, J. E., Salas, E., & Cannon-Bowers, J. A. (1991). Meeting trainees' expectations: The influence of training fulfillment on the development of commitment, self-efficacy, and motivation. *Journal of Applied Psychology, 76,* 759–769.

Taylor, S. E., & Brown, J. D. (1988). Illusion and well-being: A social psychological perspective on mental health. *Psychological Bulletin, 103,* 193–210.

Tepper, B. J. (1995). Upward maintenance tactics in supervisory mentoring and nonmentoring relationships. *Academy of Management Journal, 38,* 1191–1205.

Trice, H. M., & Beyer, J. M. (1984). Studying organizational cultures through rites and ceremonials. *Academy of Management Review, 9,* 653–669.

Tuckman, B. W. (1965). Developmental sequence in small groups. *Psychological Bulletin, 63,* 384–399.

Tuckman, B. W., & Jensen, M. A. C. (1977). Stages of small-group development revisited. *Group & Organization Studies, 2,* 419–427.

Turner, J. C. (1985). Social categorization and the self-concept: A social cognitive theory of group behavior. In E. J. Lawler (Ed.), *Advances in group process* (Vol. 2, pp. 77–122). Greenwich, CT: JAI.

Vandenberg, R. J., & Self, R. M. (1993). Assessing newcomers' changing commitments to the organization during the first six months of work. *Journal of Applied Psychology, 78,* 557–568.

Vandenberg, R. J., Self, R. M., & Seo, J. H. (1994). A critical examination of the internalization, identification, and compliance commitment measures. *Journal of Management, 20,* 123–140.

Van Maanen, J. (1978). People processing: Strategies of organizational socialization. *Organizational Dynamics, 7,* 18–36.

Van Maanen, J., & Barley, S. R. (1985). Cultural organization: Fragments of a theory. In P. J. Frost, L. F. Moore, M. R. Louis, C. C. Lundberg, & J. Martin (Eds.), *Organizational culture* (pp. 31–53). Beverly Hills, CA: Sage.

Van Maanen, J., & Schein, E. (1979). Toward a theory of organizational socialization. In B. M. Staw (Ed.), *Research in organizational behavior* (Vol. 1, pp. 209–264). Greenwich, CT: JAI.

Vaught, C., & Smith, D. L. (1980). Incorporation and mechanical solidarity in an underground coal mine. *Sociology of Work and Occupations, 7,* 159–187.

Wanous, J. P. (1989). Impression management at organizational entry. In R. A. Giacalone & P. Rosenfeld (Eds.), *Impression management in the organization* (pp. 253–267). Hillsdale, NJ: Lawrence Erlbaum Associates.

Wanous, J. P. (1992). *Organizational entry: Recruitment, selection, orientation, and socialization of newcomers.* Reading, MA: Addison-Wesley.

Wanous, J. P. (1993). Newcomer orientation programs that facilitate organizational entry. In H. Schuler, J. L. Farr, & M. Smith (Eds.), *Personnel selection and assessment: Individual and organizational perspectives* (pp. 125–139). Hillsdale, NJ: Lawrence Erlbaum Associates.

Wanous, J. P., & Colella, A. (1989). Organizational entry research: Current status and future research directions. In K. M. Rowland & G. R. Ferris (Eds.), *Research in personnel and human resources management* (Vol. 7, pp. 59–120). Greenwich, CT: JAI.

Wanous, J. P., Poland, T. D., Premack, S. L., & Davis, K. S. (1992). The effects of met expectations on newcomer attitudes and behaviors: A review and meta-analysis. *Journal of Applied Psychology, 77,* 288–297.

Wayne, S. J., & Ferris, G. R. (1990). Influence tactics, affect, and exchange quality in supervisor–subordinate dyads. *Journal of Applied Psychology, 75,* 487–499.

Weinstein, N. D. (1980). Unrealistic optimism about future life events. *Journal of Personality and Social Psychology, 39,* 806–820.

Weiss, H. M. (1977). Subordinate imitation of supervisor behavior: The role of modeling in organizational socialization. *Organizational Behavior and Human Performance, 19,* 89–105.

Whitely, W. T., & Coetsier, P. (1993). The relationship of career mentoring to early career outcomes. *Organization Studies, 14,* 419–441.

Wright, P. L. (1990). Teller job satisfaction and organization commitment as they relate to career orientations. *Human Relations, 43,* 369–381.

Yoon, J. K., Baker, M. R., & Ko, J. (1994). Interpersonal attachment and organizational commitment: Subgroup hypothesis revisited. *Human Relations, 47,* 329–351.

Zaccaro, S. J., & Dobbins, G. H. (1989). Contrasting group and organizational commitment: Evidence for differences among multilevel attachments. *Journal of Organizational Behavior, 10,* 267–273.

Zaccaro, S. J., Foti, R. J., & Kenny, D. A. (1991). Self-monitoring and trait-based variance in leadership: An investigation of leader flexibility across multiple group situations. *Journal of Applied Psychology; 76,* 308–315.

Zahrly, J., & Tosi, H. (1989). The differential effect of organizational induction process on early work role adjustment. *Journal of Organizational Behavior, 10,* 59–74.

Zalesny, M. D., & Ford, J. K. (1990). Extending the social information processing perspective: New links to attitudes, behaviors, and perceptions. *Organizational Behavior and Human Decision Processes, 47,* 205–246.

Zey, M. G. (1985). Mentor programs: Making the right moves. *Personnel Journal, 64,* 53–57.

Beyond Task and Maintenance: Defining External Functions in Groups

Deborah Gladstein Ancona* and David F. Caldwell**

Using interview and log data from 38 new product team managers and 15 team members, we identify a set of activities that group members use to manage their dependence on external groups. Team members carry out scout, ambassador, sentry, and guard activities along with immigrant, captive, and emigrant roles to manage external transactions. It is hypothesized that high team performance is associated with a fit between the level of boundary activity and the degree of resource dependence.

Teams are touted these days as a solution to many organizational ills. Whether it is product development teams at General Motors or Procter and Gamble, groups to implement manufacturing innovations in the aerospace industry (Kazanjian & Drazin, 1988), or quality circles, teams are proliferating. These teams are seen as a vehicle to shorten product development time, improve commitment and performance, and help companies compete in a global economy (Hackman & Walton, 1986; Kanter, 1986).

Unfortunately, our models of group behavior often come from the laboratory and may not reflect the changing form and role of groups in organizations today. Work groups in organizations do not exist in a vacuum. Hence their effectiveness may be as much a function of how they deal with problems in their environment as of how well the group members deal with each other.

Three factors appear to contribute to our inability to keep pace with changes in the corporate arena. First, models of group process often have failed to address the complete range of group behaviors, particularly those that describe how members of the group interact with others outside the group (Ancona, 1987). Second, researchers often do not take into account differences in the tasks that groups must complete (Goodman, 1986). Different tasks clearly require different approaches for high performance (Herold, 1979). Third, researchers

We would like to thank CIMS, the Center for Innovation Management Studies, Lehigh University, Edgar Schein, and the anonymous reviewers at *Group and Organization Studies* for their support and comments.

* Massachusetts Institute of Technology.
** Santa Clara University.

often use very general global frameworks to predict performance, rather than producing fine-grained models with clear variables and operational measures (Bettenhausen & Murnighan, 1985; Goodman, Ravlin, & Schminke, 1987).

Together, these three factors may explain why we often have difficulty predicting the performance of groups operating within organizations. Given that the tasks of many groups within organizations require interdependent action, failure to consider the external interactions required and the lack of inclusive, fine-grained models of group process make it difficult for researchers to identify the appropriate process variables related to performance.

The purpose of this article is to describe and classify a set of activities that link a group to its external environment. This external perspective assumes that the group must manage relations with outsiders because it often depends upon those outsiders for resources or information (Pfeffer, 1986). Rather than describing a complete model of group behavior, we concentrate on how groups, doing a particular task, carry on these required relations with those outside, either in other parts of the organization or external to the organization. These external behaviors can then be tested for generalizability and be incorporated into new models of group process and performance.

Functions in Groups

One aspect of group process that has received wide attention is the area of critical functions. These are behaviors or activities that must occur to some degree in order for the group to progress effectively (Schein, 1988). Most functions have been identified as falling into one of two sets: those related to accomplishing the task, and those that contribute to the maintenance of the group (Bales, 1958).

Task functions enable the group to "solve the objective problem to which the group is committed" (Philip & Dunphy, 1959, p. 162). Examples of specific task behaviors include initiating, opinion seeking, opinion giving, information seeking, information giving, elaborating, summarizing, evaluating, role and goal clarification, and developing

performance strategies (Benne & Sheats, 1948; Hackman, 1986; Schein, 1988).

Maintenance functions "build, strengthen and regulate group life" (Philip & Dunphy, 1959, p. 162). Examples of maintenance behaviors include encouraging, harmonizing, compromising, expediting, relieving tension, group observing, and diagnosing (for a more complete description of these roles, see Benne & Sheats, 1948; Schein, 1988).

The classification of group functions into task and maintenance behaviors has a long history that continues, in various forms, today (see Feldman, 1984; McGrath, 1984). This tradition does an excellent job of defining and refining critical functions within the group, but it does not address the task activities that relate to transactions with those outside the group (see Hendrick, 1987). The development of a classification scheme that excludes external activities is not surprising, given that most of the research relating to group functions has been conducted with short-term laboratory or T-groups. Research following this internal perspective consciously controls or eliminates the external context in which the group operates in order to achieve fine-grained analysis within the group.

External, Boundary-Spanning Functions

Recent research on groups in organizations has taken on more of an external approach (see Ancona, 1987) and has begun to focus on how group members interact with others outside the group. A number of studies have investigated the communication across group boundaries in R&D laboratories and have identified a set of communication roles, including stars, gatekeepers, and liaisons (Allen, 1984; Katz & Tushman, 1981; Tushman, 1977, 1979). These studies have pointed out the importance of bringing technical information into R&D groups and have established clear links between cross-boundary communication and performance (Allen, 1984). Another study of sales teams (Gladstein, 1984) has demonstrated that group members distinguish between internal and boundary activities rather than between task and maintenance activities.

Studies such as these are useful in demonstrating the relationship between external activity and group performance. So far, however, they have focused only on very specific behaviors, most particularly the transfer of technical information. Our goal is to describe a more complete set of boundary activities than these other studies have identified.

Methods

The research strategy we have chosen could be described loosely as a comparative case analysis. The reason we selected such an approach is that we believe that research on external processes in groups is at a relatively early stage of development. Because this is so, we believe that exploration and description, classification of phenomena, and attempting to identify observable patterns of activity must all precede the proposition and testing of specific hypotheses (Gladstein & Quinn, 1985).

As our goal is to describe a wide set of boundary roles in groups within organizations, we chose new product teams (NPT) in high-technology companies, which must carry out diverse forms of interaction with many external groups. New product teams are dependent upon other parts of the organization for information, resources, and support. They also must deliver products and services to others. These complex transactions are carried out with a diverse set of functional groups, including marketing, manufacturing, and top management—functions that represent other "thought worlds" (Dougherty, 1987), that is, different languages, values, and time frames, as well as different hierarchical levels.

New product teams face a highly uncertain and complex task (Ancona & Caldwell, 1987). There may be periods of creativity alternating with times when efficiency is the primary outcome of interest. Therefore most of the interaction with other groups is not clearly programmed in standard operating procedures and routines, but evolves to meet task demands. We believe that the combination of high interdependence, high uncertainty, and multiple forms of dependence with multiple groups maximizes our ability to identify a full range of cross-boundary activities.

Data Collection

During a larger study of product development, we collected data through 38 interviews with NPT managers at seven corporations in the computer, integrated circuit, and analytic instrumentation industries. Interviews ranged between one and eight hours, with an average duration of three hours. Teams were at various stages of product development: Some were just starting out while others had completed projects within the last month. Using a semistructured interview, we asked each manager to describe the activities that the manager and team members carried out with people outside the group boundaries.

In addition, 15 new product team members from two teams were asked to keep a log for a week, recording all interactions, of any kind, with people outside the team. Once the interview and log data were collected, the two authors reviewed transcripts, notes, tapes, and logs to identify all references to interactions with outsiders. Examples of these interactions included meetings, one-on-one discussions, telephone calls, and computer messages. We also reviewed the data for what might be called noninteractions; for example, a manager might speak of not wanting to meet with a member of another group until a specific part of the product had been completed. We included such noninteractions in our analysis, and we considered both interactions that were initiated by the group and those initiated by outsiders. Finally, we looked at internal group activity aimed at dealing with an external constituency; for example, group discussion regarding how to acquire external resources was considered a boundary activity.

After identifying boundary activities, we tried to cluster them into larger categories that encapsulated related sets of activities. We tried many alternative categorization schemes until settling on one that appeared to us to take into account major differences among activities, yet included all the activities that had been identified. We include here both the category schemes and the activities so that the reader can judge our work. It is important to note that the findings in this study are preliminary. We look to future research to validate our findings and their generalizability to other samples.

Results

An inspection of the reported interactions suggests that groups use, in combination, three strategies in managing their external relations. The first strategy involves initiating transactions to either import or export information, resources, or support. The second strategy consists of responses to the initiatives of those outside the group. The third strategy is slightly different in that it does not directly entail initiating or responding activity, but involves the actual definition of who is part of the group.

Each of these strategies is associated with a set of activities. We label the activity set associated with the strategy of initiating transactions as scout and ambassador activity. The activity set associated with responding to others we call sentry and guard activity. Changing the actual definition of the group involves the presence or absence of immigrants, captives, and emigrants.

Scout, ambassador, sentry, guard, immigrant, captive, and emigrant activity sets are not unidimensional. In fact, each represents multiple activities that were observed in our teams. A fuller description of the specific behaviors we discovered follows.

Scout Activities

The activities that involve bringing information and/or resources needed by the group in across the boundary we have labeled as scout activities. Scouting involves the collection of various types of information, including task-relevant information necessary for problem solution, political data about support or opposition to the group's activities, and the extent of demand for the group's output. Most previous research on external group process has focused on the import of task-relevant information. Scout activity involves the collection of a broader range of information as well as the procurement of resources necessary for group functioning, such as equipment and personnel.

The scout activity set consists of four observed activities: modeling, information and resource gathering; scanning, and feedback seeking.

Modeling. One of the boundary activities that often characterized interactions early in a team's development is modeling, or mapping the external environment. Modeling entails constructing a picture of the external environment, including predictions of future trouble spots or potential allies. Modeling represents the team's attempt to answer questions such as: "Who supports us and who doesn't?" "What do people want us to do?" "Who has information or resources that we need?" or "How can we acquire what we need?"

Modeling was sometimes done in the group using information that members had from previous experience. Other times leaders spoke of a need to update models through external observation and discussion in order to respond to changes in the organization or a new task. The quotation following illustrates modeling:

> The first thing I did was to go to talk to lots of people to find out what they thought the product was and how to get there. . . . I started out with the guy who brought me here, he sent me to someone else, and so it went that I came to talk to a lot of high- and middle-level people. . . . So I gained knowledge about details of what the product ought to be, who the players were, what they did and what they wanted.

Gathering information and resources. Throughout the life of the team the leaders and members brought in information and resources needed for current decision making, coordinating, and task progress. These activities required a fairly focused search because they flowed directly from current task demands. For example, members needed to know about the progress of other interdependent groups in order to set up schedules for themselves; they needed particular computers for certain subtasks; they needed to know the results of funding decisions in order to plan their own expenditures. More generally, this activity might be thought of as completing a shopping list of information and resources that the group must acquire to complete its task. An example of this activity follows:

> At this point we have to use the test line, which is a shared resource, so there's a lot of competition to use it. I have one guy who checks the schedule every morning so we know of any holes that we can fill.

Scanning. In contrast to the focused search described above, scanning or detecting involves the collection of information that is not immediately relevant to the task. This activity is similar to what Adams (1980) describes as seeking information about events that might occur, or that might have relevance to the group if they did occur. Here we see behaviors aimed at detecting early signs of trouble, changes in the external environment, and data that do not seem to fit into the models formed earlier in the group's history. When behavior of external entities deviates from the group's expectations and needs, it is the person doing detecting or scanning who brings this information into the group. An example follows:

> We have a kind of detector. She's very sensitive and works with the people interfaces, not the technical part. She spends time with all the groups in manufacturing to detect problems so they can be dealt with quickly.

Feedback seeking. A final example of scout activity is feedback seeking: collecting other groups' perceptions of the team's progress, product, members, or functioning. Although some of this activity was clearly geared toward acquiring additional resources to help the team complete the task, it also provided reassurance that work was done adequately, and that team members could move ahead. An example of feedback seeking follows:

> After a few weeks we had a design review with all of R&D. We just wanted to make sure that we weren't going off in crazy directions.

Ambassador Activities

Ambassadorial activities involve the export of information and/or resources to outsiders. This activity set involves developing and maintaining channels of communication in order to keep others informed and to persuade outsiders that the group's activities are valuable and should be supported. Ambassador activities include opening up communication channels, informing others of group progress, coordinating and negotiating, and activities aimed at influencing or changing the external world. The latter include attempts to mold or shape the beliefs of others.

Opening up communication channels. Early in the group's history, sometimes even before the group receives a formal charter, leaders and members are busy opening up communication channels with other groups. These interactions often do not have clear purposes or agendas other than to introduce someone from the team and begin to establish a relationship. They may be rationalized as precursors to other forms of transactions or as a means to maintain a relationship during periods when interdependence is low. Two examples follow:

> I asked my secretary to schedule one-on-one meetings with each of the senior engineering managers. I just wanted to formally tell them what they already knew, that the project had been given the green light. This got a dialogue started.

> I stop in even when there's nothing urgent, to develop a relationship with those people.

Informing. One external activity observed in every group in the study was informing other groups about the team's progress. As organizations are made up of many groups whose work is interconnected, it is not surprising that substantial effort is devoted to this activity. This generally involves using both formal and informal channels developed by the group. In many groups this activity is widely distributed. An example of informing follows:

> Then we started having meetings with all those people outside the group. There were representatives from purchasing, manufacturing, production planning, the diagnostics group, marketing, every one. . . . Everyone was informed about progress and changes. The minutes were typed on line so that the team and those who weren't at the meeting knew what was going on. The top management group also got copies.

Coordinating and negotiating. Although coordinating and negotiating appear to be separate activities, our interviewees typically discussed them together. For new product teams, coordinating typically involves resolving the issues of interdependent schedules. For example, the team needs to receive the work product of one group by a particular date in order to meet its own schedule to deliver its work to yet another group, which has its own schedule to meet. Although the focus of this activity may be integrating work activity, there is also negotiating going on. That is, there is give and take over what exchange agreements are going to exist between two units. This negotiating is particularly common because of shifting power and dependency relationships between the NPT and other groups. An example follows:

> We had to explain (to manufacturing) how certain things worked. I had lots and lots of meetings about the status of the project. We wanted some last-minute changes on the machine, but manufacturing was not able or not willing to put it in all the machines. There were great arguments and the Product Committee was involved. By April we had worked out a compromise agreement.

Molding. The activities that represent a group's attempts to influence the external environment to suit its agenda are labeled molding. The aim here is to shape the beliefs and behaviors of outsiders. Those group members trying to mold the environment often do so by presenting a view of the group they want others to share. In essence this is profile management: representing the group in extremely positive terms when resources are needed and in a less positive light if that is required. Molding involves persuading and cheerleading, influencing how much outsiders support the group and how they feel about the group. An example follows:

> I'm like a cheerleader, trying to get those guys excited about our products. . . . I went to a meeting and explained that the company was riding on this project and we were going to do it fast and do it right.

Sentry Activities

This activity set focuses on policing the boundary by controlling the information and resources that external agents want to send into the group. This means deciding from whom the group will accept input, how much of that input will be admitted, the form the input will take, and when the flow of input must stop. Sentry activity protects the group by allowing it to work with minimal distraction. Often external groups try to communicate their priorities, interests, and demands. When this input is desired, the major sentry activity is deciding when and how this will be done. When this information and other inputs are not desired, the major sentry activity is buffering the group. Buffering includes absorbing external pressures, such as political tensions, on behalf of the group. The key sentry activities are allowing entry, translating, and filtering.

Allowing entry. When outsiders have information or resources that they wish to provide to the group, allowing entry simply involves providing access so that the information or resources can be delivered. Allowing entry might mean a two-step process whereby the outsider tells a group member something and this is then relayed to the group, or it might be a direct message from an outsider. An example follows:

> We needed to get input from engineering at the beginning. We didn't want to come up with some kind of Dr. Seuss machine that had to be redesigned later so we let the engineering people in.

Translating. Many messages from outsiders require interpretation in order to be useful to the group. Due to differentiation within the organization, different subunits develop different values, jargon, and meanings for the same words. A member of the group could help outsiders to translate their messages into words that other group members would understand. This was done either by having the group member actually relay the message or by standing by when the outsider delivered it. Translating was also done after external representatives had gone and members were unclear about what had actually transpired. Translating did not always occur, even when it was needed. In some cases members were not aware that a message required translation; in other cases, no one in the group was capable of translation. An example follows:

> This guy from marketing came in and went on and on about how their research had shown that the computer was just too heavy. He kept wanting us to picture the traveling salesman going in and out of hotels every night and taking the computer with him. Marketing wanted us to know that the current machine just didn't make this an easy task. I waited until he left and explained that lighter translated into seven pounds less than our current machine and that meant we had to find a new material for the casing.

Filtering. Filtering consists of taking information from outsiders and delivering a smaller amount to the group. In other words, during filtering decisions are made as to what is appropriate for members to hear. A part of filtering is buffering, or absorbing pressure by keeping troubling information or political pressure from the team. Buffering also takes place when the volume of information or other inputs is considered too great and needs to be limited or stopped. An extreme form of buffering is actually to separate the group physically from the rest of the organization. An example follows:

> Near the end I talked to the top management group a lot. I tried to protect the group from that kind of pressure, though. It's like Tom West said, we won't pass on the garbage and the politics.

Guard Activities

This activity set involves monitoring the information and resources that others request from the group and determining how the group will respond to those demands. Outsiders may simply be curious about team activities and want information, or they may be attempting to take resources at the group's expense. Guard activities include classifying, delivering, and protecting.

Classifying. When requests for information or resources are made, group members often delay responding until they can determine the legitimacy of the request and the impact that satisfying the request would have on the team. Of course, certain requests are filled automatically because organizational or group rules determine their legitimacy.

Other requests are discussed with various group members or the group leader to determine if they will be granted. Here is an example of classifying:

> This guy from the university came by and told us he was developing a software program to PERT chart the part of the process we were working on. He wanted to know exactly what the hardware team was doing. I didn't know if we could provide that kind of access so I put him on hold.

Delivering. Once a request has been identified as legitimate and acceptable, the information or resource is simply delivered. Many external groups make requests throughout the life cycle of the group so delivering is close to a constant process. An example follows:

> Our product manager asked us if we would present our current plans to the product committee the following month. He's the one that's gotten us this far, so I readily agreed.

Protecting. When a request is not viewed as legitimate by the group, a decision may be made not to grant it. Preventing the release of information or resources is a protecting activity. Protecting could be as simple as having all group members keep certain information secret, or as difficult as explaining to top management that their constant inquiries are hampering group work. An example follows:

> Near the end people started panicking. The top guys would come down and want to know if we were making progress. I told them they had to stop, that they were having a distracting and deleterious effect on the group.

Immigrants, Captives, and Emigrants

The immigrant, captive, and emigrant are individuals who perform boundary activities. Where they are present (or absent, in the case of the emigrant) they represent changes in the membership of the focal group. The immigrant is an outsider who is induced to join the group voluntarily. Motivations to join the group may vary from needing another job, to wanting to work with a particular set of people or on a particular technology. The captive, in contrast, is assigned to the group, often despite a desire to be elsewhere. The assignment of the captive often is a precursor to internal group conflict. Finally, the emigrant is one who leaves the focal team in order to represent the group to outsiders.

These individuals carry out several functions, such as the transfer of information and resources, linking different organizational groups, and co-opting others. Immigrants and captives facilitate the transfer of information and resources into the group, either through their own information and resources or through their connections and contacts. Emigrants facilitate the transfer of the team's information to other groups.

These roles facilitate transactions by making them more efficient and also link various groups across hierarchy and function. A difficulty, however, can arise if exchange personnel are away from their original area for too long. They potentially lose their ability to represent the focal group. In some cases, emigrants came to be viewed as outsiders, and immigrants and captives, who originally represented other groups, came to be seen as members of the team. In contrast, difficulties can arise also when an immigrant or captive does not get fully integrated into the group and therefore does not supply important information or actually tries to sabotage the team. Examples of immigrant, captive, and emigrant activities follow:

> There was no problem staffing this project. As soon as word got around that we were going to do a high-end project I started hearing from volunteers. Many of them had worked with me before, but not all of them.

> They brought in this high-level guy. He has lots of connections with top management, and now it's easier to get what we need. My boss asked him to come on, I think, to get more buy-in for the project from the top guys.

> There was a lot to watch over so we decided to bring in three people from manufacturing. Later we would bring more manufacturing people in to help with the debugging, but these guys became part of the team. . . . Then we had this fight (with manufacturing). . . . Manufacturing yanked these people out.

> At this point the team has a whole different form. Those who are helping manufacturing are spending most of their time in New Hampshire at the factory.

The Complexity of the External Boundary-Spanning Functions

In describing boundary management in their new product teams, our interviewees indicated that the various boundary activities can be taken on by one individual or by many different people. For example, the group leader may assume all boundary activities with top management, performing scout, ambassador, sentry, and guard activities. Similarly, one individual may engage in an activity or it can be broadly dispersed, when, for example, the leader asks each group member to take on the guard activity of keeping certain information secret. In addition, a sequence of boundary transactions may combine elements of several activities, that is, sentry and ambassador activities.

The activity sets described here are all inter-related. For example, the scout, sentry, captive, and immigrant functions all deal with information that comes into the group. These activities therefore influence group members' perceptions of the outside world, and can shape the extent to which those perceptions are biased or distorted. The ambassador, guard, and emigrant functions influence how external groups perceive the group. Such activities define what is said and the manner in which it is said to outsiders.

Sometimes, the activity sets described here can substitute for one another; an increase in the number of immigrants or captives often means less scout and ambassador activity is required because the information or resource has been brought inside the group. Similarly, sending an emigrant to another group may mean fewer requests from that group and therefore less guard activity. Collectively scout, ambassador, sentry, guard, immigrant, captive, and emigrant activities serve to define how the group manages relations with the external environment.

Antecedents and Consequences of Boundary Activity

We have described the range of boundary activities that new product teams use to manage their external relationships. In this section, we speculate on the antecedents and consequences of these activities and why individuals, groups, and organizations

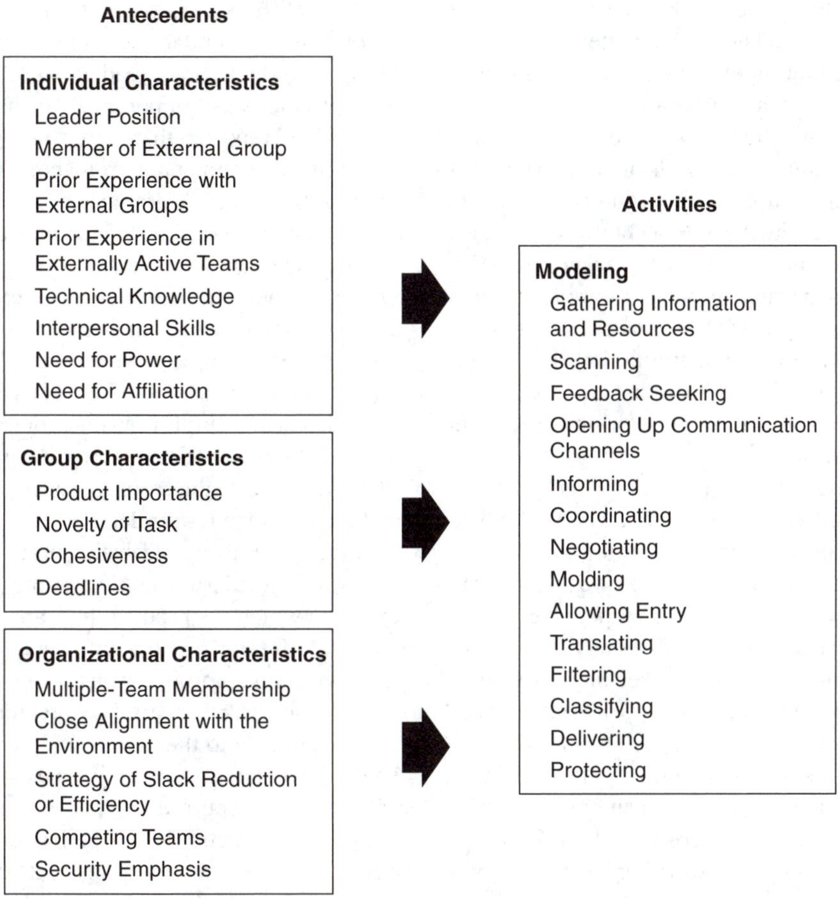

Antecedents

Individual Characteristics

Leader Position

Member of External Group

Prior Experience with
External Groups

Prior Experience in
Externally Active Teams

Technical Knowledge

Interpersonal Skills

Need for Power

Need for Affiliation

Activities

Modeling

Gathering Information
and Resources

Scanning

Feedback Seeking

Opening Up Communication
Channels

Informing

Group Characteristics

Product Importance

Novelty of Task

Cohesiveness

Deadlines

Coordinating

Negotiating

Molding

Allowing Entry

Translating

Filtering

Classifying

Delivering

Protecting

Organizational Characteristics

Multiple-Team Membership

Close Alignment with the
Environment

Strategy of Slack Reduction
or Efficiency

Competing Teams

Security Emphasis

FIGURE 26.1 ■ Antecedents of boundary activities.

show varying degrees of these activities. Here again our study is exploratory. Our goal is not to test specific hypotheses but rather to provide raw material for future research.

Our data suggest that there are individual, group, and organizational antecedents of boundary activity (see Figure 26.1 for a summary of these antecedents). In other words, people with particular roles, skills, or experiences seemed most likely to take on boundary activities. Within organizations, we also observed that certain groups with particular tasks or characteristics exhibited higher levels of boundary activity. Finally, we saw differences in organizations as to the number of group members carrying out external activities, and the percentage of time spent on these activities.

Individual antecedents. At the individual level, several factors appear to differentiate those who took on high levels of boundary activity from those who were more internally focused or isolated. First and foremost, the team leader took on higher levels of external activity, particularly upward communications and ambassadorial activities. In contrast, team members took on lower levels of external communication, and these were lateral in direction. Individuals who came from other functional groups (e.g., captives or immigrants), or those who had prior experience with other functional groups, were more likely to communicate with those other groups. Similarly, individuals who had prior experience on teams in which members had shown high levels of external activity were likely to continue that pattern. Our data suggest that these individuals had not only a better understanding of the need for input from other areas, but also more contacts on which to draw.

Another set of factors that influences individual boundary spanning is the skills and personality of the individual team member. Boundary spanners were often those with the most technical knowledge, although these individuals often lacked the interpersonal skills to negotiate and to promote the team to outsiders. In such cases team leaders might assign a specific liaison to outside groups. For this assignment, an individual with "people skills," one who had acquired a reputation for working well with others, was chosen.

Different boundary activities appear to attract people with different motives and needs. Ambassadorial activities, particularly molding and negotiating, seem to appeal to those who are motivated to influence others and to display a positive profile within the organization. Scouting activities, particularly scanning, and feedback seeking, as well as relationship building, seem to appeal to those who like interpersonal activity and believe in a consensual mode of decision making. High levels of sentry and guard activity were seen among those who had had negative experiences with outside groups and those who enjoyed working alone, in their own way, and on their own schedule.

The notion that individual differences can influence the adoption of boundary activity is not unique (Caldwell & O'Reilly, 1982; Aldrich & Herker, 1977). Similarity in values, language, and orientation toward work have been known to facilitate cooperation and communication with outsiders (Byrne, 1971; Dougherty, 1987; Festinger, 1950; Lawrence & Lorsch, 1967). Our findings are consistent with this work, but add some new variables to be considered as well as verifying the importance of these variables in the organizational setting.

Group antecedents. Our interview data suggest that a number of group variables influence the extent to which teams engage in boundary activities. Two important sets of variables seem to be (1) the nature of group's task, and (2) the group's internal process.

A key difference between teams with high and low levels of boundary activities seems to be the group's product. Team leaders who reported that their product was "important," "of high priority," or "visible" reported that there was a great deal of pressure to obtain input from other parts of the organization. These teams also reported that it was easier to contact and influence outsiders because top management had deemed their product top priority. These teams showed high levels of ambassador and scout activities, while low-priority project team members were often frustrated by their inability to carry out these activities successfully. Ironically, high-priority project teams also reported higher levels of sentry and guard activity to protect the team from excessive information and attention from outsiders.

A second task variable that seems to influence the nature of boundary spanning in the group is the extent to which the product the team was working on was "different" or "revolutionary." When teams were working on products that were very different from those the members had previously worked on or were new to the organization or the market, one of two patterns emerged. These radical innovations either spurred high levels of scout and ambassadorial activities, as members tried to find answers to the new questions and problems that emerged, or members closed ranks with sentry and guard activity to cloak their ignorance, or to work on the issues without undue interruption.

New problems require new frames (see Dewar & Dutton, 1986) and new procedures, both within the team and between the team and outsiders. Thus the internal focus may well be maladaptive. Similarly, evolutionary or small changes in products often left team members with the impression that they understood the views, inputs, and demands of other parts of the organization and they therefore did not collect new information or sufficient feedback. While these teams may have needed more scout activity to verify group assumptions and plans, this was often absent. Here, as in other group settings, group members work using the strategies learned from previous tasks, rather than necessarily updating their work patterns for the new task (Hackman & Morris, 1975; Hackman & Walton, 1986).

The second set of group variables that seems to interact with the boundary activities is the internal process of the group. In groups where the team leader described high levels of cohesiveness and internal communication, there was less mentioned about scout and ambassador activity, even when the interviewer prompted. It appears that an internal focus may inhibit external activity, or, conversely that high levels of external activity may bring alternative perspectives into the group, leading to conflict and less cohesiveness. Impending deadlines also appeared to increase the level of sentry and guard behavior while decreasing the level of ambassador and scout activity. These findings are consistent with other studies of the relationship between external relations and internal processes (Alderfer, 1976; Levine & Campbell, 1972; Sherif & Sherif, 1953).

Organizational antecedents. Finally, the results of our interviews suggest that organizations differ in degree and type of boundary activity. Of course, our informants represented a small number of organizations, so our conclusions must be limited and preliminary. Organizations in which people served on multiple teams rather than on only one team seemed to have higher overall levels of boundary activity. Perhaps multiple-team membership lessens the permeability of any one team's boundaries and makes members more comfortable working with outsiders.

Greater levels of ambassador and scout activity were seen in organizations whose strategies stressed close alignment with customers or the reduction of slack resources within the organization. In both cases, closer coordination among differentiated organizational groups was encouraged and rewarded in an attempt either to decrease the time needed to get a product to market or to reduce the formal coordination costs of product development. Higher levels of sentry and guard activity seemed to be present in organizations that used competing teams to develop the same product, or that were very security conscious, considering new products "secret."

Individual consequences. Our interviewees suggested that boundary activity has consequences both for the individual who carries it out and for the performance of the group and organization. Individuals carrying out scout, ambassador, sentry, and guard activities, as well as immigrant, captive, and emigrant roles, generally are exposed to multiple perspectives, languages, and ideas, entailing frequent interpersonal interaction and conflict. It has long been established that such situations may create stress for the individual (see Adams, 1980; Dougherty, 1987; Kahn, Wolfe, Quinn, Snoek, & Rosenthal, 1964). Our data support these findings. Interviewees reported high levels of stress attributable to the multiple loyalties created by the interactions and the high personal cost of protecting the team from outside pressure. On the positive side, high levels of external activity provide exposure to information and career opportunities that can increase the spanner's power and probability of advancement.

Group consequences. At the group level, our observations have led us to hypothesize several relationships between boundary activity and performance. First, we posit that group performance will be enhanced if the amount of external activity increases as resource dependence increases. At some level, nearly all groups in organizations must acquire resources and information externally and transfer outputs to others. In most cases, the ability of the group to accomplish these transactions successfully will influence the group's performance. When the resources that must be acquired are critical for the task, or complex, or come from multiple sources, boundary activities are likely to be a more important predictor of performance than in cases where the resources are less important, simpler, or centralized. Similarly, if the output being transferred is unique or requires specialized processing, boundary activities will be more critical than if the transfer is simple or can be routinized. Thus, while the performance of a laboratory or T-group may be predicted solely by internal behaviors, this is not true for groups that are dependent on outsiders.

Second, we posit that when a group is performing a task new to the organization or to group members, or when the environmental conditions are changing, group performance will be enhanced if there is a high level of scout and ambassador activity. Relying on old models or continuing to function according to characteristic patterns may result in inertia and an inability to update (see Gladstein & Reilly, 1985; Staw, Sandelands & Dutton, 1981), while scanning, translating, feedback seeking, and negotiating allow for the establishment of new models and new coordination agreements with outsiders.

Third, we posit that groups may become more effective if they shift their emphasis between internal and external activities. Early in the new product development process, groups often need a high degree of external scout and ambassador activity in order to determine task requirements and obtain resources. Once requirements have been determined and resources obtained, sentry and guard activity helps to buffer the group and allows it to concentrate on technical problem solving. Later, ambassador and scout activity may become critical as the group seeks out feedback and promotes its product.

Organizational consequences. As long as external activities enable a group to coordinate with other groups, get external support for internal activities, bring new ideas and information into the group, and negotiate relationships not specified by the formal hierarchy, these activities also serve organizational needs. As corporations strive to survive in a more competitive environment, they try to cut down on slack, improve internal efficiency and coordination, and get closer to the customer. For organizations moving in this direction, boundary activities become the vehicle for providing closer coupling among organizational units and between the organization and its environment.

These propositions are tentative and await testing. There has been some preliminary research in groups (Gersick, 1988), and similar propositions have been tested and supported in applications of the resource dependence perspective in organizations (see Pennings, 1980; Pfeffer, 1986). However, further group research is needed to clarify the antecedents and consequences of external activities.

Implications for Practice

If the relationships proposed here are valid, we believe that external activities in groups will become increasingly important. In the realm of new product development, as well as in many other areas, tasks are becoming more uncertain and complex. The managers in our study all saw their tasks becoming more complex and their environments becoming more volatile and more competitive. Managers want guidance on providing training and incentives that increase the levels of boundary activity required for increased external dependence in a competitive environment. In response, we have tried to articulate some implications for practice.

First, team leaders and members would benefit from a new model of group effectiveness. Nearly every book on group performance (e.g., Dyer, 1977; Zander, 1986) emphasizes internal interactions among team members and focuses on intragroup variables such as cohesiveness, trust, commitment, and conflict management (Gladstein, 1984). Our research suggests that an external perspective stressing the management of both internal and external behavior is a more appropriate model for organization groups than one that focuses on internal behavior alone (see Figures 26.2a and 26.2b).

Acceptance of this external perspective allows the team to begin diagnosing its external dependencies. The team can use this external model to identify the outsiders who could supply ideas, task or political information, support, materials, personnel, or help in obtaining other inputs and distributing the team's output. Such a process also can identify individuals and groups who might be intrusive or threatening to the team. Once such analysis has been made, team members can be identified to carry out scouting activities to model unknown aspects of the environment, verify the critical assumptions the group has made, and search for information and resources. In addition, individuals with interpersonal skills or specialized influence can be chosen or imported into the group to negotiate, translate outside demands, and inform outside groups of the team's progress. Finally, when threats are forecast or arise, the team can identify

A. Groups in Isolation

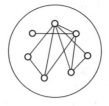

B. Groups in the Organizational Environment

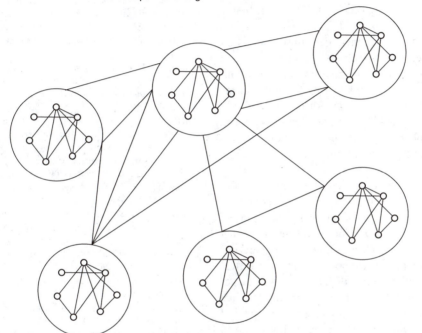

FIGURE 26.2 ■

the processes by which it can protect itself from the unwanted intrusion of outside influences.

In addition to providing an external perspective to team members, the model we propose can be useful as input to organizational human resources planning. Under conditions of increased resource dependence, the organization may need to develop broader selection, evaluation, and reward schemes. This strategy would help to ensure that teams are composed of individuals who have not only the requisite technical skills but also the abilities and motivation to work fully with others in importing information and transferring the group's outputs.

Rewards would need to change to support external activities. Team leaders and members would need to be held accountable for both internal and external performance. Performance appraisal would need to focus on intergroup as well as internal group activities, and monetary rewards would need to be tied to intergroup, not just group, products.

Conclusion

Although almost every model of group behavior refers to the functions needed for group effectiveness, most of these functions refer to behaviors inside the group. Here we have taken an external perspective, identifying those activities that link a group to other, interdependent, parts of the organization.

Support for the external perspective has been found at the organizational level of analysis. Organizations manage their external dependence through mergers, acquisitions, interlocking directorates, and boundary-spanning activity (Adams, 1980; Pennings, 1980; Pfeffer, 1972; Van de Ven & Walker, 1984). The parallel finding that organizations also manage dependence with outsiders by altering external transactions, permeability, and membership, is not surprising. Groups, like organizations, are open systems that must import information and resources, transform them into a viable product, and then export them elsewhere. There is an obvious need to interact with outsiders to manage this process at either the group or the organization level.

This research is only the first step in understanding external boundary-spanning functions in groups. We have observed and described a broad range of boundary activities in new product teams. Future research will have to compare our descriptions with other types of groups, in different settings, performing different tasks. Further steps would include performing more quantitative data collection to test whether the grouping of variables that we have performed is borne out in larger samples using more sophisticated clustering techniques. Future research must move beyond exploration and description, to classification and proposition and testing of specific hypotheses (Gladstein & Quinn, 1985).

We have identified scout, ambassador, sentry, guard, immigrant, captive, and emigrant activity sets. These newly discovered external activities now need to be integrated into models of group process and performance. We may find that external activities also fall into a task and maintenance classification, with some team members helping with task coordination and others concentrated on maintaining a workable relationship with external groups. We may find a developmental model with external activities changing in importance over time. Whatever the results, this external perspective appears to be a fruitful direction for offering better understanding of organization groups.

REFERENCES

Adams, J. S. (1980). Interorganizational processes and organization boundary roles. In *Research in Organizational Behavior 2* (pp. 321–355). Greenwich, CT: JAI Press.

Alderfer, C. P. (1976). Boundary relations and organizational diagnosis. In M. Meltzer and F. Wickert (Eds.), *Humanizing Organizational Behavior*. Springfield, IL: Charles Thomas.

Aldrich, J., & Herker, D. (1977). Boundary spanning roles and organization structure. *Academy of Management Review, 2* (April), 217–230.

Allen, T. J. (1984). *Managing the flow of technology: Technology transfer and the dissemination of technological information within the R&D organization*. Cambridge, MA: MIT Press.

Ancona, D. G. (1987). Groups in organizations: Extending laboratory models. In C. Hendrick (Ed.), *Annual review of personality and social psychology: group and intergroup processes*. Beverly Hills, CA: Sage.

Ancona, D. G., & Caldwell, D. (1987). Management issues in new product teams. *Advances in Industrial Relations*. Greenwich, CT: JAI Press.

Bales, R. F. (1958). Task roles and social roles in problem-solving groups. In E. E. Maccoby, T. M. Newcomb, & E. L. Hartley (Eds.), *Social psychology* (3rd ed., pp. 437–447). New York: Holt, Rinehart, & Winston.

Bettenhausen, K., & Murnighan, J. K. (1985). The emergence of norms in competitive decision-making groups. *Administrative Science Quarterly, 30*, 350–372.

Benne, K. D., & Sheats, P. (1948). Functional roles of group members. *Journal of Social Issues, 4*, 2, 41–49.

Byrne, D. (1971). *The attraction paradigm*. New York: Academic Press. Caldwell, D. F., & O'Reilly, C. A. (1982). Boundary spanning and individual performance: The impact of self monitoring. *Journal of Applied Psychology, 67*, 124–127.

Delbecq, A. L., Van de Ven, A. H., & Gustafson, D. H. (1975). *Group techniques for program planning: A guide to nominal group and Delphi processes*. Glenview, IL: Scott, Foresman.

Dewar, R., & Dutton, J. (1986). The adoption of radical and incremental innovations: An empirical analysis. *Management Science, 32*, 1422–1433.

Dougherty, D. (1987). *New products in old organizations: The myth of the better mousetrap in search of the beaten path*. Ph.D. dissertation, Sloan School of Management, MIT.

Dunphy, D. C. (1964). *Social change in self-analytical groups*. Ph.D. dissertation, Harvard University.

Dyer, W. G. (1977). *Team building: Issues and alternatives*. Reading, MA: Addison-Wesley.

Feldman, D. C. (1984). The development and enforcement of group norms. *Academy of Management Review, 9*, 47–53.

Festinger, L. (1950). Informal social communication. *Psychology Review, 57,* 271–282.

Gersick, C. J. C. (1988). Time and transition in work teams: Toward a new model of group development. *Academy of Management Journal, 31,* 9–41.

Gladstein, D. (1984). Groups in context: A model of task group effectiveness. *Administrative Science Quarterly, 29,* 499–517.

Gladstein, D. L., & Reilly, N. (1985). Group decision making under threat: The tycoon game. *Academy of Management Journal, 28,* 613–627.

Gladstein, D., & Quinn, J. B. (1985). Making decisions and producing action: Two faces of strategy. In H. Pennings (Ed.), *Strategic decision making.* San Francisco, CA: Jossey-Bass.

Goodman, P. (Ed.). (1986). The impact of task and technology on group performance. In P. Goodman (Ed.), *Designing effective work groups* (pp. 198–216). San Francisco, CA: Jossey-Bass.

Goodman, P. S., Ravlin, E., & Schminke, M. (1987). Understanding groups in organizations. In L. L. Cummings & B. M. Staw (Eds.), *Research in organizational behavior* (Vol. 9, pp. 1–71).

Hackman, J. R. (1986). The design of work teams. In J. Lorsch (Ed.), *Handbook of organizational behavior* (pp. 315–342). Englewood Cliffs, NJ: Prentice-Hall.

Hackman, J. R., & Morris, C. G. (1975). Group tasks, group interaction process and group performance effectiveness: A review and proposed integration. In L. Berkowitz (Ed.), *Advances in experimental social psychology* (Vol. 8, pp. 45–99). New York: Academic Press.

Hackman, J. R., & Walton, R. E. (1986). Leading groups in organizations. In P. Goodman (Ed.), *Designing effective work groups* (pp. 72–119). San Francisco, CA: Jossey-Bass.

Hendrick, C. (Ed.). (1987). *Review of personality and social psychology.* Newbury Park, CA: Sage.

Herold, D. (1979). The effectiveness of work groups. In S. Kerr (Ed.), *Organizational behavior.* Columbus, OH: Grid.

Jewell, L. N., & Reitz, H. J. (1981). *Group effectiveness in organizations.* Glenview, IL: Scott, Foresman.

Kahn, R. L., Wolfe, D. M., Quinn, R. P., Snoek, J. D., & Rosenthal, R. A. (1964). *Organizational stress: Studies in role conflict and ambiguity.* New York: John Wiley.

Kanter, R. M. (1986). The new workforce meets the changing workplace: Strains, dilemmas, and contradictions in attempts to implement participative and entrepreneurial management. *Human Resource Management, 25,* 515–539.

Kaplan, R. E. (1979). The conspicuous absence of evidence that process consultation enhances task performance. *Journal of Applied Behavioral Science, 15,* 3, 346–360.

Katz, R., & Tushman, M. (1981). An investigation into the managerial roles and career paths of gatekeepers and project supervisors in a major R&D facility. *R&D Management, 11,* 103–110.

Kazanjian, R. K., & Drazin, R. (1988, forthcoming). An empirical test of a stage of growth progression model. *Academy of Management Journal.*

Lawrence, P. R., & Lorsch, J. W. (1867). *Managing differentiation and integration.* Homewood, IL: Richard Irwin.

Levine, R., & Campbell, D. (1972). *Ethnocentrism: Theories of conflict, ethnic attitudes, and group behavior.* New York: John Wiley.

McGrath, J. F. (1984). *Groups: Interaction and performance.* Englewood Cliffs, NJ: Prentice-Hall.

McKelvey, B. (1982). *Organizational systemics: Taxonomy, evolution, and classification.* Berkeley, CA: University of California Press.

Pennings, J. M. (1980). *Interlocking directorates.* San Francisco, CA: Jossey-Bass.

Pfeffer, J. (1972). Merger as a response to organizational interdependence. *Administrative Science Quarterly, 17,* 382–394.

Pfeffer, J. (1986). A resource dependence perspective on intercorporate relations. In M. S. Mizruchi & M. Schwartz (Eds.), *Structural analysis of business* (pp. 117–132). New York: Academic Press.

Philip, J., & Dunphy, D. (1959). Developmental trends in small groups. *Sociometry, 22,* 162–174.

Schein, E. H. (1988). *Process consultation: Its role in organization development* (Vol. 1). Reading, MA: Addison-Wesley.

Sherif, M., & Sherif, C. (1953). *Groups in harmony and tension.* New York: Harper & Row.

Staw, B. M., Sandelands, L. E., & Dutton, J. E. (1981). Threat-rigidity effects in organizational behavior: A multi-level analysis. *Administrative Science Quarterly, 26,* 501–524.

Stephan, W. G. (1984). Intergroup relations. In G. Lindzey & E. Aronson (Eds.), *Handbook of social psychology: II, Special Fields and Applications* (3rd ed., pp. 599–658). New York: Random House.

Tushman, M. (1977). Special boundary roles in the innovation process. *Administrative Science Quarterly, 22,* 587–605.

Tushman, M. (1979). Work characteristics and subunit communication structure: A contingency analysis. *Administrative Science Quarterly, 29,* 82–98.

Van de Ven, A. H., & Walker, G. (1984). The dynamics of interorganizational coordination. *Administrative Science Quarterly, 29,* 591–621.

Whetten, D. (1983). Interorganizational relations. In J. Lorsch (Ed.), *Handbook of organizational behavior.* Englewood Cliffs, NJ: Prentice-Hall.

Zander, A. (1986). *Groups at work.* San Francisco, CA: Jossey-Bass.

How to Read a Journal Article in Social Psychology

Christian H. Jordan and Mark P. Zanna

When approaching a journal article for the first time, and often on subsequent occasions, most people try to digest it as they would any piece of prose. They start at the beginning and read word for word, until eventually they arrive at the end, perhaps a little bewildered, but with a vague sense of relief. This is not an altogether terrible strategy; journal articles do have a logical structure that lends itself to this sort of reading. There are, however, more efficient approaches—approaches that enable you, a student of social psychology, to cut through peripheral details, avoid sophisticated statistics with which you may not be familiar, and focus on the central ideas in an article. Arming yourself with a little foreknowledge of what is contained in journal articles, as well as some practical advice on how to read them, should help you read journal articles more effectively. If this sounds tempting, read on.

Journal articles offer a window into the inner workings of social psychology. They document how social psychologists formulate hypotheses, design empirical studies, analyze the observations they collect, and interpret their results. Journal articles also serve an invaluable archival function: They contain the full store of common and cumulative knowledge of social psychology. Having documentation of past research allows researchers to build on past findings and advance our understanding of social behavior, without pursuing avenues of investigation that have already been explored. Perhaps most importantly, a research study is never complete until its results have been shared with others, colleagues and students alike. Journal articles are a primary means of communicating research findings. As such, they can be genuinely exciting and interesting to read. That last claim may have caught you off guard. For beginning readers, journal articles may seem anything but interesting and exciting. They may, on the contrary, appear daunting and esoteric, laden with jargon and obscured by menacing statistics. Recognizing this fact, we hope to arm you, through this paper, with the basic information you will need to read journal articles with a greater sense of comfort and perspective.

Social psychologists study many fascinating topics, ranging from prejudice and discrimination, to culture, persuasion, liking and love, conformity and obedience, aggression, and the self. In our daily lives, these are issues we often struggle to understand. Social psychologists present systematic observations of, as well as a wealth of ideas about, such issues in journal articles. It would be a shame if the fascination and intrigue these topics have were lost in their translation into journal publications.

We don't think they are, and by the end of this paper, hopefully you won't either.

Journal articles come in a variety of forms, including research reports, review articles, and theoretical articles. Put briefly, a *research report* is a formal presentation of an original research study, or a series of studies. A *review article* is an evaluative survey of previously published work, usually organized by a guiding theory or point of view. The author of a review article summarizes previous investigations of a circumscribed problem, comments on what progress has been made toward its resolution, and suggests areas of the problem that require further study. A *theoretical article* also evaluates past research, but focuses on the development of theories used to explain empirical findings. Here, the author may present a new theory to explain a set of findings, or may compare and contrast a set of competing theories, suggesting why one theory might be the superior one.

This paper focuses primarily on how to read research reports, for several reasons. First, the bulk of published literature in social psychology consists of research reports. Second, the summaries presented in review articles, and the ideas set forth in theoretical articles, are built on findings presented in research reports. To get a deep understanding of how research is done in social psychology, fluency in reading original research reports is essential. Moreover, theoretical articles frequently report new studies that pit one theory against another, or test a novel prediction derived from a new theory. In order to appraise the validity of such theoretical contentions, a grounded understanding of basic findings is invaluable. Finally, most research reports are written in a standard format that is likely unfamiliar to new readers. The format of review and theoretical articles is less standardized, and more like that of textbooks and other scholarly writings, with which most readers are familiar. This is not to suggest that such articles are easier to read and comprehend than research reports; they can be quite challenging indeed. It is simply the case that, because more rules apply to the writing of research reports, more guidelines can be offered on how to read them.

The Anatomy of Research Reports

Most research reports in social psychology, and psychology in general, are written in a standard format prescribed by the American Psychological Association (1994). This is a great boon to both readers and writers. It allows writers to present their ideas and findings in a clear, systematic manner. Consequently, as a reader, once you understand this format, you will not be on completely foreign ground when you approach a new research report—regardless of its specific content. You will know where in the paper particular information is found, making it easier to locate. No matter what your reasons for reading a research report, a firm understanding of the format in which they are written will ease your task. We discuss the format of research reports next, with some practical suggestions on how to read them. Later, we discuss how this format reflects the process of scientific investigation, illustrating how research reports have a coherent narrative structure.

Title and Abstract

Though you can't judge a book by its cover, you can learn a lot about a research report simply by reading its title. The title presents a concise statement of the theoretical issues investigated, and/or the variables that were studied. For example, the following title was taken almost at random from a prestigious journal in social psychology: "Sad and guilty? Affective influences on the explanation of conflict in close relationships" (Forgas, 1994, p. 56). Just by reading the title, it can be inferred that the study investigated how emotional states change the way people explain conflict in close relationships. It also suggests that when feeling sad, people accept more personal blame for such conflicts (i.e., feel more guilty).

The abstract is also an invaluable source of information. It is a brief synopsis of the study, and packs a lot of information into 150 words or less. The abstract contains information about the problem that was investigated, how it was investigated, the major findings of the study, and hints at the theoretical and practical implications of the findings. Thus, the abstract is a useful summary of the research that provides the gist of the investigation.

Reading this outline first can be very helpful, because it tells you where the report is going, and gives you a useful framework for organizing information contained in the article.

The title and abstract of a research report are like a movie preview. A movie preview highlights the important aspects of a movie's plot, and provides just enough information for one to decide whether to watch the whole movie. Just so with titles and abstracts; they highlight the key features of a research report to allow you to decide if you want to read the whole paper. And just as with movie previews, they do not give the whole story. Reading just the title and abstract is never enough to fully understand a research report.

Introduction

A research report has four main sections: introduction, method, results, and discussion. Though it is not explicitly labeled, the introduction begins the main body of a research report. Here, the researchers set the stage for the study. They present the problem under investigation, and state why it was important to study. By providing a brief review of past research and theory relevant to the central issue of investigation, the researchers place the study in a historical context and suggest how the study advances knowledge of the problem. Beginning with broad theoretical and practical considerations, the researchers delineate the rationale that led them to the specific set of hypotheses tested in the study. They also describe how they decided on their research strategy (e.g., why they chose an experiment or a correlational study).

The introduction generally begins with a broad consideration of the problem investigated. Here, the researchers want to illustrate that the problem they studied is a real problem about which people should care. If the researchers are studying prejudice, they may cite statistics that suggest discrimination is prevalent, or describe specific cases of discrimination. Such information helps illustrate why the research is both practically and theoretically meaningful, and why you should bother reading about it. Such discussions are often quite interesting and useful. They can help you decide for yourself if the research has merit. But they may not be essential for understanding the study at hand. Read the introduction carefully, but choose judiciously what to focus on and remember. To understand a study, what you really need to understand is what the researchers' hypotheses were, and how they were derived from theory, informal observation, or intuition. Other background information may be intriguing, but may not be critical to understand what the researchers did and why they did it.

While reading the introduction, try answering these questions: What problem was studied, and why? How does this study relate to, and go beyond, past investigations of the problem? How did the researchers derive their hypotheses? What questions do the researchers hope to answer with this study?

Method

In the method section, the researchers translate their hypotheses into a set of specific, testable questions. Here, the researchers introduce the main characters of the study—the subjects or participants—describing their characteristics (gender, age, etc.) and how many of them were involved. Then, they describe the materials (or apparatus), such as any questionnaires or special equipment, used in the study. Finally, they describe chronologically the procedures of the study; that is, how the study was conducted. Often, an overview of the research design will begin the method section. This overview provides a broad outline of the design, alerting you to what you should attend.

The method is presented in great detail so that other researchers can re-create the study to confirm (or question) its results. This degree of detail is normally not necessary to understand a study, so don't get bogged down trying to memorize the particulars of the procedures. Focus on how the independent variables were manipulated (or measured) and how the dependent variables were measured.

Measuring variables adequately is not always an easy matter. Many of the variables psychologists are interested in cannot be directly observed, so they must be inferred from participants' behavior. Happiness, for example, cannot be directly observed. Thus, researchers interested in how being happy influences people's judgments must infer happiness (or its absence) from their behavior—perhaps by asking people how happy they are, and judging their degree of happiness from their responses: Perhaps by studying people's facial expressions for signs of happiness, such as smiling. While reading the method section think about the measures researchers use. Do they adequately reflect or capture the concepts they are meant to measure? If a measure seems odd, consider carefully how the researchers justify its use.

Oftentimes in social psychology, getting there is half the fun. In other words, how a result is obtained can be just as interesting as the result itself. Social psychologists often strive to have participants behave in a natural, spontaneous manner, while controlling enough of their environment to pinpoint the causes of their behavior. Sometimes, the major contribution of a research report is its presentation of a novel method of investigation. When this is the case, the method will be discussed in some detail in the introduction.

Participants in social psychology studies are intelligent and inquisitive people who are responsive to what happens around them. Because of this, they are not always initially told the true purpose of a study. If they were told, they might not act naturally. Thus, researchers frequently need to be creative, presenting a credible rationale for complying with procedures, without revealing the study's purpose. This rationale is known as a *cover story*, and is often an elaborate scenario. While reading the method section, try putting yourself in the shoes of a participant in the study, and ask yourself if the instructions given to participants seem sensible, realistic, and engaging. Imagining what it was like to be in the study will also help you remember the study's procedure, and aid you in interpreting the study's results.

While reading the method section, try answering these questions: How were the hypotheses translated into testable questions? How were the variables of interest manipulated and/or measured? Did the measures used adequately reflect the variables of interest? For example, is self-reported income an adequate measure of social class? Why or why not?

Results

The results section describes how the observations collected were analyzed to determine whether the original hypotheses were supported. Here, the data (observations of behavior) are described, and statistical tests are presented. Because of this, the results section is often intimidating to readers who have little or no training in statistics. Wading through complex and unfamiliar statistical analyses is understandably confusing and frustrating. As a result, many students are tempted to skip over reading this section. We advise you not to do so. Empirical findings are the foundation of any science and results sections are where such findings are presented.

Take heart. Even the most prestigious researchers were once in your shoes and sympathize with you. Though space in psychology journals is limited, researchers try to strike a balance between the need to be clear and the need to be brief in describing their results. In an influential paper on how to write good research reports, Bem (1987) offered this advice to researchers:

> No matter how technical or abstruse your article is in its particulars, intelligent nonpsychologists with no expertise in statistics or experimental design should be able to comprehend the broad outlines of what you did and why. They should understand in general terms what was learned. (p. 74)

Generally speaking, social psychologists try to practice this advice.

Most statistical analyses presented in research reports test specific hypotheses. Often, each analysis presented is preceded by a reminder of the hypothesis it is meant to test. After an analysis is presented, researchers usually provide a narrative description of the result in plain English. When the hypothesis tested by a statistical analysis is not explicitly stated, you can usually determine the hypothesis that was tested by reading this narrative description of the result, and referring back to the introduction to locate a hypothesis that corresponds to that result. After even the most complex statistical analysis, there will be a written description of what the result means conceptually. Turn your attention to these descriptions. Focus on the conceptual meaning of research findings, not on the mechanics of how they were obtained (unless you're comfortable with statistics).

Aside from statistical tests and narrative descriptions of results, results sections also frequently contain tables and graphs. These are efficient summaries of data. Even if you are not familiar with statistics, look closely at tables and graphs, and pay attention to the means or correlations presented in them. Researchers always include written descriptions of the pertinent aspects of tables and graphs. While reading these descriptions, check the tables and graphs to make sure what the researchers say accurately reflects their data. If they say there was a difference between two groups on a particular dependent measure, look at the means in the table that correspond to those two groups, and see if the means do differ as described. Occasionally, results seem to become stronger in their narrative description than an examination of the data would warrant.

Statistics *can* be misused. When they are, results are difficult to interpret. Having said this, a lack of statistical knowledge should not make you overly cautious while reading results sections. Though not a perfect antidote, journal articles undergo extensive review by professional researchers before publication. Thus, most misapplications of statistics are caught and corrected before an article is published. So, if you are unfamiliar with statistics, you can be reasonably confident that findings are accurately reported.

While reading the results section, try answering these questions: Did the researchers provide evidence that any independent variable manipulations were effective? For example, if testing for behavioral differences between happy and sad participants, did the researchers demonstrate that one group was in fact happier than the other? What were the major findings of the study? Were the researchers' original hypotheses supported by their observations? If not, look in the discussion section for how the researchers explain the findings that were obtained.

Discussion

The discussion section frequently opens with a summary of what the study found, and an evaluation of whether the findings supported the original hypotheses. Here, the researchers evaluate the theoretical and practical implications of their results. This can be particularly interesting when the results did not work out exactly as the researchers anticipated. When such is the case, consider the researchers' explanations carefully, and see if they seem plausible to you. Often, researchers will also report any aspects of their study that limit their interpretation of its results, and suggest further research that could overcome these limitations to provide a better understanding of the problem under investigation.

Some readers find it useful to read the first few paragraphs of the discussion section before reading any other part of a research report. Like the abstract, these few paragraphs usually contain all of the main ideas of a research report: What the hypotheses were, the major findings and whether they supported the original hypotheses, and how the findings relate to past research and theory. Having this information before reading a research report can guide your reading, allowing you to focus on the specific details you need to complete your understanding of a study. The description of the results, for example, will alert you to the major variables that were studied. If they are unfamiliar to you, you can pay special attention to how they are defined in the introduction, and how they are operationalized in the method section.

After you have finished reading an article, it can also be helpful to reread the first few paragraphs of the discussion and the abstract. As noted, these two passages present highly distilled summaries of the major ideas in a research report. Just as they can help guide your reading of a report, they can also help you consolidate your understanding of a report once you have finished reading it. They provide a check on whether you have understood the main points of a report, and offer a succinct digest of the research in the authors' own words.

While reading the discussion section, try answering these questions: What conclusions can be drawn from the study? What new information does the study provide about the problem under investigation? Does the study help resolve the problem? What are the practical and theoretical implications of the study's findings? Did the results contradict past research findings? If so, how do the researchers explain this discrepancy?

Some Notes on Reports of Multiple Studies

Up to this point, we have implicitly assumed that a research report describes just one study. It is also quite common, however, for a research report to describe a series of studies of the same problem in a single article. When such is the case, each study reported will have the same basic structure (introduction, method, results, and discussion sections) that we have outlined, with the notable exception that sometimes the results and discussion section for each study are combined. Combined "results and discussion" sections contain the same information that separate results and discussion sections normally contain. Sometimes, the authors present all their results first, and only then discuss the implications of these results, just as they would in separate results and discussion sections. Other times, however, the authors alternate between describing results and discussing their implications, as each result is presented. In either case, you should be on the lookout for the same information, as outlined above in our consideration of separate results and discussion sections.

Reports including multiple studies also differ from single study reports in that they include more general introduction and discussion sections. The general introduction, which begins the main body of a research report, is similar in essence to the introduction of a single study report. In both cases, the researchers describe the problem investigated and its practical and theoretical significance. They also demonstrate how they derived their hypotheses, and explain how their research relates to past investigations of the problem. In contrast, the separate introductions to each individual study in reports of multiple studies are usually quite brief, and focus more specifically on the logic and rationale of each particular study presented. Such introductions generally describe the methods used in the particular study, outlining how they answer questions that have not been adequately addressed

by past research, including studies reported earlier in the same article.

General discussion sections parallel discussions of single studies, except on a somewhat grander scale. They present all of the information contained in discussions of single studies, but consider the implications of all the studies presented together. A general discussion section brings the main ideas of a research program into bold relief. It typically begins with a concise summary of a research program's main findings, their relation to the original hypotheses, and their practical and theoretical implications. Thus, the summaries that begin general discussion sections are counterparts of the summaries that begin discussion sections of single study reports. Each presents a digest of the research presented in an article that can serve as both an organizing framework (when read first), and as a check on how well you have understood the main points of an article (when read last).

Research Reporting as Story Telling

A research report tells the story of how a researcher or group of researchers investigated a specific problem. Thus, a research report has a linear, narrative structure with a beginning, middle, and end. In his paper on writing research reports, Bem noted that a research report:

> … is shaped like an hourglass. It begins with broad general statements, progressively narrows down to the specifics of [the] study, and then broadens out again to more general considerations. (1987, p. 175)

This format roughly mirrors the process of scientific investigation, wherein researchers do the following: (1) start with a broad idea from which they formulate a narrower set of hypotheses, informed by past empirical findings (introduction); (2) design a specific set of concrete operations to test these hypotheses (method); (3) analyze the observations collected in this way, and decide if they support the original hypotheses (results); and (4) explore the broader theoretical and practical implications of the findings, and consider how they contribute to an understanding of the problem under investigation (discussion). Though these stages are somewhat arbitrary distinctions—research actually proceeds in a number of different ways—they help elucidate the inner logic of research reports.

While reading a research report, keep this linear structure in mind. Though it is difficult to remember a series of seemingly disjointed facts, when these facts are joined together in a logical, narrative structure, they become easier to comprehend and recall. Thus, always remember that a research report tells a story. It will help you to organize the information you read, and remember it later.

Describing research reports as stories is not just a convenient metaphor. Research reports *are* stories. Stories can be said to consist of two components: A telling of what happened, and an explanation of why it happened. It is tempting to view science as an endeavor that simply catalogues facts, but nothing is further from the truth. The goal of science, social psychology included, is to *explain* facts, to explain *why* what happened. Social psychology is built on the dynamic interplay of discovery and justification, the dialogue between systematic observation of relations and their theoretical explanation. Though research reports do present novel facts based on systematic observation, these facts are presented in the service of ideas. Facts in isolation are trivia. Facts tied together by an explanatory theory are science. Therein lies the story. To really understand what researchers have to say, you need to consider how their explanations relate to their findings.

The Rest of the Story

There is really no such thing as research. There is only search, more search, keep on searching. (Bowering, 1988, p. 95)

Once you have read through a research report, and understand the researchers' findings and their explanations of them, the story does not end there. There is more than one interpretation for any set of findings. Different researchers often explain the same set of facts in different ways.

Let's take a moment to dispel a nasty rumor. The rumor is this: Researchers present their studies in a dispassionate manner, intending only to inform readers of their findings and their interpretation of those findings. In truth, researchers aim not only to inform readers, but also to *persuade* them (Sternberg, 1995). Researchers want to convince you their ideas are right. There is never only one explanation for a set of findings. Certainly, some explanations are better than others; some fit the available data better, are more parsimonious, or require fewer questionable assumptions. The point here is that researchers are very passionate about their ideas, and want you to believe them. It's up to you to decide if you want to buy their ideas or not.

Let's compare social psychologists to salesclerks. Both social psychologists and salesclerks want to sell you something; either their ideas, or their wares. You need to decide if you want to buy what they're selling or not—and there are potentially negative consequences for either decision. If you let a salesclerk dazzle you with a sales pitch, without thinking about it carefully, you might end up buying a substandard product that you don't really need. After having done this a few times, people tend to become cynical, steeling themselves against any and all sales pitches. This too is dangerous. If you are overly critical of sales pitches, you could end up foregoing genuinely useful products. Thus, by analogy, when you are too critical in your reading of research reports, you might dismiss, out of hand, some genuinely useful ideas—ideas that can help shed light on why people behave the way they do.

This discussion raises the important question of how critical one should be while reading a research report. In part, this will depend on why one is reading the report. If you are reading it simply to learn what the researchers have to say about a particular issue, for example, then there is usually no need to be overly critical. If you want to use the research as a basis for planning a new study, then you should be more critical. As you develop an understanding of psychological theory and research methods, you will also develop an ability to criticize research on many different levels. And *any* piece of research can be criticized at some level. As Jacob Cohen put it, "A successful piece of research doesn't conclusively settle an issue, it just makes some theoretical proposition to some degree more likely" (1990, p. 1311). Thus, as a consumer of research reports, you have to strike a delicate balance between being overly critical and overly accepting.

While reading a research report, at least initially, try to suspend your disbelief. Try to understand the researchers' story; that is, try to understand the facts—the findings and how they were obtained—and the suggested explanation of those facts—the researchers' interpretation of the findings and what they mean. Take the research to task only after you feel you understand what the authors are trying to say.

Research reports serve not only an important archival function, documenting research and its findings, but also an invaluable stimulus function. They can excite other researchers to join the investigation of a particular issue, or to apply new methods or theory to a different, perhaps novel, issue. It is this stimulus function that Elliot Aronson, an eminent social psychologist, referred to when he admitted that, in publishing a study, he hopes his colleagues will "look at it, be stimulated by it, be provoked by it, annoyed by it, and then go ahead and do it better … That's the exciting thing about science; it progresses by people taking off on one another's work" (1995, p. 5). Science is indeed a cumulative enterprise, and each new study builds on what has (or, sometimes, has not) gone before it. In this way, research articles keep social psychology vibrant.

A study can inspire new research in a number of different ways, such as: (1) it can lead one to conduct a better test of the hypotheses, trying to rule out alternative explanations of the findings; (2) it can lead one to explore the limits of the findings, to see how widely applicable they are, perhaps exploring situations to which they do not apply; (3) it can lead one to test the implications of the findings, furthering scientific investigation of the phenomenon; (4) it can inspire one to apply the findings, or a novel methodology, to a different area of investigation; and (5) it can provoke one to test the findings in the context of a specific real world problem, to see if they can shed light on it. All of these are excellent extensions of the original research, and there are, undoubtedly, other ways that research findings can spur new investigations.

The problem with being too critical, too soon, while reading research reports is that the only

further research one may be willing to attempt is research of the first type: redoing a study better. Sometimes this is desirable, particularly in the early stages of investigating a particular issue, when the findings are novel and perhaps unexpected. But redoing a reasonably compelling study, without extending it in any way, does little to advance our understanding of human behavior. Although the new study might be "better," it will not be "perfect," so *it* would have to be run again, and again, likely never reaching a stage where it is beyond criticism. At some point, researchers have to decide that the evidence is compelling enough to warrant investigation of the last four types. It is these types of studies that most advance our knowledge of social behavior. As you read more research reports, you will become more comfortable deciding when a study is "good enough" to move beyond it. This is a somewhat subjective judgment, and should be made carefully.

When social psychologists write up a research report for publication, it is because they believe they have something new and exciting to communicate about social behavior. Most research reports that are submitted for publication are rejected. Thus, the reports that are eventually published are deemed pertinent not only by the researchers who wrote them, but also by the reviewers and editors of the journals in which they are published. These people, at least, believe the research reports they write and publish have something important and interesting to say. Sometimes, you'll disagree; not all journal articles are created equal, after all. But we recommend that you, at least initially, give these well-meaning social psychologists the benefit of the doubt. Look for what they're excited about. Try to understand the authors' story, and see where it leads you.

Acknowledgments

Preparation of this paper was facilitated by a Natural Sciences and Engineering Research Council of Canada doctoral fellowship to Christian H. Jordan. Thanks to Roy Baumeister, Arie Kruglanski, Ziva Kunda, John Levine, Geoff MacDonald, Richard Moreland, Ian Newby-Clark, Steve Spencer, and Adam Zanna for their insightful comments on, and appraisals of, various drafts of this paper. Thanks also to Arie Kruglanski and four anonymous editors of volumes in the series, Key Readings in Social Psychology for their helpful critiques of an initial outline of this paper. Correspondence concerning this article should be addressed to Christian H. Jordan, Department of Psychology, University of Waterloo, Waterloo, Ontario, Canada N2L 3G1. Electronic mail can be sent to chjordan@watarts.uwaterloo.ca

REFERENCES

American Psychological Association (1994). *Publication manual* (4th ed.). Washington, D.C.

Aronson, E. (1995). Research in social psychology as a leap of faith. In E. Aronson (Ed.), *Readings about the social animal* (7th ed., pp. 3–9). New York: W. H. Freeman & Company.

Bem, D.J. (1987). Writing the empirical journal article. In M.P. Zanna & J.M. Darley (Eds.), *The compleat academic: A practical guide for the beginning social scientist* (pp. 171–201). New York: Random House.

Bowering, G. (1988). *Errata*. Red Deer, Alta.: Red Deer College Press.

Cohen, J. (1990). Things I have learned (so far). *American Psychologist*, *45*, 1304–1312.

Forgas, J.P. (1994). Sad and guilty? Affective influences on the explanation of conflict in close relationships. *Journal of Personality and Social Psychology*, *66*, 56–68.

Sternberg, R.J. (1995). *The psychologist's companion: A guide to scientific writing for students and researchers* (3rd ed.). Cambridge: Cambridge University Press.

Author Index

Subject Index

Page numbers for main entries that have subheadings refer to general aspects of that topic.
Page numbers in **bold** indicate tables. Page numbers in *italic* represent figures.